SOCIOLOGY
Rules, Roles, and Relationships

The Dorsey Series in Anthropology and Sociology

EDITOR
ROBIN M. WILLIAMS, JR.
Cornell University

SOCIOLOGY

Rules, Roles, and Relationships

Everett K. Wilson
Professor of Sociology
Antioch College

1966
The Dorsey Press
Homewood, Illinois

First Printing, March, 1966

Library of Congress Catalog Card No. 65–22419

PRINTED IN THE UNITED STATES OF AMERICA

A Prefatory Note to the Instructor

To impose another introductory text upon the flooded field of primers in sociology may suggest arrogance, avarice, or both. But although I am not untouched by vice, there are loftier reasons for offering this volume to colleagues who welcome the novice to our field.

The first of these apologia is a preferred organization of materials. The discipline to which we are committed is quite variously viewed —and misconstrued. This is largely due, I think, to the potpourri often served to introduce the neophyte to sociology. As a result the student sometimes reveals amazing misconceptions if he is asked, upon completing an introductory course, what sociology is. I have tried to avoid an inchoate *omnium gatherum* by checking myself against these three criteria: clarity in defining and bounding the field, consistency in applying this definition, and simplicity in organization. On this last point, apart from the prologue and the epilogue, the book is divided into three major parts concerned, respectively, with *building, maintaining,* and *changing* systems of social relationships. If I have been successful, the teacher should find the book both tightly organized and, at the same time, providing the latitude needed for his own excursions and emphases.

I've tried, also, to demonstrate the fruitful union of theory and empirical research. It is an invidious and useless distinction that separates "pedestrians" from "intuitives." It is of course possible to trifle with trivial *ad hoc* hypotheses, compounding the error by applying million dollar tools to ten cent data. This is why Parsons, Becker, Blumer, and some European sociologists chide us. It is also possible to contrive a fuzzy conceptual edifice divorced from men's behavior and, indeed, so muddily stated as to preclude empirical testing. This is what so many have inveighed against, from Bacon, St. Simon, and Comte to Hankins, Ogburn, Bain, and Lundberg.

And while today one looks far to find the excessive empiricism recommended by St. Simon or the cloudy epistemology of Erich Fromm (to know a person is to love him; and in the loving to preclude the possibility of rational "knowing"),[1] the virtue of the union of theory and empirical inquiry is more celebrated than practiced. And so I have tried to join the two throughout this work, linking Freud with Sewell, Marx with Weber and the latter with Lenski, Durkheim's theoretical discussion of suicide with his empirical tests of the theory, Simmel with Mills's test of power relations in three-person groups, and so on for most of the topics dealt with.

A cognate aim, obviously, has been to introduce the student to the seminal ideas contributed by a few theorists—those sufficiently generative to provoke emulation, plagiarism, and rebuttal. Another related aim was to provide exposure to common methods of inquiry in sociology and related disciplines. The emphasis has been chiefly upon the general strategy of inquiry, ". . . the proof of an hypothesis (by trying) to hook up two factors into a causal relationship through the study of contrasting situations which have been controlled on all factors except the one of interest, the latter being either the hypothetical cause or the hypothetical effect."[2] I've given lesser emphasis to generic concepts bearing on methods of inquiry—concepts like validity, reliability, and sample. Finally, I have provided examples and footnotes on specific techniques wherever these were relevant to the problem under discussion.

A third aim has been to make this introduction just that: clear in expression, pruning away much of the conventional foliage without—so I hope—sacrificing core elements of the field with which the beginner should become acquainted. It is partly in self-defense that I stress simplicity and forgo encyclopedic aspirations; for it is preposterous and presumptuous to pretend competence in the score of fields embraced by our complex and growing discipline. If it is true that text writers were once constrained to provide data, concepts, and theories across the board, these to be conveyed to students by displaced housewives, reformers, and theologians, such is not the case today. The text writer need not now regard the teacher as, at best, an animated speaking tube, at worst an obstacle. Today he is

---

[1] This was a statement of Fromm's in his article "Man Is Not a Thing," in the *Saturday Review of Literature,* 40: 9–11 (March 16, 1957).

[2] Ernest Greenwood, *Experimental Sociology* (New York: King's Crown Press, 1949), p. 28.

likely to be well trained, more competent in some fields than is the writer. Today's teaching sociologists can be relied upon to fill gaps, to extend the bearing of a proposition, to challenge and correct the writer. So the student's chances are bettered, not worsened, by brevity and simplicity.

While stressing simplicity I have not been condescending. Quite to the contrary, my commitment to sociology and my respect for the often underestimated student have prompted me rather to treat the reader as an adult. The assumption of adulthood, though partially in error, is not so egregiously wrong as its opposite. For in the latter case, we miss the effect of Merton's self-fulfilling prophecy, mislead the poor student and disenchant the good one, while simultaneously boring ourselves and devaluing the discipline. I have not hesitated, therefore, to broach difficult and unfamiliar ideas, or to sample the work of a French or German writer in his own language, or to show something of the relevance to sociology of mathematics.

Most sociologists will agree that early exposure to elementary mathematical applications is desirable. They will not object to my attempt to convey, in an occasional footnote, an intuitive understanding of a few common statistical techniques. Statistically studded readings will be more intelligible when, for example, the student knows he must square r to discover what part of the variance in Y is to be explained through variance in X.

But I fear there will be less agreement about an occasional quotation in French or German. Yet it seems to me worth a try for several reasons. I draw on foreign sociologists, in their own language, because it carries the message that the life of the intellect is one of international intercourse, that sociology is not a provincial enterprise but a matter of giving and getting among thinkers wherever the accidents of birth and citizenship may place them. Furthermore, I'm persuaded (although one of the editors, Professor Whyte, disagrees emphatically on this point) that nuance and imagery are often different and more powerful in the original. I like the feel, the impact of Marx's statement: *"Die tradition aller toten Geschlecter lastet wie ein Alp auf dem Gehirn der Lebenden,"* and I like the sense of getting it directly from a titan in history without the intermediation of a linguistic midwife. A third reason is that the student, as he struggles with different formulations in English translation, may find the ideas more powerful and complex than he would were he to sail casually through the English translation (which I provide in the notes at chapters' ends, as a point of last resort).[3] A final reason is this: it seems to me important to bring several elements of a liberal education to bear upon the problems posed in sociology. For one aspect of a liberal education is to weave together relevant strands from different fields, so contriving an intellectual fabric more elegant and durable. As Louis Auchincloss has his rector of Justin say: "An equation, a Keats ode, a Gothic cathedral, a Mozart aria, the explosion of gases in a laboratory, they should be seen by [students] as related—and divine."[4] And since most of our students will never become professional sociologists, we must leave them with some appreciation of the way their interests, and ours, reciprocally illuminate each other.

One final explanation. The book is written in the first person. The tradition of scientific writing proscribes such personal communication. The third person is for matters of the mind, the first for expressions of the heart. The third person fixes on problems outside the self, conveys the objectivity of the distant and impersonal view. A text, however, is not a scientific effort, but a pedagogical one. And this book, since it is not an edited affair, is a distinctly personal piece of pedagogy. So the third person seemed to me a misleading if not a pretentious circumlocution. While most sociologists will concur in most of what I say, it would be absurd to drop a syntactical hint that matters of tone, interpretation and organization were immaculately conceived on some sociological Sinai to be antiseptically delivered by me. I hope that the direct contact of the first person does not preclude detached dealing with problems. But if it does, there is no question where the responsibility lies!

✼   ✼   ✼   ✼

The book is divided into five parts. In the Prologue I pose two questions, the obvious openers. To the first, what is the field of sociology? I answer: sociology is the controlled observation and interpretation of differing patterns of social relationships, their sources and consequences. The explication of this definition leads us easily to the second question: how do we seek answers in this field?

---

[3] Whether in weakness, weariness, or wisdom, since writing this I've bowed to others' judgments (the Asch effect at work). The English translations are now in the text, the original at chapters' ends.

[4] Louis Auchincloss, *The Rector of Justin* (Boston: Houghton-Mifflin, 1964), p. 285–86.

Here the logic of inquiry and problems of experimental design are emphasized.

Part I is called "Entering the Group." The group is endlessly built, or rebuilt, as persons are recruited to fill roles vacated through migration, social mobility, or death. A marital relationship is ritually established. Presently children enter the familial group and must, in MacIver's felicitous phrase, be inducted into the secrets of society. They enter play groups of their peers, rigidly graded age-sex groups in the school system, college and university groups, criminal and other occupational groups, neighborhood groups, political groups. In every case the definitions of modal role behavior must be learned, norms inculcated, and the legitimate range of variation specified. These shared understandings are given in the culture of the group; hence we open the discussion of entering the group by considering the concept of culture and its bearing upon the building of social relationships. But since the internalization of cultural prescriptions is not accomplished by some mystical osmosis, we are led to examine the way in which culture is mediated. We are led, that is, to consider the socialization process, especially as it is institutionalized in the family and in more formal educational agencies. It becomes relevant, also, to suggest the extent to which the groups one enters are influenced by class—the way in which, in Weber's words, life chances are conditioned by the accident of birth.

The maintenance of that system of relationships we call a group (Part II) is largely an unplanned outcome of recurrent behaviors. Recurrences and regularities in space and time contribute to the order of the social order. The ecological substructure of human relationships is seen, for example, in the spatially endogamous marriage pattern reported by Bossard. This spatial patterning is related to the moral order Park spoke of. It increases the probability of trait-homogamy in the partners. This in turn increases parental influence upon the children, promoting continuity between generations. The system is maintained, too, by a steady input of candidates, through births and immigration, for those slots vacated through death and emigration. And so our interest here shifts to the demographic substructure of the social order. The growth and composition of population is intimately related to maintenance of the group. These remarks on human ecology and demography are preface to considering those "frozen answers to fundamental questions" which, because "frozen," promote stability in the group. These answers are institutionalized. Both theory and empirical evidence suggest that the maintenance of any group hinges on the institutionalization of certain functions. In discussing socialization I spoke of two institutions performing such indispensable functions. Here, then, family and school get short shrift. Chief stress at this point is upon economy, polity, and church.

But since no social system is a closed affair, since there are strains within and stress without, we move on to a discussion of changes in systems of social relationship (Part III). While I pay some attention to planned social change, it seemed better to emphasize the implications for change lying latent in behavior patterns whose manifest functions are poles apart from their unintended consequences. A useful vantage point for assessing degree and sources of change is the rural-urban axis. It provides not merely a contrast in space, but also a dramatic transformation through time in American society. Paralleling this shift there are basic changes in the nature of the social order. The evidence clearly suggests that there are markedly different requirements for maintaining a system of relationships in primary and secondary, rural and urban, simple and complex groups.

Finally, in the epilogue, I indulge my prejudices by discussing the significance of the sociologist's role in our world, and the resistances he encounters in the pursuit of reliable knowledge about man's behavior among men.

The table of contents summarizes this summary.

❊   ❊   ❊   ❊

To dedicate a textbook is to inflate its significance. Acknowledgments are another thing. It is a good convention to acknowledge one's intellectual debts. Elizabeth Owen Wilson with her passion for contemporary literature and European history has tempered my arid sociology. Students, my despair and delight, have borne with fortitude the fumbling efforts that slowly took the form of this book. To the European greats we are all indebted—I, in particular, to Émile Durkheim and the group surrounding him in the publication of *l'Année sociologique*. Debts to Merton and Parsons are registered, not so obviously as they might be, throughout the book. Teachers and colleagues at four great American universities—Columbia, Berkeley, Chicago and Michigan—have meant much to me. In a goodly company of seekers it is hard to single out those who struck resonant chords. But among them have been Kroeber, Chatterjee, Gouldner, Angell, Hawley, Landecker, Aberle, Wilensky.

Perhaps my debts are greatest to Louis Wirth, Ronald Freedman, Heinz Eulau, and Theodore Newcomb. More by example than by precept they affirm the important things: loyalty to learning (and to the conditions that enable its free pursuit) and the friendship that binds people, even at a distance, in the common quest.

I am glad of this chance to say how much whatever strengths this book may have are due to the critical scrutiny and scholarship of Robin M. Williams, Jr., Dorsey's editor *sans pareil.* At earlier stages Peter Rossi and William Foote Whyte helped get this work off the ground. The professional criticism of Samuel Surace and Allen Grimshaw has been enormously helpful.

Let me add, finally, my sense of wonder and gratitude at the patient and knowledgeable support provided by the Dorsey Press people. They know how to put a book together and, more important to me, how to keep an author that way!

The standard exculpations are in order. All others are absolved from responsibility for my shortcomings, which are numerous. For despite the brave professions of this prefatory note, errors of omission and commission in form and substance must have crept—perhaps marched—in. But these can provide the cues for corrective surgery by the teacher, or prompt him to produce a better text.

Everett K. Wilson

Yellow Springs,
January, 1966

Table of Contents

Prologue   The Nature of the Field

Chapter 1

What Is Sociology?

What's the nature of the field?
What's the strategy of sociological inquiry?

Sociology has been so variously conceived—too often, misconceived—that we might well begin with some dogmatic denials. It is true that it has embraced such a variety of problems that laymen's misconceptions may be justified. A casual survey of the subject index to the *American Sociological Review* reveals several hundred topics on which sociologists have written. These range from the armed forces, birth control, and bureaucracy through geophagy, lumberjacks, and music to suicide, urbanism, values, war, and women. So it is not surprising that some irreverent bystanders have seen sociology as a sort of scavenger science, greedily appropriating those areas of study not already preempted by the established and legitimate disciplines. Such a welter of apparently disparate interests would seem reason enough for erroneous views of the nature of the field.

One such view is that sociology consists of a body of precepts. It is seen as the latter-day Holy Writ enjoining tolerant and humane relations among men. To this the sociologist would reply that his task is to inquire, not to require; to explore, not to implore. This is not to suggest that he is unconcerned with the values men live by: these constitute important data for him. What people believe and the behavior from which beliefs may be inferred are extremely helpful in understanding patterns of human behavior. But this is altogether different from the development of a new decalogue based upon the findings of social science.

Related to this misconception is the notion that sociology is social work. Here the sociologist's task is seen not so much as the specification of right belief as the reformation of wrong conditions and bad behavior. Delinquent and criminal must be made law-abiding, slum housing razed and replaced by wholesome housing, the divorce rate reduced, literacy increased, and tastes refined. No social scientist deprecates such objectives. He favors virtue. But his working hours are spent on a task only indirectly related to reform. This is the dispassionate description and analysis of patterns of human relationship as they actually are. To see him as a reformer is to confuse two roles. The scientist asks *what is*. The reformer asks *what ought to be*. Of course, the same man may ask both questions. Indeed, the Judeo-Christian ethic and our form of government demand he shall. What is more, for effective action it is imperative that the two be linked. "*Voir pour prévoir*," said Auguste Comte a century ago. And Herbert Spencer, writing a little later, noted that hardly a law is passed that is not a law to amend an inadequate law.[1] He meant to suggest that the loftiest motivation is not enough if the law and reform are based upon erroneous views of man and society. The man of knowledge and the man of action must somehow collaborate if social change is to be effective. But the social scientist must be scrupulous in distinguishing policy and preference from dispassionate analysis. The task of sociology is obscured when *what is* is confused with *what ought to be*.

Curiously enough, sociological is often used as an adjective synonymous with social. And sometimes—perhaps because it seems to carry collective connotations—sociology is identified with socialism. Certain of our congressmen apparently suffer from this delusion.[2]

---

[1] Auguste Comte, 1798–1857, Herbert Spencer, 1820–1903. The work of these men provides an important point of departure in the development of sociology. Comte coined the term "sociology" (although he would have preferred "social physics" had it not already been used in another connection), and is sometimes thought of as the father of sociology. The French phrase means: see in order to foresee, or more adequately translated: know in order to predict.

[2] See, e.g., the work of the Reece Committee, *Report of the Special Committee to Investigate Tax-Exempt Foundations and Comparable Organizations,* House of Representatives, 83rd Cong., 2d sess., House Resolution 217 (Washington, D.C.: U.S. Government Printing Office, 1954).

This committee, chaired by Congressman Reece of Tennessee and supported by two appropriations totaling $115,000 was authorized to investigate tax-exempt educational and philanthropic organizations ". . . especially to determine which . . . are using their resources for un-American and subversive activities." (*Op. cit.*, p. 1.) This committee's report asserts, among other things, that the "approach of the social scientists has behind it a wholly materialistic concept of life and behavior. Its natural

Close cousin to this error is the one which assumes that sociology is a discipline which develops techniques precisely for the purpose of manipulating others. The sociologist's inquiries into recurrent patterns of human conduct will enable prediction. Prediction implies control. Enter the awful "specter of predictable man." It has become very fashionable to view with alarm the alleged relapse into conformity as a result of the subtle and sinister manipulations of others, including social scientists. Erich Fromm warns against the "escape from freedom"[3] declaring for self-determination in the ambiguous assertion: "man is not a thing."[4] David Riesman conjures up the same unpalatable picture in his description of the jelly-willed "other-directed" person presumably characterizing our times in contrast to a more inner-directed past.[5] Robert Lindner, a psychoanalyst, thunders like Elijah, asking "Must You Conform?"[6] William H. Whyte, Jr. discusses the coercive influence of the corporation upon the wives of its executives;[7] and in his book *The Organization Man*[8] belabors the social scientist for providing the tools for man's greatest inhumanity to man—manipulation. The social scientist is "the hidden persuader."[9] He is perhaps the Prince of Eggheads, cavorting through the graveyard of romance and illusion. He denies the unique in man, belittles and obscures the individual as he discovers laws of behavior which enable manipulation.

This is shallow thinking. And it is consummate anti-intellectualism since it asserts that knowledge which *may* be used for purposes deemed evil by some unspecified judges should be forbidden. But unfortunately this is an elementary characteristic of all knowledge. The apple of the Garden of Eden has consequences for good and evil. Indeed, the simple knowledge which allows one to discriminate be-

---

outcome is an approach to Marxism—it is not surprising that so many of the social scientists tend to collectivism. They believe they can satisfactorily rearrange society. . . . It is a rather pitiful assumption that the springs of human behavior can be reduced to formulae." (*Op. cit.*, p. 73.)

[3] Erich Fromm, *Escape From Freedom* (New York: Rinehart & Co., 1941).

[4] Erich Fromm, "Man Is Not a Thing," *Saturday Review of Literature*, Vol. XL (March 16, 1957), pp. 9–11.

[5] David Riesman, *The Lonely Crowd* (New Haven: Yale University Press, 1950).

[6] Robert Lindner, *Must You Conform* (New York: Rinehart & Co., 1956).

[7] William H. Whyte, Jr., "The Corporation Wife," *Fortune Magazine*, Vol. XLIV (Nov., 1951).

[8] William H. Whyte, Jr., *The Organization Man* (New York: Simon and Schuster, Inc., 1956).

[9] Vance Packard, *The Hidden Persuaders* (New York: David McKay Co., Inc., 1957).

tween a ripe apple and a green one is weapon enough to impose diarrhea on the unwitting. All knowledge has this ambivalent character; and there is no evidence that ignorance necessarily entails felicity; or that perfidy invariably follows knowledge. This timid and distorted view would halt inquiry into that most significant part of nature we call *human* nature.

But what is more, such a specter obscures the very nature of man's social life. For orderly human relationships depend upon the "manipulation" and prediction of others' responses. In our daily dealings with others we are incessantly speaking and acting in ways calculated to elicit desired and expected responses. Human life and, paradoxically, freedom itself are possible only insofar as men respond predictably. The social scientist's task is to enhance our knowledge of this order and the conditions under which it changes. Through disciplined observation and imaginative analysis he seeks a more profound and accurate understanding of man's conduct among men.

Finally, there is the view that sociology is, in fact, common sense disguised, that the sociologist ("a person who dives the deepest and comes up the muddiest") puts into incomprehensible jargon what any child of twelve knows well and states clearly. Paul Lazarsfeld, a sociologist at Columbia University, discusses this viewpoint in the following paragraphs.

When the social scientist proposes that we test our commonsense notions and beliefs, he is likely to encounter serious opposition from various segments of our society. Why spend time, money, and energy doing surveys that merely verify what is already obvious? Consider, for example, the following statements from a survey of the adjustment of servicemen to military life in World War II:

Better educated men showed more psychoneurotic symptoms than those with less education. (The mental instability of the intellectual as compared to the more impassive psychology of the man-in-the-street has often been commented on.)

Men from rural backgrounds were usually in better spirits during their Army life than soldiers from city backgrounds. (After all, they are more accustomed to hardships.)

Southern soldiers were better able to stand the climate in hot South Sea Islands than Northern soldiers. (Of course, Southerners are more accustomed to hot weather.)   '

White privates were more eager to become "noncoms" than Negroes. (Lack of ambition among Negroes is almost proverbial.)

Southern Negroes preferred Southern to Northern white officers. (Isn't it well known that Southern whites have a more fatherly attitude toward their "darkies"?)

As long as the fighting continued, men were more eager to be returned to the States than they were after the German surrender. (You cannot blame people for not wanting to be killed.)

We have in these examples a sample list of the simplest type of interrelationships which provide the "bricks" from which our empirical social science is being built. But, why, since they are so obvious, is so much money and energy given to establish such findings? Would it not be wiser to take them for granted and to proceed directly to a more sophisticated type of analysis? This might be so except for one interesting point about the list. Every one of these statements is the direct opposite of what was actually found. Poorly educated soldiers were more neurotic than those with high education; Southerners showed no greater ability than Northerners to adjust to a tropical climate; Negroes were more eager for promotion than whites; and so on.
If we had mentioned the actual results of the investigation first, the reader would have labelled these "obvious" also. Obviously something is wrong with the entire argument of "obviousness." It should really be turned on its head. Since every kind of human reaction is conceivable, it is of great importance to know which reactions actually occur most frequently and under what conditions; only then will a more advanced social science develop.[10]

Sociology, then, is not a body of "correct" beliefs. Nor is it the reformation of bad behavior. Although its name suggests an interest in collectivities, it has nothing to do with collectivism or any other *ism*, including socialism. Its aim is not to develop principles for manipulating people, although to know is to predict and to predict is, sometimes, to control. As with all knowledge, it may be used well or ill. Nor can sociology be regarded as a mere restatement of common-sense knowledge. For common-sense statements often contradict one another; and are often quite contrary to scientific findings. These statements could be applied with equal force to other of the social sciences—to economics, psychology, political science, and anthropology.

DIFFERENTIATING SOCIAL FROM PHYSICAL AND BIOLOGICAL SCIENCES

We are trying to spot the problems peculiar to sociology and so to define its distinctive realm of inquiry. Now it would be redundant and confusing if we were to use two names for the same thing. As an example, if we were to accept Ralph Linton's not overly modest definition of anthropology, "The Study of Man," we would either

---

[10] Paul Lazarsfeld, "The American Soldier," *Public Opinion Quarterly*, Fall, 1949, pp. 379–80.

eliminate a dozen other disciplines or else redefine them as sub-divisions of anthropology. Now the question is whether we can differentiate sociology in any intelligible way from other of the social sciences—and here I refer chiefly to economics, anthropology, political science, history, and psychology. Or are we simply using different words for aspects of the same thing? To put the question even more grossly, we might ask if it is possible to differentiate the social sciences in any meaningful fashion from the biological and the physical sciences.

To chop knowledge into separate bits, as we do in university curriculums, is often unsatisfactory if not frustrating. Sometimes we feel, however vaguely, what the psychologists call "lack of closure." We feel that knowledge about human beings ought to have integrity; that it has, in fact, a wholeness and unity which is vitiated by curricular fragmentation. The development of a field called the behavioral sciences, combining sociology, anthropology, and social psychology perhaps provides some evidence of this urge to bring disparate and fragmentary bits of knowledge into a unified whole. Some scientists like James Miller and Ralph Gerard and Norbert Wiener and Kenneth Boulding have gone even further, hoping to build up a science of behavior which embraces physical and biological as well as social and psychological behavior.[11] For this purpose they prefer physical concepts such as *energy* and seek to establish principles of behavior which may apply to *any* system, whether physical, biological, social, or psychological, couching their analyses in terms of input and output of energy into these systems. Professor Dodd takes a similar position in developing a law of diffusion which, he suggests, applies to any situation of steady, random pairings, whether in the transmission (diffusion) of a message from person to person, the conjunction of atoms, or of molecules or of genes.[12]

This is an intriguing line of inquiry and one of the distinctive developments in contemporary social science. If ultimately the study of man is recast in this fashion, the current boundary lines between the social, the biological, and the physical sciences will be obsolete, and we shall have a new science of behavior, human and otherwise, such units of analysis—for example, a measure of input energy which, built upon more abstract and formal units of analysis. Presumably

---

[11] See, e.g., James G. Miller *et al.*, *Symposium: Profits and Problems of Homeostatic Models in the Behavioral Sciences*, Publication No. 1 (Chicago: University of Chicago Press, 1953), Introduction and pp. 2–10.

[12] Stuart Dodd, "Diffusion Is Predictable," *American Sociological Review*, Vol. XX, No. 4 (August, 1955), pp. 400 and 394.

in psychology, is now referred to as a stimulus—would be easily manipulated by mathematical techniques. We should then be able to set up mathematical models as abstract statements of the principal forms of human interaction.

There are others who take a dim view of this attempt to telescope these realms of behavior—social, biological, physical—into a single, formal discipline. The social sciences must remain distinct, they insist, since any effort to reduce the phenomena of human life to some biophysical equivalent shears away precisely those characteristics which are human or social. Thus an eminent sociologist, Émile Durkheim (1858–1917), asserts that social phenomena have emergent properties which *cannot be understood* in terms of the elements (i.e., individual human beings, to say nothing of their biological and physical properties) who are associating and interacting.[13] A social fact is a thing *sui generis* (of its own distinctive kind) and cannot be explained in other terms. Can one, Durkheim asks, from knowledge of the characteristics of two gases, hydrogen and oxygen, predict that their combination will result in a transparent, palpable fluid which is required to support life and is transformed at certain temperatures to steam and ice? Or again, he asks, what is there about the two malleable metals, copper and tin, that suggests the properties of bronze resulting from their combination? Clearly, the peculiar qualities of water and of bronze are qualities that emerge only out of the combination of elements. And so it is with the phenomena of group life. It is the fact of association which triggers certain distinctive outcomes. These provide the data for sociology. They cannot be apprehended by resorting to the more elemental units of biological or physical analyses.

Let us put it a different way. Herbert Spencer (who with Auguste Comte is regarded as marking the transition from social philosophy to the more rigorous, empirical discipline that Comte named Sociology) spoke of the realm of the *superorganic*, differentiating it from the *organic* and the *inorganic*.[14] The first would be under the

---

[13] Émile Durkheim, *The Rules of Sociological Method*, trans. Sarah A. Solovay and John H. Mueller (Chicago: University of Chicago Press, 1938).

This point of view about the emergent and extraindividual nature of the social is also seen in Durkheim's classic work on *Suicide*, in his *Moral Education* and, indeed, throughout his work.

[14] Herbert Spencer, *First Principles* (New York: P. F. Collier and Son Corp., 1901).

Although the terms are Spencer's he does not take the position that there is an insurmountable gulf between these realms, precluding explanation and terms that bridge them. Indeed, his evolutionary orientation leads him to view inorganic-organic-superorganic as a continuous series.

jurisdiction of the social sciences, the second the province of zoology and botany, and the third the realm of the physical sciences—e.g., physics and chemistry. An American anthropologist, A. L. Kroeber, represents this division of the fields of knowledge in this way:[15]

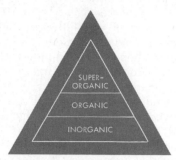

The question we are raising, of course, is whether these boundary lines are altogether arbitrary. Is it a matter of historical accident (accident here meaning unidentified influences contributing to a certain outcome) which accounts for this three-fold division of fields of inquiry? Is it a matter of economy—a calculated effort to operate efficiently through a division of intellectual labors? Or is it, as Durkheim would contend, a logical division since the phenomena of one realm, for example, the superorganic, cannot be understood in terms of phenomena at another level, the organic or inorganic?

But certainly man has a habitat, on which his very life depends. It would be naïve to suppose that man's behavior is independent of his rocks and rills, his woods and templed hills. It is equally clear that man is an animal; and there seems an element of arrogance in this separation of other animals from *homo sapiens*—the contention that man is different in kind. Quite to the contrary, a pioneer American sociologist, Hankins of Columbia, has said that the differences between man and the allegedly lower animals are matters merely of degree. There is no psychic attribute of man, contended Hankins, which is not found in at least a rudimentary state in other animals. He would contend that there is no sharp dividing line between the realms of the inorganic, the organic, and the superorganic. Through aeons of evolution man as an organism has had to adapt to the peculiarities of his physical environment. His physical environment and his biological character condition his behavior and set certain limits which, whatever his inclinations, man cannot possibly transcend. Compressing the evolutionary story, R. G. Smith wrote:

---

[15] A. L. Kroeber, *Anthropology* (New York: Harcourt, Brace & Co., Inc., 1948).

A billion years ago the Ironic Artificer brought together in magic combination those tiny electronic universes which now go by the name of carbon, hydrogen, oxygen, nitrogen, sulphur and phosphorus. Three lusty cheers resounded in Heaven as the first protozoan timidly tried out his dimpled pseudopedia in the scorching archaeozoic slime. Ages upon ages of agonizing evolution passed, and then one hot Thursday afternoon the grandfather of old Pithecanthropus Erectus climbed down from his arboreal boudoir and stood up on his hind legs. Here was the first faint intimation of the Babbitt that was to be. . . . The collective struggle of Homo Sapiens for survival and advantage, beginning in a sort of magico-religious blur, developed with incredible slowness into the complicated institutional arrangements of contemporary society, into behavior nexuses in which sense and nonsense, beauty and ugliness, tolerance and intolerance, are inextricably interlaced. However fantastic and irrational any particular culture pattern may appear, we know that its form and content do not and *cannot transcend the limits set by the biological nature of man and by the nature of this planet* on which man is doomed for a brief span to chase the will-o'-the-wisp of his funny dreams.[16]

Or consider the unity of the physical, biological, and psychic (social) implied in this statement by the naturalist, Donald Culross Peattie:

I say that it touches a man that his blood is sea water and his tears are salt, that the seed of his loins is scarcely different from the same cells in a seaweed, and that of stuff like his bones is coral made. I say that physical and biological law lies down with him and wakes when a child stirs in the womb, and that the sap in a tree, uprushing in the spring and the smell of the loam, where the bacteria bestir themselves in darkness, and the path of the sun in the heaven, these are facts of first importance to his mental conclusions and that a man who goes (unconscious) of them is a drifter and a dreamer without a home or any contact with reality.[17]

But what does it mean, in more prosaic and precise language, to suggest that the physical and the social are intimately related? That the physical is necessary for man's life is obvious but irrelevant; for we are not interested merely in living but in *different ways of living*. Or more accurately, we are interested in the different ways in which men relate themselves to one another. Are differing patterns of human relationships to be linked with variations in the physical realm (the inorganic)?

---

[16] Russell Gordon Smith, *Fugitive Papers* (New York: Columbia University Press, 1930), pp. 116–17.

[17] Donald Culross Peattie, *An Almanac for Moderns* (New York: G. P. Putnam's Sons, 1935), p. 14.

Certainly, said Montesquieu some 200 years ago in a book called *The Spirit of the Laws*. There is a right and natural "fit" between the laws describing men's relationships, their organic character, and the physical characteristics of their living place. And so, ". . . laws should be in relation to the climate of each country, to the quality of its soil, to its situation and extent, to the principal occupation of the natives. . . ."[18]

In a nation so distempered by the climate as to have a disrelish of everything . . . it is plain that the government most suitable to the inhabitants is that in which they cannot lay their uneasiness to any single person's charge. . . .[19]

In warm countries the aqueous part of the blood loses itself by perspiration; it must therefore be supplied by a like liquid. Water is there of admirable use. . . .

In cold countries, the aqueous part of the blood is very little evacuated by perspiration. They may therefore make use of spirituous liquors, without which the blood would congeal. . . .

The law of Mohammed, which prohibits the drinking of wine, is therefore fitted to the climate of Arabia; . . . Such a law would be improper for cold countries, where the climate seems to force them to a kind of national intemperance, very different from personal ebriety. . . . Go from the equator to the north pole and you will find this vice increasing together with the degree of latitude.[20]

When the Christian religion, two centuries ago, became unhappily divided into Catholic and Protestant, the people of the North embraced the Protestant, and those of the South adhered still to the Catholic.

The reason is plain: the people of the North have, and will forever have, a spirit of liberty and independence, which the people of the South have not; and therefore a religion which has no visible head is more agreeable to the independence of the climate than that which has one.[21]

A more sophisticated version of this point of view, called in its extreme form "geographic determinism," is represented in the work of certain of the human geographers. One of these, Ellen Churchill Semple, contends that:

Man can no more be scientifically studied apart from the ground which he tills, or the lands over which he travels, or the seas over which

[18] Baron de Montesquieu, *The Spirit of the Laws* (New York: D. Appleton and Co., 1900), Vol. I, p. 8. The Aldine edition in two volumes.

[19] *Ibid.*, p. 277.

[20] *Ibid.*, pp. 273, 274.

[21] *Ibid.*, pp. 520, 521.

he trades, than polar bear or desert cactus can be understood apart from its habitat. . . . Man has been so noisy about the way he has "conquered nature," and Nature has been so silent in her persistent influence over man, that the geographic factor in the equation of human development has been overlooked.[22]

These statements reveal that there are those who view human behavior—the phenomena at the level of the superorganic—as depending on or determined by the physical-geographical setting in which they live or by their biological attributes. Such persons would take strong exception to Durkheim's dictum that social phenomena must be explained *only* in social terms.

But it is probably accurate to say that most sociologists—perhaps most social scientists—lean toward Durkheim's position, despite the persuasive rhapsodies of the naturalists. Evidence from sociology and anthropology reveals that groups living under comparable conditions of terrain and climate may yet differ markedly in social structure and function. Conversely, groups whose physical-geographic habitats stand in the strongest contrast may yet be very similar in social organization and patterns of behavior. Hence we cannot grant a determinative influence to factors at the inorganic level. Nor do they have explanatory value except as they are mediated by culture and the social patterns expressing it.[23]

Similarly the sociologist would say that we cannot understand sex-linked roles which vary so markedly from one society to another simply in terms of the biological attributes of male and female; or the genetics of the X and Y chromosomes. Despite the familiar and celebrated biological differences between male and female, among the Arapesh both men and women are reported as gentle, cooperative, accommodating. The Mundugamor men and women

---

[22] Ellen Semple, *Influences of Geographic Environment on the Basis of Ratzel's System of Anthropogeography* (New York: Henry Holt & Co., Inc., 1911), pp. 1–20, *passim.*

[23] The reader might ask himself whether, in the following passage, a meaningful explanation for Lord Edward's appreciation for Bach is to be found in the physical and physiological aspects of the music. The musician's blowing, ". . . and the scraping of the anonymous fiddlers had shaken the air in the great hall, had set the glass of the windows looking on to it vibrating; and this in turn had shaken the air in Lord Edward's apartment on the further side. The shaking air rattled Lord Edward's *membrana tympani;* the interlocked *malleus, inous,* and stirrup bones were set in motion so as to agitate the membrane of the oval window and raise an infinitesimal storm in the fluid of the labyrinth. The hair endings of the auditory nerve shuddered like weeds in a rough sea; a vast number of obscure miracles were performed in the brain, and Lord Edward ecstatically whispered, 'Bach!'" (From Aldous Huxley, *Point Counter Point* [New York: Harper & Brothers, 1928], p. 32.)

are violent, aggressive, jealous, and competitive. Among the Tcham-buli the women dominate, do the fishing and manufacture impor-tant trade articles; and the men, who occupy a subservient position, do the shopping and can exchange articles only with the women's approval.[24]

Or suppose we take the matter of race, generally considered a biological phenomenon based upon genotypical characteristics re-sulting in kinky hair, differing amounts of melanin and carotene affecting skin pigmentation, epicanthic eyefold, and the like. How do the racial characteristics of a people help us to understand and predict their patterns of social behavior? Race was once defined as a category of people characterized by a cluster of biological traits inherited from common ancestors. A more adequate conception of race is that developed by physical anthropologists: a breeding population (having, therefore, a geographical locus) among whom the average incidence of specific genes varies significantly from that in other breeding populations. The former definition is the one which divided the world's population, like all Gaul, into three parts: the Caucasoids, the Mongoloids, and the Negroids. These were further dissected. The Caucasoid group included Nordics, Alpines, Mediterraneans, and Hindus. The Mongoloids were subdivided into Amerind, Asiatic, and Oceanic. The Negroid group was split among Africans, Oceanic Negroids, Negritos, and Bushmen. These cate-gories accounted for about 98 percent of the world's population, with a few problematic peoples—Polynesians, Ainus, Indo-Australoids, Australians—becoming the miscellaneous residuals.

Unfortunately, these categories were not exclusive for given traits. Most if not all differences among human beings are continuous rather than discrete. And so we find a great deal of overlapping among races for almost any trait—stature, pigmentation, hair tex-ture, etc.

But the great error was—and is—the impetuous linking of social and psychological attributes to such racially classified biological phenomena. Thus, for example, the non-Aryans according to the Nazis were inferior not only biologically but in their culture, in their intelligence, in their destiny. (The term *Aryan*, incidentally, was wrongly applied to race: it refers to a cluster of cognate languages as does, for example, the misused term *semitic*. The non-Aryans in-cluded, for Hitler, the Negroids, the Mongoloids—except for such

---

[24] Margaret Mead, *Sex and Temperament in Three Primitive Societies* (New York: Mentor paperback, 1950).

honorary Aryans as the Japanese—and, above all, a religious group belonging to the Caucasian race, Mediterranean subdivision, the Jews. Under the same regime a law was enacted forbidding the breeding of an Aryan cow to a non-Aryan bull.)

The confusion of biological and social traits is reflected in the linking of race and nationality. Certain genetic traits are presumed to be related to country of birth. We hear people refer to the Scottish race, the Italian race, the Irish race. The Scots are apparently tightfisted because of their genetic frugality. The Irish are born prodigal of their money and virtue: they are born drunkards, cops, and fighters. The English are born supercilious, reserved, and dedicated to the task of carrying the white man's burden. The Jews are a race, a nation, a religion, a culture, each or all of these linked inexorably with a nature aggressive, acquisitive, and shrewd. The Negro is simple, highly emotional, sexually potent, remarkably fertile, and innately musical. The Mongoloid is treacherous (at least in wartime, and with the exception of those who, like the Chinese, were on our side). And, of course, we except those original Americans whose "blood" we are sometimes proud to claim. Finally, there is the Caucasian (although here we exclude Indians) who is capable, intelligent, enterprising, thrifty, industrious, and ingenious.[25]

A long series of sociological inquiries demonstrates that there is probably no decisive link between racial attributes and significant social traits.[26] But reliable knowledge goes cheek to jowl with illusion. The significance of race, in social life, comes from the fact that human beings dwell, happily and in part, in a realm of fairy tales, rumor, and gossip. The significance of racial differentials for human conduct comes about as we take an insignificant biological fact (e.g., pigmentation) and blow it up into a tremendously significant social fiction. We live neither by bread nor by truth, alone. Often our lives are suspended tenuously from the gossamer threads of folklore and fancy.

Now fancy and folklore are themselves attributes of group life. They are examples of the "collective representations" which were for

---

[25] That these stereotypes are, in fact, held by a number of people is suggested by the study of the perceived attributes of various ethnic groups among Princeton students. See David Katz and Kenneth Braly, "Racial Stereotypes of One Hundred College Students," *Journal of Abnormal and Social Psychology,* October–December, 1933.

[26] See, for example, the UNESCO statement by experts on race. For the most recent and best available discussion of race, see Stanley M. Garn, *Human Races* (Springfield, Ill.: Charles C Thomas, Publisher, 1961).

Durkheim the primary focus of sociological inquiry. But we shall not get far if we look for their sources in the realm of biology. Can we explain white-Negro antagonism on biological grounds? Can we explain a race riot (an event at the superorganic level) in terms of the biological attributes of race (the organic level)? These are rhetorical questions. The answer is that we cannot: or so it seems at present.

We are led then to the position that there *is* a logical division of labor in our attempt to get at the secrets of nature; and that human nature must be understood in terms of the human—i.e., the social—sciences. (This identification of human with social we will deal with later.) I do not mean to preclude the possibility of fruitful outcomes from the efforts to bridge the social, biological, and physical sciences. I am saying that the phenomena of group life—marriage and kinship patterns, systems of belief, of infant and child training, of artistic expression, and a whole host of other behaviors—vary despite similarity of biological heritage and geographic setting; or are quite similar despite variations in biological heritage and geographic locations. That is to say, patterns of human relationships vary, within wide limits, independently of the biological and physical attributes of the actors. We have not so far devised useful ways of understanding human conduct in terms of biological and physical attributes.

DIFFERENTIATING SOCIOLOGY FROM OTHER SOCIAL SCIENCES

But suppose we confine ourselves to the level of the superorganic. What of sociology and the other social sciences? Do we have here a division of fields of inquiry which can be explained only in terms of "historical accident" or by recourse to the practical argument of efficiency through a division of labor? Or are the boundaries between the social sciences logically established on the basis of differing problems and methods of inquiry?

This is a sticky question about which the experts, as is usual, disagree; and for good reason, for the boundary lines between disciplines are shifting and uncertain. Intellectual interests are notably mercurial. It is quite impossible to confine them within the arbitrary bounds of certain disciplines. And so we find some people interested in political sociology, many sociologists (and psychologists) working in social psychology, anthropologists investigating contemporary U.S. communities, and sociologists rummaging about among peoples of underdeveloped areas formerly the exclusive province of anthropologists. Economists may be interested in the psychology of consumer behavior; and psychologists may be studying motivation, incentives, and differential response to rewards in a factory situation. Sociology may be coupled with economics—more frequently with anthropology—in the same department; and in recent years sociology, anthropology, and social psychology have been bracketed as the behavioral sciences.

Thus the boundary lines between the social sciences seem often to be very fuzzy. Yet some rough distinctions may be made between the several disciplines commonly called the social sciences. Economics might seem to provide the strongest contrast with sociology since it deals with *things* having exchange value (whereas it is ingenuously believed that sociology has to do with *people*).[27] Indeed, we can define economics as the discipline which studies the production, distribution, and consumption of goods, material and intangible, having exchange value. Thus the economist is concerned with the input of land, labor, capital, and managerial skill into a system; the output from that economic system; and its subsequent distribution and consumption. The system of interest to the economist may be arbitrarily defined: a factory, the economic system of the United States, or sometimes the system through which given products are produced and distributed on an international basis.

If the unit of analysis in economics may be said to be *value* (the exchange value of a thing—a good, or service), the unit of analysis in political science may be said to be *power*. To paraphrase an eminent political scientist, members of his clan raise the question: Who controls whom? By what means? Under what conditions? Across what sectors of life? Political scientists have traditionally been concerned with problems of government—i.e., with the formal organization of power relationships. But since power is one dimension of *any* human relationship, it becomes theoretically legitimate for the political scientist to investigate informal and nonlegal rela-

---

[27] If this view were merely ingenuous it would not much matter. Unfortunately, it misleads the newcomer to sociology, distorting his whole perspective on the field. Sociology, as I shall be at pains to state presently, deals not with persons as objects or entities, but with those aspects of their behavior—analytical elements abstracted from observed behavior—which are relevant for understanding how structures of relationship are built and maintained.

tionships in their power aspects: in the family, in business relationships, in recreation, and in religious activities. Again, this tends to blur boundary lines between the several social sciences; and in such a work as that by Eulau, Eldersveld, and Janowitz,[28] two political scientists and a sociologist collaborate in producing a work that is quite as much sociology as political science.

History might seem to present a clearer case. We commonly think of it as the chronological record of important past events. To distinguish roughly between sociology and history, Bierstedt has suggested that history is "a particularizing or individualizing discipline, [whereas sociology is] a generalizing one. History is a descriptive discipline; sociology an analytical one."[29] Again, it has been suggested that history typically deals with men and events who ride the crest of the wave, while sociology is concerned with the underlying currents of which the dramatic and visible figures are ephemeral symbols. Finally, a distinction has sometimes been made between the words *important* and *crucial,* the former referring to the historical focus, the latter to the sociological orientation. Sociology is concerned with those events necessary (though seldom if ever sufficient) to produce a given outcome. They are, therefore, crucial. On the other hand, history is preoccupied with events which loom large in the public consciousness, whether or not they are necessary antecedents for certain outcomes.

None of these distinctions is totally true. At most, they represent differing emphases. It is easy to cite historians whose investigations resemble sociologists'; and sociologists whose inquiries are barely distinguishable from those of historians. As long ago as Hume, historians were seen as seeking and providing evidence of uniformities in human conduct.

Mankind are so much the same in all times and places that history informs us of nothing new or strange in this particular. Its chief use is only to *discover the constant and universal principles of human nature,* by shewing men in all varieties of circumstances and situations, and furnishing us with materials from which we may form our observations, and become acquainted with the regular springs of human actions and behaviour. . . ."[30]

---

[28] Heinz Eulau, Samuel Eldersveld, and Morris Janowitz, *Reader in Political Behavior* (New York: Free Press of Glencoe, Inc., 1956).

[29] Robert Bierstedt, *The Social Order* (New York: McGraw-Hill Book Co., Inc., 1957), pp. 8, 9.

[30] David Hume, *Essays, Moral, Political and Literary,* edited by T. H. Green and T. H. Grose (London, 1898), Vol. II, p. 68. Italics mine.

For more recent examples, consider the historian Charles Beard, who seeks an explanation for the form and content of our Constitution in economic factors; and Frederick Jackson Turner, who writes what is essentially a social history of the development of the West. The sociologist Max Weber, on the other hand, delves into history to explain the emergence of modern capitalism.

With psychology the situation is equally complex. Psychologists study the individual personality—or perhaps more precisely, certain dimensions of personality: intelligence and problem-solving ability, the kinds, conditions, and consequences of emotional expression, perception, motivation, and attitudes. When psychology merges with biology in the investigation of the nervous system, the distinction between it and sociology is quite clear. But when we speak of social psychology, the distinction is by no means clear. Social psychology may be defined as the study of the different orientations of persons as they stem from and have an impact on the human group. Perhaps the orientation of chief interest is what we call an attitude—attitudes that vary in intensity, in content (the attributes of the object toward which the person is oriented), and in sign (positive or negative).[31] Social psychology is a major field of interest for many sociologists. Across the country, courses in social psychology are taught almost exactly half and half in departments of sociology and departments of psychology.

Of all the social sciences, anthropology is closest kin to sociology. But we might more accurately speak of anthropologies; for there are several quite distinct fields: physical anthropology which studies the physical (bodily) and physiological attributes of man; archaeology, or the prehistory of man; linguistics, the comparative study of languages; and social and cultural anthropology which is almost synonymous with sociology except that the anthropologists have typically investigated relatively primitive, often preliterate groups, whereas the sociologist has characteristically studied contemporary, complex, and literate societies. But even here the distinction is not clear-cut, and it applies chiefly to sociology in the United States rather than to French and English sociology. In England, for example, the terms "comparative sociology" and "social anthropology" have been used interchangeably. So far as sociology and anthropology go, we must regard differences as stemming from

---

[31] This is a definition of the field of social psychology that I adapt from Theodore M. Newcomb, *The Acquaintance Process* (New York: Holt, Rinehart & Winston, Inc., 1961), chap. ii, *passim*.

tradition and as being matters of emphasis rather than logical distinctions between problems, research sites, or methods of inquiry.

A DEFINITION OF SOCIOLOGY

This opening gambit may seem like the academician's characteristically devious approach to a straightforward question: What is Sociology? But to get a fix on our position—to know where we are—we have to triangulate. We do not know where we are except with reference to other points. We should add that in such matters our position is not permanently determined. The craft is moving. Today's fix is not tomorrow's. Indeed, changes in the conception of the field are already foreshadowed. So the foregoing amounts to something more than mere preliminary and academic circumlocutions. The issues are continuing ones, not yet clearly resolved.

But in the meantime, we must specify as best we can where we are and what we are about. Common definitions of the field of sociology are such as these: the scientific study of society (or of human behavior or social relationships or of the structure and function of society). Such definitions of the field are acceptable, but are yet rather ambiguous. We can be more specific and somewhat more operational—i.e., suggesting the operations which characterize sociological inquiry—if we define the field this way. *Sociology is the controlled observation and interpretation of differing patterns of human relationships: their sources and consequences.* Let me discuss the terms of this definition, one of which (human relationships) points to the subject or content of the inquiry, while the others bear on methods of inquiry. First, then, for the process celebrated by Dr. Johnson:

> Let Observation with extensive view
> Survey mankind from China to Peru.[32]

Controlled Observation

What is implied by controlled observation? Notions of discipline, order, relevance come to mind. Perhaps the first aspect of controlled observation is that it has focus. It deals with certain things to the exclusion of others. It bars the irrelevant. First attempts at careful inquiry into human behavior are characteristically diffuse, involving

---

[32] Samuel Johnson, "The Vanity of Human Wishes," *Rasselas*, chap. x.

much that is irrelevant and so confounding the hypotheses which might be tested as to make it impossible to get clear-cut and reliable answers. A global and mushy approach is sometimes justified by contending that we want to get the whole picture, see society whole, or see the whole man. It seems accurate to state dogmatically that neither in ordinary life, nor above all in scientific inquiry, do we "see things whole." Nor, indeed, do we wish to. The physician sees his patients as patients, the lawyer deals with clients, the teacher with students, the storekeeper with customers. Each of these views is very partial. Even with intimate friends we are far from seeing them as whole persons. But this clarity and specificity of focus is consciously contrived in sociological inquiry as we isolate those aspects of behavior which are relevant in testing certain notions about the nature of men's relationships with one another.

Controlled observation also implies a clear-cut definition of terms. Any body of knowledge is built through the use of abstract terms called concepts. These must refer unambiguously, in the social sciences, to forms of behavior and methods of analysis. There must be no question about what is referred to when we use such words as role, relationship, marginal utility, projection, status crystallization, displacement, and the like. If we are to see clearly, we must be able to communicate accurately about the things seen.

Closely related to this is a third feature of controlled observation: the development of increasingly adequate and refined tools, both for "seeing" and for analyzing what is seen. Adequate sampling provides such a tool since it allows us to make observations about the whole from knowledge of the part—and within measurable and specified limits of error. Bales's frame for interaction process analysis is another such device.[33] Questionnaires, interview schedules, attitude scaling devices, measures of social affinity and social distance, probability statements, measures of relationships—these and similar instruments and ever better ones are necessary for controlled observation.

---

[33] This is a set of categories for systematic observation of the interaction of persons as they deal with one another in a laboratory situation. It enables observers behind a one-way screen to record relevant behaviors on a rotating drum, synchronized with disc or tape records of audible interaction.

See R. F. Bales, *Interaction Process Analysis: A Method for the Study of Small Groups* (Reading, Mass.: Addison-Wesley Publishing Co., Inc., 1950). This work discusses Bales's complex system of role analysis. It describes a system for controlled observation of positive and negative, instrumental and expressive aspects of roles in situations of collaborative problem-solving.

Controlled observation also implies an ordering of the data. It is unthinkable that we could deal with our various worlds and the infinity of stimuli which pour in upon us daily if we did not organize and classify them. Whenever we use categorical terms like "women" or "Negroes" or "Texans" or "southerners" we are putting a number of people in given pigeonholes on the basis of certain observed characteristics. Controlled observation requires that this be done in meticulous fashion with the criteria of classification carefully specified. Linnaeus' classification of biological forms—species, genus, family, order, class, phylum—represents such an ordering of observations; so, too, does the Periodic Table classifying elements of the physical universe. Similarly, the sociologist may assign persons to classes differing in prestige, privilege, and power on the basis of such criteria as type of occupation, amount and source of income, place of residence in the community, or level of education achieved. Careful ordering of the data is an invariable aspect of controlled observation.

But the model of controlled observation is the controlled experiment. This is a way of so organizing our attack upon a problem that we are able to identify with some assurance an influence which promotes a given outcome. Ordinarily we are too cavalier in our assumptions that such-and-such, a given "cause," produces something else which we call the result. We assume, for example, that the experience of taking a certain course will result in an increase in a specified kind of knowledge. In reality, several outcomes are possible. It is at least conceivable that the student might emerge from the experience quite unaffected in any perceptible degree. It is also conceivable that the experience might be so confusing that he knows less at the end of the course than he knew at the beginning. Similarly with his affective states: he may be less favorably disposed toward the subject matter of the course; or he may have been intrigued by it, stimulated, anxious to pursue problems in the field, long after the course is concluded.

We can enter the same *caveat* about commonplace assumptions regarding any behavior assumed to have certain "obvious" consequences. Does a spanking set the child's feet in paths of righteousness, or may its only outcome be catharsis for an infuriated parent? Does greater contact with persons of other races, nationalities, and ethnic backgrounds promote friendly attitudes, or does it increase hostility? Does the work of the minister, priest, or rabbi promote moral behavior and enhance sensitivity to ethical issues, or is it a soporific enabling the parishioner to continue in his iniquities with peace of mind? Do fines or imprisonment prevent the criminal from repeating his violations and deter others from doing so? Or are the results quite otherwise? How do we know?

Now it would seem obvious, to take the first example, that if we discover through a test that students entering the course know little about the subject, and by a post-test that they know considerably more about the subject, that the intervening experiences in the class have "caused" the student to learn. Teachers seem to operate on this assumption. But clearly, taking a course is a very complex experience. Greater knowledge might be due to the teacher's brilliant exposition. It might be due almost exclusively to assigned reading in the course. It might be due chiefly to bull sessions and similar experiences which are no part of the formal program of learning in this course. But even disregarding the ambiguity of the influence accounting for increased knowledge, how can we be sure it is attributable to the influence of the course? Across the span of a semester or an academic year many other influences have been playing upon the student. He has read books, newspapers, and magazines. He has talked and listened to others, both fellow students and instructors in other courses. Radio and television have provided some of the stimuli flooding in upon him. He may even have corresponded with his parents touching on intellectual as well as financial problems. How can we attribute the change in learning represented by the difference between his post-test and his pretest scores to the experience within that course?

The fact is that unless we attack this problem with something approaching the strategy of a controlled experiment, we cannot know. And the fact is, further, that in most of those daily-life situations where we assume that A causes B—that certain patterns of behavior result in certain outcomes—we do *not* really know. We take it on faith. *In any rigorous sense it is accurate to say that we do not know what we are doing.*

How might we know? We must somehow be sure that, in our illustration, the increased learning is not attributable to some out-of-class influence. We can get such assurance if there is another group of comparable students subject to the same range of influences *except* that they are not taking the course in question. Such a group is known as a *control group*. If there is not much difference between the control group and the group actually taking the course (the *experimental group*) in the gain from pretest to post-test, then we must conclude that the course had little influence upon its unhappy subjects.[34] The control group must, of course, be like the experimental group in all relevant respects except for the presumed causal influence, or stimulus. Often our casual observations are quite wrong because the two groups compared are *not* alike in relevant respects.

For example, as you come into a major American city on a train it is quite likely that you will travel through depressed areas with slum housing and a large Negro population. You may observe that the Negro seems to be extremely prolific; for the streets and alleys and yards are full of children. This confirms certain propositions about the Negro which you may have heard: he is sexually promiscuous and an excessive breeder. By implication, Negroes are more fertile than whites. We are comparing differing patterns of human relationships (one aspect of the marital relationship) among whites and Negroes. Are the groups compared alike in all factors relevant to fertility excepting the experimental variable of race? The answer, of course, is that they are not.

But if we were to "make" them so by comparing the fertility of these Negroes with whites *in the same income category* we would find the differences in fertility fading out. But income is not the only factor known to be related to fertility. Age, education, religious affiliation, and nativity are also factors which should be alike in both groups in order to assess the influence of race upon fertility. When these factors are controlled—made comparable in both groups—we find that our original observation about the excessive fertility of Negroes is quite wrong.

This process of making the control and experimental groups sufficiently alike (except for the experimental variable) is called "holding factors, or variables, constant"; or sometimes it is called "controlling the variables." A variable, incidentally, can be defined as any attribute or characteristic of human behavior that can take on

---

[34] The foregoing is an application of J. S. Mill's method of difference: "If an instance in which the phenomenon under investigation occurs, and an instance in which it does not occur, have every circumstance in common save one, that one occurring only in the former; the circumstance in which alone the two instances differ is . . . the cause . . . of the phenomenon." (John Stuart Mill, *A System of Logic* [New York: Longmans, Green & Co., Inc., 1884].)

differing values—i.e., any attribute or characteristic that varies. The distribution of such values may be either continuous, as in the distribution of numbers from zero to infinity; or it may be discrete, as in an either-or classification (white-Negro, male-female), or as in, say, a "high-medium-low" sort of classification.

There are four general procedures for making the experimental and control groups comparable on the relevant variables. We can identify these methods as follows: (1) control through the elimination of irrelevant variables (which, were they not eliminated, would confound our hypothesis); (2) control through randomization; (3) precision control; and (4) control through frequency distribution.

As an example of the first method of control let us assume that we are testing the hypothesis that measures of the husband's authority in the household (vis-à-vis wife and children) decline when he is unemployed. Now in this case employment-unemployment is the independent variable, and *depending* on his employment status is some measure of his authority in the household (the dependent variable). But it might well be that the stability of a relationship between husband and wife or between father and child varies with race, or by religion, or by level of education of the parents. In order to test the influence of unemployment in altering a man's relationship to wife and child we *must eliminate these other possible influences.* Hence we compare employed and unemployed who are white, Protestant, and have twelve years of education, eliminating all others.

When we control by randomization we follow a procedure that aims to make control and experimental groups comparable by distributing various attributes randomly as between the two groups. Suppose, for example, that we want to find out whether chemical treatment of a kind of seed promotes successful germination. A number of factors may affect germination: exposure to sunlight, the quality of the soil, contour of the land, and so on. In order to randomize the influence of such factors as between the treated and the untreated seed (that is, to neutralize their effects so as to be able to assess the influence of the experimental or independent variable), we might superimpose a grid upon the field, planting first a treated seed and then an untreated seed in adjacent squares.

Similarly, if we were trying to assess the influence of a propaganda film on attitude toward birth control, we might use such a procedure as the following. Knowing that religion, education, and a number of other factors are related to this matter, we might randomly divide the group into two parts. This could be done by listing all persons alphabetically, numbering them, and then assigning all the odd-numbered (or even-numbered) persons to the control group and the others to the experimental group, which would be subjected to the supposed influence of the film. Having pretested both groups on the subject matter of the film, if on the post-test the experimental group showed greater change in attitude, we might then conclude that the film had had some influence.

In precision control, a person in the experimental group having a given cluster of traits—male, college graduate, Protestant, etc.—is matched in the control group by a person having the same attributes.

In control by frequency distribution, the frequency with which a given trait appears in the experimental group is made approximately the same as its frequency in the control group. Thus, for example, if

BEFORE MEASURES		AFTER MEASURES

EXPERIMENTAL GROUP  EXPERIMENTAL TREATMENT

CONTROL GROUP  (WITHHELD FROM CONTROL GROUP)

A model for controlled observation of differing patterns of human relationships.

in the experimental group 20 percent are Catholics and 40 percent are college graduates, the same percentages must characterize the control group. But this does not require that *the same person* be both Catholic and a college graduate. In precision control, the attributes of one individual are matched by those of another. In the second case (control by frequency distribution), it is the group as a whole which is matched with another.

Interpretation

But sociology does not stop—nor indeed does it begin—with controlled observation. It also involves interpretation. Contrary to common-sense nonsense, the facts do not speak for themselves. What is seen is always affected by the see-er. What is known is transformed by the knower. "No man," says Benedict, "ever looks at the world with pristine eyes. He sees it edited by a definite set of customs and institutions and ways of thinking. Even in his philosophical probings he cannot go behind these sterotypes; his very concepts of the true and the false will still have reference to his particular traditional customs."[35]

But true as it is that everything we see is filtered through the screen of tradition and training, and that this must seem at first blush a serious limitation, it does serve to emphasize the fact that neither in everyday life nor in disciplined inquiry do "facts" speak for themselves. They must be interpreted. And this is the juncture at which imagination enters. Nearly two centuries ago St. Simon remarked that there are two sources of knowledge: observation and imagination. He deprecated imagination because he thought men's minds were clouded by shoddy theological fantasies. And St. Simon's secretary, August Comte, systematically developed the idea that man had undergone an intellectual evolution in the course of which undisciplined imagination gave way to hardheaded observation of the facts of social life. Here is Comte, speaking:[36]

---

[35] Ruth Benedict, *Patterns of Culture* (New York: Mentor paperback, 1952).

[36] This isn't quite true. He spoke, of course, in French. If the reader would like to see how Comte *really* said it, he should refer to Original Texts, Note 1 at chapter's end.

I would like to step aside, occasionally, to let better informed, more literate and more distinguished persons speak to the reader, even when they speak a different language. A university is a place of many ideas and many tongues. Important ideas are better conveyed in their own tongue than through the awkward intervention of an interpreter. Where the student can do so independently, or with another's help, he is urged to read the original statement, given at the end of chapters, rather than, or in addition to the translation provided in the text.

. . . In my inquiry into the whole course of intellectual development from its simple beginnings up to the contributions of our day, I believe I have uncovered the underlying law that, by an invariant necessity, governs the development of men's minds. This law states that each of our major ideas, every branch of knowledge, passes through three different theoretical stages: the theological (or fictitious), the metaphysical (or abstract) and the scientific (or positive). . . . Hence three sorts of philosophies or three mutually exclusive conceptual systems. The first is the necessary point of departure for the human mind. The third is its clearly destined state. And the second stage is peculiarly suited to serve as transition between them.

The terms "positive philosophy" and "positive method" are ambiguous ones in English. Comte used the term "natural philosophy" synonymously with "positive philosophy." He meant that human behavior was to be regarded and investigated as natural phenomena; that theory ("interpretation" in our definition) was the handmaiden of observation and subject to its test; and that the notion of the *relative* was to be substituted for the old *absolutes,* testable hypotheses for unquestioned dogma.

Yet despite the emphasis upon observation, Comte's position should not be construed as being hostile to interpretation, to the development of theories and those sub-theses we call hypo-theses.

. . . if all positive theory must necessarily be based on observation, it is equally clear that, if the mind is to make anything of what is observed, it must be furnished with some sort of theory. Were we to deal with phenomena without promptly linking them with some abstract categories (*principes*), not only would it be impossible to combine disparate observations (and, consequently, to make any use of them) but we would be utterly incapable of remembering them. Indeed, for the most part we could not see things right under our noses.*

To celebrate the imaginative—i.e., the interpretive, or theory-building—aspect of sociology is not to minimize the first term in our definition, observation. Upon occasion there have been spurious, sterile, even acrimonious debates between those who thought that one or the other of these aspects of inquiry was being overdone. Those stressing tough-minded observation, treating social phenomena rigorously (as though they were things—"comme des choses," in Durkheim's words) have sometimes appraised the theorist as a

---

* See Original Texts, Note 2 at end of chapter.

woolly-headed dreamer, out of touch with reality, while the latter, in his turn, has spoken derisively of raw empiricists, figure-fiddlers, and machine manipulators.

My view is that neither of these positions is right because each emphasis is literally indispensable. "Neither the naked hand nor the understanding left to itself can effect much," Bacon remarked.[37]

> Those who have handled sciences have been either men of experiment or men of dogmas. The men of experiment are like the ant; they only collect and use; the reasoners resemble spiders, who make cobwebs out of their own substance. But the bee takes a middle course; it gathers its materials from the flowers of the garden and of the field, but transforms and digests it by a power of its own . . . experience, when it wanders in its own track is mere groping in the dark, and confounds men rather than instructs them. But when it shall proceed in accordance with a fixed law, in regular order, and without interruption, then may better things be hoped of knowledge.[38]

It is, of course, a facile resolution and a counsel of perfection to recommend the bee as a model. Sociologists differ in capacities and preferences. But here we are concerned with sociology rather than sociologists. And from the perspective of the discipline, observation and interpretation are twin necessities. If for the moment I am stressing the importance of interpretation, the second term in our definition, it is because the popular view tends to minimize the part played by disciplined imagination. Science is reduced to routine formulas and techniques employed by passionless, white-coated robots with the aid of esoteric gadgets. The humanists have been the unwitting collaborators of the toothpaste ads in purveying the utterly false notion that imagination is alien to science, especially to social science. The truth is quite the contrary. The theoretical aspect

---

[37] Francis Bacon, *Novum Organum,* "Aphorisms Concerning the Interpretation of Nature and the Kingdom of Man," (London: George Routledge and Sons, New Universal Library, n.d.), pp. 60, 64

[38] *Ibid.,* p. 121.
Dualisms are dangerous, and this as much as most. In reality, the "men of experiment" do not pose their problems or select their data in random fashion. Nor are "men of reason" able to divorce themselves from the concrete events in which they are implicated. The former are theorists by default; the latter empiricists because they are sensate, more or less integrated beings. Whether desirable or not, I doubt that we can achieve that schizoid separation of interpretation from observation implied in the statement attributed to Darwin: "It is a fatal fault to reason whilst observing, though so necessary beforehand and so useful afterward." (*The Autobiography of Charles Darwin 1809–1882,* edited with an Appendix and Notes by his granddaughter Nora Barlow [New York: Harcourt, Brace & Co., Inc., 1959], p. 159.)

of sociology involves the insightful and imaginative treatment of observations. For this reason poetry, literature, and philosophy are closely related to first-rate scientific work.

But to assert that the imaginative, yet disciplined, interpretation of things observed is a *sine qua non* for sociology is simply to state a virtue. We should ask in the good American tradition how virtue pays off. What good is theory, for theory is what we build and use in interpreting a set of observations. And there is the prior question: what is meant by theory?

> In sociology, as in most scientific fields, theory is an intellectual creation, explaining the sum of the observed facts by means of a general principle from which these observations can be deduced as consequences. Theory, furthermore, provides the guidelines for future research.*

What sort of intellectual creation (*construction de l'esprit*) is this? A theory consists in a set of logically interconnected, general propositions which interpret the phenomena under investigation in such a way as to lead to testable hypotheses. These general propositions result from describing, ordering, and relating classes of concrete events.

This aspect of sociological inquiry is most important for these reasons. First, it involves a public statement of the assumptions underlying a study and so makes appraisal and criticism possible. It leads to endless revision of theory, sometimes to outright rejection. Thus Freudian theory emphasizes the crucial importance of the child's early years, especially the struggle which ensues as imperious biological impulses are confronted with the repressive demands of culture. The battlefield lies within the framework of the mother-father-child triangle. Related propositions suggest that an affectionate, permissive, and supportive relationship takes much of the devastating edge off this conflict, leading to a better adjusted personality in the child. Such a relationship might be expressed in easy and late toilet training, breast feeding, avoidance of corporal punishment, and so on. I will discuss Professor Sewell's test of these notions in Chapter 3. Here I merely note the use to which the theory is put: it gives rise to a testable hypothesis which states that, as between two groups of comparable children, those treated in one

---

* See Original Texts, Note 3 at end of chapter.

way will differ significantly in their personal adjustment, in their subsequent relationships with others.

Second, theory provides us with a set of categories, concepts, and questions with which we confront a problematic world. It is, as it were, a pair of glasses through which we select and inspect relevant social events, classifying and relating them in such a way as to enhance our understanding of them. What we see through these glasses is governed by the key terms in a theory, those words we call concepts. These are abstract terms which summarize the relevant aspects of a rich variety of concrete beliefs and behaviors. Sociological theory makes frequent use of such concepts as culture, role, status, class, stratification, bureaucracy, attitude, mobility, structure, and institution.

Third, since theory involves general propositions, it is both economical and powerful in its interpretive capacity. It is economical in saying much with few symbols. To say "class conditions life chances" is to embrace a world of events touching all age categories across a broad spectrum of experiences. Theory is powerful to the extent that its general propositions allow us to predict to a wide variety of specific instances. If, for example, we can make a general statement about minority group members, it means that we can predict what will happen, under specified conditions, not only in the case of Negroes, but also where Catholics, Puerto Ricans, Jews, or orientals are involved.

Fourth, sociological theory, the interpretation of social phenomena, is useful because it helps us see the similarities in apparently unlike events; and the dissimilarities in apparently similar events. Max Weber, in *The Protestant Ethic and the Spirit of Capitalism,* develops a theory which finds a necessary feature of capitalist enterprise at the heart of a church doctrine. Durkheim's theory of suicide bridges the family, the military, and the church— i.e., finds the same causal factors operating in these disparate social settings. Later on I shall have occasion to remark about the similarities between child rearing and brainwashing. A theory of effective induction into a group may reveal similarities between boot training, entering a convent, becoming a prison inmate, or joining a business organization. To the extent that interpretation of apparently disparate events allows us to embrace them in a single theory (the rusting nail and the burning wood, both cases of oxidation), our understanding is enhanced. Adam Ferguson, an early sociologist

and a member of the productive school of Scottish moral philosophers (which included Adam Smith) put the point well about two
hundred years ago:

> The faculties of penetration and judgment are . . . employed to
> unravel intricacies of this sort; and the degree of sagacity with which
> [a person] is endowed is to be measured by the success with which
> [he] is able to find general rules applicable to a variety of cases that
> seemed to have nothing in common, and to discover important distinc-
> tions between subjects which the vulgar are apt to confound.[39]

Let me underline this critical contribution of theory with one more
statement, this from Cohen and Nagel: "It is the isomorphism found
in diverse subject matter which makes possible theoretical science as
we know it today."[40]

I will note, finally, what must be obvious in discussing the
essential part played by interpretation through theory, namely, that
it is this feature of sociology which allows our findings to be
cumulative. Theory provides a general framework, constantly revised and enriched. It is unthinkable, in any science, for the findings
of various investigators to be scattered and separate, never being
joined together or mutually confronted for the building of a
structure of knowledge. Knowledge is by its nature general. We do
not know, in any intelligible or communicable sense, the literally
unique. Theory is, as it were, the repository of general knowledge—
general in the sense of being abstract, and general in the sense of
being a common storehouse which is the beginning and the end of
inquiry. A principal reason for such professional organizations as the
American Sociological Association is to provide the resources for
bringing together[41] the work of various investigators and so building
more adequate interpretations of social phenomena.

Differing

The distinguished University of Chicago sociologist, Louis Wirth,
used to say: "If there isn't any difference, it doesn't make any difference." Problems arise out of differences. I underline this term in
our definition as a reminder that the controlled experiment is simply

---

[39] Adam Ferguson, *An Essay on the History of Civil Society* (8th ed.; Philadelphia:
A. Finley, Publisher, 1819), p. 49.

[40] M. R. Cohen and Ernest Nagel, *An Introduction to Logic and the Scientific
Method* (New York: Harcourt, Brace & Co., Inc., 1934), p. 139.

[41] In the *American Sociological Review*, the chief official publication of the society.
See also the *American Journal of Sociology*.

a way of analyzing the factors which make for such differences. "An experiment," in Greenwood's definition, "is the proof [meaning "test"] of an hypothesis which seeks to hook up two factors into a causal relationship *through the study of contrasting situations* which have been controlled on all factors except the one of interest, the latter being either the hypothetical cause or the hypothetical effect."[42] That is to say, we manipulate a situation so as to induce *differences* in one group while a comparable group is not so manipulated. Or, if we are unable to manipulate the situation, we may simply observe differences in behavior between two groups or categories of persons, proceeding then to ferret out another factor which *differentiates* the two groups and which might, therefore, be regarded as causal (the groups remaining comparable in other respects).

> The late Professor Kurt Lewin used to express the experimentalist's credo by saying that if you want to improve your understanding of something you will observe it as it changes [i.e., as *differences* emerge] and preferably as it changes under conditions that you yourself have created. . . . Basically . . . any procedure is an experimental one if it systematically observes the emergence of phenomena under conditions which have been designed to make them emerge.[43]

It may well be that the rapid development of sociology in the last century is due to our increased exposure to differences. Both in space and in time, contrasts are now more apparent than ever before. Change occurs so rapidly that within the span of a person's lifetime there are sharp points of contrast. Whereas "around the world in eighty days" was once a breathtaking feat, as many hours would, today, be onerously slow. Hence the comparison of different forms of social organization has become both frequent, easy, and inevitable.

Nonetheless, most of us are so deeply immersed in the familiar forms of our own societies, or even restricted segments of them, that it is not easy to detect the differences. There is, therefore, an injunction involved in this term of our definition. Sociology requires us to sharpen our capacities for asking, especially with respect to customary, taken-for-granted behaviors: "Why this instead of that?" "Why this type of relationship rather than a different one?" We are asked to cultivate a heightened sensitivity to the possibility of differences.

---

[42] Ernest Greenwood, *Experimental Sociology* (New York: King's Crown Press, 1949), p. 28.

[43] Cited in Theodore M. Newcomb, *The Acquaintance Process* (New York: Holt, Rinehart & Winston, Inc., 1961), p. 3.

Patterns

This term is introduced in our definition to suggest two characteristics of social phenomena: recurrences in time and concurrences in (social) space. If we are concerned with differences, they are patterned differences. Different patterns of relationship—employer-employee, priest-communicant, parent-child, buyer-seller, governor-governed—persist through time. In the individual's relatively short life span the sequence of novel experiences promotes the illusion of inconstancy. But the condition of the social order is stability through predictable recurrences. In sociology we are concerned with recurrent conditions yielding predictable effects. This concern with regularities in conduct does not, of course, distinguish sociology from other disciplines. None of them is concerned with the unique, the idiosyncratic. Even in applied psychology, in diagnosing and prescribing for the unique individual, the therapist does so only against the background of a general knowledge of those *patterns* of individual behavior embodied in psychological theory. All knowledge is general and so implies patterns in the phenomena dealt with.

From another perspective, the patterning of conduct is seen cross-sectionally, as it were, in complementary forms of behavior. Effective induction into an organization may be a concomitant of low turnover. Ordeals and tests of physical fortitude for the young may go along with a rejection of corporal punishment of children. A high level of participation in decision making may be associated with low rates of absenteeism. Adverse attitudes toward minorities may be a concomitant of conventional religious orientations. Restricted access to male roles in a female-dominated group may be associated with delinquency among juveniles. That is to say, there is an interweaving of behaviors in the social order that reveals a pattern. It is these patterns which we seek to identify and understand.

Human Relationships: Their Sources and Consequences

I have used the term, human relationships, in the definition of the field rather than social relationships, to emphasize their identity. For outside a social context, the attributes we call human do not develop or mature. These are the objects of our inquiry: the building, maintaining, and changing of human relationships. And certainly nothing could be of greater personal concern to us; for aside from sheerly visceral pleasures, all the satisfactions of life are bound up with making, maintaining, and sometimes breaking, human relationships.

We are concerned here, however, with the scientific rather than the personal import of human relationships. This being the case, it is well to suggest more exactly what the concept means. A relationship is an inference derived from the behaviors of two or more people. It may be represented, not by person A or person B, but by the double-headed arrow joining them and indicating its existence. More precisely, this inferred bond grows out of the interaction of persons-in-roles: student-teacher, husband-wife, worker-employer. Roles, then, may be regarded as the unit elements in a human relationship. By role I mean the culturally prescribed performance of any person in a given position within a group. It is legitimate to infer the relationship only on the basis of direct or indirect observation. That is to say, our inference may be based on the behavior of the persons as they interact with one another in their respective roles; or it may, for example, be based on our reading of a job description which states the expectations of and by employer and employee.

To state the polar roles involved in a relationship is scarcely a beginning, and a crude one at that. The same roles (parent-child roles, for example) may be defined quite differently by different groups (Israeli Kibbutz and French peasant family); and by different categories (U.S. middle- and lower-class families). There are, furthermore, different dimensions in terms of which performance in these roles may be analyzed. The range of claims that A may make of B may be very great (as in the child's relationship to its mother), or quite restricted (as in the relationship between patient and physician). The role may be infused with emotion, or coldly calculated. The right to perform in the role and appraisal of the performance may be based upon demonstrated capacity (passing a civil service examination) or on considerations irrelevant to performance (kinship). The roles may be immediate or mediating, carried out face to face or remotely, unwittingly, anonymously. They may be analyzed as they range from conflict to reciprocal support. Matters are further complicated because a relationship often involves the same people in a variety of roles. This was particularly so in the early American rural family.

Of course, no relationship stands alone. It is implicated in an extended network of relationships, as in a large industry. There are, then, structures of interlocking relationships which, as they differ or change, become grist for the sociologist's mill. We want to describe different sorts of groups (seen as structures of human relationships). And we want to know how they got that way and what their consequences are. Man is not like the lowly mule, without pride of ancestry or hope of posterity. Human relationships have both ancestry and posterity. They derive from antecedent relationships (the husband-wife relationship is, presumably, not independent of the antecedent parent-child relationships). And they have consequences. (How, for example, does the great increase in the number of relationships in a bureaucratic organization affect the redistribution of types of roles?) To belabor an earlier point, whether we are dealing with sources or consequences of a given pattern of relationship, there is always the contrast, implicit or explicit, with a *different* structure of relationships.

Orientation and Growth of Sociology

Since the world is full of human relationships, the data for sociological inquiry are in good supply everywhere—in factories, on farms, in government and business, in church and school, wherever human beings act in concert. Its material crosscuts every walk of life and intersects the special fields of other social sciences. With such a vast terrain, with so many points of relevance, it is not surprising that the field has grown enormously in recent years. The rate of increase in personnel and publication has increased, likewise the range of activities with which sociologists have concerned themselves. They are at work not only in university teaching and research; but also in business, in industry, in government at all levels including such international agencies as UNESCO, in labor, the military establishment, in hospitals and medical societies, social work agencies, and virtually every other field of the world's work.

The wonder is not, indeed, that sociology has flourished so in recent years, but rather that the flowering was so long delayed. The explanation of the emergence of a discipline (or a dominant philosophy, a school of painting, styles in poetry) is a problem in a subdivision of sociology called the sociology of knowledge. (The central problem of the sociology of knowledge is this: what are the social conditions for the emergence of a given body of knowledge?) Putting this question to sociology itself, I can offer some plausible but unsupported suggestions. Two such notions have already been offered: First, there must be sufficiently rapid social change so that within the span of a person's lifetime there will be problem-raising points of contrast; and second, there must be enough contact, communication with differing forms of social organization, elsewhere, to provide points of comparison. These conditions have increasingly obtained in recent years.

A third condition for the emergence of a discipline like sociology is the availability of tools, the most elementary of which is literacy. The written record reveals change, stimulates criticism, reduces duplication, promotes the accumulation of knowledge. Another set of basic tools is provided in mathematics which, until recent years, was both ill-adapted and too infrequently used by sociologists despite the example of such illustrious forebears as Comte, Spencer, and Pareto. A fourth condition is a viewpoint which might be called secular. Many human relationships are vested with an aura of sanctity and, so long as they cannot be questioned, so long as one point of view has a monopoly over men's minds, sociology cannot function effectively. The secular view is taken, here, as the antithesis of sacred. It implies a concern with proximate rather than ultimate (and therefore unknowable) causes; a willingness to suspend judgment, to consider alternatives; an acceptance of "human nature" as falling within the realm of natural science; and an incessant drive to know with more precision the conditions and consequences of patterns of human relationships. I think these are the conditions, increasingly fulfilled, of sociology's growth.

Such conditions are not easily achieved. Some have ingenuously believed that human behavior is unpredictable because of the "free will" of the actor.[44] They disregard the obvious fact that freedom to choose a given course of action depends on stable (predictable) conditions for achieving the desired end. They fail to account for the fact that the goals we seek vary systematically from group to group. The ends we "freely" choose do not vary randomly. Others have thought the realm of human relationships too complex to be ordered

---

[44] On this objection to sociological inquiry, and others, George Lundberg makes some trenchant observations in his early book, *Social Research* (New York: Longmans, Green & Co., Inc., 1929). This misconception persists, obdurately. Mr. Thomas Murray of the U.S. Atomic Energy Commission wrote, in 1952, that "it is all but useless to investigate the inner and higher life of man. You can't examine free will in a test tube." For a keen analysis of this paralyzing fantasy see Adolf Grünbaum, "Science and Man," *Perspectives in Biology and Medicine*, Vol. 5, No. 4 (Summer, 1962), pp. 483–502.

and apprehended by reason. This timid view disregards the rich
fund of practical knowledge which informs our everyday manipulation of human relationships. It also confuses the (fortunate) existence of problems with intellectual impotence. There is another view
which asserts that human relationships have certain ineffable qualities which are sadly distorted, if not contaminated, by inquiry. This
is a special case of the antiscience bias expressed in verse by poets as
different as Dickinson and Cummings.

> Arcturus is his other name—
> I'd rather call him star!
> It's so unkind of science
> To go and interfere
>
> I pull a flower from the woods—
> A monster with a glass
> Computes the stamens in a breath
> And has her in a class.[45]

Cummings, too, sees science as the enemy:

> O sweet spontaneous
> earth how often have
> the
> doting
>
>   fingers of
> prurient philosophers pinched
> and poked
>
> thee
> ,has the naughty thumb
> of science prodded
> thy
>   beauty . . .[46]

There have, then, been resistances. Especially have attempts at
clearer and more precise statements through quantification exercised some ill-informed skeptics. The attempt to gain reliable knowledge about human relationships and to state it with precision would
seem an innocent if not a laudable enterprise. This leads us to
measurement, to quantification. Often, for example, in describing

---

[45] Emily Dickinson, *The Complete Poems of Emily Dickinson,* edited by Thomas
H. Johnson (Boston: Little, Brown and Co., 1960).

[46] E. E. Cummings, "O Sweet Spontaneous Earth," in *Poems, 1923–1954* (New
York: Harcourt, Brace & World, Inc., 1954).

some aspect of human behavior, we try to summarize a wealth of observations in a single figure, the mean $(\overline{X})$, qualified by a statement of the dispersion of the observed values around this figure. Likewise we often try to make a clear statement of the extent to which two variables, two varying aspects of human relationships, change in a consistent fashion under specified conditions. But for those who make a sharp distinction between the qualitative and the quantitative, putting matters of human relationship in the former category, these are futile efforts which confuse two exclusive and exhaustive categories of things. Quantification is, at the least, abortive; and at the most, it is dangerous distortion of social reality. And so again the poet (W. H. Auden) sounds off:

> Thou shalt not answer questionnaires
> Or quizzes upon world affairs
>   Nor with compliance
> Take any test. Thou shalt not sit
> With statisticians nor commit
>   A social science.[47]

Contrast this with Lord Kelvin's view.

> I often say . . . that when you can measure what you are speaking about, and express it in numbers, you know something about it; but when you cannot measure it, when you cannot express it in numbers, your knowledge is of a meagre and unsatisfactory kind; it may be the beginning of knowledge, but you have scarcely, in your thoughts, advanced to the stage of science, whatever the matter may be."[48]

This is a little closer to the sociologist's position. His aim, at any rate, is to be as precise as possible; and constantly to increase the precision of his statements by developing more adequate measures. He sees no special virtue in ambiguity. Nor is he persuaded by the obscurantists that this or any other realm should be closed to inquiry lest the mysteries be disturbed.

But this is not a matter of pride or ingenuous cocksureness. Like other scientists, the sociologist is keenly aware of his ignorance. This, of course, is a principal reason for the public side of science. The sociologist, in reporting his research, heeds Pope's injunction:

---

[47] W. H. Auden, *Nones* (New York: Random House, Inc., 1951).

[48] An abbreviated version of Lord Kelvin's statement is inscribed in stone, as I recall it, on the Social Science Research Building, 1126 East 59th Street, at the University of Chicago.

> Trust not yourself; but your defects to know.
> Make use of ev'ry friend—and ev'ry foe.[49]

The humility and tentativeness associated with sociological inquiry do not preclude vigorous debate and criticism touching all phases of the reported study: the underlying assumptions and the theoretical framework of the inquiry; the derived hypotheses (the *if . . . then* statements which assert a determinate relationship between two variables under specified conditions); the validity of the indices used to get at these variables (validity referring to the extent to which a measure does in fact get at what it purports to be measuring); the manner of collecting the data; the reliability of the observations (reliability referring to the extent to which measures and measurers agree in their "readings" of the same data on the same instrument); the study design and techniques used in manipulating the data; the interpretation of the data and projected next steps in the research.

Sociology is, then, an active and a vigorous enterprise. Like all vital realms of inquiry, it is more *becoming* than *being*. It involves the excitement of the chase, but tempered by the demands of systematic method and the discipline—indeed the drudgery—required to discover order in the data.

This order, this patterned predictability of human relationships, is embedded in the cultural prescriptions of a group. As microorganisms are sustained in the culture of a Petri dish, so is the network of human relationships articulated and sustained in the context of human culture. This is the matter to which we now turn as we consider the way in which culture defines the ends and stipulates the means enabling the new arrival to join the human group.

ORIGINAL TEXTS

1. Auguste Comte, *Cours de Philosophie Positive: Discours sur l'esprit Positive*, avec une introduction et un commentaire par Ch. Le Verrier (Paris: Librairie Garnier freres, n.d.) pp. 4, 5. Comte writes:
   En étudiant . . . le développement total de l'intelligence humaine dans ses diverse sphères d'activité, depuis son premier essor le plus simple jusqu'à nos jours, je crois avoir découvert une grande loi fondamentale, à laquelle il est assujetti par une nécessité invariable . . . Cette loi consiste en ce que chacune de nos conceptions principales, chaque branche de nos connaissances, passe successivement par trois

---

[49] Alexander Pope, *Essay on Criticism* (Boston: Houghton Mifflin Co., 1903), line 13 *et seq.*, p. 70.

états théoriques différents: l'état théologique, ou fictif; l'état méta-physique, ou abstrait; l'état scientifique, ou positif. . . . De là, trois sortes de philosophies, ou de systèmes généraux de conceptions sur l'ensemble des phénomènes, qui s'excluent mutuellement; la première est le point de départ nécessaire de l'intelligence humaine; la troi-sième, son état fixe et définitif; la seconde est uniquement destinée à servir de transition.

2. *Ibid.*, pp. 14, 15 (italics mine) The original reads:

. . . si d'un côté toute théorie positive doit nécessairement être fondée sur des observations, il est également sensible d'un autre côté, que, pour se livrer à l'observation, *notre esprit a besoin d'une théorie quelconque.* Si, en contemplant les phénomènes, nous ne les rattachions point immédiatement a quelques principes, non seulement il nous serait impossible de combiner ces observations isolées, et, par conséquent, d'en tirer aucun fruit, mais nous serions même entièrement incapables de les retenir; et, le plus souvent, les faits resteraient inaperçus sous nos yeux.

3. J. J. Maquet, *Sociologie de la Connaissance* (Louvain: Institut de Re-cherches Economiques et Sociales, 1949) p. 305

Une théorie en sociologie, comme dans la plupart des autres disci-plines scientifiques, est une *construction de l'esprit* qui explique la synthèse des résultats observés en postulant un principe dont on peut déduire ces résultats à titre de conséquences. Par ailleurs, elle sert de principe directeur pour les recherches ultérieures.

SELECTED SUPPLEMENTARY READINGS

*BARTON, ALLEN H., AND LAZARSFELD, PAUL F. "Some Functions of Qualitative Analysis in Social Research," *Frankfurter Beiträge Zur Sociologie*, 1955, pp. 321–61.

*BECKER, HOWARD S. "Problems of Inference and Proof in Participant Observation," *American Sociological Review*, 1958, pp. 652–60.

BERELSON, BERNARD, AND STEINER, GARY A. "Methods of Inquiry," in *Human Behavior: An Inventory of Scientific Findings*, pp. 15–33. New York: Harcourt, Brace & World, Inc., 1964.

*BIERSTEDT, ROBERT. "A Critique of Empiricism in Sociology," *American Sociological Review*, 1949, pp. 584–92.

LAZARSFELD, PAUL F. "Problems in Methodology," in Robert K. Merton, Leonard Broom, and Leonard S. Cottrell, Jr. (eds.), *Sociology Today*, ch. ii. New York: Harper & Row—Harper Torchbooks, 1965.

*———. "Evidence and Inference in Social Research," *Daedalus*, Vol. 87, No. 4 (Fall, 1958), pp. 99–130.

*Lundberg, George. "The Concept of Law in the Social Sciences," *Philosophy of Science*, 1938, pp. 189–203.

*Meadows, Paul. "Models, Systems and Science," *American Sociological Review*, 1957, pp. 3–9.

*Merton, Robert K. "Sociological Theory," *American Journal of Sociology*, 1945, pp. 462–73.

*———. "The Bearing of Empirical Research upon the Development of Social Theory," *American Sociological Review*, 1948, pp. 505–15.

———. "Notes on Problem-Finding in Sociology," in Robert K. Merton, Leonard Broom, and Leonard S. Cottrell, Jr. (eds.), *Sociology Today*, Vol. I, pp. ix–xxxiv. New York: Harper & Row—Harper Torchbooks, 1965.

Riley, Matilda White. *Sociological Research: A Case Approach* (especially Unit 1, "Introduction to Sociological Research"; Unit 11, "Experimental Design"; and Unit 12, "Special Problems of Sociological Analysis"). New York: Harcourt, Brace & World, Inc., 1963.

*Sewell, William H. "Some Observations on Theory Testing," *Rural Sociology*, 1956, pp. 1–12.

*Solomon, Richard L. "An Extension of Control Group Design," *Psychological Bulletin*, 1949, pp. 137–50.

*Stouffer, Samuel A. "Some Observations on Study Design," *American Journal of Sociology*, 1950, pp. 355–61.

*Swanson, Guy E. "Some Problems of Laboratory Experiments with Small Populations," *American Sociological Review*, 1951, pp. 349–58.

*Weber, Max. "Science as a Vocation," in H. H. Gerth and C. Wright Mills (eds.), *From Max Weber: Essays in Sociology*, pp. 128–56. New York: Oxford University Press, 1946.

Zelditch, Morris. "Some Methodological Problems of Field Studies," *American Journal of Sociology*, 1962, pp. 566–76.

---

* Articles marked with an asterisk are available as reprints from the college division of the Bobbs-Merrill Company, Indianapolis, Indiana.

Part 1 **Entering the Group**

THE TRANSMISSION OF RULES
THE FORMATION OF ROLES

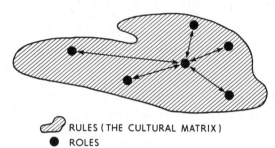

RULES (THE CULTURAL MATRIX)
● ROLES
◄──► RELATIONSHIPS

Chapter 2

The Cultural Context of Human Relationships

*What's the nature of
a human—i.e., a social—relationship?*

In this chapter I shall try to make two points. First, culture provides the *rules,* that define the *roles* that make the *relationships* that constitute the group. Second, acquiring the appropriate culture is, therefore, a prerequisite for entering the group. Incidental to these points is the matter of clarifying the concept of culture and noting ways of getting at it.

A set of relationships is not a happenstance, a "sometime thing." It is contrived, an artifact, the most significant of all human artifacts. That set of interlocking relationships which we call a group is a creation. An enduring group is a continuous re-creation. Groups are built and continuously rebuilt. The sociologist sees this process from two general perspectives: new members *are recruited* and new members *choose* the groups they join. But whether we view this process from the passive or the active perspective, we gain little by seeing it simply as the addition of one person to a number of others.[1]

---

[1] The addition of members to a group constitutes a necessary but not a sufficient condition for certain significant changes. George Simmel (1858–1920), a distinguished German sociologist, points out in his insightful way that the addition of a

This simple conception of the group diverts our attention from its essential and significant characteristics. For if we think of the group simply as two or more persons, we neglect certain facts of overriding importance. First, the group may outlast a given membership and so have an existence independent of particular persons. Second, in any single group "the whole person," whatever this misleading cliché may mean, is only partially involved. Third, membership means learning to perform in a particular role which is then meshed with others' roles. Fourth, membership requires and presupposes shared understandings of what is and what ought to be in members' dealings with one another. Fifth, it follows that, on the basis of such understandings, there is a predictable interplay between the *roles* which comprise the *relationships* that constitute the *group*.

Even apparently simple groups—families, gangs, college roommates—involve an intricate network of understandings which require certain learnings before a person can become a full-fledged member. The newcomer must understand and accept the group's goals and the agreed-upon means for achieving them. Until he is privy to the obligations of membership—accepting certain aims, acquiring requisite skills (language, for example)—he cannot be considered by others a normal or legitimate group member. In the vernacular, he doesn't know the score.

Knowing the score means acquiring the group's *culture*. Linton[2] conveys the meaning of this term by suggesting that society (or a group) is an orchestra in which the musical score represents culture. Each musician (person) must learn and follow the score in his particular role. Of course, his performance may not be altogether predictable from the score. For he has his own interpretation, due largely to the idiosyncrasies of his particular background (training). At a given moment in time he is the repository of a set of experiences and stands at the center of a network of relationships which, in their combination, have never been duplicated anywhere else or at any other time. So he may improvise a bit on the score. His crescendos and diminuendos may have a touch of the idiosyncratic about them. Yet he cannot so depart from the score, from the

---

third person affords the possibility of majority decision, makes possible a coalition of two against one, or enables one to play the other two against one another. (See *The Sociology of George Simmel*, translated and edited by Kurt Wolff [New York: Free Press of Glencoe, Inc., 1950]). But what I stress here is that the person joining a group is not a neutral, colorless unit, but rather represents a complex of culturally specified traits enabling him to mesh his behavior with that of others.

[2] Ralph Linton, *The Study of Man* (New York: Appleton-Century, 1936).

expectations of conductor and fellow musicians as to jeopardize their collective effort. Should this happen, he will be dropped from the group. But it is worth noting that he must be replaced. For his part (role) is indispensable in the performance of the score. Conversely, it is impossible for the individual to realize the score independently. For the score is realized only in concert: culture emerges only within the framework of human relationships. It is not a case of a C and an E and a G, but of a chord which results only from collective effort and common purpose.

Thus the shared understandings (both of what is and what ought to be) *embodied in culture make a social relationship possible.* Indeed, a social relationship can be said to exist only when, *as a result of their common culture,* one person's behavior elicits a dependable and expected response from another.[3] Were it not so—if in answer to A's query or greeting B might respond in any way, randomly, from coitus to combat—human life would be utterly impossible. Human beings cannot live without order.

A system of ordered relationships is a primary condition of human life at every level. *More than anything else it is what society means.* Even an outlaw group, a pirate ship, a band of brigands, has its own code of law, without which it could not exist.[4]

Professor MacIver's point is driven home in a book edited by a sociologist (criminologist), E. H. Sutherland, and entitled *The Professional Thief.*[5] So also Professor Whyte reveals an intricate and effective ordering of relationships in the kind of slum area which is sometimes ingenuously called "disorganized."[6]

Now order presupposes standards.

Group standards often seem arbitrary to members of other groups— and indeed they are and must be, in the literal sense, for in many areas of life it is the *fact* of consensuality, not its content, that matters. One needs to know, dependably and in advance, what kinds of behavior

---

[3] This is the core of Max Weber's definition of a social relationship. A social relationship exists, he said, in ". . . the behavior of a plurality of actors in so far as, in its meaningful content, the action of each takes account of the other and is oriented in these terms. The social relationship thus consists entirely and exclusively in the . . . probability that there will be an anticipated course of action." (Max Weber, *The Theory of Social and Economic Organization,* translated by A. J. Henderson and Talcott Parsons [New York: Oxford University Press, 1947], p. 118.)

[4] Robert MacIver, *The Web of Government* (New York: Macmillan Co., 1948), p. 61.

[5] Edwin H. Sutherland, *The Professional Thief* (Chicago: University of Chicago Press, 1937).

[6] William Foote Whyte, *Street Corner Society* (Chicago: University of Chicago Press, 1943). See especially pp. 269–72.

will and will not be rewarded. Such standards come to have the psychological impact of ineluctability, and are sometimes referred to as "social reality."[7]

However unpalatable it may be to those who imagine themselves emancipated and free to follow vagrant whims of the passing moment, human society depends for its existence on recurrences and continuities. Lacking the order which enables prediction, a relationship founders. To reply in anatomical detail to a person's casual query, "How are you?" is, at the least, to put the questioner off. Such a response reveals a divisive lack of common understandings. But culture, as Ruth Benedict has put it, is "that which binds men together" rather than separating them. A society is an ordered or organized set of relationships maintained by common adherance to the culturally specified rules, and roles, of the game. We have to know them if we are to enter the group.

For the human group is to be conceived as a system of relationships sustained by generally shared cultural prescriptions. A culture is the condition of a social system. This term, system, is often used to convey the idea of differentiation and unity—unity through the dovetailing of differentiated parts. It is in this sense that we speak of an atomic system, an economic system, a molecular system, a cultural system, a political system, a social system. They are often represented in such ways as shown in the accompanying illustration.

The unity of a social system, and of other systems, is an outgrowth of differentiation of parts, interdependence between the parts, and predictability in the connections between the parts.[8] Consider as an

---

[7] Theodore M. Newcomb, *The Acquaintance Process* (New York: Holt, Rinehart & Winston, Inc., 1961).

[8] These characteristics of a social system are sometimes hard to grasp in concrete situations, often because the connections between parts of the system are indirect and complex. Lincoln Steffens provides an illustration:

Why were these law-breakers so strong? And why was there such an opposition to the simple, superficial reforms of Dr. Parkhurst? [Why] the opposition of good, prominent citizens who had no apparent connection with the underworld? As Dr. Parkhurst forced such results as the voluntary closing of some saloons, he was hated more and more openly by people whom one might expect to see approving his course: bankers, business men, and even other clergymen. There was something to find out about the organization of society. I asked my friends in Wall Street to justify their indignation at Parkhurst, but all they would say was that his crusade "hurt business." That was the first time I heard that expression. "How can the closing of saloons hurt business in Wall Street?" I asked James B. Dill, who knew everything. He kicked my shin, hard, and when I exclaimed, he answered my question: "Why does your mouth cry out when only your shin is hurt?" That was the answer . . . (Lincoln Steffens, *The Autobiography of Lincoln Steffens* [New York: Harcourt, Brace & World, Inc., 1931], pp. 219, 220.)

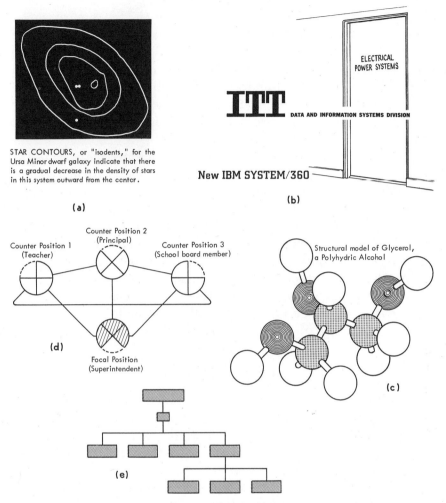

STAR CONTOURS, or "isodents," for the Ursa Minor dwarf galaxy indicate that there is a gradual decrease in the density of stars in this system outward from the center.

(a)

ELECTRICAL POWER SYSTEMS

ITT DATA AND INFORMATION SYSTEMS DIVISION

New IBM SYSTEM/360

(b)

Counter Position 1 (Teacher)

Counter Position 2 (Principal)

Counter Position 3 (School board member)

(d)

Focal Position (Superintendent)

Structural model of Glycerol, a Polyhydric Alcohol

(c)

(e)

Sources: (a) Paul W. Hodge, "Dwarf Galaxies," *Scientific American*, Vol. 210, No. 5 (May, 1964), p. 81; (c) A. B. Garrett, J. F. Haskins and H. H. Sisler, *Essentials of Chemistry* (New York: Ginn and Co., 1951), p. 347. ;(d) Neal Gross, Ward S. Mason, and Alexander W. McEachern, *Explorations in Role Analysis* (New York: John Wiley & Sons, 1958), p. 53.

FIG. 2–1. Representations of systems: (a) galactic, (b) information and data-processing systems, (c) a molecular system, (d) and (e) microsocial systems.

example of a social system a family of four. We might represent the system of social relationships in some such fashion as shown in (*d*) in Figure 2–1. The lines represent relationships; the circles, roles. Each of these persons is linked with three others by common understandings, reciprocal obligations, and privileges. Whether the wife is to be decorous, docile, and an adornment for her husband or a career woman commuting to work while her children are consigned to the care of a sitter depends largely on the role prescribed by the culture inherited by members of her group.[9] Her conceptions of the wife's obligations, her notions of beauty, and even her idea of a desirable weight are culturally conditioned. And so, also, with the is's and ought's of her relationship to son and daughter. The integrity of a social system is rooted in the culturally given consensus.

And so to raise the question: How do we enter the group—the human group, first of all, or any of the smaller and particular groups thereafter—is to ask: How do we get culture? For to become a member of society, of a family, a community, to join a church, to enter school, to become a citizen, to join a club, to enter military service, to get married, to join a union, a civic organization, a play group—*to enter any group* requires that we know, believe, and feel "properly." Only when we know the score can we articulate our behavior effectively with others. How do we come to know the score? How do we become encultured, and able to take on various roles in the groups of which we are members?

THE MEANING OF CULTURE

But let us be clear, first, what we mean by the word *culture*. It is a central concept in anthropology and indeed for some anthropologists, anthropology *is* culturology, the science of culture. It is also central for sociology, for it embodies the rules that define the roles which make the relationships that make the group. Hence we must be clear about its meaning. The commonest and simplest definition of culture consists of two words: social heritage (or social legacy). It is ". . . the total life way of a people," says Kluckhohn.[10] It is ". . . that part of the environment that is the creation of man." But "social heritage" and "life way" are spongey phrases, conveying just enough meaning to engender a premature sense of having grasped an idea, yet not enough to put it to use. And the notion of a man-made environment conveys the false notion that culture consists in perishable hardware. I find the classic definition of culture

---

[9] In a society so complex as ours the wife's role will vary, of course, by subcultures. Different regions, different classes, rural and urban settings may represent subcultures differing in conception of the woman's role.

[10] Clyde Kluckhohn, *Mirror for Man* (New York: McGraw-Hill–Whittlesey, 1949), p. 17.

by Tylor rather more satisfactory, yet not so from another point of view. In his *Primitive Culture,* Tylor wrote:

> Culture or civilization, taken in its wide ethnographic sense, is that complex whole which includes knowledge, belief, art, morals, law, custom and any other capabilities and habits acquired by man as a member of society.[11]

While this seems a good beginning for grasping the meaning of culture, it makes a bad ending. For it is an enumerative definition. (What is a mammal? A mammal is Sophia Loren, an opossum, a whale. What is fruit? Fruit is kumquats, tomatoes, mangoes.) The question remains: What is it that all these things have in common? That which all manifestations of culture have in common, I suggest, is knowledge; and I propose, therefore, this definition: Culture is socially shared and transmitted *knowledge,* both existential and normative, symbolized in act and artifact.[12]

That is to say, first of all—and here I follow Professor Murdock[13] —culture is learned: it is socially transmitted from parents to child, from elders to youth, from drill sergeant to inductee, from priest to novitiate, from generation to generation.

> Every new generation has to learn to accommodate itself to an order which is defined and maintained mainly by the older. Every society imposes some sort of discipline upon its members. Individuals grow up, are incorporated in the life of the community, and eventually drop out and disappear. But the community, with the moral order which it embodies, lives on.[14]

Now what is learned is, in one way or another, taught. What is generally taught to the young is what is commonly thought to be *necessary.* Culture is forcefully inculcated. There is a mandatory element in it. It is not a *comme çi, comme ça* affair. As we are instructed in *South Pacific,* "You've got to be taught, before it's too

---

[11] E. B. Tylor, *Primitive Culture* (New York: Henry Holt & Co., Inc., 1889).

[12] Since writing this I have run across an old note recording Robert Redfield's definition of culture. It is so similar to mine that I fear I may have unintentionally borrowed it. He defines culture, somewhere, as ". . . an organized body of conventional understandings manifest in art and artifact which, persisting through tradition, characterizes a human group." In my definition I mean, by "existential," that which is conceived to exist, what *is,* and by "normative" that which is deemed appropriate or desirable, what *ought* to be.

[13] George Peter Murdock, *Social Structure* (New York: Macmillan Co., 1949).

[14] Robert E. Park, "The Urban Community as a Spatial Pattern and a Moral Order," in E. W. Burgess (ed.), *The Urban Community* (Chicago: University of Chicago Press, 1926), p. 12.

late / Before you are 6, or 7 or 8 / to hate all the people your relatives hate / You've got to be carefully taught."* One *must* learn his mother tongue. He must learn enough arithmetic to do the shopping, pay the bills, and balance a checkbook. He must become domesticated. Culture has this coercive element. Culture, being generally shared, represents the expectations that large numbers of powerful adults have of the newcomer. It exercises constraint upon him. It has the characteristics of what Durkheim called the "social fact": *generality, exteriority,* and *constraint.* This may seem a dismal doctrine, denying what must seem apparent to every casual observer, that man is an active innovator rather than a passive conformist. One need not gainsay man's creative capacity to assert that culture sets the conditions for creativity.

> Man makes his own history, but he does not do so independently or under conditions of his own choice. The tradition of all past generations weighs like a mountain on the mind of the living.†

Reflecting this characteristic of culture is the term "press" introduced by Henry Murray[15] to refer to the impact of cultural influences upon the person. Similarly, Pace and Stern[16] attempt to get at the press of the college culture through their College Characteristics Index. How does the college subculture, its regulations, standards, its patterns of reward and punishment exercise leverage on the learning behavior of the student?

What is taught requires a teacher, whether or not formally designated as such—which is to say that the transmission of culture is a social matter, as is the fact of its being shared. The social character of enculturation must be set over against geographical and biological factors. Culture is not determinatively linked to a geographic base or to such biological factors as race, age, or sex. Manhattan is not a fishing village despite its location. And so far is culture from being biologically rooted that it would be more plausible to reverse the relationship, suggesting that biological characteristics stem from cultural factors.

---

* From "You've Got to Be Carefully Taught." Copyright © 1949 by Richard Rodgers and Oscar Hammerstein, 2nd. Used by permission of the publisher, Williamson Music, Inc., New York, New York.

† See Original Texts, Note 1, at end of chapter.

[15] Henry Murray, *Explorations in Personality* (New York: Oxford University Press, 1939).

[16] C. Robert Pace and George C. Stern, *College Characteristics Index* (New York: Psychological Research Center, Syracuse University, 1958).

Prof. Stanley Garn illustrates the point: "In what other animal does a railroad track serve as an effective barrier to gene flow?"[17] He goes on to point out that what is eaten, how much and how often, is affected by our culturally conditioned eating patterns. Again, the level of fertility in a population may be affected by such culturally conditioned factors as mean age at marriage and the culturally conditioned extent of sexual activity, including ritual taboos. He gives further illustrations: The ". . . middle class American child, reared by moderately authoritarian and relatively apprehensive parents, is protected from over-exertion"—play periods, naps, etc. There is sufficient contrast with lower-class behavior, on this score, so that even if caloric intake in the two groups were comparable, "the caloric expenditure is not. And the difference, caloric intake minus caloric expenditure, represents the energy reserve available for tissue maintenance and growth."

> . . . the high October-through-April temperatures of the American household (which distress visiting Europeans so markedly) may have a hothouse effect on the children allowing the maximum usage of the energy intake for growth.
> . . . practices affecting one sex alone. In many parts of the world, women eat apart from the men, girls get the soup while boys get the meat. Or both sexes may eat with the women until puberty, with the boys transferring to the men's table thereafter. Boy babies may be suckled longer (to make them strong), or weaned earlier (to make them independent). Such child-rearing practices may be expected to have a marked effect upon stature and weight, producing growth curves markedly different from those customarily encountered.

When in our definition we say that culture is knowledge of what is and what ought to be, we emphasize its *ideational* character. Culture is not to be confused with the acts and artifacts that symbolize it. Buttons, bowlers, and bikinis are not culture: they are indexes of culture. They symbolize the extensive knowledge in agriculture, manufacture, chemistry, animal husbandry, merchandising, advertising, metallurgy, bookkeeping, accounting, and corporate organization which enable their production. Not only do they symbolize the *what is* sort of knowledge. What *ought to be* is implicit in the choice of this garment over another (trousers instead of a kilt); and the implied constraint when, for a given occasion, this

[17] This and the two following quotations are from Stanley M. Garn, "Cultural Factors Affecting the Study of Human Biology," *Human Biology*, Vol. 26, No. 2, May, 1954, by permission of the Wayne State University Press.

clothing is preferred to that. I would not speak, therefore, as Ogburn[18] does, of material and nonmaterial culture as though they were coordinate. This jumbles together jet planes, toothbrushes, steel and concrete, the ideal of monogamous marriage, baked beans, razor blades, and the commitment to decisions by majority vote. Such a bifurcation, material and nonmaterial, confounds the concept.

Again, what these things have in common is the ideational element. Act and artifact are symbols of common understandings which include: (1) discrimination of the object, and knowledge of its meaning; (2) knowledge of the techniques of production and/or use; (3) knowledge of its worth. Nor would I say that the rate of growth in material culture outstrips that of the nonmaterial culture. This is an Alice-in-Wonderland race between creatures of different realms. A better statement would be that the accumulation of culture (knowledge) is irregular in both its existential and normative aspects: sporadic in time and uneven as between various realms of human activity. The result is that elements of culture are variously distributed. In some cases they may differ to the extent of being incompatible, even contradictory, as Professor Lynd will presently illustrate.

If culture is ideational, if it resides in our knowledge of what is and what ought to be, then it must be conveyed symbolically. "Of all aspects of culture, it is a fair guess that language was the first to receive a highly developed form and that its essential perfection *is a prerequisite* to the development of culture as a whole."[19] The significance of language in and for culture is stressed by Dewey. "Society not only continues to exist *by* transmission, *by* communication, but it may fairly be said to exist *in* transmission, *in* communication. There is more than a verbal tie between the words common, community, and communication."[20] The sense and reality of a common culture are given in language. The objects of life and our experiences with them are shaped by a prefabricated system of symbols, a legacy from the past, influencing both perceptions and conceptions. The terms, the gestures, the inflections and associated

---

[18] William F. Ogburn, *Social Change* (New York: Viking Press, 1930).

[19] E. Sapir, "Language and Culture," *Encyclopedia of the Social Sciences* (New York: Macmillan Co., 1930), Vol. IX, pp. 155–68 (italics mine).

[20] John Dewey, *Democracy and Education* (New York: Macmillan Co., 1921), p. 5.

affect, the range and richness of vocabulary—these vary with age and sex, time, place, and circumstance.[21] The shared definitions of the situation implicit in language have both a selective and a directive influence on man's conduct. Relevant objects are indicated to the exclusion of other objects: a piece of obsidian, a carburetor, cow dung, manioc.

But the symbol also embraces the social meaning of the object. The obsidian is for a knife, useful among other things in competitive destruction with rival Indians. The carburetor is an essential part of our civilization on wheels, providing an air-and-fuel mixture for controlled explosions in most internal combustion engines. The dung is to be made into patties for warmth, in India; or in the U.S.A., to be loaded on the manure spreader to fertilize the fields. The manioc is to be eaten although, being poisonous, it must be artfully leached to render it edible. The word, its inflection, the frequency with which it is used, the number of words used to describe an object—these give us some clue as to its importance to those who use the object, speak the word. The more language devoted to a given object, the greater its cultural significance for the group.[22] Cases in point are the great number of terms for Buffalo and parts of this animal among the Plains Indians; the great number and diversity of terms referring to maize and its uses among the agricultural Indians; or the highly refined discrimination between kinds of snow among Eskimo groups. Thus language, the chief carrier of culture, reveals its symbolic and ideational character.

To mention three such groups as the Pueblos, the Plains Indians, and the Eskimos is to remind ourselves of the enormous variation between cultures—and of certain related matters: the process of diffusion as a way by which cultures are diversified, the ethnocentrism displayed in rejecting other varieties of culture, and the inconsistencies likely to emerge in a variegated culture or between subcultures. Consider these matters briefly: the diversity in the range of culture, ethnocentrism, and inconsistent elements in culture.

People's behavior—and the products of their behavior—reveal the great range of the cultural spectrum: from the queer conduct of

---

[21] See, or rather hear, Professor Walter Goldschmidt's useful recording for the National Association of Educational Broadcasters, entitled "A Word in Your Ear."

[22] See, e.g., the pleasant essay by Weston LaBarre, entitled "Social Cynosure and Social Structure," in which he discusses the remarkable preoccupation, in the U.S., with the nubile female. (*Journal of Personality*, Vol. XIV, pp. 169–83.)

the Snacirema[23] to our own cultural patterns which seem so much more plausible to us, from our alleged monogamy to others' polygyny and polyandry, from our "conspicuous consumption" to the conspicuous destruction of Kwakiutl and Tlingit, from our cult of romance and cheesecake to unions quite terrestially ordained by parents (sometimes before the birth of one of the partners), from snakehandling protestant sects to Zen Buddhism, from space ships to Missouri mules.[24]

But cultural diversity can be seen even within our own country. There is marked regional variation revealed in dialect, habits, and preferences. The D.A.R. has taken special interest in one variant, the culture of small Appalachian enclaves where isolation has preserved in purer form the Anglo-Saxon heritage. Some are convinced that culture, in the vulgar sense of the term, is bounded on the west by the Hudson river; and that the center from which refinement radiates is in "the home of the bean and the cod" where the Lowells, the Cabots, and God form an exclusive trinity. In any case, many traits vary widely within the United States. For example, East and West Coast dwellers were found by Stouffer[25] to be more tolerant than mid-Westerners of atheism, communism, and socialism. City dwellers have been shown to vary quite consistently in their beliefs and behavior from rural residents. It is at least conceivable that modes of life and norms of conduct so differentiate urban from rural that we have here, symbolized in space, the schizoid character of contemporary life: the split between an expressive and an instrumental orientation, between the world of the heart and that of the head, between giving and getting, between a world of social and one of physical objects. But the contrast, which I've exaggerated here, is diminished with greater mobility, extension of mass media, national standards and controls.

Our cultural diversity results largely from imports—and this despite a propensity to view our beliefs and behaviors as indigenously American (or French, German, Irish, or Russian), ours by ordinance of God and nature. Conversely, other peoples' ways are

---

[23] Horace Miner, "Body Ritual Among the Snacirema," *American Anthropologist,* Vol. LVIII (June, 1956), pp. 503–7.

[24] This diversity is best documented in the Human Relations Area Files begun some years ago at Yale. Duplicates of this file are found at major universities throughout the country. They provide comparative data on hundreds of tribes around the globe, classified by type of behavior.

[25] Samuel A. Stouffer, *Communism, Conformity and Civil Liberties* (New York: Doubleday & Co., 1955), pp. 60–62 *passim*.

often seen as unnatural and barbarous. This tendency to depreciate others' ways and to appreciate our own is called ethnocentrism. Ethnocentrism is doubtless a universal characteristic, a function of isolation and a concomitant of the loyalty which is necessary for self-identification and persistence of the group. For DeGaulle's France there is the mystique of the world's civilized core to reassert, the grandeur of *La Patrie*. Hence a poor showing at the Olympics becomes a *catastrophe d'état*. For Hitler's Germany there was the primacy of the "Aryan" dominated heartland, a sacred trinity of blood, soil, and culture. "I have seen the phenomena at every level," Granville Hicks wrote,

> . . . the snobs disdaining the lower classes; the intellectuals with their scorn for the booboisie; the communists rubbing out the capitalists, and (at certain stages) the reactionary middle class and the un-class-conscious proletariat. I know all the words that shut people out: intelligentsia, liberal, progressive, right-thinking, Nordic, Gentile, 100% American. What is dangerous in these words is not that they imply "I'm right and you are wrong," for that can be argued about and should be. No, the danger lies in the assumption, "I exist and you don't."[26]

In the United States, our ethnocentric predispositions are likely to be revealed in our esteem of 100 percent Americanism. Ralph Linton has commented so effectively on the fiction of native self-sufficiency, that he is worth quoting at length, especially since he helps peg the point about cutural diversity.

> There can be no question about the average American's Americanism or his desire to preserve this precious heritage at all costs. Nevertheless some insidious foreign ideas have already wormed their way into his civilization without his realizing what is going on. Thus dawn finds the unsuspecting patriot garbed in pajamas, a garment of East Indian origin; and lying in a bed built on a pattern which originated in either Persia or Asia Minor. He is muffled to the ears in un-American materials: cotton, first domesticated in India; linen, domesticated in the Near East; wool from an animal native to Asia Minor; or silk whose uses were first discovered by the Chinese. All these substances have been transformed into cloth by methods invented in Southwestern Asia. . . .
>
> On awakening he glances at the clock, a medieval European invention, uses one potent Latin word in abbreviated form, rises in haste, and goes to the bathroom. . . . But the insidious foreign influence pursues him even here. Glass was invented by the ancient

[26] Granville Hicks, *Small Town* (New York: The Macmillan Co., 1946), p. 261.

Egyptians, use of glazed tiles for floors and walls in the Near East, the porcelain in China, and the art of enameling on metal by Mediterranean artisans of the Bronze Age. Even his bathtub and toilet are but slightly modified copies of Roman originals. The only purely American contribution to the ensemble is the steam radiator. . . .

[And so on, through his dressing, his breakfast, his dishes, to the point of his departure for the commuter's train.]

Breakfast over, he places upon his head a molded piece of felt, invented by the nomads of Eastern Asia and, if it looks like rain, puts on outer shoes of rubber, discovered by the ancient Mexicans, and takes an umbrella, invented in India. He then sprints for the train—the train, not the sprinting, being an English invention. At the station he pauses for a moment to buy a newspaper, paying for it with coins invented in ancient Lydia. Once on board he settles back to inhale the fumes of a cigarette invented in Mexico, or a cigar invented in Brazil. Meanwhile, he reads the news of the day, imprinted in characters invented by the ancient Semites by a process invented in Germany upon a material invented in China. As he scans the latest editorial pointing out the dire results to our institutions of accepting foreign ideas, he will not fail to thank a Hebrew God in an Indo-European language that he is a one hundred percent (decimal system invented by the Greeks) American (from Americus Vespucius, Italian geographer).[27]

Of course it would be surprising if, in a culture so diverse in its origins, so complex and so rapidly changing, certain inconsistencies and antitheses did not appear. Professor Lynd highlights some of these antithetical elements in the culture of the United States:[28]

Individualism, "the survival of the fittest," is the law of nature and the secret of America's greatness; and restrictions on individual freedom are un-American and kill initiative.

BUT: No man should live for himself alone; for people ought to be loyal and stand together and work for common purposes.

. . . . .

Hard work and thrift are signs of character and the way to get ahead.

BUT: No shrewd person tries to get ahead nowadays by just working hard, and nobody gets rich nowadays by pinching nickels. It is important to know the right people. If you want to make money, you have to look and act like money. Anyway, you only live once.

Education is a fine thing.

BUT: It is the practical men who get things done.

. . . . .

---

[27] Ralph Linton, "One Hundred Percent American," *The American Mercury*, Vol. XL (April, 1939).

[28] Reprinted from *Knowledge for What?* by Robert Lynd by permission of Princeton University Press, copyright 1939. All rights reserved.

Patriotism and public service are fine things.

BUT: Of course, a man has to look out for himself.

Poverty is deplorable and should be abolished.

BUT: There never has been enough to go around, and the Bible tells us that "The poor you have always with you."

No man deserves to have what he hasn't worked for. It demoralizes him to do so.

BUT: You can't let people starve.

One such antithesis in our culture presented the problem, the theme, and the title of Gunnar Myrdal's important volume, *An American Dilemma.*[29]

Such discrepancies—in Myrdal's work, *de jure* equality vs. *de facto* inequality—imply stress. Antithetical principles are invoked to support incompatible policies and contradictory proposals. The attempt to resolve the issue, in practice and principle, involves strain. There is, William Graham Sumner[30] suggested in his classic work, *Folkways,* a strain toward consistency in the mores. The Supreme Court decision on the integration of schools is one example of this tendency to move toward a position consistent with other elements of American culture. It was a partial resolution of the antithesis: (1) all men are created equal; and (2) the white man is genetically superior (and, *sotto voce,* should be accorded, in custom and in law, privilege consonant with his superiority).

Yet despite the gaps and gulfs, sociologists and anthropologists have both assumed and found prevailing themes, certain motifs which thread their way through the score of a culture. The underlying assumption is that ". . . the ideas of every epoch in history are related, usually with one dominant concept setting the key-tone for the others."[31] In her *Patterns of Culture,* Ruth Benedict[32] tried to isolate just such basic cultural configurations, summarizing them in such words as Dionysian (for the Kwakiutl) and Apollonian (for the Pueblo Indians). Such efforts telescope too many diverse observations in general terms of some obscurity. Geoffrey Gorer errs egregiously in this direction as he interprets the American character in terms of rebellion against the European

---

[29] Gunnar Myrdal, *An American Dilemma* (New York: Harper & Bros., 1944).

[30] William Graham Sumner, *Folkways* (Boston: Ginn & Co., 1940); first published in 1906.

[31] J. B. Bury, *The Idea of Progress* (New York: Dover Publications, Inc., 1955).

[32] Ruth Benedict, *Patterns of Culture* (New York: New American Library–Mentor Books, 1953); first published in 1934.

father image.[33] David Riesman seeks to uncover the design in American culture and its implications for the modal character in *The Lonely Crowd.*[34] Such brave attempts to crystallize, with conceptual parsimony, the diversity of a complex culture suffer the defects of hyperbole. Yet they have that primary scientific virtue of being provocative—in the case of Riesman, sufficiently provocative to stimulate significant research. Sociologists prefer verifiable statements about the cultural context of American society. This is why they are amused and disheartened, although occasionally enlightened, by the sweeping and confidently proclaimed generalizations about the modal character of a people made by the literati. (See the cavalier characterization of our culture in Mrs. Trollope's *The Domestic Manners of the Americans.*) But she is only one of many variously persuasive writers who spoke with commanding assurance on American society. Charles Dickens[35] was one of these—as was the more perceptive Alexis de Tocqueville, whose *Democracy in America*[36] has become a classic document in social history. And the tradition continues, even among members of the clan that gets most exercised about the social determinism of the social scientist and his disposition, as they say, to "pigeonhole" people. For example, Lawrence Durrell is only one of the latest among those who find a stable, culturally conditioned national character:

> Just as one particular vineyard will always give you a special wine with discernible characteristics so a Spain, an Italy, a Greece will always give you the same type of culture—will express itself through the human being just as it does through its wild flowers. We

---

[33] Geoffrey Gorer, *The American People* (New York: W. W. Norton & Co., Inc., 1948).

[34] David Riesman, Nathan Glaser, and Reuel Denny, *The Lonely Crowd* (New Haven: Yale University Press, 1950). The literature in the field of the national character is enormous, short on evidence and long on impressions, especially adverse ones. Recognizing that a few suggestions must be unrepresentative, it might nonetheless be well to supplement the references to novelists, travelers, sociologists and anthropologists with the work of an historian and a political scientist. For an historian's view of the American character (and American culture) see Henry Bamford Parkes, *The American Experience* (New York: Alfred A. Knopf, Inc., 1947). Here the white southerner is characterized on pp. 211, 212; and American character in general on pp. 236, 115, 45 and, indeed, throughout the book. See also Richard Snyder and H. H. Wilson (eds.), *Roots of Political Behavior*, "The American Character," pp. 645–50 (New York: American Book Co., 1949).

[35] See Una Pope-Hennessy, *Charles Dickens* (New York: Howell, Soskin, Publishers, Inc., 1946), especially chap. xii, "Sampling America."

[36] Alexis de Tocqueville, *Democracy in America* (New York: Alfred A. Knopf, Inc., 1945).

tend to see culture as a sort of historic pattern dictated by the human will, but for me this is no longer absolutely true.

I don't believe the British character, for example, or the German has changed a jot since Tacitus first described it; and . . . if you want a bit of real, live Aristophanes, you have only to listen to the chaffering of the barrowmen and peddlers in the Athens Plaka. . . .[37]

There *is* this sort of stability in culture, a continuity in time linking past and future, and a pattern as between elements which damps out outrageous discrepancies. Culture tends to be conservative. Our trivial span of seventy years yields a false impression of change as we recapitulate, through the intervention of parents and teachers, aeons of cultural development. And even though we deal with surface features which had no exact prototype in past generations, the innovation rests, like the manifest portion of an iceberg, on an enormous submerged portion. For,

> . . . ideas, no less than the living beings in whose minds they arise, must be begotten by parents not very unlike themselves, the most original still differing but slightly from the parents that have given rise to them. Life is like a fugue, everything must grow out of the subject and there must be nothing new.[38]

This continuity of culture was stressed by Durkheim—the way in which

> Early generations are replaced by later ones, and meanwhile society remains with its own structure and its own particular character. . . . There is an identity between France of the middle ages and contemporary France that one cannot fail to recognize. And so while generations of individuals succeed one another, throughout this perpetual flux of particular personalities there is something that persists, society [culture] with its own mode of thought, its particular temperament. . . .*

The constancies of culture sometimes convey the impression of a supernatural force acting independently of persons. If we speak metaphorically about the "power" of culture, or say that culture "specifies" appropriate conduct for various roles, it is not to be taken as a new supernaturalism. Culture resides in persons. Customs in the group are habits in the individual. Cultural specifications of desirable

---

[37] Lawrence Durrell, "Landscape with Literary Figures," *New York Times Book Review*, June 12, 1960, Section VII, p. 1. Reprinted by permission of the Author. © 1960 by The New York Times Company.

[38] Samuel Butler, *The Way of All Flesh* (New York: Macmillan Co., 1925), p. 220.

* See Original Texts, Note 2, at end of chapter.

conduct are represented as norms of behavior. The word is made flesh! Professor Burgess has suggested that personality is the subjective aspect of culture. This definition of personality leaves out of account certain biophysical attributes which may be relevant in understanding personality.[39] But it points to an important idea. Common elements of culture are introjected by members of the group, becoming central parts of their personalities. Thus there is provided a framework of common meaning enabling relationships between members of the group. Common meanings assigned to objects (including other human beings and their behaviors) creates a high probability that anticipated responses will, in fact, occur. If I am blistered with epithets, it is because I have known how to arouse antagonism and because the offended person knows how to retaliate in such a way as to hurt or infuriate me. We share a body of culturally provided meanings which allow us to manipulate others' responses, to elicit predictable behavior. Since these meanings must be conveyed symbolically, the significance of language for human relationships is apparent. Incidentally, as Weber suggests in his definition of a social relationship, the meanings involved are not "true" meanings in any metaphysical sense. The meaning is given, arbitrarily, by the culture and forcefully inculcated in each person entering the group. And so friendship, hostility, superordinate-subordinate relationships may not be defined in the same way by an observer as by the people so related. It is also true that the subjective meanings may not be identical for the persons related. This is implied, of course, when we say that people have had a misunderstanding.

Nevertheless, there is no enduring group so cavalier in the transmission of its culture as to allow great variation in the meanings attached to important acts and objects. Custom in the cultural realm has its parallels in habits and norms, in the psychological and social realms, respectively. There is, of course, deviation. In wartime, a few men are conscientious objectors. Some students are "grinds" and others "goof off." But in mundane matters of everyday life and especially where public sentiment is strong, deviation is negligible. Commonly held views and values give rise to similar behaviors under similar circumstances. We must infer widely shared stand-

---

[39] See, for a stronger biopsychological conception of personality, Clyde Kluckhohn and Henry Murray, *Personality in Nature, Society and Culture* (New York: Alfred A. Knopf, Inc., 1953).

ards for behavior (norms) that underly these patterns of conduct.

Norms, then, are revealed in modal[40] behavior and reflect elements of the culture commonly shared and internalized by members of the group. Such was the norm revealed by the production mode of 6,600 units among a group of workers observed by Roethlisberger and Dickson at a plant of the Western Electric Company in Cicero, Illinois.[41] To produce more was to be a rate-buster; to produce less, a chiseler. There is, as it were, a golden mean which best fits the cultural prescriptions. This is characteristic of many dimensions of many behaviors. Take the dimension of goodness as defined by honesty. Somewhere in between a compulsive truthfulness and unreliable mendacity there seems to lie the approved norm in American society. Gordon Allport has investigated this tendency for behaviors to "peak" in their frequencies, so revealing norms of conduct characteristic of our culture.[42]

CULTURAL CHANGE

If culture provides those common understandings registered in norms, making for predictability in men's relationships and so promoting stability in the social order, it also has a potential for

---

[40] **An Aside on Methods: Three Measures Providing Summary Descriptions of Group Characteristics**

Modal is the adjective, mode the noun referring to the most frequent value in a distribution. It is one of three sorts of summary statements often used to give a partial description of a series of values. The other two are the mean ($\bar{X}$) and the median. The median is the value of that term which is midway in the distribution. The mean is the arithmetic average, the value obtained by adding all values in the distribution and dividing by the number of such values. As an illustration, suppose that we have this record of the weekly production of units of something or other by

	Mon.	Tues.	Wed.	Thurs.	Fri.
Man A	6,600	5,700	6,700	6,800	6,600
Man B	6,500	6,700	6,600	6,600	6,600
Man C	6,800	6,600	6,400	6,600	6,700

three men. The most frequently occurring value, the mode, is 6,600 units. The mean, the sum of these values divided by the number of them (15) is 6,566. The median, the midpoint in the distribution of values is 6,600 (midway between the 1st and the 15th values, arranged in ascending or descending order).

[41] F. J. Roethlisberger and W. J. Dickson, *Management and the Worker* (Cambridge, Mass.: Harvard University Press, 1940).

[42] Gordon Allport, "The J-Curve Hypothesis of Non-Conforming Behavior," in G. E. Swanson, T. M. Newcomb and E. L. Hartley (eds.), *Readings in Social Psychology* (2d ed.; New York: Henry Holt & Co., Inc., 1952), pp. 231–42.

generating change. This is so to the extent that there lie latent in the cultural backlog elements whose combination would constitute an innovation. The cultural backlog is made up of the sum of that knowledge, existential and normative (knowledge of what is and what ought to be) available to the society under consideration. Since ideas are mercurially mobile, especially in the modern world, this means in effect that the cultural stockpile of a given people is a worldwide body of knowledge. And since the availability of complementary ideas is a prime condition of cultural elaboration, the persistence, unmodified, of most beliefs and behaviors is unlikely. As one isolated example, knowledge (conceptions of what ought to be, as well as of what is) was markedly affected by the development of atomic fission: religion, the industries affected by extraction of fissionable materials, business, obviously the military, medicine, research, the power industry, national government, and international relations including the work of the United Nations, NATO, and the like. Knowledge is, as the Garden of Eden demonstrated, remarkably disruptive. Of such disruptions there is no end because of the crescive character of culture. Few elements of culture are really lost (although both meaning and use may be radically changed): many are added.

And so, if culture provides the meanings that inform human relationships, and if the cultural system is continuously altered by novel inputs (new infusions), the meanings change and the network of relationships must change. It is claimed that atomic power has changed the meaning of war. As a consequence we must either reconstruct our warmaking patterns (the notion of brush-fire wars) or our peace-preserving patterns, or both. Either of these alternatives involves significant changes in the patterning of human relationships, first of all in political and military networks, but with obvious repercussions throughout all spheres of social life.

Having attested the significance of this aspect of culture, we might raise in passing the question of the conditions and character of cultural change. Gilfillan[43] and Ogburn[44] have written instructively on the conditions of invention. The crucial condition is the fructifying interplay of complementary ideas. This condition is best fulfilled in scientific disciplines; for they recognize it, explicitly,

---

[43] S. C. Gilfillan, *The Sociology of Invention* (Chicago: Follett Pub. Co., 1935).

[44] William F. Ogburn, Gene L. Adams and S. C. Gilfillan, *The Social Effects of Aviation* (Boston: Houghton Mifflin Co., 1946).

and institutionalize means for exchanging ideas. Chase[45] gives some conception of the importance of this condition in the following report which highlights some of the stages in the elaboration of our knowledge of atomic fission.

> The inevitable bond, bridging time and space and linking men in common enterprise is clearly seen in the development of atomic energy. In 1870, the great French chemist Lavoisier determined the difference between elements and compounds and laid down the principle of the conservation of matter. Twenty-eight years later, Dalton formulated early atomic theory stating that all atoms of a given element, like iron, are alike and combine with atoms of other elements to form molecules. Then in 1869 Mendeleev, a Russian chemist arranged the 75 known elements into the famous periodic table and predicted a total of 92 elements on the basis of blanks in the table. He was presently confirmed by experiment. About this time, J. J. Thompson discovered the existence of charges which he called electrons. In 1895, the German, Roentgen, discovered X-rays. A year later, Becquerel found that uranium was radioactive. Soon it was announced that the French scientists, Pierre and Marie Curie had found radium. The Englishman Rutherford then exploded the notion that the atom was like a billiard ball. Instead, he suggested that the atom was like a solar system—a nucleus surrounded by revolving electrons. Presently the Swede, Bohr, worked out the electron circuits of various atoms. Successive contributions were made by Soddy, Aston, Urey and Chadwick; and then, in the 1930's Einstein's equation $E = MC^2$ was brought in to explain the loss of mass when protons and neutrons combine to form helium. Matter was transformed into energy. . . . Other contributions were made by Hahn and Strassman and by Lise Meitner. . . . She evolved the revolutionary hypothesis that a chain reaction could be developed. This idea was confirmed by Frisch, Fermi, Szilard in March 1939; and finally, in 1940, Chadwick was certain that anyone could make an atomic bomb with the published knowledge available provided he wanted to spend the time and money.

A condition of cultural accretion, then, is contact. Innovation is a product of shared enterprise and intellect; it is a social matter, often transcending national boundary lines and covering indefinite time spans.

Of course contact is not always so consciously contrived, nor is change so consciously directed as in the case of atomic fission. In Bali, Indonesia, for example, the culture is undergoing radical changes as it combines, in varying degree, with elements from the

---

[45] Stuart Chase, *The Proper Study of Mankind* (New York: Harper & Bros., 1956).

Western world. Young nationalists are, as they say, "modernizing" Bali. This involves new schools, a new language (Indonesian and English rather than Balinese), the denial of old beliefs called "superstitions," the intrusion of Hollywood movies revealing Western technology together with the film versions of American love and crime. The traditional gamelan orchestras (the gamelan is a kind of xylophone) are being gradually modified, reflecting cultural diffusion. "Recently, a rajah in North Bali included violins and an accordion in the performance of his gamelan orchestra. The new instruments discreetly were placed behind a screen."[46] Similarly, hereditary rajahs were retained as administrative heads in a government being gradually westernized. It is probably true that most cultural elaboration has been a consequence of unwitting rather than planned contact in support of cultural growth. For example, in Linton's discussion of traits in American culture imported from other societies (I count over fifty such culture traits in his article, including pajamas, silk, glass, coffee, rubber, cigarettes, coins, a conception of God, eleven sorts of cultivated plants—and coming from more than twenty-five sources), few if any were contrived additions to the culture as is the case in the collaborative growth of science.

The elaboration of a culture depends, then, upon contact. But contact itself is conditioned by means, motivation, and resistances. The means are those available in terms of the present state of knowledge. Our means of transport and communication are today adequate to penetrate every known society. But whether energy shall be invested in new products and new ideas depends on normative elements in the culture, on what we value. In any society, culture is selectively cumulative. Early Americans borrowed with gratitude from the Indians (Amerinds) their corn, methods of cultivation and fertilizing, and their snowshoes. They did not borrow much of their family, political, or religious systems. I hope this illustration does not convey the wrong notion. The motivation to seek or accept cultural innovation does not arise solely—or even chiefly—from man's efforts to adapt himself to his habitat. His desires go far beyond visceral satisfactions. His tastes are, as we say, cultivated. Human nature, like the culture of which it is a product, is a thing created, an artifact. It is not, then, to be regarded as something

---

[46] *New York Times*, October 28, 1951.

irrevocably set at birth. "The conventional statement that human nature does not change is plausible only so long as attention is focused on those aspects of it which are least distinctively human."[47] As human nature changes, the motivation for adaptive cultural change emerges.

A third condition of contact, and hence of cultural growth, is the degree of resistance to innovation. We think, for example, of the resistance to the adoption of insurance among members of certain religious groups, a practice viewed as gambling with God; or the resistance to the Copernican view of the solar system which Galileo encountered; the antipathy to the development of powerful and effective instruments of international control on the grounds that sovereignty is challenged; the withholding of inventions which would injure investments; resistance to contraceptive programs on religious grounds. It is to be assumed that any cultural innovation will be disruptive to some extent. For example, automobile manu- facturers must weigh with care the possible adverse effects an innovation may entail—in sales for their agents throughout the country, in making certain mechanics' skills obsolete, in eliminating the supplier of the part no longer needed, and the like.

But whatever the resistances, the fact of cultural accretion and growth is incontrovertible. In 1767, one of the founding fathers (Adam Ferguson) wrote:

> When nations succeed one another in the career of discoveries and inquiries the last is always the most knowing. Systems of science are gradually formed. The globe itself is traversed by degrees, and the history of every age, when past, is an accession of knowledge to those who succeed. The Romans were more knowing than the Greeks; and every scholar of modern Europe is, in this sense, more learned than the most accomplished person that ever bore either of those celebrated names.[48]

Each generation has what preceding generations had, *plus*. Indeed, the rate of increase seems to be increasing in many realms of culture. (Note the ever upward slope of lines tangent to the curve in the figure on page 68.) And this is what we would expect as the increments of knowledge provide an ever larger base to build on; for

---

[47] R. H. Tawney, *Religion and the Rise of Capitalism* (New York: Mentor Pocket Books, 1948), p. 19.

[48] Adam Ferguson, *An Essay on the History of Civil Society* (8th ed.; Philadel- phia: A. Finley, Publisher, 1819), p. 48.

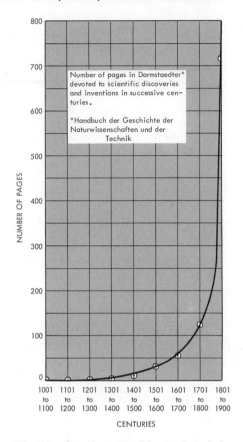

FIG. 2–2. Growth curve of human knowledge.

the larger the cultural base, the greater the number of possible permutations among the elements. This should give rise to the kind of curve found when one plots, over time, the number of pages used to record scientific discoveries and inventions (see Figure 2–2).

This figure conveys the impression that man is tied to the kitetail of a continuing technological revolution. There may be a bit of hyperbole in this figure. But cultural changes in the sphere of science and technology have been, to say the least, dramatic—and this within a relatively short period of time. Changes in other realms are doubtless less impressive, although woman suffrage, double-entry bookkeeping, contraception, neo-orthodox theology, the communal Kibbutzim of Israel, self-service merchandising, social security and other forms of insurance—such cultural increments have left their mark.

Efforts to chart the growth and fluctuations in culture have not been notably successful or useful. Early social theorists like Condorcet, St. Simon, Comte, and Spencer tied to the plausible observation of man's increasingly complex culture the evaluative notion of progress. Man's intellectual growth, Condorcet claimed, showed his potential for perfectibility and the irreversible nature of this cultural trend. Kant, Hegel, Marx, and Spengler tried their hands at tracing the course of cultural evolution. Among these, Marx made the most notable contribution, discerning the drive toward a redistribution of wealth, power, and opportunity but mistaking both the movers and the means. In the U.S., Lewis H. Morgan, pioneer anthropologist, identified, as he supposed, a unilinear cultural development as the form of the family, shifting from promiscuity, mother clans, father clans, and polygyny to patriarchal monogamy, reflected the triumph of democratic forms. So also has Sorokin provided some suggestions as to the nature of cultural growth and change. And although Sorokin, in particular, adduces illustrative data from a great variety of sources, such efforts have generally been too far removed from empirical reality and, by their nature, preclude empirical research. Hence they remain in the realm of speculative reconstructions of questionable validity.

THE CULTURE CONCEPT AS A TOOL OF INQUIRY

But the same stricture, it would seem, must apply to the concept of culture itself. Is it not too nebulous, abstract, fuzzy? Does it do more than provide us with a general set of assumptions: the diversity of human ways, the flexibility of human nature, the notion that conceptions of *what is* and *what ought* are systematically inculcated in those entering the group by persons responsible for such teaching, that there is a tendency to iron out discrepancies between elements of culture, that culture, being ideational, is readily diffused when communication is good and resistances are minimal, that it is selectively accumulative and in some realms of life grows at an amazing rate . . . ? Of course it is no little contribution if a concept is so fruitful that its explication provides a general framework of assumptions on which the structure of inquiry can be hung. Nonetheless, the question persists with this concept, as with any other tools in our theory kit: can the concept of culture be walked down the abstraction ladder to touch the realities of concrete behavior? If so, how do we do it? How do we "get at" culture? To answer these questions, it will be useful to come at them from three angles: (1) *dimensions* of analysis of culture; (2) the *content* of culture; and (3) some specific *techniques* of analysis as illustrations.

Dimensions of Analysis of Culture

Culture has been analyzed in several dimensions: in *space,* in the *time* dimension, in terms of the *generality* of culture traits, and in terms of their *complexity.* A culture area is a geographical region within which we find a trait or a cluster of traits characterizing persons and groups. Such traits may be the use of obsidian blades or woodpecker scalps, the complex of traits associated with maize or the buffalo, a given dialect, the igloo house or the teepee. When plotting the distribution of such culture traits in space, we often find that the boundaries are not clear-cut, a given trait simply becoming less and less characteristic until, finally, it fades away.

The matter of plotting culture areas is complicated, too, since frequently a practice, although apparently similar in two groups, may have different meanings. Pre-Columbian culture areas have been charted for the United States and for considerable portions of the rest of the world. Nor have we dealt exclusively with preliterate peoples. In 1917, F. J. Galpin wrote his research bulletin on "The Social Anatomy of an Agricultural Community."[49] In this study he tried to define the limits of an agricultural community, a culture area, in terms of boundaries that embraced common activities: the area through which people subscribed to a given paper, used the same banking facilities, were drawn to central shopping areas, and the like. Although Wissler has suggested that there are only two clear-cut modern culture areas, that embracing oriental culture and that of Euro-American culture, it is clear that many smaller cultural areas are distinctive such as rural French Quebec,[50] or the Ozark and Appalachian regions of the United States. The delimitation of such areas yields some clues as to cultural diffusion in the past, and provides a bench mark for the analysis of subsequent inputs

---

[49] F. J. Galpin, "The Social Anatomy of an Agricultural Community" (University of Wisconsin Agricultural Experiment Station Research Bulletin No. 34, 1915).

[50] Horace Miner, *St. Denis, A French-Canadian Parish* (Chicago: The University of Chicago Press, 1939).

affecting the indigenous culture. But of more significance is the way in which area analysis sets the stage for detecting concomitant variation, for discovering what traits fit together, for posing the problem of functional connections.

In the time dimension, we are concerned with such things as significant seasonal celebrations and the temporal structuring of behaviors which memorialize central convictions and commitments of the group.[51] I would distinguish two sorts of ceremonies, although these categories are not exclusive and I doubt that they are exhaustive.

There is the ceremony that reaffirms traditional beliefs and behaviors. Christmas, Veterans Day, Yom Kippur, Easter, Mother's and Father's Days, Memorial Day, Sunday and Sabbath services, funerals—these are principally occasions for affirming the virtues embedded in tribal traditions and for recommitment to them. These are some of the institutional safeguards which assure that a man's mortality will not jeopardize the immortality of men.

There is a second sort of ceremony that serves to redefine the person's role, revealing the culturally prescribed structuring of the life span. Such ceremonies occur at pivotal points in the life history: at confirmation, at graduation, when the Australian, the Hopi, the Zuni, or American joins his fraternity or his religious organization, at marriage, at childbirth. In some groups these stages are clearly defined, in others ambiguously. It has been suggested that in U.S.

---

[51] A dramatic example of the temporal structuring of culture is reported by Marcel Mauss in his *Essai sur les Variations Saissonières des Sociétés Eskimos.* He writes:

In summer, members of the group live in widely dispersed tents. In winter, they live in tightly clustered houses. While the tent contains only one family, the winter dwelling usually contains several. . . . While the summer provides an almost limitless field for hunting and fishing, in winter, on the contrary, the hunting area is greatly restricted. . . . Religion among the Eskimos goes through the same cycle as the rest of their social organization. There is, so to speak, a summer religion and a winter religion: the private domestic cult of summer and the general state of religious fervor in the winter.

But this contrast between style of summer and winter living is seen not only in rites, celebrations and religious ceremonies of all sorts. It has an equally telling impact on ideas, collective representations—in a word, on the whole mental life of the group. In certain tribes during a series of festivals we see everybody divide into two groups. In one are all those born in winter: in the other, those born in the summertime.

Thus the very pattern of life is classified, men and things bearing the mark of this cardinal contrast between the two seasons. Each season serves to define a whole species of beings and things. One might say that the conceptions of winter and summer are like two poles around which the whole Eskimo thought system gravitates. [See Original Texts, Note 3, at end of chapter.]

society, adolescence is just such an ill-defined, never-never land, and that this ambiguity accounts for certain of the problems associated with adolescence. In any case, this sort of culturally prescribed temporal structuring of the person's life provides a clear-cut distinction between past and future, between duties and privileges of the previous stage and those of the succeeding stage. "When I was a child I spake as a child, I understood as a child, I thought as a child; but when I became a man I put away childish things." Observation of these rites of passage[52] provides clues as to the things deemed significant in a given group; and the appropriate means for achieving them. Consider a high school graduation, the themes expressed in invocation and benediction, the statements of salutatorian and valedictorian, the main speaker's analysis of the crisis we confront and what must be done to preserve the things we esteem. Consider the mottoes chosen to represent the spirit of the group: *Ad Astra per Aspera, Ad Summa Contendimus*, and the like.

Linton has suggested that a relevant dimension in the analysis of culture is the generality of the trait. There are some traits which are *universals*. Everyone does it, thinks it, believes it. Certain of the clothing habits of men and women, respectively, come close to being universals within a given group. At a second level of generality there are *specialties*. People are sharply discriminated in terms of their special training and particular talents. This is reflected in the specialization which is a concomitant of the division of labor. But specialties are also seen in different styles of life distinguishing categories of persons who would be incompetent to swap roles. At much expense and a world of trouble M. Jourdain finds it quite impossible to become a "gentleman";[53] and similarly, the provincial, middle-class, college-educated man finds it quite impossible to think, believe, or act in the role of a lower-class person. Again, there are *alternatives*—ways of thinking, believing, and acting which allow a wider range. One may do it this way, or he may do it that way. And finally, there are the *idiosyncracies* of personal behavior which are quite outside the culture pattern. We might observe in passing that this is not a clean, undimensional ordering of this

---

[52] The person who coined this phrase is often done the honor (so common has it become) of not being recognized as its author. See Arnold van Gennep, *The Rites of Passage* (Chicago: University of Chicago Press, 1960).

[53] The reference is, of course, to the enterprising hero of Molière's *Bourgeois Gentilhomme*.

dimension. In particular, the generality of the trait is confounded with the extent to which it is mandatory.

The commonest way of breaking down the concept of culture has been to see it in terms of level of *complexity:* traits, complexes, institutions, and themes. Traits refer to behavior focused on an object and the knowledge, existential and normative, involved in such behavior. The production and use of a football is a culture trait, characteristic of, but varying within, the Euro-American culture. It involves the knowledge that it is to be used chiefly in the autumn, in the context of team rivalry, conveys overtones of strength, virility, and associated prestige, techniques of handling, passing, kicking, and the like. Sumner referred to such specific customary acts and artifacts which can be discerned in a group as *folkways*.[54] They include all manner of customary behaviors, not for the most part mandatory, but traditionally handed down and carried out automatically, unreflectively: three meals a day, the use of cosmetics, cuffs on trousers and buttons on sleeves, applauding by clapping, shaking hands, the kiss to show affection, shaving, engagement and wedding rings, flowers and tombstones on graves, wearing ties, using the color black for adult funerals, white for children's, men removing hats in elevators, and the like.

Such elementary behaviors and their associated ideas pervade our lives. Indeed, "John Dewey has said in all seriousness that the part played by custom in shaping the behavior of the individual as over against any way in which he can affect traditional custom, is as the proportion of the total vocabulary of his mother tongue over against those words of his own baby talk that are taken into the vernacular of his family."[55] This view seems to render the individual impotent in the face of the folkways. But in reality, the extensive control of behavior through the folkways is fortunate since they represent ready-made decisions with which we need not preoccupy ourselves. While folkways are moderately binding, they are at the same time liberating. We would never get to bed—or, almost as disturbing, never get out of it—lacking those customary definitions and prescriptions which free us from solving every problem anew.

A second sort of culture trait is distinguished from the first in being charged with a sense of public welfare, moral rightness and,

---

[54] William Graham Sumner, *Folkways* (Boston: Ginn & Co., 1940).

[55] Cited in Ruth Benedict, *Patterns of Culture* (Boston: Houghton Mifflin Co., 1961), p. 2.

therefore, personal necessity. Such a trait is called a *mos* (plural, *mores*), after Sumner's use of the term. It involves such traits as the belief of some in segregating Negroes and whites, saluting the flag, standing up for the national anthem, uncovering in the presence of the dead, the male ostensibly taking the lead in dating-courting conduct, an attitude of reverence in church, and the commitment to universal suffrage (in the U.S.). We must be clear that such beliefs and behaviors thought to be right, good, and necessary, are likely to be so only within a given group. The sacred cow in India is a case in point, a creature ill-sustained on inadequate forage which may not be used for its meat by undernourished people. The mores are not necessarily right or true from some transcendental and objective point of view. They may be objectively detrimental. They are nonetheless thought, within the context of the culture, to be both necessary and desirable. Whether objectively right or wrong and regardless of the content of the behaviors and beliefs, from the standpoint of the group the folkways and mores have this beneficial effect: they identify the like-minded, right-thinking people, promote a sense of solidarity, provide a basis for reciprocal support and for mutual protection against those beyond the pale.

The folkways and the mores do not stand alone, as isolated traits. Any given belief or behavior is intricately bound up with a whole network of knowledges, symbolized in act and artifact. That football mentioned above can be used illustratively. It symbolizes knowledge of butchering and skinning, the chemistry of tanning hides, knowledge of valves and the metallurgical and manufacturing skills involved, knowledge of rubber extraction and fabrication—or knowledge of the chemistry of synthetic rubber. It symbolizes stadia, school spirit, ranking systems reflected in the statuses of players among themselves from varsity through scrubs and between players and nonplayers. It involves professional and amateur gambling, the sports goods industry, the alumni association, musicians and cheerleaders—and schools and clinics for training them. It involves the administration and faculty of major universities in one of their largest budget items. It involves leagues of competing teams, bowl games, television, journalism, conceptions of education, recruitment for professional teams, local townspeople whose businesses are affected by the gladiatorial display. It involves rallies and bonfires, stirring speeches by players, coaches, deans, and miscellaneous dignitaries, cross-country travel, hotels, special food at train-

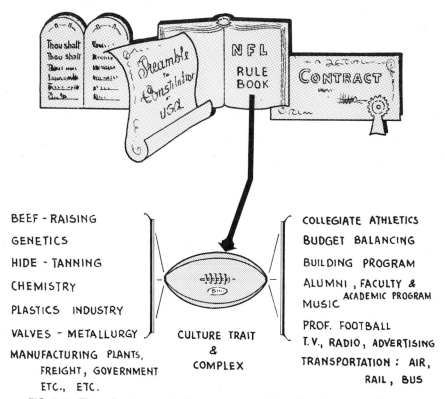

FIG. 2-3. The cultural context of human relationships: the rules that underlie roles and relationships, and their exemplification in clusters of conduct.

ing tables, advertising over the mass media which report the games.

This partial enumeration[56] suggests that the football (and other culture traits) can be seen as the focus of a whole complex of activities. And to this cluster of interconnected traits we give the name, *culture complex*. The maize complex, the football complex, the buffalo complex, the automotive complex refer to just such

[56] Under the lead, "Buckeyes Should Show $28,000 Profit" a sports writer says: Television has made the Rose Bowl game a genuine million-dollar attraction . . . The television sponsor is paying $500,000 for the rights to the game and that . . . plus gate receipts of about the same amount, goes into the main pot from which the sponsoring Tournament of Roses committee, the Pacific Coast conference and the Western conference share the booty. . . . After deduction of basic expenses, the Rose Bowl Committee keeps approximately 15 per cent for year-round operational costs . . . the president of the [Ohio State] university interjected a thought . . . "there actually is no profit motive in a trip of this kind. . . . We consider this Rose Bowl trip an investment in public relations. . . . We agree it is educational for the boys and also for the university administrators here. . . ." [Si Burick in the *Dayton Daily News*, January 2, 1955.]

clusters. Their spread and their dominance give us more adequate understanding of the behavior of people in a given group.

For those functions deemed indispensable by members of the group, regular ways of behaving must be *institutionalized*. Institutions are, then, enduring social structures operating for the achievement of culturally prescribed ends: the care, rearing, and indoctrination of the young, the propitiation of the Gods and the support of public morality, the production and allocation of wealth and power, the search for reliable knowledge, the care of physical, mental, and criminal dependents. Behavior in these realms is so vested with a public interest that societies are disposed to specify with precision and to sanction, rigorously, rights and duties informing the relationships in these social structures. That is to say, law steps in. Thus if parental care is inadequate, the courts have the power of appointing a guardian and so breaking the parent-child relationship. If a merchant defrauds his customers, his license may be revoked. Institutions, as I shall suggest in Part II, are, in fact, the gyroscope of the social and cultural systems. Someone has suggested that they are "frozen answers to basic questions." The very word, institutionalize, carries this connotation of conservative stability. And since all enduring groups have beliefs and ways of life they cherish, arrangements must be made for conserving them in the face of changing personnel and changing circumstance. The analysis of institutional patterns will carry us close to the central characteristics of a culture.

Some investigators have tried to get at such core characteristics by crosscutting institutions and less formal behavior patterns in the search for some theme or motif assumed to thread its way through all aspects of group life. The Mundugamor, the Tchambuli, the Arapesh, the Zuni, the Kwakiutl, and the Dobu have been described in such terms.[57] And so indeed have the peoples of more complex cultures: the Americans, the British, the Germans, and the French. Because the problem is so broadly posed and the data so uncertain, this is a very hazardous undertaking. I shall mention some of the ways of attacking it in the discussion of techniques.

Content of Culture

We have been thinking about *dimensions* of analysis of culture. But the dimensions of an object—length, breadth, height—are

---

[57] Ruth Benedict, *op. cit.;* Reo Fortune, *Sorcerers of Dobu* (London: George Routledge & Sons, Ltd., 1932); Margaret Mead, *Sex and Temperament in Three Primitive Societies* (New York: New American Library—Mentor Books, 1950).

different from the thing itself (a table, for example). We may attempt to describe and understand a culture in terms of the space dimension, the time dimension (the temporal structuring of culture through periodic affirmations), along the dimension of generality or in terms of complexity (trait, complex, institution, theme). But what is the concrete thing we look at? What is the content in a study of culture? The answer is given in our definition. We look at the *acts and artifacts that symbolize the knowledge,* both existential and normative, which constitutes culture. We look at men's behavior and the products of that behavior. The anthropologist in the field lives with his group, maintaining a dawn-to-dusk surveillance over his subjects in an unobtrusive, participant-observer style. The sociologist may observe behavior through a one-way screen, recording conversations, coding gestures and relating these to the problem dealt with and other relevant aspects of the situation. He may live in the neighborhood seeing, listening, working, playing—and recording—as Whyte did in "Cornerville" and as Hollingshead did in "Elmtown." Or he may sit quietly in one department of a business organization, observing and recording as Homans did. That is to say, first of all, his data may derive from people's acts. Or the observations may have to do with the products of men's acts—the things they write, the themes they use, the nature of their heroes and villains, the records of the patent office, the Sears, Roebuck catalog, the federal budget, popular plays and novels, Holy Writ, the law as it bears on the whole intricate network of men's dealings with one another. What the relevant data are, and what concrete observations should be made will obviously depend upon the problem posed.

Techniques of Analysis

The techniques involved in getting at culture are, roughly, these: direct observation, or analysis of others' observations. Direct observation is a very complicated business requiring both skill and wisdom. The categories of things to be observed must be set in the context of the problem and the problem in the context of relevant theory. The observer must be astute in picking up and recording both the objective act, the gestures and inflections, and, separated from this, the inferred subjective state of the actor. He must, if he is a participant observer, take care to observe the schizoid requirements of the role, identifying in a genuine way with his fellows in the situation, yet maintaining a degree of distance allowing him to appraise the behavior in objective fashion. He must not allow himself to become all participant or all observer. He must keep in mind the requirements of analysis: the sorting and manipulating of the data, and so make his observations as to meet these requirements.

Indirect observation requires the selection of reliable, relevant, and representative observations made by others. It then demands careful manipulation of the data in order to derive general summarizing statements, and statements revealing the interdependence of selected variables. Consider this example: McGranahan and Wayne compared American and German traits by analyzing the forty-five most popular plays in each country for a given year.[58] Although theater audiences could not be taken as representing the populations of the two countries, the investigators assumed that they could be thought of as literate and influential. If plays are successful because they give forceful expression to the thoughts and feelings of their audiences, then such data as these might be expected to tap basic themes in German and American culture. Criteria were carefully specified for determining the most popular plays.

> It was found that the structure of nearly all dramas could be described in terms of the pattern of conflict, the interplay of opposing forces, that underlay the plot; conflict between youthful lovers and parents, between honest folk and criminals, between revolutionary and reactionary political forces, between moral and immoral impulses within the individual . . . it was further found that these conflicts could be classified into six major categories called the "love" theme, the "morality" theme, the "idealism" theme, the "power" theme, the "career" theme, and the "outcast" theme.

Ninety summaries of these plays, with authors and titles deleted and settings disguised were analyzed by nine judges. Their task was to classify plays by theme, by type of ending, and the like. Examples of their findings are given below.

We find the American plays focusing on love and morality, the German plays on idealism and power. Personal goals and their pursuit, celebrated in American plays "are frequently portrayed as the root obstacle in the German plays, the materialism against which the idealist must fight. . . . While the American plays carry the

---

[58] Donald V. McGranahan and Ivor Wayne, "German and American Traits Reflected in Popular Drama," *Human Relations,* Vol. I, pp. 429–55, *passim.*

The Basic Themes: Distribution in Percent*

	U.S.	GERMANY
Love	60%	31%
Morality	36	9
Idealism	4	44
Power	2	33
Outcast	0	18
Career	11	9
Disagreement among judges	13	2

* These percentages do not add to 100 percent because some plays were classified as having two or more themes.

Level of Action (in Percent, as Coded for 45 Plays)

	U.S.	GERMANY
Ideological	4%	51%
Personal	96	47
Disagreement among judges		2

lesson that virtue [pays off], the lesson to be found in the German plays is that success in worldly conflicts is won through power and ruthlessness." Thus from men's artifacts (their plays, in this case) we can infer their views and values, their knowledge of what is and ought to be—i.e., their culture.

Similarly, the mass media—newspapers, radio programs, television, magazines—provide data amenable to content analysis aimed at identifying central themes and emphases in the culture. Such analyses may involve frequency counts of words, phrases, assertions pro and con, measures of intensity of statements, recurrent themes, and the like.

Many other techniques are available (some of them, like projective tests, fairly recently developed) for teasing out the judgments, beliefs, feelings, opinions, characteristics of a people. With the development of opinion polling and, in recent years, the use of carefully drawn probability samples, we are accumulating a wealth of data bearing on prevailing and changing cultural themes.

In contemporary societies, much detailed information must be gathered for administrative purposes. These data, too, may provide useful clues as to the nature of a people's culture.[59] The figures on

[59] See the publications of the U.S. Bureau of the Census, the U.S. Office of Vital Statistics, and those of the Department of Health, Education, and Welfare; as well as the publications of insurance companies and trade associations; the United Na-

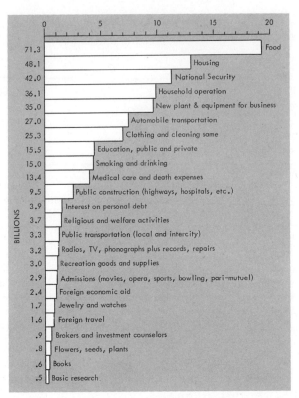

Source: Edwin L. Dale, Jr., "Are We Americans Going Soft?" *New York Times*, Magazine Section, December 1, 1957. © 1957 by The New York Times Company. Reprinted by permission.

FIG. 2–4. Approximate national expenditures, 1956.

the following pages, for example, allow us to make some tentative inferences as to the kind and extent of knowledge, existential and normative, characterizing our society.

Statistics may also be helpful in checking on inferences we make about a given culture. Suppose that we are dealing with what appears to be a very stable, traditionally oriented group among whom the cultural universals predominate.[60] The system is patrilineal with the son inheriting privileges, wealth, rank, obligations together with the symbols of status transmitted from his father. We

tions Demographic Survey; the *Sociological Almanac for the United States* by Gendell and Zetterberg; and a host of other data collected by business, industry and government at every level.

[60] This illustration (although he used it in a different connection) I owe to Professor W. F. Ogburn. But he should not be held responsible for any lack of lucidity in my argument.

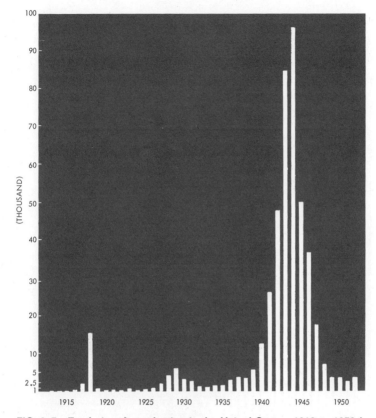

FIG. 2-5. Total aircraft production in the United States, 1913 to 1952.*

* Figures for 1941–45 include U.S.-financed aircraft produced in Canada. In the years 1943–44 there was no production other than military. For 1948–52, there is no information on military aircraft production available. Data from: *Historical Statistics of the United States, 1789–1945*, and *Continuation to 1952 of Historical Statistics of the United States, 1789–1945* (Washington, D.C.: Bureau of the Census, U.S. Department of Commerce, 1949 and 1954, respectively).

have a hunch that the lineage is of great importance and that much of the stability in the system relates to this traditional pattern. If this is so, then we might suppose that there would be marked emphasis on having male heirs. Conversely, a strong emphasis upon male heirs should be something of an index of the significance, in a given group, of transmission in the male line and the strength of traditionalism.

Now if we were to consider only two-child, two-sex families in this group (disregarding boy-boy and girl-girl combinations), we could state two differing predictions, one based on biology and the other on the inferred cultural emphasis. On the basis of genetics we

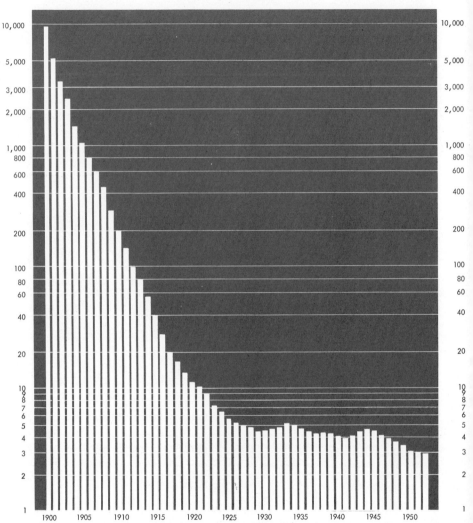

Source: *Historical Statistics of the United States, 1789–1945,* and *Continuation to 1952 of Historical Statistics of the United States, 1789–1945* (Washington, D.C.: Bureau of the Census, U.S. Department of Commerce, 1949 and 1954, respectively).

FIG. 2-6.   Relative change in number of persons per car in the United States, 1900 to 1952.*

* Note: These data are presented on a logarithmic scale. Thus, e.g., the persons-per-car value for 1921 is just half of that for 1912.

would expect that the first-a-boy, then-a-girl combination would be about as frequent as the first-a-girl, then-a-boy combination; i.e., B then $G = G$ then B. The contrary prediction stems from the inferred behavior conditioned by this particular culture. We would expect to find on the basis of these observed cultural characteristics (in a

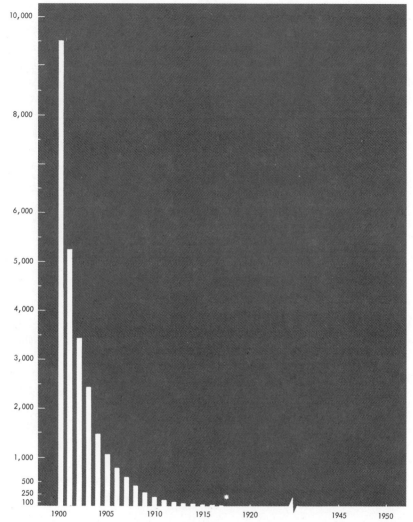

Source: *Historical Statistics of the United States, 1789–1945*, and *Continuation to 1952 of Historical Statistics of the United States*, (Washington, D.C.: Bureau of the Census, U.S. Department of Commerce, 1949 and 1954, respectively).

FIG. 2–7.   Change in number of persons per car in the United States, 1900–1952.*

* From 1918 to 1952 number of persons per car ranges from 16.97 to 2.98—figures too small to represent accurately.

traditionally oriented, patrilineal society) a significant excess of the first-a-girl, then-a-boy combination over the first-a-boy, then-a-girl combination; i.e., G then $B > B$ then G; or, briefly:

Genetic hypothesis: $BG = GB$

Cultural hypothesis: $GB > BG$

The first hypothesis is supported by theory and empirical evidence confirming the notion of the random assortment of genes, specifically the sex-determining XX genes of the mother and the XY genes of the father and resulting in a near equivalence of the two sexes. It is conceivable that some couples, starting with a boy, would intend to stop there, yet accidentally reproduce a girl. But the reverse is equally likely: that is, accidental reproduction can be assumed to be equivalent as between the two combinations. The theory underlying the cultural hypothesis of nonequivalence would go something like this: We start with the assumption of equivalence of the two combinations where only the number, and not the sex, of the children is important to the parents. But some couples having first had a daughter would have another child expressly in order to have a male heir. In roughly half of the cases, this second child can be assumed to be male, in half the cases female. Those in the first category can call a halt to reproduction at this point, whereas the others, persisting in the attempt to get a male heir, will have a third child and thus no longer belong to the two-child, two-sex category we are considering. Thus, if our reasoning is correct, we should be able to check on the inference about one cultural characteristic by comparing what happens under the presumed cultural influence with what would happen if biological factors alone affected the sex sequence among children in two-child, two-sex families. If the statistical analysis of the difference between them shows that the two outcomes are so far apart as to be inconceivable on a chance basis, we may conclude that the difference is not accidental.[61] It is attributable to some regular influence. And of course, in the preceding argument we think we have identified that influence, the value traditionally placed upon patrilineal transmission.

There are, then, ways of using this important concept, culture. We can analyze it within a spatial or temporal framework, in terms of its generality or its complexity, as folkway, mos, complex, institution, or theme. We concentrate upon the particular content most relevant for our problem: adages and aphorisms, literature, indexes of science and technology, indexes of the state of medical knowledge—the group's *materia medica* or its infant mortality rate —kinship networks, religious conduct, juridical lore and processes. And there are available techniques which I have crudely classified as direct and indirect observation, while providing a few cursory examples.

---

[61] See "An Aside on Methods: Some Tactics of Problem-Solution," p. 85.

An Aside on Methods: Some Tactics of Problem-Solution

Let us take this occasion to make a short sortie into the realm of tactics—the tactics of problem-solution. The specific problem in this case is whether the difference in frequency of the two combinations $f_{(G \text{ then } B)} - f_{(B \text{ then } G)}$ is significantly greater than 0, the value that the genetic hypothesis would suggest. Now if we were to take a sample of two-child–two-sex families and if, according to our genetic hypothesis, one combination should occur as frequently as another, then the sampling error for 100 such families (selected by probability sampling) is given by the formula: s (standard error of the sampling distribution) $= \sqrt{n\,p\,q}$ where $n = 100$ (the sample size), $p =$ the probability of one combination (first G-then-B $= \frac{1}{2}$), and $q = 1 - p$ (all other possibilities). Thus $s = \sqrt{100 \cdot \frac{1}{2} \cdot \frac{1}{2}}$, or $s = \sqrt{25} = 5$.

This formula is derived deductively and may be sensed inductively. It represents the way in which random errors distribute themselves. Their distribution follows what is called a "normal curve," most of the values, heaping up in the middle around the true value for the population, while a few values range farther above and below the true value. This formula says that in a large number of samples having the characteristics of this one (100 cases with the probability of the event, as stipulated in the hypothesis $= \frac{1}{2}$), we could be confident that two thirds of the time our observed value would lie within the range: 50-plus-or-minus-5.

That is to say, 50, plus or minus 5, would be the number among 100 such randomly chosen families which we would usually expect to find having either the first-B-then-G or the first-G-then-B combination if they are, as biology might dictate, equal in number in the general population. "Usually," here means two thirds of the times such samples are taken.

Now suppose that in fact we find 65 two-child families, in our sample of 100, in which we have the first-G-then-B combination (and 35 with the other combination). Is such a sample likely to occur in a population in which, in fact, there is a 50–50 distribution of these combinations? The answer is: No. Why so? How can we say "no" with any assurance? Because what we observe is quite far away (three standard errors away) from what we might expect on the basis of the assumption of no (culturally induced) difference in the proportion of these two combinations. That is to say, 65 (our observed number) minus 50 (expected number on the basis of sheerly genetic assumptions) is equal to three standard errors: $\dfrac{65 - 50}{5} = 3$. Or, if we were to put this graphically, in a large number of samplings in which we drew each time 100 (two-child, two-sex) families from a population in which the probability of $GB = BG$, i.e. $= \frac{1}{2}$, we should expect such a distribution as the following.

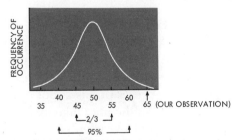

In two thirds of the samples we would expect, on a sheerly chance basis, that the first-G-then-B combination would occur between 45 and 55 times in a sample

An Aside on Methods: Some Tactics of Problem-Solution (continued)

of 100 (i.e., 50, plus or minus one standard error, which $= 5$). In 99 percent of the cases (samples) we would expect that the first-G-then-B combination would occur between 40 and 60 times in a sample of 100—i.e., 50 plus or minus two standard errors). Or more to the point, in only one case out of 100 would we expect an observed value to be fewer than 40 or more than 60 in a sample of 100 cases. But what we observed was 65 cases of this combination, a number that could be expected to occur on a chance basis only very rarely. We conclude, therefore, that this finding is *not* a chance occurrence, but probably reflects a cultural peculiarity of this group. "Probably" is, however, too strong a word here. We have probably rejected the null hypothesis, the assertion of equivalence, or no difference between the combinations. We have *not* demonstrated that we have the correct explanation—in our definition of the field, the correct *interpretation*—of the difference between these two combinations. But as Samuel Stouffer used to put it, we have narrowed the range of ignorance a bit. We are fairly confident it is not a chance effect. We are on the track of something.

❊ ❊ ❊ ❊

But let us be clear about the connection between the concept, culture, and the general topic of Part I, "Entering the Group." To enter a group means, we have said, to mesh one's beliefs and behaviors with those of others in a system of relationships. Relationships imply reciprocal communication. Such communication presupposes shared understandings, enabling us to predict others' responses. These shared understandings constitute the core of culture which I have defined as socially shared and socially transmitted knowledge, symbolized in act and artifact. Culture, therefore, is the necessary and sufficient condition for entering the human group: and special sectors of the culture are prerequisite for entering specialized subgroups—age and sex groups, occupational groups, fraternities, friendly cliques, government services, the pool hall gang, and the like.

The network of relationships which is a group is built upon a foundation of prefabricated cultural prescriptions. So I have been contending. This is perhaps a plausible assertion. But taken alone it leaves unanswered two important questions. First, what is the process by which these prescriptions about appropriate conduct are built into the person so that he may take up the roles required by his relationships with others: How is culture transmitted? And second, what or who are the effective agents in this process? In the next chapter we turn to the first of these two questions, focusing especially on the socialization process and bringing to bear the support of reason and the evidence of experience.

ORIGINAL TEXTS

1. Karl Marx, *The Eighteenth Brumaire of Louis Napoleon* (New York: International Press, n.d.), p. 1

   In Marx's words, "Die Menschen machen ihre eigene Geschichte, aber sie machen sie nicht aus freien Stücken, nicht unter selbstgewählten, sondern unter gegebenen und überlieferten Umständen. Die Tradition aller toten Geschlechter lastet wie ein Alp auf dem Gehirn der Lebenden.

2. Emile Durkheim, *L'Education morale* (Paris: Librairie Félix Alcan, 1925), pp. 71, 72.

   Durkheim puts it this way: "Les générations premières, elles, sont remplacées par des générations nouvelles, et, cependant la société reste avec sa physionomie propre et son caractère personnel . . . entre la France actuelle et celle du Moyen age, il y a une identité personelle que nul ne peut songer a méconnaître. Ainsi, tandis que des générations d'individus succédaient à d'autres générations, par-dessus ce flux perpetuel des personalités particulières, il y avait quelque chose qui persistait, c'est la société avec sa conscience propre, son temperament personnel . . .

3. Marcel Mauss, "Essai sur les variations saissonières des sociétés eskimos," *Année sociologiques* (Paris: Librairie Félix Alcan, 1904–05), Vol. IX.

   The original reads as follows: En été, les membres qui le composent habitent dans des tentes et çes tentes sont dispersées; en hiver, ils habitent des maisons resserrées les unes près des autres. Tandis que la tente ne comprend qu'une famille, l'habitat d'hiver en contient normalement plusieurs . . . Tandis que l'été étend d'une manière presque illimitée le champ ouvert à la chasse et à la pêche, l'hiver, au contraire, le restreint de la manière la plus étroite . . . La religion des eskimos passe par le même rythme que leur organization. Il y a, pour ainsi dire, une religion d'été et une religion d'hiver . . . le culte privé, domestique [d'été] et l'état d'exaltation [d'hiver].

   Mais cette opposition de la vie d'hiver et de la vie d'été ne se traduit pas seulement dans les rites, dans les fêtes, dans les cérémonies religieuses de toute sort; elle affecte aussi profondement les idées, les représentations collectives, en un mot la mentalité du groupe. Dans certaines tribus, au cours d'un complexus de fêtes, on voit tous les gens du groupe se diviser en deux camps. L'un comprend tous ceux qui sont nés en hiver; dans l'autre, se trouvent tous ceux nés en été.

   Ainsi la manière même dont sont classés et les hommes et les choses porte l'empreinte de cette opposition cardinale entre les deux saisons. Chaque saison sert à définir tout un genre d'êtres et de choses. On peut dire que la notion de l'hiver et la notion de l'été sont comme deux poles autour desquels gravite le système d'idées des eskimos.

SELECTED SUPPLEMENTARY READINGS

ALLPORT, GORDON. "The J-Curve Hypothesis of Non-Conforming Behavior," in G. E. Swanson, T. M. Newcomb, and E. L. Hartley (eds.), *Readings in Social Psychology*, pp. 231–42. New York: Holt, Rinehart & Winston, Inc., 1952.

BARNETT, JAMES H. "The Sociology of Art," in Robert K. Merton, Leonard Broom, and Leonard S. Cottrell, Jr. (eds.), *Sociology Today*, ch. viii. New York: Harper & Row—Harper Torchbooks, 1965.

GOLDSCHMIDT, WALTER (ed.). *Ways of Mankind*. Boston: Beacon Press, 1954. Hear, also, the National Association of Educational Broadcasters' recordings under the same title.

HONIGMANN, JOHN J. *The World of Man*. New York: Harper & Row, 1959.

*MCGRANAHAN, DONALD V., AND WAYNE, IVOR. "German and American Traits Reflected in Popular Drama," *Human Relations*, 1948, pp. 429–55.

*MINER, HORACE. "Body Ritual Among the Snacirema," *American Anthropologist*, 1956, pp. 503–7.

*WHORF, BENJAMIN LEE. "Science and Linguistics," in John B. Carroll (ed.), *Language, Thought and Reality, Selected Writings of Benjamin Lee Whorf*, pp. 207–19. Cambridge, Mass.: The Technology Press, Massachusetts Institute of Technology, 1957.

WILLIAMS, ROBIN M. *American Society*, ch. x, xi. 2d ed. New York: Alfred A. Knopf, Inc., 1960.

* Articles marked with an asterisk are available as reprints from the college division of the Bobbs-Merrill Company, Indianapolis, Indiana.

Chapter 3

Transmitting Culture: the Socialization Process

How does the newcomer enter the group?
How is culture transmitted?
What's the nature of the socialization process?

Entering a group is a complex matter and so is the theory which tries to interpret it. Let me, therefore, outline the argument in a first paragraph and develop it throughout the rest of the chapter. The elements of culture are inculcated in the newcomer through a process called socialization. We shall be concerned chiefly with the child as newcomer to the human group. But the principles of the socialization process come into play whenever a person enters a new group, for there is always the problem of so shaping his behavior (in its covert as well as its overt aspects) that it meshes effectively with others' behavior. If this is to happen, the newcomer must learn the appropriate score—how he is expected to act toward all the objects of his particular world. These expectations are conveyed in the symbols of speech (or writing, or gestures). As symbols, they are internalized, retained in memory, representing both the communicator and the matter communicated, teacher and things taught. As symbols, or images, the other and his expectations of us become part of us. Since the reality of things consists in the images we have of them, we are able to deal with them at a distance. That is to say, we are freed from the world of tangible things which, were we to deal with them in their endless concrete detail, would make a "big, buzzing, booming confusion" of our lives.

But if we are freed from the concrete event, we are bound by the introjected meanings which become part of us. These are the meanings, derived from symbolic interaction with others, of those objects (physical, abstract, and social) with which we must deal. In the category of social objects, the self is certainly the most signifi- cant. Indeed, we can think of the socialization process as one in which the person's identity is established. One does not establish his identity without identifiers, and in this process the meaning of *self* is gradually revealed through the responses of *others*. Knowledge of self and of other is the critical, dual outcome of the socialization process. This knowledge is indispensable not only because A and B (for example, child and parent) triangulate on X (the objects of life) and reveal their meaning; but also because in this process the bonds of mutual agreement are established. Indeed, in many cases the nature of X may be less important than the fact that A and B agree on it (and perhaps erroneously). For in seeing things alike, in making common cause, group as well as personal identity is established. The limits of allegiance, rights, and duties are defined. The culturally framed knowledge of self, of other, and of the relationship between the two—this is the outcome.

Socialization, then, is the process of entering the human group— of being inducted, as Professor MacIver put it, into the secrets of society. It is a process in which a number of minor miracles occur: the animal becomes a human being, sheer behavior is transformed into conduct, the individual as an organic unit becomes a person, self-aware and able to guide his conduct in terms of the increasingly subtle cues that signal others' expectations.

The induction of a person into his society may cover a long period of time. Indeed, in one sense it is a process that continues through- out life. When we go to a new school, enter upon our first job, join a new club, enlist in the armed services, change a field of work, enter upon marriage and parenthood, retire to join the oldsters on St. Petersburg's green benches—whenever we enter a new social context we are being further inducted into the secrets of society. We travel toward death through peopled time and space. The several legs of the trip are differentiated in part by our induction into various groups.

But the first entrance is by all odds the most dramatic and the

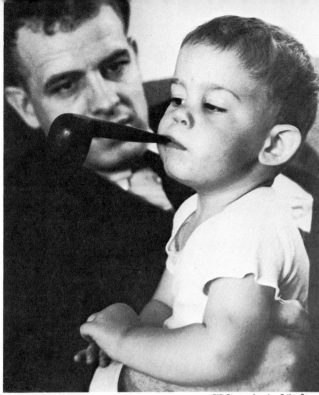

Symbolic
identification
of self and
other

most significant. The newcomer to the human group finds himself an alien in the hands of utter strangers. Both physically and mentally he is almost powerless. In some groups his impotence is underlined by the *patris potestas*, the right (sometimes exercised) of life and death over the infant. There is an infinite distance between his age (zero) and that of his parents (say, 25) in extent of knowledge. By the time he is 25 and they 50, he will have cut down his parents' lead considerably. (In some respects he will have outdistanced them.) But when he enters the human group, he is quite at the mercy of parents and siblings. They determine both what and when he shall eat and wear, when he shall sleep and wake, what he shall think and feel, how he shall express his thoughts and feelings (what language he shall speak and how he shall do it), what his political and religious commitments shall be, what sort of vocation he shall aspire to.[1]

Not that parents are ogres. They give what they have to give: their own limited knowledge, their prejudices and passions. There is no alternative to this giving of themselves; nor for the receiver is there any option. Neither can withhold the messages conveyed to the other. Before the age of six the personality of the child has been deeply marked by the introjected images provided chiefly by parents and siblings. These images (ideas, signs, impressions) conveyed by parental word and gesture are, in fact, the parent. For the reality of the other consists not in his corporeal self but in the symbolic messages it emits. In this sense we incorporate others— they become quite literally part of us. The Biblical statement, "Ye are severally one of another," reflects this conception as does the communion service. Indeed we might say that the process of socialization is the process of becoming severally one of another, of fusion, a merging of self and other.[2] John Donne's overquoted

---

[1] "From the moment of his birth the customs into which he is born shape [the individual's] experience and behaviour. By the time he can talk, he is the little creature of his culture, and by the time he is grown and able to take part in its activities, its habits are his habits, its beliefs his beliefs, its impossibilities his impossibilities. Every child that is born into his group will share them with him, and no child born into one on the opposite side of the globe can ever achieve the thousandth part." (Ruth Benedict, *Patterns of Culture* [Boston: Houghton Mifflin Co., 1961], p. 2.)

[2] This is a common insight among religious and literary people. Consider the following: "'You are a brave man, Rifleman Quigg,' said King George pinning the Victoria Cross on the Irishman. 'I am, King,' said Quigg. Notice the dignity of the reply—no beating about the bush, no impudent blushes, no batting a modest eyelid, just a calm acceptance of a superior fact. As if it were a cold, impersonal point, which

statement conveys the same notion of merging, identification of one person with another: ". . . every man's death diminishes me because I am involved in mankind. Therefore never seek to know for whom the bell tolls: it tolls for thee."

It would be strange if it were otherwise. For when we reflect on it we find it hard to say with precision where the boundaries lie separating us as concrete individuals from the physical and the biological realms, to say nothing of the social. When are the air we breathe, the light and sound waves impinging on us—when are these us, and when non-us? Or the food we ingest and excrete— when is it us and when non-us? If there is some problem in asserting a clearly bounded identity here, how much more so is it to be expected in the realm of human interchange. Or if, as Locke contended,[3] a man's title to his product derives from the fact that it is a thing invested with his energy, his sense of craftsmanship and beauty—vested, in short, with elements of himself—how infinitely more so must the self be fused with its product when that product is a person as in the case of teacher-student, parent-child, employer-employee relationships. In human relationships a theory of unqualified individualism is both spurious and dangerous.

There is, then, a kind of permeability of the human psyche by virtue of man's capacity to symbolize. Here the crucial significance of language is obvious.[4] It provides the symbols from which the image of the other is formed. Symbols make light luggage. We can carry a great freight of them around with us. And since many of them represent the people with whom we deal, the person carrying them becomes a society in microcosm. Marcel Mauss says:

> Other people need not be there, physically, corporeally distinguishable from us; for we always carry with us and in us a number of clearly identifiable others.[*]

---

of course it was. How different from John Bunyan who, when a churchman said to him, 'That was a fine sermon you preached today, Mr. Bunyan,' replied, 'So the devil told me before I went into the pulpit.' An impudent reply. Why? *Because it was an exclusively personal one. After all, we are more than ourselves, and to belittle one's self is to belittle all men.*" (W. A. Rodgers, "Impudence and Dignity," *Vogue,* Vol. 15 [October, 1954].)

[3] John Locke, *Second Essay on Civil Government* (New York: E. P. Dutton & Co., Inc., 1924), chap. v.

[4] See, e.g., the work *Social Psychology* by Alfred R. Lindesmith and Anselm Strauss in which language is treated as the crucial characteristic of the human group and the matter of prime concern in social psychology. (New York: Holt, Rinehart & Winston, Inc., 1956.)

[*] See Original Texts, Note 1 at the end of the chapter.

So it was that Charles Horton Cooley said, "a separate individual is an abstraction unknown to experience, and so likewise is a society when regarded as something apart from individuals."[5] Cooley's views, on which I draw heavily, are particularly germane to the problem of socialization, especially as he developed them in his classic work on *Human Nature and the Social Order*. His central theme is that the solid reality of social life consists in the images people have of one another, and that these images are built up through the process of symbolic interaction.

> So far as the study of immediate social relations is concerned, the personal idea is the real person. That is to say, it is in this alone that one man exists for another, and acts directly upon the mind. . . . *The immediate social reality is the personal idea.* . . . Society, then, in its immediate aspect, is a relation among personal ideas.
>
> Thus the imaginary companionship which a child of three or four years so naïvely creates and expresses, is something elementary and almost omnipresent in the thought of a normal person . . . [for] we have no higher life that is really apart from other people. It is by imagining them that our personality is built up; to be without the power of imagining them is to be a low-grade idiot; and in the measure that a mind is lacking in this power it is degenerate. Apart from this mental society there is no wisdom, no power, justice, or right, no higher existence at all. The life of the mind is essentially a life of intercourse.[6]

What I have been emphasizing, then, is that there is reason to think that self and other are deeply and indivisibly implicated in one another. This has special significance for the socialization process because it means that, willy-nilly, the child must incorporate, internalize his parents (and the others to whom he is regularly exposed). The ability to manipulate symbols which enables this internalization has interesting and ambivalent consequences. It means that the person is freed from bondage to the concrete reality and can deal with objects at a distance or in their absence. This is what we do when we turn things over in our memories, solve problems, reflect on certain matters. The power of a relationship may be felt even—sometimes especially—in the absence of the other. But if we are emancipated from dependence on the immediate and tangible reality, we are not, on the other hand, free to

---

[5] Charles Horton Cooley, *Human Nature and the Social Order* (New York: Charles Scribner's Sons, 1902), p. 84.

[6] *Ibid.*, pp. 61, 62. Italics mine.

shake the symbols of it which we have internalized. The very core of Freudian theory relates to these deeply buried images persisting in the subconscious. Even to deal, however unsatisfactorily, with a violent and tyrannical father, a child must come to "understand" him. In doing so, in making the father intelligible, he must bring that father within himself. And despite firm and understandable resolutions that he will never behave in such a manner toward *his* child, the internalized and latent father represents a capacity for action which may, years hence, be realized spontaneously. Similarly, although it is not a good one, there is perhaps something to the syllogism of which the first two terms are: "Wars are made in the minds of men. The minds of men are made at mother's knee. Therefore. . . ." There is a terrifying power exerted by the elders— the internalized elders—in the socialization process. It is a long-lasting power by virtue of the symbolic character of human interaction.[7]

The symbolic interpenetration of self and other, of parent and child in the socialization process, results in the transmission of knowledge of what is and what ought to be. The other who becomes part of us is a congeries of knowings, feelings, and believings which become ours as he becomes us. Put more abstractly, as A and B interact, culturally prescribed definitions of X emerge and become fixed. In this process we learn the significance of certain objects: of *physical objects*—cabbages and cornflakes, crucifix and cadillac, TV and vitamins, pens, planes, and pencils; of *social objects*—mother and father, playmate and preacher, teacher and employer, insider and outsider, and, among all social objects that which is above all

---

[7] Perceptive writers have long capitalized on the power of the socialization process and its enduring and remote consequences. Samuel Butler's *The Way of All Flesh* (New York: Modern Library, Inc., 1950), is heavy with this theme. In Jerome Weidman's book, *The Enemy Camp* ([New York: Random House, Inc., 1958], p. 497), the hero, George Hurst, cannot shake the deeply inculcated fear and hostility toward the *shkutzim* (gentiles) and the sense of a necessary and exclusive identity with his fellow Jews. Adopted and reared by Aunt Tessie, Hurst acted upon the advice of Uncle Zisha who said: "Don't make a hole for yourself and creep into it. Don't make yourself a private Ghetto. Do what your heart says, not your religion. To be a man is more important than to be a Jew. Without listening to your heart you'll never be a man. You like this girl? She likes you? It says in your heart I want to marry her? So marry her."

Aunt Tessie had a different view of the matter. "If you marry this girl," [she] said slowly, "I don't want to see you, I don't want to hear, nothing, never again. It'll be by me like twenty-eight years ago I never went to the Henry Isaacs Orphan Asylum to find you." He *did* marry the girl. What he was *unable* to do was to free himself of the fear and passion of Aunt Tessie's attitude toward the *shkutzim* (one of whom he married).

significant for us, the self; and third, of modes of conduct symbolized by such *abstract objects* as are suggested by the words justice, equality, republican, democratic, socialist, communist, playing square, being a "square," Catholic, Protestant, Jew, etc.

It seems probable that these objects are crystallized for the person as the smooth, ongoing tenor of his life is interrupted, as action is impeded. A complete, unimpeded satisfaction of wants would tie us to the level of sensory perception. But some interference, some interruption or intrusion, an obstacle thrown in our path, creates the life of imagination, prompts us to isolate the object, to hold it in suspension, as it were, while possible alternatives are considered. For the young just entering a strange group, such blocking is a very familiar experience. The very nature of things is carved out of a refractory world in which the elders are constantly interposing obstacles. The objects of the world are not "out there" possessing some intrinsic character which will reveal itself when an independent mind is mature enough for the knowing. The objects of the world are gradually revealed to us as we act upon them and they upon us through the mediation of the elders. To know is to experience, selectively, those objects deemed relevant within a culture, and to interpret such experiences in terms dictated by the culture as mediated in the socialization process.

A television set, for example, is a physical object toward which we act, with which we have experiences. It represents a complicated set of knowings, both about what is and what ought to be. It is not available to all people. From the user's point of view it involves learning some things about entertainment, business (advertising), citizenship (campaign speeches). Some programs are "worthwhile" and others are not. There are times when one must yield in his preference for a given program to the desires of others and do the things he *ought* to do, such as studies. Thus a physical object gains meaning as we experience it within a cultural frame under the tutelage of significant others. Even though physical objects might be thought to be essentially alike for all persons, this is so—if it is so— only within the realm of immediate sensory perception. As regards function, the object is different for different groups, and the person entering the group must learn the appropriate functions. The Christian cross is a physical object, but a very different one to the devout Christian than to the Jew whose family was killed by "Christians" in an antisemitic pogrom.

Especially with abstract objects such as communism, what is learned is learned not so much in direct physical contact with the sounds and sights of communist activity, but in interaction with others whose conception of, and attitudes toward, the object we internalize. Many of our most important attitudes are learned in contact with others' attitudes, rather than in contact with the object of the attitude. This is especially true as the child picks up from his parents the attitudes deemed appropriate within the group he is entering.

The social object, a person, is rather a complicated problem for the newcomer because such objects are so complex. In the one case he is male, in another female, each requiring different responses. The person may be husband or wife, cousin, uncle, aunt, brother, sister, grandparent, teacher, preacher, clerk, doctor, salesman, policeman. A great variety of roles must be identified, along with certain dimensions of the roles (he's a bad boy; "cheese it, the cops"; Dr. Carter is an able surgeon). Now what we act toward, with social objects, is not the corporeal or physical object but rather the image which each of us has of another.[8] Indeed, the corporeal aspect of another may remain the same while the image changes. ("When I first met him, a year ago, I found him witty and entertaining; but having heard the same stories ten times over, an evening with him is a dismal prospect." Or consider the case of the Negro who has "passed" and then, somewhere along the line, is "unmasked.") Conversely, a person may change in physical appearance, yet still be seen and dealt with as before. It is, therefore, not the physical aspect but the image of the social object and its transmission that is the

---

[8] This is perhaps too strong a statement, although the emphasis is right. There are times when we transform persons, social objects, into physical objects and treat them as such. In the Army, in all large organizations where things are done "by the numbers," there is a tendency to treat people as things. And this may be appropriate, depending upon the group, its personnel and purposes. It might, for example, be very bad for the patient and for everyone involved in the healing processes if a person having an "appendectomy" were to be treated as a "whole" person, as anything but a case of appendicitis. Isidor Thorner gives an illuminating treatment of the necessarily restricted role of the nurse, which is the point here, the limited number of attributes of the patient which become relevant in this relationship. This lack of range and depth of attributes is characteristic of physical, in contrast to social, objects. ("Nursing: The Functional Significance of an Institutional Pattern," *American Sociological Review*, Vol. XX [October, 1955], pp. 531–38.)

The converse is true, too: occasionally we treat physical objects as social objects. Walking through a dark room in the middle of the night we bark our shins against a chair. Now we may act toward the chair as though it were a social object, reproaching it vigorously and even kicking it back "to teach it a lesson."

significant thing. Since for the rest of his life the person must be acting in and dealing with social objects, learning how to act in and toward such roles comes close to the center of the socialization process.

But the most important, the crucial social object about which the person must learn and toward which he must act is himself, or his self. The socialization process may be thought of as directed above all toward answering the question for the newcomer: "Who am I?" Even to pose the question of self-recognition implies something of the nature of the process: to recognize or identify the self implies the position of an outsider. It suggests that the subject must come to think, feel, and act toward himself as object. But the person does this only to the extent that he can stand in another's position, seeing and appraising himself through another's eyes. Thus the ability to take the role of the other and self-consciousness are twin-born. To "be" another and to be one's self are cognate matters. The self as a social object emerges as the images of other social objects emerge.[9]

Because this process of self-realization requires seeing one's self reflected in others' eyes, Cooley used the phrase, the "looking-glass self."

> In a very large and interesting class of cases the social reference takes the form of a somewhat definite imagination of how one's self. . . . appears in a particular mind, and the kind of self-feeling one has is determined by the attitude toward this, attributed to that other mind. A social self of this sort might be called the reflected or looking-glass self:
>
> > Each to each a looking-glass
> > Reflects the other that doth pass.
>
> A self-idea of this sort seems to have three principal elements: the imagination of our appearance to the other person; the imagination of his judgment of that appearance; and some sort of self-feeling, such as pride or mortification.[10]

As we think in terms of the parent-child relationship in the socialization process, we can paraphrase Cooley's three elements of the self-idea in these questions: (1) How does the child imagine he

---

[9] This would suggest that insight (self-knowledge) and empathy (capacity for feeling in and with another and presumably understanding another) ought to go together. Indeed this is what R. F. Dymond found in her work on the conception of self. (R. F. Dymond, A. S. Hughes, and J. L. Raabe, "Measurable Changes in Empathy with Age," *Journal of Consulting Psychology*, Vol. XVI [1952], pp. 202–6; also, C. R. Rogers and R. F. Dymond [eds.], *Psychotherapy and Personality Change* [Chicago: University of Chicago Press, 1954].)

[10] Cooley, *op. cit.*, pp. 151, 152.

appears to his mother and father? (2) How does he suppose they judge the picture they have of him? And (3) how does he react to the judgment of his appearance which he imputes to his parents? In its dissection this analysis makes the process much too rational, conscious, and calculated. Cooley means rather to suggest a constant interplay between persons in terms of the images they present to one another, and their evaluations of such images.[11] It is instructive to recall the etymology of the word, person: it comes from the Greek and originally meant mask. (We use the word in its literal significance on playbills, *dramatis personae.*) In this sense it conveys precisely the proper notion that becoming a person involves learning to wear the right masks at the right times, learning to define situations and enact the appropriate roles correctly. It also conveys the correct notion that underneath the mask there are other elements of the personality which must be understood if we are to grasp a person's motives, the meaning of his act, and his expectations of us.

This interpretation of the nature of self-awareness, the interpenetration of self and other and the emergence of a conception of self as the reflexive product, was perceptively developed in a story by Edward Bellamy.[12] The people referred to in the following paragraphs were, so the story goes, descendants of some Persian mystics who were shipwrecked 2000 years ago on an isolated island. During the centuries they had become able to read each others' minds completely.

> . . . the very knowledge that my mind was overlooked by others operated to check thoughts that might be painful to them, and that, too, without more effort of the will than a kindly person exerts to check the utterance of disagreeable remarks. As a very few lessons in the elements of courtesy cures a decent person of inconsiderate speaking, so a brief experience among the mind-readers went far in my case to check inconsiderate thinking. . . . Among the mind-readers, politeness never can extend to the point of insincerity, as among talking nations, seeing that it is always one another's real and inmost thought that they read. . . . For the very reason that the mind-reader reads all your thoughts, particular thoughts are judged with reference to the general tenor of thought. Your characteristic and habitual frame of mind is

---

[11] For an insightful development of this theme, see Erving Goffman, *The Presentation of Self in Everyday Life* (New York: Doubleday & Co., Anchor Books, 1959).

[12] Edward Bellamy, "To Whom This May Come," found in *The Blindman's World and Other Stories* (Boston: Houghton Mifflin Co., 1898) and cited in Arthur E. Morgan, *Nowhere Was Somewhere* (Chapel Hill: University of North Carolina Press, 1946), pp. 142, 143.

what he takes account of. No one need fear being misjudged by a mind-reader on account of sentiments or emotions which are not representative of the real character or general attitude.

Despite the connotations of the occult, mind reading of sorts is the accomplishment of every adequately socialized person. The result is knowledge of three sorts: knowledge of others, the reflexive knowledge of self, and knowledge of those objects (including persons) with which self and other must deal.

But socialization involves not only agreement as to the nature of these three sorts of objects but also *the recognition that we are agreed.* In the process of learning to discriminate, identify, understand, and evaluate the objects with which our worlds are furnished, we learn to see them *as others see them.* We do not learn what these objects are in any immutable, absolute, or metaphysical sense. We agree with others first of all because the powerful elders insist we do. But underlying the coercion of the elders is the unarticulated requirement of common cognition if we are to communicate—and hence, to live—and common values if we are to live in some degree of harmony. If this is a requisite for personal survival, it is also mandatory from the perspective of the group. A high degree of consensus is required if the person is to fulfill his role as a member of the group. It is the perception of consensus on matters deemed essential by the group that defines the person's allegiance and the group's boundaries. Those who agree with us are our kind.

It is important, then, in building relationships, that we "see" given objects in essentially the same way as do other members of the group. In daily life we would be more distressed than amused by the excessive flexibility of Polonius as he tries to adapt himself to Hamlet's view of an object:

> HAMLET.   Do you see yonder cloud that's almost in shape of a camel?
> POLONIUS.   By the mass, and 'tis like a camel indeed.
> HAMLET.   Methinks it is like a weasel.
> POLONIUS.   It is backed like a weasel.
> HAMLET.   Or like a whale?
> POLONIUS.   Very like a whale.

But this strain to see things as do our significant others is something which must appeal both to our own experience and our reason. For we deal with most of the objects of life in the company of others. We *triangulate* on objects: persons A and B oriented toward, concerned about, arguing over, collaborating with respect to an object, X.

Failure to identify and appraise X (a thing, an idea, another person) as do our friends, our employers, our fellow worshippers and fellow citizens—such failure would mean a failure in communication, a threat to relationships. We tend, then, to "see" alike and to associate with those who see as we do. We read papers expressing the "right" editorial views, switch off radio and television programs expressing the "wrong" sentiments. And especially in the socialization process, the child is constrained to view X in the same light as do his parents, his neighbors, people of the same community and the same communion. This may be easy to achieve since, not being exposed to alternatives, he simply and literally has no choice. Or, the parents, aware of alternative views of an object, X, and inclined in one direction, may use their power to bring the child's views of X into line. But we should not overlook the tendency and the desire, from the child's side, to see the world as respected and powerful parents see it. All his rewards lie in this direction. Professor Newcomb suggests a principle (which fits certain experimental observations made in his study of the acquaintance process) to the effect that there is a force felt by A (the child, in our case) toward maintaining a constant relationship between (A→X) and (B→X), a force which varies with the attraction B (the parent) has for A, and with the importance and relevance of the object, X. This could be put, illustratively, in this fashion:

1. I love my fiancé (or Picasso's art, or the *Chicago Tribune*, or artichokes).
2. I love my parents.
3. Therefore my parents *must* (or should) share my passion for. . . .

A stable A-B-X system is one in which there is "minimal perceived discrepancy." Where there is discrepancy—either between A's fondness for B and B's for A, or between assessments of the importance and relevance of X—then there is strain in the relationship and a force working to reduce the strain. Referring to the following diagram, we can suggest that the value of the bond A↔B (a measure of the strength of this bond) is a function of the extent to which BX = AX: or, as the difference BX − AX approaches zero, the value of the bond A↔B increases.

A←——→B

X

Human socialization necessarily includes the acquiring of many attitudes that are consensual with others' (especially adults') attitudes. To survive requires the acquiring of unfavorable attitudes (like those of adults) toward possibly drowning waters, or devouring beasts, or macerating machinery. To adapt comfortably to a stabilized family, community, or social order one must acquire the right attitudes (i.e., attitudes like those of one's associates who have already adapted comfortably to family, community, etc.) towards cabbages and kings, and all else that is culturally sanctioned. *Socialization, in short, includes the building in of danger signals when attitudinal discrepancies with trusted others are perceived.* Some signals may, of course, prove to be false alarms, and with experience one learns to discriminate among them—a process that is also included in the socialization process. But there are few, presumably, in whom the acquired drive is ever totally extinguished, and for most of us it continues—under the stipulated conditions of strong attraction and intense attitude—to be a source of discomfort.[13]

Achieving consensus on all these matters relating to life's essential objects is not a simple matter in our day. It takes much time, enormous expenditures, and the combined efforts of many people. Family, school, church, and government are prominently involved in the process of socialization, the first two being explicitly charged with it. Business participates in many ways. Also implicated are the Boy Scouts (and Girl), summer camps, the Catholic Youth Organization, the P.A.L. (Police Athletic League), 4-H Clubs, and a host of other agencies. The process, once narrowly defined, clearly focused, and fairly achieved by the early teens, now requires many more years.

To mention various agents of socialization must not mislead us. It is not a process wholly conscious and calculated. Outcomes are often unintended, produced by a cryptic mix of influences typically unidentified and unassessed: family size, sibling position, region, religion, parental prejudices and pathologies, relatives and guests, class and crises—factors ad infinitum. In the process, attitudes and values are shaped, becoming, like cognitions, the essential person. To challenge them is to affront the person: for his conceptions of what ought to be lie at the center of his being. Slowly, often imperceptibly, the newcomer picks up his culture.

---

[13] Theodore M. Newcomb, *The Acquaintance Process* (New York: Holt, Rinehart & Winston, Inc., 1961), p. 14.

STAGES IN THE PROCESS OF SOCIALIZATION

I have said *imperceptibly* the individual becomes a person, behavior becomes conduct. Yet it is possible to establish some benchmarks along the way, less arbitrary than Shakespeare's seven ages of man. Some of the more penetrating suggestions as to stages in the socialization process come from George Herbert Mead, from Jean Piaget, and from Sigmund Freud.[14]

Mead was concerned with the development of the self-concept and the relationship between self and society.[15] We gain some understanding of these matters, he suggests, if we think of socialization as proceeding through three stages: an early stage of haphazard emulation, a play stage, and a game stage. The first stage, characteristic of the child under two or three years, is one in which he copies others' activities without understanding the meaning of the activities. This is an elementary step in his learning to take the role of the other. He "reads" the paper—upside down. He paces the floor, hands behind back, "reflectively." He repairs a mirror, with a hammer. Such activities Mead conceives as a prelude to the stage when the child actually takes on different roles meaningfully. This is the play stage when he plays father or physician and in doing so, puts himself in the position of being able to act back toward his Self. He looks upon himself as a patient when he assumes the doctor's role, as a child when he assumes the father's role. .

This capacity of the subject for treating itself as object is sometimes revealed when the child refers to itself in the third person: not "I want water," but "Mary wants a glass of water," Mary being the speaker. Here in the play stage the social character of selfhood is clearly revealed. The child's conception of self conforms to the way it is conceived by others. The role is rehearsed in terms of another's expectations. It is roughly correct to say, then, that the way in which a child conceives himself is conditioned by the roles which he takes; and that these roles are defined by others' treatment of him. This is the perception contained in Shaw's astute statement

---

[14] On the applied side, and with a strong biological orientation, we have the work by Ilg and Gesell at Yale, and many of the advisers to parents, Dr. Spock, for example, detect certain stages in development which require differentiated behaviors and responses.

[15] George Herbert Mead, *Mind, Self and Society* (Chicago: The University of Chicago Press, 1934). See especially Part III, "The Self," pp. 135–226.

to the effect that the difference between a Duchess and a flower girl lies not so much in the way they act as in the way they are treated.[16]

But if the child takes on various roles, he develops a series of discrete selves, wavering and perhaps inconsistent. It is in the third or game stage that Mead sees a more or less consistent self-conception emerging. He uses the word "game" to express the requirement faced by the child of reconciling diverse expectations and meeting common ones. Like a member of a team he must develop a self-concept and a pattern of conduct consistent with the expectations of all other members. Instead of taking the role of *the* other, he must take the role of *all* others, the "generalized other" as Mead calls it. A given situation will elicit from every member of the team/group the same (actual or potential) response. Situation: man on first base, the hit goes between second and third. Solution (an actual one for the shortstop, and potential for other members of the team): shortstop fields ball, throws to second baseman who moves up to take the throw and sends it on to first for a double play. Every man on both teams—and the spectators, too—expect this behavior of any person (shortstop) in this situation. And so it is with any adequately socialized person who, for example, respects his parents, is loyal to his country, works conscientiously at his job, outwits a shrewd adversary, but is indulgent with children, women, and other dependents. That is to say, he takes the role and meets the expectations of the generalized other. We have a generalized other when we internalize the shared prescriptions for conduct in commonly encountered situations.

Mead's third stage has something in common with the fourth and last stage which Piaget has distinguished in mastering the rules of the game. This is the stage which he calls that of the *codification of rules*. "Not only is every detail of procedure in the game fixed, but the actual code of rules to be observed is known to the whole society."[17] This clearly implies the sense of the generalized other: for a sense of the rules is an acknowledgment of the common expectations.

Piaget and his Swiss group have been working for some 35 years

---

[16] George Bernard Shaw, "Pygmalion," in *Four Plays* (New York: Modern Library, Inc., 1953).

[17] Jean Piaget, *The Moral Judgment of the Child* (New York: Free Press of Glencoe, Inc., n.d.), pp. 16–18, *passim*.

in the attempt to unravel the mysteries of the socialization process. Much of his work has only recently been read in the United States (because only recently translated).[18] But for some time his study of *The Moral Judgment of the Child* has been known throughout the world as a pioneer effort in understanding this significant aspect of socialization. Morality is a matter of adherence to rules; and Piaget distinguishes four stages in the development of the child's conceptions of the rules of the game: first, a stage of erratic and ephemeral individualism, with strong motor activity; second, the egocentric stage (roughly, ages two to five), "combining imitation of others with a purely individual use of the examples received"; third, between ages seven and eight, Piaget distinguishes an age of

---

[18] Relevant statements on some of Piaget's later work on *stages in the development of cognition* come from a Social Science Research Council report by Professor William Kessen:

> Stage I, *sensory-motor operations* characteristically develops through the first ten months of life. During this time the child learns that physical objects are stable and durable and he builds a "geometry" of the space immediately around him. Stage II, *operations of concrete thought*, extends from the middle of the second year until the eleventh or twelfth year. During this period children find out about the relations of negation and reciprocity (reversibility) . . . Stage III, which begins at about eleven or twelve years, is characterized by the development of *formal abstract* (adult) *operations of thought* . . . marked by experimental procedures on the part of the child in the solution of problems and by his use of algorithms (i.e., generalized mathematical methods that can be applied in a standard way) in the solution of physical problems.

See William Kessen, "Report on a Conference on Intellective Development in Children: A Conference on Piaget's Contributions in Relation to Other Theories of Children's Thinking," in *Items*, Vol. XIV, No. 3 (New York: Social Science Research Council, September, 1960).

Complete references for the English translations of Piaget's recent works (since 1950) are as follows:

The Psychology of Intelligence (London: Routledge & Kegan Paul, 1950).

Play, Dreams and Imitation in Childhood (New York: W. W. Norton & Co., Inc., 1951).

The Origins of Intelligence in Children (New York: International University Press, 1952).

The Child's Conception of Number (London: Routledge & Kegan Paul, 1950).

The Construction of Reality in the Child (London: Routledge & Kegan Paul, 1950).

The Child's Conception of Space (London: Routledge & Kegan Paul, 1950).

The Growth of Logical Thinking from Childhood; trans. Ann Parsons and Stanley Milgram (New York: Basic Books, 1958).

The Child's Conception of Geometry (with Bärbel Inhelder and Alina Szeminska) (London: Routledge & Kegan Paul, 1960).

For a good example of the interchange and refinement of ideas through cumulative research, see the extension of Piaget's work represented in Anselm L. Strauss and K. Schuessler, "Study of Concept Learning by Scale Analysis," *American Sociological Review*, Vol. XV (December, 1950), pp. 752–62.

incipient cooperation with an agreement on rules which may last the length of a single game but do not have an existence independent of the particular game; and finally, fourth, the stage mentioned above in which there is a codification of rules known to all members of the group and thus conveying the same notion as Mead's generalized other.

Piaget distinguishes three stages in the child's growing awareness of the rules: first a stage in which the rules do not have any mandatory quality, being taken as interesting examples rather than as obligatory realities; a second stage in which rules come to be seen as sacred, immutable, emanating from powerful adults and lasting forever; and a third stage in which a rule is looked upon as a law stemming from mutual consent, which should be respected but, also, which may be changed if the change is in accord with general sentiment. These correspond almost exactly to Newcomb's terms for describing the stages of personal growth and development: autism, absolutism, and reciprocity.[19]

For Freud, the socialization process was, at its core, the struggle to redirect primal impulses into culturally required and approved channels of conduct; for man is, first of all, an organism propelled by deep-rooted and preemptory drives. The confrontation with a repressive culture generates conflicts which may be resolved in a number of ways, among them by the use of psychic defense mechanisms: repression, sublimation, displacement, projection, and the like.[20] As diffuse sexual and aggressive drives seek expression within the constraining context of human society, determinate stages of the socialization process may be distinguished: infancy, latency, and puberty. Infancy covers the period up to about age five with satisfactions focused in the erotogenic zones, mouth, anus, and genitals, while culturally prescribed controls over feeding and elimination are imposed on the child. The second, or latency stage bridges, roughly, ages six to twelve, a period during which the child's great dependence on and attachment to the mother is attenuated—that is to say, œdipal inclinations are masked and a sense of the rules of the game begins to crystallize (in Freudian

---

[19] Theodore M. Newcomb, *Social Psychology* (New York: Dryden Press, 1950).

[20] The student who lacks familiarity with Freudian terminology and theory should consult such references as the following: Healy, Bronner, and Bowers, *The Structure and Meaning of Psychoanalysis* (New York: Alfred A. Knopf, Inc., 1930); Anna Freud, *The Ego and Mechanisms of Defence* (New York: International Universities Press, Inc., 1946); and Gordon S. Bloom, *Psychoanalytic Theories of Personality* (New York: McGraw-Hill Book Co., 1953).

terms the superego, or conscience, gains in strength). In the third, the puberty stage, starting at approximately age thirteen, the focus of gratification is on the genitals and heterosexual impulses gain in strength, once again controlled and deflected by the constraining cultural context mediated by the elders.

Now Freud was disposed to view man as endowed with a quantum of energy which, if not allowed to flow directly toward its goal, would seek alternative or compensatory outlets. Like a child's balloon, if constricted at one point it would billow out elsewhere. On the whole, the more restrictive the cultural context and the more repressive the socialization process, the greater the likelihood that this psychic energy would flow out in aggressive and damaging fashion, both for the person concerned and for others. This being so, it becomes extremely important that the relationship between parent—particularly mother—and child be a supportive one, gentle and affectionate. Thus the child has secure anchorage during this turbulent business of becoming socialized. In its popular and somewhat distorted version, this principle has often become a prescription of permissiveness.

What we have been discussing, quite obviously, is different (although by no means contradictory) interpretations of the socialization process—various theories as to the way in which the child enters the human group. But before we go on, let us pin down some of these ideas by looking at a piece of concrete research. This will allow us to tie the idea of socialization to the field of sociology as we discussed it in the introductory chapter: the controlled observation and interpretation of differing patterns of human relationships, their sources and consequences. Using Professor Sewell's study to which I alluded earlier,[21] consider these questions: (1) What are the "differing patterns of human relationships" that we are observing? (2) What interpretation is involved? (3) How is the observing done and in what sense is it controlled observation? (4) How is the problem formulated as an hypothesis? (5) How are the data manipulated in order to test the hypothesis? Take them seriatim.

WHAT ARE THE DIFFERING PATTERNS?

Although people in various roles share in the transmission of culture to the child—father as well as mother, siblings, relatives,

---

[21] William Sewell, "Infant Training and the Personality of the Child," *American Journal of Sociology* (published by The University of Chicago Press), Vol. XLVIII (September, 1952), pp. 150–59.

friends, and neighbors—the early and elemental aspects of socialization fall predominantly within the mother's sphere. Sewell is investigating the significance of different training practices such as breast versus bottle feeding, self-demand nursing schedules in contrast to a more rigid and regular schedule, the use or nonuse of punishment in toilet training, and the like. Hence it seems accurate to say that we are dealing here with differing patterns of mother-child relationships, relationships which differ along the dimension of leniency-severity. Our interest, then, is focused on the behavior of four persons: two persons (mother and child) in each of two categories. In the one category the mother trains the child in a way we call rigid, or rigorous, or demanding. In the other group the mother behaves indulgently, permissively. We might put the contrasting relationships, schematically, in this way:

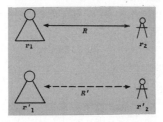

(where R and R' represent the differing patterns of relationship built from the articulation of r_2 and r'_2 (children's roles) and r_1 and r'_1, the mothers' roles, lenient and demanding, respectively). The differing (and, let us remind ourselves, *inferred*) relationships, indulgent and demanding, are represented by broken and solid lines, respectively.

WHAT IS THE INTERPRETATION INVOLVED HERE?

The interpretation to be tested is built upon the theory of socialization just mentioned above. Psychoanalytic prescriptions derived from Freudian theory emphasize such things as breast feeding, frequent sucking periods, casual and unforced toilet training. Karl Menninger, for example, asserts that every child should be guaranteed seven things:

1. He should have the opportunity for frequent sucking periods not

limited in time, not artificially interrupted, and preferably at the mother's breast.

2. There should be no attempt to train the functions of excretion in accordance with adult standards until the child can sit alone securely, until he has acquired a primitive sign language by means of which he can make known his bodily need, and until he shows some autonomous inclination to learn. . . .

3. There must be a long and uninterrupted period of consistent and skillful "psychological mothering" by one individual. This brings about a biological and psychological symbiosis in which two organisms with essentially different needs profit mutually. . . .*

4. He should have a father and a mother in harmonious relationship with one another to set a consistent pattern for his love development.

5. He should be spared reproaches, intimidations, threats, warnings, and punishments regarding physical manifestations of his sexuality. . . .

6. He should be accorded the dignity of a separate individual possessed of his own needs, rights, and feelings. . . .

7. In all communications with the child, truthfulness, honesty and sincerity on the part of the parents are unequivocally essential.[22]

* These first three recommendations, wholly in line with the thought of this entire chapter [reference is to Menninger's book], are paraphrased and elaborated from Margarethe A. Ribble ("Disorganizing Factors of Infant Personality," *American Journal of Psychiatry*, 98:459–463, November, 1941).

Such plausible prescriptions as these have dominated our thinking, if not our practice, for some time. But persuasive as such reasoning may be, the sociologist insists on testing it. This is the only defense we have against the tendency to use a theory to justify our preconceptions. The psychoanalysts, of course, are not working exclusively in the realm of speculation. They have their clinical observations. But typically the client is an adult whose difficulties must, in terms of the theory, be traced back through time to origins in infancy. Sewell points out two dangers in this procedure which make testing mandatory: first, the reconstruction of infant experiences may be erroneous; and second, there is no way of knowing whether the psychoanalysts' clients differ from the rest of the population in the infant training they have undergone. That is to say, the psychoanalyst may be disposed to make his inferences on the basis of inadequately controlled observations.

[22] From pp. 39–40 of *Love Against Hate* by Karl Menninger, copyright, 1942, by Karl Menninger and Jeanetta Lyle Menninger. Reprinted by permission of Harcourt, Brace & World, Inc.

HOW DOES SEWELL MAKE CONTROLLED OBSERVATIONS?

First of all, he must specify those behaviors of the mother which allow us to make the inference of an indulgent—or a demanding—mother-child relationship. His independent variable is some measure of degree of severity in child-training practices among mothers of Wisconsin farm children. Degree of severity is registered in manner and timing of nursing, weaning, bowel and bladder training, punishment for toilet accidents, sleep security (sleeping alone or with mother during the first year of life).

The information on these training practices was obtained from the mother by highly trained interviewers. These practices were measured simply by dichotomizing them in accordance with degree of severity. For example, weaning was abrupt or gradual, bowel training early or late, nursing by bottle or breast, etc. The dependent variable, measures of adjustment presumed to depend upon severity or indulgence in child training, came from three major sources: parents, teachers, and personality or behavior inventories. There were measures on aggression, arguing, fighting, nail-biting, finger-sucking, stuttering, fears, eating troubles, crying, sleep disturbances, etc.—thirteen such component scores on the tests of general adjustment and measures on twenty-six behavior manifestations bearing on level of adjustment.

Because no great claim can be made for either the precision, the validity or the reliability of any of the personality tests, indexes, or items, and because the sample size is not great, no attempt is made in this study to use any of them as quantitative measures. Rather, each is used only as a crude indicator. Thus, in the case of the tests and components, the child's score on each of the personality indexes was computed, an array[23] of scores was cast for each measure, and

---

[23] **An Aside on Methods: Using a Frequency Distribution to Describe a Group Attribute**

An "array" is a distribution of values, in descending or ascending order, together with their frequencies. Suppose, for example, that we were dealing with total adjustment scores on the California Test of Personality (one of the instruments used by Sewell). For 20 persons, an array of data might fall in this fashion:

Score	Frequency (Number of Persons Scoring within the Specified Category)
80–100	2
60– 79	4
40– 59	7
20– 39	5
0– 19	2

two relative score groups of approximately equal size were established. The only assumption was that those who made scores or ratings in the top half of the distribution were better adjusted as a group than those who made scores which placed them in the lower half of the distribution.

Now we have two sets of observations: one set on child training practices and one on adjustment. Since both training and adjustment have two values (strict-lenient and adequate-inadequate), we can represent the way in which the findings will be summarized in a four-celled table such as that in the figure below. Note in passing that when we dichotomize our data—when, for example, we take an

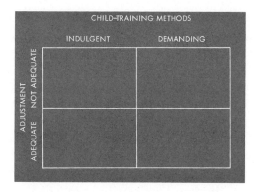

array of adjustment scores ranging, theoretically, from 100 to 0 and split the distribution so that half our subjects have higher scores than the other half—there are two outcomes from the point of view of accuracy. First, when we make an error in classification it is going to be a whopper. It will not be a matter of being slightly wrong, but completely wrong. Second, fewer errors in classification are likely to be made with only two categories in which to sort the data, since every additional category or division represents an additional problem in classification.

Before we leave this matter of controlled observation, we must raise the question as to how Sewell can know that differences in adjustment (adequate and inadequate) are attributable to differences in socialization practices *rather than* to differences in parental income, occupation, race, and the like. As his report indicates, he tries to control other variables which might otherwise confound his hypothesis *by eliminating them.* That is to say, he eliminates all mother-child pairs except persons who are white, members of farm families, in Wisconsin, native born, with children between five and six years of age who are products of unbroken and never broken unions. Hence differences in race, or income, or occupation, or nativity, or marital status, or age of child *cannot* account for any differences in adjustment observed between children experiencing indulgent and those experiencing demanding child-training practices.

HOW IS THE HYPOTHESIS FORMULATED?

Now if the interpretation of the mother-child relationship in the socialization process is as Menninger describes it, then all of Sewell's cases should fall into the lower left and the upper right cells. Thus we might state the hypothesis: the indicated measures of indulgent child training are positively related to specified measures of better adjustment. Or we might pose the logically prior hypothesis of *no relationship* between these child-training practices and these measures of adjustment. This is called a *null hypothesis* (H_0) and is commonly set up to serve as a target, as it were. If we can reject it, then an alternative hypothesis to account for the results is that hypothesis (H_1) derived from our theory which asserts a determinate relationship between the variables. If we cannot reject the null hypothesis, then we are probably badly off the track somewhere—anywhere—along the line between the original formulation of the problem and the statement of results.

HOW IS THE HYPOTHESIS TESTED? THE DATA MANIPULATED?

In manipulating his data on 162 cases, Sewell uses a device often encountered in sociological research, called the chi-square test (χ^2). This compares the distribution of cases actually observed with the distribution which would obtain were there no relationship between the independent and the dependent variables. As an illustration, assume that we have 100 mother-child pairs, of which 50 represent an indulgent relationship and 50 a rigid and demanding relationship. Suppose also that half of these pairs involve children who have made a satisfactory adjustment on such measures as Sewell used, the other half being children whose adjustment scores are low. Now if there is no relationship between extent of indulging-demanding on the one hand and adequacy of adjustment on the other, the distribution of cases (the frequencies we would expect) should look like this:

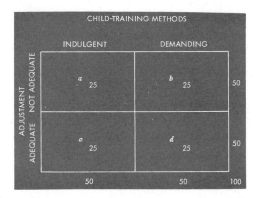

The extent to which this is not true, the extent to which the frequencies of our actual observations (f_o) differ from the frequencies, above, which we would expect on the assumption of no relationship $(f_e =$ frequencies to be expected on this assumption)[24] gives us some clue as to the significance of our findings. If the $(f_o - f_e)$ values are large—if, that is, the distribution of observed frequencies is such that it could not reasonably be attributed to chance—then it is a nonchance, a systematic relationship which we have uncovered and which wants explaining. And, of course, since the observations are testing an hypothesis derived from a theory, in this case Freudian theories of socialization, we have that explanation ready at hand.

Having followed Professor Sewell so far, we have earned a right to his findings; and he the right of a final *caveat*.

Of the 460 chi square tests, only 18 were significant at or beyond the .05 level. Of these, eleven were in the expected direction and seven were in the opposite direction from that expected on the basis of psychoanalytic writings. Such practices as breast feeding, gradual weaning, demand schedule, and easy and late induction to bowel and bladder training, which have been so much emphasized in the psychoanalytic literature were almost barren in terms of relation to personality adjustment as measured in this study. . . .

Finally a word . . . about the limitations of this study. First, it must be admitted that the controls employed, although better than in most studies of this type, were very crude. . . . Second, the data

---

[24] See "An Aside on Methods: Calculating Expected Frequencies to Compare with Observed Frequencies," pp. 114–15.

An Aside on Methods: Calculating Expected Frequencies to Compare with Observed Frequencies

The calculation of f_e (expected frequencies) is simple. The total number of cases and the marginal frequencies are taken as given. Our job is to find out how they would distribute themselves within the cells on the assumption of no relationship between the two variables (H_0). Take, for example, the cell representing children whose measured adjustment was "inadequate" and who were subjected to "demanding" child-training practices. Fifty out of 100 children ($50/100$, or $1/2$) fall in the first category; and $50/100$ in the second category. Now the probability that a child will have *both* of these attributes (inadequate adjustment *and* demanding training) is given by the product of these separate probabilities—i.e., by $50/100 \times 50/100$ or $(.5) (.5) = .25$. This tells us that in one fourth of the cases we should find this particular combination of traits, severe training and inadequate adjustment *if* the two are not related. Since there are 100 cases, $(.25) (100) = 25$ as our expected frequency (f_e) for the upper right hand cell.

χ^2 itself is *a measure of the difference—between observed and expected frequencies* (f_o and f_e, respectively). The formula for χ^2 is

$$\sum \frac{(f_o - f_e)^2}{f_e}$$

This should be simplified for ease in calculation.
Expanding, we get:

$$\sum \frac{(f_o{}^2 - 2f_o f_e + f_e{}^2)}{f_e} \quad \text{or} \quad \sum \frac{f_o{}^2}{f_e} - 2\sum \left(\frac{f_o f_e}{f_e}\right) + \sum \left(\frac{f_e}{f_e}\right)^2.$$

Then: $\sum \left(\frac{f_o}{f_e}\right)^2 - 2\Sigma f_o + \Sigma f_e$ and, since $\Sigma f_o = N$ and $\Sigma f_e = N$,

$$\chi^2 = \sum \left(\frac{f_o}{f_e}\right)^2 - 2N + N, \text{ or } \sum \left(\frac{f_o}{f_e}\right)^2 - N.$$

To continue with our illustration of Sewell's method of manipulating the data, let us assume that the observed frequencies (f_o) in the four cells a, b, c, and d were 40, 10, 10, and 40 respectively. Now having already calculated the expected frequencies on the assumption of the null hypothesis (no relationship between the variables), and having found them to be 25, 25, 25, and 25, we are ready to calculate χ^2. Following our formula,

$$\chi^2 = \sum \left(\frac{f_o}{f_e}\right)^2 - N,$$

we arrange the data and calculate:

Cell	f_o	f_e	$f_o{}^2$	$f_o{}^2/f_e$
a	40	25	1600	64
b	10	25	100	4
c	10	25	100	4
d	40	25	1600	64

$$\text{and} \quad \sum f_o{}^2/f_e = 136$$

$$\text{Now, } \chi^2 = \sum f_o{}^2/f_e - N$$
$$= 136 - 100$$
$$= 36$$

An Aside on Methods: Calculating Expected Frequencies to Compare with Observed Frequencies (continued)

Now what does a χ^2 value of 36 mean? We must remember that it is a measure of the difference between what we observe and what we might expect were there no relationship between the variables jointly observed. Now we compare the value which we obtained (36) with other values in a Table of χ^2 values to determine what the probability is that a difference of this order would appear. In reading the table two matters must be considered: the χ^2 value and the "degrees of freedom." In this case, where we have a 2×2 table, only one of the cell values is free to vary independently; for once the marginal values are given plus the value in *one* cell, all the other cell values are determined. There is, then, one degree of freedom in this table. Now a χ^2 value of 36 is comparable to a probability less than .001 ($p < .001$). That is to say, the observed and expected frequencies are sufficiently different so that one would expect such a distribution as that which we have observed to occur by chance fewer than once in a thousand times. Hence we reject the null hypothesis of no relationship between the two variables. (Note that these are concocted data. Sewell's findings were quite different.)

---

on training experiences, although gathered and treated with care, may be inadequate for reasons cited or unknown. Third, the measures of personality employed in the study are far from perfect in relation to either their validity or their reliability. Consequently, the possibility remains that the results may be different when the children are tested at later periods in their development and with more satisfactory measures. But despite these and other limitations, the results of this study are unequivocal for the sample covered, and their generality must be affirmed or denied by means of better-designed and executed empirical studies, not by dialectic.

SIGNIFICANCE OF DIFFERENT PATTERNS OF SOCIALIZATION

These contrasts in socialization which we have been discussing are fairly mild ones when we consider the intercultural range of practices. The mothers of Alor are quite indifferent to Dr. Menninger's good counsel. From their second week of life the Alorese youngster learns to do without its mother, who goes back to the fields. "Mothers, even when present, seem to provide only casual and disinterested care, and as the child grows older his lot continues to be one of neglect and rebuff."[25] The child is roughly, often precipitously weaned, incited to anger and jealousy (the mother

---

[25] Taken from Cora DuBois in Abram Kardiner, *Psychological Frontiers of Society* (New York: Columbia University Press, 1945), and quoted in T. M. Newcomb, *Social Psychology* (New York: Dryden Press, 1950), pp. 442, 443.

may deliberately take another infant to feed), intimidated ("a boy often has . . . fingers and arrows poked into his distended abdomen. . . ."), frightened, threatened, punished and rewarded inconsistently, kept awake at night. It seems a reasonable inference that this child is being prepared for adult roles differing markedly from those of the middle-class American. Some notion of the contrast is brought home to us when we read between the lines of this chant, or poem, sung in his bathtub every evening by an American four year old. Not only the solicitous care focused on this youngster but also the fond delight of the mother who recorded it comes through clearly.

> He will just do nothing at all,
> He will just sit there in the noonday sun.
> And when they speak to him, he will not answer them,
> Because he does not care to.
> He will stick them with spears and put them in the garbage.
> When they tell him to eat his dinner, he will just laugh at them
> And he will not take his nap, because he does not care to.
> He will not talk to them, he will not say nothing.
> He will just sit there in the noonday sun.
> He will go away and play with the Panda.
> He will not speak to nobody because he doesn't have to.
> And when they come to look for him they will not find him.
> Because he will not be there.
> He will put spikes in their eyes and put them in the garbage,
> And put the cover on.
> He will not go out in the fresh air or eat his vegetables.
> Or make wee-wee for them, and he will get thin as a marble.
> He will do nothing at all.
> He will just sit there in the noonday sun.[26]

Such contrasts in child rearing interest us for many reasons. Among other things, they are a chief source of personal uniqueness. As an organism (and with the exception of single-egg twins) each individual is unique as a result of the independent segregation and assortment of genes received from his parents. But *with no exceptions whatsoever,* each child stands at the hub of a social context quite peculiar to himself and generating that particular constellation of attributes which distinguish him as a personality. (On the other hand, such personal uniquenesses will not be permitted to interfere with the inculcation of the general knowledge, normative and existential, characterizing the group of which the mediators, parents

---

[26] *The New Yorker,* July 1, 1939. Reprinted by permission; Copr. © 1939 The New Yorker Magazine, Inc.

and teachers, are members. He will have to know and follow the score, holding idiosyncratic interpretations to an insignificant minimum.)

But differences in ways of socialization between or within societies are significant, for our purposes, from a social rather than an individual perspective. Different methods of rearing, training, educating lead to different slots in a complex social structure. Beliefs and behaviors have consequences; and different ways of inducting the newcomer affect his destiny as a social creature, as a group member. Depending on his early socialization he will have the inclination and the ability to enter subsequent groups. Depending on his early socialization he will be acceptable or unacceptable to groups he enters later. For socialization is a continuous process and the later stages are necessarily conditioned by aptitudes and attitudes learned earlier.

Consider joining a national group—immigration to the United States. To enter this group is clearly hard or easy depending upon the likenesses between the culture earlier inculcated and the culture of the new land (group). Command of the language, familiarity with the style of life, a generally high appraisal of things American, ease the way into the new group. And these features derive from antecedent socialization. Emma Lazarus expressed a kindly sentiment, inscribed on the statue of liberty:

> . . . Give me your tired, your poor,
> Your huddled masses yearning to breathe free,
> The wretched refuse of your teeming shore.
> Send these, the homeless tempest-tossed to me,
> I lift my lamp beside the golden door.

But while we applaud such charitable sentiments, Lazarus' invitation is misleading. For we are not typically hospitable to those regarded as "refuse." Every group is selective in its recruitment, including even the family which controls both the quantity and the quality of its recruits. (The number of children is controlled and so, in the rearing, is the newcomer made "qualitatively" acceptable.) All groups select, indoctrinate (socialize), and eliminate the unfit and undesirable—each group, obviously, in terms of its own standards. The group which is the national society is no exception. This is not to claim either wisdom or righteousness for the Walter-McCarran immigration act (the "Immigration and Nationality Act of 1952). But I would suggest that with the nation as with other groups, those who seek and most readily gain admission are those congenially encultured. Thus in the U.S., until 1966, of the 154,657 persons annually admittable, 96.8 percent were Europeans. Closer still to the culture of the group they were entering, 81.6 percent were from northern and western Europe. But the most significant figure is this: 70 percent of the total immigrant quota was assigned to three nations: the United Kingdom, Germany, and the Irish Free State. In general, the 40 million immigrants who have entered the U.S. were culturally qualified to enter the group—or the subgroup, in the case of orientals and southeast European immigrants, many of them illiterate and destitute who came to do the most menial labor. What they had to offer has been well articulated with what the group needed. One evidence of this is the similarity of curves representing business activity or, inversely, unemployment, and the curve representing flow of immigrants.

Doubtless the input into any organization never makes a perfect match with the requirements of the group. Where there is little self-selection, as in a drafted army or a state university, the problem of assimilation is acute. And so we have indoctrination programs, orientation programs, in-service training, Americanization schools, and the like.

But self-selection figures significantly in the immigration process. And immigration quotas are ostensibly designed to promote self-selection, so encouraging only those who are "best qualified" to join a new nationality group. Yet with all this, it is not easy to achieve the aim of bringing the newcomer to understand and participate in the life of the new group he has entered. We spend fifteen to twenty years effecting the induction of the child to the first group he must enter. It is not surprising, then, that the later entrance into a different nationality group entails a host of problems, despite self-selection. Sometimes the immigrant wives remain resistantly immured at home. There are problems of recertification and re-qualification of professionals like lawyers and physicians. Similarly with technicians, new and different standards may be required in their trades, compelling them to undergo adaptive training.

C. A. Price estimates that one out of three of the 900,000 persons migrating to Australia between 1945 and 1954 required instruction in English.[27] Where immigrants settle in colonies it is easier for the

---

[27] C. A. Price, "The Education of Immigrants in Australia," *Some Studies in Education of Immigrants for Citizenship,* No. 16 in UNESCO Educational Studies and Documents Series (Paris: UNESCO Workshops, 1955).

host government to reach them (for training purposes and supposing there is either need or interest in doing so); but such colonies also offer the newcomer a refuge within his own national enclave which may so effectively isolate him from the larger group that he never actually enters it. (This appears to have been the case in some German communities in Brazil.[28]) Dispersed settlement, on the other hand, makes the newcomer harder to reach formally, but implicates him more effectively in the life of local communities where informal agencies of assimilation may take over. Above all, there is the problem, from the perspective of the group, of achieving unity in the face of diversity.[29] "Ninety-eight percent of Canadians are transplanted Europeans," notes Mr. Joseph Kage.[30] The newcomer at birth poses the same problem of assimilation. But the devices and time available are much more adequate in this earlier socialization.

A dramatic illustration of the problem of entering the group and the problem of assimilating diverse newcomers to the group is provided in the recent history of immigration to Israel which was, in 1950, about 80 percent foreign born. Prime Minister Ben Gurion declared:

> We shall bring into the country a nation of unusual character, spread all over the world, speaking many languages, influenced by many cultures, divided into various communities and sects. It is our duty to cast this differentiated and colourful people, into the mould of a reformed nation. We have to uproot all the geographical, cultural, social and linguistic divisions which separate them and give them one language, one culture and one citizenship.[31]

The dimensions of this socialization problem are suggested by the two figures on the following pages.

In Israel's first ten years (1948–1958), her population almost tripled. The Law of Return, passed by the Knesset in July, 1950, granted to every Jew the right to immigrate to Israel, should he so choose. This "open door" policy brought over a million Jews from

---

[28] Manuel Diegues, Jr., "The Education of Immigrants in Brazil," UNESCO, *op. cit.*

[29] Let us be clear that this is not a matter of celebrating conformity and deprecating diversity. It is simply to note that certain common understandings are necessary for the concerted action characterizing any group.

[30] Joseph Kage, "The Education of Immigrant Workers in Canada," UNESCO, *op. cit.*, p. 22.

[31] Joseph Shaked, "The Education of New Immigrant Workers in Israel," UNESCO *op. cit.*, p. 32.

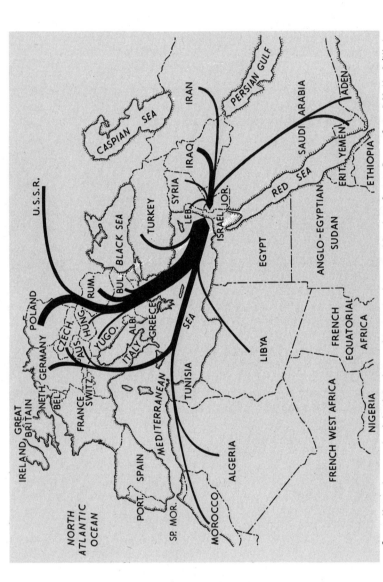

Source: Norman Lawrence, Israel: *Jewish Population and Immigration. International Population Statistics Reports,* Series P-90, No. 2 (Washington, D.C.: U.S. Government Printing Office, 1952), p. 20.

FIG. 3–1. Origin of principal streams of Jewish immigrants to Israel and Palestine: 1919 to 1952.

seventy different countries within ten years. Fewer than 2 percent of the immigrants entering after 1948 had any agricultural experience. More than half lacked vocational or professional training of any kind. Most were poor. Included were children, the sick and the aged. Many were illiterate. Few spoke Hebrew. They had to be woven, culturally, into the fabric of Israeli society.

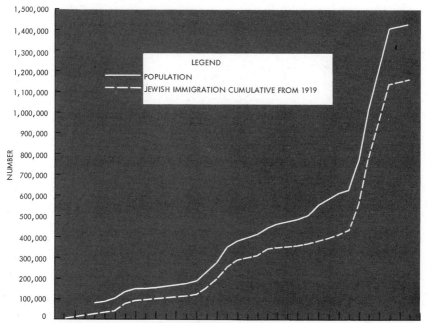

Source: Norman Lawrence, *Israel: Jewish Population and Immigration*. International Population Statistics Reports, Series P-90, No. 2 (Washington, D.C.: U.S. Government Printing Office, 1952), p. 4.

FIG. 3–2. Jewish population and Jewish immigration for Israel and Palestine: 1919-1952.

Their assimilation hinged on the development of Israel's resources. The first wave of immigrants (1948–1950) for which the warring new nation was unprepared, remained in reception camps maintained by the Jewish Agency[32] until arrangements were completed for the final settlement. The result was months of enforced idleness, demoralizing dependence, and delay in participating in the life of the group. Beginning in July, 1950, immigrants were transferred to transitional settlements—*ma'bara*—in rural or urban

[32] The Jewish Agency is an international organization formed to promote the development of Israel through contributions of Jews throughout the world.

areas where work was available on the site of a planned village or city. They were provided with tents or huts, but were dependent on their own resources for furniture, food, and clothing. Newcomers in *ma'bara* earned their living by working on nearby public works, on afforestation, reclamation, and irrigation projects, in factories, on road construction, etc. In 1954, a "ship to settlement" policy was initiated, providing for the planned direction of every immigrant to a specific agricultural settlement or industrial development area where work was available. As far as possible, immigrants were settled away from larger towns, and money was invested in creating new villages in rural, especially border, areas. Native Israeli farmers went as instructors to the new settlements. These new settlements were dependent on the Jewish Agency until economically on their feet. This "ship to settlement" made the immigrant self-sustaining as soon as possible, enabling him to become a productive member of his new country without much delay.

Many immigrants knew so little Hebrew when they arrived that they could not pronounce the name of the village which was to be their new home. The government (through the Ministry of Education and Culture) is trying to impart at least an elementary knowledge of Hebrew to every adult Jew. Instruction in the language includes intensive residential courses (*Ulpanim*) and day and evening classes. A daily Labor Federation newspaper is printed in simplified and "vowelled" Hebrew. Most newspapers print a column of hints on correct Hebrew. Lessons and news bulletins in easy Hebrew are broadcast over the State Broadcasting Service, Kol Israel. Elementary, high, and vocational schools have been built for the education of immigrants. (Education is compulsory for children five to fourteen years of age.)

There is, of course, the greatest disparity in cultural backgrounds of the immigrants. Such Israeli values as the defense of the country, the Hebrew language and literature, the Jewish family with the mother and child at its center—these and other elements of a new national culture must be inculcated in the newcomer.

The great number of persons involved, their diversity and the rapid rate of their immigration make Israel a forceful illustration of the problems and process of entering the group (later socialization). But it does not come as close to home for most people as the more mundane matter of entering a (new) school group; or joining a work group. In his study of "The Military Academy as an Assimilating Institution,"[33] Professor Dornbusch reveals some of the principal elements of socialization in a school group. As in the case of *The Nun's Story* or in the matter of entering a prison group, effective socialization depends upon a rejection or a renunciation of the past and a commitment to the present.

The rejection of the past is accomplished in various ways. The "swab" at the Coast Guard Academy is effectively isolated from the past since he is not allowed to leave the base; nor is he permitted to have dealings with noncadets. The use of uniforms (and sometimes standardized campus clothing achieves the same end) erases signs of differentials that might be linked to the past. They emphasize the common condition and common destiny of members of the group. Sometimes letters from home are forbidden. Sometimes receipt of money from outside sources is forbidden. This pattern of isolation is a common phase of the socialization process. (It is, of course, unnecessary with the infant since there are no antecedent experiences except those of the intrauterine period to be extinguished.) The newly inducted inmate of a federal prison undergoes a period of quarantine for about a month. The newly inducted G.I. has a period of basic training during which his outside contacts are restricted. During her novitiate the nun may not be allowed to leave the convent, so cutting contact with family, friends, the past. Such severance from the past is certainly promoted by acquiring a language peculiar to the new group. Parents sometimes get a slight sense of this effect when their children return from school for the holidays.

The obverse side of the coin is commitment to the present, identification with the current group. Learning the language, the slang, the mystic symbols of the group helps to achieve this end. Isolation in the present situation is also achieved by an exhausting schedule, so preempting time and energy that nostalgic retrospection is almost impossible. Camp counselors are aware of this device and put it to effective practice. Uniforms, badges, pins emphasize, not only the distinctiveness of the group, its separation from other groups, but the identity of those within the group. And here the only status differences are those relevant to the value system of the current group. Group solidarity, identification with it, is enhanced by common sharing and survival through bad experi-

---

[33] Sanford M. Dornbusch, "The Military Academy as an Assimilating Institution," *Social Forces*, Vol. XXXIII, No. 4 (May, 1955).

ences such as hazing. (Dornbusch notes that if one cadet is unable to answer the teacher's question, it is mandatory for others to respond to the same question by saying: "I don't know, sir.")

Commitment to the group is enhanced where there is a clear-cut gradation of experiences with plenty of opportunity for imaginal role-rehearsal, in preparation for the next stage. One knows where he is going and the destination is desirable. Not only is it desirable, but however difficult of attainment, it is possible. Dealings—especially informal ones—with admired upperclassmen enhance both the desirability of achieving group goals and the probability of doing so. For the upperclassman is what the newcomer will become. The single-minded pursuit of the goal deemed desirable is made easier if there are such models available, especially models who can be put in dramatic focus. This is an important reason for celebrating our heroes. Lincoln, Churchill, Garibaldi are persons not merely to venerate but to emulate. The exemplary nun referred to in *The Nun's Story* as *"la règle vivante"* performs this function for the novitiates.

In the service of this imaginal role-rehearsal ("anticipatory socialization"), rites of passage are useful. They provide clear-cut gradations of experience, separating past from future, emphasizing the new role requirements and providing evidence of progress toward the goal.

Finally, we should note the importance, for the socialization process, of the rigorous weeding out of the defectors, the delinquents, the disenchanted, the disabled, the disaffected. The fewer the alternative views of the group, of its goals and procedures, the more effective the socialization process. Perhaps it is an enervating academic view that wholehearted commitment to anything is a function of ignorance. But as a principle in socialization it is doubtless true that the newcomer becomes a loyal old-timer more readily when he is denied the luxury of skepticism. Some American groups having a conception of democracy based on the Biblical injunction to forgive seventy times seven find it difficult to apply this last principle of socialization. In consequence, they may retain as members of the group a number of skeptics, critics, or subversives. But one result of constant concern for the aberrant individual is an attenuation of group strength. Tolerance of the apathetic or indifferent, to say nothing of the deviant, may compromise organizational ends and means. Put positively, such tolerance promotes change, the re-formation of the structure of relationships that constitutes the group

Work groups are likely to be more rigorous in their recruitment and socialization of new members; for the caculus of profit provides a yardstick and exerts pressure for continuously improved selection and training. But always supplementing the selective recruitment practiced by the group is the self-selection practiced by those entering it. Neither sort of selection produces a perfect fit between the role to be filled and the aptitudes and attitudes of the newcomer. Indoctrination procedures are usually necessary. Nonetheless, the two selective processes work together to sort individuals into slots in the work-system in a way sufficiently effective to enable perform-ance of a task and, indeed, to enable the recognition of occupational types. Henry Fielding, in 1742, seems to have thought the lawyer a recognizable type. And the novelist Robertson Davies thinks it plausible to portray a lawyer whose professional style is modeled, nature imitating art, on fictional forebears created in books and plays.

> I question not but several of my readers will know the lawyer in the stage-coach the moment they hear his voice. . . . I declare here once for all, I describe not men, but manners; not an individual, but a species.[34]

> In the nineteenth century . . . many lawyers were dry and fusty men, of formal manner and formal dress, who carried much of the deportment of the courtroom into private life. Novelists and play-wrights . . . put many such lawyers into their books and upon the stage . . . Mathew Snelgrove . . . seized upon this lawyer-like shell eagerly, and made it his own . . . until . . . he was not only a lawyer in reality, but also a lawyer in a score of stagey mannerisms; a lawyer who joined the tips of his fingers while listening to a client; a lawyer who closed his eyes and smacked his lips disconcertingly while others talked; a lawyer who tugged and polished at his long nose with a very large handkerchief; a lawyer who coughed dryly before speaking; a lawyer who used his eyeglasses not so much as aids to vision as for peeping over, snatching from the nose, rubbing on the lapel, and wagging in his listener's face. He was a master of legal grimace—the smile of disbelief, the smile of I-pity-your-igno-rance, the smile of that-may-safely-be-left-in-my-hands, as well as a number of effective frowns, signifying disapproval, impatience and

---

[34] Henry Fielding, *Joseph Andrews* (London: F. C. and J. Rivington, 1820).

disgust. Like many another professional man, Mr. Snelgrove had become the prisoner of a professional manner. . . .[35]

Sartre provides another insight: the realization of self in a role, the role of a waiter, by meeting the expectations of the public. Having commented on his dexterity, the exaggeration of pace and posture, he suggests that the waiter:

> . . . is playing at being a waiter in a cafe. . . . The game is a kind of marking out and investigation. The child plays with his body in order to explore it, to take inventory of it: the waiter in the cafe plays with his condition in order to *realize* it. The obligation is not different from that which is imposed on all tradesmen. Their condition is wholly one of ceremony. The public demands of them that they realize it as a ceremony; there is the dance of the grocer, of the tailor, of the auctioneer, by which they endeavor to persuade their clientele that they are nothing but a grocer, an auctioneer, a tailor. A grocer who dreams is offensive to the buyer, because such a grocer is not wholly a grocer. Society demands that he limit himself to his function as a grocer, just as the soldier at attention makes himself into a soldier-thing with a direct regard which does not see at all, which is no longer meant to see. . . . There are indeed many precautions to imprison a man in what he is, as if we lived in perpetual fear that he might escape from it, that he might break away and suddenly elude his condition.[36]

Sometimes what the public demands is not formally specified if, indeed, it is known. The expectations and understandings transmitted may be chiefly within the organization, and sometimes implicitly rather than explicitly. Breed discusses the way in which the tyro learns a newspaper's policy.[37] Even though this policy is seldom explicitly stated, he gradually picks it up as part of the socialization process in which he adapts to his co-workers and superiors.

The aptitudes, attitudes, attributes in general which condition the match between newcomer and the needs of the group he is entering are built upon in his *initial socialization*. There is much evidence that the family group which the person first enters has an emphatic

[35] Robertson Davies, *Leaven of Malice*. Reprinted by permission of Willis Kingsley Wing. Copyright © 1954, by Clarke, Irwin & Co., Ltd.

[36] Jean-Paul Sartre, *Being and Nothingness*, translated by Hazel E. Barnes (New York: Philosophical Library, 1956), p. 59.

[37] Warren Breed, "Social Controls in the Newsroom: A Functional Analysis," *Social Forces*, Vol. XXXIII (1954), pp. 326–35.

influence on the occupational group which he later enters. Consider the following data:[38]

	DISTRIBUTION OF OCCUPATIONS OF FATHERS OF MEN LISTED IN AMERICAN MEN OF SCIENCE	DISTRIBUTION OF THESE OCCUPATIONS IN THE GENERAL POPULATION (Data Refer to Situation c. 1906)
Professional	43.1%	3.0%
Commercial	35.7	34.1
Agricultural	21.2	41.1

Similarly, Bernard Barber makes the point that there appears to be a connection between the person's religion, inculcated in early socialization, and the probability of his entering one of the scientific professions. Catholics in the United States—disregarding other relevant variables, such as class—are not proportionately represented among scientific workers in the United States.

Father Cooper says he "would be loathe to have to defend the thesis that five percent or even three percent of the leadership in American science and scholarship is Catholic. Yet we Catholics constitute something like twenty per cent of the total population."[39]

As for American Jews, we have no figures at all, but it is very probable that they are at least proportionately represented in science and learning, at least in the universities. This is what we might expect for two reasons. First, the Jewish values seem to favor learning and empirical rationality. And, second, there is an important relevant factor in the American social system. The Jews have been remarkably socially mobile in the U.S., and the free professions, including science, have been more open to them than large industry and many areas of business.[40]

That persons enter groups appropriate in terms of the attitudes and values they bring to them is supported by some evidence

---

[38] These data are reprinted with permission of The Free Press of Glencoe from *Science and the Social Order* by Bernard Barber, pp. 134, 135. Copyright 1952 by The Free Press, a corporation. The data came originally from *Science*, Volume XXIV (1906), pp. 732–44.

[39] Bernard Barber, *op. cit.*, p. 136. He is quoting J. M. Cooper, "Catholics and Scientific Research," *Commonweal*, Vol. XLII (1945), pp. 147–49.

[40] Morris Rosenberg, "Factors Influencing Change of Occupational Choice," reprinted with permission of The Free Press of Glencoe from *The Language of Social Research* by Paul F. Lazarsfeld and Morris Rosenberg. Copyright 1955 by The Free Press, a corporation.

provided by Rosenberg. He questioned a group of students who planned to become businessmen, dividing them into two categories, "very conservative" and "not very conservative," depending on their responses to these statements.

> Democracy depends fundamentally on the existence of free business enterprise.
> The "welfare state" tends to destroy individual initiative.
> The laws governing labor unions today are not strict enough.
> Labor unions in this country are doing a fine job.

Those who answered these four questions "yes," "yes," "yes," and "no," respectively, were called "very conservative" and those who answered any other way were called "not very conservative." The question we are raising is whether students' orientations on these matters will predict the occupational group they choose to enter. Here are Rosenberg's data:

PLANS IN 1952	ORIENTATION IN 1950		
	VERY CONSERVATIVE	NOT VERY CONSERVATIVE	
Remained businessmen	73%	36%	
			$p = .01$
Changed occupational choice	27%	64%	
	N = (22)	(56)	

Consider comparable data for medical students who were asked about the things from which they expected to gain most satisfaction in their lives:

IN 1952	MAIN LIFE SATISFACTION (1950)		
	CAREER OR OCCUPATION	FAMILY RELATIONSHIPS	
Still chose medicine	80%	33%	
			$p = .01$
Left medicine	20%	67%	
	N = (20)	(27)	

Rosenberg combined his teachers and businessmen in relating dominant value complex to the occupational group entered. Again, the data are revealing:

	TEACHERS AND BUSINESSMEN	
IN 1952	AGREEING WITH DOMINANT VALUE COMPLEX IN 1950	DISAGREEING WITH DOMINANT VALUE COMPLEX IN 1950
Remained in occupation	57%	27%
Changed occupation	43%	73%
N =	(124)	(64)

p = .01

Here then is evidence of the sorting into occupational groups of persons whose prior socialization has so shaped their attitudes as to make them proper recruits. Clearly one of the most significant developments of the socialization process is the shaping of these orientations whose repercussions flow throughout life affecting, among other things, the groups we enter.

       ❄   ❄   ❄   ❄

Let us review, briefly. The first and critical part of the socialization process occurs as we enter the human group. It involves such an interpenetration of self and other that the other's expectations, expectations reflecting cultural prescriptions, become one's own. The process is a long and arduous one for the human child and the stages of development have been charted in various ways. The interpretations of Mead, Piaget, and Freud provide useful insights.

To illustrate how a theory of early socialization might be tested by a sociologist we reviewed Sewell's test of the hypothesis that indulgent rather than demanding infant training practices promote good adjustment in the child's subsequent relationships.

But as we noted, this first entry into the human group is only one of many. Some people migrate to new countries and enter new nationality groups. All of us enter school groups, since it is a legal requirement. And most of us enter work groups, worship groups, play groups, and a variety of other groups. In each case adaptive or socializing processes are involved and those subcultural emphases picked up in prior socialization influence the choice of, and success in these groups later entered. (As Rosenberg's study illustrated, thing-oriented persons tend to give up their plans to become teachers: person-oriented students stay with it.)

In discussing culture in Chapter 2, I emphasized the social aspect of culture. Culture is learned and taught, there is a "student" and a "teacher." But why is what is taught, taught? For apparently the transmission of core cultural elements is mandatory. Much, no doubt, is unwittingly transmitted. But the proper induction of the newcomer is a matter of such import that no enduring group leaves it to chance. And so we look to the leverage applied by the group and the evidence for its coercive influence, attending especially to family and school as agents of cultural transmission.

ORIGINAL TEXTS

1. Marcel Mauss, "Mémoire et société," *L'Année sociologique,* 3rd series, Vol. I, (1940–48) (Paris: Presses Universitaires de France, 1949), pp. 3–177.

    Mauss's words are as follows: Il n'est pas nécessaire que d'autres hommes soient là, qui se distinguent matériellement de nous: car nous portons toujours avec nous et en nous une quantité de personnes qui ne se confondent pas.

SELECTED SUPPLEMENTARY READINGS

*BECKER, HOWARD S., AND STRAUSS, ANSELM L. "Careers, Personality, and Adult Socialization," *American Journal of Sociology,* 1956, pp. 253–63.

*BENEDICT, RUTH. "Continuities and Discontinuities in Cultural Conditioning," *Psychiatry,* 1938, pp. 161–67.

BERELSON, BERNARD, AND STEINER, GARY A. "Behavioral Development," in *Human Behavior: An Inventory of Scientific Findings,* pp. 37–85. New York: Harcourt, Brace & World, Inc., 1964.

*HOMANS, GEORGE C. "Social Behavior as Exchange," *American Journal of Sociology,* 1958, pp. 597–606.

LINDESMITH, ALFRED R., AND STRAUSS, ANSELM L. *Social Psychology.* New York: Dryden, 1949.

SHIBUTANI, TAMOTSU. *Society and Personality.* Englewood Cliffs, N.J.: Prentice-Hall, Inc., 1961.

STRAUSS, ANSELM (ed.). *The Social Psychology of George Herbert Mead.* Chicago: Phoenix Books, The University of Chicago Press, 1956.

* Articles marked with an asterisk are available as reprints from the college division of the Bobbs-Merrill Company, Indianapolis, Indiana.

Chapter 4

The Group as the Agent of Cultural Transmission

How are people induced to take up a given role?
What's the evidence of the group's influence?
What are the means of, the agents for, socialization?

U p to this point we have been thinking about the *process* through which a person becomes a member of a group. We see this process in the training of the infant, in the rearing of the child to meet the requirements of his particular society. We see it in the indoctrination of the immigrant, culminating, from the legal standpoint, in naturalization and from a social standpoint, in assimilation. We see this process in the puberty rites marking the transition from youth to adult responsibilities, the induction of a student into college, into his fraternity, into the armed forces; and in the hiring and in-service training of the new employee.

These are merely illustrative. For all our lives we grow and develop by means of the novel and stimulating interchange involved in entering new groups. When we fail a little in this process we are dull. When we fail flagrantly we are mad. When we suspend it temporarily we sleep. When we give up the attempt altogether we vegetate—almost the equivalent of death. This is the process by which, as Reuter once put it, "individuals are taught to function in the group in which *their wishes are created and realized.*"[1] It is the process through which one comes to prefer majority vote to concurring in a dictator's mandate (or vice versa), of becoming Methodist rather than Catholic, of preferring roast beef to escargots, gefilte fish to roast pork, of becoming a Republican rather than a Democrat. It leads one to read the little mags. and wear a beard rather than joining the clean-shaven philistines with *Harper's* and the *Atlantic.* It disposes one to enter the clan of lawyers rather than the ranks of the physical scientists, etc., etc.

United Press Photo

The power of the elders through example and tutelage.

Now we cannot understand how such preferences, capacities, attitudes, and judgments emerge except as we come to appreciate

[1] E. B. Reuter, *Handbook of Sociology* (New York: Dryden Press, 1946). Italics mine.

the extent to which others, in transmitting culture, exert enormous influence on us. And so we turn now to the *agency* of cultural transmission, the group, and to the evidence of its influence upon the person. Such an influence we have implied in our characterization of the concept, culture. Culture is social, it is learned, it is inculcated. So much is this so, so imperative are the demands of others upon us to abide by the dictates of Emily Post and the mandates of democratic beliefs, that we both anticipate and suffer severe sanctions for nonconformity. The group, through its agents, shapes the person. There is no "natural" unfolding of the personality without human intervention. Men are made. Motherhood is revered, wherever it is understood, as the consummately creative role, the work of ultimate artistry. Parents and teachers, in their institutional workshops, are the recreators of groups through the making of persons. They wield a powerful influence, at once liberating and restrictive. The effect is to liberate the person's potential as a human being while restricting it to those channels appropriate to the group. (For most mortals the potential is but partially realized and it may, of course, be for ill as well as good.)

These are the matters, then, with which this chapter is concerned: the influence of the group, considered in the abstract; and, in the concrete, family and school as groups primarily responsible for making men and re-creating groups.

THE INFLUENCE OF THE GROUP

One way of appreciating the influence of the group—of others—is to raise the question: What would happen if there were no others? Or, to put it more plausibly, if interaction with others is reduced, what happens?[2] There is a great body of evidence which bears in various ways on this question. I offer in the following paragraphs but a few scattered pieces of this evidence.

Others' Absence

The very absence of others, the effect of which we wish to investigate, makes it almost impossible to get reliable data. For this reason there has been much controversy over so-called "wolf

---

[2] The writers of fiction, like Kilroy, have already been here. Writing an introduction to two of Joseph Conrad's short pieces, Albert J. Guerard says: ". . . His is one of the greatest portraits in all fiction of *moral deterioration and reversion to savagery as a result of physical isolation.*" (Introduction to Joseph Conrad, *Heart of Darkness* and *The Secret Sharer* [New York: Signet Books, 1957], p. 13.)

children," feral creatures supposedly reared outside the human circle.[3] But Professor Kingsley Davis has given us one fairly well-documented case of extreme isolation from human contact: that of an illegitimate child discovered at six and one half years of age who had been kept in seclusion from the age of two.[4] The mother was a deaf mute. Both she and the child spent most of their time together in a dark room shut off from the rest of the mother's family. Characteristics of the child, when discovered, that seem to stem from this isolation, are the following: a mental age test score (Stanford-Binet) of nineteen months;[5] behavior like that of a child of six months, but more hostile and erratic; an initial diagnosis of deafness that, when shown to be wrong, was supplanted by a diagnosis of feeblemindedness. But with intensive help, this youngster's I.Q. score trebled in a year and a half. Presently she reached what appeared to be a normal level.

This, it will be observed, is a before-and-after case. There is no carefully contrived control group of matched youngsters experiencing normal human contacts. But normal rearing is so clearly different in the matter of human intercourse and this child's "recovery" so dramatic, it seems legitimate to infer the deleterious consequences of isolation and to assert the presence of others as a necessary and sufficient cause of socialization.

Extreme but fortunately more transient cases of isolation are seen in recent laboratory work on the effects of sensory deprivation. Dr. John Lilly has reported on some relevant psychological outcomes when external stimuli are cut off.[6] The procedure is to suspend the

---

[3] See, e.g., the article by William F. Ogburn, "The Wolf Boy of Agra," *American Journal of Sociology*, Vol. LXIV, No. 5 (March, 1959).

[4] Kingsley Davis, "Extreme Social Isolation of a Child," *American Journal of Sociology*, Vol. XLV (January, 1940), pp. 554–65; and "Final Note on a Case of Extreme Isolation," *American Journal of Sociology*, Vol. LII, No. 5 (March, 1947), pp. 432–37.

[5] An intelligence test score is calculated by relating mental age, in months (given by the test score) to chronological age, in months; thus:

$$\frac{\text{MENTAL AGE}}{\text{CHRONOLOGICAL AGE}} \times 100 = \text{INTELLIGENCE QUOTIENT.}$$

In this case the values are $\frac{19}{78} \times 100 = 20$.

[6] John C. Lilly, "Effects of Physical Restraint and of Reduction of Ordinary Levels of Physical Stimuli on Intact, Healthy Persons," (New York: Group for the Advancement of Psychiatry, 1790 Broadway, 1956), *Symposium No. 2*, pp. 13–20. See also reports of his testimony before a Congressional Committee, *New York Times*, April 15, 1956.

subject in a tank of slowly flowing water kept at body temperature, face down, wearing only a head mask for breathing. An initial feeling of great comfort and relaxation gradually gives way to some curious effects. Lacking all sensory input, the subject finds his thoughts going around, becoming magnified, distorted. Anxiety mounts as he becomes increasingly disoriented. He may begin to suffer hallucinations.

Dr. Milton Meltzer draws upon his experiences as Chief Medical Officer at Alcatraz to make these observations on the effect of isolation from others:

> . . . the prison experience in general and solitary confinement in particular, threatens the inmate's integration by depriving him of stimuli and various sets of reaction patterns or things in the environment towards which he can orient himself and constantly *redefine himself in the service of knowing who he is.* As these are withdrawn he tends to regress towards an infantile ego state of split and paired good-bad objects. . . .
> To the degree that the basic state is achieved so is the man vulnerable to forceful indoctrination . . . at this point he is capable of massive incorporation, introjections and identifications.[7]

We might note in passing a deduction drawn from the theory of socialization discussed in the last chapter and bearing on this matter of personal disorganization under conditions of extreme isolation. If it is true that becoming a human being entails incorporating or introjecting the other—if by virtue of our capacity for symbolic interaction the single person becomes a group in microcosm—then, the more integrated the group, the greater its cohesiveness, the clearer its goals and the better rationalized the means for achieving them, the better integrated the person. The better integrated person should be better able to survive conditions of sensory deprivation, of isolation. He should be less readily "brainwashed," better able to maintain his personal integrity. Such a theory and such a prediction are consonant with the findings on mental illness among the Hutterites.[8] They are consonant with the observation that political prisoners had emphatically better survival rates than criminal prisoners among Danish inmates of a German concentration camp.

---

[7] Milton Meltzer, "Factors Used to Increase the Susceptibility of Individuals to Forceful Indoctrination: Observation and Experiments" (New York: Group for the Advancement of Psychiatry, December, 1956), *Symposium No. 3,* p. 103.

[8] Joseph Eaton, "Controlled Acculturation: A Survival Technique of the Hutterites," *American Sociological Review,* Vol. XVII, pp. 331–40.

Of the former, 13 percent died; of the latter, 30 percent. "The consciousness that one is not imprisoned because of an occasional transgression of the law for the sake of gain but that one suffers the misery and humiliation *for the sake of a common cause* seems to be a life-sustaining factor of unsuspected importance . . . the inner bond with the world outside the concentration camps is maintained."[9]

Other relevant data are provided by Mandel Sherman and Cora B. Key in their investigation of the intelligence of isolated mountain children.[10] Calculating the percent of a community's children having lower than average intelligence test scores, they found that this percent increased with isolation, declined with accessibility. The more isolated the community, the simpler its style of life, the less the contact with the outside world, the lower the level of its children's scores on measures of intellectual development.

One final illustration of the meaning of the absence of others is found in René Spitz's study of "hospitalism."[11] Here we have a contrast between the degree of the child's isolation in a foundling home and in the nursery of a penal institution. Conditions in the foundling home were antiseptically proper, both physically and socially. The children were well fed and cared for but had relatively little contact with one another, with staff, or with their mothers. In strong contrast, the prison nursery was rather more loosely run. But if it was less sterile in a bacteriological sense, so was it less sterile socially. The children were less isolated, had frequent contact with mothers, peers, and staff. Under these *different patterns of relationships,* the contrast in the children's development was startling. The prison nursery children, in contrast to their matched counterparts in the foundling home, weighed more, were taller, had better health in general, had emphatically lower mortality rates, were more responsive, and far superior in their developmental quotients.[12]

---

[9] See H. B. M. Murphy, *Flight and Resettlement* (Paris: UNESCO, 1955), p. 38. The quotation is from Hedwig Larsen, H. Hoffmeyer, *et al.,* "Famine Disease in German Concentration Camps." *Act. Neur. et Psychiat.* Scand. supp. 83, 1952. Italics mine.

[10] Mandel Sherman and Cora B. Key, "The Intelligence of Isolated Mountain Children," *Child Development,* Vol. III (1932), pp. 279–90.

[11] René Spitz, "Hospitalism," in *The Psychoanalytic Study of the Child* (New York: International Universities Press, Inc., 1945), Vol. I, pp. 53–72. The citation is taken from Ronald Freedman, *et al.* who use this report in their textbook, *Principles of Sociology* (New York: Holt, Rinehart & Winston, Inc., 1961), pp. 85 *et seq.*

[12] This term, developmental quotient, refers to the average level of the child's development (calculated on the basis of norms for a given age) in six sectors: de-

Others' Presence: the Group's Influence on Thought and Perception, on Normal and Abnormal Behavior

These examples point in a negative fashion to the power of the group. They stress the harmful outcomes of the *absence* of others.[13] Let us turn now to the significance of others' *presence*, the impact of the group upon the person.

Consider, first, the influence of his group upon the way a person thinks. Crudely put, we may suggest that what people think and the way they think it are conditioned by the sort of group they belong to. What problems are raised, how solutions are sought, the kind of evidence brought to bear, the extent of reliance upon the supernatural for solutions, what sorts of solutions are likely or tolerable— these are matters in which the person's thinking is emphatically under the influence of the group.

Professor Lucien Lévy-Bruhl in a series of studies on the mentality of primitive peoples[14] commences with the assumption I have suggested: Mental processes must be understood relative to the group in which they operate.

> Mental processes will vary as groups vary. This is especially brought home to us when we recognize that institutions, our very customs are, at bottom, only our common imagery, our ideas, so to speak, concretely registered.*

velopment of perception, body mastery, memory, social relations, relations to inanimate objects, and intelligence.

While the direction of the differences observed is incontestable, difficulties in research design require the sociologist (and this is often the case) to hold these results tentatively. For example, the two groups of infants were in different countries of the western hemisphere. And before the follow-up study, the N (number of cases) for the Foundling Home dropped from 91 to 21, due to deaths and adoptions.

[13] Many other observations suggest the dehumanizing effects of isolation. For example, reports on U.S. prisoners of war in Korea highlight three important features of the process popularly called "brainwashing:" isolation from the past, punishment in the present, and rewards held out for the future. The withholding and manipulation of mail, the prohibition of group meetings, playing men off against one another, and the segregation of men by race, nationality, and rank together with the substitution of Chinese leaders—these isolating devices proved effective in severing familiar bonds, reducing the person to the naked impotence of an unsupported individual, and so preparing the way for indoctrination. "The most significant feature of Chinese prisoner camp control was the systematic destruction of the prisoners' formal and informal group structure." (Edgar H. Schein, discussing POWs in Korea. See *Symposium No. 4, Methods of Forceful Indoctrination: Observations and Interviews* [New York: Group for the Advancement of Psychiatry, July, 1957].)

[14] *Mental Functions in Primitive Societies* (1910), *Primitive Mentality* (1922), and *The Soul of the Primitive* (1927).

* See Original Texts, Note 1, at end of chapter.

Lévy-Bruhl would assume as wide a range of mental processes as there are determinate differences between societies. But as a crude test of his notion that the primitive was not simply an undeveloped twentieth-century Frenchman or American, he lumped a group of mildly differing societies together under the label "primitive," and called another group of moderately differing societies "civilized." Thus he hoped to reveal the strongest possible contrast in ways of thought corresponding to differing social orders. (The contrast, as it turned out, was so strong as to distort the difference between primitive and civilized.)

The primitive mentality is not to be seen, Lévy-Bruhl thought, as "simply a rudimentary form of ours, as infantile, almost pathological." It is rather to "be seen as normal under the conditions in which it is exercised."[15] In this elementary form of social organization in which man often stands impotent before the unknowns of the universe, his pattern of thought follows what Lévy-Bruhl calls the "law of participation." Thus the primitive does not distinguish, as we do, the animate from the inanimate,[16] the picture from the thing pictured,[17] the person's name from him who bears it,[18] the shadow from the body that throws it,[19] dream from reality.[20] To both parts of these coupled terms they attribute the same properties and they believe that the one is always affected by the other. We see the portrait identified, materially and spiritually with its model.[21] And in *The Soul of the Primitive*, we see exactly this same sort of fusion:

> The picture is not a reproduction of some original, and distinct from it. It is it, itself. Resemblance between things is not simply a connection apprehended in thought. By virtue of the intimate fusion or participation of things, the picture, the image, the representation has as much reality as the thing itself. My image, my shadow, my reflection, my echo, . . . each is literally me. Whoever possesses

---

[15] Lucien Lévy-Bruhl, *Mentalité Primitive*, from the Bibliothèque de Philosophie *Contemporaine* (Paris: Félix Alcan, 1915), pp. 14–16.

[16] This and the following footnotes refer to works of Lévy-Bruhl, as indicated, but are cited from Georges Davy, *Sociologues d'hier et d'aujourd'hui* (2d ed.; Paris: Presses Universitaires de France, 1950), p. 168. The reference here is to Lévy-Bruhl, *Fonctions mentales* (Paris: Presses Universitaires de France, 1951), p. 33.

[17] *Ibid.*, pp. 40–43.

[18] *Ibid.*, pp. 44–49.

[19] *Ibid.*, pp. 50–52.

[20] *Ibid.*, p. 56.

[21] *Ibid.*, p. 44.

an image of me holds me in his power. Hence the universal practice of sorcery.[22]

Rather than say that primitives believe what they see in dreams *despite* the fact that they are dreams, I would say that they believe *because* they are dreams.[23]

. . . among the Gabon a dream offers more convincing evidence than a witness.[24]

And so Lévy-Bruhl concludes that the mental processes in primitive societies are characterized by mysticism, by the fusing of self with other persons and things. There are things which "belong" to one, appurtenances which are as much a part of one's self as one's own body or mind. One *participates*, merges with, these things. Participation means to be implicated in a complex network of mystic alliances or identities, sharing elements of other group members, living and dead, animal and vegetable life, the earth itself and occult powers protecting the group and the individual. The person is a *"lieu de participations,"*[25] the intersection of things and beings that are animate through him. He may be quite unpersuaded by sensory experience. What we regard as a causal influence is simply the occasion and instrument of occult forces. Hence Lévy-Bruhl arrived at the conclusion that primitive and modern societies were distinguished by two quite different thought patterns: prelogical and logical, mystical and rational, dominated by the principle of participation and that of contradiction, respectively.

As he reflected on it and as he considered the criticisms he had invited from fellow sociologists, Lévy-Bruhl changed his position on a sharp, qualitative difference between primitive and modern. He later wrote:

As I moved ahead [in this investigation] the original hypotheses were markedly modified. The idea of a logic differing from ours, which in any rigorous sense appeared unsupported [by the data] gave way in my mind to the notion of a prelogical mentality—a word which I use for lack of a better one—that is to say a thought pattern which is neither anti-logical . . . nor a-logical . . . but one which is, in certain cases, indifferent to the matter of contradiction because it is mystical and follows the law of participation as well as the principle of contradiction.[26]

---

[22] *Ame primitive,* p. 186.

[23] *Fonctions mentales,* p. 56.

[24] *Mentalité primitive,* p. 99.

[25] *Ame primitive,* p. 251.

[26] *Bull. de la Société française de philosophie,* February 15, 1923, p. 22.

Where Lévy-Bruhl ploughs a great gulf between prelogical, primitive thought and ours, Durkheim sees it as a first stage in the development of modern thought patterns. In any case, the basic point seems indisputable: both form and content of thought vary from group to group. The problems central to primitive life are not ours, nor their modes of solution. Their omens, dreams, oracles, and ordeals, their divinatory practices aimed at revealing malevolent and invisible forces, the hidden, mystical source of the visible misfortune—these suggest, as M. Davy points out, that words like "accusation," "judgment," "innocence," and "guilt" carry very different meanings for them than for us.

We have been discussing the influence of the group upon the *process,* the *logic,* of thought. Consider now the matter of group influence upon the *content* of the person's thought, upon *what* rather than *how* he thinks.

Newcomb, in his study of attitudes toward public affairs, finds evidence that views on such issues are shaped as the person relates himself to some group or category of persons. "In many cases (perhaps in all) the referring of social attitudes to one group negatively leads to referring them to another group positively, or vice versa, so that the attitudes are dually reinforced."[27]

With Charters, Newcomb pursued the matter of group influence upon attitudes in a study which varied level of awareness of their religious membership group for Catholics, Jews, and Protestants (chiefly Lutherans).[28] Catholic students—I report only on this category for simplicity's sake while noting in passing that the hypothesis was not supported for Jews and Protestants—were randomly divided into experimental and control groups. One control group, whose members were unaware that they were involved in the experiment, met in the auditorium along with other university students in the class. A second control group consisted wholly of Catholic students, but their awareness of this fact was not underlined as was the case with the experimental group. With the latter, their common faith was emphasized by the investigator as he

[27] Theodore M. Newcomb, "Attitude Development as a Function of Reference Groups: The Bennington Study," in Eleanor E. Maccoby, T. M. Newcomb, and Eugene L. Hartley (eds.), *Readings in Social Psychology* (New York: Henry Holt & Co., Inc., 1958), p. 275.

[28] W. W. Charters, Jr., and Theodore M. Newcomb, "Some Attitudinal Effects of Experimentally Increased Salience of a Membership Group," in Maccoby, Newcomb and Hartley, *op. cit.,* p. 276.

requested their help in developing a questionnaire on religious beliefs. That is to say, a sharp awareness of their common group membership was aroused in the experimental group, in contrast to the treatment of the control groups where Ss (subjects) were simply asked to fill out a questionnaire (the same one, of course).

The responses of Catholics in the two control groups were very much alike despite the fact that in one control group Catholic students were part of an auditorium lecture group of 500, while the other control group comprised a separated group of students, all Catholic. On questionnaire items dealing with the Catholic faith, with the church, or with religion in general, there were significant differences between the control groups and the experimental group (in which consciousness of group membership had been purposely aroused). In the latter group for whose members "the potency of religious group membership was deliberately increased," responses "more closely approximated the orthodox Catholic position" than was the case with "control subjects whose awareness of membership was not increased."[29]

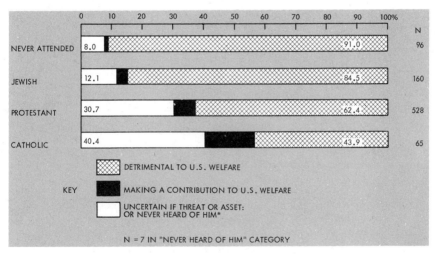

FIG. 4–1. Relationship between religious identification and appraisal of Senator McCarthy, 849 college students, Autumn, 1953.

A link between the way one thinks on a political issue and the religious group with which he identifies is suggested in Figure 4–1. Students at a private college, their families can be taken as relatively homogeneous in income and education. Even so, the observations

---

[29] *Ibid.,* p. 278.

reported here are inadequately controlled. We do not know that these members of different religious groups are alike in all respects relevant to attitude toward Senator McCarthy, other than their religious identification.

Bearing on this question: How does group membership affect a person's thinking? is the classical experiment by Mustafer Sherif. He posed the problem: How are standards or guideposts established for judging certain characteristics of physical objects? How does the person make a judgment in an utterly unstructured situation, when he is alone? How does he do it as a member of a group?[30] To create a situation in which points of reference were completely lacking, Sherif made use of the autokinetic phenomenon, the "false" perception of movement in a visual object seen in an unstructured field— i.e., outside any frame of reference. To achieve this effect, Sherif exposed his subjects to a pinpoint of light in a room completely dark. The results, when he was dealing with individual subjects, alone, Sherif summarized in these two sentences:

> When individuals repeatedly perceive movement which offers no objective basis for gauging the extent of movement, there develops within them, in the course of successive presentations [of the apparently moving pinpoint of light] a standard (norm or reference point). This subjectively established standard or norm serves as a reference point with which each successive experienced movement is compared and judged to be short, long, or medium—within the range peculiar to the subject.[31]

A second phase of Sherif's study raised the question: How are individual judgments (already having been formed as described above) influenced when in company with others each subject is asked again to judge the distance moved by the pinpoint of light. There were two subjects in each of eight groups, and three subjects in each of eight other groups. The findings are summarized in Sherif's conclusion:

> When the individual, in whom a range and a norm within that range are first developed in the individual situation, is put into a

---

[30] Mustafer Sherif, "Group Influence upon the Formation of Norms and Attitudes," in Newcomb, Hartley, *et al.*, *Readings in Social Psychology* (New York: Henry Holt & Co., Inc., 1947), pp. 77–90. See also Mustafer Sherif, *The Psychology of Social Norms* (New York: Harper & Bros., 1936), and "An Experimental Approach to the Study of Attitudes," *Sociometry*, Vol. I (1937), pp. 90–98.

[31] Sherif, "Group Influence upon the Formation of Norms and Attitudes," *op. cit.*, p. 80.

group situation, together with other individuals who also come into the situation with their own ranges and norms established in their own individual sessions, the ranges and norms tend to converge. But the convergence is not so close as when they first work in the group situation, having less opportunity to set up stable individual norms.[32]

Bearing on the same point I am making here—the influence of the group upon perception and judgment of certain dimensions of physical objects—is another important study, this one by Solomon Asch.[33] A central theme of his book, *Social Psychology,* is that "in society we become dependent on others for understanding, feeling and the extension of the sense of reality."[34] In the experiment I am reporting, Asch raises the question: To what extent is the individual's judgment distorted under the influence of other group members' erroneous judgments? He asked his subjects to judge which of three lines on one card was the same length as a standard comparison line on a second card. Judgments were orally expressed, seriatim, by members of groups of seven to nine persons, one of whom was a naïve—i.e., uninstructed—subject, while the others had been told to make occasional, palpably wrong judgments. Thus the naïve subject was caught between two contradictory and irreconcilable forces: the evidence of his own senses and the unanimous testimony of a group of peers. The results of one phase of this study are given in the Table 4–1. To test the extent to which such findings depart from outcomes that might be expected if there were no

TABLE 4–1

Estimates of Experimental and Control Groups

EXPERIMENT	N	TOTAL NUMBER OF ESTIMATES	CORRECT ESTIMATES f	%	PRO-MAJORITY ERRORS f	%
Minority of one vs. a unanimous majority	31	217	145	66.8	72	33.2
Control	25	175	162	92.6	13	7.4

Source: Solomon E. Asch, *Social Psychology* (Englewood Cliffs, N.J.: Prentice-Hall, Inc., 1952), p. 450.

---

[32] *Ibid.,* p. 83.

[33] Solomon E. Asch, *Social Psychology* (Englewood Cliffs, N.J.: Prentice-Hall, Inc., 1952), chap. xvi, "Group Forces in the Modification and Distortion of Judgments," pp. 450–501.

[34] *Ibid.,* p. 450.

relationship between group influence and accuracy of judgment, we can arrange the data in a four-celled table and apply the chi-square test as in Table 4–2 (see Chapter 3, pp. 113–15). Expected frequencies, on the assumption that the incidence of error would be as great in the one group as in the other, are given in parentheses.

TABLE 4–2

Applying the Chi-Square Test to Asch's Data

		JUDGMENTS			
		Correct		Erroneous: Conforming to Errors of the Instructed Majority	
Experimental group	a)	(170) 145	b)	(47) 72	217
Control group	c)	(137) 162	d)	(38) 13	175
		307		85	392

The formula to be evaluated is $x^2 = \Sigma(f_o^2/f_e) - N$, and the data are as follows:

CELL	f_o	f_e	f_o^2	f_o^2/f_e
a)	145	170	21,025	124
b)	72	47	5,184	110
c)	163	137	26,244	192
d)	13	38	169	4
			$\Sigma(f_o^2/f_e) =$	430

Thus $x^2 = 430 - 392 = 38$ and, where degrees of freedom $= 1$ and $x^2 = 38$, $p < .001$.

Here we see, in Asch's subjects, a marked distortion of judgment conforming to the erroneous estimates of the majority. A third of all estimates made by the naïve subjects were errors identical with or in the direction of the distorted estimates of the majority. Those who yielded fell into three categories: those who "saw" wrongly, who judged wrongly, and who reported wrongly. One person apparently came to see lines wrongly matched, in length, as being of the same length. Most subjects were ambivalent, knowing that their eyes saw one thing while their judgment told them, erroneously, that the majority must be right. The third category of subjects knew they saw a different line-matching solution than did the majority, felt their judgment was correct, but yielded "because of an overmastering need not to appear different from or inferior to others. . . ." Asch underlines one point that is worth repeating here.

> The distortions . . . in action, judgment, and, to some extent, perception were a consequence of pressures from the social sphere, not of tendencies whose source is in the individual himself. . . . The effects we have observed had their start in a prior contamination of the social field [that is, the majority in a group of Ss had been instructed to answer erroneously on some line-matching problems]— evidence of the profound difference, from the standpoint of the individual, between being in a group that possesses an adequate view and being in a group whose view is distorted.[35]

Of course, what we must realize is that in the significant groups in which most of us achieve our humanity—the family, school, work, and military and play groups—there is *always* "a prior contamination of the social field." Furthermore, if people's judgments are distorted under the influence of the group where the matter at issue is a fairly unambiguous one of physical perception, how much more might we expect to find people yielding to the prevailing sentiments of an already "contaminated social field" on matters of politics, race, religion, and matters of morality in general!

We have been discussing the influence of the group upon the process of problem-solution, upon the content of our thought and upon our perceptions. There is also evidence of the way in which norms of behavior emerge under group influence, and are maintained, when they are central to group operations, within a fairly narrow range of tolerance. One of the best illustrations of the influence of the group in the establishment of such norms comes from the well-known study of the bank-wiring room (wiring for telephone relays) at the Hawthorne Works of the Western Electric Company in Chicago. Among these workers there was a clearly specified norm: 6,600 completed connections was a day's work. One maverick named Mueller was very fast in his work and tended to "overproduce." He said:

> Right now I'm turning out over 7,000 a day, around 7,040. The rest of the fellows kick because I do that. They want me to come

---
[35] *Ibid.,* p. 495.

down. They want me to come down to around 6,600; but I don't see why I should.[36]

Homans summarizes the norms of the group—norms imposed upon its members—in the following statements:[37]

1. You should not turn out too much work. If you do, you are a "rate-buster."
2. You shouldn't turn out too little work. If you do, you're a "chiseler."
3. You shouldn't tell a supervisor anything that will react to the detriment of an associate. If you do you are a "squealer."
4. You should not attempt to maintain social distance or act officious. If you are an inspector, e.g., you should not act like one.
5. You should not be noisy, self-assertive, and anxious for leadership.

While we can appeal to our own experience for confirmation of the group's influence upon behavior (consider, for example, the group-linked constraint we feel when, among a group of worshipers, we find it mandatory to mute our conversation), the influence of the group upon memory may not be so obvious. Yet consider these questions: *Why* do we remember what we do? *How* do we commemorate? *What* do we remember? What determines the accuracy with which we remember? Certainly, as Maurice Halbwachs has suggested,[38] the answers to these questions lead us to recognize the way in which the person's remembering is influenced by his group membership. Remembering is useful in preserving common values. As its etymology suggests, it *brings back to mind* acts and events we should guard against ("Remember the Maine," "Remember Pearl Harbor") and celebrates those deeds that we should emulate ("My only regret is that I have but one life to give for my country"). Our heroes and villains provide common memories, common points of reference for reaffirming our convictions and commitments. Professor Klapp says:

> While hero worship in America ranges from the adulation of entertainers and other celebrities to such diverse things as the celebration of legendary heroes, the decoration of military heroes, and the

---

[36] George Homans, *The Human Group* (New York: Harcourt, Brace & World, Inc., 1950), p. 123. Homans' quotation is from F. J. Roethlisberger and W. J. Dickson, *Management and the Worker* (Cambridge, Mass.: Harvard University Press, 1939), p. 417.

[37] Homans, *op. cit.,* p. 79.

[38] Maurice Halbwachs, "Mémoire et Société," *Année sociologique,* Vol. I (Third Series, 1940), republished as *La Mémoire Collective* (Paris: Presses Universitaires de France, 1950).

cult of saints, we believe that it represents a generic process which expresses itself in many aspects of life as the tendency to select certain individuals as collective ideals, to accord them special status, and to surround them with behavior characterized as "hero worship."

Hero worship in America expresses our characteristic values. It reveals not only the traits we admire most but also our fields of interest. While one age may emphasize strenuous piety, another emphasizes war or athletics. Through the heroism of all societies, no doubt, run certain common threads: great achievement, heroism in war, martyrdom, and the like. The hero worship of American society reveals the run of our interests and consequently the fields in which heroes emerge.[39]

Amplifying his thesis in another study,[40] Klapp suggests that the tribe's memorializing of its heroes, villains, and fools yields several significant outcomes. Such figures serve as simplified symbols dramatically pinpointing conceptions of good and evil. For the person, they provide "norms of self-judgment and roles for emulation or avoidance." They heighten the we-feeling, the solidarity of the group, perpetuating certain common values, nourishing and maintaining

> certain socially necessary sentiments—pride in great men, admiration of courage and self-sacrifice, hatred of vice, contempt for folly, a sense of national destiny, the historic continuity of a church militant . . . the memory of a great hero or anti-hero . . . is like an heirloom.[41]

Memories of significant historical events are either learned from others or stem from personal experience. If the former, then they are external to the person and his experiences. They are transmitted by others who have evaluated these events, committing to our minds and memories the significant past in affect-laden terms. If our memories relate to experiences we have lived through, either directly or indirectly, then their salience and intensity will depend on concurrent social events (war, depression) and others' evaluation of such events.[42]

---

[39] Orrin E. Klapp, "Hero Worship in America," *American Sociological Review* (published by The American Sociological Association), Vol. XIX, No. 1 (February, 1949), pp. 53, 62.

[40] Orrin E. Klapp, "Heroes, Villains and Fools as Agents of Social Control," *American Sociological Review* (published by The American Sociological Association), Vol. XIX, No. 1 (February, 1954), pp. 57–62.

[41] *Ibid.*, p. 62.

[42] Others' influence on one's memory is suggested by Darwin. "My mother died in July, 1817, when I was a little over eight years old, and it is odd that I can remember hardly anything about her except her death-bed, her black velvet gown and

What is memorable will, then, vary from group to group. There are as many calendars, Halbwachs points out, as there are different groups, the division of time expressed sometimes in religious terms (as in Saints' days) or in business terms (market and exchange days).[43] One group can't use another's calendar. Its requirements are different: its memories are different.

I have been offering some suggestive evidence on the influence of the group upon the person. When I speak of the "group's influence," incidentally, I speak figuratively and ambiguously. The group is not animate, sensate, psychic as is the human actor. I mean more precisely certain characteristics or dimensions of the group—its size, its salience, its voting or preference structure (for example, size of the majority)—are clearly related to individual and aggregate characteristics of its members. This point will become clear in a final illustration. There are many other studies which provide supporting evidence;[44] but Durkheim's classic study of suicide[45] will serve us

---

her curiously constructed work-table. I believe that my forgetfulness is partly due to my sisters, owing to their great grief, never being able to speak about her or mention her name; and partly to her previous invalid state." (Charles Darwin, *The Auto-biography of Charles Darwin* [New York: Harcourt, Brace & World, Inc., 1959], p. 22.)

[43] Halbwachs, *op. cit.,* p. 120.

[44] Sociologists agree that the complex of skills, knowledge, and attitudes necessary for systematic criminal behavior depend upon effectively organized criminal groups. See Edwin H. Sutherland, *Principles of Criminology* (Philadelphia: J. B. Lippincott Co., 1939), *The Professional Thief* (Chicago: University of Chicago Press, 1937), and *White Collar Crime* (New York: Dryden Press, 1949). Also Albert K. Cohen, *Delinquent Boys* (New York: Free Press of Glencoe, Inc., 1955), and Richard A. Cloward and Lloyd E. Ohlin, *Delinquency and Opportunity* (New York: Free Press of Glencoe, Inc., 1961).

William Foote Whyte in his study of a young men's gang found an interesting parallel between individuals' bowling scores and their relative standing in the gang. But, he points out, these bowling scores "did not fall automatically into this pattern. There were certain customary ways of behaving which exerted pressure upon the individuals. Chief among these were the manner of choosing sides and the verbal attacks the members directed against one another." *Street Corner Society* (2d ed.; Chicago: University of Chicago Press, 1955), p. 23.

Not only may membership in a given group mean the inculcation in the person of certain attitudes. It may mean the inculcation of attitudes or beliefs that are erroneously founded—e.g., the Negro is "by nature" inferior. But further, not only may such erroneous beliefs be inculcated. They may lead to actions creating the conditions which confirm them (denial of equal educational, civic, and occupational opportunities). Thus the influence of the group is exercised at a further remove. See, e.g., Robert K. Merton's delightful and penetrating essay, "The Self-Fulfilling Proph-ecy," *Antioch Review,* Summer, 1948, republished in *Social Theory & Social Struc-ture* (New York: Free Press of Glencoe, Inc., 1957).

[45] Émile Durkheim, *Suicide,* trans. John A. Spaulding and George Simpson (New York: Free Press of Glencoe, Inc., 1951).

especially well. For aside from illustrating the influence of one aspect or dimension of the group, it will introduce us to one of sociology's founding fathers and underline a point or two bearing on methods of inquiry.

The general problem posed is this: Why do people commit suicide? This is a very fuzzy formulation of the problem. We might put it this way to emphasize our concern with differences: Why do some people commit suicide while others do not? But clearly, since we use the word "people," we mean to seek some general explanation which applies to types or categories of persons. Thus we might rephrase the question this way: Why is it that suicide rates vary consistently as between different categories of persons? Let us be clear about this. It is not a question of explaining *a* given person's suicide, exploring that conjuncture of circumstances leading to the frame of mind prompting self-destruction. If we interpret suicide A in terms of a given motive, suicide B in terms of some other psychological quirk, we may conceivably provide two suggestive interpretations of two separate acts. But we have not enlightened ourselves as to the predisposing condition common to both—i.e., we have achieved no insight as to the nature of suicide. If, on the other hand, our inquiry reveals that A and B can be described as suffering some psychosis—a monomania, manic-depressive spells—we have restated the problem, not answered it. The question as reformulated still awaits an answer: what accounts for the quite predictable development of such psychoses which register themselves in a remarkably regular suicide rate? Durkheim's problem is to explain *suicide in general* as it characterizes a given group in contrast to other groups. And as he observes, there are indeed characteristic and quite stable suicide rates. "Each society," he notes, "is predisposed to contribute a definite quota of voluntary deaths."[46]

But if we are to inquire into the causes of suicide, we had better know what we are talking about. A central requirement of controlled observation is an unambiguous definition of our central terms. This is not so simple as might appear. For example, we must decide whether to include under the heading of suicide only those acts where the intent was clear. Shall we take account of the means by which it was accomplished? Does it make a difference whether

---

[46] Reprinted with permission of The Free Press of Glencoe from *Suicide,* by Émile Durkheim, translated by John A. Spaulding and George Simpson. Copyright 1951 by The Free Press, a corporation.

the act was a positive one, carried out with some lethal weapon, or a negative one, as where death results from refusal to eat? Do we consider it a case of suicide when a person volunteers for a mortal mission, knowing full well that his death is foreordained? Durkheim considers these problems and concludes by defining suicide as "any death which is the direct or indirect result of a positive or negative act accomplished by the victim himself."[47]

The next step is to consider the common and current interpretations of such behavior. One such explanation likely to be offered by the alienists of Durkheim's day was simply that the suicide was psychopathic. Here Durkheim underlines the selective—and so, distorted—evidence with which the psychotherapist characteristically deals, and the importance of the negative case. "From the suicides they [the alienists, or psychotherapists] have known who were, of course, insane, no conclusion can be drawn as to those not observed who, moreover, are much more numerous."[48]

He proceeds to check further on this notion of a relationship between nervous disorders in general (neurasthenia) and suicide. And here we get some evidence of the typical sophistication of his thinking. Using insanity as an index of the extent of neurasthenia in a group, he finds that it varies directly with suicide. But it also varies with urban-rural residence. To assume a causal connection would be sloppy thinking, confounding our hypotheses. A third variable may underlie both of these factors which vary in the same direction. We can only untangle the influences by holding constant one of the variables. Still pursuing the matter, he notes that rates of insanity are higher among women than among men. Hence, if there were a relationship between insanity and suicide, we would predict higher suicide rates for women. But this is exactly contrary to the facts. Suicides are disproportionately male.

Furthermore, if we order the data on insanity by the three major

---

[47] *Ibid.*, p. 42.

[48] *Ibid.*, p. 62. Compare this with Professor Sewell's criticism of psychoanalytic theory as the basis for prescribing child-training practices (see Chapter 3, page 109). We should remember that *Suicide* was first published in 1897 and that theory and practice in psychotherapy were embryonic. So, also, was sociology. Statistics were undeveloped, Durkheim's data were poor, and many of his measures were simple *ad hoc* inventions. But with these precautions, the main points should be kept in mind: (1) Durkheim reveals the influence of the group—more accurately, one of its dimensions, degree of cohesiveness—as it affects what common-sense erroneously sees as an altogether idiosyncratic, personal act. (2) The strategy of his inquiry (in contrast to the tactics) is a ground-breaking example of controlled observation.

religious faiths (the data are from European countries and provinces: Silesia, Mecklenburg, Bavaria, Prussia, etc.), we find that
"insanity is evidently much more frequent among the Jews than
among the other religious faiths . . . ," yet there is relatively little
suicide among Jews. "In this case . . . suicide varies in inverse
proportion to psychopathic states, rather than being consistent with
them."[49] Further inquiry brings him to the conclusion that,

> . . . no psychopathic state bears a regular and indisputable rela-
> tion to suicide. A society does not depend for its number of suicides
> on having more or fewer neuropaths or alcoholics. . . . Admittedly
> under similar circumstances, the degenerate is more apt to commit
> suicide than the well man; but he does not necessarily do so because
> of his condition. This potentiality of his becomes effective only through
> the action of other factors which we must discover.[50]

In similar fashion Durkheim disposes of other popular notions:
that suicide is related to racial or ethnic characteristics, or that it is
to be explained by what he calls "cosmic factors" (variations in
temperature and the like), or simply by imitation.

Now he turns to the matter of social causes. Can we find
something in the nature of the group, some attribute or dimension of
the group, which helps us to understand those differing patterns of
behavior registered in contrasting suicide rates? "We shall try," he
says,

> . . . to determine the productive causes of suicide directly, without
> concerning ourselves with the forms they can assume in particular in-
> dividuals. Disregarding the individual as such, his motives and his

---

[49] *Ibid.*, p. 72.

[50] *Ibid.*, p. 81. Let me enter several *caveats* here. First, the archaic use of such
a term as "degenerate" should remind us that, in 1897, psychology, to say nothing
of sociology, was little developed. Second, there is a danger of concluding prema-
turely that psychic states have nothing to do with suicide. But we must remember that
Durkheim was dealing with *rates* for areas (regions, nations) and categories of persons (Protestants, Catholics, Jews). He is *not* dealing with the convergence of two
or more traits in a single person, as a psychologist would. The latter would raise the
question: what constellation of personality traits in this person accounts for an inward
turning of aggression resulting in suicide? Durkheim would ask: what are the attributes of groups, registered in certain rates, that vary concomitantly with suicide
rates? Thus psychologists and sociologists address themselves to different questions.
Third, it should be noted as C. S. Robinson does in an important study of "Ecological
Correlations and Behavior of Individuals" that measures based on aggregates—proportions, ratios and the like—give very different results from those relating individuals' attributes. Robinson demonstrates that "there need be no correspondence
between the individual correlation and the [correlation of aggregate measures]. Indeed, it is possible for the direction of the relationship to be *reversed!* (*American
Sociological Review*, Vol. XV, No. 3 [June, 1950], p. 354.)

ideas, we shall seek directly the states of the various social environments (religious confessions, family, political society, occupational groups, etc.), in terms of which the variations of suicide occur. Only then returning to the individual shall we study how these general causes become individualized so as to produce the homicidal results involved.[51]

Turning first to the data revealing a consistent and continuing difference between Catholic and Protestant suicide rates (emphatically higher for the latter), Durkheim writes:

> . . . both [Protestantism and Catholicism] prohibit suicide . . . penalize it morally . . . teach that a new life begins beyond the tomb where men are punished for their evil actions [and that] these prohibitions are of divine origin; they are represented not as the logical conclusions of correct reason, but God Himself is their authority.
>
> [Now the] essential difference between Catholicism and Protestantism is that the second permits free inquiry to a far greater degree than the first.
>
> All variation is abhorrent to Catholic thought. The Protestant is far more the author of his faith.
>
> We thus reach our first conclusion, that the proclivity of Protestantism for suicide must relate to the spirit of free inquiry that animates this religion. [Now] free inquiry develops only if its development becomes imperative, that is, if certain ideas and sentiments which have hitherto adequately guided conduct are found to have lost their efficacy. Then reflection intervenes to fill the gap that has appeared. . . . if it is correct to say that free inquiry once proclaimed, multiplies schisms, it must be added that it presupposes them and derives from them. So if Protestantism concedes a greater freedom to individual thought than Catholicism, it is because it has fewer common beliefs and practices.
>
> The more numerous the manners of action and thought of a religious character are, which are accordingly removed from free inquiry, the more the idea of God presents itself in all details of existence, and makes individual wills converge to one identical goal. Inversely, *the greater concessions a confessional group makes to individual judgment, the less it dominates lives, the less its cohesion and vitality.*[52]

This is a general statement, an interpretation, based upon such observations as Durkheim could make with the data available to him. First he observes higher suicide rates for Protestants than for Catholics. Then he develops this interpretation of the data: high

---

[51] *Ibid.*, p. 151.

[52] *Ibid.*, pp. 157–59, *passim.*

suicide rates are related to lack of consensus, to a high degree of individualism, to low group cohesion. Now a third step: he deduces an hypothesis as to the relationship between education and suicide: (1) Protestants, compared with Catholics, have higher suicide rates. (2) Liberated from clerical tradition, Protestants seek answers from secular sources and favor education. (3) Level of education should, therefore, be positively related to suicide rates.

> . . . if the progressive weakening of collective and customary prejudices produces a trend to suicide and if Protestantism derives thence its special predisposition to it, [then] (1) the desire for learning must be stronger among Protestants than among Catholics; (2), in so far as this denotes a weakening of common beliefs, it should vary with suicide, fairly generally.[53]

To test this prediction, Durkheim uses data on three clusters of Italian provinces, thus holding constant the factor of religion (all

TABLE 4–3

GROUPS OF PROVINCES	AVERAGE PERCENT OF MARRIAGES WITH BOTH PARTNERS LITERATE	SUICIDE RATE (SUICIDE PER MILLION INHABITANTS)
I*	39.09	41.1
II	15.23	32.5
III	6.23	14.7

* The provinces are the following: I, Piedmont, Lombardy, Liguria, Rome, and Tuscany; II, Venice, Emilia, Umbria, Marches Campana, and Sardinia; and III, Sicily, Abruzzi, Apulia, Calabria, and Basilicata.
Source: Émile Durkheim, *Suicide*, trans. by John A. Spaulding and George Simpson (New York: Free Press of Glencoe, Inc., 1951).

Catholics). The percent of marriages in which both husband and wife were literate provides him with an index of education. The data are shown in Table 4–3.

Since suicide rates vary with level of education achieved, and since in his day any extended education was almost a male monopoly, Durkheim suspects that the same factor underlies the difference in suicide rates between men and women.

He also finds a higher rate of suicide in times and groups that are politically unstable, in smaller in contrast to larger families, and among single persons in contrast to married.[54]

---

[53] *Ibid.*, p. 162.

[54] As to this last finding, let us take a brief detour on the matter of controlling variables. Suppose we were to check Durkheim's assertion that the married have

Now we are finally ready for Durkheim's conclusions. He has shown that family size is inversely related to suicide rates, that such rates are directly related to degree of political instability, that they vary directly with proportion of population which is Protestant, that there is a higher incidence of suicide among the single than among married persons.

> . . . this is due not to a special characteristic of each [of these spheres of life] but to a characteristic common to all. Religion does not owe its efficacy to the special nature of religious sentiments, since domestic and political societies both produce the same effects when strongly integrated. . . . It is not the specific nature of the domestic or political tie which can explain the immunity [from suicide] they confer, since religious society has the same advantage. The cause can only be found in a single quality possessed by all these social groups, though perhaps to varying degrees. The only quality satisfying this condition is that they are all strongly integrated social groups. So we reach the general conclusion: suicide varies inversely with the degree of integration of the social groups of which the individual forms a part.
>
> . . . The bond that unites [people] with the common cause attaches them to life and the lofty goal they envisage prevents their feeling personal troubles so deeply. There is, in short, in a cohesive and animated society a constant interchange of ideas and feelings from all

significantly lower rates of suicide than do single persons. Let us get our data from New York City and tally our findings in the following table. What would we find?

Suicide Rate	Married	Single
High	XXX	
Low		XXX

Apparently Durkheim is wrong! Or perhaps his statement is too sweeping and needs to be restricted to Europe in the late nineteenth century. (Or, conceivably, we are wrong!) What other factor conceivably related to suicide might be disguised behind marital status? One factor comes to mind immediately: the married are generally older than single persons. Is age related to the suicide rate? Let us check, tallying the data in this table:

	Age	
Suicide Rate	Old	Young
High	XXX	
Low		XXX

Age is, indeed, associated with suicide rates. And so, when married and single people *of the same age group* are compared, the apparent relation between suicide and marital status is *reversed!* That is to say, the effect of family life is to reverse the relationship which would obtain were age the only factor:

	Age group 30–39	
Suicide Rate	Married	Single
High		XXX
Low	XXX	

to each and each to all, something like a mutual moral support, which instead of throwing the individual on his own resources, leads him to share in the collective energy and supports his own when exhausted.[55]

And so, according to Durkheim, as one dimension of the group varies (its integration or cohesiveness), the consequences are felt by the person and reflected in variations in the suicide rate.

We have been dealing with the general question: whence the leverage, the power that accounts for the inculcation of the requisite culture, enabling the person to enter the group? And we have looked first at certain evidence of the group's influence considered in the abstract. The data indicate that the isolated individual never becomes a person, never achieves a self, never acquires culture, never learns the score, never becomes a human being in any intelligible sense of the word. On the other hand, the evidence points to the way the group conditions our thought processes: its salience affects our degree of conformity, it influences our opinions and political views, our perception of physical objects, our norms of behavior. It sets the framework for the person's thinking and remembering. And finally, Durkheim's work suggests that one dimension of the group, its cohesiveness,[56] affects even such an apparently idiosyncratic sort of behavior as suicide.

But let us turn now to specific groups, the two groups chiefly charged and consciously invested with the task of cultural transmission. These are the family and the school.

THE FAMILY AS AGENT OF CULTURAL TRANSMISSION

The face-to-face group is the nucleus of all organization, remaining, in a modified form, within the most complex systems. It is, as it were, the unit of all the social structure. *It is the group which, in the form of the family, initiates us into the secrets of society.* It is the group through which, as comrades and playmates, we first give creative expression to our social impulses. It is the breeding ground of our mores, the nurse of our loyalties. It is the first and always remains the chief

---

[55] *Ibid.*, pp. 208–10, *passim.*

[56] In a recent study of 228 work groups where degree of cohesiveness was also the independent variable, Seashore found measures of anxiety inversely related to group cohesiveness. In productivity there was less intragroup but more intergroup variation among high cohesive groups. (Stanley E. Seashore, *Group Cohesiveness in the Industrial Work Group* [Ann Arbor, Mich.: Survey Research Center, Institute for Social Research, 1954].)

form of our social satisfactions. It is the group in which we really can reveal our social nature.[57]

The family is so central as an inducting agency that the wider society makes matters of reproduction and rearing a matter of prime concern. For parents leave their impress upon the newcomers: their name, their standing, their prejudices and anxieties, their relatives, religion, politics, attitudes, beliefs and practices, their manners and their mannerisms. And so the influence of the larger group is exercised upon the family—through law, through custom, and the mores. Church, state, and business combine to assign responsibility to the parents for these newcomers to the human group. Sirjamaki reminds us that

> The state [in the United States] was thus conceived to be a third party at every marriage ceremony, representing the public interest by imposing its legal and ethical standards upon an otherwise private undertaking.[58]

State and local laws set minimum ages for marriage, define incest, set the conditions for divorce. Our federal government, too, touches the family in many ways. It taxes the family income, favors reproduction by labeling children "deductibles," provides aid to dependent mothers, protection for women and children through labor legislation, and the like.

The public interest in the competence of the partners as prospective parents extends to control over who enters the family group; for this implies, again, an influence over the way in which the family exerts *its* influence. That is to say, the wider society conditions entrance into the family group; and the family group conditions entrance into society. If this seems circular, it is. The model to bear in mind is that of a closed system in which a fairly constant input of material (infants) is, cyclically, indoctrinated and indoctrinator. This is not, of course, the real picture. For the input of persons varies in space and time and the system of ideas to which they are exposed varies—on the whole, slightly—with the parental "mix." But the tendency toward a repetitive cycle is real and necessary, both for the sanity of the person and the functioning of the social order.

---

[57] Robert MacIver, *Society: A Textbook of Sociology* (New York: Holt, Rinehart and Winston, Inc., 1937), pp. 236, 237. Italics mine.

[58] John Sirjamaki, *The American Family in the Twentieth Century* (Cambridge: Harvard University Press, 1953), p. 33.

Who Marries Whom? Influences Making for Partner Homogamy and Strength of Parental Influence

Because of the public interest in the children who will be entering the group, marriages are controlled in the United States by law, by values commonly held, and by sheer accessibility of the partners. Let me illustrate.

Among the more emphatic controls exercised by the state—aside from those over age at marriage and health—are restrictions on so-called interracial marriages. Professors Simpson and Yinger summarize the situation as of 1965:

> Altogether, 21 states now prohibit, through constitutional provision or statutory law or both, the marriage of white persons and those who are defined in . . . varying ways as "Negro." . . . Nine states have laws which expressly or impliedly prohibit the marriage of Caucasians and Mongolians, four states do likewise for whites and Malays, and three prohibit the marriage of whites and Indians. Louisiana and Oklahoma prohibit unions of Indians and Negroes, and North Carolina has placed a ban on the marriage of Cherokee Indians in Robeson County with persons of Negro ancestry to the third generation, inclusive. Although statistically the chances of marriages between Malays and Negroes would not seem to be great in Utah and Wyoming, those states take no chances and forbid them.[59]
>
> The United States Supreme Court has never ruled on the constitutionality of state laws forbidding intermarriage, but lower courts have held that such statutes do not violate the Fourteenth Amendment.[60]

But quite aside from such legal restrictions, people's personal preferences in mating seem to lead to similar results. And here, let us remind ourselves, we are still discussing the influence of the family group upon the person, of parents upon the newcomer—*an influence which is greatly strengthened by homogamy in marriage.* Homogamy means similarity of traits among marriage partners. To the extent that marriages are homogamous, the probability of common premises, prejudices, and preferences is increased. To the extent that such common commitments do in fact obtain, the child confronts an effective coalition. His not to reason why, his simply to comply—with the unanimous mandates of his world of powerful adults. The evidence suggests that this does, in fact, tend to happen.

---

[59] George Eaton Simpson and J. Milton Yinger, *Racial and Cultural Minorities* (New York: Harper & Row., 1965), pp. 375, 376.

[60] *Ibid.*, p. 374.

Like tends to marry like is the general rule: marriages do not ordinarily occur between persons of different race, creed, or ethnic origin, nor between those widely separated in age, job, education, or social class, nor even between those dissimilar in their somatic or psychosomatic defects.[61]

Now marriage, with few exceptions, is contingent on meeting. And so we may ask: Who is likely to meet whom? Is it probable that someone will meet and marry someone within his own class, or someone outside it? Someone within his own educational stratum, or someone with much more, or less, education? Someone within his own neighborhood or someone far afield? Data from a study by Professor Bossard are quite characteristic of the answers we have found to these questions. Checking the court records of marriages of 5,000 Philadelphia couples for place of residence prior to marriage, he found the following: 17 percent had lived within two blocks of one another, 34 percent within five blocks, and 52 percent within a mile of one another.[62] Now neighborhoods are something more than mere spatial entities. In neighborhoods people neighbor—i.e., they deal with one another, help one another, quarrel with one another, ally themselves with one another. They have a sense of community because they share a number of things in common. Neighborhood dwellers tend to be more like their neighbors than like outsiders. Thus intraneighborhood marriages increase the trait-homogamy of the partners. And so the impact of each in the socialization process is reinforced.

One might suppose that the richer or better educated would cut a wider swath in their spouse-hunting activities. But even if they are not quite so restricted to a given area, travel more, have distant summer places, go away to college, nonetheless the familiar and the preferred tend to influence marriage choices. During the academic year 1954–55, a sample of students at a liberal arts college was asked whether they would be willing to admit to close kinship by marriage, people of various ethnic groups. This is what they said. (The data should be read this way: 90 percent of these students reported in 1954–55 that they would be willing to admit native white Americans to close kinship by marriage. This percentage is

---

[61] John Sirjamaki. *op. cit.*, p. 66.

[62] James H. S. Bossard, "Residential Propinquity as a Factor in Marriage Selection," *American Journal of Sociology*, Vol. XXXVIII (September, 1932), pp. 219–24. The figure is from Meyer Nimkoff, *Marriage and the Family* (New York: Houghton Mifflin Co., 1947), p. 412.

subject to a calculable sampling error.) The population sampled was 4 percent Negro, 96 percent white. Protestants made up 57 percent of the group, Jews 31 percent and Catholics 12 percent (identification, not church membership). The unlovable Pirenians are a fictitious group.

	PERCENT
Native white Americans	90.1
English	87.3
Jews	84.5
Germans	80.3
Russians	70.4
Italians	70.4
Ukrainians	69.0
Spaniards	62.0
Mexicans	59.2
Turks	56.3
Roman Catholics	49.3
Japanese	49.3
Chinese	46.5
Pirenians	33.8
American Negroes	31.0
Africans	29.6

Source: This is an adaptation of the Bogardus Social Distance Scale. While the percentages accepting to close kinship by marriage are higher, the rank order of ethnic groups is very similar to that found by Bogardus in 1928. See Emory S. Bogardus, *Immigration and Race Attitudes* (Boston: D. C. Heath & Co., 1928).

The power of the parents over the child derives not only from homogamy of traits, a homogamy required by law, resulting from propinquity or from a preference for the comfortably familiar. It stems, too, from the notions of filial piety which still obtain, though doubtless in attenuated fashion. The relationship between child and socializing agent is suffused with emotion. What might otherwise be an intolerable dictatorship is often tempered with tenderness. And so the newcomer emulates his parents, the group's agents of socialization, not only because he is powerless to do otherwise, not only because, being similar in many traits they present him with a single, reinforced set of expectations, but also because they are "worthy" and loved models. As the physician is for the medical student, as the older nun is *la règle vivante* ("a living rule book") for the novitiate, so the mother is for the daughter, the father for the son. An annual mother-daughter party at a Protestant church in a small town illustrates this affective element of the relationship. It is reported in the abbreviated version of the observer.

ANNUAL MOTHER-DAUGHTER PARTY
May 6, 1954
SODOMVILLE PROTESTANT CHURCH

Invocation

Welcome—A mother.

Response—A daughter.

Vocal Trio—Mother and two daughters (one of them a married daughter)

"I Light My Candle" (9- and 10-year-olds recited verses emphasizing courage, honesty, love . . . with piano music in background. At the end of each poem, girl lit candle).

Piano Duet—"A Polonaise Barcarole"—mother and daughter.

Reading by a Mother—Story about a little Negro boy who wants an ice cream cone, mother says can't afford it . . . he has 2 cents, works hard to get the additional 3 cents; but one day when he's accumulated his pile, ice cream wagon shifts its route and he goes after it . . . gets lost . . . winds up in Police Station. . . . Police can't understand his repeated, plaintive requests for ice cream cone but finally identify him, call mother who scolds. He finally persuades her to cease and desist, impresses her with fix on cone, shows 5 cents to buy same. She asks: *where* did you get all that money . . . he explains hard toil to earn same . . . she admits never realized how much he wanted/needed ice cream cone and vows to go without something she needs so that he may have a cone once a week.

Clarinet Duet—Two girls about high school age.

Mother's Day Reading—Man, bootstrap success now M.D., about to be married . . . old mother shows up. He disconcerted, she not in his class now, shows it. Next morning mother disappears. M.D. abashed, his bride exclaims, "I never had a mother; we will find her." Postpone wedding to find aged one. She succeeds in remaining at large for a year. One day, Dr. in hospital drops flower from his lapel, patient in nearby bed grabs same, clutches to bosom . . . nurse tries to separate blossom from bosom. M.D. turns to see what hassle's about, finds elderly patient is his mother. She's lost memory, however. Announces mother is his, tells nurse she's to be taken to his home, given every care. Bride-to-be hovers about, they transfer mother but she dies.

Solo: "My Mother"; "Mother of Mine."

Special Honors to:

> Mother with largest family.
> Youngest mother.
> Youngest grandmother.
> Newest mother.

Here then we celebrate filial piety, motherly love and sacrifice, the extended family, fertility, the traditional virtues of honesty, courage, and love, the bootstrap version of success—all of these linking parent and child together within a religious setting. As you know, we have the male counterpart of such rites in father-and-son banquets.

We might note in passing that in our society there is no such neat, bisexual symmetry in the socialization of the child as the reference to father-son and mother-daughter relationships might have suggested. Quite to the contrary, whereas for the daughter sex identification and person-identification involves the same person, this is not so with the son.[63] The son's sex identification is, of course, with the father; but he is often an absentee parent. For the early years of his life the American male has typically a predominantly female exposure, both at home and at school. The case is otherwise with the daughter. Her socialization involves no sharp discontinuities. She can model herself on her mother from infancy to maturity. But the son must at some point wrench himself from the nurturant-expressive female figure on whom he has depended and fit his future to some masculine model.

I suggested first that law, propinquity, and preferences geared to class and background lead to homogamy of traits in the parents, so confronting the child with an unbeatable coalition. Then I pointed to the emotional depth of the parent-child relationship as facilitating the socialization process. All this makes for parental power. Indeed, at the risk of offending sacred sentiments attaching to home and mother, I would suggest that becoming a member of the human group is a process much resembling brainwashing. The family setting provides the conditions for a totalitarian government. The child is close to state zero, inexperienced, relatively impotent, an easy target for indoctrination. The parents are omniscient and omnipotent. They are gods and dictators. They have available to them most of the conditions that have made brainwashing and reindoctrination an effective totalitarian technique. Indeed, parents have the advantage of not having to extinguish the experience of decades before commencing indoctrination.

And so the child is scolded, spanked, shamed, humiliated, embarrassed, nurtured, fed, encouraged, praised, taught. Typically he is isolated, although not necessarily by design, from counter

---

[63] Talcott Parsons and Robert F. Bales, *Family, Socialization and Interaction Process* (New York: Free Press of Glencoe, Inc., 1955), p. 99.

influences—at least during the preschool years. His mentors, his parents, are likely to have moved in the same circles, have had similar education, have experienced similar background within the same social class; and their continued intercourse will be unwittingly selective, barring contact for their children with most of the spectrum of human attributes available in their culture. His indoctrination involves onerous repetition of the party line. And unlike academic learning, which consciously eschews one of the most effective of all the levers for learning, the child's indoctrination within the family is heavily laden with emotion.

Ascribed Traits and Attitudes Transmitted from Forebears to Progeny

Aside from conscious parental indoctrination, the child acquires certain familial attributes willy-nilly. Nativity, place of residence, parental income, father's occupation, religion, education—these are family traits and automatically become those of the newcomer. They represent influences characteristically felt by all persons who, by virtue of their families' positions, fall at birth into given categories. Thus Ericson, Bronfenbrenner, Kohn, and others have found middle-class children exposed to influences quite different from their lower-class counterparts.[64] They are more often controlled through reasoning, an inculcated sense of guilt, or the threat of love to be withheld. The working-class parent more readily resorts to physical punishment. For middle-class parents punishment hinges on the child's intent, while the lower-class parent fixes on the tangible outcomes of misbehavior. A subtle mix of child-rearing practices differentiates parental impact, by class. The critical outcome is a replication of parental experience. And of course, this conservative strain toward intergenerational repetition may be viewed as a stabilizing influence, sustaining the social order.

I will set down a tale as it was told to me by one who had it of his father, which latter had it of *his* father, this last having it in like manner had it of *his* father.[65]

[64] Martha C. Ericson, "Social Status and Child-Rearing Practices," in T. M. Newcomb, Eugene L. Hartley, *et al.*, *Readings in Social Psychology* (New York: Henry Holt & Co., Inc., 1947), pp. 494–501; Urie Bronfenbrenner, "Socialization and Social Class Through Space and Time," in Eleanor E. Maccoby, Theodore M. Newcomb, and Eugene L. Hartley (eds.), *Readings in Social Psychology* (New York: Henry Holt & Co., Inc., 1958); Melvin Kohn, "Social Class and Parent-Child Relationships," *American Journal of Sociology*, Vol. LXVIII, No. 4 (January, 1963).

[65] Samuel L. Clemens, "Foreword," *The Prince and the Pauper*.

And so the culture, the knowledge of what is and what ought to be, is transmitted, remarkably similar in substance and form, from generation to generation through the family.

Thus Herbert Hyman in his review of what we know about the political socialization of the child can say that intergenerational political preferences "are so similar that one can conclude that social differentiations in voting preference [and above all in party preference] are almost complete at the pre-adult level."[66]

We know that favorable attitudes toward labor, toward unions, and "collectivism" are characteristic of lower-class, rather than upper-class, persons. And the children of the poorer classes reflect this orientation, being more favorably disposed toward unions than their middle- and upper-class counterparts.[67]

Professor Hyman reviews past studies of extent of agreement between parent and children on attitude toward war and its likelihood, view of the New Deal, attitude toward Communist and Fascist positions, ethnocentrism, liberalism, conservatism, the USSR, and party preferences. A few inquiries report no great similarity between parents' and children's views. But about three fourths of the studies do report finding marked agreement between political views of the two generations.

"The political homogeneity of the family may extend over several generations," report Berelson, Lazarsfeld, and Gaudet.[68] "Our panel members were asked, 'Do you consider that your family (parents, grandparents) have always been predominantly Democratic or Republican?' Fully three fourths of the respondents . . . followed the political lead of their families." Thus the link between generations in political views is quite clear. And since it is unlikely that political attitudes flow from children to parents, we must assume that the filial loyalties stem from parental commitments. But the moderate size of the correlations between attitudes of father and son suggest that parents are not the only agents transmitting political preferences and other views. Indeed, in one early study of resemblances in moral knowledge between children and five socializing agents, the correlation (r) between parents and children was only

---

[66] Herbert Hyman, *Political Socialization* (New York: Free Press of Glencoe, Inc., 1959), p. 36.

[67] *Ibid.*, p. 39.

[68] Bernard Berelson, Paul Lazarsfeld, and Hazel Gaudet, *The People's Choice* (New York: Columbia University Press, 1948), p. 142.

.55;[69] that is, variance in parental views accounted for something around 30 percent of the variance in children's views (although this influence was greater than that of any other of the agents studied: friends, club leaders, school, and Sunday school teachers).[70] The relative impact of other agents of socialization seems to increase through time. The influence of the school increases over time, and this in two senses. Political and other attitudes have been shown to change with further years of schooling. And the average number of years of schooling achieved has increased over the years. (It was on this basis that Samuel Stouffer, having found greater concern for civil liberties among the better educated, and an increasing proportion of the population achieving higher levels of education, predicted an increased concern to preserve our Bill of Rights and to tolerate various sorts of deviants.)[71] It is to this matter of the school's influence that we now turn, seeing it, after the family, as the principal agent for inducting the newcomer into the group.

THE SCHOOL AS THE GROUP'S AGENT OF CULTURAL TRANSMISSION

Formal education is the most powerful of the tools consciously and consistently used to bring the influence of the group to bear upon the person.[72] The teacher is delegated by the group to inculcate the knowledge (the elements of culture) necessary for satisfactory group membership. Like parents, teachers are vested with a public responsibility. Like parents they share in the task of "fabricating" human beings. And to some extent they are able to work, like parents, upon relatively malleable material—upon persons much of whose behavior has not yet been irreversibly channeled.

---

[69] We run across the Pearsonian *r*, or the product moment correlation coefficient, so frequently in the social sciences, it is worth stopping briefly to illustrate its meaning. See "An Aside on Methods: the Pearsonian Correlation Coefficient," pp. 165–67.

[70] H. Hartshorne, M. May, and F. Shuttleworth, *Studies in the Nature of Character, III* (New York: Macmillan Co., 1930), p. 98.

[71] Samuel A. Stouffer, *Communism, Conformity and Civil Liberties* (New York: Doubleday & Co., Inc., 1955), p. 92.

[72] This is a strong statement. But recall that law requires every normal person to submit to this influence, a mandatory exposure to indoctrination which is true of no other human association save the family and the state. Consider, also, the way in which this influence is standardized (again, by law) in contrast to the broadly varying influences of different families. I speak here only of the U.S., obviously. In other societies newcomers to the group may be inducted—i.e., educated—chiefly through other agencies.

An Aside on Methods: the Pearsonian Correlation Coefficient

In Figure A, below, as the measure of father's conservatism increases one unit, so likewise does the son's. A measure of the extent of the relationship between these two variables is the correlation coefficient, r; and its value here is $+ 1.0$.

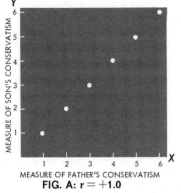

FIG. A: $r = +1.0$

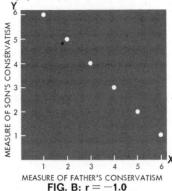

FIG. B: $r = -1.0$

Given the value on X (father's conservatism score) we can predict always and accurately what the value on Y (son's conservatism score) will be. The relationship here is *positive*, i.e., with an increase of one unit in X there is an increase of the same degree in Y. Were the converse true, if as in Figure B, above, with every increase of one unit in X there were a corresponding *decrease* in Y, the relationship would be *inverse*, or negative.

When we use r, we are usually trying to get a fuller understanding of the dependent variable (Y). Now in the figures, above, we can describe sons' conservatism by calculating the mean score made by 6 sons on some measure of conservatism. This would be 3.5 ($21 \div 6$). It tells us what conservatism score each person would have if each had the same score. But of course they don't have the same score, and the extent to which they don't is the extent to which the $\overline{Y}$ gives us a false impression. We might, then, calculate a measure of dispersion, typically s, the standard deviation, to take account of the spread and to correct mis-impressions conveyed by the mean of Y ($\overline{Y}$). (In this case, $s =$ the square root of the sum of the following values, squared and divided by N, or 6: 1–3.5, 2–3.5, 3–3.5, 4–3.5, 5–3.5 and 6–3.5. It is $\sqrt{17.5/6}$ or 1.7, in this case.) Now combining these two measures gives us a better *description* of sons' conservatism. But it doesn't help us much in understanding why some sons are more, others less conservative. It doesn't help explain the difference.

Such differences are presumably linked with conditions or influences that shape the son's political and economic convictions. Put this way we are treating son's conservatism scores as the dependent variable and we'll put this dimension along the Y axis. These scores depend at least in part, we think, on variations in some other factor—in this case the influence of the father.

Note, now, that if there were no variation in the sons' conservatism scores, there'd be nothing to explain. If there isn't any difference, it doesn't make any difference. The problem is posed precisely because there are differences. These are variations in degree of conservatism. Statistically we call measures of these differences the *variance*. The fact that there is variance indicates the existence of a problem. It represents what we don't know, what we have to explain. Variance, then, can be viewed as a measure of error, or ignorance. Thus s_Y^2, the variance

An Aside on Methods: the Pearsonian Correlation Coefficient (continued)

around $\overline{Y}$ is a *measure of our original ignorance* or our total ignorance. Let's represent it by 1, or unity, the whole of anything.

Now we have a hunch that we can reduce our ignorance or, to put it positively, we can increase our understanding of differences in conservatism if we have some notion of factors linked with, perhaps largely responsible for it. Parental influence, in this case the father's, seems one plausible source of influence on the son's attitudes. If this is in fact the case we might be able to reduce the variance (our ignorance) represented by the dispersion around $\overline{Y}$ by relating or connecting values on Y (sons' conservatism scores) with the other variable suggested by our interpretation (fathers' conservatism scores). The latter then becomes our independent variable. Our attempt, now, is to see how much of our ignorance (s_Y^2, variation in the dependent variable) can be dealt with or reduced by linking it with variance of the independent variable (s_X^2).

And so we relate the two variables. For each value of Y we find the corresponding value of X and the data fall, let us say, as illustrated in the fictional figures above. If we plot a line through these points (it is called a regression line), we get a graphic impression of the relationship between the two variables. If we can so construct a line through the data that a reading on it for X will give us a precise, or even an approximate value for Y, then we have improved our knowledge considerably. This regression line, or line of least mean squares, is one that minimizes the dispersion of the data from themselves. The line in our diagram is one from which the sum of the deviations equals 0. Put another way, whereas at first we could only describe son's conservatism as represented by a mean score of 3.5 and a standard deviation of 1.7, we can now use father's score to predict the son's score precisely and can describe the perfect relationship between these two variables by saying that $r = +1.0$. We can think of the dispersion around the mean of Y as our original ignorance about the son's conservatism. The dispersion around our regression line can represent our remaining ignorance (after taking father's conservatism into account). If there is no dispersion, as in our illustration, there is no ignorance; for we can predict perfectly from the father's score.

Now using 1, as we often do to represent the whole of something, let 1 stand for all the variation in Y—i.e., 1 = variance we've "explained" by relating Y to X + the residual variance that is not "explained" by relating Y to X. Or

$$1 = \begin{array}{c}\text{Proportion of variance} \\ \text{in } Y \text{ that } can \text{ be attrib-} \\ \text{uted to variance in } X\end{array} \quad + \quad \begin{array}{c}\text{Proportion of variance} \\ \text{in } Y \text{ that } cannot \text{ be attrib-} \\ \text{uted to variance in } X\end{array}$$

$$\text{and } 1 - \begin{array}{c}\text{Proportion of variance} \\ \text{in } Y \text{ that } cannot \text{ be attrib-} \\ \text{uted to variance in } X\end{array} \quad = \quad \begin{array}{c}\text{Proportion of variance} \\ \text{in } Y \text{ that } can \text{ be attrib-} \\ \text{uted to variance in } X\end{array}$$

and, in conventional symbols:

$$1 - \frac{s_{Y_c}^2 \; [\text{Variance around computed regression line on } Y]}{s_{\overline{Y}}^2 \; [\text{Variance around the mean of } Y \; (\overline{Y})]} = r^2.$$

The Function of Public Education

Education is the means by which the group models persons to fit
its requirements. (This is not, of course, the common view of
education; and I shall point out presently why I think the common
view illusory and this view correct.) Formal education consists in
sets of standardized roles defined in law—federal, state, and local—
in custom and in the credos of professional organizations. We think
ordinarily of such roles as those associated with the public schools,
colleges, academies, and universities: teachers, professors, students,
principals, superintendents, presidents, regents, and the like. But
education, even where as in Western societies it is separately
institutionalized, is not confined to the school. Helvétius was right
when he said:

> . . . everyone . . . has for teachers both the form of government un-
> der which he lives, and his friends and his mistresses, and the people
> about him, and the books he reads and, finally, chance, that is to say
> an infinite number of events whose connection and causes we are un-
> able, through ignorance, to perceive.[73]

Priest and parent and peers have educational roles; and so do fellow
workers, actors, employers, and grandparents. Wherever there is

---

[73] Claude Adrien Helvétius, *de l'Esprit* (Paris, 1758), discours iii, chap. i.

systematic instruction in skills, knowledge, and attitudes, "teachers" are at work. Learning the multiplication table or Shamanistic secrets, the notions of fair play or the arts of mendacity, pressure chipping of flint or metallurgy, people are learning and being taught. Suggesting that we think too much in terms of formal education, delegating the task to the school while failing to exploit the possibilities of informal education, George A. Pettitt writes:

> We cannot read deeply in ethnological literature without being struck by the fact that primitive education was a community project in which all reputable elders participated at the instigation of individual families. The result was not merely to focus community attention on the child, but also to make the child's education a constant challenge to the elders to review, analyze, dramatize, and defend their cultural heritage.[74]

So it is, too, with the school today. The task is to preserve the cultural heritage. The end of the process is to contrive a "proper" human being who embodies the core elements of that heritage. Durkheim says:

> That is the task of education, and thus we see it in all its greatness. Education does not restrict itself to developing the individual in accordance with his [genetic] nature, teasing out those hidden capacities that lie there, dormant, asking only to be revealed. *It creates a new being.*[*]

Durkheim has perfectly expressed this view that education is the instrument of the group to induct succeeding generations into their appropriate roles in the group. "Education, far from having as its unique or principal object the individual and his interests, is above all the means by which society perpetually recreates the conditions of its very existence."[75] But the professional educators and public spokesmen take a contrary position. Education, they say, is the process of developing as far as possible the particular potential of the individual. This conventional view of education is hopelessly myopic. It sees only the cherished individual, wallowing in tender loving care. Indeed, this egocentric view has so long prevailed—we

---

[74] George A. Pettitt, *Primitive Education in North America.* University of California *Publications in American Archaeology and Ethnology,* Vol. XLIII (1946).

[*] See Original Texts, Note 2, at end of chapter.

[75] Emile Durkheim, *Education et sociologie* (Paris: Librairie Felix Alcon, 1922), p. 123. See also Professor Sorokin's similar statement. The school is "primarily a testing, selecting and distributing agency . . . allocating people to the niches necessary to perform their social function." *Social Mobility* (New York: Harper & Bros., 1927), p. 188.

have been so long misled by an individualistic, psychologically distorted view of education—that it is now almost subversive to view education from a social perspective. Our clichés about developing the individual, cultivating the whole personality of the child, the democratic respect for the individual, the Christian emphasis upon the dignity of the individual, our God who is conscious of the single swallow's fall—these pieties have at once blinded us to the reality and barred its consideration as heretical. For this reason— and in support of my general thesis, the influence of the group upon the person entering it—I shall stress here the necessarily coercive influence and the conformist product of public education.

Winston Churchill once declared that he did not become Prime Minister of England to preside over the dissolution of the British empire. So it is with our Boards of Education in the United States. They do not see themselves as having been elected to promote change in the community through novelties in education purchased with tax dollars. Their task is to see that education preserves the community. For this reason public education is and must be essentially a conservative force, the "means by which [the group] perpetually recreates the conditions of its very existence." We should not, therefore, be surprised if teachers disposed to encourage independent thought are regarded as subversive; for quite literally that is what they are. Even at the university level, the school can encourage innovation with impunity only in those realms—for example, engineering—where the material consequences are "more of the same" (bigger and better) and where the social consequences are remote and obscure.

Through education, then, we induct persons into the group in ways that respond to the needs of the group. In a nation in which it is possible for a Secretary of Defense to say: "What is good for General Motors is good for the U.S.," it is to be expected that "driver education" will have an important part in the curriculum.[76] In an

---

[76] The *New York Times* reports that "High Schools in U.S. Trained 1,338,246 to Drive in 1958–59."

As a result of a "marked advance" in their programs, Delaware, New Jersey, N. Carolina, Utah, and the District of Columbia received Progress Awards in the 12th annual evaluation by the Association of Casualty and Surety Companies . . . insurance companies give discounts ranging as high as 10% from the extra premiums charged to "unmarried male drivers under 25 years" if a youth has successfully completed such a program. The insurance report showed that 63% of the 21,000 public high schools in the country offered some kind of driver training to 67.7% of the eligible students . . . the insurance group said that "the revolt

increasingly complex society the fragmentation of the curriculum will reflect the specialized needs of the group. This tendency is indicated in Table 4–4, which, since it applies only to the elementary school level, is an emphatic understatement.

The increased emphasis in recent years upon language, mathematics, and the physical sciences is, again, a response through education to the need felt by the group (in the United States) to

TABLE 4–4

Expansion of Elementary School Curriculum from 1775–1900

1775	1825	1850	1875	1900
Reading	Grammar	History	Drawing	Physiology & Hygiene
Spelling	Reading	Language &	Civics	Literature
Arithmetic	Spelling	Grammar	History	Drawing
Writing	Arithmetic	Reading	Language &	Civics
Bible	Writing	Spelling	Grammar	History
	Conduct	Arithmetic	Reading	Language & Grammar
	Bookkeeping	Writing	Spelling	Reading
	Geography	Object	Writing	Spelling
		Lesson	Arithmetic	Writing
		Bookkeeping	Physical	Arithmetic
		Geography	exercise	Play
		Conduct	Nature study	Nature study
			Geography	Geography
			Music	Music
			Conduct	Physical training
				Sewing
				Manual training

Source: O. W. Caldwell and S. A. Courtis, *Then and Now in Education* (New York: World Book Co., 1924), p. 119.

strengthen itself vis-à-vis the U.S.S.R. Similarly, formal education serves the needs of the group in undeveloped rural areas by reducing its demands upon the child—a shortened school year, the common withdrawals during planting and harvesting seasons, a disregard for the letter of the school law.

It follows, clearly, that what is appropriate education for entering one group will not be appropriate in another. The educational patterns of one society cannot be successfully imposed on another having a different congeries of beliefs and behaviors. This is why, as

against frills in the secondary school curriculum" had not forced a reduction in driver training—an implied criticism of New York City [where] complete driver training is offered only in 6 vocational schools, largely because members of the school administration feel that such training in academic high schools is unnecessary and difficult to give. (*New York Times*, October 5, 1959.)

Kingsley Davis points out, the attempt to transplant British education in India was necessarily such a thumping failure. "The western
model collides with two great realities in Hindu life—*ruralism* and
caste."[77] An educational program drawn from a group (the English)
having a single language, a complex technology, elaborate industry
with its concomitant organization and bookkeeping systems, was
scarcely appropriate for a poor agricultural population. The result,
Davis points out, was great waste as nine out of ten students gave up
what was for them an irrelevant education before achieving effective literacy. Of course this is by no means a lasting situation in
India. As a new and independent nation, seeking unity through a
common language and striving to advance the level of living for its
people, the group now requires something other than its traditional,
informal modes of education. These changing needs are reflected in
the growth of literacy and school enrollment in India. On this score
British education was not a failure. If it was ill suited to sustain the
old society, it was well suited to support the Western patterns being
imported.

Before leaving Davis' data on India and Pakistan, it is worth
noting that the minority groups, the Parsis, Jews, Jains, and Christians were those with highest literacy rates according to the figures
for 1931.[78] It is at least plausible that effective membership in a
minority group demands the weapons of literacy, training in rare
skills which compensate to some extent for the handicaps of
minority status. Similarly, one gets some idea of the peculiar and
particular significance of school for immigrant Jews in the United
States from Alfred Kazin's telling account of his childhood school
experiences.

> It was never learning I associated with that school: only the ne-
> cessity to succeed, to get ahead of the others in the daily struggle to
> "make a good impression" on our teachers. . . .
> All teachers were to be respected like gods, and God himself was
> the greatest of all school superintendents. Long after I had ceased to
> believe that our teachers could see with the back of their heads, it
> was still understood, by me, that they knew everything. They were
> delegates of all visible and invisible power on earth—of the mothers
> who waited on the stoops every day after three for us to bring home
> tales of our daily triumphs; of the glacially remote Anglo-Saxon prin-
> cipal whose very name was King; of the incalculably important Super-

[77] Kingsley Davis, *The Population of India and Pakistan* (Princeton: Princeton
University Press, 1931), p. 159.

[78] *Ibid.*, Figure 40, p. 155.

intendent of Schools who would some day rubberstamp his name to the bottom of our diplomas in grim acknowledgment that we had at last given satisfaction to him, to the Board of Superintendents, and to our benefactor the City of New York—and so up and up to the great Lord Jehovah Himself. . . .[79]

In inducting the child into the group, the school is in an intermediate position. In the person's life line it stands between the family of orientation and the family of procreation, between his past and his future, between one generation and another. Between the varied backgrounds of its students and the equally varying futures they will experience, public education tends to emphasize the necessary communal learnings, the cultural universals. For persons still unacceptable in the general labor market yet too old for constant parental supervision, the public school serves a quasi-custodial function. It is perhaps intermediate between home and job in the demands it makes: personal attributes are occasionally judged relevant ("A" for effort), not yet being entirely superseded by general standards impersonally applied to the performance of the task (as supposedly obtains in the rational setting of the workaday world). It is also intermediate in the same sense that a personnel department mediates between labor supply and vocational placement. In this connection, it can be seen as a kind of institutional sieve, sorting out persons of different backgrounds, aptitudes, and prospects into appropriate slots in the social structure. This is what Sorokin meant in describing the school as "primarily a testing, selecting and distributing agency . . ." This is apparently a recognized function of education in England.

> Until just now the universities acted as a final sieve—a means of turning out enough people to man the civil service, the upper ranks of business, and the professions, but not many more. This manufactured aristocracy roughly tallied with the jobs thought suitable to it; as lately as 1952 the University Grants Committee, the nearest thing to a policy making body for all the universities, said that universities ought to expand only if there were enough "appropriate" jobs for the extra graduates.[80]

We have often seen free public education as the instrument par excellence of a democracy. That is to say, form of government and

---

[79] From *A Walker in the City,* copyright, 1951, by Alfred Kazin. Reprinted by permission of Harcourt, Brace & World, Inc.

[80] John Rosselli, "English Education: More Room at the Top," *The Reporter,* Vol. XXIV, No. 9 (April 27, 1961). Copyright 1961 by The Reporter Magazine Company.

type of education are seen as necessarily interconnected. Thus we assert that if the suffrage extends to all citizens, it is imperative to provide universal, "free" education. (Democratic revolutionaries have agreed with Danton: *"Après le pain, l'éducation est le premier besoin du peuple."*)[81] The assumptions of our form of government require that education provide that equality of opportunity which guarantees both personal fulfillment and the disclosure of socially useful *in*equalities. To an indeterminate extent this has been true. Much of the imagery of education has made it, from the person's perspective, a social escalator, the proper instrument for improving one's standing. This has probably led us to underemphasize the extent to which education responds to differentials in the group, tending in general to reproduce them. Especially have we over-looked the extent to which other socializing agencies such as the family have already set the conditions of knowledge and aspiration that qualify the school's influence. Consider in this connection the bearing of the class of the student's family upon various aspects of his education.

EDUCATION AND CLASS

The relationship between student and teacher is strongly affected by the class position of the student's family. The data suggest one overriding tendency. This is for the student's performance and prospects to approximate those of his parents. The best prediction we can make is that the school will help to induct the student into a niche in the social order not differing markedly from that of his family of orientation.

The over-easy assumption might be that "h'it's the rich what gets the gryvey; h'it's the poor what gets the blyme." Differentials in income, one index of class, play an important part in determining whether, where, and how long the child goes to school. The data[82] given in Tables 4–5 and 4–6 support this notion.

---

[81] This statement is from the base of Danton's statue at the *carrefour de l'Odéon*, Paris (Georges-Jacques Danton, 1759–94). Translation: "After bread the people's first need is for education."

[82] These data are for 1937 and 1938. The Bureau of the Census reports that median income, 1960, for professional, technical and kindred male workers was $6,619.00. Note that the median, rather than the mean, is used as a measure of central tendency for income. The mean is affected by extreme values, and since the income distribution is heavily skewed the mean is pulled toward the high values, giving a distorted impression of this characteristic of the group.

TABLE 4–5

Relationship of Parental Income to Full-
Time College Attendance of Superior
Milwaukee High School Graduates

PARENTAL INCOME	PERCENT IN COLLEGE FULL-TIME
$8,000 plus	100.0
5,000–7,999	92.0
3,000–4,999	72.9
2,000–2,999	44.4
1,500–1,999	28.9
1,000–1,499	25.5
500– 999	26.8
under $ 500	20.4

But beyond and behind the matter of wealth and poverty lie more
subtle but perhaps equally influential factors. There is the matter of
problem-solving ability as measured by intelligence test scores. In
his study of 507 high school students in "Elmtown," Hollingshead
found the following distribution of I.Q. scores by class.[83] I have

TABLE 4–6

Median Parental Income
and Type of College Course Pursued

COLLEGE COURSE	MEDIAN PARENTAL INCOME
Law	$2,118
Medicine & Dentistry	2,112
Liberal Arts	2,068
Journalism	1,907
Engineering	1,884
Teaching	1,570
Commercial	1,543
Nursing	1,368
Industrial trades	1,104

Source (Tables 4–5 and 4–6): Helen Bertha Goetsch,
Parental Income and College Opportunities, Teachers College
Contributions to Education, No. 795 (New York: Bureau of
Publications, Teachers College, Columbia University, 1940);
cited in W. Lloyd Warner, Robert Havighurst, and Martin B.
Loeb, *Who Shall Be Educated?* (New York: Harper & Bros.,
1944), pp. 53, 72.

[83] A. B. Hollingshead, *Elmtown's Youth* (New York: John Wiley & Sons, Inc.,
1949), p. 175.

converted his data into percentages for ease in seeing the direction
of the relationship (Table 4–7).

TABLE 4–7

I. Q. TEST SCORES	CLASS				
	1 & 2	3	4	5	
120–139	23%	13%	5%	0%	
111–119	43	47	36	12	N = 507
91–110	34	39	56	77	
70–90	0	1	3	11	p < .01
	100	100	100	100	

Whether or not I.Q.[84] is a genetic legacy, we can be sure that the
problem-solving capacity of a child will be affected by his social
setting; by the ease with which his parents handle symbols; by the
stimuli provided (or lacking) through radio, television, books,
papers, friends; by the kinds of concerns and the level of conversation in which they are discussed; by the extent of family travel; by
the range of family friends. We are not then surprised to find, in
comparing high- and low-achieving Negro students of comparable
ability, that 20 percent of the high achievers had parents in
professional or white-collar occupations while this was true of only 5
percent of the low achievers.[85] Among the high achievers, only 10
percent had parents who themselves had less than a seventh grade
education. The figure was 50 percent among the low achievers.

Income differentials, then, somewhat disguise the influence of
parental occupation and education as they condition the parent-
child relationship. And out of this relationship, in turn, emerges the
value placed upon education and the qualifications and attributes
necessary to achieve it. Professor Stouffer writes: ". . . among
bright working class children, family income is not the only or
possibly even the most important factor" in the decision about
college. "Many of the poorest of these children go to college; many

---

[84] Useful as it is, the measure of problem-solving capacity, the I. Q. test, is a
culture-bound instrument whose items fit the middle-class, schoolish child better than
his lower-class counterpart.

[85] Raymond E. Schultz, "A Comparison of Negro Pupils Ranking High with
Those Ranking Low in Educational Achievement," *Journal of Educational Sociology,*
Vol. XXXI, No. 7 (March, 1958), pp. 265–70. The number of students studied was
originally 100, fifty in each group; but the N was dropped to 91 in the attempt to
make the groups comparable in ability.

of the relatively better off do not."[86] Stouffer, Kluckhohn, and Parsons think that the basic determinant lies in "differences in the value orientations of the parents and in ways of implementing these orientations." Sometimes, "there seems to be a lack of serious belief that college would be possible—'in the cards'—for their own child, even though he is bright and even though other bright children at the same economic level do go to college." Or they may fail in providing effective motivation, in manipulating rewards and punishments. "Such skill is particularly necessary in neighborhoods where there are high alternative rewards available to the child, especially to the boy, in play groups and gangs of his age mates."

Whether or not it is a realistic assessment, the generally more modest aspirations of the lower-class child are translated not only into a rejection of college as a live option, but also in terms of humbler vocational choices. Professor Hollingshead again provides us with some data on this matter (see Table 4–8). The last figure in the right-hand column is particularly interesting. I believe it represents the indecision of the lower-class child caught between the onward-and-upward injunctions of his culture as mediated by middle-class teachers, and what he regards as the realities of the situation.

TABLE 4–8

Vocational Choices of 735 Elmtown High School Students (in Percent)

CHOSEN OCCUPATION	CLASS				
	1 & 2	3	4	5	
Professional or Businessman	77.1	36.1	23.1	7.0	
Clerical	5.7	20.3	20.5	10.9	
Craftsman	.4	12.0	17.3	13.9	N = 735
Farmer	11.4	10.1	6.4	2.6	
Miscellaneous & undecided	.4	21.5	32.7	65.7	

Source: Adapted from A. B. Hollingshead, *Elmtown's Youth* (New York: John Wiley & Sons, Inc., 1949), p. 469.

If we collapse this table, calling the first two occupational categories "white-collar" and the others "blue-collar," and separating classes 1 and 2 from the others, we get the picture given in Table 4–9.

---

[86] This and the following quotations are from Samuel A. Stouffer, "The Study of Social Mobility," n.d., dittoed, pp. 3 *et passim*.

TABLE 4–9

	CLASS		
	1 & 2	3, 4, 5	
White-collar	83	38	
Blue-collar	17	62	N = 735
	100%	100%	

The case would be still more striking were we to assume, as seems reasonable, that students in classes 1 and 2 who plan to become "farmers" mean that they will manage their fathers' farms—that is to say they are, in effect, white-collar workers.

Now if goal and motivation are thus differentiated by class, we would be justified in predicting parallel differences in school performance. This is indeed what we find.

TABLE 4–10

Percent of Elmtown High School Students Failing, by Class

CLASS	PERCENT FAILING	
1 & 2	2.9	
3	2.7	N = 390
4	10.0	p < .01
5	23.1	

TABLE 4–11

Grades Achieved by Elmtown High School Students, by Class

	PERCENT WITH MEAN GRADE OF		
CLASS	50–69	70–84	85–100
1 & 2	00.0	48.6	51.4
3	1.3	63.2	35.5
4	12.4	69.2	18.4
5	25.0	66.7	8.3

Source (Tables 4–10 and 4–11): A. B. Hollingshead, *Elmtown's Youth*, (New York: John Wiley & Sons, Inc., 1949) pp. 172, 173.

Recall our definition of the field. We have here the controlled observation of differing patterns of human relationships (differing by class); and the bearing such differences may have, directly or indirectly, upon the teacher's assessment of student performance. It will be useful to remind one's self of this definition and to try fitting it to various studies reported.

Let us digress for a moment, also, to be certain we make the necessary distinction between presenting the facts and interpreting them. This is as good an occasion as any to remind ourselves that the facts never speak for themselves. The same set of data (facts) may suggest quite different sorts of interpretations. Here are four very different interpretations of Table 4–11.

First, we might speculate that these data reveal the tendency of the privileged (middle-class Board of Education people) to maintain their position through the agency of teachers whom they "buy." We need not take the word "buy" literallly. The purchase of minds and wills may be quite a subtle process in which both buyer and seller act, so far as they know, honestly, independently and in good faith. There may be, nonetheless, a remarkable coincidence between the interests of the employer and the "independent" inclinations of the employee.

A second interpretation of these data might run to the effect that the relationship between good grades and high class standing masks the underlying connection between class and native intelligence. (The rich and the well born are, in fact, the able.)

A third interpretation suggested by Professor William Foote Whyte is this: middle-class teachers understand better and communicate more effectively with middle-class students.

A fourth interpretation would emphasize the fact that middle-class teachers are dealing with students whose goals, motivation, and background, deriving from their families' class-linked style of life, necessarily make for different behaviors, in school work as elsewhere, resulting in differences in grades.

Such data represent controlled observation in the sense that the inquiry is clearly focused, terms are defined with care, and the variables are measured. But aside from the two variables dealt with —class and I.Q. score, class and drop-out rate, class and school grades—there are others which should be controlled, or held constant lest we attribute a causal influence unjustifiably to that cluster of factors represented by the concept, class. Such a variable, obviously, is intelligence. The data in Table 4–12 give us some indication of the influence of the student's father's class status when we compare boys and girls *with comparable I.Q. scores.*

Pursuing the same problem, Sewell, Haller, and Straus compared the percent of students having high-level educational aspirations among different classes (as measured by the North-Hatt scale of occupational prestige) while holding constant the variables of I.Q. scores and sex.[87] Their results are the same as Stouffer's. And so we seem justified in saying with Sibley that ". . . as a boy passes through the educational sifting process, his parents' status assumes

---

[87] William H. Sewell, Archie O. Haller, and Murray A. Straus, "Social Status and Educational and Occupational Aspiration," *American Sociological Review,* Vol. XXII (February, 1957). See Tables 1 and 2, pp. 70, 71.

TABLE 4–12

How College Plans of Students in a Massachusetts High School Vary
by I.Q., Social Status, and Sex (in Percent)

	NOT IN COLLEGE PREPARATORY COURSE & NOT PLANNING ON COLLEGE	IN COLLEGE PREPARATORY COURSE & PLANNING COLLEGE	TOTAL	N
Two Highest I.Q. Deciles:				
White-collar fathers:				
Boys	30	70	100	34
Girls	46	54	100	41
Working-class fathers:				
Boys	58	42	100	41
Girls	58	42	100	33
Next Two Highest I.Q. Deciles:				
White-collar fathers:				
Boys	62	38	100	24
Girls	59	41	100	
Working-class fathers:				
Boys	75	25	100	32
Girls	87	13	100	42

Source: Samuel A. Stouffer, "The Study of Social Mobility," n.d., dittoed. The time is spring, 1951, the place an industrial suburb of Boston.

increasing importance, both absolutely and in comparison with his own intelligence, as a factor influencing his chances of continuing his preparation for one of the more advantageous vocations."[88]

Such sociological inquiries give us a different perspective on education. The function of public education, both formal and informal, is to assure the survival of the social order through differential transmission of the culture. The principal influence of the school, working with children whose families span the community class structure, is to induct the student into a niche in the social order not differing greatly from that of his family of orientation.

This suggests that the role persons come to assume in the social order is influenced not only by their personal interests and aptitudes; but also by characteristics ascribed to them on the basis of their family's class position. There are, then, two sorts of attributes

---

[88] Elbridge Sibley, "Some Demographic Clues to Stratification," *American Sociological Review*, Vol. VII (June, 1942) p. 330.

that jointly determine what a person shall become as he enters the group: those *ascribed* to him and those *achieved* by him. (The distinction is a little too neat since these two types of criteria for role allocation are interdependent: the ascription of favorable traits promotes achievement, and achievement entails ascription.) The significance of ascribed traits we have seen in our discussion of the interplay of class and public education. But that cluster of influences that the sociologist subsumes under the concept of class is so significant in conditioning the person's entrance into the group—the human group and all subsequent groups—that it merits our further attention. To the matter of class, then, we now turn—most particularly the class of parents, peers, and pedagogues as they condition the groups entered by the newcomer.

ORIGINAL TEXTS

1. Lucien Lévy-Bruhl, *Fonctions Mentales* (Paris: Presses Universitaires de France, 1951), p. 19.

    In Lévy-Bruhl's own words: À des types sociaux différents correspondront des mentalités différentes, d'autant plus que les institutions et les moeurs mêmes ne sont au fond qu'un certain aspect des représentations collectives, que ces représentations, pour ainsi dire, considérées objectivement.

2. Èmile Durkheim, *Education et sociologie* (Paris: Librairie Félix Alcan, 1922), p. 51.

    Durkheim writes: Voilà quelle est l'oeuvre de l'éducation, et l'on en aperçoit toute la grandeur. Elle ne se borne pas à développer l'organisme individuel dans la sense marqué par sa nature, à rendre apparentes des puissances cachées qui ne demandaient qu'à se révéler. *Elle crée dans l'homme un être nouveau.* (Italics mine.)

SELECTED SUPPLEMENTARY READINGS

HYMAN, HERBERT. *Political Socialization.* (New York: The Free Press of Glencoe, Inc., 1959.

INKELES, ALEX. "Personality and Social Structure," in Robert K. Merton, Leonard Broom, and Leonard S. Cottrell, Jr. (eds.), *Sociology Today,* ch. xi. New York: Harper & Row—Harper Torchbooks, 1965.

NEWCOMB, THEODORE M. *Personality and Social Change.* New York: Holt, Rinehart & Winston, Inc., 1957.

Chapter 5

Class Differences in the Transmission of Culture

How does socialization vary by class?
How does class affect the groups we enter?

Let us extend an idea broached in preceding pages. In discussing the school as the group's formal agent of induction, we saw that class affects the sort of education gotten, the motivation to get it, and the ends for which education is thought to be the means. Now, going beyond the effect of class on educational category or school group entered, the more general notion of this chapter is this: class influences the groups we enter (and, therefore, the elements of culture transmitted).

Class points to the hierarchical ordering of roles along the scale of a group's values. Men characteristically value. This means that they prefer, discriminating between better and worse. And class always conveys the notion of differences among men in the extent to which they possess things valued by the group: virtue, wealth, wisdom, virility, grace, valor, skill, saintliness. The term commonly connotes more or fewer possessions, more or less prestige, greater or lesser power, higher or lower standing: differences, in short, among things valued by the group.

Roles differentiated along the scale of group values imply relationships similarly differentiated. Roles characteristic of a given class (parental roles, work roles, the roles of communicant, citizen,

EVERYDAY TASTES FROM HIGH-BROW T

	CLOTHES		FURNITURE	USEFUL OBJECTS	ENTERTAINMENT	SALADS
HIGH-BROW	TOWN Fuzzy Harris tweed suit, no hat	COUNTRY Fuzzy Harris tweed suit, no hat	Eames chair, Kurt Versen lamp	Decanter and ash tray from chemical supply company	Ballet	Greens, olive oil, wine vinegar, ground salt, ground pepper, garlic, unwashed salad bowl
UPPER MIDDLE-BROW	TOWN Brooks suit, regimental tie, felt hat	COUNTRY Quiet tweed jacket, knitted tie	Empire chair, converted sculpture lamp	Silver cigaret box with wedding ushers' signatures	Theater	Same as high-brow but with tomatoe avocado, Roquefo cheese added
LOWER MIDDLE-BROW	TOWN Splashy necktie, double-breasted suit	COUNTRY Sport shirt, colored slacks	Grand Rapids Chippendale chair, bridge lamp	His and Hers towels	Musical extravaganza films	Quartered icebe lettuce and store dressing
LOW-BROW	TOWN Loafer jacket, woven shoes	COUNTRY Old Army clothes	Mail order overstuffed chair, fringed lamp	Balsam-stuffed pillow	Western movies	Coleslaw

Class conditions the groups we enter, and their differing styles of life.

LOW-BROW ARE CLASSIFIED ON CHART

DRINKS	READING	SCULPTURE	RECORDS	GAMES	CAUSES
A glass of "adequate little" red wine	"Little magazines," criticism of criticism, avant garde literature	Calder	Bach and before, Ives and after	Go	Art
very dry Martini with lemon peel	Solid nonfiction, the better novels, quality magazines	Maillol	Symphonies, concertos, operas	The Game	Planned parenthood
bourbon and ginger ale	Book club selections, mass circulation magazines	Front yard sculpture	Light opera, popular favorites	Bridge	P. T. A.
Beer	Pulps, comic books	Parlor sculpture	Jukebox	Craps	The Lodge

Copyright, 1949, by Russell Lynes.

and the like) build into characteristic class-linked relationships. Thus we have much evidence (some of which I reviewed in Chapter 4) on the way parent-child relationships differ by class. And since interaction tends to be intra-class, relating one's self to similar others reinforces the attributes that establish the class category. Such outcomes are implied in familiar sayings: "To him that hath shall be given, and from him that hath not shall be taken away even that which he hath." "The rich get richer and the poor get—children."

Roles and relationships differentiated by class imply, too, differences in rules, the standards guiding behavior and belief. This whole invisible structure of rules, roles, and relationships shapes the world of newcomers to the group. Their induction and their destiny, while not irrevocably set, are yet emphatically affected by conditions of class.

CLASS AS A SET OF RULES, ROLES, AND RELATIONSHIPS TRANSMITTED FROM THE PAST AND SHAPING THE FUTURE

Thus class-linked differences in life style—in occupation, aspirations, possessions, prestige, values, view of self, and others—set the stage for socialization in differing patterns of conduct and conviction. This is especially the case since a person's class standing stems first of all from that of his family of orientation.

> A family shares many characteristics among its members that greatly affect their relationship with outsiders: the same house, the same income, the same values. If a large group of families are approximately equal to each other and clearly differentiated from other families, we call them a *social class*.[1]

Looking backward in time we see the newcomer, along with others in similar circumstances, exposed to a set of conditions affecting his values, motivations, attitudes, his knowings and believings. Thus class-linked sets of influences launch members of different classes on differing social trajectories.[2] This notion is crudely represented in Figure 5–1.

---

[1] Joseph A. Kahl, *The American Class Structure* (New York: Rinehart & Co., 1957), p. 12.

[2] This is a loose and metaphorical use of the word "member." Classes do not have rosters of members, presidents, chairmen, secretaries, and treasurers. That is to

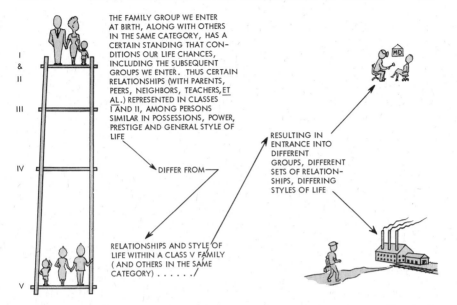

THE FAMILY GROUP WE ENTER AT BIRTH, ALONG WITH OTHERS IN THE SAME CATEGORY, HAS A CERTAIN STANDING THAT CONDITIONS OUR LIFE CHANCES, INCLUDING THE SUBSEQUENT GROUPS WE ENTER. THUS CERTAIN RELATIONSHIPS (WITH PARENTS, PEERS, NEIGHBORS, TEACHERS, ET AL.) REPRESENTED IN CLASSES I AND II, AMONG PERSONS SIMILAR IN POSSESSIONS, POWER, PRESTIGE AND GENERAL STYLE OF LIFE

DIFFER FROM

RESULTING IN ENTRANCE INTO DIFFERENT GROUPS, DIFFERENT SETS OF RELATIONSHIPS, DIFFERING STYLES OF LIFE

RELATIONSHIPS AND STYLE OF LIFE WITHIN A CLASS V FAMILY (AND OTHERS IN THE SAME CATEGORY) . . . . . . /

FIG. 5-1. The class structure is here represented as A. B. Hollingshead found it in Elmtown. But the particular division into classes is irrelevant for the point made here. More generally this figure says that different antecedent human relationships have differing consequences. It serves to remind us of our definition of the field: sociology is the controlled observation and interpretation of differing patterns of human relationships: their sources and consequences.

Looking forward, now, we find the destiny-defining aspect of class (one I am stressing in connection with the general theme, entering the group) suggested in Max Weber's view of class, a

say, they are not organized as groups. They are discerned and their boundaries specified by some observer. If he is a casual member of a small community, the observer will assign others to class categories in terms of certain locally relevant but ill-defined criteria. If he is a sociologist undertaking controlled observation he will specify his criteria with care and stratify his population in these terms. But in either case those falling in a given category are unlikely to know or be aware of all others assigned to that category by the observer. They need not have dealings with one another. Their relationships vis à vis one another *are not organized.* A class category is most likely to approximate a group—having internal coherence, mutual recognition and promotion of common objectives—where numbers are small. In a small community of but a few hundred families, class categories might approximate groups. For the United States as a whole this could only be the case with the upper sector of the elite, the heads of the establishment. A German observer says of this category:

"Perhaps the most influential members of the power elite are the legal consultants to the investment bankers, or the investment bankers themselves, who have the best knowledge of the key personnel in the economy and an overall view of the industrial potential. They are key figures in the interlocking of the political, industrial and military hierarchies. Men like McCloy, Clay, Allen Dulles, Dillon, Dewey, Brownell and Acheson belong to this group as did the late John Foster Dulles." (Herbert Von Borch, *The Unfinished Society,* trans. from the German by Mary Ilford [New York: Hawthorn Books, Inc., 1962], pp. 74–75.)

category of persons having similar life chances.[3] When people's life chances are set at birth, when they are ascribed to them exclusively on the basis of the class to which parents belong, we have caste. In the extreme case this means that each generation precisely recapitulates the pattern of its predecessor.

> O let us love our occupations
> Bless the squire and his relations,
> Live upon our daily rations
> And always know our proper stations.[4]

> The rich man in his castle,
> the poor man at his gate,
> God made them, high or lowly
> and order'd their estate.[5]

When beliefs and behaviors are thus immutably set by the accident of birth—when whom one marries, works with, eats, plays, and worships with is predetermined by the position in the social structure of the family of orientation—the central principle of order is that of caste. Caste, to rely on Weber again, is the fixing and legitimation of social distance by a religious principle. It is prescribed by God and in nature that the son's pattern of roles and system of relationships shall parallel the father's. Such a situation, only remotely approximated in most societies (as, for example, in white-Negro relationships in the United States) may be thought of as the limiting case. In actuality, the characteristics of class affecting the person's destiny are a complex amalgam of traits, those taught as well as those caught (from the family).

---

[3] What he says is this: a class consists in a category of persons having a ". . . typical chance for a supply of goods, external living conditions, and personal life experiences, in so far as this chance is determined by the amount and kind of power . . . to dispose of goods or skills for the sake of income in a given economic order." Or, again, "We may speak of a 'class' when (1) a number of people have in common a specific causal component of their life chances, in so far as (2) this component is represented exclusively by economic interests in the possession of goods and opportunities for income, and (3) is represented under the conditions of the commodity or labor markets." (H. H. Gerth and C. Wright Mills, *From Max Weber: Essays in Sociology* [New York: Oxford University Press, 1946], p. 181.)

[4] Charles Dickens, *The Chimes*, second quarter.

[5] Mrs. C. F. Alexander, "All Things Bright and Beautiful." These lines in the *Church Hymnal for the Christian Year* are to be excised, according to a *New York Times* news article. The Church of England, seeking to "keep up with the times," wishes to eliminate lines "thought to smack of feudalism. A committee headed by the Vicar of Christchurch, Orpington, Kent, is carrying out the revisions." *New York Times*, September 20, 1963.

STANDARDS FOR STANDING: ASCRIPTION AND ACHIEVEMENT

The criterion at work here, conditioning one's class standing and so, in turn, affecting the groups that he enters, is that of ascription. The person's standing is ascribed, and in some measure his several roles prescribed, on the basis of qualities inferred from his prior group memberships or his categorical identification. In Chapter 4 we saw how certain conditions linked with class of the student's family came to bear on the educational process. For we found that drop-out rates, grades, scores on intelligence tests, curriculum (whether college preparatory, commercial, or vocational), college attendance, course failure, vocational aspirations—these matters were related to the class standing of the student's family. Such data suggest that motivation, aspiration, expectation—and the resources appropriate to them—are fundamental features of class, conditioning the roles the person is to play (which is to say, the groups that he will enter). But here the person's standing derives from that of his family. It is not something that he has achieved, but rather something that has happened to him. He is, as it were, the passive recipient of a set of conditions on the basis of which certain characteristics are *ascribed* to him. (Candide remained a bastard, you may recall, because his mother, the sister of monsieur le baron de Thunder-ten-tronckh, could not bring herself to marry a local squire; for he could trace his family back only seventy-one generations!)[6]

The criterion of ascription runs counter to the stress upon equality of opportunity in a democratic creed. "The citizen in a democratical government," wrote Ferguson, ". . . cannot conceive [as do the European nobility] how a man that is born free should be inferior to another, who does not excel him in parts, integrity, or in service performed to his country."[7] Yet even in a "democratical"

---

[6] Voltaire, *Candide,* in *Romans et Contes* (Paris: Éditions Garnier Frères, 1960), p. 137.

[7] Adam Ferguson, *Principles of Moral and Political Science* (Edinburgh, 1792), Vol. I, pp. 244 *et seq.* The contrast between criteria of ascription and criteria of achievement is made in this passage.
". . . . Ask a gentleman of the continent of Europe what it is to be noble. He will answer, it is to be descended through a certain number of generations of noble ancestors. Cannot merit compensate the want of birth? The answer is that merit may recommend a gentleman in his rank, but no merit can ever entitle a peasant or a burgher to the reception that is due a gentleman. Ask him to discuss the evidence of these opinions: He will reject the proposal with contempt. The citizen,

country such as ours, standing may be ascribed on the basis of traits irrelevant to performance. For example, veterans of military service automatically get ten points preference on civil service examinations. This reward for service to the country approaches the nature of a contract, a calculated quid pro quo. But the quid (service as a G.I.) may have nothing to do with the quo. Just as my being your brother provides, in itself, no compelling reason for appointing me attorney general, so my service in the infantry would not seem a logical qualification for a position in, say, the Bureau of Internal Revenue. Religion, race, length of time lived in the community, nativity, lineage, parental occupation—these are categories on the basis of which ascriptions are made that influence our destinies. Cleveland Amory illustrates the point when he states that:

> Boston is 2,350,000 people [but] Boston society according to the *Boston Social Register* is 8,000 people. Yet to the Proper Bostonian this volume which admits only one Jewish man and, in a city now 70 per cent Catholic in population, less than a dozen Catholic families, is impossibly large.[8]

But it would be naïve to suppose that it is the person rather than the principle that is not democratic, or to leap to the conclusion that the preferred position of an upper-class person is totally undeserved. For ascription interacts with achievement. What is caught (parental position and opportunities conferred by family membership) affects what is taught and learned, that is to say, achieved. Some children of the "rich, the well-born and the able" may have the motivation and knowledge, the skills and values (for example,

---

in a democratical government, on the contrary cannot conceive how a man that is born free should be inferior to another who does not excell him in parts, integrity, or in service performed to his country."

The eminent English historian, A. L. Rowse, in his study of *The Early Churchills, An English Family,* provides a vivid illustration of the same point.

". . . the Drakes of Ashe were one of the leading families of Devon, a medieval family that had been going on for generations, intermarried with the oldest Norman gentry of Devon, Granvilles, Fortescues and such. Sir Bernard Drake, Sir John's grandfather, had been a foremost figure in the country in the reign of Queen Elizabeth. He had had an angry pass with Sir Francis Drake, on the latter's assuming the Drake coat of arms on his return from the Voyage Round the World, the most celebrated Englishman of his day. This was not good enough for Sir Bernard, who thought him an upstart and is said to have boxed the upstart's ears. *This is the kind of thing that is important to human beings: birth of more consideration than being the first circumnavigator of the globe."* ([New York: Harper & Bros., 1956], p. 20. Italics mine.)

[8] Cleveland Amory, "The Proper Bostonians," *Harper's Magazine,* September 1947, p. 201.

dedication to public service) to merit through achievement the high standing ascribed to them through their families. Differences in ascribed status make for differences in achievement. And conversely, what is taught (achieved through the person's own efforts) may modify or supersede what is caught (ascribed to him through his family's standing), so distinguishing the person's position and prospects from those of his family of orientation. In the United States personal achievement through education is for some an important way of altering the social trajectory implicit in the family's position. Education may modify the impact of ascription in three ways: by responding to the unique set and sequence of experiences endowing each person with his individuality, by inculcating cultural universals that mute class-linked differences, and by teaching/training in a great range of specialties. Consider the second and third points.

While much of what is taught varies by class, the elementary aspects of culture are transmitted to all. For some learning has to do with achieving capabilities universally required of all members of the group. Certain common learnings—among us, the three R's, a general morality, the common meanings of a common citizenship—must be achieved by all to be identified as citizens of the United States. One sort of criterion for entering the group—the human group and that society defined by nativity or naturalization—is, then, the *achievement* of the minimal elements of culture necessary to the survival of the group. Such common learnings tend to mute or mask class differentials.

But beyond these common achievements there is, in a complex society like ours, an extraordinary specialization in subgroups, chiefly occupational ones. Doctors, lawyers, merchantmen, chiefs, rich men, poor men, beggarmen, thieves—these are but the faintest intimation of the range of our better than 20,000 occupational specialties. Beyond the acquiring of a minimal common culture, the achievement of finely differentiated knowledge, attitudes and skills is a condition of entrance into these subgroups or categories. The achievement of these specialized learnings works against ascriptive classifications, making for social mobility and altering class lines.

Depending on what is caught and what is taught, on ascription and achievement, we enter different sorts of groups. And since not all sorts and degrees of achievement are equally valued in any human society, the rewards conferred by group membership will vary. They vary, too, along the road to some terminal role. Typically, membership in one group requiring lesser achievement and conferring slighter rewards is prerequisite to membership in another involving more achievement and greater rewards. In the case of scouting we have the tenderfoot, the second-class scout, first-class, star, life, and eagle scouts. In the United States civil service we have ratings from G-1 to G-14, with power, responsibility and income differentiated accordingly. In academic ranks we have student assistants, instructors, assistant, associate and full professors. In the military there is a lengthy hierarchy ranging from privates, PFC's, corporals, sergeants of several varieties up to master sergeant, warrant officers, second and first lieutenants, majors, lieutenant colonels, colonels, brigadier, major, lieutenant, and full generals, capped by the top ranking General of the Army. Battle and campaign ribbons, the Congressional Medal, decals on fuselage of plane or prow of ship are also symbolic of a sort of collective rank and achievement. Chairmen of the board, directors of the corporation, presidents, vice presidents, staff officers, plant managers, superintendents, and so on down the ladder, with rewards ostensibly geared to demonstrated achievement. So also in the church, from postulant to mother superior, from parish priest to Pope. In each case we have the hierarchical ordering of roles along the yardstick of some scale of values with a corresponding differentiation in possessions, power, prestige, privilege, and duties.

CLASS AND THE INTERGENERATIONAL REPETITION OF ROLES AND RELATIONSHIPS

Several aspects of American society tend to qualify clear and sharp class lines: the number of discernible levels, alternate paths to success, the numerous ways in which persons are ranked, the common training of group members in the "universals," the education of specialists, technological innovation, and a changing occupational structure. Given motivation, education, and persistent industry, class position need not follow automatically from that of the parental family. But these attributes, despite the Horatio Alger ethos, are not readily given. It is probably accurate to say that the tendency in a social order, even one so rapidly changing as ours, is toward intergenerational repetition.

> A hundred little things make likenesses
> In brethren born, and show the father's blood.[9]

If parents provide the model for the child, if class characteristics are mediated through family and school, if "the childhood shows the man, as morning shows the day,"[10] then the social order is maintained. And on the whole there does seem an inertia in social systems making such recapitulation the rule rather than the exception.

Of course I do not mean that a given generation impresses, in intricate detail, its mold upon its successor: that the son of a Methodist, Republican plumber invariable echoes his father's religious and political sentiments while fitting and repairing pipes. But the data do indicate that professionals are largely drawn from the ranks of professionals; and that the plumber's son is likely to have less expectation of, aspiration for and access to, the preparation necessary to become a professional. The dominant tendency toward intergenerational recapitulation stems from an early differentiation of life chances in the context of family, friends, neighborhood, and school. The fortunes, like "the sins of the father, are to be laid upon the children."[11] For example, Natalie Rogoff shows in her doctoral dissertation how roles emptied of the fathers tend to be refilled by the sons.

> One of the recurrent findings in . . . research on occupational mobility is that sons are more likely to enter their father's occupation than to enter any other single occupation. This is upheld, without exception, by the data in this study. . . . Stability is always greater than average mobility into or out of an occupation. However, there are variations in these measures from one occupation to another.[12]

Rogoff's Indianapolis data for 1910 and 1940 are given in the Tables 5–1 and 5–2. The like-father-like-son diagonal figures are circled. They should be read as follows: whereas professionals were 3.8 percent of the labor force in Indianapolis in 1910, 21 percent of those entering professional occupations had fathers who were

---

[9] Euripides, *Electra,* Line 642.

[10] John Milton, *Paradise Regained,* Book IV, Line 220.

[11] William Shakespeare, *Merchant of Venice,* Act III, Scene 5, Line 1.

[12] Natalie Rogoff, "Recent Trends in Urban Occupational Mobility." Reprinted with permission of the Free Press from *Cities and Society* by Paul K. Hatt and Albert J. Reiss, Jr., (editors). Copyright 1951, 1957 by The Free Press, a corporation.

TABLE 5–1

Occupational Mobility, Indianapolis, 1910: Proportion of Sons in Each Occupation According to Their Fathers' Occupation

FATHER'S OCCUPATION	SON'S OCCUPATION											
	PROFESSIONAL %	SEMI-PROFESSIONAL %	PROPRIETORS, MANAGERS, OFFICIALS %	CLERKS AND SALESMEN %	SKILLED %	SEMI-SKILLED %	UNSKILLED %	PROTECTIVE SERVICE %	PERSONAL SERVICE %	FARMING %	ALL FATHERS %	NUMBER OF FATHERS
Professional	21.0	3.7	12.2	24.1	21.8	10.9	3.2	0.5	2.1	0.5	100.2	377
Semi-professional	4.1	27.0	9.5	21.6	13.1	13.5	5.4	2.7	2.7	..	100.0	74
Proprietors, managers, officials	7.3	2.8	21.1	27.5	20.2	10.5	5.0	1.0	3.8	1.0	100.2	1,253
Clerks and salesmen	5.6	2.9	7.4	43.7	22.0	10.6	3.6	0.5	2.4	1.2	99.9	659
Skilled	1.9	1.6	4.1	15.2	48.7	16.9	7.0	0.8	3.2	0.7	100.1	2,720
Semi-skilled	2.4	1.5	3.6	13.7	31.8	37.6	10.3	0.7	3.3	1.0	99.9	940
Unskilled	0.8	0.7	2.8	10.9	26.8	19.0	34.2	0.9	3.3	0.6	100.0	1,256
Protective service	1.3	0.6	10.6	21.3	32.5	19.4	8.8	2.5	3.1	..	100.1	160
Personal service	0.8	3.1	3.9	17.8	26.4	20.9	11.6	0.8	14.7	..	100.2	129
Farming	3.4	1.2	6.1	14.6	27.8	16.7	14.0	1.3	4.3	10.7	100.1	2,685
Sons of all fathers	3.8	1.9	7.1	18.2	32.0	17.1	12.0	1.0	3.7	3.4	100.2	....
Number of sons	389	190	731	1,869	3,280	1,753	1,225	98	374	344	10,253	10,253

TABLE 5-2

Occupational Mobility, Indianapolis, 1940: Proportion of Sons in Each Occupation According to Their Fathers' Occupation

SON'S OCCUPATION

FATHER'S OCCUPATION	PROFESSIONAL %	SEMI-PROFESSIONAL %	PROPRIETORS, MANAGERS, OFFICIALS %	CLERKS AND SALESMEN %	SKILLED %	SEMI-SKILLED %	UN-SKILLED %	PRO-TECTIVE SERVICE %	PER-SONAL SERVICE %	FARMING %	ALL FATHERS %	NUMBER OF FATHERS
Professional	28.3	6.3	7.6	27.9	15.4	9.5	2.5	0.8	1.5	0.2	100.0	474
Semi-professional	15.8	19.3	3.5	17.5	23.7	12.3	2.6	1.8	3.5	..	100.0	114
Proprietors, managers, officials	7.7	3.4	17.6	30.6	14.3	19.8	2.5	1.6	2.1	0.5	100.1	1,203
Clerks and salesmen	7.7	5.2	7.6	42.2	15.1	16.4	2.4	1.3	1.9	0.2	100.0	1,092
Skilled	3.3	2.9	4.3	19.1	32.3	26.9	5.6	2.1	3.0	0.6	100.1	2,729
Semi-skilled	2.5	2.1	4.1	17.3	18.4	43.2	5.3	2.2	4.3	0.6	100.1	1,520
Unskilled	2.4	1.5	2.8	13.1	15.4	30.0	28.6	2.4	3.6	0.3	100.1	720
Protective service	2.5	0.8	6.6	22.8	17.0	31.5	8.7	8.3	1.2	0.4	99.8	241
Personal service	4.9	4.3	5.5	17.1	22.6	29.9	3.7	1.8	10.4	..	100.2	164
Farming	3.8	1.6	5.9	15.2	23.1	28.7	8.9	3.6	5.1	4.2	100.1	1,635
Sons of all fathers	5.5	3.1	6.6	22.1	21.9	27.1	6.9	2.3	3.4	1.1	100.0	....
Number of sons	548	307	656	2,188	2,163	2,678	684	229	334	105	9,892	9,892

TABLE 5–3

Intergenerational Stability and Mobility between Occupational Categories,
1950 (in Percent)

	SON'S OCCUPATION, 1950				
FATHER'S OCCUPATION	PROFESSIONAL AND BUSINESS	CLERICAL, SALES AND SKILLED	SEMISKILLED SERVICE AND LABORERS	TOTAL %	(N)
Professional and business	47	31	22	100	(532)
Clerical, sales, and skilled	21	40	39	100	(1073)

Source: Adapted from Herman P. Miller, *Income of the American People* (New York: John Wiley & Sons, Inc., 1955), pp. 31–33; and Gladys L. Palmer, *Labor Mobility in Six Cities* (New York: Social Science Research Council, 1954).

professionals.[13] In each case, as we look at the columns, we can say that the greatest number of persons in a given occupation had fathers in the same occupational category. More recent data confirm this tendency.

The tendency for son to recapitulate father's occupational experience is important in itself as it bears on the issue of stability in the social organization of work, hence stability in the social order. But for our purposes it is simply an indication of the way a family's class position may condition the newcomer's destiny. While occupation is only one component in an index of class position, Rogoff's occupational categories are broad enough to suggest distinctive, class-linked styles of life.

---

[13] Let me call your attention to the way Dr. Rogoff controls her observations. ("Sociology is the *controlled observation* and interpretation. . . .") She is comparing type of occupation of father and son. She seeks an answer to the question: do sons move above (or below, or simply recapitulate) their fathers' positions in the occupational ranking system? Which occupations show more and less mobility? etc. But how can she answer such a question when, as we know, occupational opportunities differ from generation to generation, indeed, from decade to decade. (For example, farming cannot now absorb the 80 percent of the workers engaged in it around 1800. A mere 10 percent of the United States labor force is now engaged in farming.)

Apparent occupational mobility may simply be a reflection of changing opportunities. How does Dr. Rogoff control the factor of variations in opportunity from generation to generation? Consider the category "Professional." In 1910, 3.8 percent of the labor force were professionals. Of all the persons so engaged, 7.3 percent had fathers who were proprietors, managers or officials. And 7.3/3.8 shows that nearly twice the proportion of professionals in the general labor force came from this particular background. Or, to illustrate again, 21.0/3.8 tells us that five times as many (as the proportion in the general labor force) were sons of fathers who themselves were professionals. Now when we say "twice the proportion in the labor force of 1910," or "five times the proportion in the labor force," we can compare such statements with similar statements for 1940. Thus the ratio 7.7/5.5 tells us that in

CLASS SHAPES AND REFLECTS GROUP MEMBERSHIP AND LIFE STYLE

Differing life styles connected with class are revealed in many ways. The way a person spends his money may well indicate where his heart lies and what his head dictates. It seems reasonable to assume that his budget discloses conceptions of need, and of costomary behavior, offering a clue to style of living. "The budget of an individual or family," says Warner, is in part a symbol system, or a set of collective representations that expresses the social value of a person's membership in a group life."[14] Style of living, in turn, provides that cultural matrix in which roles and status crystallize for the newcomer, pointing him in the direction of certain affiliations. So Warner's study of budgets, by class, in Yankee City (see Table 5–4) suggests the necessary preoccupation of the lower-lower's with matters of the body;[15] the focus of the upper-upper's on matters

1940, sons of proprietors, managers, and officials became professionals 1.4 times the proportion of professionals in the general labor force. Similarly, 28.3/5.5 tells us that the proportion of professionals whose fathers were also professionals is five times the share of this category in the total labor force. Thus we can conclude that, *despite whatever changes may have occurred in the occupational structure*, the category of professional fathers is contributing about as many professionals (and a disproportionate share) to the next generation in 1940 as was so in 1910; while the mobility from the ranks of proprietors, managers and officials to professional status seems to have declined somewhat between these dates.

The use of ratios, proportions or percentages to control certain variables—i.e., to enable controlled observation—is a common and necessary device in sociology. Thus we can compare birth or death rates of two quite different communities (a village of a few thousand and New York city) by relating the absolute number of births (which, taken alone, would leave differences in size of breeding population uncontrolled) to the size of population, then moving the decimal point for convenience.

[14] W. Lloyd Warner (ed.), *Yankee City*, abridged, one-volume edition (New Haven: Yale University Press, 1963), p. 93.

[15] George Orwell provides grim details of the necessary preoccupation of the poor with matters of sheer bodily sustenance in his *Down and Out in Paris and London* (London: Secker and Warburg, 1960). Orwell is writing of those whom Warner would call the lower-lowers. Warner elaborates the familiar trichotomy of class categories (upper, middle and lower), subdividing each into three classes: hence the nine-fold set of categories. These are: upper-upper, middle upper and lower upper, upper middle, middle-middle and lower middle, upper lower, middle lower and lower-lower. (These labels have prompted the irreverent reference to their users as the dental plate school of stratification.)

Of course the investigator may not find, in a given community, families that fit all of these categories. Means of determining class position are varied. Some indexes that have been used are: (1) appraisal and ranking of the family's living-room furnishings, (2) the rating of one or more of the following characteristics: occupation, size and source of income, area of residence, type of dwelling, (3) subjective appraisals of a family's relative standing in the community by respondents themselves, or knowledgeable locals. For a good review of measures of class standing see Joseph A. Kahl, *The American Class Structure* (New York: Rinehart & Co., 1957), pp. 32–47.

TABLE 5–4

Classes Spending Highest and Lowest Proportion of Their Total Budget for Specified Items in Yankee City, 1930's

| | CLASS HIGHEST AND LOWEST IN EXPENDITURE ON GIVEN ITEM, WITH PERCENT OF BUDGET SPENT ON IT | | | |
| | HIGHEST | | LOWEST | |
BUDGET CATEGORY	CLASS	% SPENT	CLASS	% SPENT
Clothing	UU*	11.25	LU	8.53
Formal education	UU	9.8	LL	0.1
Taxes	UU	9.8	LM	0.3
Medical	UU	5.2	LU	3.0
Gifts	UU	3.7	UL	1.4
Charity	UU	3.6	LL	0.5
Business-travel	UU	1.3	LL	—
Unclassified	UU	3.7	UL, LL	—
House operation	LU	18.9	LL	9.0
Automobile	LU	17.2	LL	1.3
House equipment	LU	4.3	UU	1.8
Associations	LU	3.3	LL	0.5
Vacation travel	LU	2.3	LL	—
Postage	LU	0.6	LL	0.1
Legal expenses	LU	0.3	LM, LL	—
Sporting equipment	LU	0.2	LL	—
Personal appearance	LM	1.2	LU	0.8
Amusements	LM	1.2	LL	0.5
Informal education	UL	2.4	LL	0.5
Tools, Professional and technical equipment	UL	1.1	LL, UL	—
Food	LL	45.4	UU	11.8
Rent and shelter	LL	20.8	UU	10.4
Tobacco	LL	1.8	UU	0.3

Source: Adapted from W. Lloyd Warner (ed.), *Yankee City*, abridged, one-volume edition (New Haven: Yale University Press, 1963), Table 2, p. 100.

* Classes are designated as follows:

UU = upper-upper.
LU = lower-upper.
UM = upper-middle (missing in the table above since there was no budget item on which their expenditure was either highest or lowest).
LM = lower-middle.
UL = upper-lower.
LL = lower-lower.

moral, civic, intellectual, and interpersonal; the concern of the lower-upper's with the furniture of life: houses, cars; and with those memberships that provide a useful stage, together with the stamp of proprietorship and legitimacy conveyed through the authority of the legal profession. The prominence of vacation travel and sporting equipment might be interpreted as the necessary cost of a taut and stressful life oriented toward peak achievement.

In more detail we see that the lower-lower's spend proportionately four times as much for food as do members of the elite; about twice as much for rent and shelter as do the upper-uppers (who spend less than any other class, relative to their total expenditures, on this item). On the other hand, among the six class categories, the upper-uppers spend a larger proportion of their budget on clothing than any other (although the range on this item is not great, the upper-lowers and the lower-lowers spending 8 percent of their budget on clothing, the upper-lowers and the lower-middles spending 9 percent and the upper-middles 10 percent). The upper-uppers also invest a much larger proportion of their budget in formal education than the other classes: 70 times as much as the proportion spent by the lower-lowers, about 11 times the proportion spent by the lower-uppers, 9 times that spent by the upper-lowers, 6 times that spent by the lower-middles and 4 times the proportion spent by the upper middles. The spread on proportion spent on medical expenses, taxes, gifts and charity was not so great. (For charity, the upper-uppers spent 7 times as large a part of their total budget as did the lower-lowers.)

The average class incomes supporting these expenditures are given in Figure 5–2. Figure 5–3 provides a base point for comparison on certain expenditures. (But it should be noted that the data are for 1951.)

Analysis of Warner's data on occupation and income suggest that style of life may differ chiefly as between three categories, differentiated by two breaks in the data. There is, first of all, a break in the class structure between occupations pursued by the upper-middles (and the two classes above them) and the lower-middles (and the two classes below them). In the high-income occupations, those conferring most prestige, privilege and power, we find 83 percent of the upper-uppers, 86 percent of the lower-uppers and 62 percent of the upper-middles. By contrast, at the lower end of the occupational scale, 79 percent of the lower-lowers are semiskilled workers; and

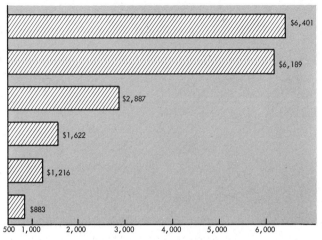

Source: Adapted from W. Lloyd Warner (ed.), *Yankee City* (New Haven: Yale University Press, 1963), pp. 94–97, *passim*.

FIG. 5–2.   Distribution of average family incomes among Warner's six classes in Yankeetown, 1933.

among upper-lowers and lower-middles, 61 and 27 percent, respectively. Table 5–5 brings out the point clearly.

Similarly, when we look at savings we find the results given in Table 5–6.

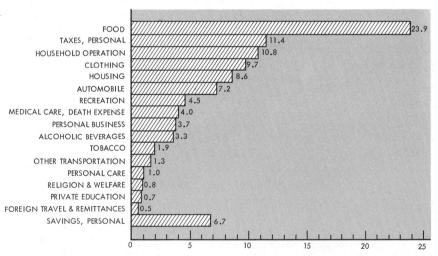

Source: Adapted from Elizabeth Hoyt, *et al.*, *American Income and Its Use* (New York: Harper & Bros., 1954) and cited in Joseph Kahl, *The American Class Structure* (New York: Rinehart & Co., 1957), p. 114.

FIG. 5–3.   Percent distribution of expenditures among Americans in 1951.

TABLE 5–5

Occupation and Class (in Percent) Yankee City

OCCUPATIONAL TYPE	CLASS					
	UU	LU	UM	LM	UL	LL
Professional and proprietary	83.33	85.72	62.16	13.74	2.78	0.73
Wholesale and retail dealers		7.14	15.38	10.87	5.88	2.74
Clerks and kindred workers	16.67	7.14	15.08	28.80	9.19	3.66
Skilled workers			5.23	17.32	12.71	4.57
Semiskilled workers			2.15	27.12	61.53	79.16
Unskilled workers				2.15	7.91	9.14
	100.0	100.0	100.0	100.0	100.0	100.0

Source: W. Lloyd Warner (ed.), *Yankee City* (New Haven: Yale University Press, 1963), p. 90. I have circled certain figures and drawn the dotted line to highlight the cleavage referred to above.

Here again a chief distinction in style of life would seem to lie along the line separating lower-middles from upper-middles.

But there is another break revealed in Warner's data (and in other stratification studies), suggesting an important distinction between a small hereditary elite at the top—hereditary in the sense of inherited wealth and power-enhancing family connections) and the stratum immediately below it. Warner's data tell us that,

TABLE 5–6

Average Balance between Income and Expenditures, Yankee City Families, c. 1933

CLASS	NET END-OF-YEAR BALANCE
Upper-uppers	$388.00
Lower-uppers	870.00
Upper-middles	467.00
Lower-middles	19.00
Upper-lowers	−22.00
Lower-lowers	−57.00

Source: Calculated from data on average family income given in Warner (ed.), *Yankee City*, pp. 96, 97.

occupationally, the upper-uppers were the most homogeneous of all his classes. In this as in other matters, the upper-uppers seemed to constitute a group sufficiently small and with such similarity of background, interests, and way of life that a category became, virtually, a group. They not only knew one another quite intimately but created fictions of biological kinship to express their sense of identity and belonging to the appropriate stratum and, conversely, to emphasize the social distance between themselves and others.

The break between upper-uppers and the lower-uppers is also signalized by the fact that they save less of their annual income than do the lower-uppers, thus disrupting what would otherwise be a smooth progression from size of debt to size of savings as one mounts the income-power-prestige scale. Also the per-person income and expenditures among the upper-uppers is less than that among the lower-uppers. Now since the total family income for upper-uppers is more than that of any other class, one might infer that it must be spread among a larger number of persons. If family size of upper-uppers is larger, a plausible interpretation might be that birth control among lower-uppers, their larger per capita expenditures, and their greater savings all suggest a level of striving and perhaps insecurity, placing them in strong contrast with the top group—and the latter with every other category except, perhaps, the lower-lowers.

Class and the Ecology of Life Styles

Style of life is registered spatially. There is an interplay between attributes of people and their habitat. The rich and the wellborn commute from Long Island to the city by private launch, while those less able to buy distance live closer in and use conventional commuting techniques. Styles of life, then, come to be reflected in differing locations, differing habitats. Styles of living are not randomly distributed in space. As a consequence, the newcomer to the group is exposed, not to the spectrum of cultural possibilities, but to those peculiar to his district, his zone, his neighborhood. And so to revert to the classic study by Warner, we have the Merrimac river serving to mark the least desirable neighborhood, the down-by-the-tracks area in Newburyport; and Hill street, at a higher elevation, is reserved for those of more elevated status. (The relation between physical and social altitude is an interesting question. Clearly the relationship is inverse for James West's subjects in *Plainville*.[16] On the other hand, casual observation would suggest that in cities, distance from industrial sites and transportation routes would prompt those able to bear the costs to seek the altitudes of urban America's Nob Hills.)

Figure 5–4 gives us some impression of the ecology of class, the geography of life styles. Table 5–7 offers supporting data. What concerns us here is the way in which these sequestered subcommunities provide a seedbed for differential induction into the social order.

Class and Marriage

Class touches life patterns in innumerable ways. For example, there is a tendency for marriage to be intraclass.[17] This may be enforced by law where race (Negroes, Indians) reinforces other class attributes. Warner found that class affected the age at which people in Yankee Town entered marriage—or, to stress our theme, entered a new group. For the six classes from upper-upper to lower-lower, the median ages at marriage were 28, 27, 26, 25, 24 and 23.[18]

Class and Interaction Patterns

Modes of life are shaped and reinforced not only by the class of the family entered at birth and by endogamous marriage by class, but also by social and spatial barriers between classes.[19] Thus

---

[16] James West, *Plainville, U.S.A.* (New York: Columbia University Press, 1945. A Columbia Paperback edition was published in 1961). In this community the good— and more costly—farm land lies low, along the river. The poorer families are higher, literally, although lower in standing, occupying the less desirable land.

[17] The generality of this pattern is suggested by Lévi-Strauss when he writes that ". . . each [Bororo] clan is subdivided into three groups: upper, middle, and lower. One regulation takes precedence over all others: that an 'upper' should marry another 'upper,' a 'middle' another 'middle,' and a 'lower' another 'lower.' Despite, that is to say, all the appearances of institutionalized brotherhood, the Bororo village is made up in the last analysis of three groups, each of which always marries within its own numbers." (Claude Lévi-Strauss, *Tristes Tropiques* [Paris: Librairie Plon, 1955], p. 230.)

[18] W. Lloyd Warner, *op. cit.*, p. 61. I have rounded Warner's data, given to two decimal points, to the nearest year. For example, his figure for median age at marriage for the upper-uppers is 27.90.

[19] Social barriers are erected and sustained through adverse stereotypes. People on the wrong side of the tracks, down by the canal (Elmtown) or down by the river, the "Riverbrookers" (Yankee City) are those with whom the "right" people prefer not to associate, at least beyond the requirements of commercial transactions. "Riverbrookers," Warner writes, "were contemptuously referred to by all, their sexual

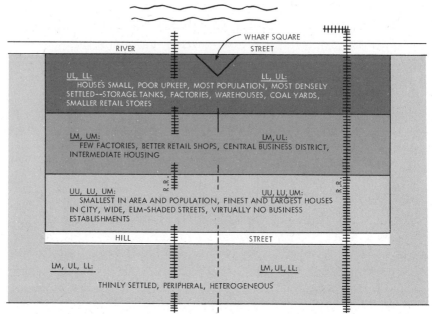

Source: Adapted from W. Lloyd Warner (ed.), *Yankee City* (New Haven: Yale University Press, 1963), p. 364.

FIG. 5-4. Residential configuration of Yankee City: the ecology of life styles.

TABLE 5-7

Relationship between Class and Area Lived in: Elmtown

AREA LIVED IN	CLASSES				TOTALS
	1 & 2	3	4	5	
"The 400," the Old Residential, & The West End	28 (8.1)	85 (30.9)	41 (64.5)	4 (54.7)	158
Down by the Mill, The Mill Addition, & Down by the Canal	0 (15.0)	20 (57.8)	158 (120.4)	117 (102.1)	295
North of the Tracks, & Below the Canal	0 (4.9)	3 (19.4)	26 (40.2)	70 (34.2)	99
Totals	28	108	225	191	552

Source: Adapted from A. B. Hollingshead, *Elmtown's Youth* (New York: John Wiley & Sons, Inc., 1949), Appendix Table IX, p. 462. Figures in parentheses are the frequencies that might be expected *were there no relationship* between class and place of residence. If the reader wishes to assess the significance of the difference between these and the observed frequencies, he can apply the χ^2 test discussed and illustrated in Chapter 3, pp. 114–15.

Among other things this table tells us that all members of classes 1 and 2 live in the preferred sections of Elmtown. They share these areas with 80 percent of the class 3's, 18 percent of the 4's and 2 percent of the 5's.

interaction comes to be predominantly intraclass. Stratification studies show repeatedly that this is the case. In their study of 199 male
respondents, aged 30–49 in Cambridge, Massachusetts, Kahl and
Davis found close correspondence between respondents' status
(occupational prestige as measured on the North-Hatt scale) and
the average status of their three best friends.[20] Hollingshead's data
on Elmtown show a strong tendency for clique relationships to be
intraclass.[21] Warner found Yankee Town cliques were formed with
persons of the same or adjacent classes,[22] the intraclass-only tendency being strongest at the top and bottom of the class hierarchy.

This being the case, the impact on the person tends to be
consistent and persistent—the attitudes, values, expectations, and
aspirations to which he is exposed. We have seen, in Chapter 4,
some of the evidence of the power wielded by his associates over the
person's views and values. We would predict, therefore, as a result
of the channeled interaction associated with class position, a series
of class-linked behaviors and beliefs. Consider as illustrations such
subtle and diverse concomitants of class as mental health, aesthetic
preference, and—immediately germane to the question as to who
enters what groups—educational and occupational aspirations.

Some Subtle Correlates of Class: Mental Health and Aesthetic Preference

If psychic attributes are socially conditioned and if class is a
significant social variable, then indices of mental health should vary
with class position. If we take as an index of class the income and
prestige associated with various occupations,[23] we find an inverse

morals were considered low, and their behavior was usually looked upon as ludicrous
and uncouth . . . depreciatory stories were told despite the fact that it was easily
verifiable that they were no more true of Riverbrookers than they were of other
classes . . . The 'low' behavior was attributed to [the Riverbrooker] . . . *because*
of his low social position. . . ." (*Ibid.*, p. 39.)

This points to the probability that class may cause an unfavorable reputation as
well as—or rather than—an unfavorable reputation causing lowered class status.
But the point here is that such barrier-creating stereotypes reduce interclass and
intensify intraclass interaction.

[20] Joseph A. Kahl and James A. Davis, "A Comparison of Indexes of Socio-
Economic Status," *American Sociological Review*, Vol. XX (June, 1955), reported in
Kahl, *op. cit.*, pp. 137, 138.

[21] A. B. Hollingshead, *Elmtown's Youth* (New York: John Wiley & Sons, Inc.,
1949), p. 214.

[22] W. Lloyd Warner, *The Social Life of a Modern Community* (Vol. I in the
Yankee City Series) (New Haven: Yale University Press, 1941), p. 354.

[23] Kahl and Davis report that occupation makes the best scale for "a measure of
the over-all complex of class behavior." (Joseph A. Kahl, *op. cit.*, p. 46.)

relationship with a number of psychotic conditions. In 1949 Professor Clark summarized his findings on white male first admissions for psychoses, admissions between 1922 and 1934 in the Chicago area, as shown in Table 5–8.

TABLE 5–8

Rank Order Correlation Coefficients Calculated over 17 Occupational Groups between Various Psychoses Rates for White Male First Admissions and Occupational Income and Prestige

	OCCUPATIONAL FACTOR	
TYPE OF PSYCHOSIS	INCOME	PRESTIGE
Schizophrenia (all types)	−.71	−.81
Manic-depressive	−.02	−.01
Alcoholic psychoses	−.78	−.92
General paralysis	−.75	−.73
Senile psychoses and psychoses with arteriosclerosis	−.57	−.50
All psychoses	−.75	−.83

Source: Robert E. Clark, "Psychoses, Income, and Occupational Prestige," *American Journal of Sociology*, published by The University of Chicago Press, March, 1949.

Similar findings came from a study of the diagnosis and treatment of persons under psychiatric care, either with a psychiatrist, a psychiatric clinic, or a mental hospital in the New Haven area. Figure 5–5 confirms and extends these findings. The complex linkage between class, a pattern of living, the ailments accompanying it and their expression is suggested in this statement by the investigators.

> Psychosomatic reactions . . . are related inversely to class. The class IV's and the class V's somatize their complaints to a greater extent than class I, II and III patients. On the other hand, obsessive-compulsives are concentrated in classes I and II. The gradient for hysterical patients runs in the opposite direction; in this illness there is an extreme concentration in class V.[24]

Differing aesthetic preferences—although there are fewer data available—as well as mental illnesses, reflect differences in life patterns varying by class. The presence and kind of books on the shelves, pictures hung, magazines, newspapers and journals, flower

[24] August B. Hollingshead and Fredrick C. Redlich, *Social Class and Mental Illness: A Community Study* (New York: John Wiley & Sons, Inc., 1958), p. 226.

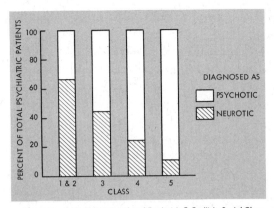

Source: August B. Hollingshead and Frederick C. Redlich, *Social Class and Mental Illness: A Community Study* (New York: John Wiley & Sons, Inc., 1958), p. 223.

FIG. 5–5.   Percentage of neurotics and psychotics among total psychiatric patients, by class.

arrangements, objets d'art, music and musical instruments—these may be conceived as instructive indexes of class-conditioned styles of life.[25] One test of the link between class and musical preference was made by Professor Karl Schuessler. With the exception of popular music he found strong (nonchance) associations between socioeconomic background and preference for various sorts of music: classical, jazz, hill-billy and popular.

> These findings may be tentatively interpreted as follows: socioeconomic position operates to channelize experiences in such a way that a given individual tends to form a favorable attitude toward certain kinds of music, and music training . . . has a pronounced influence on musical taste. Likewise, familiarity affects musical taste, and socioeconomic position may cause an individual to be *regularly exposed to some kinds of music and remain virtually isolated from other kinds.*[26]

I mean to suggest by such illustrations the pervasive influence of that complex of factors denoted by the concept, class. These

---

[25] Such items (although the emphasis was more heavily on material possessions) were items the interviewer was to observe, record, and score following the Chapin Social Distance Scale. (F. Stuart Chapin, "The Social Status Scale," copyright, 1933, by the University of Minnesota.)

[26] Karl F. Schuessler, "Social Backgrounds and Musical Taste," *American Sociological Review,* published by The American Sociological Association, Vol. XIII, No. 3 (June, 1948), p. 333, italics mine.

influences affect the probability of birth, of survival, of death. (Family size, infant mortality, death rates, and longevity vary inversely with indexes of class position.) Motivation to learn, school achievement, the length and type of formal education—these, too, are related to class position. So also are religious affiliation, political preference, and occupational roles. And class-linked differences in the institutional structure—family, school, church, and work—entail differences in beliefs, attitudes, motivation, aspiration.[27] Class, to reiterate the theme, conditions the groups we enter, the hopes and expectations of entering them and the development of psychic states appropriate for entering them.

Two such groups, the school group and the work group are crucial for everyone in our society. So we will do well to look at two examples of research testing the influence of class on school and work groups entered, and stressing those psychological concomitants of class position that affect entrance into these groups.

A RESEARCH ILLUSTRATION: CLASS AND THE SCHOOL GROUP ENTERED

Let me allude, first, to a study by Sewell, Haller and Straus touched on, glancingly, in Chapter 4 (page 178).[28] Investigating a population of 4,167 nonfarm, Wisconsin high school senoirs (both public and private schools), these sociologists asked whether there was a connection between class (as indexed by prestige of parental

---

[27] The best leads to such studies in stratification are, of course, the indexes of the *American Journal of Sociology* and the *American Sociological Review*. A good collection of studies in stratification is in the Reader edited by Bendix and Lipset, footnote 29 below, although it needs updating. Other sources worth looking into are: Paul F. Lazarsfeld, Bernard Berelson, and Hazel Gaudet, *The People's Choice* (New York: Columbia University Press, 1948), on the connection between class (socioeconomic status) and political preference; Floyd Hunter, *Community Power Structure* (Chapel Hill: University of North Carolina Press, 1953); W. Lloyd Warner, *et al., Democracy in Jonesville* (New York: Harper & Bros., 1949) and W. Lloyd Warner, *et al., Social Class in America* (Chicago: Science Research Associates, 1949); Allison Davis, Burleigh B. Gardner, and Mary R. Gardner, *Deep South: A Social-Anthropological Study of Caste and Class* (Chicago: University of Chicago Press, 1941); John Dollard, *Caste and Class in a Southern Town* (New York: Harper & Bros. 1937, 1949); Gerhard Lenski, *The Religious Factor* (New York: Doubleday & Co., 1961).

[28] William H. Sewell, Archie O. Haller, and Murray A. Straus, "Social Status and Educational and Occupational Aspiration," *American Sociological Review*, Vol. XXII (February, 1957).

occupation on the North-Hatt Scale[29]) and the students' educational aspirations. Level of aspiration, the dependent variable, was simply dichotomized: those planning to enter a regular four-year college program were classified as the high aspirers, the rest as lower aspirers. Since subjects were nonfarm, Wisconsin high school seniors, level of education achieved, region and, to a degree, rural-urban factors were controlled. The data were analyzed separately for males and females thus controlling the variable of sex. But more important, level of measured intelligence was controlled by relating the independent and dependent variables only within a restricted range of problem-solving ability.[30] (The measure for this critical control variable was the Henmon-Nelson Test of Mental Ability.)

---

[29] This scale was developed by Paul K. Hatt and C. C. North for a NORC (National Opinion Research Center) study carried out for the President's Scientific Research Board. The survey sought to tap and order public attitudes toward various occupations. Interviewers asked a probability sample of Americans how they rated ninety different jobs. Cautioned not to "judge a job according to your own opinion of some one person you know who has such a job," respondents were presented with this rating card for each occupation.

"For each job mentioned, please pick out the statement that best gives *your own personal opinion* of *the general standing* that such a job has:

1. *Excellent* standing   4. *Somewhat below average* standing
2. *Good* standing   5. *Poor* standing
3. *Average* standing   X. I don't know where to place that one."

Eighty-three percent of the respondents accorded an "excellent" rating to U.S. Supreme Court justices, 71 percent to the job of state governor, 67 percent to that of physician, etc. The top ten and the bottom ten rated occupations, in rank order, were as follows: U.S. Supreme Court justice, physician, state governor, cabinet member in the federal government, diplomat in the U.S. Foreign Service, mayor of a large city, college professor, scientist, U.S. representative in Congress and banker . . . dock worker, night watchman, clothes presser in a laundry, soda fountain clerk, bartender, janitor, sharecropper, garbage collector, street sweeper, and shoe shiner. A 1963 replication of this study revealed great stability in prestige scores of occupations. Correlation of scores for 1947 and 1963 yielded an $r = +.99$! Scattered evidence from other studies back to 1925 indicates very little change in the relative standing of occupations. See Robert W. Hodge, Paul M. Siegel, and Peter H. Rossi, "Occupational Prestige in the United States, 1925–1963," *American Journal of Sociology*, Vol. LXX, No. 3 (November, 1964). (National Opinion Research Center, "Jobs and Occupations: A Popular Evaluation," in Reinhard Bendix and Seymour Martin Lipset (eds.), *Class, Status and Power: A Reader in Social Stratification* [New York: Free Press of Glencoe, Inc., 1958], p. 412 *et seq.*) The final report on occupational prestige, as estimated from the North-Hatt Scale, is that by Albert J. Reiss, Jr., *Occupations and Social Status* (New York: Free Press of Glencoe, Inc., 1961).

[30] Variations in mental ability were controlled by dealing separately with each intelligence *quintile*. Quintiles divide the total number of measures—in this case the mental ability test scores on 1,917 boys—into five equal parts. Casting an array of test scores from highest to lowest we find the top fifth (384 subjects) have mental ability test scores from 119 to 139. These are high scores and they are relatively homogeneous in problem-solving ability compared with the total range of test scores stretching from 139 to 59.

Findings on the link between class and educational aspiration are given in Table 5–9

TABLE 5–9

Percent of 1,917 Nonfarm, Wisconsin High School Seniors Expressing High-Level Educational Aspirations, by Prestige of Parental Occupation and Intelligence Test Scores (Males)

	PARENT'S OCCUPATIONAL PRESTIGE, IN QUINTILES					
	V	IV	III	II	I	
	(CORRESPONDING NORTH-HATT OCCUPATIONAL PRESTIGE SCALE VALUES)					TOTAL PERCENT
INTELLIGENCE SCORE QUINTILES	93–72	72–67	67–60	60–55	55–39	(N)
V (I.Q., 139–119)	90	79	79	71	66	79 (384)
IV (I.Q., 119–113)	71	70	53	57	61	63 (384)
III (I.Q., 113–109)	58	62	51	55	43	54 (383)
II (I.Q., 109–102)	66	45	32	31	24	40 (383)
I (I.Q., 102–59)	34	35	23	26	32	30 (383)
Total: Percent (N)	68 (384)	59 (384)	47 (383)	48 (383)	43 (383)	53 (1,917)

Source: William H. Sewell, Archie O. Haller, and Murray A. Straus, "Social Status and Educational and Occupational Aspirations," *American Sociological Review*, published by The American Sociological Association, Vol. XXII (February, 1957), Table 3, p. 72, slightly modified.

Reading along the rows we see that, with measured intelligence and sex controlled, high school students' aspirations for college education tend to vary directly with class (as represented by prestige of parental occupation). The proposition is confirmed by findings in a number of other studies, among them, Herbert Hyman's.[31]

But to link class position with other social attributes is not

---

[31] Herbert H. Hyman, "The Value Systems of Different Classes: A Social Psychological Contribution to the Analysis of Stratification," in Bendix and Lipset, *op. cit.*, pp. 426–42.

enough. Hyman would say, as Samuel Stouffer used to: to stop with a correlation coefficient is to acknowledge defeat. We have to interpret an observed relationship. We need to uncover the connecting links between independent and dependent variables if the relationship is to be intelligible. X (the independent variable) gives rise to a, b and c (intervening variables) that promote certain outcomes registered in Y (the dependent variable). Now it is Hyman's assumption that "an intervening variable mediating the relationship between low position and lack of upward mobility is a system of beliefs and values within the lower classes which in turn reduces the very voluntary actions which would ameliorate their low position."[32] And so he poses the question: Do beliefs and values vary by class in such a way as to limit upward mobility?[33] For example, do lower-class values restrict educational aspirations? Do they reduce the desirability of a college education? Figure 5–6 helps us answer this question.

For each of four indices of class standing we find that those having least aspire least (insofar as recommending a college education is a clue to level of aspiration). These data are the more telling since, when dealing with such an unexceptionably virtuous matter as education, variance in response is reduced. (When the desire for a college education becomes a commonplace piety, expressions of impiety—contrary or variant beliefs—might be expected only infrequently. And of course if one of our variables doesn't vary, there can be no connection between them—in this case between class and belief in the need of college education.) But however great the agreement on college education, there is a consistent positive relationship between class standing and the desirability of college.

---

[32] *Ibid.*, pp. 426, 427.

[33] Upward mobility means a change in role that advances one's position along the scale of things valued by the group. Malcolm Bradbury suggests a useful enterprise to assist the upwardly mobile:

"You don't know anyone who'd put up a bit of money for an interesting commercial speculation?" he [Oliver, a student] asked.

"I don't think I do," said Treece. "What is it?"

"Well, I was thinking of starting a correspondence course for people who are socially mobile. It's called 'Room at the Top, Limited.' It's to enable people to fit easily into any socket in the social scale—what shoes to wear, what books to read, whether to be sado-masochistic or anal-erotic, whether to know what words like that *mean*. Things to say for all occasions at different class levels. . . .

"I don't know who'd help, I'm afraid."

"Might interest the Sociology Department," said Oliver. "They could probably get a Rockefeller Grant." (Malcolm Bradbury, *Eating People Is Wrong* [New York: Alfred A. Knopf, Inc. 1960], p. 145.)

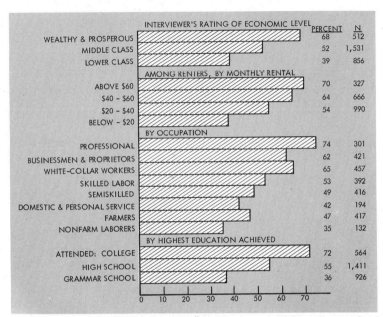

Source: Adapted from Table I, Chapter IV, "The Value Systems of Different Classes: A Social Psychological Contribution to the Analysis of Stratification," by Herbert Hyman. Reprinted with permission of The Free Press from *Class, Status and Power: A Reader in Social Stratification* by Reinhard Bendix and Seymour Martin Lipset (eds.). Copyright 1953 by The Free Press, a corporation.

FIG. 5–6.   Percent of a national sample of respondents (NORC) deeming college education desirable in order for a young man to get along in the world, by four indices of class.

This relationship holds when age and sex are controlled. And in dealing separately with age and sex categories, we find that females and the younger respondents consistently place more emphasis on higher education than do males and older respondents. In one of his summary statements Hyman writes:

> Implicitly, these findings demonstrate that the individual in lowly position sets his strivings and expectancies for success in the light of the established social hierarchy of groups and a belief in differential opportunities within the hierarchy.[34]

A RESEARCH ILLUSTRATION: CLASS AND OCCUPATIONAL GROUP ENTERED

Studies of occupational aspiration and of rewards sought in the job yield similar findings. Occupational aspiration tends to vary

[34] *Ibid.*, p. 438.

directly with class. (Sewell gets measures on the independent variable, you'll recall, by scoring parental occupation on the North-Hatt scale. Similarly the vocational choices of his Wisconsin non-farm high school students were assigned values on the same scale.) Occupational choice also varies strongly with measures of intelligence, or problem-solving ability. But holding constant the factor of intelligence (by making intraquintile comparisons by class—i.e., by prestige of parental occupation—we find that class, independent of intelligence, affects aspiration to enter occupational groups. The findings are reproduced in Table 5–10.

The relationship is not as clear with intelligence test score

TABLE 5–10

Percent of 1,386 Nonfarm Wisconsin High School Seniors Having High-Level Occupational Aspirations* by Parental Occupational Prestige Status and Intelligence: Males

INTELLIGENCE QUINTILES	PARENT'S OCCUPATIONAL PRESTIGE, IN QUINTILES					TOTAL PERCENT (N)
	V	IV	III	II	I	
	(CORRESPONDING NORTH-HATT SCALE VALUES)					
	93–73	73–67	67–60	60–55	55–39	
V (IQ: 139–119)	84	48	55	64	45	63 (278)
IV (IQ: 119–113)	54	51	51	37	35	45 (278)
III (IQ: 113–109)	41	42	43	29	32	37 (278)
IV (IQ: 109–103)	45	36	21	27	22	29 (278)
I (IQ: 103– 59)	25	19	16	18	17	18 (277)
Total: Percent (N)	57 (278)	38 (278)	36 (278)	33 (278)	27 (277)	39 (1,389)

Source: William H. Sewell, Archie O. Haller, and Murray A. Straus, "Social Status and Educational and Occupational Aspiration," *American Sociological Review*, published by The American Sociological Association, Vol. XXII (February, 1957), p. 72.

* High-level occupational aspiration was defined as choosing an occupation having a prestige rating on the North-Hatt scale equal to or higher than that of public school teacher.

controlled as it is without this control. (Percent having high occupational aspirations declines as prestige of parental occupation descends: 57, 38, 36, 33 and 27 percent.) But to leave this variable uncontrolled confounds our hypothesis: we don't know whether to attribute high occupational aspirations to class, to native ability or, as these data indicate, to some combination of these and other factors. Controlling, then, for measured intelligence we see that with the exception of the third intelligence quintile there is a tendency for aspiration to be linked to class, here represented by prestige accorded parents' occupation.

The same connection between class and occupational aspiration is seen in Table 5–11. The data come from an NORC survey.[35]

TABLE 5-11

Types of Occupations Recommended by Youth of the Different Classes

	PROFESSIONAL OCCUPATION	SKILLED MANUAL WORK	N
	PERCENT RECOMMENDING		
Males Between 14–20			
Wealthy or prosperous	76	5	39
Middle Class	52	6	100
Lower Class	21	27	62
Difference between wealthy and poor	+55%	−22%	
Females Between 14–20			
Wealthy or prosperous	81	4	45
Middle Class	64	5	128
Lower Class	42	18	73
Difference between wealthy and poor	+39%	−14%	

Similarly, Hollingshead's findings reveal the link between class and the occupational group young people aspire to enter (see Figure 5-7).

Not only does class condition the occupational groups we aspire to enter: it is also related to attitude toward work. Upper-class persons value the entrepreneurial spirit and will accept career risks to an extent not true of the more security-minded members of lower classes. Work features having appeal vary by class. For example, Hyman reports that an NORC survey revealed among wealthy or

---

[35] Hyman, *op. cit.*, p. 435.

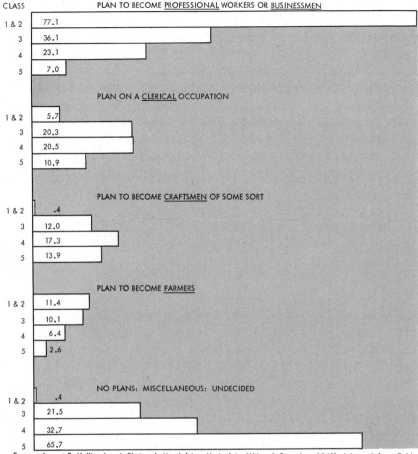

Source: August B. Hollingshead, *Elmtown's Youth* (New York: John Wiley & Sons, Inc., 1949). Adapted from Table XIX, Appendix, p. 469.

FIG. 5–7. The vocational aims of 735 Elmtown youth, by class—i.e., the occupational groups they plan or hope to enter. Figures are percentages. Let me make two comments. First, among those planning to become farmers, there are probably a number of class 1 and 2 persons who mean by this that they plan to manage family-owned farms operated by tenants. Second, the emphatic relationship between class and indecision should be noted. A plausible interpretation might be that these high school students in classes 4 and 5 respond in this way to a dilemma: the pressure to echo appropriate middle-class aspirations, on the one hand, and the felt unreality of such aspirations on the other.

prosperous men, aged 21–39, four times as many emphasizing personal congeniality as the most important desideratum in choosing one's life work as those emphasizing economic rewards. The ratio of congeniality answers to economic answers was 3 for middle-class and 1 for lower-class respondents. Comparable findings for young women aged 21 to 39 give a ratio of congeniality to economic desiderata in vocational choice for wealthy, for middle- and for lower-class respondents of 10.0, 2.2, and 1.2 respectively.[36] Thus the evidence indicates that class conditions the groups people enter, or aspire to enter and that, beyond this, class is linked with a set of beliefs, subjective states that alter people's plans and expectations. And so the person "in lowly position sets his strivings and expectancies for success in the light of the established social hierarchy of groups and a belief in differential opportunities within the hierarchy."[37] To know the class structure is to know, then, something about the objective probability of differing group memberships, about the subjective states (motivations and attitudes) of persons identified with different classes and about different life styles and the differing transmission of culture to the infant, the neophyte entering the human group.

I have suggested before that the clarity, rigidity, and immutability of a class system depends upon such things as: the number of ranking systems (paths to success, related in turn to the complexity of the value system), the number of strata, amount and generality of education, extent of scientific innovation and related changes in technology, the occupational structure, and the like. The groups a person enters, the style of life and values he espouses, are related to the class system; therefore, the definiteness of his destiny, the rigidity and immutability with which it is specified, must depend on such things as I've enumerated above.

CLASS, CASTE AND COLOR

In the United States, as we know, that attribute (with the ascribed and often fictitious traits associated with it) most firmly fixing destiny, values, style of life, is race. This attribute is the one above all others that contributes to a caste-like definition of destiny for the newcomer, prescribes an enculturation differing from that of whites. Figure 5–8 provides a graphic description of the relation between class and a caste-like racial division (white and Negro).

The first figure might be taken to represent something close to the pre-Civil War class and "caste" structure in the United States with the most privileged Negro yet more deprived than the lowest-class

---

[36] Hyman, *op. cit.*, Table V, p. 433.

[37] *Ibid.*, p. 438.

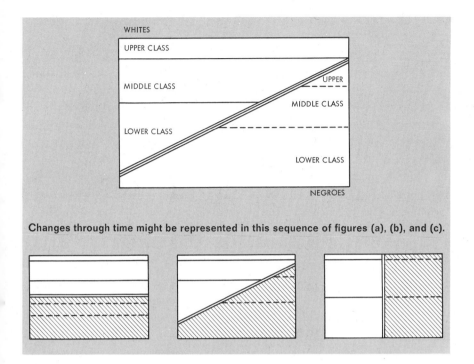

Changes through time might be represented in this sequence of figures (a), (b), and (c).

(a) **Stage 1.**   (b) **Stage 2.**   (c) **Stage 3.**

Source: Allison Davis, Burleigh B. Gardner, and Mary R. Gardner, *Deep South: A Social-Anthropological Study of Caste and Class* (Chicago: University of Chicago Press, 1941), p. 10. Copyright 1941 by The University of Chicago.

FIG. 5–8. Class and caste-like racial divisions.

white. Figure 5–8 (c) shows the caste-line axis having been rotated to a vertical position with property, prestige, and power equitably distributed between two separate but equal categories. This is the "apartheid" solution advocated by the nationalist descendants of the Boers in South Africa. This is an incongruous solution since, as Kahl points out, if members of two groups are in fact thought of as equal, nobody would bother to keep them apart. It is the solution rejected as spurious in the 1954 Supreme Court decision on segregation in the schools.

In our social order the tendency through time has been to diminish the significance of race as a criterion of status and opportunity. The democractic ethos, the findings of social scientists[38]

[38] I do not mean to suggest that there are no differences between race-labeled categories. We know that sickle-celled anemia is linked with Negroid attributes. But the differences of social significance—such as ability to perform in various work roles—appear to have social and cultural, not biological roots. Such differences may therefore be eliminated by social and cultural changes.

and the requirements of a competitive, instrumentally oriented culture shift the emphasis away from ascription and toward achievement as the criterion of status.

To the extent that this is so we might expect occupational opportunities for Negroes to multiply. Conversely, insofar as it is not so, in our society, Negroes might be expected to have to do menial work, and the more of them in a given population the larger the servant sector of the labor force. Figure 5–9 provides some interesting data on these questions.

It is clear, especially in the 1940 urban data, that the larger the part Negroes are of southern state populations, the larger the servant sector in the labor force. This is not quite so true of village populations in 1940, although a linear relationship does seem to obtain. But the point I want especially to note is that *the slope of the regression line is reduced in the 1950 data.* And as the slope is reduced, the extent of relationship between two variables is reduced.[39] We might infer, therefore, that a caste-like restriction of the Negro to menial occupations is being lifted: and on other grounds, of course, we know this to be true.

But differences in destiny—in the groups we enter, in the elements of culture transmitted to newcomers through these groups —stem not only from traits ascribed on the basis of race. As we have seen, parental occupation, education, religion, nativity, psychic states, language—these and a host of other attributes vary by class, both reflecting and reinforcing the position and prospects of the newcomer. The interplay of racial and cultural features is suggested by Warner in a table that I have modified (Table 5–12). Crosscutting 6 cultural and 5 racial types we get 30 categories whose positions, in declining rank and readiness of assimilation to native, Yankeetown culture read from left to right and top to bottom. Thus the cell C-1:R-1 is at the top, C-2:R-1 in second position and C-6:R-5 at the bottom of the prestige-power-property scale.

Warner deals here with attributes in terms of which people in Yankeetown are ranked: *language* (whether English-speaking or not), *religion* (Protestant, Catholic, non-Christian), and *race* (Caucasoid, Mongoloid, and Negroid). But this is to oversimplify reality for two reasons: first, people use other, additional attributes to rank one another (occupation, education, income), and, second, this

---

[39] See "An Aside on Methods: Scatter Diagrams and Regression Lines," pp. 218–19.

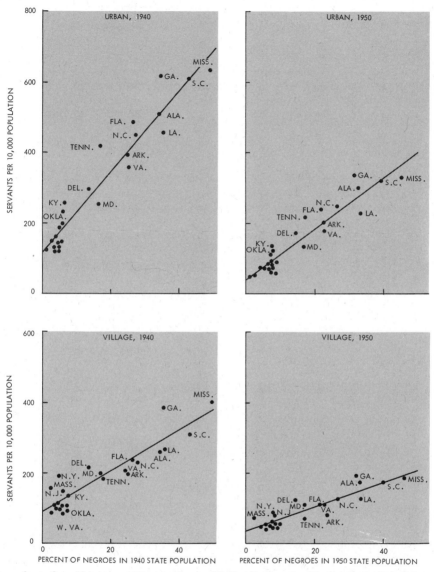

Source: C. Arnold Anderson and Mary Jean Bowman, "The Vanishing Servant and the Contemporary Status System of the American South," *American Journal of Sociology*, published by The University of Chicago Press, November, 1953, p. 217.

FIG. 5–9.   Relationship between proportion of state population that is Negro and number of servants per 10,000 population in the South, and selected northern states, village and urban, 1940 and 1950.

An Aside on Methods: Scatter Diagrams and Regression Lines

This is a good point for another methodological excursion on the meaning of the slope of a regression line. If you will revert to the discussion of the meaning of *r*, the correlation coefficient (see p. 165), you will see that in the left-hand scatter diagram, $Y = X$. That is to say, if we had a value of 3 as a measure of father's conservatism, we could predict that the value of a measure of son's conservatism would also be 3. The relationship is described by a straight line. We often plot such regression lines *to provide a graphic summary of the relationship between two variables.*

In Figure 5–9 values on the dependent variable (servants per 10,000 population) are plotted against values on the independent variable (percent of Negroes in the state population, urban and village). And as in the earlier illustration, the relationship between father's and son's conservatism, a straight regression line sometimes makes a useful summary of the direction and extent of the link between two variables.

The equation for a straight line is $Y = a + bX$ where $a = $ the value on the Y axis where it is intercepted by the regression line and b is the value (a second constant) representing extent of slope of the regression line. In the illustration on p. 165, $a = 0$ and $b = 1$. Thus $Y = 0 + 1(X)$, or $Y = X$. Consider these three sets of values for two variables.

I		II		III	
X	Y	X	Y	X	Y
0	1	0	1	0	1
2	2	1	2	1	3
4	3	2	3	2	5

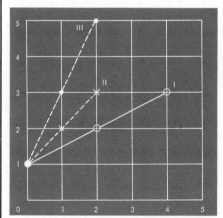

Plotting these points and joining them we have the three regression lines, as shown. And if we evaluate the formula for each of these regression lines we have the following:

for I, $Y = 1 + .5(X)$
for II, $Y = 1 + 1(X)$
for III, $Y = 1 + 2(X)$.

We see, then, that the value of b increases with increasing slope of the regression line. Anderson's data (Figure 5–9) indicate that the value of b for both urban and village areas has declined in the decade 1940 to 1950.

Now suppose that, where $Y = $ servants per 10,000 population and $X = $ percent of Negroes in the state population we got the following set of data.

X	Y	
1%	100	servants/10,000 population
2	100	
3	100	
4	100	

An Aside on Methods: Scatter Diagrams and Regression Lines (continued)

The graphic representation of these data would look like this. Evaluating the formula for a straight regression line $Y = a + b(X)$, we get $Y = 100 + 0$. Thus in a situation in which b, the slope of the regression line, is 0, there is no relationship between percent of state population that is Negro and the ratio, servants-per-10,000 population. Or, to put it differently, we can say that a decline in the value of b is an index of declining rigidity of the caste-like race line in determining probability of employment as a servant. More generally stated, when there is no variance in one of the variables there can be no relationship between it and a second variable.

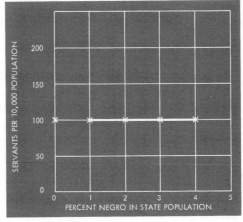

vertical dimension—higher-lower, more-less, better-worse—is not the only one conditioning aspiration, groups entered, and culture transmitted.

TABLE 5–12

Degree of Subordination and Assimilability by Racial and Cultural Type, Yankeetown

	CULTURAL TYPE					
RACIAL TYPE	ENGLISH-SPEAKING PROTESTANT	NON-ENGLISH-SPEAKING PROTESTANT	ENGLISH-SPEAKING CATHOLIC	CATHOLIC AND NON-PROTESTANT SPEAKING ALLIED INDO-EUROPEAN LANGUAGE	ENGLISH-SPEAKING NON-CHRISTIAN	NON-ENGLISH-SPEAKING NON-CHRISTIAN
	C-1	C-2	C-3	C-4	C-5	C-6
Light caucasoid R-1						
Dark caucasoid R-2						
Mongoloid and caucasoid mixed with caucasoid dominant R-3						
Mongoloid and caucasoid mixed with mongoloid dominant R-4						
Negroes R-5						

Source: W. Lloyd Warner (ed.), *Yankee City* (New Haven: Yale University Press, 1963), Table 8, p. 416.

ANOTHER DIMENSION: CONSISTENCY OF RANK ACROSS SEVERAL STATUS SCALES

Another dimension is that of consistency, the consistency of level of a person's standing across various ranking scales. What this means may be clearer if we ask such a question as this: if we had a common measure of people's standing in education achieved, occupation, income, and ethnic status, would it make any difference that for some, standing was the same on each of these four ranking scales while for others the four measures of status varied markedly? (This question is rather like asking if, among communities having the same average income there would be important differences associated with differing values of the standard deviation of the income distribution. We know that we can get the same $\overline{X}$, say 10, with very different distributions of five scores: 10, 10, 10, 10 and 10; 1, 2, 3, 4, and 40; or 20, 5, 20, 4, and 1.) What we are after, then, in this nonvertical dimension of social status, is the degree to which overall standing, or class, has *crystallized*.

This is the term used by Lenski in one of the first empirical studies of the significance of status crystallization. Working with a probability sample ($N = 749$) of the Detroit Metropolitan area, Lenski tested the hypothesis that "individuals characterized by a low degree of status crystallization differ significantly in their political attitudes and behavior from individuals characterized by a high degree of status crystallization, when status differences in the vertical dimension are controlled."[40]

His first job was to get measures of status on each of four ranking scales. We can think of these four scales as thermometers, one each for income, education, occupation, and ethnic standing. But clearly they are not, like thermometers, measuring the same thing. Hence the problem of commensurability. Lenski solved this by ranging respondents' scores from high to low, converting these distributions into cumulative frequencies and then calculating scores for a person depending on his position in the cumulative distribution. For example, he found 29 respondents with incomes of $10,000 or more

---

[40] Gerhard E. Lenski, "Status Crystallization: A Non-Vertical Dimension of Social Status," *American Sociological Review*, published by The American Sociological Association, Vol. XIX, (August, 1954), pp. 405–6.

per year while 95.3 percent got lesser incomes. These top incomes were received by the top 4.7 percent. Taking the midpoint of this range, 95.4 to 100.0, the score for people falling in this top income category was, then, $95.4 + .5(4.6) = 95.4 + 2.3 = 97.7$ or, rounded off, 98. So it was that each respondent was scored on each of the four scales.

The second task was getting a measure of crystallization, the measure of extent of sameness or congruence among these four scores. The measure contrived was this: the square root of the sum of the four squared deviations from their respective means, subtracted from 100—i.e., $100 - \sqrt{\Sigma(\overline{X} - x)}\,^2$. Thus where the second term, the measure of deviation $= 0$, the crystallization score would be 100, and the greater the value of the deviation measure the lower the crystallization score.[41]

Now we come to the central questions. (1) Does behavior (such as voting or expression of political preference) vary with degree of status crystallization? (2) Do high and low status crystallization predict to differing political behavior even when members of these two categories have similar incomes, educations, similar mean occupational and ethnic scores? (Here again is the need for controlled observation. To attribute some influence to degree of status crystallization we must control by eliminating those influences known to obtain between position on ranking scale, such as education or occupation, and such dependent variables as political preference.) (3) For given scores on status crystallization, does it make any difference *which* ranking scales a person is high or low on? Whether, for example, occupation is high, education low, or vice versa?

The answer to the first question is given in Figure 5–10 relating voting behavior (1948, 1950) and voting preference (1952) to

---

[41] Lenski's reasoning in support of this measure of status crystallization will give you some sense of the sociologist at work. He writes:

"The use of squared deviations from the mean rather than simple deviations was employed to emphasize the effect of larger deviations and to minimize the effect of smaller deviations. This was considered desirable since the techniques employed in quantifying positions (or intervals) in the several hierarchies were sufficiently crude so that no great importance could be attached to small deviations.

"The technique of subtracting the resulting figure from one hundred was employed so that respondents whose status was highly crystallized would have numerically higher crystallization scores than those whose status was poorly crystallized. This was done solely to avoid semantic difficulties." (*Ibid.*, p. 408, footnote 14.)

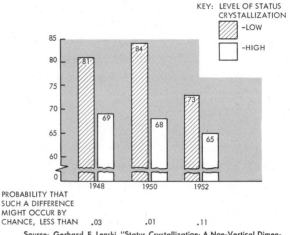

Source: Gerhard E. Lenski, "Status Crystallization: A Non-Vertical Dimension of Social Status," *American Sociological Review*, published by The American Sociological Association, Vol. XIX (August, 1954), Table 2, p. 408.

FIG. 5–10.   Percent of voters favoring the Democratic party, by degree of status crystallization, in 1948, 1950 (voting behavior) and 1952 (expression of party preference).

degree of status crystallization.[42] This last, the independent variable, was simply dichotomized, high crystallization being defined as scores of 53 or more and low crystallization as those of 52 or less. As the figure shows, occupying discrepant statuses in four ranking systems (lack of status crystallization) does appear to be related to political preference.

Now consider the second question. Suppose we were to deal with

---

[42] It is worth noting that Lenski puts the hypothesis without telling us why it's plausible. The "interpretation" in our definition of the field—controlled observation and interpretation of differing . . .—is missing. We cannot know how Lenski might argue the case, but it might go something like this. (1) Rewards are typically conferred in accordance with the conscientiousness and competence with which an incumbent performs in roles valued by the group. (2) When, as between two or more ranking systems, rewards are high in one (occupation of physician) but low in others (nativity, religion: immigrant, Catholic, and Mexican), there is a strain to lift rewards in all ranking systems to the level of the highest. For if prestige, power, and income accorded a physician are high, reflecting both competence and conscientious performance in role, why, the incumbent must ask, should Catholicism, immigrant status, and Mexican nativity lower his overall standing? (3) To the extent that response is overt, the strain to "level up" to the rewards of the highest status translates itself into efforts to induce social change. (4) In the political sphere, persons of discrepant statuses (low status crystallization) will favor parties identified with change. (5) Since the early 1930's with their wave of social welfare legislation, the Democratic party has been identified as the party of change. (6) Low status crystallization will be associated, therefore, with preference for the Democratic party.

two groups[43] so similar that differences in political preference could
not be accounted for by differences in income, education, occupation, or ethnicity. Would the group having low status crystallization
still show Democratic preferences? By eliminating 34 cases Lenski
was able to get a fair approximation between high and low
crystallization groups on these four variables. The resulting mean
scores left the low crystallization group slightly higher (in income,
education, etc.) than the high crystallization group. And since
higher income, higher ranking occupation, and the like we know to
be associated with Republican preferences, Lenski was, in effect,
stacking the cards against the hypothesis that low status crystallization would be related to Democratic political preferences. Now with
the differences in the vertical dimension controlled (high and low
income, etc.), his findings showed smaller differences in political
behavior between the two crystallization categories. For the 1948
election, 82 percent of his low crystallization category voted Democratic in contrast to 71.4 percent in the high crystallization category
($p < .05$). In 1950 the figures were 84 and 71 percent, respectively
with $p < .04$. And on the expression of political preference in 1952
the figures were 72 and 68 percent respectively, with $p \leq .46$. On
three controversial issues the low crystallization category gave the
more liberal responses. The differences in percent giving liberal
responses, low-minus-high crystallization categories, were as follows: on government health insurance, $+ 12$ percent ($p < .02$), on
the extension of government powers, $+ 13$ percent ($p < .02$) and on
price controls, $+ 5$ percent ($p < .35$).

The third question, you will recall, was whether, among those
having low crystallization, it made any difference what the pattern
of discrepant statuses was. Analysis of the data enables two tentative
conclusions. The tendency for Democratic party preference and
political liberalism to be linked with low status crystallization
persists despite variations in the pattern of status inconsistencies.
But, secondly, certain patterns of low status crystallization yield
more liberal responses than others. For example, where income is
high and occupation is low, only 4.8 percent of a subsample were
strongly liberal in their responses. But in the reverse situation,
occupation high and income low, 29.4 percent gave strong liberal
responses.

---

[43] Let me note, again, that I am using the word "group" loosely here. We are in
fact dealing with categories.

Lenski concludes his study of this dimension of social status with the following statement. Note that it offers us an important clue in assessing the stability of a social order (or conversely, its vulnerability to change).

> Conceivably a society with a relatively large proportion of persons whose status is poorly crystallized is a society which is in an unstable condition. In brief, under such conditions *the social system itself generates its own pressures for change.*[44]

*   *   *   *

The theme of this chapter was that class conditions the groups we enter. Different groups entered means difference in culture transmitted and reflected in distinctive styles of life. Thus: class⟶ groups entered⟶culture (style of life), or class-defined roles⟶ differentiated relationships⟶differentiated rules.

A chief influence of class is seen in the way sons recapitulate fathers' experiences. Not that mobility is lacking. This does occur, and the rigidities of class are softened through several social mechanisms: extended education, training in specialties, shifts in the occupational structure of society rendering old skills obsolete, failure of upper classes to reproduce themselves. But the dominant tendency—and from the standpoint of stability in the social order, a necessary one—is for one generation to repeat its predecessors' experience.

This experience includes distinctive life styles: buying patterns, differences in group affiliation, in goals and motivation to achieve them. Such differences, as we saw, are registered spatially. Spatial clustering isolates the person from other life styles, other subcultures, and of course enables more effective (unchallenged) socialization. (This is an important characteristic of effective indoctrination.) The tendency toward endogamy by class also reinforces the peculiar and parochial character of class influence. This influence is seen not only in the externalities of life, but also in its subjective aspects: in aesthetic preferences, political judgments, types of mental illness, and in educational and other sorts of aspiration.

We noted that the limiting case in the determination of the newcomer's destiny is called caste: a fixing at birth of occupational, marital, and other prospects. In the United States, as the Negro's style of life and prospects have improved, we have moved away

---

[44] *Ibid.*, p. 412.

from a caste-like system. One index of this we saw in the declining slope of the regression line relating a menial occupation to the percent of Negroes in the population.

Class is a complex phenomenon. In our social order, in particular, there are many paths to power, prestige, and property. Furthermore, because there are many ranking systems, the possibility arises that a person may not have the same status in each of them. Were his position identical on each we might say that his statuses had crystallized at a given level. We might further suppose that where this is not the case there would be come strain to level up to that status carrying most kudos. Which is to say, a lack of status crystallization might be expected to be linked with change. We have seen that Lenski's study of status crystallization and political preference tends to confirm this notion.

The group's class structure, then, has a profound influence on the person entering it. Persons in a given class category receive, through the socializing agencies of family and school, similar aspects of the culture. There is a complex social alchemy involved in that mix of influences converging in the person. From this perspective we can see the person as product: and to a consideration of this product we turn in Chapter 6, a short addendum to this section on "Entering the Group."

SELECTED SUPPLEMENTARY READINGS

BENDIX, REINHARD, AND LIPSET, SEYMOUR MARTIN (eds.). *Class, Status and Power: A Reader in Social Stratification.* New York: The Free Press of Glencoe, Inc., 1953.

BERELSON, BERNARD, AND STEINER, GARY A. "Social Stratification," in *Human Behavior: An Inventory of Scientific Findings,* pp. 453–90. New York: Harcourt, Brace & World, Inc., 1964.

BROOM, LEONARD. "Social Differentiation and Stratification," in Robert K. Merton, Leonard Broom, and Leonard S. Cottrell, Jr. (eds.), *Sociology Today,* ch. xix. New York: Harper & Row—Harper Torchbooks, 1965.

*INKELES, ALEX, AND ROSSI, PETER H. "National Comparisons of Occupational Prestige," *American Journal of Sociology,* 1956, pp. 329–39.

KAHL, JOSEPH A. *The American Class Structure.* New York: Holt, Rinehart and Winston, Inc., 1957.

---

* Articles marked with an asterisk are available as reprints from the college division of the Bobbs-Merrill Company, Indianapolis, Indiana.

KAHL, JOSEPH A. "Educational and Occupational Aspirations of 'Common Man' Boys," *Harvard Educational Review*, 1953, pp. 186–203.

LIPSET, SEYMOUR MARTIN, AND BENDIX, REINHARD. *Social Mobility in an Industrial Society*. Berkeley: The University of California Press, 1958.

MILLS, C. WRIGHT. *White Collar: The American Middle Classes*. New York: Oxford University Press, 1951.

REISS, ALBERT J., JR. *Occupations and Social Status*. New York: The Free Press of Glencoe, Inc., 1962.

*———, AND RHODES, ALBERT LEWIS. "The Distribution of Juvenile Delinquency in the Social Class Structure," *American Sociological Review*, 1961, pp. 720–32.

Chapter 6

The Person as Product: The Fixing of Role and Status

How does the process of entering the group
come to a head in the crystallizing of role and status?[1]

As he travels through peopled space and time, the newcomer to the human group is rewarded and punished, rebuffed and accepted, stopped and started, directed and redirected. The usual outcome is a person rehearsed to take his part in a number of plays: for the male, dual roles as husband and father in the domestic drama; in the work theater, fellow worker to some, subordinate and superordinate to others. Rehearsals have been scheduled over a long period in the parental family, in the school, in the neighborhood. The first two, as I have stressed, are the chief formal socializing agencies. But crucial also are the informal rehearsals with one's peers, the local neighborhood gang. Family, school, and gang collaborate on the script, working through the lines and the plot that we call culture.

But families differ in their styles of life, differ in the prospects they hold out for their children. Such differences in life ways and life chances distinguish categories of persons identified by the sociologist as belonging to a given class. And class, too, we can say, conditions the groups the newcomer will enter. To put it a different

---

[1] The terms "fixing" and "crystallizing" perhaps convey an unintended finality and immutability. I mean to suggest, rather, a progressively narrowed range of options and alternatives (as antecedent experience conditions the future) or, more positively, an increasingly specific definition of appropriate roles worked out by the person in collaboration with others sharing his "life space." This is the idea I've tried to convey in the shishkebab illustration that sounds this chapter's theme.

way, the intertwining influences of family, school, and class convey a set of expectations registered in a self-conception and a gradual shaping of one's destiny. In these early and elementary social circles —at least by the time he has completed his formal schooling— continuous exposure to a limited and reinforcing set of influences has led the understudy to achieve a fair fix on his part in the play, his roles and statuses.

In this process, absence is as significant as presence, omission as commission. The entrant's influences are unintentionally limited to the themes of his culture as interpreted in his community. Ruth Benedict makes the point of selective limitation when she writes:

> It is in cultural life as it is in speech; selection is the prime necessity. The numbers of sounds that can be produced by our vocal cords and our oral and nasal cavities are practically unlimited. . . .
> In culture, too, we must imagine a great arc on which are ranged the possible interests provided either by the human age-cycle or by the environment or by man's various activities. A culture that capitalized even a considerable proportion of these would be as unintelligible as a language that used all the clicks, all the glottal stops, all the labials, dentals, sibilants and gutturals from voiceless to voiced, from oral to nasal. Its identity as a culture depends upon the *selection of some segments of this arc*. Every human society everywhere has made such selection in its cultural institutions.[2]

The exclusion of other influences is carried further in regional and local enclaves with their variations on the theme. Because of what he is not, as well as what he *is* taught, the person becomes an accepted member of the group, crystallizing with ever greater precision the roles required in support of the relationships that constitute the group.

THE MEANING OF THE CONCEPT, ROLE

But let us be clear about what we mean by this term, *role;* for it is a critical, elemental concept in sociology. It refers to a regular way of acting, expected[3] of all persons occupying a given position in the social order and confronting specified categories of others. Thus, the parental role consists in behavior expected of an adult confronting

---

[2] Ruth Benedict, *Patterns of Culture* (Boston: Houghton Mifflin Co., 1961), pp. 21, 22.

[3] Sometimes it's expected in the sense that it is obligatory. Sometimes this aspect is minimized, and it may be loosely and descriptively used to refer to a type or class of conduct, as when we speak of a "square," a "hipster," or a "schlemiel."

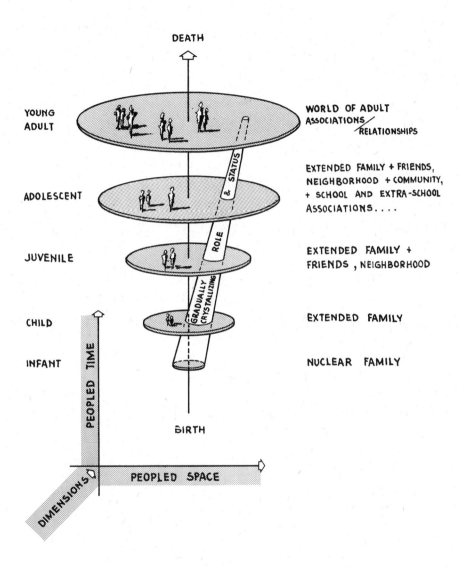

The trip from birth to death through peopled space and time: the shaping of role and status.

his/her children. (The role includes indirect, as well as direct confrontations as, for example, when the parent consults the physician, or the teacher, or the policeman *about* this child.) The employer role involves the conduct appropriate when dealing with or about employees. The role of the communicant is that appropriate to the person when confronting his God, a priest, or fellow communicants—and so on across the spectrum of life's activities. In short, a role is the culturally specified behavior for dealing with classes of social objects.

PERFORMANCES IN ROLE: VARIATION AND STABILITY

Behavior in a given role has two components. One stems from the unique ancestry of the incumbent, a set of social influences, diverse and unduplicated, converging in the person. The other consists in commonly held conceptions of performance appropriate to a given position. Which is to say that explanations of differences in role performance—especially deviant conduct—must be sought at the intersection of personal characteristics and common cultural prescriptions (knowledge of what ought . . .). Since those characteristics that lend identity to the person are themselves derived largely from unique constellations of social influences, it might be better to restate the proposition: differences in role performance result from discrepancies between social exposures peculiar to the person and those common to most members of the group. To put it differently, the incumbent of a given role—student, for example—is the focus of (1) a set of expectations common to most members of the group, and (2) a set of predispositions peculiar to him and stemming from his unique social (and biological) ancestry. In the study of social structure, we can generally disregard the significance of genetic and biologically traumatic variations between persons. After discarding the biologically unable and disabled, people are sorted into various positions in the social order largely on the basis of the attributes ascribed to, or achieved by, them.

The positions into which they are sorted are those in which public and personal definitions of the role are reasonably compatible. But seldom, if ever, does the person's social ancestry provide a perfect preparation for the roles he will carry as an adult. As he enters a new school, a new job, achieves a new position in the company, joins the church, allies himself with wife, he undergoes supplementary socialization, in-service training, as it were. This is simply an extension of his social ancestry, effecting a more adequate fit between the expectations characterizing a new position and the trained capacities brought to it.

Variations in role performance are due not only to differences in the social ancestry of incumbents; they also stem from the existing set of group affiliations peculiar to each person. Even within a single group, others' expectations are not uniform, either as to behaviors expected or as to the rigidity with which the incumbent is expected to adhere to these behaviors, and these alone. Uniformity and rigidity of expectations vary from group to group and from role to role. A great range of behavior is accepted among those called "parents" but a more restricted range is expected of those called "teachers."

But I should not convey the notion of endless variation in role performance. The contrary is the case. Roles refer to behavior in publicly recognized positions or "slots" in the social order. They endure through time, being successively filled by one incumbent after another. That they are publicly recognized implies that the expectations establishing norms of conduct are general and to a degree coercive. Indeed, the expectations are often stated in the law.

Role, then, is a distinctly social concept rooted in the requirements of the social order. It does not refer to the psychological idiosyncracies of the incumbents. It is accurate to say that most of the difference in behavior of persons in different roles is due to the roles, not to the particular personalities of the incumbents. Conversely, the similarity of behavior of persons in the same role is a function of the socially sanctioned demands of the role, not the coincidental similarity of incumbents' personalities.

Indeed, there is some folk wisdom in the view of the disgruntled citizen who says it makes no difference which candidate one votes for. Yet if, to a degree, he is right, it is for the wrong reason. In his view, both candidates will act alike because they are equally unreliable, if not corrupt. But if their behavior is so very much alike, it is rather because each is the focus of essentially the same set of expectations. It is, of course, true that as one mounts toward the apex of a power pyramid—toward bank president, university president, United States President—two different incumbents will surround themselves with different advisers and, therefore, different sets of expectations. Yet the numbers subtended by such social pyramids are greater the higher one goes, and the greater, therefore, is the pressure to meet the common demands of the dependent many. Napoleon's statement was perceptive: "I am their leader; therefore I must follow them." Furthermore, it is toward the peak of the pyramid that persons in leadership roles confront others who incorporate the demands and expectations of *their* followers. Eisenhower as well as Truman, Johnson as well as Kennedy confront Castro, Khrushchev and Kosygin, Roger Blough and George Meany, Macmillan and Wilson and Pearson, de Gaulle and Thant, the governors of Mississippi, Alabama, and 48 other states, the American Legion, the NAM and AMA. Whether I mention the name of a man, a nation, or a voluntary association, a persisting point of view, an enduring interest is implied. It is an interest and a point of view corporately held, outlasting the membership or lifetime of an individual. No matter who the incumbent of a peak position, he confronts a set of pressures very like those his predecessor dealt with and those his successor will deal with.

In this view, then, we see the conduct of the person largely defined by his position in the group, the role he is called upon, after appropriate socialization, to take. So faithfully do normal persons reflect the expectations defining their roles that, if we wish to know a stranger, we spar with him initially until we have discovered the groups and categories he's identified with: Negro or white, old or young, male or female, doctor, lawyer, beggarman, thief. . . . These give us clues to the roles he will take—which is to say, the kind of person he is.

THE SHAPING OF ROLE AND STATUS: A CLASSIFICATION OF INFLUENCES

We can see the process of entering the human group, the process of socialization, as one in which the newcomer first learns—and is identified by—categories shared with major sectors of the population. With time, his identity is narrowed and specified, as classification in additional categories, and membership in additional groups, gives him a particular configuration of attributes shared by fewer people. In the person's developmental sequence, successive experiences serve to define life chances and aptitudes, to channel interests, to specify the prospects—in short, to fix the positions and roles that define the person.

To help tidy up our thinking on this matter let me suggest that there are three sorts of categories and groups that contribute to the crystallizing of role.[4] There are, first, the socially significant biological traits. Second, there are various categories with which the person's family is identified. Third, there are the groups in which the person is directly implicated. The outcome, the precipitate, is seen in a long roster of personality variables. Let me be more explicit in the following outline.

1. Biological attributes having social meaning because certain expectations as to belief and behavior are typically, or stereotypically linked with them: sex, age, race.
2. Social characteristics stemming from the categories describing the parental family: occupation, class, religion. . . .
3. Personal characteristics stemming from membership in extrafamilial groups in which the person participates: his job, his educational achievement, his income, his views and values.

This classification makes a sort of developmental scale in which the value for a given variable implicates a cluster of antecedent variables. Thus, the groups with which the person voluntarily affiliates are conditioned by antecedent categories describing his family, and these, in turn—as in the case of parental occupation or class—are conditioned and implicated in the categories of sex, age, and race.

I've suggested that this classification follows two sequences: the temporal sequence of personal development, and a second sequence from gross and general influences (embodied in prescriptions attached to age, sex or race) to a wide range of specific influences shaping roles and conferring personal identity. (Almost everyone is male or female, and each person shares this attribute with about half the population. But considerably fewer than half the population are existentialists, Seventh Day Adventists, or Presbyterians.)

There are other sequences implicit in this classification of role-shaping influences. The classification moves, roughly, from ascribed to acquired or achieved attributes. The former involve attributes typically dealt with as discrete distributions (gross differentiation:

[4] I am relying in the following few paragraphs on the argument set forth in Theodore M. Newcomb and E. K. Wilson (eds.), *The Study of College Peer Groups: Problems and Prospects for Research,* chap. iii, "The Entering Student: Attributes and Change Agents" (Chicago: Aldine Publishing Co., 1965).

male-female, white-Negro). But as we move toward outcomes in the person, we find attributes whose measures fall in a continuous distribution, implying a refined differentiation in measures of knowledge or problem-solving ability, position on a scale measuring religious behavior or belief, political or aesthetic preferences, income and the like.

One other sequence I've implied before, the sequence involved in role-spotting, in identifying the other. It is a sequence in assessing the probability of another's responses, a sequence, that is, in the building of relationships. For do we not, in coming to know another, typically gain initial impressions from such gross externalities as sex, race, age, language, or accent? And do we not tend then to discover other categories to which the person may be assigned on the basis, for example, of his occupation or his place of residence? And only later, having "cased the joint," as it were, do we know the more particular and personal details enabling us, if we are so disposed, to establish the reciprocal interchange, between now-established roles, that makes a human relationship.

Socially Relevant Biological Traits: Race, Age, Sex

The categories with external visibility, the socially significant biological traits, are early and crucial in their role-shaping influence. Anyone with normal hearing, sight, and sensitivity during the 1950's and 1960's cannot fail to have some faint appreciation of the significance of race in shaping roles. For a tenth of the population of the United States, there is throughout their lives no role, no relationship, untouched by the fact of race. (The same can be said of the white 90 percent of the population, although, obviously, they are not so keenly aware of the benefaction conferred by the accident of birth, coupled with prevailing racial stereotypes.)

Age—and I shall mention only race, age, and sex in this discussion of the biological hooks for role prescription—age is a universal criterion for assigning expectation-sets. Clearly, different roles must be assigned to dependent young and old, and independent middle age. For dependence and independence are in part biological facts of the life cycle. But how the roles are defined is a cultural matter, varying widely from group to group. Consider that age category for which we have coined the maudlin euphemism, "senior citizen."

The definition of old age as a state and as a role varies greatly. In the United States we have a legal definition of old age: 65 is a common age of retirement and full social security benefits commence at this time. But

> . . . among the Bontoc Igorot in the Philippines a woman reaches "her prime" at 23, while at 30 she is "getting old," before 45 she "is old," and by 50, if she is so fortunate as to live that long, she is a mass of wrinkles from foot to forehead.[5]

In his analysis of the role of the aged, Leo Simmons studied 71 tribes scattered around the globe: 16 in North America, 10 in Central and South America, 14 in Africa, 3 in Europe, 16 in Asia and 12 in Oceania and Australia.[6] A few of his findings help us to grasp the complexity and variation in the role definitions attached to age —in this case, old age.

The control of property rights by older people varies with the type of economy and with the form of family organization. For example, aged women tend to enjoy control over property more in groups gaining their living from collecting, or hunting or fishing, and where the family organization is matrilocal or matrilineal, whereas aged men consistently control property to a greater degree in farming and herding groups and where family organization is patriarchal. With a shift from gathering economies toward herding and agriculture, there is a decline in communal sharing of food and a tendency for preplanned and organized help for the needy aged. The aged are often accorded respect, sometimes bordering on reverence (they are often the custodians of sacred lore), but seldom continuing when the oldster becomes a senile dependent.

Respect for aged women appears to be linked with elemental economic forms and with matriarchal family systems, but men seem to command more respect in stable social orders whose economies turn on herding or agriculture. The oldsters often become men Fridays to vigorous younger ones, making themselves as useful as they can (although in magic and sorcery they may retain control). But if the diviner is likely to be a senior citizen, so also may his victim be. For in the event of disaster, an older rather than a younger person is likely to be found responsible, or so it is among the Xosa. There are a few cases of cannibalism where, under pressure of adversity, the older persons may be served up. More

---

[5] Leo W. Simmons, *The Role of the Aged in Primitive Society* (New Haven: Yale University Press, 1945), p. 17.

[6] *Ibid.*, pp. 6–10.

common, apparently, is the practice, as among the Chippewa, of an exit from this vale of tears agreed upon by the aged person and his kinfolk, and effected by the latter.

One gets the impression from Simmons' data that where eminence does not depend upon demonstrable achievement but rather upon occult powers in controlling the mystic unknowns of the universe, distinction (rather than extinction) may inform the role of the aged. The aged are, he says, the "guardians of life's emergencies, the custodians of (esoteric) knowledge, and the directors of ceremonies and pastimes . . . they have been the chief conservators of the status quo. And finally, after death, they have become supernatural agents. . . ."[7]

Dealing as he does with 71 widely distributed groups, Simmons is able to tease out of the data (by means of a coefficient of association)[8] some suggestions as to uniformities in the role of the aged. But we notice also in his data the frequent need to discriminate between old men and old women. Sex makes a difference in role prescriptions far beyond the point of its reproductive significance.

Some intimation of the significance of sex in role definition is suggested by an experiment in role-taking in which James C. Brown tested the notion that ". . . there exists a partial disjunction between the cultural worlds of males and females, in contemporary American society, which gulf is greater than that between any other such pair of status-categories." For sex is an exclusive status[9] and "more durable, more pervasive and more universal than any other."[10] Race and age may approximate the visibility of sex, but they lack the legibility of clothing, coiffure, and distinctive naming.

To test the disjunction between sex roles, Brown had eight boys

---

[7] *Ibid.*, p. 176.

[8] See "An Aside on Methods: A Simple Coefficient of Association between Variables," p. 237.

[9] The term, status, refers to those labels we use to tell where a person stands, relative to others, in the social structure. (The word is borrowed directly from the Latin, meaning circumstance, condition, or state.) For example, in the category sex, we have male and female. Similarly as to employment: employed and unemployed; or for race: Caucasoid, Negroid, Mongoloid; or for marital status: single, married, widowed, divorced; or for location in the labor force: unskilled, semiskilled, skilled, clerical, etc. Such position labels connote the complex expectation-sets we call roles, typically the more institutionalized roles.

[10] James C. Brown, "An Experiment in Role-Taking," *American Sociological Review*, published by The American Sociological Association, Vol. XVII, No. 5 (October, 1952), p. 588.

An Aside on Methods: A Simple Coefficient of Association between Variables

It will be worth our while to take another detour into methods, reporting on a simple coefficient of association used by Simmons—he reports 1,146 such coefficients!—to determine whether a relationship obtains between certain aspects of the role of the aged and other conditions in the social order. The device used is Yule's Q. It is used in fourfold tables (2×2 tables with 4 cells) in which, if there is a perfect positive association, all the cases fall in the upper left- and lower right-hand cells; or, if there is perfect negative association, in the other diagonal cells, lower left and upper right. Simmons finds, for example, that this measure gives him a coefficient of association of -1.00 between hunting economies and the property rights of aged men. But the relationship between herding and property rights of old men is $+.76$. Here are some of his data in a 4-celled table.

		Tribes in which herding is:	
		Dominant or tends to prevail	Absent or little practiced
Property rights vested in aged men	Dominant or often found	a 23	b 22
	Absent or generally lacking	c 3	d 21
		26	43

Thus an inspection of the table suggests that where herding is the main economic activity, the old men almost always have rights in property, whereas in the absence of herding this set of expectations as to older males occurs about half the time and half of the time not.

Now a perfect relationship would be one in which, wherever we found herding we would always find old men dominating property; and in the absence of herding we would never find this characteristic in their roles. All the cases would fall in the upper-left-to-lower-right diagonal. Thus we can see in the formula for Yule's Q

$$Q = \frac{ad - bc}{ad + bc}$$

that, for a perfect positive association, $bc = 0$ and in a perfect negative association $ad = 0$. In the usual, intermediate cases, the value of ad (and hence the value of a positive coefficient of association) is reduced by the extent to which we find cases falling in cells b and c.

Applying Yule's Q to the data provided by Simmons for herding and property rights among the aged (above) we have the following:

$$Q = \frac{ad - bc}{ad + bc} = \frac{483 - 66}{483 + 66} = +.76 \;.$$

and eight girls role-play 64 performances. These performances had to do with four situations, two of them oriented toward the male role (a blow-out on an automobile trip, and being insulted in a rough neighborhood), and two oriented toward female roles (a meeting of a girls' sewing club and a Ladies' Aid meeting). Two boys and two girls performed in each situation, in half of them playing their own sex roles and, in the other half, performing just as he/she would behave in the opposite sex role. The person whose role was being

TABLE 6–1

Estimated Accuracy of Role-Taking in Same- and Opposite-Sex Roles, in Situations Oriented toward Male and Female Roles

	SEX OF ROLE-TAKER	SEX ROLE TAKEN	SEX ORIENTATION OF SOCIO-DRAMATIC SITUA-TION	MEAN SCORE ON ACCURACY OF PERFORMANCE
	(1)	(2)	(3)	(4)
	m	m	f	3.50
Playing same-sex	f	f	m	3.13
roles	m	m	m	2.88
	f	f	f	2.50
	m	f	m	2.50
Opposite-sex role-	f	m	f	2.25
playing	m	f	f	2.00
	f	m	m	1.88

Source: Adapted from a summary in James C. Brown, "An Experiment in Role-Taking," *American Sociological Review*, published by The American Sociological Association, Vol. XVII, No. 5 (October, 1952), p. 592.

taken rated the performance of the role taker on a 4-point scale as to accuracy of performance: poor, fair, good, and excellent (1, 2, 3, and 4, respectively). Certain of the results are summarized in Table 6–1.

There are problems with this study: the accuracy-of-performance rating by the young subjects, the inadequacy of the sample for the population to which generalizations are extended, the effect of previous trials on subsequent role-playing. But these things can be said for this population. (1) Sex roles *are* emphatically discriminated. (2) The interaction of three factors—those situational factors heading the first three columns of Table 6–1—accounts for 60 percent of the variance in accuracy of role performance. (3) There are individual differences in role-taking skill and perceptiveness, but the joint effect of these psychological variables is less than that of just two (among many) situational, or social, variables. (4) The problem, as usual, is more complicated than at first appeared. Two examples: the male role was most readily perceived in female-oriented situations and the female role in male situations, and males were slightly more skillful perceivers of others than females.

Race, age, and sex are critical pivots for role definition in our society. Their relevance for sociological inquiry is forcefully suggested in a set of tentative propositions about age and sex roles offered by Leonard S. Cottrell, Jr.

1. The degree of adjustment to roles which a society assigns to its age-sex categories varies directly with the clarity with which such roles are defined.
   i. The degree of clarity is determined by the proportion of the social situations in which the individual is called on to act for which there are explicit definitions of the reciprocal behavior expected.
   ii. Clarity of definition of role is reduced by:
      (1) Discrepancies between what is given verbally and what is demonstrated in practice.
      (2) Contacts among members of subculture groups which have different roles for the same age-sex categories.
      (3) Inconsistency in the response and expectations exhibited to the individual by members of his social world.
2. The degree of adjustment to specified age-sex roles varies directly with the consistency with which others in the individual's life situations exhibit to him the response called for by his role.
3. When a society assigns or permits more than one role to a given age-sex category, the degree of adjustment to the roles varies directly with the compatibility of the roles.
4. When incompatible roles belong to a given age-sex category, the degree of adjustment varies directly with the extent to which means exist for minimizing the overlap of situations calling for incompatible roles.
5. The degree of adjustment varies indirectly with the discrepancy between the abilities of the individual and those required in the roles of a given age-sex category.
6. The degree of adjustment to the roles of specified age-sex categories varies directly with the extent to which the role permits the individual to realize the dominant goals set by his sub-cultural group.
7. When the role represents an excess of deprivation or frustration of dominant goal satisfactions, adjustment varies directly with:

    i. The extent to which the frustrating role is defined as a path to another role which promises the desired gratifications, and/or

    ii. The accessibility of substitute gratifications.

        (The remaining propositions have to do with adjustment to transitions from one role to another.)

8. The degree of adjustment to a future role varies directly with the degree of clarity with which the future role is defined.

9. The degree of adjustment to a future role varies directly with the amount of opportunity for:

    i. Emotionally intimate contact which allows identification with persons functioning in the role.

    ii. Imaginal or incipient rehearsal in the future role, and

    iii. Practice in the role through play or other similar activity.

10. The degree of adjustment to a future role varies directly with the degree of importance attached to and the definiteness of the transitional procedures used by the society in designating the change in role.

11. The degree of adjustment to a future role varies directly with the completeness of the shift in the responses and expectations exhibited by the society to the individual in his new role.

12. Adjustment to more mature roles is aided rather than handicapped by occasional sanctioned regressions to less demanding roles.[11]

These propositions might apply with equal force to other roles. But since age and sex refer to universal statuses, they have their widest possible bearing here.

Traits Ascribed to the Person through His Family of Orientation

Let us turn from these socially relevant biological traits to a second category of characteristics (refer to page 233) shaping men's roles. These are attributes of the parental family ascribed to the person. He is born to a family of a given faith, a certain occupation, a certain social class. We need not dwell long on this point, for the preceding chapter was devoted to it. But it's worth recalling that the cluster of familial attributes telescoped in the term, class, entail a wealth of role-shaping influences, influences on husband-wife roles, parental roles, work roles, roles as citizen, communicant, and

---

[11] Leonard S. Cottrell, Jr., "Individual Adjustment to Age and Sex Roles," *American Sociological Review*, published by The American Sociological Association, Vol. VII, No. 5 (October, 1942), pp. 618, 619.

See, also, in the same issue of the *Review*, Ralph Linton on "Age and Sex Categories," and Talcott Parsons, "Age and Sex in the Social Structure of the United States."

A later issue of the *Review* carried seven articles on age and sex roles, Vol. XXIX, No. 4 (August, 1964).

student. Here is a very partial miscellany of illustrations largely drawn from Berelson and Steiner's useful inventory of scientific findings:[12] As to the spouse role, class endogamy (intraclass marriage, implying compatible role definitions) is linked with measures of better adjustment in marriage. The higher the class, the more unmarried women and the later the age at marriage. Lower and upper classes exhibit most instability in marriage (divorce, separation, and abandonment), the middle class least. Affecting parental roles, the higher the class, the lower the fertility rate (an inverse relationship, now becoming weaker), the more likely parents are to follow experts' prescriptions on child rearing, and the more likely the use of psychic rather than physical punishment. Touching work roles, the higher the class of parental family, the more likely the children to achieve a preferred white-collar position, higher income, and to assume an entrepreneurial, or risk-taking posture. As to student—and by implication, teacher—roles: the higher the class, the likelier a college education (even holding measured intelligence constant), the better the grades, the more compatible the interests of teacher and student (although the emphasis on achievement and prestige is likely to be less among upper- and lower-class persons than middle-class). Class conditions personality factors affecting role performance. People from lower-class families are more resigned to their positions in life, more distrustful of authority, more likely to feel inferior, and, in their political and religious orientations, more likely to be, respectively, radical and conformist. These, let me stress, are scattered and roughly stated examples of role-conditioning factors rooted in the social location of the person's family.

On a scale of range of influence we might say that our first category, biological traits emerging at the confluence of two genetic streams, offers least option or range. Less rigid, less prescriptive are the role-forming influences that stem from the ascribed characteristics of the parental family, such as class. Most opportunity for individuation, for personal role creation, comes from membership in groups outside the family: school, camp, travel, guests and visitors from different backgrounds, and the like. In a way the building of a role-set defining a unique personality is a matter of progressive

---

[12] Bernard Berelson and Gary A. Steiner, *Human Behavior: An Inventory of Scientific Findings* (New York: Harcourt, Brace & World, Inc., 1964), chap. xi, *passim*.

emancipation from restrictions of the first two categories of role conditioners. But of course it also means, once the choices are made, a narrowing or fixing or crystallizing of roles. This is, indeed, what makes the person discernible.

Participation and Achievement in Extrafamilial Groups

For our third category of role influences, those groups in which the person participates directly, as an individual, and achievement in which shapes the role to be played, the school provides a good example. To illustrate the influence of education in shaping the civic role, and, beyond that, to show something of the dynamics of the role-fixing process, let me draw on an intriguing study by Theodore Newcomb. In his *Personality and Social Change*[13] he shows how one aspect of the civic role, the attitudes supporting civic behavior, are formed in the course of a college career. About thirty years later, in another study of the same population he asks: have these attitudes conditioning the civic role persisted? And if so, what accounts for their persistence?

These are important questions, since the learning and fixing of a role implies the persistence of attitudes supporting performance in that role. To the first question posed above—and let me put it more generally: do attitudes tend to persist?—the answer is yes. To the second question as to the mechanisms promoting persistence, we might offer the following set of propositions:

1. Attitudes are shaped in an intricate dialectic between self and other. They only emerge, that is to say, out of a social context. Thus:
    1.1 Personality can be seen as the subjective aspect of culture.
    1.2 Outside of a social context, attitudes toward objects would not be formed.
    1.3 Personal integrity, or unity, or balance is some function of the unity and integrity of the person's socio-cultural setting.
2. His attitudes once shaped, the person tends to associate with others whose attitudes are compatible with his. He seeks a social context, not always consciously, whose effect is to support and reinforce his attitudes. This means that:
    2.1 When we are successful in joining compatible groups (finding a congenial husband or wife, a school setting, a work or religious group responding to our views, interests and abilities), "an

---

[13] Theodore M. Newcomb, *Personality and Social Change* (New York: Dryden Press, 1957). This study on the political posture of Bennington students was carried out between 1935 and 1939, the report being first published in 1943.

*intra*personal state of balance comes to correspond with [a state of] interpersonal" balance.[14]

2.2 When we find ourselves out of harmony with others, we seek to achieve intra- and interpersonal balance through inducing changes in the relationship.

". . . an imbalanced state, under conditions of continued interaction, is likely to be an unstable one simply because, when it is discovered, it arouses *intra*personal imbalance on the part of one or more interactors, and this state arouses forces toward change."[15]

2.3 We may achieve balance, psychically and socially, so arriving at relatively stable role definitions, by various devices: avoiding incompatible attitudes held by others (restricting communication with them, developing hostility toward them), by persuading others to our attitudes, by changing our own attitudes in accord with others', or by changing the situation. This often means changing our affiliations—i.e., entering new and different groups.

The fixing of roles and the attitudes appropriate to them is a gradual process. We can conceive of it as a funneling process, the person gradually zeroing in on supportive and reinforcing social environments as he selects appropriate others for interaction. In Newcomb's study of the acquaintance process, "expressions of interpersonal attraction during the first week or two were highly unstable, but after about the fifth week they showed only slow and slight changes."[16]

The persistence of attitudes and the fixing of roles through selection of appropriate (reinforcing) environments—social environments, and specifically in this case, husbands—is well illustrated by Newcomb's two studies of Bennington College women, once in the 1930's and again in the 1960's. His original data show a clear and regular change in the direction of "political and economic progressivism" (PEP) on the part of many Bennington women during their college careers in the 1930's. Thus attitudes were shaped. The question, then, is whether they persisted, and if so—our second question—what the mechanism of persistence was. One of Newcomb's findings, represented in Figure 6-1, speaks to the first

---

[14] Theodore M. Newcomb, "Persistence and Regression of Changed Attitudes: Long-Range Studies," *Journal of Social Issues*, Vol. XIX, No. 4 (October, 1963), p. 12.

[15] *Ibid.*, p. 12.

[16] *Ibid.*, p. 5. The reference is to *The Acquaintance Process* (New York: Holt, Rinehart & Winston, Inc., 1961).

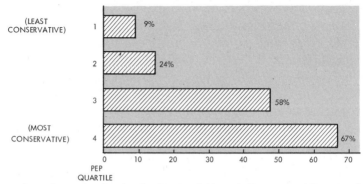

Source: Figure is based on data from Theodore M. Newcomb, "Persistence and Regression of Changed Attitudes: Long-Range Studies," *Journal of Social Issues*, Vol. XIX, No. 4 (October, 1963), Table 1, p. 7.

FIG. 6–1. Percent preferring Nixon for president in 1960, by PEP (Political and Economic Progressivism) scores registered in the late 1930's by 130 Bennington College women.

question. The data tell us that, by knowing their PEP scores in the late 1930's, one could predict remarkably well these Bennington College graduates' presidential preferences in 1960! Thus, were you to predict that those in the least conservative quartile (on their PEP scores in the 1930's) would all vote for Kennedy in 1960, you would incur only a 9 percent error. Or in predicting that those in the most conservative quartile would all vote for Nixon, one would be right in two thirds of the cases. Attitudes did persist.

Now for our second question: what was the mechanism? If, as suggested above, attitudes persist through the conscious or unwitting selection of attitude-reinforcing environments, we must look at those with whom these women associated to see if, in fact, they selected others supporting such attitudes as those reflected in their PEP scores. Above all, one might ask, what sorts of husbands did they select? (Or, to put it in our somewhat awkward terms: what sort of marital group did they enter/form?) Newcomb found that the husbands, despite the disproportionate share of them from Ivy League schools and from wealthy and conservative backgrounds, were *less* conservative than their backgrounds would indicate.

> Our Bennington graduates of the late 1930's found their husbands in the kinds of places where their families expected them to be found, but they selected somewhat atypical members of these "proper" populations of eligibles; they tended not to have conservative attitudes that were then typical of these populations.[17]

---

[17] *Ibid.*, p. 9.

Thus, we get some notion of the way in which the psychic concomitants of a person's role become fixed: initial attitude formation under the tutelage of parents, peers, and pedagogues, the selection (often unwitting) of reinforcing social environments and the avoidance or conversion of those presenting incompatible attitudes, a firmer fixing of attitudes and the roles in which they're implicated, and so on around the circle.

THE SHAPING OF ROLES THROUGH GROUP REQUIREMENTS

But it would be erroneously simple to think of the crystallizing of roles as a process through which a person systematically selects like-minded, right-thinking others to deal with, thus fixing his patterns of behavior. Roles are fixed in large measure as a result of organizations' requirements. Restaurants, legal firms, department stores and colleges, churches, fraternities, and political parties stipulate the role requirements thought desirable for performance as waitress, lawyer, salesman and teacher, priest, "brother," and Republican, respectively. Such role prescriptions doubtless develop from the trial and error of daily experience, an experience later codified in job descriptions by product- and profit-minded employers. But more sophisticated notions of the role requirements for meeting organizational goals come from sociological theory.

Parsons has suggested that groups—different structures of relationships—vary in the role patterns required to meet their objectives. For example, take a very simple, two-person group involving nurse and patient. They are a part of that set of relationships we call a hospital. Now, *how is a person's role fixed by her work with such a group?* How is the role patterned so as to maintain the diadic subsystem of nurse-and-patient, and to achieve the goal of the patient's health? Isidor Thorner raises these questions and, in offering an answer, uses a set of concepts proffered by Parsons for analyzing the various ways in which roles are patterned to meet social system requirements.[18] Let us look at Thorner's suggestive analysis of role requirements imposed by the nature of nurse-patient relationships.

The situation is a common one, nurse and patient constituting an

[18] Isidor Thorner, "Nursing: Functional Significance of an Institutional Pattern," *American Sociological Review*, published by The American Sociological Association, Vol. XX, No. 5 (October, 1955).

elementary social system with roles geared to the restoration of health. The objective reflects an almost unqualified value, health. The predicament is a delicate one, with the patient helpless and vulnerable, yielding himself to bodily intrusions not ordinarily tolerated. Now what are the concepts that help us understand how, in this situation, the nurse's role is necessarily patterned?

The first of these concepts, describing the orientation of nurse to patient is *universalism*. This means that the nurse sees the patient, not as a unique person, but as a case—not in terms of his particular and unduplicated constellation of attributes, but as an appendectomy, as the preoperative gallstone case in room 38. He is treated as a member of a category all of whom have similar symptoms, similar diagnoses, similar treatment and prognoses. Now in the treatment of the sick we confront problems of cause and effect. Given a set of symptoms, we infer a cause and manipulate matters so as to produce the effect of health. Identification and diagnosis imply a cognitive orientation. A cognitive orientation implies discrimination among classes of objects. And classes and classification imply generalization, an orientation toward objects (in this case, the patient) in terms of one or more attributes shared with *all* members of the same class. This is quite in contrast to a cathectic orientation which suggests a fix on the gratificatory potential of the object. If the nurse regards the patient as a member of a class, patient, and subclass, gallstone case, we describe the orientation as universalistic. On the other hand, if she finds the patient distinctively handsome, brave, buoyant, humorous, and wealthy, we're on the way to a *particularistic* performance. So, also, when he begins to respond to the nurse, not as a member of the class, nurse, but as an attractive woman, the patient is about to become a person. Both transformations, Thorner suggests, alter role and relationship, frustrating performance in the service of healing.

Speaking in quite general terms, Parsons says of these two terms, describing one dimension of a person's role orientation:

> The primacy of cognitive values then may be said to imply a *universalistic* standard of role-expectation, while that of appreciative values implies a *particularistic* standard. In the former case the standard is derived from the validity of a set of existential ideas, or the generality of a normative rule, in the latter case from the particularity of the cathectic significance of an object, or of the status of the object in a relational system. Thus definitions of role-expectations in terms of a uni-

versally valid moral precept, e.g., the obligation to fulfill contractual agreements, an empirical cognitive generalization, or a selection for a role in terms of the belief that technical competence in the relevant respects will increase the effectiveness of achievement in the role, are universalistic definitions of roles. On the other hand, definitions in such terms as "I must try to help him because he is my friend," or of obligations to a kinsman, a neighbor, or the fellow-member of any solidary group *because of this membership as such*, are particularistic.[19]

To return to Thorner's discussion of the nurse's role, a second requirement is that it be oriented toward the *performance* of the patient. She is not, supposedly, concerned with *who* he is, but with *what he does:* changes in temperature, pulse beat, a relapse, recovery. In a word, the nurse's role is contingent upon and varies with the performance of her charge as he makes the transition from patient to person. The emphasis is upon *achieved* states of the patient, not upon *ascribed qualities*.

> Achievement-oriented roles are those which place the accent on the performances of the incumbent, ascribed roles, on his qualities or attributes independently of specific expected performances. [In the former case] the expectation is that the actor is committed to the achievement of certain goals or expressive performances and that expectations are oriented to his "effectiveness" or "success" in achieving them. . . .
>
> On the other hand . . . all objects have attributes, they not only *do* this or that, but they *are* such and such. They have attributes of sex, age, intelligence, physical characteristics, statuses in relational systems. . . . The focus of orientation then may be what the object *is* in this sense, e.g., that he is ego's father, that he is a physician, or that he is over six feet tall.[20]

A third aspect of role performance is the range, or scope of relevance, that one role incumbent has for another. This is what Parsons calls the *specificity-diffuseness* dimension. In the case of the nurse, she is both entitled and obliged to restrict the scope of her relationship to the patient, as patient.

> The nurse, like the mother in relation to the infant, caters to the patient's needs and, therefore, presents the most convenient "object of cathexis" on whom he may discharge his craving for response as well as aggressive impulses. This is the situation which predisposes the patient to the transference phenomenon ("falling in love" with the

---

[19] Talcott Parsons, *The Social System* (New York: Free Press of Glencoe, Inc., 1951), p. 62.

[20] *Ibid.*, p. 64.

nurse) and provides not only the condition for willing conformance to the nurse's authority, but also the opportunity for exploiting the patient's vulnerability. In this complex situation the interests of all . . . must be safeguarded so that therapeutic measures may be undertaken with maximum effectiveness. . . .

Hence it is a functional prerequisite [of the nurse's role] that all concerned take for granted that the exclusive focus of interest is not the unique person, but the patient. . . . The mutuality of privileges and obligations is *functionally specific* in that it only applies while the nurse is on duty and insofar as the patient is defined as such.[21]

The division of labor in the contemporary working world tends to emphasize this functional specificity of role. On the other hand, in the child's relationship to its mother, an extremely broad and diffuse range of expectations is regarded as legitimate.

Finally, in Thorner's analysis, the nurse's role is one of affective neutrality. Contrived expressions of personal concern—"And how are we feeling this morning?"—should not be construed as violations of this norm. The significance of affective neutrality in the nurse's role may be better appreciated by considering its opposite, especially, say, in the case where the nurse marries her patient. To this suggestion, Thorner reports his respondents reacting with something bordering on revulsion. Commenting on this, he says:

Marrying a patient is disapproved because it implies that the nurse has taken advantage of the patient's vulnerability and placed the gratification of private interest and emotional expression above professional obligation and loyalty. It is *prima facie* evidence to the profession . . . that discrimination has occurred among patients [contrary to universalistic expectations], that affective neutrality has broken down, and finally, that segregation of emotional relationships (other than what is therapeutically indicated) to the private sphere, outside working hours has failed.[22]

Thus, the nurse-patient relationship depends for its maintenance upon certain characteristics of the nurse's role. Through recruitment, training, and the reinforcement of professional organizations, these role requirements become fixed in the incumbent we call nurse.[23] These requirements of the nurse's role are, in summary: affective neutrality and functional specificity as attitudinal varia-

---

[21] Thorner, *op. cit.*, p. 532.

[22] *Ibid.*, p. 533.

[23] We must suppose that characteristics of the role are more readily fixed in the novice for the consistency with which others provide a common professional model. And this consistency among the novice's models is in part a function of the systematic separation of the maladapted. This implies assessing performance and shearing off the lower end of the performance scale.

bles, and universalism and performance as standards in terms of which the patient's demands upon the nurse may be assessed and responded to.

Thorner points to what is required in the nurse's role. I use his study as complement to Newcomb's. Newcomb's Bennington students built up, in the course of their college careers, a set of attitudes defining certain aspects of their roles as citizens. Their definition of the civic role persisted, largely because their associates —in particular, their husbands—reinforced their views.

This is to start with the person who builds a Weltanschauung and buttresses it by dealing, selectively, with those who think, feel, and act as he does. But if we start with the group—say an occupational group like that of nurses—we can discover dimensions of role performance that must be fixed if the group's goals are to be achieved. In both cases, performance in the role results from actions of the individual, achievement of skills, knowledge and attitudes through education, rather than a role definition stemming from traits ascribed to the person on the basis, say, of class of parental family, or expectations based on such biological attributes as race, age and sex.

INCOMPATIBILITIES OF ROLES AND STATUSES: PERSONAL AND SOCIAL CONSEQUENCES

In the course of the socialization process, the newcomer to the group gets an increasingly firm fix on his positions and roles. But in the roles that are their elemental units, social structures built by men lack the precision and clarity of a wooden Chinese puzzle. Within limits, definitions of and performances *in* roles do vary. Beyond this, we may find stress *between* roles, due to ambiguity of reciprocal expectations or incompatibility of two or more roles. In concluding this brief discussion of the fixing of role and status, let us consider the matter of inconsistent expectations in our dealings with others.

Role incompatibility cuts two ways, affecting the integrity both of person and group. Thus, the study of role compatibility opens up two significant lines of inquiry: (1) effects on the person of counterdemanding roles, stemming from multiple group membership, and (2) effects on social integration of role-sets differing in degree of compatibility.

A normal adult will have several significant group affiliations simultaneously (and in each, a set of expectations defining his role):

a family, a church, a job, a few congenial others with whom he enjoys his leisure. "He is determined, socially, in the sense that [such] groups intersect in his person by virtue of his affiliation with them."[24]

This situation can be graphically expressed in this way.

where 1 = student, or teacher   or, worker
        2 = peers   prof'l ass'n   union member
        3 = parents   faculty   employee

As the individual leaves his established position within *one* primary group, he comes to a stand at a point at which many groups "intersect.". . . The security and lack of ambiguity in his former position gives way to uncertainty in the conditions of his life. This is the sense of an old English proverb which says: He who speaks two languages is a knave.[25]

Membership in two or more groups need not always entail role incompatibility. Yet in a complex social order this may often be the case. We recognize it in the phrase, "conflict of interest," as when a government official has, simultaneously, some affiliation with a company which could profit from a connection in government. Some roles are especially susceptible to incompatible expectations. The foreman may find that management's and workers' expectations of him are in conflict. Like the foreman, the noncommissioned officer may be caught in the middle. Engaged in research on the military in World War II, Professor Stouffer says of the noncom that, on the one hand, he

. . . had the role of agent of the command and in case the orders from above conflicted with what his men thought was right and necessary, he was expected by his superiors to carry out the orders. But he also was an enlisted man, sharing enlisted men's attitudes, often hostile attitudes, toward the commissioned ranks . . . the system of informal controls was such as to reward him for siding with the men in a conflict situation and punish him if he did not . . . on the other hand, open and flagrant disobedience by him of an order from above could not be tolerated by the command.[26]

---

[24] Georg Simmel, *Conflict and The Web of Group-Affiliations,* trans. Kurt H. Wolff and Reinhard Bendix (New York: Free Press of Glencoe, Inc., 1955), p. 150.

[25] *Ibid.,* p. 141.

[26] Samuel A. Stouffer, "An Analysis of Conflicting Social Norms," *American Sociological Review,* published by The American Sociological Association, Vol. XIV, No. 6 (December, 1949), p. 707.

TABLE 6–2

Percentage Who Attribute Given Role Expectations on the Part of Authorities and/or Students with Respect to Each Specific Act (N = 196)

	PERCENTAGE DISTRIBUTION FOR EACH SPECIFIC ACTION					
	A	B	C	D	E	ALL ACTIONS
Case of Ordinary Student						
Think given action would be approved by:						
Authorities only	28	12	3	—	—	9
Both authorities and students	68	81	19	4	2	35
Students only	1	6	55	48	24	27
Neither authorities nor students	3	1	23	48	74	29
	100	100	100	100	100	100
Case of Roommate-Friend						
Think given action would be approved by:						
Authorities only	63	44	9	1	—	24
Both authorities and students	33	53	25	6	4	24
Students only	—	—	49	66	48	33
Neither authorities nor students	4	3	17	27	48	19
	100	100	100	100	100	100

Source: Samuel A. Stouffer, "An Analysis of Conflicting Social Norms," *American Sociological Review*, published by The American Sociological Association, Vol. XIV, No. 6 (December, 1949), p. 712.

Let us look at the study from which this quotation is taken as an example of inquiry into conflicting roles. Our standpoint is that of a person confronted by expectations to some degree irreconcilable.

One hundred and ninety-six Harvard and Radcliffe students were asked how they would act, and which sort of action fellow students and authorities would approve if, while proctoring an examination, they found (1) a fellow student cheating, and (2) a roommate and close friend cheating. Respondents were offered five solutions, or action choices, ranging from harsh to lenient, as follows:

A. Take away his notes and exam book, dismiss him and report him for cheating.
B. Take away his notes, let him finish the exam, but report him for cheating.
C. If he can be led to withdraw from the exam on some excuse, do *not* report him for cheating; otherwise report him.

D. Take away his notes, but let him finish the exam, and *not* report him for cheating.

E. Act as if nothing had happened and *not* report him for cheating.

The drift of the data from upper left to lower right (Table 6–2) shows that these students saw the authorities as generally favoring the more severe, their fellow students the more lenient solutions. Discrepancies in expectations are graphically represented in Figure 6–2. We may infer that some students would be torn when, in a situation like this, they sense incompatible expectations. This was true in 28 percent of the cases. For these people, "the range of acts approved by the authorities did not overlap in any way with the

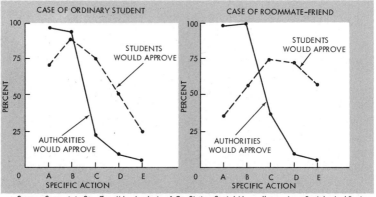

Source: Samuel A. Stouffer, "An Analysis of Conflicting Social Norms," *American Sociological Review*, published by The American Sociological Association, Vol. XIV, No. 6 (December, 1949), p. 711.

FIG. 6–2. Percentage saying that a specific action as proctor would be approved by authorities and by fellow students, respectively.

range of acts approved by the students. For them, simultaneous conformity to both was impossible."[27]

For another, small group of respondents (11 percent of the total), there was no problem at all. For them the range of approved acts was identical for the authorities and the students.

Most (61 percent) perceived a difference in the range of expectations of authorities and students but were able to find at least one action, one solution, that would be approved by both. Perhaps it is just such compromises that are most commonly invented to resolve the problem of incompatible rules, roles, and relationships that most members of complex societies sometimes confront.

---

[27] *Ibid.*, p. 716.

Now consider the matter from the perspective of the group. Insofar as people have similar life experiences—which means, in large measure, having overlapping group memberships or common constellations of positions (statuses)—we might expect role incompatibility to be minimized, social integration enhanced. Put the other way around, measures of *mal*integration should be inversely related to the extent to which members of a group share in common a cluster of statuses with the relatively institutionalized roles that define them.[28]

Furthermore, it seems reasonable to assume that, in the process of adjusting to a social and biophysical environment, compatible sets of statuses/roles sort themselves out, the flagrantly incompatible elements in these constellations being discarded. This is what Professors Gibbs and Martin argue when they assume

> . . . that the actual occupancy of statuses in a society reflects the degree of compatibility among statuses. If two statuses have conflicting roles, thereby making them incompatible statuses when occupied simultaneously, it is assumed that these two statuses would be less frequently occupied simultaneously than would two statuses with roles that do not conflict.[29]

If this seems plausible, we need to ask: What are the mechanisms for eliminating incompatible roles and statuses? Gibbs and Martin mention three: social taboos on simultaneous incumbency, personal dissatisfaction, and personal incapacity. Social disapproval varies, depending on the role-pair we're considering. Woman and physician make a more congenial pair of statuses in the U.S.S.R. than in the United States, as do woman and street cleaner. Woman and engineer are a socially incompatible role- and status-pair in our country, as Emily Hahn discovered. Male and nurse are attributes joined only at risk of social disparagement. The small-town teacher moonlighting as grocery clerk might find himself under pressure to

---

[28] See William J. Goode, "A Theory of Role Strain," *American Sociological Review,* Vol. XXV, No. 4 (August, 1960), p. 485, footnote 7, where he says: "I distinguish role and status on the basis only of 'degree of institutionalization': all role relations are somewhat institutionalized, but statuses are more fully institutionalized." This is the sense in which I am using the concept, status, a term too variously and fuzzily used. You will note that in my illustrations on page 233, all refer to formal, relatively institutionalized roles.

[29] Jack P. Gibbs and Walter T. Martin, "A Theory of Status Integration and Its Relationship to Suicide," *American Sociological Review,* published by The American Sociological Association, Vol. XXIII, No. 2 (April, 1958), p. 142.

relinquish one or the other of these two roles. Taking as cue the large percentage of divorced bartenders, Gibbs and Martin suggest that, here, the "demands of an occupational status may create dissatisfaction with a particular marital status."[30] Finally, there is the matter of incapacity. Old age may not go with the status "profitably employed."

If, as these investigators argue, role or status compatibility is reflected in the frequency with which certain clusters of statuses and roles appear in a population, then it might be argued that the commoner such clusters, the greater the group's integration. Conversely, the less such clusters cohere in a population, the lower the group's integration and the higher such indices of *mal*integration as suicide. And this is the hypothesis proposed by Gibbs and Martin: the greater a measure of status integration (i.e., the more frequently clusters of statuses and roles cohere in a population), the lower the suicide rates.[31] The underlying theoretical argument goes like this.

Postulate 1: The suicide rate of a population varies inversely with the stability and durability of the social relationships within the population.

Postulate 2: The stability and durability of social relationships within a population varies directly with the extent to which individuals in that population conform to the patterned and socially sanctioned demands and expectations placed upon them by others.

Postulate 3: The extent to which individuals in a population conform to the patterned and socially sanctioned demands and expectations placed upon them by others varies inversely with the extent to which individuals in that population are confronted with role conflicts.

Postulate 4: The extent to which individuals in a population are confronted with role conflicts varies directly with the extent to which individuals occupy incompatible statuses in that population.

Postulate 5: The extent to which individuals occupy incompatible statuses in a population varies inversely with the degree of status integration in that population.

---

[30] *Ibid.*, p. 142.

[31] We are on the way, as we shall see, to a test of Émile Durkheim's most general and most important proposition in his classic work, *Suicide*. He writes, "So we reach the general conclusion: suicide varies inversely with the degree of integration of the social groups of which the individual forms a part." Trans. by John A. Spaulding and George Simpson (New York: Free Press of Glencoe, Inc., 1951), p. 209.

From the above postulates there follows the major theorem: *The suicide rate of a population varies inversely with the degree of status integration in that population.*[32]

What is needed now is a measure of status integration, the extent to which, given one status—for example, marital status: widowed—other statuses cohere with it. Gibbs and Martin provide two hypothetical sets of data and show (Table 6–3) how they may be handled to get three measures of status integration: one yielding intergroup comparisons, a second yielding intercluster comparisons and a third providing intracluster comparisons. These will become clear after we examine the hypothetical tables and look at some findings.

You will notice that ΣX^2, as a measure of common status and role configurations, varies from 1.00 down toward 0.00. The minimal value is approached as the number of statuses in a category increase and the spread among them is greater. To take the first column of Table 6–3, all members of the group who are widowed *share the same* age, religious, racial, occupational, sex, and parental statuses. Now if each of these clusters, or status configurations, is weighted by the proportion of the total population in each, and if, then, we sum them, we get the case of complete status integration and a value of 1.00 ($\Sigma\{P(\Sigma X^2) = 1.00$) If, on the other hand—consider the second part of Table 6–3—the status clusters were evenly spread among the four marital statuses, .25 in each, the sum of the five X^2's, appropriately weighted by proportions of population in each of the five clusters, would yield a measure of status integration of .06. The actual value for this hypothetical society is .54.

Before leaving this matter of role compatibility measured through an index of status integration, it will be interesting to report Gibbs and Martin's preliminary findings. First, there is the matter of comparisons between societies. Using their hypothetical second society with a status integration measure of .54, their prediction is that any society having greater measured status integration will have a lower suicide rate, any society with a lower value on this index will have a higher suicide rate. At the time of this study, they

---

[32] Here the investigators drop to a footnote worth repeating. "An alternative theorem making use of the concept of role conflict can be stated: The suicide rate of a population varies directly with the degree of role conflict in that population. [But] . . . no quantitative measure of the amount of role conflict in a society or population has been developed. Consequently such a proposition remains untestable." (Gibbs and Martin, *op. cit.*, p. 143.)

TABLE 6-3

The Integration of Marital Statuses with Selected Status Configurations in a Hypothetical Society Where Marital Integration Is at a Maximum

MARITAL STATUS	ALL OCCUPIED STATUS CONFIGURATIONS (%)				
	CLUSTER 1	CLUSTER 2	CLUSTER 3	CLUSTER 4	CLUSTER 5
	$R_1, A_1,$* $Re_1, O_1,$ S_1, P_1	$R_2, A_2,$ $Re_2, O_2,$ S_2, P_2	$R_1, A_3,$ $Re_3, O_3,$ S_1, P_1	R_1, A_4 $Re_1, O_4,$ S_1, P_3	$R_2, A_5,$ Re_3, O_5 S_2, P_2
Single	.00	.00	.00	1.00	.00
Married	.00	1.00	.00	.00	1.00
Widowed	1.00	.00	.00	.00	.00
Divorced	.00	.00	1.00	.00	.00
ΣX	1.00	1.00	1.00	1.00	1.00
ΣX^2	1.0000	1.0000	1.0000	1.0000	1.0000
Proportion of population	.0700	.4300	.0300	.1500	.3200

Status integration measure for given cluster weighted by proportion of population occupying that status configuration

e.g.,
$$\begin{array}{r}.0700 \\ \times\ 1.0000 \\ \hline \downarrow \end{array}$$

$\Sigma\{P(\Sigma X^2) =$ .07 $+$ .43 $+$ .03 $+$ .15 $+$ .32
$= 1.0$

* Key:
R = race
A = age
Re = religion
O = occupation
S = sex
P = parental status
And 1, 2, 3, 4 = particular positions, or statuses within these categories

And, for a Hypothetical Society Where Marital Integration Is Less than Maximum

Single	.15	.05	.00	.35	.05
Married	.05	.75	.05	.25	.90
Widowed	.60	.15	.25	.20	.05
Divorced	.20	.05	.70	.20	.00
ΣX	1.00	1.00	1.00	1.00	1.00
ΣX^2	.4250	.5900	.5550	.2650	.8150
Proportion of population	.1435	.3825	.0870	.1970	.1900

Status integration measure for given cluster weighted by proportion of population occupying that status configuration

e.g.,
$$\begin{array}{r}.1435 \\ \times\ .4250 \\ \hline \downarrow \end{array}$$

$\Sigma\{P(\Sigma X^2) =$ .06 $+$ .23 $+$ .05 $+$ .05 $+$ .15
$= .54$

Source: Jack P. Gibbs and Walter T. Martin, "A Theory of Status Integration and Its Relationship to Suicide," *American Sociological Review*, published by The American Sociological Association, Vol. XXIII, No. 2 (April, 1958).

had no data on genuine societies, but tried the measure on 30 states "for which the necessary data were available for a measure of the integration of occupation, with age, sex and color in 1950."[33] The coefficient of correlation (recall our discussion of this measure in Chapter 4) between this measure of status integration (independent variable) and suicide rates (dependent variable), for 30 states, was —.57.

Now a second way of testing the link between measures of status integration and suicide rates is to make intercluster comparisons. For if the argument and the hypothesis presented on page 254 is correct, the value of ΣX^2 should vary inversely with suicide rates. Thus in the second part of Table 6–3, the highest suicide rate should

TABLE 6–4

Mean Annual Suicide Rates per 100,000 Population, 1949–51, and Measures of Occupational Integration for Six Race-Sex Status Configurations in the U.S., 1950

RACE-SEX STATUS CONFIGURATION	OCCUPATIONAL INTEGRATION		SUICIDE	
	MEASURE	RANK	RATE	RANK
Negro female	.2473	1	1.5	6
White female	.1828	2	5.3	5
Other female	.1416	4	5.9	4
Negro male	.1588	3	6.1	3
White male	.1295	5	18.5	2
Other male	.1243	6	21.3	1

Source: Jack P. Gibbs and Walter T. Martin, "A Theory of Status Integration and Its Relationship to Suicide," *American Sociological Review*, published by The American Sociological Association, Vol. XXIII, No. 2 (April, 1958), p. 146.

be found for persons exhibiting the configuration of statuses represented in cluster 4, for which the value of ΣX^2 is .2650. (And the lowest suicide rate should be found among persons in cluster 5, where the value of ΣX^2 is high, .8150). Now, taking six race-sex combinations, Gibbs and Martin studied their coherence with each of 11 occupational statuses. Then, rank-ordering the suicide rates and the measures of status integration, they got the results shown in Table 6–4. (In their original worksheet, to relate this test to the presentation in Table VI–3, the 11 occupational statuses would be in the left-hand stub, the race-sex status configurations, or clusters, heading the columns. The measures reported are the ΣX^2 values.) The rank-order correlation coefficient (rho) for these data gives a

---

[33] *Ibid.*, p. 146.

value of —.94, corresponding to p < .01. These data clearly support the hypothesis: the more occupational status coheres with race and sex statuses, the lower the suicide rates.

Finally, we can make intracluster comparisons, in this case a comparison of suicide rates for persons falling in various status configurations *within* a cluster. For example, in the second part of Table 6–3, first column, the predicted rank order of suicide rates from low to high would be: widowed, divorced, single, and married. (Remember that the data in this table are fictitious.) Now when Gibbs and Martin actually did this for U.S. males, aged 60–64 in 1950, for four marital statuses, they found the following:

TABLE 6–5

Percent of Males Aged 60–64 (1950) and Average Annual Suicide Rates (1949–51), by Marital Status

MARITAL STATUS	PERCENT OF MALES AGED 60–64	AVERAGE ANNUAL SUICIDE RATE
Married	.793	36.2
Widowed	.096	64.7
Single	.086	76.4
Divorced	.025	111.1
	1.000	

Source: Jack P. Gibbs and Walter T. Martin, "A Theory of Status Integration and Its Relationship to Suicide," *American Sociological Review*, published by The American Sociological Association, Vol. XXIII, No. 2 (April, 1958), p. 147.

Again, these data support the notion that, when statuses within a group cohere—when roles are compatible and status integration is high—measures of malintegration, such as suicide, are low. Gibbs and Martin stress the exploratory nature of this initial study, the lack of adequate data, and the oversimplified index of integration. In a subsequent test using Ceylonese data and relating measures of marital integration, by sex and ethnic status, to suicide rates, these sociologists get qualified confirmation of the earlier findings. ("Out of 18 rho's computed, 14 were in the predicted direction."[34]) This later study has special interest as it detects isomorphisms—similar forms and relationships—among people whose cultures differ markedly.

But lest we be bemused and deflected by the illustration, let me

---

[34] Jack P. Gibbs and Walter T. Martin, "Status Integration and Suicide in Ceylon," *American Journal of Sociology*, Vol. LXIV, No. 6 (May, 1959), p. 590.

recall the central point. Role incompatibility has consequences for the person and for the group. From the person's perspective, Stouffer's study illustrates the dilemma of student official (proctor) straddling two sets of dissimilar expectations. His position is sometimes awkward because two roles "intersect" in his person, faculty and student. Other positions—for example, noncom and foreman—may be similarly subject to counterdemanding roles.

From the perspective of the group, we have seen how roles and statuses vary in their coherence. Such variations in cohesiveness, or integration, may be expected to entail predictable outcomes, one of which, the suicide rate, is the object of inquiry for Gibbs and Martin.

❊   ❊   ❊   ❊

Now a cursory backward glance before we move on to consider the means of group maintenance. In Part I we dwelt on the person, his learning of the cultural score through the socialization process and the offices of peers and elders. Over time, and at some pains, a social alchemy works to transform an organism of near-infinite potential into a person with the particular skills, knowledge, attitudes, and values appropriate to the roles he must play. In this constraining-liberating process, the product of a genetic encounter with uncertain outcomes, a callow, asexual, illiterate, uncommitted organism becomes a mature man (or woman), variously facile in symbolic manipulation (of the King's English, or Mandarin or Hindi), dedicated to Judeo-Christian (or Buddhist, or Moslem) ideals, and to secular salvation through the Republican Party (or Democratic, or Labor, or Socialist, or Communist). The renewal of the group depends on his becoming a person: his becoming a person depends on his implication in the group.

The gradual fixing of role and status is a process contingent on many things. The shaping of self, and its roles, hinges on such factors as race, sex, and age—biological attributes given crucial definition in the group's culture. It also depends on the attributes ascribed to the person by virtue of his parents' position. And it depends, finally, on personal choice and achievement.

Roles are fixed, as we have seen, because attitudes early inculcated are reinforced through selective exposure, largely unwitting, to those whose views and values are like our own. Our choice of newspapers, television shows, friends, and spouses tends to be restrictive—as we doubtless think, discriminatingly so. But beyond this, roles are fixed through organizational requirements. And so, as we saw, using the hospital and the nurse for illustration, role characteristics are shaped to the means and goals of the group. (In the fixing of the nurse's role, she is trained in standards that are universalistic and oriented to the patient's performance, developing attitudes toward her charges that are emotionally neutral and specific to the healing task.) Thus, personal predisposition and group needs converge in the fixing of role and status.

But to assume a simple, easy convergence from a broad and ambiguous set of possibilities at birth to a sharply focused adult personality would be to oversimplify, and so distort, the case. Multiple group memberships open the possibility of incompatible roles with dual outcomes: a challenge to the integrity of the person and to the integrity of the group. I've offered empirical examples in Stouffer's study of conflicting social norms, and that by Gibbs and Martin on correlates of status integration.

Up to this point I have directed our attention at the person who acquires his humanity as he acquires his culture, through fruitful transactions with others. The focus (which might be represented as in Figures 6a, 6b) has been not so much upon the group entered as upon the person entering it. The problem was: How does the individual become a person, the animal become human? How does the person pick up the culturally given role prescriptions that enable him to establish satisfactory relationships with a, b, c, d, and e (in Figure 6–3b)? How does he enter the human group, first of all, and the various subgroups that ultimately provide the matrix for his conduct?

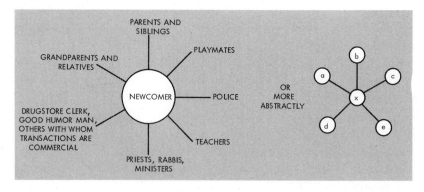

FIG. 6–3a   FIG. 6–3b

But now our attention shifts. Our concern is not now with the *articulation of roles* that comprise a relationship, but with the *articulation of relationships* that comprise the group. We might illustrate the shift by contrasting Figure 6–3b with Figure 6–3c. Now we have a closed, a bounded system of relationships, direct and indirect, that constitutes a group. Now the concepts of culture and socialization are not our prime focus, but rather the concept of institution (Chapters 9 through 13). Now we move from the fields of cultural anthropology and social psychology to the heart of the matter, the structure and functioning of the social order: the institutionalizing of the ties that bind, as men organize their efforts to perform those tasks without which the group could not be maintained. These tasks include not only the hard necessities of breeding and rearing, of producing and distributing goods, of

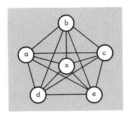

FIG. 6–3c

allocating power. Also required are the institutionalizing of ways to answer proximate and ultimate questions (in science and religion, respectively). There is, further, the need to reaffirm and reinforce the social bond, both through the common communion of religion and through membership in those voluntary associations that fill in the interstices of the institutional building blocks.

But underlying the forms of interaction that are institutionalized are other factors conditioning the maintenance of groups. There is the matter of replacing the raw material of social life, the input through birth and migration and changed longevity to match output through death and emigration. Also affecting the stability, the maintenance of the group, are the ecological aspects of human populations—the spatial and temporal ordering of man's dealings with his fellows.

To these matters we turn in Part II.

SELECTED SUPPLEMENTARY READINGS

*FIELD, MARK G. "Structured Strain in the Role of the Soviet Physician," *American Journal of Sociology*, 1953, pp. 493–502.

* GOODE, WILLIAM J. "A Theory of Role Strain," *American Sociological Review*, 1960, pp. 483–96.

*HUGHES, EVERETT C. "Social Change and Status Protest: An Essay on the Marginal Man," *Phylon*, Vol. X (First Quarter, 1949) pp. 58–65.

NEWCOMB, THEODORE M.; TURNER, RALPH H.; AND CONVERSE, PHILIP E. "Complex Role Demands," in *Social Psychology*, ch. xiii. New York: Holt, Rinehart & Winston, Inc., 1965.

---

* Articles marked with an asterisk are available as reprints from the college division of the Bobbs-Merrill Company, Indianapolis, Indiana.

Part **2** **Maintaining the Group**

STRUCTURES OF RELATIONSHIPS:
BUILDING AND MAINTAINING THEM

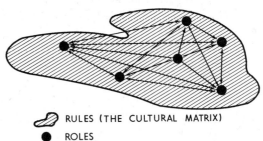

RULES (THE CULTURAL MATRIX)

ROLES

RELATIONSHIPS

Chapter 7

The Ecological Substructure of Human Relationships

How are human relationships ordered in space and time?
How are spatial and temporal patterns reflected
in social patterns—and vice versa?

Like other approaches to the mystery of man, human ecology probes hidden sources and unrecognized connections. Consider two parallels. Marxist theory links psychic and social products—religious beliefs, law, political forms, class, family structure—with their alleged source in patterns of economic organization. Freudian theory connects overt psychic symptoms, normal and abnormal, with their hidden sources in infancy when, in the matrix of the mother-father-child triangle, imperious organic impulses are warped to meet the stipulations of culture. So, likewise, the theory of human ecology connects social and cultural characteristics with the distribution of men and their activities in time and space, as a result of competitive processes largely unplanned and unwitting.

Biologists have long studied the order that emerges in plant and animal communities through competitive adaptation to the environment. Building on their work, sociologists have studied the maintenance of symbiotic ties in the social order as they are registered in the spatial and temporal patterning of human communities. From the plant and animal ecologists, the human ecologist borrows the term, symbiosis, to convey the notion of unplanned interdependence. It describes a unity arising from the interlocking of complementary differences. Durkheim used the words "organic solidarity" to describe this same unity, deriving from the division of labor. (We will discuss this source of unity, functional integration, in Chapter 9.)

Neither the unwitting character of such relationships nor the biological analogy should be overdrawn. With man, sentiment, tradition, preference enter in to modify a strictly anonymous competition that better describes the world of plants and animals. Man has a culture. He is not like the lowly mule, without pride of ancestry or hope of posterity. He has a body of knowledge, symbolized in act and artifact, and including especially knowledge of what *ought* to be. (He can, for example, establish restrictive housing covenants that alter the distribution of population as it would be were impersonal competition the sole determinant.) And if the sort of relationship I'm discussing is largely unwitting and uncontrived, it is not entirely so. People know the first links in the relationship chains and act, wilfully, to alter them.

THE FAR-FLUNG WEB OF UNPLANNED BUT PATTERNED HUMAN RELATIONSHIPS

Yet it is clear that we do not know either the nature or extent of the relationships we have with most of the people with whom we are linked. We are necessarily ignorant of our widespread involvement in others' affairs (and theirs in ours): I say "necessarily" because connections with most others are indirect, ramified, and complex. Yet despite our ignorance of these bonds, a surprisingly short series of indirect linkages is enough to connect us with the rest of the world. Suppose that you know fifty persons, each of whom knows an additional fifty. How many links in this chain of acquaintanceship would be required to embrace the world's population? Taking the world's population as 3 billion we can state the problem in this fashion: $50^x = 3{,}000{,}000{,}000$. We find that in six short steps we would have indirect connections with 15.6 billion persons, roughly five times the world's population. Or, suppose we were more conservative and estimated that each person knew or dealt with only ten (nonduplicating or nonoverlapping) others. In this case if we solve for x in the equation $10^x = 3{,}000{,}000{,}000$ we find that the value of x lies between nine and ten.

Human relationships patterned in space.

The stipulation of nonoverlapping acquaintances is, of course, unrealistic. Those we know are more likely to know many of the same others as do we. National, religious, ethnic boundaries tend to set limits beyond which dealings are formal and official. But if reality only approximates this limiting case, it is nonetheless impressive to sense the rapid spread of involvement far beyond the conscious contrivance of the person. Far-flung as it is, the hidden network of relationships is there, conditioning our choices, altering our conduct, affecting our attitudes. No sense of social man is perceptive or adequate that neglects this essential characteristic of modern society: the unwitting, indirect interlocking of men's destinies.

But let us be concrete. The dairy farmer may be generally aware that anonymous others exist—others with whom his work is linked. But the interdependence is unplanned, its full extent and character unknown. With those who set freight rates for transporting raw milk to the plant he has no direct connections. He may be conscious of a consequence—the fact that volume production of cheaper milk (lower butter fat content) is better adapted to areas close in to the city while higher butter fat milk from Jerseys and Guernseys can better support the greater time-cost distance from the outer rim of the milkshed area. Thus vaguely apprehended competitive influences condition land use and the distribution of men and functions. But certainly our farmer is but dimly aware of those others whose influence is registered in a pattern of land use and occupancy. Nor is he intimate with suppliers; manufacturers; laborers producing tractors, binders, harrows, stanchions, milking machines and refrigeration equipment; the trucking companies; railroads; power suppliers; and, behind them, the engineers, designers, chemists, metallurgists, *et al.*—all of them linked with him in his daily work.

Or suppose your father works for General Motors (as 605,000 persons do, including 114,000 outside the United States). With how many others, and where, are you connected through him? Beyond the .6 million employees there are over a million shareholders in GM residing in fifty states, in eighty foreign countries, and in every province in Canada. Moreover, GM gets parts, materials, and services from more than 30,000 other firms. Hence you would be linked, indirectly, with all the employees of these firms. Nor have we begun to exhaust the linkages—with government, the military, the medical and legal and teaching professions, and a host of others.

But this is enough to suggest the unplanned emergence of a web of relationships built on differentiated but complementary activities.

Ecological conditions then, both reflect and set the conditions for human relationships. This is why we can speak of the ecological substructure of the social order. The possibility and type of access to another person and the probability of an encounter with him—these constitute elementary preconditions for the culturally defined give and take that makes a human relationship. Encounters are social events strung like beads along the axes of space and time. When in the adjustment to their habitat people bind themselves in space and routinize their encounters through time, a persisting structure of relationships emerges. Regularities in space, continuities through time, set conditions for bounding and maintaining a social order.

THE TIMING OF HUMAN RELATIONSHIPS

Consider some garden variety examples of the temporal patterning of relationships. The whole urban network of transport and communication is contrived to enable the encounter of the right persons at the right time. (Transport, indeed, might be subsumed under communication, since it is a principal device for achieving face-to-face communication among members of the group.) This temporal structuring controls encounters, conditions the intersection of experience, strengthens or attenuates relationships. Student and teacher, priest and communicant, official and citizen, husband and wife, worker and boss—all the relationships implied by these role labels are sustained by the New Haven, the Pennsylvania, the I.C., and the Long Island Railroad, the subway, underground and metro, by the highways and sidewalks that convey A to B's side, enabling each to meet the reciprocal expectations that define the relationship.

And there is, especially in city life, an exquisite timing in these encounters. Not everyone meets everyone else at the same time and place. Professor Wirth facetiously described the timing of the commuting pattern this way: in the morning, first the workers, then the clerkers, and, finally, the shirkers, the pattern being reversed at end of day. Banking hours, hours for factory and shop, theater and restaurant hours, train, plane, bus, and boat schedules, the stop and go of traffic lights—these time the ebb and flow of human contacts and the relationships that depend on them. Consider the timing of radio and TV programs: the early morning union-sponsored broadcasts with economic and political commentary in support of union policy directed at blue-collar workers, the midmorning soap opera for the vulnerable housewife, the after-school programs geared to children's interests, the "adult" programs of later evening. The timing of events often reflects differing role requirements by age, sex, occupation, class.

The dimensions of space and time intersect like the hairlines on a telescopic sight to fix the chances of encounter, suggesting the type and range of influence brought to bear on the person. For example, they promote discriminable differences in conduct between a United States senator and a congressman. The senator's district (a state) subtends a larger area than the congressman's. (Congressmen-at-large are obviously an exception.) The senator runs for office every six years, his counterpart in Congress every two. Being relatively liberated from confines of time and space, the senator might be expected to be more liberated in his views, to enjoy a wider range of discretion. Congressmen, their reference groups being more limited, their views more often reviewed and reinforced by their parochial constituencies, might be expected to display more provincial passions. And disregarding for the moment other contributory factors such as margin of victory, race, religion, region, this is in fact what we find. When we say that a person is able to take "the long view" it means, literally, a view embracing greater social space and time.

Time is significant as a frame for human relationships in many ways. Cultural accretion depends on it. Different generations step into the cultural stream at different time points, complicating parent-child relationships. Every culture has its calendar, a temporal map locating significant, recurrent events. "No people," Professor Hughes notes, "has for long lived without some established group ways which turn with the sun."[1] Temporal intervals bound statuses. After periods of time infants become children, children adolescents, and adolescents adults, and, at 62 adults become the aged by fiat (when they are eligible for social security). After so long in role a worker gains seniority, the captain his majority, the recruit his PFC stripe. Time symbolizes the strength and demands of a relationship, as suggested in the pledge " 'til death do us part." Time is a frame enabling a systematic, recurrent affirmation of common values and

[1] Everett Hughes, *Men and Their Work* (New York: Free Press of Glencoe, Inc., 1958), p. 13.

reinforcement of relationships. It is these timed encounters that interest us here: the routinization of contact. The significance of space stems from the numbers and propinquity of those occupying it. But before we turn to the spatial dimension let me offer one more illustration of the significance of time as a population accommodates itself to the conditions of its habitat. The example comes from Marcel Mauss's classic essay on "Seasonal Variations in Eskimo Societies."[2] (See Chapter 2, pp. 71 and 87.) In this work he describes structural changes in the social order that are linked with the seasonal dispersion and concentration of Eskimo groups. Contrasting patterns of summer and winter life stem from the habits of their game, and from methods of pursuing them. And so, Mauss points out, there emerges a cyclical rhythm in their religious and familial life, in their moral and judicial patterns.

In the summer, settlements are sparse, in winter dense and clustered. From summer to winter their shelter shifts from tents to houses. A summer dwelling houses a single family while in winter time as many as six to nine families live in a single dwelling. And so Mauss sees here a genuinely symbiotic phenomenon. As the game concentrate or disperse, according to the season, there is a concomitant expansion and contraction of the social structure.

This is reflected in religious practices. These are minimal in summer, limited to domestic rites: rituals of birth and death and the observance of certain proscriptions. But the winter is a time of continuous religious excitement. It is the time when the myths and tales are transmitted from one generation to the other. The slightest event requires the more or less serious intervention of magicians. In sum, one can see the whole of the winter life as a sort of extended religious festival.

The contrast between summer and winter life, he goes on to say, extends to ideas: peoples' birth dates, summer or winter, serve to classify them. "Each season serves to define a whole order of beings

---

[2] Marcel Mauss (1872–1950) is probably best known for his work on gift-giving as an elementary form of exchange (*le Don, forme archaïque de l'échange*). His interest was in the way gift-giving defined and supported human relationships. His chief contribution to sociology—aside from his teaching at Bordeaux, the Collége de France, Harvard and elsewhere—came through his work with the group surrounding Durkheim (his uncle) in publishing the *Année sociologique*. This was the principal medium not only for publishing his own work, chiefly in ethnology and the sociology of religion but, in his capacity as editor, for developing and preserving the often unfinished work of his colleagues killed in World Wars I and II.

and things." Laws affecting family relationships and property follow the same temporal cycle.

> Eskimo social life undergoes, then, a sort of regular rhythm. It is not the same at different seasons of the year. Now if this curious alternation is most clearly seen among the Eskimos it is not peculiar to or exclusive with them. Social life is not sustained at the same level throughout the year but rather goes through regular and successive phases of increasing and decreasing intensity, of rest and activity, of expenditure of energy and restoration.[3]

SPACE: PROPINQUITY, ISOLATION AND FREQUENCY OF INTERACTION

Let us turn from the time to the space dimension. Despite our ability to communicate via Telstar and less dramatic electronic means, sheer physical propinquity remains a potent factor in creating and maintaining a community. Other things equal, spatial propinquity → social propinquity → an articulation of interdependent roles → psychic propinquity: common attitudes and values that identify and bound the group. Put another way, a common habitat enables frequency of interaction, frequency of interaction is associated with people's attractiveness and accommodation to one another, and common conceptions of a range of objects are developed and reinforced. This yields what Durkheim referred to as "moral density," a consistency of viewpoint, a uniformity in the cultural fabric that enhances group solidarity. Perceiving familiar, friendly others as having the same view of things, persons, and symbols makes for maintaining the network of relationships that is the group. The reverse of this situation weakens group bonds.

Let me illustrate. Newcomb finds in his data evidence that there is a force working on the person, a strain toward identifying and evaluating objects in the same way as one's friends do.[4] (I assume here that one's friends and familiars are commonly those physically close enough to interact with frequently.) The more frequent the interaction between A and B and the more attractive B is for A, the more accurate is A in assessing B's orientation toward some object, X (for example, another person). This means of course that A's

---

[3] Marcel Mauss, "Essai sur les variations saisonniéres des sociétés eskimos: étude de morphologie sociale," *l'Année sociologique*, Vol. IX (1904–5), pp. 39–132, *passim.*

[4] Theodore M. Newcomb, *The Acquaintance Process* (New York: Holt, Rinehart & Winston, Inc., 1961).

expectations of B's behavior are likely to be fulfilled. A expects B to act in a given way. He does so. A's image of B is reinforced. The relationship is predictable, which is to say, stable. To recall Weber's definition of a social relationship, there is a high probability that, in its meaningful content, an anticipated course of action will ensue. And conversely, the evidence indicates that accuracy in estimating others' behavior and belief *declines* with reduced frequency of interaction and attractiveness. Thus, as to a person with whom I deal infrequently, my expectations of his conduct are much more likely to be wrong. My anticipations are more often unfulfilled, my "predictions" unrealized. He does not behave as he "should," and this is unsettling. Such erratic behavior arouses uncertainty and distrust. We are disposed to call such an other irresponsible. Hence we are inclined to have as little as possible to do with him, resulting in future estimates of him and his conduct that may then be more inaccurate than ever.

These are, respectively, the virtuous and vicious circles. But both outcomes, though contradictory in content, have the same effect: they tighten the drawstrings of the inner circle and hold the "outsider" at a distance. For at the psychic level there is the regular reinforcement from like-thinking, "right-minded" others. We know the person we detest is untrustworthy, has execrable tastes, while our friends are exquisite in their sensibilities, penetrating in their judgments, and thoroughly reliable. On the social side it increases the stability of a social order to know and to predict, as we do daily and with high accuracy, the other's responses. Thus the social bond is strengthened in our intercourse with those near to us: and near commonly means physical as well as affective nearness. There is a clear connection between frequency of dealing with others (generally implying propinquity: same firm, factory, union, office, family, church, neighborhood) and common definitions of roles and objects. To share such views is to strengthen the bonds of the group and so to maintain it.

Consider the extent of agreement between those who are "close" and those who are not so "close" to one another. (Again, I mean to imply the probability of physical as well as social and psychic propinquity.) Table 7–1 has to do with the extent of agreement between friends and nonfriends as to a characteristic (attractiveness or nonattractiveness) of seventeen objects (other persons living in a student residence). These data suggest that people who often deal

TABLE 7–1

Physical, Social and Psychic Propinquity and Extent of Agreement in Assessing Others' Attractiveness

EXTENT OF AGREEMENT (RHO†) VALUES) ON ATTRACTIVENESS OF 17 OTHER HOUSE MEMBERS		PERCENT OF A's ESTIMATES AND 2 PERSONS MOST ATTRAC- TIVE TO HIM FALLING AT INDI- CATED LEVEL OF AGREEMENT (N = 34: A AND B WITH RE- SPECT TO 17 OBJECTS AND SIM- ILARLY WITH A AND C)	PERCENT OF A's ESTIMATES AND TWO PERSONS LEAST AT- TRACTIVE TO HIM FALLING AT INDICATED LEVEL OF AGREEMENT (N = 34: A AND X WITH RE- SPECT TO 17 OBJECTS AND SIM- ILARLY WITH A AND Y)
.75	High	47	0
.50–.74		38	29
.25–.49	EXTENT OF AGREE- MENT	15	15
.00–.24		0	18
.00	Low	0	38
	Total	100	100

Source: Adapted from Theodore M. Newcomb, *The Acquaintance Process* (N.Y.: Holt, Rinehart & Winston, Inc., 1961), p. 99–102, passim.

† See "An Aside on Methods: Measuring Degree of Association between Two Sets of Rank-ordered Observations," pp. 276–77.

with one another are likely to be friendly and to see the world through like lenses. A primary predisposing factor is physical propinquity, location in shared space. Thus the spatial, the social, and the moral order are likely to be coterminous, the first setting the conditions of frequency of interaction, hence conditioning the strength of the social bond and the extent to which the significant objects of life carry similar values.

Thus, as Newcomb's inquiry shows, locus and likings (and the language to express them) are linked. The world of significant objects with which we deal is formed not so much by experience with the objects themselves as by contact with our friends and neighbors. From this point of view certain nations, groups, races, categories of persons are enemies not because they have distasteful traits. Rather they have distasteful traits because they are defined by colleagues, friends, family as enemies. Thus the Republican depreciates the Democratic position (and vice versa) not because the policy is stupid and coincidentally Democratic but because it is Democratic and *ipso facto* stupid. When the wrong policy is taken over by the "right" party it promptly becomes the course of wisdom. Attraction and agreement are reciprocally reinforcing: distaste and disagreement strengthen one another. Spatial propinquity favors the first, supports social propinquity. Spatial distance favors the second.[5]

If propinquity favors interaction, if it tends to sustain definitions of enemy and friend, out-group and in-, so supporting a given network of relationships, its opposite should have a contrary effect. But if physical isolation promotes an opposite effect, social distance, it produces a complementary effect within the group, setting boundaries and reinforcing group identity. Isolation from others adversely evaluated means that additional inputs of information cannot challenge derogatory stereotypes. Thus the network of relationships that is based, in part, on a defensive posture, is not altered. The spatial segregation of differentiated modes of life—of differing social patterns—helps us to draw the boundary lines between groups. Under these circumstances roles and relationships are more likely to remain constant, less likely to be contaminated by external challenges. Physical barriers, reinforced by cultural barriers (which themselves encourage the retention of physical barriers, as when anti-Negro prejudice promotes segregated communities), sustain a relationship of organism to habitat that *maximizes access and encounter among the like-minded.* We might call this the mechanism of differential exposure, or selective isolation. We see it operating in our choice of newspapers and editorial policies, in the choice of certain radio and TV programs and rejection of others. Throughout our lives we erect these belief- and behavior-protecting ramparts, these Berlin walls that maintain our identity and protect

---

[5] I say "favors" because this physical dimension is not a *sufficient* condition for reinforcing or attenuating human relationships. A southern anglophile may feel closer to his far-distant British cousins than to his nearby Latin neighbors. Physical distance $\neq$ social or cultural distance. Nor should propinquity and frequency of interaction be seen as strengthening relationships and so maintaining the group simply through enhanced attractiveness of the persons interacting. Repeated interaction is likely to involve reciprocal obligations, contractual relationships, the felt requirement of response. Gift-giving, whatever the balance in value of things exchanged, maintains a relationship always in disequilibrium; for only one of the partners has last thought of the other. The time dimension is relevant here. Gift-giving is a relationship that always leans into the future. It sets the requirement of restoring a balance of affect-plus.

But this is not to minimize propinquity as a powerful influence affecting frequency of interaction, the probability of attractiveness and reciprocal influence. See, in addition to Professor Newcomb's study cited above, the work of L. Festinger, S. Schachter and K. Back, *Social Pressures in Informal Groups: A Study of a Housing Project* (New York: Harper & Bros., 1950); and recall the study by James H. S. Bossard cited in Chapter 4, "Residential Propinquity as a Factor in Marriage Selection," *American Journal of Sociology,* Vol. XXXVIII (September, 1932).

An Aside on Methods: Measuring Degree of Association between Two Sets of Rank-ordered Observations

Measures of relationship between rank-ordered observations are especially important to the sociologist. This is because his data are often crude, preventing him from treating them as though they formed equal-interval or zero-point scales. Let me make this clearer. We can distinguish several sorts of scales—several ways in which data can be usefully ordered in some sort of progression. There is the nominal scale that has no inherent order, no ostensible progression. A nominal scale is one in which the points are simply labels (nominal means name): male-female, Democratic-Republican-Dixiecrat-Socialist-Birchite, etc. We might, for example, wish to discover if there was any relationship between sex and voting preference, so constructing and crosscutting two nominal scales as indicated in this 2 × 2-celled table.

	Male	Female
Democratic		
Republican		

But the ordinal scale, as its name suggests, does have an order, a succession. Thus, in the illustration used above, there is a succession from "most liked" to "least liked" among our acquaintances. But much less seldom do we have data that can be arranged so that the intervals between two points on the scale are equal. With income we know that the distance between $1,000 and $2,000 is the same as that between $17,000 and $18,000. With family size we know that the "distance" between two and three children is the same as that between four and five; and that four children is twice as many as two, just as six is twice as many as three. But to treat the numbers in the two tables, above, as cardinal (rather than ordinal) numbers would involve quite untenable assumptions. Can I demonstrate that I like Jones *twice as much* as Smith? or that the two points in social distance ("attractiveness") between Jones and Doaks are equivalent to the two points between Smith and White? Unfortunately not. But I *can* deal with them in terms of more or less, relying on ordinal measures.

Let us attempt to clarify the meaning of Rho. (This is a measure of agreement, in the population studied, of two series of *rank-ordered* observations. The measure of such agreement in the sample is commonly designated as r_s, the Spearman rank correlation coefficient.)

In our illustration, here, we wish to know whether two persons, A and B, rank 17 others with whom they live, in the same order of attractiveness. Thus if A says Jones is his best friend (ranks highest in attractiveness), Smith his next best, and so on through the 17th person, and if B ranks these people in precisely the same order of attractiveness, r_s (or Rho, if we're dealing with the whole population) = +1.0 Perfect *dis*agreement would yield a rank order correlation coefficient of −1.0.

An Aside on Methods: Measuring Degree of Association between Two Sets of Rank-ordered Observations (continued)

The formula for calculating r_s is:

$$r_s = 1 - \frac{6\Sigma D^2}{N(N^2 - 1)}, \text{ where}$$

$N =$ the number of paired observations, and
$D =$ the difference between the ranks assigned to each of a given pair of observations.

Suppose, for example, that we were to do what Professor Newcomb did: the investigator asks me and my friend to rank the attractiveness of five acquaintances. The following fictitious and oversimplified data are worked through to show the way of calculating the Spearman rank correlation coefficient.

THE (SOCIAL) OBJECT: MY FRIEND'S AND MY ACQUAINTANCES	RANK ORDER OF AT- TRACTIVENESS OF 5 ACQUAINTANCES, BY		D	D^2
	ME	MY FRIEND		
Jones	1	1	0	0
Smith	2	3	-1	1
Doaks	3	2	1	1
White	4	5	-1	1
Brown	5	4	1	1
			0	4

$$r_s = 1 - \frac{6\Sigma D^2}{N(N^2 - 1)} = 1 - \frac{24}{120} = 1 - .20 = .80 \, .$$

If on the other hand we were calculating the rank correlation on agreement between me and my *least* liked acquaintance, the data and outcome might be as follows:

THE (SOCIAL) OBJECT: (OUR ACQUAINTANCES— MINE AND MY LEAST- LIKED ACQUAINTANCE'S)	RANK ORDER OF AT- TRACTIVENESS OF 5 ACQUAINTANCES, BY		D	D^2
	ME	MY LEAST- LIKED AC- QUAINT- ANCE		
Jones	1	5	-4	16
Smith	2	4	-2	4
Doaks	3	3	0	0
White	4	2	2	4
Brown	5	1	4	16
			0	40

$$r_s = 1 - \frac{6\Sigma D^2}{N(N^2 - 1)} = 1 - \frac{6(40)}{120} = 1 - 1 = 0 \, .$$

The Spearman rank correlation coefficient has been used for some time and is doubtless still better known than other rank correlation methods. But others, for example, Kendall's tau (τ) are in various ways more useful.

our predispositions within a favored group having, often, a specific *locus*. Class and caste-like barriers, differences in religion, education, occupation (and these categories are neither exhaustive nor exclusive) are ways in which we isolate ourselves, limit the range of our exposures and continuously reinforce our conceptions of others and of the objects of life with which we must deal. In this process, *identification with place* is constantly reinforced, common commitments regularly reaffirmed, animosities sustained at a functionally useful pitch. When geographic terms are used to identify persons having different life chances (the Riverbrookers and the Hillstreeters in Yankee City,[6] the Four Hundred and those in "squatters paradise" below the canal in Elmtown,[7] prairie dwellers and hill folk in Plainville[8]) physical boundaries appear to coincide with social boundaries. This indeed is what Robert Park asserted in his classic essay on "The Urban Community as a Spatial Pattern and a Moral Order."[9] Restricted access and limited encounter tend to convert an aggregate (a spatially identifiable collectivity) into a clearly defined if loosely organized group. Repeated encounter among the like-minded makes for what the psychologists call "reinforcement": the fixing of behaviors and their supporting beliefs through reward and punishment. The effect is to produce a constancy of character persisting through time and lending a discriminable identity to particular quarters. When we use terms like Wall Street, or LaSalle Street, Harlem or the Black Belt, Brooklyn or Brookline, Nob Hill or Little Italy, the Bowery, the Village, the garment, fur, and theater districts, we refer to such spatially defined areas that retain their character (persist in the structure of relationships) through time despite continuous changes in population.

It is because geography, occupation, and all the other factors which determine the distribution of population, determine so irre-

---

[6] Professor Warner reports: "In the expressions about wealth and occupation to which higher and lower valuations were attached, we noticed that certain geographical terms were used not only to locate people in the city's geographical space but also to evaluate their comparative place in the rank order . . . These designations were terms of rank employed . . . to refer obliquely to higher and lower social statuses in the community." (W. Lloyd Warner [ed.], *Yankee City*, abridged edition [New Haven: Yale University Press, 1963], pp. 38, 41.)

[7] A. B. Hollingshead, *Elmtown's Youth* (New York: John Wiley & Sons, Inc., 1949).

[8] James West, *Plainville, U.S.A.* (New York: Columbia University Press, 1945).

[9] Robert E. Park, "The Urban Community as a Spatial Pattern and a Moral Order," in Ernest W. Burgess (ed.), *The Urban Community* (Chicago: University of Chicago Press, 1926). Copyright 1926 by The University of Chicago.

sistibly and fatally the place, the group, and the associates with whom each one of us is bound to live that spacial relations come to have, for the study of society and human nature, the importance which they do.[10]

This is Robert Park, speaking in his presidential address to the American Sociological Society. He went further than this in linking the spatial and the social, suggesting that ". . . all we ordinarily conceive as social may eventually be construed and described in terms of space and the changes of position of the individuals within the limits of a natural area; that is to say, within the limits of an area of competitive cooperation."[11] This was a speculative statement, an idea that Park held lightly because of the self-aware and self-transforming nature of human beings. But that human beings contrived particular relationships, sustained by particular norms of conduct and *characteristic of particular areas* he had no doubt. Nor have we; for a number of studies stimulated by the work of Cooley, McKenzie, and Hawley at the University of Michigan and by Park, Burgess, and Wirth at the University of Chicago bear out the emergence of "natural areas."

NATURAL AREAS AND SOCIAL STRUCTURE

Natural areas are areas of unplanned growth whose inhabitants are subject to the informal controls of common behaviors and beliefs. Such areas emerge as a result of competition for space, a competition conditioned by such cultural factors as the level of technology (controlling transport and communication) and sentiment (preserving in nonrational uses areas like the Boston Common or Central Park; and affecting the competitive capacity of Catholic, Negro, native white Protestant and Jew). No one, no authority, plans the location of cities at breaks in transportation[12] and in such a place as to serve and control a sector of the rural hinterland. No one

---

[10] *Ibid.*, p. 18.

[11] *Ibid.*, p. 12.

[12] The term is Cooley's. His argument (and that of others) was:
"Population and wealth tend to collect wherever there is a break in transportation. . . . By a break is meant an interruption of the movement at least sufficient to cause a transfer of goods and their temporary storage. If this physical interruption of the movement is all that takes place we have what I may call a mechanical break; but if on account of the close relation between transportation and exchange . . . the physical interruption causes a change in the ownership of the transported goods, we have a commercial break." (Charles Horton Cooley, *Sociological Theory and Social Research*, chap. ii, p. 76; originally published as "The Theory of Transportation," *Publications of the American Economic Association*, Vol. IX [May, 1894].)

controls the overall growth of the city, nor the expansion of central business district facilities. Despite after-the-fact zoning, no one really plans the changing patterns of land use made possible by shrinking time-cost distance of city centers from satellites, suburbs, and hinterland. Nor do we plan the speculative holding of land adjacent to the growing central business district, the minimal investment in property that is held for gain rather than specific use, its consequent deterioration and relative undesirability making it available to categories of persons—immigrants, Negroes, Puerto Ricans—who will and must filter into such areas because they cannot compete for more desirable ones. No one contrived a scheme to make the central city increasingly and disproportionately Negro while the suburbs become disproportionately white. And no one contrived the special location of editorial and advertising offices, the used car district, or the Ghetto. Yet without designing, a design emerges. As a result of unwitting, symbiotic processes a spatial structure emerges, a nonrandom mosaic of relationships, beliefs, and values. The elements of this spatial structure have been called "natural areas."

One of the first studies of the human community as a natural area whose population adapts itself to the conditions of life, establishing relationships and occupying space quite independent of the political boundaries, was that of Galpin. In 1915 he published a study of trade areas in Walworth County, Wisconsin, under the telling title, "The Social Anatomy of an Agricultural Community."[13] Mapping the areas in which people dealt with one another (in such activities as banking, use of libraries, church and high school attendance, distribution of local newspapers), Galpin defined the unrecognized boundaries of human intercourse. Other studies of the natural frontiers established by communities show the great discrepancy between the legal unit and the social reality. The legal unit leaves out an aspect of reality suggested by the stretch of the viewing and listening area embraced by the city's radio and TV stations, the reading area for the city's newspapers, the retail store delivery area, the area served by central banks—that area, in short, through which people interlace their roles in relationships that develop like Topsy. ("I 'spect I growed. Don't think nobody never made me.")[14]

---

[13] C. J. Galpin, "The Social Anatomy of an Agricultural Community" (Madison, Wisc.: University of Wisconsin Agricultural Experiment Station Research Bulletin 34, 1915).

[14] Harriet Beecher Stowe, *Uncle Tom's Cabin*, chap. xx.

Professor Burgess was one of the first to offer a scheme describing in an abstract and general fashion, subject to local influences, the ecological tendencies registered in city structure. His model, the "concentric zone scheme," is represented in Figure 7–1. There have

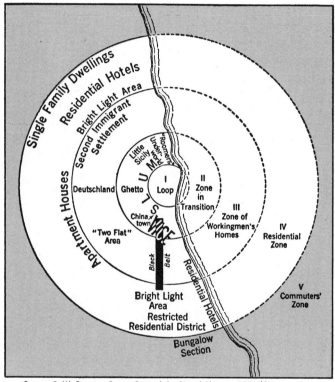

Source: E. W. Burgess, *Census Data of the City of Chicago, 1920* (Chicago: University of Chicago Press, 1920). Copyright 1920 by The University of Chicago.

FIG. 7–1. The concentric zone principle of urban growth, as formulated by Burgess. This chart, which applies specifically to Chicago, also shows the segregation of different cultural and racial areas of the city.

been a number of variations on this model: stellate patterns, sector modifications, multinucleated urban patterns (see Figure 7–2) Each qualification of the Burgess zonal theory has responded to careful observations of patterns of human settlement. But whatever the variants on this spatial model, these things are agreed upon:

1. A determinate, nonrandom pattern of settlement, land use, of social and psychic characteristics emerges.
2. The market place, the downtown shopping area, or retail business

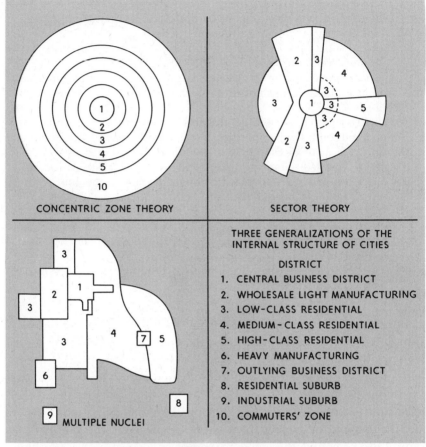

CONCENTRIC ZONE THEORY

SECTOR THEORY

MULTIPLE NUCLEI

THREE GENERALIZATIONS OF THE
INTERNAL STRUCTURE OF CITIES

DISTRICT

1. CENTRAL BUSINESS DISTRICT
2. WHOLESALE LIGHT MANUFACTURING
3. LOW-CLASS RESIDENTIAL
4. MEDIUM-CLASS RESIDENTIAL
5. HIGH-CLASS RESIDENTIAL
6. HEAVY MANUFACTURING
7. OUTLYING BUSINESS DISTRICT
8. RESIDENTIAL SUBURB
9. INDUSTRIAL SUBURB
10. COMMUTERS' ZONE

Source: Reprinted with permission of The Free Press from "The Nature of Cities," by Chauncy D. Harris and Edward L. Ullman, in *Cities and Society* by Paul K. Hatt and Albert J. Reiss, Jr. (eds.). Copyright 1951, 1957 by The Free Press, a corporation.

FIG. 7-2. Generalizations of internal structure of cities. The concentric zone theory is a generalization for all cities. The arrangement of the sectors in the sector theory varies from city to city. The diagram for multiple nuclei represents one possible pattern among innumerable variations.

district is consistently at a central location, a point of maximum accessibility.

3. Adjacent to an expanding central business district and along rail, river, and shore lines are areas of deteriorated housing, cut-rate commercial outfits, rescue missions, and wholesale and storage facilities.

4. Single-family housing, more costly and in better repair, tends to be at the outer reaches of the corporate area with apartment houses, dual or duplex housing, and tenements at points successively nearer the center—nearer commercial and industrial uses.

5. The relative status of various ethnic groups is registered in their differing capacity to compete for preferred residential areas.
6. The growth of human settlements tends to be from the original, central settlement outwards, with population and supporting institutions pressing toward the peripheries.
7. Where movement or transiency is greatest and where, in consequence, relationships are ·unstable, a social order is ill-defined and ill-sustained.
8. In deteriorated residential districts which are alone available to poor migrants and minorities low in status, having slight opportunity to achieve the goals of middle-class America as described and diffused through the mass media—in such districts the social order tends to be integrated through deviant norms and rates of illegal and aberrant activities are high.
9. Increases in number of persons in a human settlement entail increased diversity of belief and behavior leading to the substitution of formal (governmental) controls for the informal controls of custom and tradition.
10. This spatial patterning of people and their behaviors develops as men accommodate through competitive processes to their environment.

Burgess's paper presenting the zonal theory of urban settlement[15] stimulated a series of inquiries into the spatial patterning of human settlements. As a model of land use in urban settlements Burgess had suggested, first a zone embracing the central business district (see zone 1, in Figure 7–3). Here are the services and businesses requiring maximum accessibility to the largest possible population; and the center of a circle is the point that minimizes the stretch of its radii. (But of course the ecological center need not be—and seldom if ever, is—the geographical center.) Empty at night, it is the daytime focal point of urban settlements. This zone, as Professor Earl Johnson points out, is the point of transport terminals, the locus of the goods and service market and, especially, the money market.[16] From this zone radiate directives to and controls over the hinterland. From this zone in Chicago[17] 25 percent of the local telephone calls, 33 percent of the regional calls, are charged to the less than 6 percent of the city's telephone accounts located in this zone. It is the

[15] Ernest W. Burgess, "The Growth of the city," in Robert E. Park and Ernest W. Burgess, *The City* (Chicago: University of Chicago Press, 1925).

[16] Earl S. Johnson, "The Function of the Central Business District in the Metropolitan Community," in Paul Hatt and Albert J. Reiss, Jr. (eds.), *Cities and Society* (New York: Free Press of Glencoe, Inc., 1957), pp. 248–59.

[17] The date for these figures is not given. It was probably in the late 1930's.

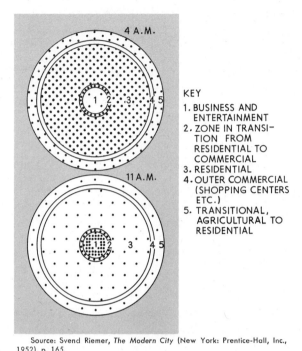

KEY
1. BUSINESS AND ENTERTAINMENT
2. ZONE IN TRANSI-
   TION FROM
   RESIDENTIAL TO
   COMMERCIAL
3. RESIDENTIAL
4. OUTER COMMERCIAL
   (SHOPPING CENTERS
   ETC.)
5. TRANSITIONAL,
   AGRICULTURAL TO
   RESIDENTIAL

Source: Svend Riemer, *The Modern City* (New York: Prentice-Hall, Inc., 1952), p. 165.

FIG. 7–3. Urban population distribution: different hours of the day (schematic).

political as well as the financial and commercial control center. And it is the locus of narrowly defined professional specialties and esoteric services.

The second zone, the zone in transition, is the one being gradually preempted by the functions of the central business district. Since such uses are more intense than residential uses and command larger rentals, owners of land in the zone of transition tend to withhold any major investment in their properties, minimize maintenance costs, and await the day when the encroachments of business uses will enable profitable sale or rental. In the meantime, as an ill-maintained and deteriorating area it has marginal uses for warehouses, cheap transient residences, is the locus of hobohemias and of Rescue Missions for homeless men and wayward girls.

Beyond this, an area of immigrant settlement provides tenement homes, cold-water walk-ups to the newly arrived and the economically impotent. Encapsulated in this area and the zone of transition and bordering the central business district are the Black Belts and the Harlems. For the Negro, of course, the cultural fact of prejudice leads to limited education and occupational skills lowering his capacity to compete for space. And so he is filtered into the least desirable residential areas, showing up on ecological maps in tightly bunched and segregated clusters (see Figures 7–4 and 7–5).

While ties of church, language, and common status may cement the bonds making for a cohesive group among immigrants, the same

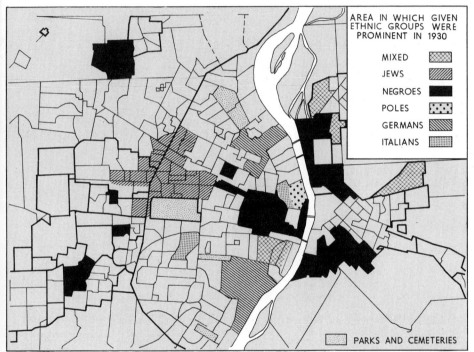

AREA IN WHICH GIVEN
ETHNIC GROUPS WERE
PROMINENT IN 1930

MIXED

JEWS

NEGROES

POLES

GERMANS

ITALIANS

PARKS AND CEMETERIES

Source: From *The American City* by S. A. Queen and D. B. Carpenter. Copyright 1953. McGraw-Hill Book Company. Used by permission.

FIG. 7-4.   Ethnic groups in metropolitan St. Louis.

is not true for the rural-urban migrant. And even in the case of the immigrant, the strain is to forsake the past, to become assimilated in order to get onward and upward as these directions are defined in the host culture. And so this area, along with the zone of transition, tends to claim the rootless, the mobile, those with tentative and tenuous positions and relationships. Such areas seem to give rise to different but related social conditions: cohesive groups whose members share a depressed destiny and who express themselves,

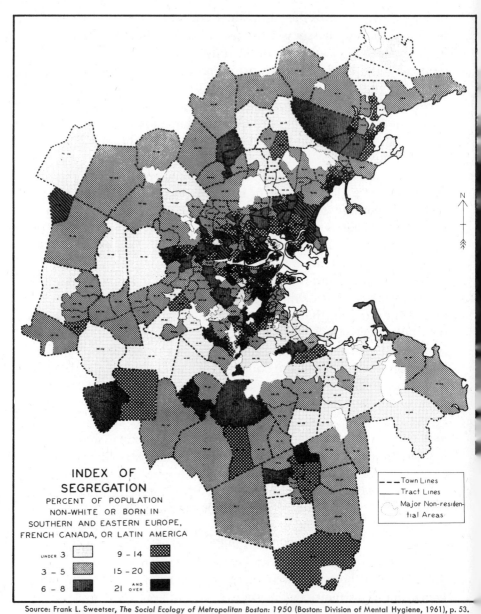

INDEX OF
SEGREGATION
PERCENT OF POPULATION
NON-WHITE OR BORN IN
SOUTHERN AND EASTERN EUROPE,
FRENCH CANADA, OR LATIN AMERICA

UNDER 3		9 – 14	
3 – 5		15 – 20	
6 – 8		21 AND OVER	

Town Lines
Tract Lines
Major Non-residen-
tial Areas

Source: Frank L. Sweetser, *The Social Ecology of Metropolitan Boston: 1950* (Boston: Division of Mental Hygiene, 1961), p. 53.

FIG. 7-5. Segregation in Metropolitan Boston, by census tracts, 1950.

occupy themselves, in illegal or illicit conduct; and a second social outcome, the normlessness that goes with bondlessness expressing itself in unusually high rates of mental disorder and suicide. Typical data on these dual outcomes are offered in Figures 7–6 through 7–8.

Beyond these first three zones lie those of apartment dwellers, the single-family homes farther out, shading into suburbia, truck farming, peripheral rural slums, the dairy belt, and cereal farming.

Following Burgess' lead in trying to uncover a social pattern emerging on the basis of an unconsciously contrived spatial pattern, Ernest Mowrer inquired into the distribution of urban family types.[18] According to his scheme, zone 1 is the nonfamily area. Principally devoted to commerce, it has few permanent residents, some hotel dwellers plus a few in old family homes long since engulfed by the spread of the city. Zone 2 he characterizes as that of the "emancipated family," with liaisons casually entered into and left, typically childless, the relationship as transient as the population of this area. In the third zone he finds the patriarchal family, a type linked with the large proportion of foreign-born whites—often of rural background—living here. In the fourth zone, the apartment-house area, he speaks of the equalitarian family, one in which wife, as well as husband, is likely to be a clerical or professional worker. This small, or childless family might be described by Dorothy Parker's squib: "although in wedlock/he and she go/ each maintains/ a separate ego." Finally at a farther remove, in zone five and in suburbia, Mowrer speaks of the matricentric family. It is mother-centered both because of the characteristic absence of a commuting father and because of the civic and educational concerns of relatively well-educated middle-class mothers. This mother is chauffeur, tutor to the children, cook and housekeeper, PTA participant, chancellor of the family exchequer, responsible for family social obligations, civic representative for the family, shopper. She is, in short, executive officer in a complex family operation: hence the term "matricentric family."

Such a scheme—nonfamily, emancipated family, patriarchal, equalitarian, and matricentric—is not precise. But it does help us recognize that in the process of man's accommodations to his

---

[18] Ernest R. Mowrer, *Family Disorganization* (Chicago: University of Chicago Press, 1927). See chap. v on "The Ecology of Family Disorganization."

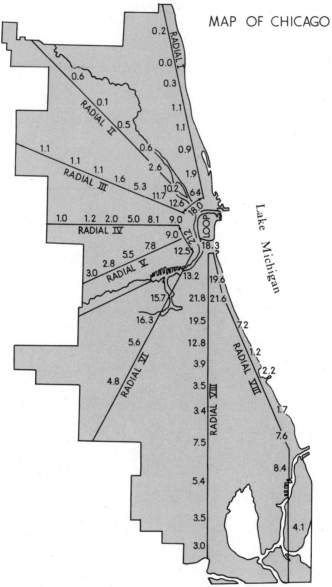

Source: Clifford R. Shaw and others, *Delinquency Areas* (Chicago: University of Chicago Press, (c) 1942 by The University of Chicago, p. 69. By permission.

FIG. 7–6. Delinquency rates in representative mile square areas in Chicago, 1927.

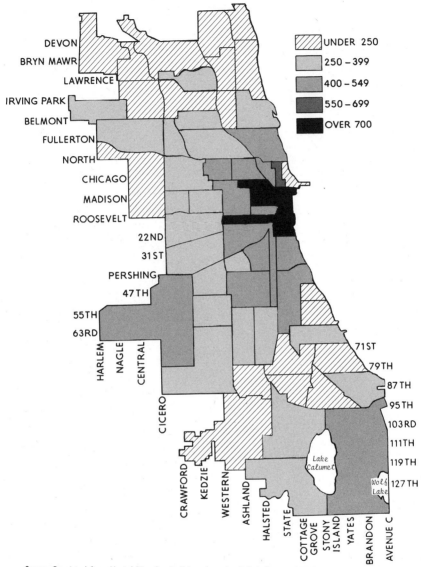

Source: Reprinted from *Mental Disorders in Urban Areas* by R. E. L. Faris and H. W. Dunham by permission of the University of Chicago Press. (c) 1939 by The University of Chicago.

FIG. 7-7. Distribution of schizophrenia cases in Chicago from 1922 to 1931.

habitat, competitive forces distribute persons, their roles and relationships, in space, in a patterned, a nonrandom fashion.

Other of men's social arrangements adapt to his shifting, spatial distribution. Urban churches tend to follow the outward, expansive movement of population which accompanies the growth of the city.

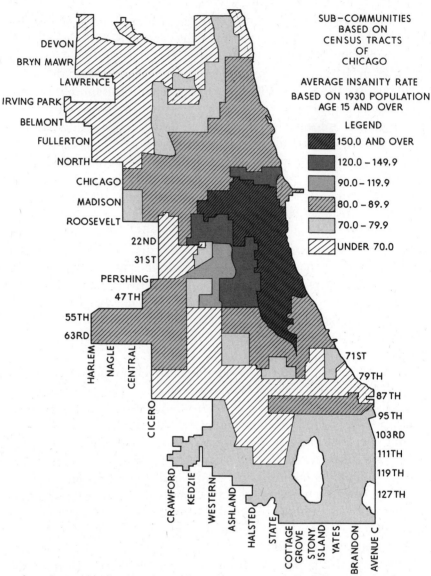

SUB–COMMUNITIES
BASED ON
CENSUS TRACTS
OF
CHICAGO

AVERAGE INSANITY RATE
BASED ON 1930 POPULATION
AGE 15 AND OVER

LEGEND

150.0 AND OVER
120.0 – 149.9
90.0 – 119.9
80.0 – 89.9
70.0 – 79.9
UNDER 70.0

Source: Reprinted from *Mental Disorders in Urban Areas* by R. E. L. Faris and H. W. Dunham by permission of the University of Chicago Press. (c) 1939 by The University of Chicago.

FIG. 7–8.   Rates of mental disorders in districts of Chicago, 1922–34.

This is illustrated in Figure 7–10. Or, if we raise the question as to type of religious organization, as Mowrer did for family organization, we find spatially discriminable types.[19] In the central city, aside

[19] These comments on the spatial distribution of religious organizations are drawn from E. K. Wilson's study, *"Criteria of Urbanism Applied to Religion in Chicago,"*

from the "First" churches that remain as monuments and centers for special services—in Boston, Trinity and Tremont Temple; St. Patrick's and St. John's in New York; St. Mary's, the Methodist Temple in Chicago—there are two types of religious, or quasi-religious, organizations. First, there is the platform church, providing eloquent speakers (not necessarily clergymen), good music, free parking, and informed discussions of domestic and international issues that are, as are all issues, instinct with moral dilemmas. The second type characteristic of the central city is the cult, the fringe or splinter group. The appeal is to a few, widely dispersed communicants for whom such a central location, like the mean $(\overline{X})$, minimizes distance between them. Spiritualist groups, national societies of healing, near- and far-eastern cults, and fundamentalists meet here for their services. The future is divined through crystal balls. Animate ouija boards and ectoplasmic wraiths give answers and assurance. Names unusual in the roster of traditional American churches are seen here: Christadelphians, l'Église Évangelique Française de Chicago, the Christian Catholic Apostolic Church, Fraternal Spiritualist Church, the Unity Fellowship of Practical Christianity, Rosicrucians, etc.

In Burgess' zone of transition the most characteristic religious organization is the mission church or rescue mission. The missions advertise with catchy signs and slogans, with electric bulbs in cross-formation, with loudspeakers, and often with a man at the entrance issuing personal invitations to passersby. Food and shelter are important drawing features. Mission churches, Salvation Army posts, Volunteers of America, and similar groups appeal to a transient constituency through a fundamentalist theology and agrarian symbols (Shepherd, blood of the lamb) that suggest the rural past of these rootless wanderers in the inhospitable city.

In zone 3, the area of workingmen's homes, the typical religious organization in the past has been the Catholic church. Here, at the several masses, there is likely to be standing room only. The Catholic church with its universal rites (and its universal language) was better able to minister to the needs of the many immigrants who moved into such areas in American cities, especially after the World War I. Here also, we find the foreign-language churches established for non-English-speaking immigrants. Chicago had more than sev-

an unpublished Master's Thesis (Chicago: The University of Chicago, 1942), pp. 107–98.

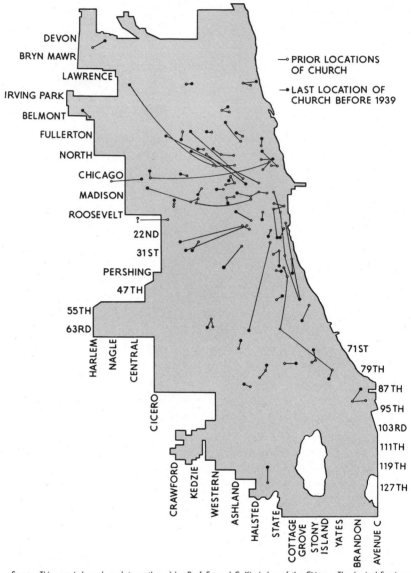

DEVON
BRYN MAWR
LAWRENCE
IRVING PARK
BELMONT
FULLERTON
NORTH
CHICAGO
MADISON
ROOSEVELT
22ND
31ST
PERSHING
47TH
55TH
63RD

○─ PRIOR LOCATIONS
       OF CHURCH

─► LAST LOCATION OF
       CHURCH BEFORE 1939

71ST
79TH
87TH
95TH
103RD
111TH
119TH
127TH

HARLEM
NAGLE
CENTRAL
CICERO
CRAWFORD
KEDZIE
WESTERN
ASHLAND
HALSTED
STATE
COTTAGE GROVE
STONY ISLAND
YATES
BRANDON
AVENUE C

Source: This map is based on data gathered by Prof. Samuel C. Kincheloe of the Chicago Theological Seminary. Some of these churches merged, died, or disbanded. The larger dot only indicates last location prior to 1939.

FIG. 7–9. Movements of fifty-seven Baptist churches from date of organization to 1939.

enty such churches in 1940 ministering to various nationalities ranging, alphabetically, from Armenian, Assyrian, and Bohemian to Roumanian, Russian Slovak, and Spanish.[20]

---

[20] Chicago Church Federation, *Chicago Church Federation Yearbook, 1940* (Chicago, 1940), p. 94.

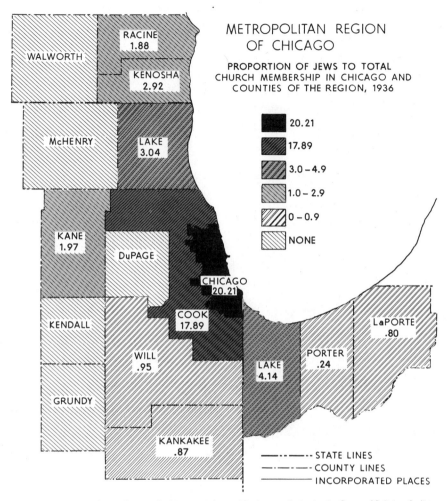

METROPOLITAN REGION
OF CHICAGO

PROPORTION OF JEWS TO TOTAL
CHURCH MEMBERSHIP IN CHICAGO AND
COUNTIES OF THE REGION, 1936

■	20.21
▨	17.89
▧	3.0 – 4.9
▦	1.0 – 2.9
▨	0 – 0.9
▨	NONE

WALWORTH

RACINE
1.88

KENOSHA
2.92

McHENRY

LAKE
3.04

KANE
1.97

DuPAGE

CHICAGO
20.21

KENDALL

COOK
17.89

LaPORTE
.80

WILL
.95

LAKE
4.14

PORTER
.24

GRUNDY

KANKAKEE
.87

——··——·· STATE LINES
——·——·— COUNTY LINES
———————— INCORPORATED PLACES

Source: Map based upon data supplied in a special prepublication compilation by the Census of Religious Bodies,
U.S. Bureau of the Census.

FIG. 7-10. Proportion of Jews to total church membership in Chicago and
counties of the region, 1936.

Of religious behavior in the apartment house area (the zone of
Mowrer's equalitarian families) we know little. It has been assumed, perhaps accurately, that this area "selects" a relatively large
portion of the religiously uncommitted or indifferent. "The minister
who must make calls in a large apartment house, often receiving a
rebuff through the speaking-tube, has a problem which the small-
town pastor never faces."[21] To such people the church can offer little

---

[21] Murray Leiffer, *City and Church in Transition* (Chicago: Willett, Clark and
Co., 1938), p. 13.

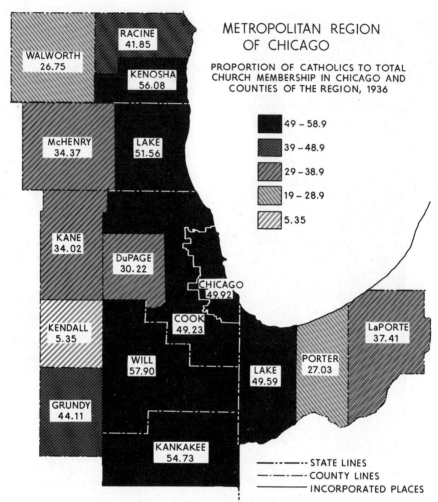

FIG. 7–11. Proportion of Catholics to total church membership in Chicago and counties of the region, 1936.

Source: Map based upon data supplied in a special prepublication compilation by the Census of Religious Bodies, U.S. Bureau of the Census.

in the way of material or social services. Those who can afford to live in this area tend to be among the more privileged in education and material things. They have probably "tuned out" orthodox theology, are not responsive to supernatural sanctions, and tend toward what Niebuhr called a "prudential morality" that determines the good by its payoff.

Finally, in the farther reaches of the urban settlement we find the

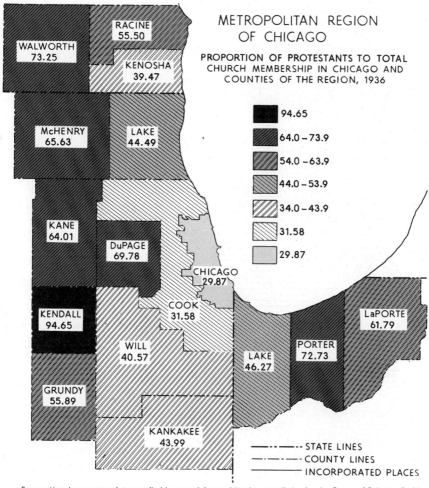

FIG. 7–12. Proportion of Protestants to total church membership in Chicago and counties of the region, 1936.

traditional Protestant groups operating with more or less success in relatively cohesive and self-conscious communities. The Protestant outer rim of Chicago's metropolitan area is shown in Figure 7–12. The urban-industrial Catholic center and, especially, the concentration of Jews in the central city are shown in Figures 7–10 and 7–11. Once again we see here an unplanned but highly patterned distribution of social characteristics.

PATTERNS OF CHANGE IN SPATIAL
DISTRIBUTION AND SOCIAL STRUCTURE

This distribution of social traits is not a fixed matter. The human settlement grows from the center outward. In its expanding thrust there is a predictable change in land use and occupancy, a predictable change in the spatial and the social patterns. To put it very generally, more intense land use/occupancy tends to drive out less intense. Residential uses displace agricultural uses. Multiunit dwellings displace single-unit dwellings, commercial and industrial uses displace residential uses. In the realm of plant and animal ecology we say that one species invades and displaces another's domain. When we refer to a Negro invasion of a hitherto segregated white district we use the word in the same sense. But here, of course, the competitive space-seeking process is modified by the culturally given stereotypes that condition people's behavior. The process of invasion is most readily accomplished, where residence is at issue, by those groups that are culturally most similar to the population hitherto residing there. Thus, distance from the center of the city, or ease in invading remoter areas is an index of the assimilability of a foreign group and its likeness to the culture of the host.

If we think of the changing spatial and social structure of a human settlement as impulses moving toward peripheral points, we may also conceive of the regular replenishing of the city's population as a series of waves originating in rural places and setting toward the city. The migratory succession of persons moving cityward was noted more than seventy-five years ago by E. G. Ravenstein. Having tested Ravenstein's laws of migration in the United States, the sociologist T. Lynn Smith concluded that, as formulated below, they describe correctly this process of successive occupancy:

1. Most migrants move only a short distance.
2. The process of absorption is like this: inhabitants of the immediately surrounding area flock to the city, creating gaps in the rural population which are filled by persons from more remote districts, which in turn creates other gaps, until the attractive force of the city makes itself felt step by step in the most remote corners of the nation.

3. Each main current of migration sets up a compensating counter-current and the process of dispersal is the reverse of the process of absorption.
4. Long-distance migrants go immediately to the great centers of trade and industry.[22]

Especially among superrural and depressed groups, the man often moves alone, followed later by his wife and family. Often this is a leapfrog process of the sort implied by Ravenstein, with the migrant moving toward an urban center in successive stages. In the process he may stay with friends or relatives who have already established beachheads. In the Belgian Congo, for example, the movement toward the city of Stanleyville has been shown to be of this order (see Table 7–2).

TABLE 7–2

Number of Moves Made by Migrants in Converging on Stanleyville, Belgian Congo, by Sex, in Percent

NUMBER OF MOVES	MALES	FEMALES	TOTAL
1	23.7	41.9	32.1
2	33.8	32.4	33.2
3	21.2	13.9	17.8
4	10.0	6.4	8.3
5 or more	11.3	5.4	8.6
	100.0	100.0	100.0
N = 1,902	1,632	3,534

Source: V. G. Pons, N. Xydias, and P. Clements, *Social Effects of Urbanization in Africa South of Sahara* (Paris: UNESCO, 1956), p. 257.

SYMBIOTIC TIES BETWEEN HUMAN COMMUNITIES

Here, then, we have predictable changes in a spatial pattern and the concomitant social order, both within the urban settlement and in the environing region. But beyond this, the social order is

---

[22] T. Lynn Smith, *The Sociology of Rural Life* (3d ed.; New York: Harper & Bros., 1953). The original statement by E. G. Ravenstein was published as "The Laws of Migration," in the *Journal of the Royal Statistical Society*, Vol. LXVIII (1885), pp. 167–235.

conditioned by the development of unplanned interregional and intercommunity relationships. The web of social life, to modify Darwin's phrase, embraces regions and nations. If the decisions of myriad individuals in their competitive struggle is registered in a structure of settlement, so are the linkages of these structures registered in larger symbiotic networks. Without conscious planning, a division of labor and a hierarchy of influence develops between interlocked communities. A network of communities becomes integrated, some dominant, others subordinate in a complex set of interlocking functions.

> McKenzie used the language of ecology to describe the competitive struggle *among great cities* for dominance and the adjustment process by which those that lost out in the process tended either to become integrated to the dominant metropolis by specialization or to die out, a symbiotic competition for survival similar to that in plant and animal "communities."[23]

Now to get some notion of this intercommunity network, of metropolitan dominance and integration among southern cities, Vance and Smith studied twenty-nine metropolitan areas in the South, ranking them on six indexes. (The indexes used were (1) wholesale sales, (2) business services receipts, a measure of specialized services used in the given city, (3) number of branch offices linked with a city, (4) retail sales, (5) bank clearings—as an index of business activity, and (6) value added by manufacturing. The array of 29 values on a given index was used to strike the mean ($\overline{X}$) and calculate the standard deviation. A score was calculated (called a Z score) for each city on each index, and these were combined to give an overall score so that the twenty-nine cities could be ranked according to the extent to which they served these six metropolitan functions.[24]

---

[23] Reprinted with permission of The Free Press from "Metropolitan Dominance and Integration," by Rupert B. Vance and Sara Smith, in *Cities and Society* by Paul K. Hatt and Albert J. Reiss, Jr. (eds). Copyright 1951, 1957 by The Free Press, a corporation. Reference is to R. B. McKenzie, *The Metropolitan Community* (New York: McGraw-Hill Book Co., 1933). Italics mine.

[24] **An Aside on Methods: the Use of Z Scores**

What is a Z score? First let us put another question: How can one combine, for a given city, scores on these six indexes? Isn't this rather like trying to combine can openers, partridges, and blubber? What have they in common? How can one add stars and starfish, or multiply limes by limousines? Impossible, of course. We must ask: what do these six scores have in common that *can* be combined? For each city we can measure the difference between its score and

The average Z scores, giving us a ranking on the extent to which these cities serve metropolitan functions, are given in column (2), Table 7–3. We see that this regional intercommunity web is maintained through a gradation of dominance, two cities serving as regional nuclei and linking their subdominant communities with other regional networks through their focal communities (see Figure 7–13). There emerges, that is to say, and in quite uncontrived fashion, an organization of relationships and activities stemming from intercommunity competition. The relationship between the size of the population, on the one hand; and dominance or high fulfillment of metropolitan functions on the other is clear from a comparison of columns (2) and (3). Let us take advantage of these two rank-ordered series to calculate the Spearman rank order coefficient discussed earlier in this chapter. This measure of the relationship turns out to be .84.

Thus inter- as well as intrasettlement patterns develop through time. Commenting on the figure, above, Vance and Smith write:

> . . . the constellation of cities has been moored to territory so that it is possible to trace the major lines of integration. The great Appalachian barrier set the spatial pattern early in the South's history. Transportation lanes run south to north, toward New York in the east and toward Chicago west of the mountains. The Dallas–Fort Worth metropolitan region is oriented to the Chicago–New York axis through St. Louis and Kansas City. On this map-like diagram, one can also see the vacuum out of which Memphis was able to carve a hinterland. The orientation of the South's great ports—like Houston and New Orleans —to intercoastal traffic is indicated by broken lines.[25]

❀   ❀   ❀   ❀

I've been trying to show how the social order rests on a framework of temporal and spatial arrangements that condition the interaction, the relationships of human beings. Both within and between communities there emerges, on the basis of unplanned, competitive adaptation to the environment, a routinizing in time, a

---

the average score for all twenty-nine cities expressed in standard (deviation) units. Using the mean ($\overline{X}$) as a benchmark each city gets a standard rank among all twenty-nine, on each of these six indexes. Thus, on wholesale sales, we take the value of such sales in Atlanta, subtract the average value of wholesale sales for all twenty-nine cities and express this difference in standard deviation units. Z, then, $= (X - \overline{X})/s$. And the sum of the Z's/6 gives us a combined score that ranks a given city relative to all others on a common trait: distance above or below the average.

[25] Hatt & Reiss, op. cit., p. 117.

TABLE 7–3

Cities of Over 100,000 in the South, Ranked by Size and Metropolitan Function: and Calculation of the Spearman Rank-Order Correlation Coefficient for These Two Variables

(1) CITY	(2) RANK SCORE ON METRO- POLITAN FUNC- TION	(3) RANK SCORE ON SIZE	(4) RANK ORDER MET FN	(5) RANK ORDER SIZE	(6) D	(7) D²
SECOND ORDER METROPOLISES						
Atlanta	9.91	6.67	1	3	− 2	4
Dallas	9.71	6.38	2	4	− 2	4
THIRD ORDER METROPOLISES						
Houston	8.10	7.43	3	1	− 2	4
New Orleans	7.36	6.77	4	2	2	4
Memphis	6.62	5.67	5	9	− 4	16
Louisville	6.43	6.18	6	5	1	1
Birmingham	5.94	6.07	7	6	1	1
SUBDOMINANTS with METROPOLITAN CHARACTERISTICS						
Richmond	5.34	4.83	8	14	− 6	36
Forth Worth	5.24	5.00	9	12	− 3	9
Oklahoma City	5.02	4.81	10	15	− 5	25
*Miami	4.90	5.71	11	8	3	9
Charlotte	4.80	4.11	12	22	−10	100
Jacksonville	4.79	4.70	13	17	− 4	16
Tulsa	4.60	4.40	14	18	− 4	16
Nashville	4.59	4.79	15	16	− 1	1
Little Rock	4.54	4.09	16	23	− 7	49
*San Antonio	4.48	5.75	17	7	10	100
*Norfolk-Portsmouth	4.42	5.28	18	10	8	64
El Paso	4.38	4.12	19	21	− 2	4
SUBDOMINANTS						
Tampa-St. Petersburg	4.18	5.26	20	11	9	81
Chattanooga	4.11	4.38	21	19	2	4
Knoxville	3.84	4.88	22	13	8	64
Shreveport	3.62	4.00	23	24	− 1	1
Mobile	3.54	4.29	24	20	4	16
Savannah	3.46	3.87	25	28	− 3	9
Corpus Christi	3.30	3.94	26	25	1	1
Montgomery	3.25	3.79	27	29	− 2	4
Baton Rouge	3.25	3.90	28	27	1	1
Austin	3.19	3.92	29	26	3	9
						$\Sigma D^2 = 653$

$$\text{and } r_s = 1 - \frac{6\Sigma D^2}{N(N^2 - 1)} = 1 - \frac{6(653)}{29(29^2 - 1)} = 1 - \frac{3,918}{24,360} = .84$$

Source: Adapted with permission of The Free Press from "Metropolitan Dominance and Integration," by Rupert B. Vance and Sara Smith, in Cities and Society by Paul K. Hatt and Albert J. Reiss, Jr. (eds.), p. 114. Copyright 1951, 1957 by The Free Press, a corporation.

* Miami because of its resort function and San Antonio and Norfolk-Portsmouth because of military installations probably rank somewhat higher than their basic metropolitan function would place them. They are essentially Sub-dominants.

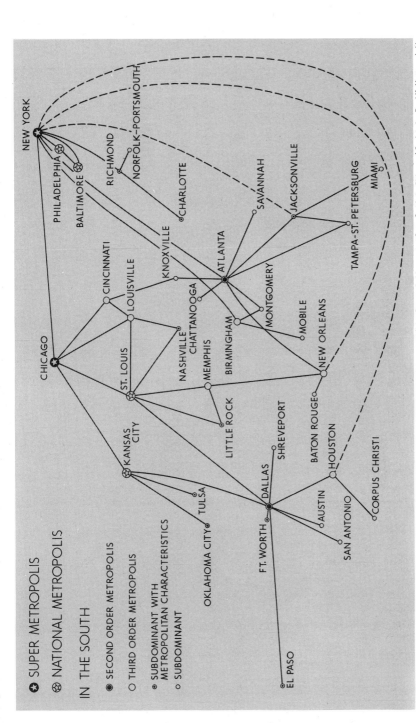

SUPER METROPOLIS

NATIONAL METROPOLIS

IN THE SOUTH

● SECOND ORDER METROPOLIS

○ THIRD ORDER METROPOLIS

◉ SUBDOMINANT WITH
   METROPOLITAN CHARACTERISTICS

○ SUBDOMINANT

Source: Reprinted with permission of The Free Press from "Metropolitan Dominance and Integration," by Rupert B. Vance and Sara Smith, in Cities and Society by Paul K. Hatt and Albert J. Reiss, Jr. (eds.), p. 118. Copyright 1951, 1957 by The Free Press, a corporation.

FIG. 7-13. Metropolitan organization of the South, with orders of dominance and major lines of integration.

patterning in space. None of us is fully aware (except, perhaps, in a poetic sense—"I am involved in mankind") of the vast reach of this network of interdependence. So the sociologist borrows from plant and animal ecology the term "symbiosis" to describe these relationships. He sets himself the task of exploring the hidden sources and unrecognized connections of the social order as competitive processes sort people out in time and space.

Minimizing time-cost distance, populations tend to gather, as Cooley and others point out, at "breaks in transportation." (In the past, as a quick circuit of the globe suggests, these spots have often been at breaks between sea and land or river transport: Tokyo, Osaka, Yokohama, Peiping at the Huang ho and Yellow Sea, Shanghai, meaning literally, on the sea, Singapore, Rangoon, Calcutta and Bombay, Cairo and Alexandria, Athens on the Piraeus, Rome on the Tiber, Paris on the Seine, London on the Thames, New York and Chicago at their breaks in transportation.)

Subsequently, with division of labor, comes differentiation in space and time: differentiation in types of land use, types of activities, and types of belief, the moral order reflecting, and reflected in, the spatial order. Neighborhoods become relatively homogeneous. Within them people resemble one another more nearly than they resemble those of other neighborhoods. Frequency of encounter is increased within, decreased without. Thus a patterning of land use emerges, of residential types, ethnic, familial, religious types. Nor are deviant behaviors randomly distributed in human settlements. Vice, crime, and delinquency follow a spatial pattern as do mental disorders. Even variations in birth and death rates are spatially differentiated.

But space and time, let us be clear, are clues, not causes. They are clues to the culturally conditioned competition among men for a favorable position in goods and status. The unplanned patterns of human relationships that emerge, registered in space and time, may be viewed as substructure of the social order.

If time and space are fundamental categories in analyzing the social order so, also, are numbers and their composition. It is to this matter of demographic phenomena—population, its growth and composition—that we turn in the following chapter.

SELECTED SUPPLEMENTARY READINGS

*CLAUSEN, JOHN A. AND KOHN, MELVIN L.   "The Ecological Approach in Social Psychiatry," *American Journal of Sociology*, 1954, pp. 140–51.

*FIREY, WALTER.   "Sentiment and Symbolism as Ecological Variables," *American Sociological Review*, 1945, pp. 140–48.

*GRIMSHAW, ALLEN D.   "Urban Racial Violence in the United States: Changing Ecological Considerations," *American Journal of Sociology*, 1960, pp. 109–19.

*HAWLEY, AMOS.   *Human Ecology*. New York: Ronald Press Co., 1950.

*————.   "Ecology and Human Ecology," *Social Forces*, Vol. 22 (May, 1944), pp. 398–405.

*HELM, JUNE.   "The Ecological Approach in Anthropology," *American Journal of Sociology*, 1962, pp. 630–39.

*MACK, RAYMOND W.   "Ecological Patterns in an Industrial Shop," *Social Forces*, 1954, pp. 351–56.

PARK, ROBERT E.   *Human Communities*. New York: The Free Press of Glencoe, Inc., 1952.

THEODORSON, GEORGE A. (ed.).   *Studies in Human Ecology*. Evanston, Ill.: Row, Peterson, 1961.

---

* Articles marked with an asterisk are available as reprints from the college division of the Bobbs-Merrill Company, Indianapolis, Indiana.

Chapter 8

The Demographic Substructure of Human Relationships

How do growth and composition of population reflect and influence the ordering of human relationships?

It makes sense, in one way, to think of demographic phenomena (the growth and composition of populations) as substructure of the social order. For birth and death are biological events, and life itself is a precondition of socially differentiated forms of living. Or in the case of migration we are dealing with a physical event (the movement of the body through space) which is antecedent to the social and cultural effects on the losing and receiving communities. Population matters are substructure, then, first in the sense that biological and physical events are fundamental, and second because the input of newcomers must *precede* the socialization processes that transform a new organism into a human being about to be integrated into some social order. Finally, demographic phenomena are basic since a regular input of individuals is required to man the ship—of state, or any other sector of the system; to staff a business, a factory or school, a gang, department, or community.

But on the other hand it would be misleading to conceive the link between biological and social events as a one-way street. There are social antecedents that go before those biological outcomes that are registered in birth and death rates. We have only to think of Catholic and communist doctrines which agree, for quite different reasons, in opposing contraceptive techniques that would limit

Input and output in the social order.

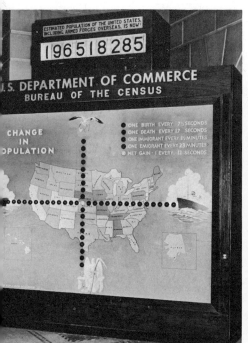

U. S. Department of Commerce, Bureau of the Census

Magnum Photo, by Ernst Haas

Courtesy, Abbott Laboratories

population growth. So it is that births, deaths, and migration may be seen as outcomes, direct or indirect, of a given social and cultural context. Demographic characteristics reflect the nature of the social order as well as setting conditions that must be met through social arrangements. So in India a rigidly stratified society, low levels of literacy, a highly developed religious life, a weak central government, subservience to foreign interests, subsistence agriculture— these social characteristics were in part, in the past, both cause and effect of high birth and death rates.[1] Population characteristics may be more properly viewed, then, as in between social antecedents and social consequences.

And so this chapter is chiefly addressed to these two problems in sociology: (1) What conditions are set for the social order by demographic phenomena? and (2) How do demographic phenomena reflect conditions of the social order?

We turn first to the general effects upon society of changes in birth, death, and migration rates; for replacement of parts is a requisite for maintaining a system. And we shall consider briefly, in passing, the disruptions of the system occasioned by over- and underreplacement. But the problem of system maintenance is more complex than this. For if we look at the occupational structure of a community, its division into men and women, religious distinctions, such as Protestant, Catholic, and Jew, categories like Negro and white, it becomes clear that the problem is not simply replacement but finely differentiated replacement of parts having different weight and meaning for the system. (How do we maintain the requisite number of shepherds? Senator McCarran saw to the importing of Basques just as previous statesmen had seen to the importing of Chinese for unskilled labor on western railroads. How do we maintain the supply of physicians? Whether consciously or

---

[1] The interplay of demographic and social factors is splendidly brought out by Kingsley Davis in his *The Population of India and Pakistan* (Princeton, N.J.: Princeton University Press, 1951).

Demographic studies typically use social phenomena for one variable, dependent or independent and demographic phenomena for the other. Since births, deaths, numbers, density, migratory movements have sources and consequences in aspects of the social order, the sociologist is disposed to consider population phenomena either as intrinsically social, in themselves, or as indexes of significant social variables. I take the latter position, making two observations. First, demographic data are particularly potent as indexes, because they point to phenomena indispensable for maintaining a social order and because they deal with events of central importance to the person. (They have high social and psychological relevance.) Second, using these data as indexes, any complete sociological study must at least acknowledge *both* the social sources and social outcomes that flank the demographic event.

otherwise we encourage the upward mobility of middle- and lower-class males, etc.) Finally we turn to the significance of numbers, density, and heterogeneity as they affect the social structure.

Then we must look at the other side of the coin: the reflection of the social order in population data. For population not only has effects as it feeds newcomers into a social structure. It also *reflects* certain latent aspects of the social structure helping us to anticipate future social conditions. Let me repeat: from the sociologist's point of view the appropriate way of viewing vital phenomena is to see them as representing variables lying in between their social and cultural antecedents and their social and cultural consequences. Here I will draw on the discussion by Davis and Blake[2] to suggest the many points at which the social order sets the conditions for fertility and, therefore, for its own maintenance. And Mr. Nathan Keyfitz will help us see how fertility (family size) is both consequence and indicator of cultural diffusion.[3]

DEMOGRAPHIC CONDITIONS AFFECTING THE SOCIAL ORDER

The crucial notion in understanding the link between demographic and social phenomena is this: an input of human organisms (presently to be socialized) is essential to staff the system—i.e., for the maintenance of any social order. And it is not simply that people—or, more accurately, culture carriers—must be fed into the system: they must be fed into it in appropriate numbers, balancing losses from death and emigration with births and immigration. Furthermore they must be fed into appropriate sectors of the system; for how they are to be socialized depends in large measure upon whom they are born to. For as we saw in our discussion of class, patterns of rearing still depend in marked measure upon birth. So it is that birth and death, immigration and emigration become important considerations for the maintenance of the group.

When we have a fair match between input and output we have a basic condition for a stable system. When a community's population grows markedly and rapidly—or declines—strains are introduced. These are periods of rapid change. The contrary system, a stable

[2] Kingsley Davis and Judith Blake, "Social Structure and Fertility: An Analytic Framework," *Economic Development and Cultural Change,* published by The University of Chicago Press, Vol. IV, No. 3 (April, 1956), pp. 211–35.

[3] Nathan Keyfitz, "A Factorial Arrangement of Comparisons of Family Size," *American Journal of Sociology,* Vol. LVIII (March, 1953), pp. 470–79.

social order, can be oversimply represented by a football team. A condition for its continuance as a group is the regular replacement of lost parts. There are eleven distinct roles (barring for the moment the scores of satellite roles now involved in this institutionalized form of tribal recreation. Were we to classify ends, tackles, guards, and halfbacks together we might settle for seven distinct roles.) Fatigue or injuries, like deaths in the larger social order, *require replacements, part for part.* If this proves impossible, the team, as we say, falls apart. The group is destroyed.

Similarly our labor force in American society requires regular replacements for its maintenance. But beyond this, if the order is to sustain itself, as is, we must have a regular recruitment and re-placement of Catholics, Protestants, and Jews; Negroes and whites; old, middle-aged and young; men and women; foreign- and native-born; the law-abiding and criminals of various sorts. . . . To take the last category as an example, if we are to maintain that web of relationships represented in a police force of given size, insurance salesmen and the customers they protect against losses from theft; the Pinkerton people and sundry "private eye" outfits; all those employed in the lock, bolt and safe business; tool and weapon, car and radio manufacturers; lawyers, judges, and the clerical apparatus of the courts, and the taxpayer who supports them; prison personnel and the sociologist specializing in criminology—if we are to main-tain the relationships implied by these role labels, then we must have a regular input of criminals into the social order.[4]

This immediately suggests that a social system is never literally maintained. Quite aside from unplanned change, we are always trying to alter certain aspects of it deemed by some to be undesira-ble. Stability of the system is not necessarily to be viewed as a good in itself. But from the sociologist's point of view, the unreal condition of a stable system is a most useful heuristic device (a thinking tool). For it provides a base point, a point of comparison. We can then ask the question: how much does what we observe differ from what would have occurred under conditions of stability, of a balanced input and output? And then the second and intriguing question, what accounts for this difference?

---

[4] Regular replacement of our criminal population is, of course, different from sheer replacement of bodies through birth. But the former entails the latter. This is why, as I've been saying, the sociologist must concern himself with the demo-graphic substructure of the social order.

The General Problem of Population Replacement

Births and Deaths. The extent of balance between input and output in a human population can be crudely measured by the rate of natural increase (disregarding net migration for the moment). The crude rate of natural increase (CRNI) is given by the difference between the crude birth rate and the crude death rate ($CBR - CDR = CRNI$). The CBR is measured by dividing the number of births in a given community over a period of one year by the number of persons living in that community.[5] This gives us a statement of births per person. It is typically modified to make it a more intelligible and manipulatable figure by changing it to births per thousand persons. So the CBR is defined, for a given community, as

$$\frac{\text{Number of Births in a Year}}{\text{Population of Given Community}} \times 1000 \, .$$

The death rate (the CDR) is similarly defined. The difference between the two, then, is a measure of input, of natural increase. For the United States in 1960 the CBR was 23.8 and the CDR was 9.4. Thus the Crude Rate of Natural Increase was 14.4 or 1.44 per hundred, or about 1.4 percent per year.

These rates, incidentally, are called crude because they represent unrefined and possibly misleading observations. If we compare two communities, observing that in one the CBR is 30.0 and the other 0.0, we are likely to miss the boat—despite the fact that the observations are "correct"—if we blithely accept common conclusions as to differences in leisure time, or in fecundity, or in race. We cannot begin to interpret differences in population input until we have controlled or taken account of such variables as differences in age distribution, religion, median income, occupational structure, and education. For the hypothetical communities cited, we might find, in the first, people who are predominantly between ages 17 and 35; and in the second—say a war-ravaged community—only the very young and the very old. For this reason it is common to gather age-specific data. Thus when we compare two populations we can be sure

---

[5] Since this number changes from time to time throughout the year, the number of persons estimated to be residing in that community, state, or nation at year's midpoint is often taken as the denominator.

that differences in fertility[6] are not simply due to differences in age. That is to say, we control the variable of age.[7] And so, also, with other variables that must often be controlled for adequate interpretation of demographic data.

When input exactly matches output—i.e., when $CBR - CDR = 0$ —we have a stable population of a special sort: a *stationary* one. (A population may also be stable when the rate of growth or decline persists from generation to generation. Social conditions may then be geared to regular change rates in population.) The situation of a stationary population, where input provides precisely and continuously the personnel necessary to man the social structure may be viewed as a theoretical limit which does not, in fact, occur. Normally, growth exceeds or falls short of demands or resources of the social order. This is what exercised the Reverend Thomas Malthus, "a kindly, gentle, sensitive and sincere Christian minister [whose name nonetheless] stands for a cruel, mechanical doctrine of despair."[8] He saw population growth constantly threatening to outstrip resources. Responding to what he deemed an almost irresponsible naïveté on the part of a fellow cleric, William Godwin,[9] Malthus felt it imperative to confront the reality of man's two primal, and irreconcilable, biological drives: the sexual and the abdominal. He wrote:

> . . . the power of population is indefinitely greater than the power in the earth to produce subsistence for man.
>
> Population, when unchecked, increases in a geometrical ratio. Subsistence increases only in an arithmetical ratio.[10]

. . . . .

---

[6] The word "fertility," as the sociologist uses it, does not refer to reproductive capacity (for which "fecundity" is used). It means the actually observed rate and pattern of reproduction characteristic of a population.

[7] See "An Aside on Methods: One Way of Controlling Certain Demographic Observations," p. 311.

[8] Kenneth E. Boulding in his "Foreword" to Thomas Robert Malthus, *Population: The First Essay* (Ann Arbor, Mich.: University of Michigan Press, 1959), p. v.

[9] Godwin's *Enquiry Concerning Political Justice* (1793) reflected a yeasty optimism that pervaded his times, supported in part by social Darwinism and the heady political climate of the American and French Revolutions. It was clear, Godwin thought—as did Condorcet, in France, sketching out the *Progress of the Human Mind*—that man had the world by the tail on a downhill drag. His ideal society, an anarchistic one, was grounded in equality, cultivated individualism and, through the ascendance of reason, would eliminate error, vice, and violence. Godwin's son-in-law, Percy Bysshe Shelley echoed these sentiments in poetry and pamphlet.

[10] Malthus, *op. cit.*, p. 5.

An Aside on Methods: One Way of Controlling Certain Demographic Observations

Let us take a brief detour, once again, on the matter of methods of inquiry—here, specifically, means of controlling our observations.

In comparisons of the fertility of any two groups, age is clearly a critical variable. Youngsters and oldsters are low reproducers. Until we eliminate the effect of this variable—until we control it—we cannot be sure that causal influence attributed to other factors is not spurious. Consider, for example, two communities, Jonesville and Plainville whose CBRs are 24.6 and 8.4, respectively. How shall we understand this? Is the first community Negro, the second white? The first Catholic, the second Jewish? The first a rural-agricultural community, the second an urban-industrial one? Consider these fictitious data.

	JONESVILLE			PLAINVILLE		
AGE CATEGORY	NUMBER OF PERSONS	AGE-SPECIFIC BIRTH RATE	NUMBER OF BIRTHS	NUMBER OF PERSONS	AGE-SPECIFIC BIRTH RATE	NUMBER OF BIRTHS
Young	100	5	.5	400	5	2.0
Middle-aged	800	30	24.0	200	30	6.0
Old	100	1	.1	400	1	.4
	1,000		24.6	1,000		8.4

It becomes apparent when we have age-specific data that much of the difference in the input of the two communities (the natural increase) is due to differences in the age composition of the two groups. How much of it is due to age? This we can tell very easily. For the extent to which the difference between the two CBR's would change, *were the two communities to have the same age composition*, is a measure of the influence of this variable. (How much difference would there be left, between these two birth rates, if there were no difference in age composition?) And so we can give Jonesville the same age composition as Plainville (or vice versa) and then see what the CBR's would be. In the concocted data I have offered here, it is clear that the two communities would then have precisely the same CBR's. All the difference in fertility between the two communities is, then, attributable to the difference in age composition. (The apparent difference in fertility between the two communities is in a way spurious; for it derives exclusively from differing age distributions in Jonesville and Plainville.) Now we can ask the critical question: what characteristics of these communities explain the composition?

There is another way of controlling the variable of age in order to compare more usefully the fertility of two communities. Instead of giving community A the same age composition as community B, or vice versa, we can give them both the same age composition as that of a third community, C. We then apply the age specific birth rates (which will differ as between the two communities rather than, as with my concocted data, above, being identical). Then, summing the births for all age categories—say, from 15–19 to 45–49, by five-year age categories (although we might make our calculations for single years of age)—and relating them to population units of 1,000, we can compare the two communities with the age variable controlled. We have, in effect, prevented its variation by holding it constant as between the two communities. When it becomes conventional for investigators to use a standard community as the base line for age composition, comparisons may then be made very generally—indeed, internationally—by many people at different times and places. Such a base "community" has been accepted. It is called the "standard million of England and Wales."

Taking the population of the world at any number, a thousand millions, for instance, the human species would increase in the ratio of—1, 2, 4, 8, 16, 32, 64, 128, 256, 512, &c. and subsistence as—1, 2, 3, 4, 5, 6, 7, 8, 9, 10, &c. In two centuries and a quarter, the population would be to the means of subsistence as 512 to 10: in three centuries as 4096 to 13, and in two thousand years the difference would be almost incalculable, though the produce in that time would have increased to an immense extent.[11]

. . . . .

By that law of our nature which makes food necessary to the life of man, the effects of these two unequal powers must be kept equal.

This implies a strong and constantly operating check on population from the difficulty of subsistence. This difficulty [of matching reproductive performance and available food] must fall somewhere and must necessarily be severely felt by a large portion of mankind.[12]

The "constantly operating check(s)" were those disasters that periodically decimate populations: war, plague, famine. Another sort of check, a preventive one that Malthus called "moral restraint," offered scant hope of warding off the catastrophic knife thrusts of the positive checks. We could predict, then, that any population, given a certain subsistence base, would increase, at first slowly and then with increasing speed until, reaching the point of saturation, numbers would level off, before long being cut back to size through disease and death. The picture Malthus paints is much the same as the often demonstrated growth of the fruit fly, *Drosophila melanogaster* on a limited subsistence base. The growth curve that emerges was first given prominence mathematically by Raymond Pearl and Lowell J. Reed. It looks like the accompanying illustration, and it may indeed represent the situation of culturally crude accommodation of organism to environment. *X* marks the spot in this figure at

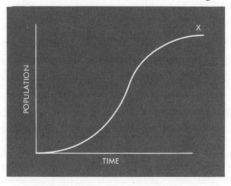

[11] *Ibid.*, p. 9.
[12] *Ibid.*, p. 5.

which malnutrition, epidemics, the aggressive ravaging of foreign territories occur, decimating the population, which then begins, slowly, to repeat the cycle.

So far as we can estimate past populations—and the data are poor —over most of the centuries past world population has remained sparsely distributed and at a low level. Major and enduring increases are recent. (It is estimated that the world population

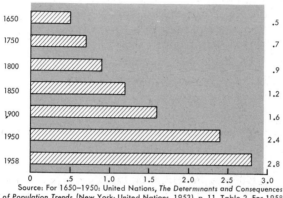

Source: For 1650–1950: United Nations, *The Determinants and Consequences of Population Trends* (New York: United Nations, 1953), p. 11, Table 2. For 1958 data: United Nations, *Demographic Yearbook 1959* (New York: United Nations, 1960), p. 127, Table 2. Note that elapsed time between the last two bars is *eight* years not, as with the time between all others, fifty years.

FIG. 8–1.   Estimated world population for selected years, 1650–1958 (in billions).

doubled between 1600 and 1800; and once again between 1800 and 1930.) Malthusian theory suggests a fairly stable population, periodically adjusted, by disaster, to the limited supply of foods and fibers. But as Figure 8–1 suggests, the recent growth of world population has been enormous. While it is true that populations have periodically been reduced by wars, the wars themselves were not precipitated by simple lack of subsistence.[13]

But under conditions, especially prehistoric, where culture was little elaborated, approaching, to a degree, the condition of nonhuman organisms, Malthus' conception of a miserably monotonous and monotonously miserable pattern of population growth and decline

[13] It is true that some, like Germany before World War II, cried for *lebensraum*. But it is instructive to note that while demanding, as a right, a larger resource base, Germany promoted a population policy that effectively reduced her *lebensraum*. For example, the Nazi regime encouraged young couples to reproduce by offering loans at marriage, loans canceled a fourth at a time with the advent of each child. Other national policies encouraged the multiplication of "Aryans."

may have had some substance. Sounding this somber note and insisting that no conceivable advances in agriculture could possibly offset the ultimate curse of man's reproductive propensities, Malthus was twitted by his contemporaries:

> Come, Malthus, and in Ciceronian prose
> Show how a rutting population grows
> Till all the produce of the soil is spent
> And brats expire for lack of aliment.
>
> Science finds out ingenious ways to kill
> Strong men, and keep alive his weak and ill—
> That these a sickly progeny may breed,
> Too poor to tax, too numerous to feed.[14]

---

[14] This was a popular version of Malthusian theory. It is cited by F. L. Schuman in his *International Politics* (New York: McGraw-Hill Book Co., 1933), p. 336.

Perhaps you will recall Jonathan Swift's solution to the Malthusian dilemma (although he saw its source in an evil English colonialism rather than in irremediable biological impulses). His solution for a burgeoning population entailing death and deprivation for the Irish is found in *A Modest Proposal for Preventing the Children of Poor People in Ireland from Being a Burden to Their Parents or Country, and for Making them Beneficial to the Public* (1729).

"It is a melancholy object to those who walk through this great town [Dublin] or travel in the country, when they see the streets, the roads, and cabin doors, crowded with beggars of the female sex, followed by three, four, or six children, all in rags and importuning every passenger for an alms. . . .

"I think it is agreed by all parties that this prodigious number of children in the arms, or on the backs, or at the heels of their mothers, and frequently of their fathers, is in the present deplorable state of the kingdom a very great additional grievance; and, therefore, whoever could find out a fair, cheap, and easy method of making these children sound, useful members of the commonwealth, would deserve so well of the public as to have his statue set up for a preserver of the nation. . . .

"I do therefore humbly offer it to public consideration that of the 120,000 children already computed, 20,000 may be reserved for breed, whereof only one-fourth part to be males . . . one male will be sufficient to serve four females. That the remaining 100,000 may, at a year old, be offered in sale to the persons of quality and fortune throughout the kingdom; always advising the mother to let them suck plentifully in the last month, so as to render them plump and fat for a good table. A child will make two dishes at an entertainment for friends; and when the family dines alone, the fore or hind quarter will make a reasonable dish, and seasoned with a little pepper or salt will be very good boiled on the fourth day, especially in winter. . . .

"I believe no gentleman would repine to give 10 shillings for the carcass of a good fat child, which, as I have said, will make four dishes of excellent meat, when he has only some particular friend or his own family to dine with him. Thus the squire will learn to be a good landlord, and grow popular among the tenants; the mother will have 8 shillings net profit, and be fit for work till she produces another child." Taken from Paul Robert Lieder, Robert Morss Lovett and Robert Kilburn Root, *British Poetry and Prose* [New York: Houghton Mifflin Co., 1928], pp. 495–99, *passim.*

But of course whether a theory of population input into a social order is somber or distasteful is irrelevant. The sociologist cannot prefer the "sweet mirage" to "bitter, barren truth."[15] We have to ask: Is it accurate? (not: Is it pleasant?) Does it fit our observations? Or, under what conditions is it true? And when not true? For example, we can look at the growth of population in the United States (as Malthus himself did, noting that the population was doubling every twenty-five years). How does it happen, then, that this population on a virgin continent has not continued to expand at the rate predicted by Malthus' theory (see Figure 8–2); or that it has not been cut back to size despite a fairly sizable growth? How does one explain the fact that Eire's population is today half of what it was 100 years ago, yet without the intervention of Malthus' positive checks? Is it due simply to gut and glands that certain Americans who threatened to vanish are no longer "vanishing Americans" but are reproducing at a rapid rate? Why does it happen that peoples with about the same reproductive potentials and having available similar resources vary so emphatically in their population growth?

Our general answer must be that we are not feeding new elements into a cohort of organisms, but into a social order. It is differences between social orders that condition differences in input, just as differences in input affect the nature of the social order. Not, of course, that there is a perfect fit between input and the requirements of the system. Currently obtaining rates of fertility and mortality may be out of phase with changing conditions in the social order: changes in the labor force, in the distribution of wealth, in commonly held religious views bearing on contraception, in political conceptions and practices. Certainly non-Malthusian possibilities emerge when we look at the changed distribution of children per family in Great Britain, contrasting the situation in 1860 with that in 1925. The data are presented in Figure 8–3.

The flat curve in 1860 suggests the random influence of a number of unknown factors influencing the growth of population (and excluding, generally, the intent of the marriage partners). But the dramatically different curve for 1925 showing that 67 percent of British married couples had one, two, or no children reveals purpose and planning. Such general limitation of family size means commonly held values—a standard of living to be maintained, a status

[15] William Wetmore Story, "Girolamo, Detto Il Fiorentino, Desponds and Abuses the World," in *Poems* (New York; Houghton Mifflin & Co., 1896), Vol. I, p. 115.

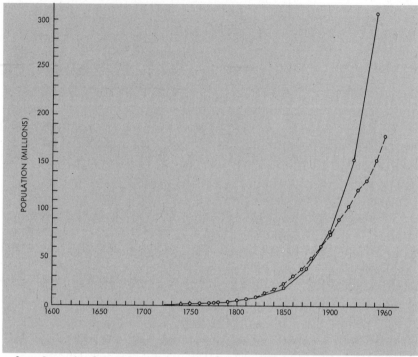

Source: Bureau of the Census, *Historical Statistics of the United States, 1789–1945;* and *Continuation to 1952* . . . and *United States Census of Population, 1960: United States Summary* (Washington, D.C.: U.S. Government Printing Office, 1949, 1954, 1961), Tables B 1–12 in first two sources, pp. 25 and 1; and Table 42, p. 1–143 for 1960 data.

FIG. 8–2. The growth of United States population, 1790–1960: actual, for continental U.S. (– – – – –) and as Malthus' geometric increase formula would predict it, doubling every 25 years from 1750 (————). The data are as follows (in millions):

YEAR	U.S. CENSUS	MALTHUS' FORMULA	YEAR	U.S. CENSUS	MALTHUS' FORMULA
1650	.05		1820	9.6	
1660	.08		1825		9.6
1670	.1		1830	12.9	
1680	.2		1840	17.1	
1690	.2		1850	23.2	19.3
1700	.3		1860	31.4	
1710	.4		1870	39.3	
1720	.5		1875		38.6
1730	.6		1880	50.2	
1740	.9		1890	62.9	
1750	1.2	1.2	1900	76.0	77.2
1760	1.6		1910	92.0	
1770	2.2		1920	105.7	
1775		2.4	1925		154.5
1780	2.8		1930	122.8	
1790	3.9		1940	131.7	
1800	5.3	4.8	1950	154.2	309.0
1810	7.2		1960	179.3	

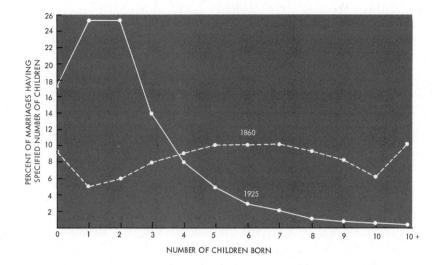

Source: Based on data reported in Dennis H. Wrong, *Population and Society* (New York: Random House, Inc., 1961), p. 53, and coming originally from Table XVII of Command Paper 7695 *Royal Commission on Population* (London: His Majesty's Stationery Office, 1949), p.26.

FIG. 8–3. Distribution of family size in England and Wales (1860) and in Great Britain (1925).

to be achieved, the desire to invest more in fewer children, general support given medicine and biological science so reducing mortality and making possible three survivors out of three births rather than three out of six, etc. Let us put it this way: rate and type of population growth reflect people's values. People's values reflect the nature of the social order. The fact that actions or decisions bearing on population growth are individually made tends to obscure both their cumulative social effect and their source in the conditions of society. Even in groups where no preventive measures are commonly undertaken to control the growth of population (contraception, postponement of marriage, esteem of celibacy) or where there are practices unplanned but promoting control (protracted military service, hazardous male occupations like fishing that promote an unbalanced sex ratio) "curative" measures may be practiced: abortion, infanticide, and the like. Very generally, that is to say, the link between population and the social order is tacitly acknowledged in behaviors that have the latent function of adjusting input to system requirements.

But such an adjustment is a matter of extraordinary intricacy—

more so than Henry Pratt Fairchild's formula explicitly states:

$$\text{Population} = \frac{T \times R}{LL}$$

(where T means technology, R stands for resources, and LL refers to level of living). Thus to maintain the balance between the two sides of the equation, an increase in population would require an increase in the value of T or R or both. Conversely—and this is more clearly seen if we convert the equation to

$$LL = \frac{T \times R}{P}$$

—a decline in population enables an increase in the level of living. (One is reminded of Carlyle's statement in Sartor Resartus: "The fraction of life can be increased in value not so much by increasing your numerator as by lessening your denominator. . . . Make thy claim to wages zero, then; thou hast the world at thy feet.")[16] But what is implied in such a formula? Both T and R depend on the rate of savings and investment, on invention and scientific work, and these upon the available cultural backlog and the means and interest in diffusing scholarly knowledge. All of these depend on the extent and quality of education. This latter will vary depending on the level of economic development and the complexity of the culture. The level of economic development is linked with the form of government, with modes of production and distribution. In Marx's view these were so fundamental that we cannot properly speak of population problems, but rather of problems of economic organization. Various modes of economic organization have population problems peculiar to them. In his own day he insisted that

> The laboring population . . . produces—along with the accumulation of capital produced by it—the means by which itself is made relatively superfluous [i.e., it creates of itself a surplus population]— and it does this to an always increasing extent. This is a law of population peculiar to the capitalist mode of production; and, in fact, every special historic mode of production has its own special laws of population, historically valid within its limits alone. An abstract law of population [like Malthus'] exists for plants and animals only, and only in so far as man has not interfered with them.[17]

---

[16] Thomas Carlyle, *Sartor Resartus*. See Lieder, *et al.*, *op. cit.*, p. 959.

[17] Karl Marx, *Capital: A Critique of Political Economy* (Chicago: Charles H. Kerr & Co., 1921), pp. 692, 693.

In recent years Communist China has vacillated between this orthodox Marxist position and the desperately felt need to limit the growth of the largest nation, now numbering nearly 700 million, about a quarter of the world's population.

Marx's correction of Malthus lies not only in stressing the error of a sheerly biological view of population growth, but in asserting that variations in the biological realm are themselves outcomes (as well as reinforcing sources) of the social order. But if it is right to assert that population input is influenced by the nature of the economy, it is wrong to regard the economic subsystem as the only one relevant to population problems. The socializing institutions, family and school, the church and the values there affirmed, the political system, the extent and mode of institutionalizing scientific development—all of these institutions with everything they imply, including their complex interweaving, affect and are affected by rate of population growth.

Now the supply or replenishing of a social order is clearly not a mere matter of input, of balance between birth rate and agricultural productivity. Nor, indeed, is it a matter solely of social factors conditioning the birth rate. The maintenance of a social order depends upon length of life or, more grimly, upon death. If ten men remain on the job in one factory for ten years but in a second factory the average tenure is five years, then, other things being equal, we will need twenty men—twice as many—to staff the second plant. We need, so to speak, to double the birth rate to compensate for a doubled death rate. It makes a difference, in staffing a society, that the infant mortality rate is over 150 in Egypt and under twenty in Sweden. It makes a difference that, at birth, a male child in the United States may expect to live better than twenty years longer than his counterpart in Guatemala.[18] Deaths as well as births, mortality and longevity as well as fertility, must be taken into account in study of the conditions for maintaining a social system.

Imagine a society in which men were immortal, each role permanently, and with consistent competence, filled by the same person. Obviously this society would require no input. We would have a stable, an unchanging social order. This limiting case is not closely approximated in reality.

But why not? Because of death, emigration, and internal role-

---

[18] See, for such data as these, the *Demographic Yearbook* published annually, in New York, by the statistical office of the United Nations.

shifting. Our attention here is focused on death (or on any disability rendering a person incompetent to perform as parent, worker, communicant, citizen, learner, etc.). Death or disability represent output. Birth is the input counterpart.

Now one might suppose that where the death rate is high there must likewise be a counterbalance in the birth rate if the role structure is to be maintained (apart from migration or some internal rearrangement of roles). This should be the case since either lack or oversupply of role incumbents places stress on the social network. An oversupply may mean such things as unemployment, schools operating in shifts with inadequate facilities and hastily certified teachers, erstwhile-teachers-then-mothers leaving their families in response to a flood of school-age children, inadequate housing, a strain on public services. An undersupply may entail the flight of factories, a loss of tax base for public services, redefinition of parental and spouse roles, an emphasis on technology to supply mechanical hands to substitute for the missing human hands, and a score or more of other outcomes. Thus the tendency would be, one might suppose, for birth rates and death rates to vary together. Certainly if there is any tendency toward equilibrium in a social system, or conversely if there is any stress induced when certain roles fail to be fulfilled (or are oversupplied), then we would expect that birth and death rates would not vary randomly but would tend to move together. Let us test this notion by looking at the connection between birth and death rates in the United States from 1915 through 1951.

A first look at Figure 8–4 would seem to refute the notion of positive concomitant variation between birth and death rates in the service of maintaining a social order. But if we make allowance for the abnormal fluctuations introduced by the flu epidemic following World War I and for the deferred marriages and births connected with the decade of depression and World War II, the idea is perhaps not so farfetched. Had it not been for these demographically disruptive events it is at least plausible that the slope of the curve would have been gently—rather than precipitously—downward, paralleling rather neatly the consistent decline in the death rate.

But let us make a more direct check by plotting birth rates against death rates. If they tend to move together a scatter diagram should reveal some linear order; and there should be a reasonably high

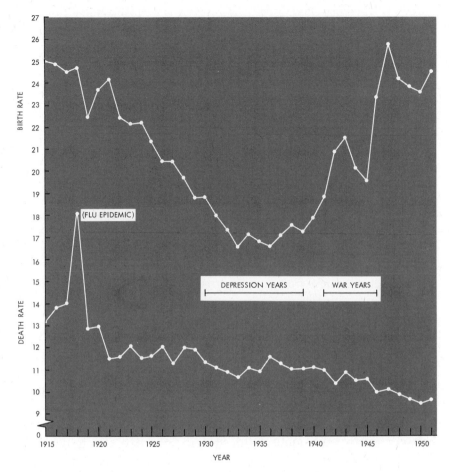

Source of data: U.S. Bureau of the Census, *Historical Statistics of the United States, 1915–1945* and *Continuation to 1952 of Historical Statistics* (Washington, D.C.: U.S. Government Printing Office, 1949 and 1954, respectively). Tables: Series C 45–54, p. 47 and C24, C45, pp. 6 and 7, respectively.

FIG. 8-4. Birth and death rates for the total population in the United States, 1915 through 1951.

product-moment correlation between the two sets of data. Figure 8–5 gives the picture for the total U.S. population, and the relationship between input and output is clear and marked. (This is especially so when we remind ourselves that maintenance of a social order through balanced output and input is a function of immigration and emigration as well as of births and deaths; and that a lack of relationship between births and deaths might be partly accounted for by social and technological innovations requiring more, or fewer, hands to be trained to staff the system.)

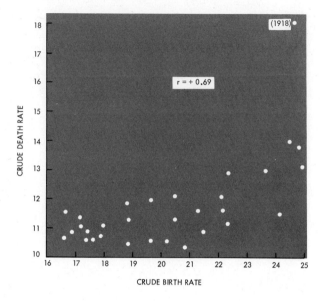

Source of data: U.S. Bureau of the Census, *Historical Statistics of the United States, 1789–1945* (Washington, D.C.: U.S. Government Printing Office, 1949). Table: Series C 45–55, p. 47.

FIG. 8–5. Relationship of birth and death rates in the United States (all races), 1915–45.

Data are provided separately for whites and nonwhites (the latter category referring chiefly to Negroes, of course) in Figures 8–6 and 8–7. What is of special interest is the utter lack of relationship between input and output for Negroes in the United States ($r = +.16$). One might explain this by suggesting that Negroes are in a state of transition, of instability in the United States; and this condition is reflected in the erratic connection of their birth and death rates. It might be as with certain African, Asian, and Latin American countries that the mortality rates of American Negroes have tardily dropped as they become more fully integrated into American society while their fertility rates continue high, reflecting the generally high fertility of rural-agrarian southeastern United States. The social structure of the Negro population in the United States is changing very rapidly. Birth and death are part of a larger pattern of life, linked with occupation, income, education, religion, region, aspiration. As these characteristics change, at different rates in different places and with greater or less rapidity we might .well expect Negroes' vital characteristics to change erratically. But as they migrate increasingly to urban America, as they involve them-

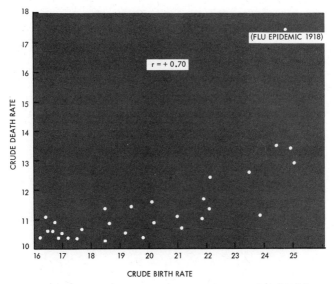

Source of data: U.S. Bureau of the Census, *Historical Statistics of the United States, 1789–1945* (Washington, D.C.: U.S. Government Printing Office, 1949). Table: Series C 45–55, p. 47.

FIG. 8–6. Relationship of birth and death rates for whites in the United States, 1915–45.

selves increasingly across the spectrum of American life, as their status shifts first from that of subservient caste to that of predominantly lower class and then to modes of life that spread across the class structure, input and output from year to year may tend to stabilize.

The extent to which birth and death rates are so adjusted that the deaths of the fathers are made up for by the births of sons[19] is suggested in a demographic device called the net reproduction rate (NRR). It tells us, given certain assumptions about persistence of birth and death rates (and the factors promoting their persistence) the extent to which one generation is replaced by its successor.

---

[19] This is a good place to remind ourselves that the group need not be maintained exclusively by a balance of births and deaths. In a moment we will turn to immigration and longevity as means of staffing the social order. But in addition it may be that an imbalance in one social sector may compensate for a complementary imbalance in another. For example, a relatively low death rate and continuing high birth rates in one category may provide the blue-collar workers that low birth rates in another category fail to provide. Thus the very fact that there is not a stable input-output relationship in the Negro sector of the population could be a prime factor in maintaining balance in the system as a whole.

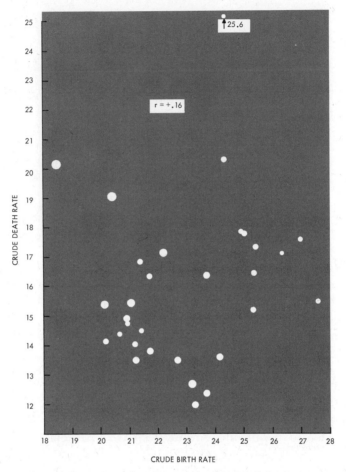

Source of data: U.S. Bureau of the Census, *Historical Statistics of the United States, 1789–1945* (Washington, D.C.: U.S. Government Printing Office, 1949). Table: Series C 45–55, p. 47.

FIG. 8-7.   Relationship of birth and death rates for nonwhites in the United States, 1915-1945.

Exact replacement gives us a net reproduction rate of 1.00. That is to say, at N years after their birth (the number of years being the average age of their mothers at the time they gave birth), the number of daughters will equal the number of mothers, so that the one divided by the other equals 1.00. This, as you might expect, is seldom the case. Let me illustrate the calculation of the NRR with data for 1950. These data indicate a 40 percent excess over exact replacement between generations (on the assumption that the conditions then prevailing would persist over several decades).

TABLE 8–1

Calculation of the Net Reproduction Rate: a Measure, Based on Certain Assumptions, of Inter-generational Replacement

AGE OF MOTHER	SURVIVING TO INDI- CATED AGE FROM ORIG- INAL COHORT OF 100,000*	1950 BIRTH RATES†	NUMBER OF BIRTHS
(1)	(2)	(3)	(4)
15–19	96,638	79.1	7,644
20–24	96,304	192.5	18,538
25–29	95,890	163.0	15,630
30–34	95,362	101.5	9,679
35–39	94,633	51.2	4,845
40–44	93,562	14.6	1,366
45–49	91,941	1.0	92

Total number of births for females in the child-bearing age group............... $\overline{57,794 \times 5\ddagger}$ = 288,970 and since females are about 48.5% of all births, 288,970 × .485 yields the number of females born to a cohort of 100,000 prospective mothers, or

$\dfrac{140,150}{100,000}$ daughters are born to prospective mothers, i.e., NRR = 1.40

---

* These data come from Public Health Service, National Office of Vital Statistics in the U.S. Department of Health Education, and Welfare, *United States Life Tables, 1949–51*, Vol. 41, No. 1 (November 23, 1954), Table 6, p. 18. Figures in this column represent the mean number of females living through the five-year period.

† Birth rates are taken from the U.S. Bureau of the Census, *Continuation of Historical Statistics, 1789–1945: 1946–1952* (Washington, D.C.: U.S. Government Printing Office, 1954), Series B 331–C37, Table 1, p. 6. As usual, these are births per thousand. Thus if there were 100,000 mothers having a birth rate of 79.1 (per thousand), 7,910 children would be born to them.

‡ These rates are annual rates—births/thousand/annum, while the age categories cover five-year periods; hence the need to multiply by five.

Unaware or careless of the assumptions underlying the NRR the novice is likely to overinterpret or overextend an NRR like 1.40. (The professional is sensitive to the limitations of his data, more conscious of his ignorance, than the layman. "The wise man knows himself to be a fool," but "fools rush in where angels fear to tread"— to lay Shakespeare and Pope end to end.) In interpreting these figures we must remember that they are projections, indicating *what would happen if* the birth and death rates then obtaining—and related conditions like age composition, marriage and divorce rates —were to continue over a period of years. But with this caveat in mind the NRR yields useful clues to the ebb and flow of population, the challenges to stable role replacement inherent in the current demographic situation. For growth or decline of populations is the common case, just as change—social change—is the chronic condition. And the two, population change and social change, are certainly connected. Rapidly increasing numbers impose new, sometimes excessive, demands on the existing role structure. Declining numbers render existing roles useless or obsolete.

In our appraisal of the strains upon the social order stemming from changing population input, the intergenerational estimates provided by the NRR are very useful. In the depression years the NRR was commonly below unity in European and American countries. In the United States, the NRR was .96, or 4 percent below

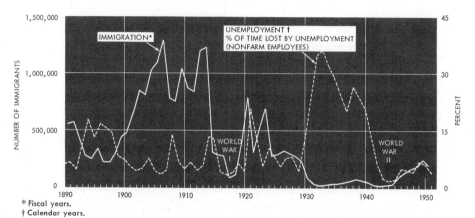

* Fiscal years.

† Calendar years.

Sources: Immigration—U.S. Immigration and Naturalization Service: Employment—Stanley Lebergott, "Earnings of Non-farm Employees in the U.S., 1890–1946" in *Journal of the American Statistical Association*, March, 1948. Taken from the President's Commission on Immigration and Naturalization, *Whom We Shall Welcome* (Washington, D.C.: U.S. Government Printing Office, 1953), p. 28.

FIG. 8–8. Immigration and unemployment

replacement level in 1940. In France, the Scandinavian countries, and England a similar situation obtained. And in our urban areas in this country the threatened decline was even more marked, with the NRR at about .75 or an indicated deficiency of 25 percent. By contrast the *United Nations Demographic Yearbook* reports a NRR for Israel (1940) of 2.17!

Immigration and Emigration.   But as I observed before, a social order does not live by births alone. A second source of supply for staffing the group's role structure is immigration. Emigration is, of course, its counterpart. Our society, endowed with great natural resources, enjoying a standard of living based in part upon a growing population,[20] stressing optimism, inventiveness, and enter-

---

[20] Note the chagrin, if not skeptical indignation on the part of civic leaders when the decennial census reports their communities as not having grown in population.

prise as a triad of prime virtues, has welcomed immigrants in the past. An expansionist immigration policy fitted very well the requirements of a burgeoning industrial society. Immigrants were typically youthful, therefore low in mortality and high in reproductivity as well as productivity. And their coming and going was well geared to the economic conditions of our society. For example,

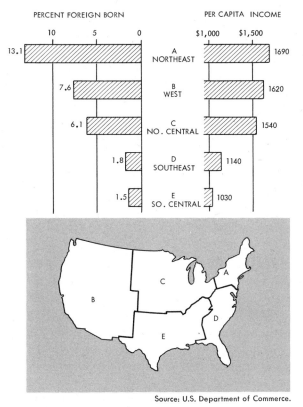

Source: U.S. Department of Commerce.

FIG. 8-9   Immigration and income.

during the depth of the depression years, 1932 through 1935, more persons left than entered the United States. The relationship between immigration and unemployment is suggested in Figure 8–8.

A similar link between input-through-immigration and the conditions of production is seen in Figure 8–9 presenting data on the connection between per capita income and the proportion foreign born in five regions of the country.

Finally it is of some interest to note the legally determined input-through-immigration as it operated in the United States from 1921

TABLE 8–2

Group Maintenance via Input-through-Immigration: Annual Quotas, by Country, under Successive United States Immigration Laws: 1921–51

	1921 ACT 3 PERCENT 1910	1924 ACT 2 PERCENT 1890	1929 NATIONAL ORIGINS ACT*	1952 IMMIGRATION AND NATIONALITY ACT†	
				N	%
TOTAL	375,803	164,667	153,714	154,657	100.0
Asia	492	1,424	1,423	2,990	1.9
Africa and Oceania	359	1,821	1,800	2,000	1.3
Europe	356,952	161,422	150,491	149,667	96.8
Northern and western Europe:					
Belgium	1,563	512	1,204	1,297	
Denmark	5,619	2,789	1,181	1,175	
France	5,729	3,954	3,086	3,069	
Germany	67,607	51,227	25,957	25,814 ⎫	
Grt. Britain & N. Ireland	77,342	34,007	65,721	65,361 ⎬ 70.0	
Irish Free State	——	28,567	17,853	17,756 ⎭	
Netherlands	3,607	1,648	3,153	3,136	
Norway	12,202	6,453	2,377	2,364	
Sweden	20,042	9,561	3,314	3,295	
Switzerland	3,752	2,081	1,707	1,698	
Total northern and western Europe	197,630	140,999	127,266	126,131	81.6
Southern and eastern Europe:					
Austria	7,342	785	1,413	1,405	
Czechoslovakia	14,357	3,073	2,874	2,859	
Greece	3,063	100	307	308	
Hungary	5,747	473	869	865	
Italy	42,057	3,854	5,802	5,645	
Poland	30,977	5,982	6,524	6,488	
Portugal	2,465	503	440	438	
Rumania	7,419	603	295	289	
U.S.S.R.	24,405	2,248	2,784	2,697	
Turkey	2,654	100	226	225	
Yugoslavia	6,426	671	845	933	
Total southern and eastern Europe	155,585	20,423	23,235	23,536	15.2

Source: Report of the President's Commission on Immigration and Naturalization, *Whom We Shall Welcome* (Washington, D.C.: U.S. Government Printing Office, 1953), pp. 76, 77.

* The general formula for admitting aliens to citizenship was this: the quota for a given country was that part of a total of 150,000 represented by the proportion their nationality constituted of the white population of 1920.

† The population base on which these quotas are calculated is the white population of the United States (excluding, that is, Negroes and Indians).

to the abolition of the national origins scheme in 1965. (See Table 8–2.)

The percentages that I have entered in the right-hand column indicate the extent to which our legislators tried to arrange for input to match output. (The demise of persons of west-European background was to be compensated for by admitting such others, in disproportionate share, under our quota system.) Indeed, this was the central notion underlying our national origins system of immigration. The Senate Judiciary Committee in supporting our Immigration and Nationality Act of 1952 wrote:

> Without giving credence to any theory of Nordic superiority, the subcommittee believes that the adoption of the national origins formula was a rational and logical method of numerically restricting immigration in such a manner as *to best preserve the sociological and cultural balance in the population of the United States.*[21]

Length of Life

There is a third demographic factor, length of life, that affects the maintenance of a social order. The longer a person's life the greater his span of parenthood, the longer his period of employment, the more votes he will cast (and otherwise act in role of citizen), the longer his participation as a communicant in some religious group— and the less the need, to maintain the social order, of input through births. The likelihood is that a system characterized by great longevity (other things equal) will have achieved solutions to problems of survival, will have fixed its roles and institutionalized its relationships. Its turnover is slow. It can rely on answers given in tradition, can indoctrinate, or socialize, slowly and surely. A prosaic contrast is offered by the summer camp that admits new groups every two weeks to a strange way of life. Here socialization must be

---

[21] President's Commission on Immigration and Naturalization, *Whom We Shall Welcome* (Washington, D.C.: U.S. Government Printing Office, 1953), p. 89. Italics mine. I cannot forebear signalizing this sloppy and thoroughly erroneous use of the word *sociological*. The good senators have fallen into the common illiteracy of substituting "sociological" for "social." The first refers to a field of inquiry. The second refers to a class of phenomena, a class to be distinguished from psychological, biological, physical phenomena, etc. While for pomp and circumstance "sociological" has the advantage of four syllables, it has the disadvantage of the wrong referent and of obscuring the meaning. This is the sort of word butchery that prompted Shakespeare's clown in *Twelfth Night* to lament: ". . . words are grown so false I am loath to prove reason with them."

(Speaking of Shakespeare, the quotations on page 325 are from *As You Like It*, Act V, scene I, line 35 and Alexander Pope's *Essay on Criticism*, Part III, line 66.)

swift, clear, intense, systematic—and often ineffective. And so longevity has much to do with the character of the social order.

Wherever we have records of birth and death, they show that, through the years, man's longevity has increased. From these records we know that out of a given number—say 100,000—so many will survive to any specified age. For a given cohort, then, we know the number of people living to a given age and the total number of years lived by them. We can then calculate the average number of

TABLE 8–3

Expectation of Life at Age 20, by Color and Sex, in the United States, 1939–41 and 1962

	AVERAGE NUMBER OF YEARS OF LIFE REMAINING	
	1939–41	1962
White males	47.8	50.2
White females	51.4	56.4
Negro males*	39.5	45.6
Negro females	42.0	50.2

* The 1964 *Abstract* uses the term nonwhite.

Source: United States Bureau of the Census, *Statistical Abstracts of the United States* (Washington, D.C.: U.S. Government Printing Office, 1950 and 1964), pp. 80 and 55 respectively.

years lived by each. It is upon such calculations, of course, that insurance companies depend for determining the premiums charged to cover their risks.

Longevity varies greatly through time and space. In Shakespeare's day average life expectancy, at birth, was about 35 years, and at age twenty a person had traveled, on the average, a little more than a third of the way to the grave. At the same age, in 1940 and 1962, expectation of remaining years to live would be as indicated in table 8–3.

Input to Subsectors of the Social Order

But I have been talking about the replenishing of the social order taken as a whole. This is to oversimplify the problem; for there must be different inputs into different sectors of the social order. The maintenance of any group structure requires differential inputs so as to retain its age and sex composition, the distribution of religious affiliation among the population, the race and nativity composition, the relative educational achievement of college, high school, and elementary school graduates, the rural-urban distribution of population, and occupational structure. And of course these various dimensions of society change with time. (In 1900 a third of the population was under age fifteen and 4 percent over sixty-five: fifty years later the figures were 12 and 8 percent respectively. In 1900 about a third of the labor force was employed in agriculture: in 1950 a little over 10 percent.) Again, the demands of this differentiated structure can be met by variations in the balance between births and deaths, between immigration and emigration, by shifts in longevity or by internal role shifts (for example, the Welsh tailor's son becomes a professor of physics).

Let us take this last instance and consider the way in which differences in fertility enable or require compensatory shifts in the role structure. And let us use the case of class, since class embraces a number of social characteristics relevant for maintenance of the social order, such as income, education, and occupation.

The problem is this: *How does differential fertility entail certain characteristics in the social order* (mobility, in this case) *that have the effect of maintaining the order?* Now in the United States the upper classes have typically had reproduction rates below replacement.[22] Assuming that their roles must be replenished if the system is to be maintained, it becomes necessary for such categories of persons to be supplied from other sources. Table 8–4 gives us some notion of the significance of social mobility in rectifying inadequate population replacement by the upper classes which, in this illustrative table, are deficient by 20 percent in replacing themselves.

Numbers and Patterns of Interaction

I have been trying to show how population factors—birth and death rates, length of life, the ebb and flow of migrants, shifts from one sector, one category of the population to another—affect the stability of a social order.

But important as this is, there is a matter beyond the sheer quantity of persons available to man the role structure: there is the effect of numbers on the quality or character of interaction. For, as

---

[22] While this was the characteristic situation in the past, there is some evidence that the long-standing inverse relationship between breeding (cultural) and breeding (biological) is weakening. Professor Freedman's data suggest a convergence on an ideal family size with the rich having more, the poor fewer children. (Ronald Freedman, Pascal K. Whelpton, and Arthur A. Campbell, *Family Planning, Sterility and Population Growth* [New York: McGraw-Hill Book Co., 1959], pp. 402–4.)

TABLE 8–4

Differential Fertility, by Class; and Necessary Replacements through Recruitment
from Next Lower Class if Structure Is to Be Maintained:
(Estimates Based on Fertility Conditions Existing 1920–1940)

				IF PROPORTIONS ARE TO REMAIN THE SAME			
SOCIAL CLASS	NUMBER IN EVERY 100 ADULTS	NRR*	NUMBER IN NEXT GEN- ERATION IF NO MOBIL- ITY OCCURS	NUMBER NEEDED IN NEXT GEN- ERATION	NUMBER WHO MUST BE UPWARDLY MOBILE	PERCENT IN EACH CLASS WHO ARE UPWARDLY MOBILE	PERCENT OF TOTAL MOBILITY DERIVING FROM EACH CLASS
0	i	ii	iii (ii × i)	iv (i × 108.7)	v (iv − iii plus mobility losses from next higher class)†	vi (v /iii)	vii: (no. mobile in given class/ 13.2)
Upper	3	.80	2.4	3.3	0	0	0
Upper-middle	8	.80	6.4	8.7	0.9	14	7
Lower-middle	30	1.00	30.0	32.6	3.2	11	24
Upper-lower	39	1.15	44.9	42.4	5.8	13	44
Lower-lower	20	1.25	25.0	21.7	3.3	13	25
TOTALS	100		108.7	108.7	13.2	12	100%

Source: Adapted from Robert J. Havighurst and Bernice L. Neugarten, *Society and Education* (Boston: Allyn and Bacon, Inc., 1962), Table 16.5, "Relations between Natural Population Increase, Differential Fertility, and Upward Mobility (Estimates)," p. 422. The table title is changed here, column vii is added along with column-identifying numbers and explanations of derivation of the figures in columns iii through vii. It is important to remember that upward mobility may be due to factors other than differential fertility which is the only matter we are considering here.

* The estimates of column ii are derived, one supposes, from known differentials in fertility by occupation, income, and other class-related variables. The net reproduction rate (NRR) is a rate that takes age-specific fertility and mortality into account, estimating the survivors to the next generation on the assumption that the birth and death rates used in the calculation continue to apply over that period.

† For example, if the net reproduction rates give us, from 100 persons (i) a total of 108.7 in the next generation (iii); and if these 108.7 persons are distributed among the several classes as were their forebears in the preceding generation (i), then we would have 3.3 persons in the upper class, 8.7 in the upper-middle, etc. But they do not distribute themselves in this way because the fertility of the several classes differs and the upper classes fail to reproduce themselves. The extent of this under- or overreproduction is indicated by the difference between columns iv and iii. Thus the number of upper-class persons needed (3.3, column iv) minus those available (2.4 in column iii) gives us the number that must be recruited from the next lower class if the upper class is to maintain its position in the structure (3%, column i). This is simply 3.3 minus 2.4 in the case of the upper-class category, indicating that 0.9 persons must be recruited from the upper-middle category to compensate for their failure to reproduce themselves. In the case of the upper-middle class the discrepancy is 2.3 (8.7 − 6.4) to which must be added the 0.9 lost to this category as a result of their movement into the upper-class category—i.e., 2.3 + .09 or 3.2 represents the number who must be upwardly mobile from the lower-middle class to fill out the ranks of the upper-middle class, etc.

Column vi suggests that it may be the upper-middles who tend to be most mobile (14%); although the difference between them and the lowers is certainly not great. Indeed the surprising thing here is the comparative equality of upper mobility due to differential fertility among the several classes.

Taking all who are mobile, 13.2, as the base we find in column vii that 44% of all those who are upwardly mobile are the upper portion of the lower class, followed by the lower-lower and the lower-middle classes, each of these accounting for about a fourth of the total upward mobility.

population increases, there is a change in the structure of relationships that constitutes a group. This is the matter to which we now
turn, leaning heavily, first of all, on Simmel's discussion of two- and
three-person groups; and then raising the question: What is it about

population increase that accounts for these changes in the social network?

This, then, is the first point: an increase in numbers, in size of group, can transform the nature of its constituent relationships. But then we must ask: how so? What is it about population increase that accounts for such changes? In answer to this question I shall point to three outcomes of population increase: a disproportionate increase in the number of relationships, an increased heterogeneity or diversification of roles and finally, a significant increase in the proportion of coordinating roles—administrative, supervisory, mediating.

We betray some sense of the significance of numbers for human relationships when we deplore the impersonality entailed by the growth of a business, a club, or a college; or, conversely, when we shudder at the goldfish-bowl character of the small community where one's innermost secrets may be ruthlessly disseminated through the rumor-gossip network; or when we savor the comfortable anonymity of a large city; or when Reinhold Niebuhr speaks of *Moral Man and Immoral Society*[23] (the moral individual or small group and the a-moral mass); or when David Riesman associates with numbers and density of population differing personality types: the tradition-, inner-, and other-directed person.[24]

Georg Simmel was especially intrigued with the way in which different relationships emerge with an increase in numbers. He asks us to consider the nature of a two-person group, a dyad.[25] It has this peculiar characteristic shared by no other group: the loss of one party destroys the relationship. This extreme vulnerability, the complete dependence of each upon the other for the maintenance of the group may explain why (in addition to society's obvious interest in the protection and appropriate rearing of offspring) the husband-wife relationship is hedged about with conventional and legal prescriptions. Being such a fragile relationship, this dyad requires the support of socially devised buttresses.

But, Simmel says, note what happens when the dyad is increased by one. The conversion to a triad (a three-person group) makes possible a majority: two against one. Now we have, also, the

---

[23] Reinhold Niebuhr, *Moral Man and Immoral Society* (New York: Charles Scribner's Sons, 1932).

[24] David Riesman, *The Lonely Crowd* (New Haven: Yale University Press, 1950). This book is available in paperback edition, abridged but with a very useful preface reviewing the odyssey of the ideas expressed in the book.

[25] Georg Simmel, *The Sociology of Georg Simmel*, trans. and ed. by Kurt Wolff (New York: Free Press of Glencoe, Inc., 1950), Part II, chaps. iii, iv.

possibility of a delegation of authority and responsibility. With three instead of two we have a more refined division of labor. There is, also, the possibility of mediation, arbitration, as the third seeks to resolve some difference between the two. But the third may profit from the difference between the two, playing one off against the other. Thus the shrewd child advances his interest by pitting parent against parent; and the student by contriving differences between teachers to his own advantage. Nor need it be a matter of individuals manipulating two others. A special case of the *tertius gaudens* (the third who profits—at the expense of the other two) is that of "divide and rule" (*divide et impera*) as where a colonial ruler creates or encourages factional disputes among the ruled. Thus the unbridged gulf between Moslem and Hindu in India made it possible for the English Raj to sit more firmly on the imperial throne.

Simmel speaks suggestively of the difference numbers make as between small and large groups. Here is a sample of his thinking on this matter:

> . . . socialistic societies . . . have been possible only in very small groups and have always failed in larger ones. The principle of socialism—justice in the distribution of production and reward—can easily be realized in a small group and, what is surely quite as important, can be safeguarded there by its members. The contribution of each to the whole and the group's reward to him are visible at close range; comparison and compensation are easy. In the large group they are difficult, especially because of the inevitable differentiation of its members, of their functions and claims.[26]

Distinctive religious groups, too, can preserve their identity only so long as their numbers remain small.

> Where dogma forbids oath, military service and occupancy of offices; where very personal affairs, such as occupation, daily schedule, and even marriage, are regulated by the community; where a specific dress separates the faithful from the others and symbolizes their belonging together; where the subjective experience of immediate rapport with Christ constitutes the real cohesion of the community—in

---

[26] Reprinted with permission of The Free Press from *The Sociology of Georg Simmel,* translated and edited by Kurt Wolff. Copyright 1950 by The Free Press. The reference here is not to "socialism" as the term is used in the U.S.S.R., but rather to the sort of communal group represented by the Hutterites or various utopian groups. That it be small is not, of course, the only relevant criterion for group survival as Robert Owen's experience at New Harmony, Indiana, indicated.

such situations, extension to large groups would evidently break the tie of solidarity which consists to a large degree precisely in the position of being singled out of larger groups and being in contrast to them.[27]

Or again, with an increase in population size, ideas held in common must be reduced to their simplest terms. For ". . . large masses can always be animated and guided only by *simple* ideas: what is common to many must be accessible even to the lowest and most primitive among them."[28] Or conversely, if the beliefs that distinguish a group, that establish its cultural identity and define its boundaries are to be maintained, then its population must not get out of bounds. This is especially so with deviant or radical groups. For:

> It is the unconditional solidarity of elements on which the . . . possibility of radicalism is based. *This solidarity decreases in the measure in which numerical increase involves the admission of heterogeneous individual elements.* For this reason, professional coalitions of workers, whose purpose is the improvement of labor conditions, know very well that they *decrease in inner cohesion as they increase in volume.* . . . on the other hand, the numerical extension has the great significance of freeing the coalition, through each additional member who joins it, of a competitor who might otherwise have undersold it and thus have threatened its existence.[29]

In such seminal remarks as these Simmel raises important questions about the connection between population size, on the one hand, and the effective functioning and maintenance of the group on the other. Is it through some subliminal appreciation of this connection that the Hutterites limit their settlements to about 100 persons? Is it this connection that we sense when we make our estimates for the optimum size of the classroom group under specified conditions? How large should a department, a working group in a factory, be?

The group cannot be maintained, I am suggesting, when increases in its population change the nature of the relationships that define the group. This, indeed, is tautological. The question is: How do increases in population alter the nature of relationships and thus jeopardize the maintenance of the group? Let me suggest three ways in which this occurs: (1) by increasing disproportionately the

[27] *Ibid.*, pp. 89, 90.
[28] *Ibid.*, p. 93.
[29] *Ibid.*, Part II, p. 95. Italics mine.

number of relationships to be articulated in the social structure of the group, (2) by increasing the heterogeneity of the group, and (3) as one consequence, by increasing the division of labor, or specialization, entailing an increase in coordinating or administrative roles.

First, an increase in numbers entails a disproportionate increase in relationships—the parts that must somehow be shaped into a whole social structure. We can illustrate what happens, as population increases, by noting how many simple, bilateral relationships we have with two persons, three persons, four, five, six, and so on. The following figure will help:

x = Number of actors-in-roles	2	3	4	5	6	7
y = Number of relationships	1	3	6	10	15	21

Graphic representation of actors-in-roles and relationships

Figure 8–10 shows another way of representing this elementary idea about the linkage between size of population and number of simple, bilateral relationships. The relationship graphically represented in these two figures can be expressed algebraically in this formula:[30]

---

[30] This is the formula expressing what the sociologist James H. S. Bossard called "The Law of Family Interaction." (*American Journal of Sociology,* published by the University of Chicago Press) Vol. L [January, 1945], pp. 242–94. This he stated as follows: "With the addition of each person to a family or primary group, the number of persons increases in the simplest arithmetical progression in whole numbers, while the number of personal interrelationships within the group increases in the order of triangular numbers." Bossard was especially impressed by the increased potential for tension with the disproportionate growth in relationships as families grew larger. He reports on the case of one youngster "who at five years of age, appears nervous, high strung, and over-stimulated, with spells of nervous vomiting. Helen is an only child, but in her two-and-a-half-story home of moderate size there live, in addition to her father and mother, two grandparents, one paternal, the other maternal. Also two servants are in the house daily. With seven persons in the house, there are twenty-one sets of personal relationships. In at least ten of the twenty-one, there is some emotional strain and tension. Helen is the most constantly present person in the household [and hence most regularly exposed]." Clearly, there are dimensions other than numbers that might be relevant in understanding this child's behavior: number of generations present, employer-employee as well as intrafamilial relationships, etc. Yet we must agree with Bossard that an increase in population involves a disproportionate increase in the potential heterogeneity of the group and in potential tensions.

Baker and Traphagen, with whose work Bossard was apparently unacquainted,

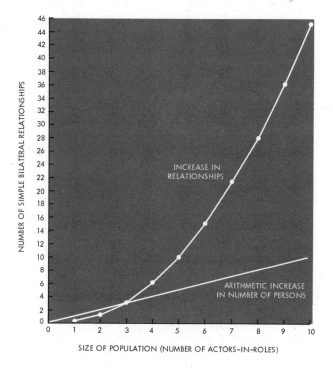

FIG. 8-10. The relationship between increase in numbers of persons (size of population) and simple, bilateral social relationships.

$$y = \frac{x}{2}(x - 1).$$

Thus where we have a group of six persons, we evaluate the formula as follows:

$$y = \frac{6}{2}(6 - 1) = 15.$$

If a student were living in a fraternity house or a dormitory section numbering twenty men we would see, by evaluating this formula,

suggested some years earlier the significance of this dimension in analyzing personality and problems of adjustment. (Harry J. Baker and Virginia Traphagen, *The Diagnosis and Treatment of Behavior Problem Children* [New York: Macmillan Co., 1936], pp. 284–85.) Baker and Traphagen deal not with *a* relationship between two people but with the orientation of each toward the other. Hence where there is one relationship there are two orientations, and their formula would read $Y = x^2 - x$.

that he was involved in a network of 190 simple, bilateral relationships. But this is a minimum statement of the way in which number and complexity of human relationships increase with a growth in population. For obviously, in a three-person group there is the possibility not only of bilateral relationships between A and B, B and C, C and A; but also of A leading B and C (or mediating between them, or being in a minority position vis-à-vis their majority), or of B confronting a united A and C, or of C differentiated somehow from A and B. Which is to say, once again, that the shift from a two- to a three-person group opens up a richly varied set of new relationships. And while we have six bilateral or symmetrical relationships with four actors-in-roles ($A \leftrightarrow B$, $A \leftrightarrow C$, $A \leftrightarrow D$, $B \leftrightarrow C$, and $C \leftrightarrow D$) there are, in addition four combinations, four three-and-one permutations suggesting leader-led, alliances, majorities or divisions-of-labor: $(A, B, C) \leftrightarrow D$; $(B, C, D) \leftrightarrow A$; $(C, D, A) \leftrightarrow B$; $(D, A, B) \leftrightarrow C$. But beyond this there are the two-and-two combinations (contending factions, collaborators in teams of two, split votes, etc.): $(AB) \leftrightarrow (CD)$, $(AC) \leftrightarrow (BD)$, $(AD) \leftrightarrow (BC)$.

This, then, is the first point: as population grows, the number and form of potential human relationships are vastly elaborated at a rate far in excess of the sheer increase in number of persons.

Now heterogeneity comes into the picture in two ways: culturally and socially. First, other things being equal, it seems accurate to assume that the greater the number of persons, the greater the portion of the cultural range likely to be represented within the expanded group. Thus American society includes scores of religious groups: denominations, sects, and cults. Other things being equal, the larger the population of an area, the broader the representation of the religious spectrum is likely to be.[31] In 1936, the last time we had a census of religious bodies, Chicago in the process of its growth had accumulated 111 different religious groups ranging from the

---

[31] Things are not, of course, equal. Such an assumption would suggest the random selection of persons from some larger whole to swell the population of a designated group. But populations do not grow, either "naturally"—as we erroneously put it—or by migration on a random basis. It is not a chance matter that Detroit has the largest Lebanese population outside of Lebanon; or that there are better than half a million Puerto Ricans living in New York City. Yet even despite the fact that groups—associations, communities—tend to select their newcomers and that newcomers sort themselves into comfortable and appropriate niches, there is strong empirical evidence for an increase in heterogeneity with an increase in population size. This is an important matter as it effects changes in the group; and we shall have to pay some attention to it in Chapter 14 when we raise the question: What are the sources of change in patterns of human relationships?

"big seven" (Catholics, Jews, Lutherans, Baptists, Methodists, Presbyterians, and Episcopalians) comprising 91 percent of the city's church membership to the rare and esoteric groups, 104 of them, whose membership taken together made up only 8.5 percent.[32]

But increase in numbers entails social as well as cultural diversity. I tried to indicate above how increase in numbers made possible new group formations: majorities and minorities, alliances, mediation and arbitration, differentiation between leader and led, contending factions, division of labor. In his book on *The Division of Labor in Society*, Durkheim traces a whole sequence of social effects having their roots in an increase in numbers. Assuming no extension of the area occupied, increase in numbers means increased density. Increased density heightens the probability of interaction with one's neighbors. Through such interaction common commitments are buttressed. Physical density thus leads to "moral density." What is significant in this awkward term is this: the reinforcement, the regular reaffirmation of particular views and values. But as a result of the "moral density" competition arises. For since "moral density" implies similarities in skills and occupations and the values attached to them, people are unwittingly brought to compete by the same means for the same limited supply of food, fibers, and frivolities. Then differentiation, a splintering off of occupational specialties, emerges as the structural mechanism for reducing competition and conflict. Such differentiation, or specialization, or division of labor runs counter to the relatively undifferentiated antecedent state of "mechanical solidarity." It reduces the common content of the *conscience collective*. Men's relationships are increasingly regulated by formalized legal codes. Increasingly the mortar of human relationships comes to be people's interdependence based upon differences rather than their common cause founded in likenesses.

But let us turn to an empirical test of this notion that an increase in population affects the social structure of the group. As one significant illustration of a social effect of increasing numbers, let us consider the division of labor between that part of an organization carrying out the coordinating, or supervising or administrative role, and all other sectors of the organization. Frederic Terrien and Donald Mills pose the problem: when numbers increase (in this case, numbers of persons involved in the operation of school

---

[32] E. K. Wilson, "Criteria of Urbanism Applied to Religion in Chicago." Unpublished Master's thesis, University of Chicago, 1942.

districts), what happens to the size of the administrative compo-nent?[33] They start with the assumption represented in Figure 8–10, showing the link between increased population and number of relationships.

> If the point be taken as axiomatic that the number of potential intra-group relationships increases at a greater rate than does the size of the group, then it would seem logical to suppose that those relation-ships would require at least a moderately increasing amount of super-vision.[34]

Let me emphasize that what an administrator administers is relationships, not persons. He helps define appropriate roles to achieve the group's mission; and he tries to link these roles in productive relationships—productive of whatever it is that the group is set up to achieve: health, wealth, happiness—or, in this case, informed children. And so these investigators state as their hypothesis to be tested: ". . . the larger the size of the containing organization, the greater will be the proportion given over to its administrative component." They got their data from a sample drawn by (1) taking just under half of the state's fifty-eight counties, rank ordered in eight strata according to total yearly budgets; and (2) adding all districts having an average daily attendance of 2,000 or more students, where such districts were not already in the sample. Thus the larger districts were overrepre-sented; and this is especially so since districts having fewer than ten employees were not dealt with. Their findings for three types of districts, elementary, high school, and unified and city school districts are summarized in Table 8–5.

It would, of course, be absurd to suggest, even in this relatively simple type of organization, the school district, that the dispropor-tionate increase in administrative roles is simply a consequence of increased population. What the division of labor shall be, how much of the total pool shall be vested in coordinating roles depends as well on other factors. Are the connections between the organization and sectors of the environing social order increasing or decreasing? If the school district administrators are extending their adult education efforts, strenuously cultivating PTA concerns, wooing the service organizations in the county, and stepping up public relations

---

[33] Frederic W. Terrien and Donald L. Mills, "The Effect of Changing Size upon the Internal Structure of Organizations," *American Sociological Review*, published by The American Sociological Association, Vol. XX, No. 1 (February, 1955).

[34] *Ibid.*, p. 12.

TABLE 8–5

Average Size of the Administrative Component* in California School Districts
Varying in Number of School System Employees, 1951–52

TYPE AND NUMBER OF DISTRICTS	SIZE OF DISTRICT ORGANIZATION	N	AVERAGE $(\overline{X})$ SIZE (%) OF ADMINISTRATIVE COMPONENT	S
264 elementary school districts	10–49 (Small)	178	9.5	4.1
	50–149 (Medium)	60	12.6	3.2
	150–626 (Large)	26	13.9	3.0
96 high school districts	10–49 (Small)	55	11.4	4.0
	50–149 (Medium)	25	12.3	4.4
	150–859 (Large)	16	17.6	4.9
68 unified and city school districts	13–249 (Small)	31	13.7	3.7
	250–999 (Medium)	27	14.3	2.5
	1,000–4624 (Large)	10	15.6	1.7

Source: Frederic W. Terrien and Donald L. Mills, "The Effect of Changing Size Upon the Internal Structure of Organizations," *American Sociological Review*, published by The American Sociological Association, Vol. XX, No. 1 (February, 1955).
  * Administrative personnel were defined to include "the superintendent, his assistants and immediate staff, principals, business managers and the like." *Ibid*, p. 12.

programs in anticipation of a bond issue—then the administrative component may be increased for reasons other than internal growth in the organization. Or it may be that with the electronic processing of data and the proliferation of ingeniously contrived business machines the administrative component can decline despite an increase in size of organization. Again, it may be that an ingenuous conception of democracy and bureaucracy, deprecating empire-building, defining organizational size in terms of numbers of persons rather than in terms of an increasingly intricate tangle of roles and relationships, and emphasizing Jacksonian conceptions of government by laymen rather than specialists—that such considerations as these may lead to a stable administrative component despite increase in population size.

But if other factors *may* be at work in increasing the administrative component of an organization (the coordinating roles in a group), it is clear that increased population *is* such a factor. Now before leaving this matter of changes in the structure of relationships stemming from increases in the size of the group, let us take one more case: the link between variations in size of urban populations and variations in costs of police protection. The data are given in Figure 8–11. Now the increased per capita cost of police with increasing size of city would seem most obviously to be explained, as Whittaker Chambers explained it: by the iniquity of the city.[35] And this is the interpretation placed upon the data by a distinguished sociologist dealing with problems in the sociology of urban life. "The large city," Duncan says, "not only experiences a greater relative amount of crime, but also pays proportionately more

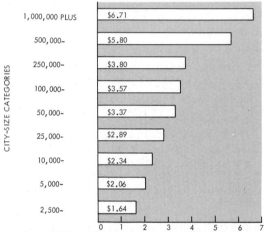

CITY-SIZE CATEGORIES

1,000,000 PLUS	$6.71
500,000–	$5.80
250,000–	$3.80
100,000–	$3.57
50,000–	$3.37
25,000–	$2.89
10,000–	$2.34
5,000–	$2.06
2,500–	$1.64

0 1 2 3 4 5 6 7

Source: This figure is based on data presented in Otis Dudley Duncan, "Optimum Size of Cities," in Paul K. Hatt and Albert J. Reiss, Jr. (eds.), *Cities and Society* (New York: Free Press of Glencoe, Inc., 1959), p. 765. The data are drawn from U.S. Bureau of the Census, *City Finances: 1942*, Vol. III; and *Finances of Cities Having Populations Less than 25,000: 1942* (Washington, D.C.: U.S. Government Printing Office, 1944).

FIG. 8-11. Per capita expenditures for police force, by size of city, United States, 1942.

heavily for it."[36] But he also notes that the differences between cities of differing populations, differences in police effort and expenditure, are greater than the differences in most sorts of crime. In any case, to establish the relationship is not to explain it. To speak of the evil city is to revert to unenlightening epithets.

Let me suggest that an increase in city size leads, as we have seen, to an enormously increased complex of relationships, and that this

[35] Whittaker Chambers, *Witness* (New York: Random House, Inc., 1952), p. 88. Chambers writes: "I returned to the land and undertook that second life, which was not only an experience in creative labor, but first and foremost a way of bringing up my children in close touch with the soil and hard work, and apart from what I consider the false and vitiating influence of the cities."

[36] Otis Dudley Duncan, "Optimum Size of Cities," in Paul K. Hatt and Albert Reiss, Jr. (eds.), *Cities and Society* (New York: Free Press of Glencoe, Inc., 1959), p. 764.

development has two plausible outcomes. First there is the impossibility of knowing all the others with whom one's destiny is linked. Relationships become increasingly superficial, specialized, and anonymous. In contrast to relationships in smaller groups, it is easier to convert a social object into a physical object. There is, that is to say, an increased instrumentalism in man's dealing with man.

But also, and in addition, there is a vastly more complex set of relationships that must be coordinated, chiefly through the market place, the exchanges, the agencies of government. This coordination can be seen as an important function of the police, standing as in-between agents: between driver and pedestrian, driver and driver, between Birch Society rightists and left-wing pickets, between union members and the management they condemn, between law-abiding and the criminal, between local criminals and those who would muscle in on their territory.

If, then, my argument is cogent, we can see demographic phenomena as substructure of the social order. For birth and death, in- and out-migration, changes in the length of life mean changes in numbers available for role replacement. To maintain the group requires a balance between population input and output. But demographic and social phenomena are linked in other ways. It is not merely a matter of filling (or over- or underfilling) a role structure. Changes may be wrought in the nature of the group itself as a result of increases in population. Simmel, as we have seen, commented perceptively on this. The triad, he suggested, is not as vulnerable to dissolution as the dyad. With the advent of the third —and more—the possibilities of a majority, of a more refined division of labor, of leadership, mediation, arbitration, and of the instrumental use of others to promote one's own purpose—these possibilities emerge. Furthermore I have suggested that with increased numbers we have a disproportionate increase in relationships, increased heterogeneity and division of labor and the ever increasing significance of the white-collar coordinating role.

SOCIAL CONDITIONS AFFECTING DEMOGRAPHIC VARIABLES

Now let us reverse the perspective. I have been pointing to variations in demographic factors that generate repercussions throughout society. But the reverse is true. Social and cultural variables promote population changes. Births, deaths, migration, and longevity have a posterity *and* an ancestry in aspects of the social order. Let us see how this social ancestry is revealed in certain demographic data.

Take birth rates which, in western Europe and the United States,

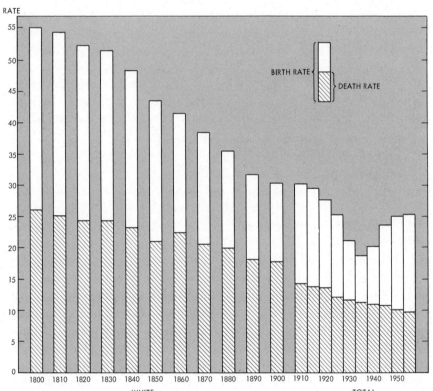

Source: Ronald Freedman, Pascal K. Whelpton, and Arthur Campbell, *Family Planning, Sterility and Population Growth* (New York: McGraw-Hill Book Co., 1959), p. 4.

FIG. 8–12. Crude birth and death rates, United States, 1800–1955 (rates are five-year averages centering on year indicated).

declined from various points in the nineteenth century to a low point in the mid-thirties.

This general decline has been recapitulated in countries like Bulgaria, Poland, and Czechoslovakia, the change being compressed within a much shorter time period. Now why this decline over the past 75 to 100 years? Our evidence suggests that, except in Ireland, it cannot be attributed to lower marriage rates or an increase in age at marriage. Nor can it be attributed to a change in age distribution such that there were fewer women in the reproductive age period. Other speculations seem inadequate to explain the decline: an increase in veneral disease, sybaritic living, dietary changes inhibiting conception, or the practice of women bathing with soap (a spermatocide).[37] Most of the decline appears to be due to the increasing and increasingly effective spread of contraception. In a landmark study of family planning in the United States, Freedman, Whelpton, and Campbell found that in a national sample of 2,713 married women, aged eighteen to thirty-nine inclusive, 65 percent who had been married for fifteen or more years (and 70 percent of all women) had used some measure to prevent conception.[38] Among fecund couples the figure was higher: 83 percent for all fecund couples and 92 percent for those who had been married fifteen or more years. But such data then require us to rephrase the question: How account for the spread of contraceptive practices? Or, to put it in terms of our second major question in this chapter: what underlying social influences are reflected in the decline in fertility (and mortality) in our society?

To answer this question let us inspect the data on those categories of American society registering the lower rates and the larger declines, raising the question: What do these low fertility (and, by implication, high fertility) categories have in common that might promote such an outcome? During the few decades that we have had adequate data on these matters the results have been quite consistent. Urban dwellers have had lower fertility rates than rural nonfarm residents; and the latter lower rates than farm populations. Rates for higher-income, white-collar workers have been lower than for poorer, blue-collar workers. Higher levels of education achieved are associated with low fertility. The fertility of Jews has been quite consistently lower than that of Protestants, and Protestants in turn, have had lower fertility rates than Catholics.

Some years ago Samuel Stouffer found both Catholic and non-Catholic fertility declining in certain midwestern cities, the former at a faster rate than the latter, suggesting a point of convergence at

---

[37] United Nations, Department of Social Affairs, Population Division, *The Determinants and Consequences of Population Trends* (New York: United Nations, 1953), pp. 74, 75.

[38] Ronald Freedman, Pascal K. Whelpton, and Arthur Campbell, *Family Planning, Sterility and Population Growth* (New York: McGraw-Hill Book Co., 1959), Table 3–2, p. 65.

some future date.[39] Freedman, Whelpton, and Campbell found that the Catholic women in their national sample were married, on the average, 1.5 years later than the Protestant wives.[40] Furthermore, "thirty percent of all Catholics. . . . had adopted either withdrawal or appliance methods (of birth control), that is methods unacceptable to the church."[41] This would support the expectation of converging rates anticipated in Stouffer's study. Yet despite delayed marriage and fairly extensive control of conception (among fecund Catholics 70 percent practiced some means of control), Catholic wives in this national sample expect and have more children than their Protestant counterparts—but not as many more as their favorable attitudes and expectations would indicate. Why is this so? There is, of course, the underlying instruction of the church, abjuring mechanical and chemical means of contraception. Further, there are fewer divorces among Catholics and, although most divorced women remarry, they do not have as many children as their nondivorced counterparts. Also, births to Catholic women are more closely spaced: between marriage and first birth an average of 23 months for Catholic women and 27 months for Protestant women, between first and second births 33 months for the former and 36 for the latter.[42] While reduced, the Catholic-Protestant-Jewish differences in fertility persist.

Second, we find in the Freedman study (which I continue to cite because of its recency and its ground-breaking character in providing us with the first set of nationwide data) a confirmation of the inverse relationship between years of schooling and size of family. Women of lower educational attainment expect and have more children than those with more extensive education. If it were assumed that advanced education is related to superior mental ability, then the inverse relationship between fertility and education achieved would suggest a decline in the general level of problem-solving ability in the United States. This is, indeed, the argument of Huntington and Whitney in their *Builders of America*.[43] With others, they see the offspring of the well-born and able being

---

[39] Samuel A. Stouffer, "Trends in Fertility of Catholics and Non-Catholics," *American Journal of Sociology*, Vol. XLI, pp. 143–66.

[40] Freedman, Whelpton, and Campbell, *op. cit.*, p. 281.

[41] *Ibid.*, p. 182.

[42] *Ibid.*, pp. 281, 282.

[43] Ellsworth Huntington and Leon F. Whitney, *Builders of America* (New York: William Morrow & Co., Inc., 1927).

supplanted by those of the ill-born and incompetent. The reproductive failures of Vassar girls and Princeton men are viewed as alarmingly dysgenic. But I think there is no evidence that the less educated have not been able to provide, from among the children in their larger families, enough capable offspring to meet the demands for professionals, executives, and technicians, demands unfulfilled by highly educated but underreproducing parents. This is one reason, of course, why public in contrast to private and familial agencies of education are so significant in our society. But this is not to deny that "better educated parents are likely to provide a more stimulating and more constructively oriented environment for their children than are the less educated."[44]

Differences in fertility are also registered between different income and occupational categories. Both the number and spacing of children tend to be planned more among high income than lower income families, although differences in the number of children they expect to have are slight. The relationship between income and family size is strongest for the older persons, weaker among the younger, suggesting that this differential may disappear in time. Occupational differences, too, are less marked for younger than for older families suggesting, again, a narrowing of differentials. The average number of births in the 2,700 families studied by Freedman, *et al.*, broadly classified as to type of occupation, was as follows:[45]

TYPE OF OCCUPATION*	NUMBER OF BIRTHS AT TIME OF INTERVIEW (1955)
Upper white collar	1.9
Lower white collar	1.9
Upper blue collar	2.1
Lower blue collar	2.2
Farmers	2.7

* Families were classified as follows by husband's occupation:

Upper-white-collar workers:	Proprietors, managers, officials and professional workers
Lower-white-collar workers:	Salesmen, and clerical and kindred workers
Upper-blue-collar workers:	Craftsmen, foremen, and kindred workers
Lower-blue-collar workers:	Operatives and kindred workers, service workers and laborers (nonfarm)
Farm workers:	Farm managers, and farm laborers, Farmers

(See Freedman, *et al., op. cit.*, p. 132.)

---

[44] Freedman, Whelpton, and Campbell, *op. cit.*, p. 288.
[45] *Ibid.*, p. 306.

Among wives who were working, there was an inverse relationship between length of time worked and number of children expected or had.

Let me mention one final differential, that between the fertility of urban and rural residents. The progression of the average number of births by place of residence as Freedman found it in 1955 was as follows: for the twelve largest cities, then other large cities, small cities, suburbs of the largest cities, other suburbs, rural nonfarm residents, and farm families: 1.7, 1.9, 1.9, 2.1, 2.1, 2.3, and 2.8 respectively. Essentially the same differentials were found as to the expected total number of children to be born. Again these investigators observe that the differentials appear to be narrowing. There is ". . . a rising trend in the expected fertility of wives living in urban and suburban areas and a downward trend in the expected fertility of farm wives."[46]

The differences in fertility often found between income, educational, occupational, and race categories are, in our cities, disguised place-of-residence differentials. For migrants to the city carry their fertility patterns with them. Professor David Goldberg has pointed out that among two-generation Detroit families there are only insignificant differences in fertility between different socioeconomic categories.[47] It is the migrant, selectively recruited or self-recruited to urban communities who accounts for the link between high fertility (a rural-agrarian, place-of-residence import) with low level of education achieved, unskilled occupation, low income, a fertility level characteristic of the Negro refugees and poorer whites from the South, Irish Catholic immigrants to major cities, etc.

Now let us return to the question: what social characteristics, what aspects of the social order are revealed in the general decline in fertility and the differences in fertility rates between such categories as those I have mentioned? We are now moving from observation to interpretation. This is to live, to think, rather more dangerously. And I shall be out-generalizing the data. Yet there is something to Professor Bruner's statement: "Better to be flat-footed and wrong than guardedly indeterminate."[48] To be as flat-footed as

---

[46] *Ibid.*, p. 313.

[47] David Goldberg, "Family Role Structure and Fertility." Unpublished Ph.D. thesis, The University of Michigan, 1958.

[48] Jerome S. Bruner, "Theorems for a Theory of Instruction." Dittoed working paper, n.d., received 1963.

possible, let me say at the beginning that I interpret these changes in fertility as revealing a revolution in culture and a dramatic transformation in the social order. The cultural revolution consists, first, in changed conceptions (knowledge) of what *ought* to be. In the physical realm it seems we should not regard ourselves as limited by this globe, by this provincial atmospheric envelope. So entrancing are our lunar fantasies that we're willing to invest vast amounts in sending migrants to the moon. In the biological realm we think it good, do we not, to uncover the meaning of the genetic code, to unlock the secrets of ribonucleic acid. So far have we moved from submission to instinct and somatic necessities as to plan to achieve our genetic preferences.

Whereas the flood and ebb of population was a matter, once, of ill-controlled mortality it is becoming a matter, chiefly, of well-controlled fertility. And we have no question about the goodness or oughtness of these advances in control over our destiny. Socially and psychologically the decline and differentials in fertility seem to mean not merely a sense of the possibility and practicality in balancing income and output, but of pride in supplanting quantity with quality (calories, clothing, and college for a few, rather than a thinner gruel distributed among more children).

The cultural transformation consists, further, in changed conceptions (knowledge) of *what is.* Figure 2–1 gave us some conception of the constant, crescive character of this cultural treasure hunt. The exponential rate of development in all the sciences, and their derivative technologies, provides both impulse ("better things for better living") and the means (biochemical knowledge and contraceptive techniques) of fertility control. As we view these cultural accretions we see man progressively banishing the gods of indeterminacy. Not for us the "bludgeonings of chance." The child of the late twentieth century can say, with evidence beyond Henley's conceiving: "I am the master of my fate; I am the captain of my soul."[49] (But he had better note at the same time, with Donne, that he is so "involved in mankind" that apparently private matters are increasingly clothed with a public interest; and self determination, taken literally, is a dangerous illusion.) Our studies of fertility suggest, then, that man is shaping his world so as to match personal demands with changing cultural norms by means of innovations—

---

[49] William Ernest Henley, "Invictus," in Arthur Quiller-Couch, *The Oxford Book of English Verse, 1250–1900* (Oxford: Clarendon Press, 1921), p. 1019.

sometimes artfully contrived, more often not—in social organization.

What of his social organization? What changes in it are revealed by these fertility data? The high-fertility society (and such remaining high-fertility groups as the Hutterites and the Catholics of rural Quebec with an average family size of better than ten children) was a rural one. It was sparsely populated. Its people were in agrarian occupations. They profited from many "hands." For not only were large numbers required to counterbalance a heavy death rate; many children were also needed since there was almost no other form of productive energy save for low-efficiency domestic animals. Their education was chiefly, if not exclusively, outside the classroom and provided a near-perfect fit for the world of work: direct relevance, honest motivation, learning on the spot at the moment of necessary performance, role models readily available, emotional involvement and bodily participation in the learning process, alternative paths closed or unknown. It was a traditional society. Answers to persisting problems were simply and strongly given within the institutions of the church, the extended family and traditional practices. Family, school, church, civic participation were woven together on the loom of blood ties. Religious model and communicant, teacher and pupil, father and son, employer and employee, elder statesman and younger citizen—these were the same two persons. Thus were beliefs and behaviors continuously reinforced, and without contending or distracting alternatives.

This is to assemble, in somewhat exaggerated form, a number of the characteristics of groups having high fertility (and high mortality) rates. The contrasting low-fertility groups are typically those living in cities, or under the far-reaching influence of urban centers. Such populations have increasing proportions employed in industry, commerce, the professions, and service trades. Their energy is multiplied by mechanical, electrical, and chemical processes and, with the matter of ·crude power or energy well in hand, more attention is accorded social inventions—the corporation, the holding company, the stock exchanges—to match the efficiency of the inanimate with that of collaborating humans. The employment of women rises, that of children declines. Legislation precluding child labor; required school attendance outside the home for longer periods of time and at great cost; higher standards of nutrition and medical care, have made of children an increasingly costly commodity. A reduction in family size is consonant with these developments in the social order, especially since large numbers of children are not required to offset high mortality rates. The aleatory aspects of a mysterious universe are fewer in number and the realm of the sacred is increasingly secularized. The church devotes less of its energies to cosmology and theology, more to matters of ethical theory and moral issues, less to celestial and more to terrestial problems (see, for example, Pope John XXIII's *Pacem in Terris.*)

Points at Which Social and Cultural Factors Influence Fertility

But we can be more specific than this. If we refine the notion of fertility, isolating those points at which social and cultural factors can influence the reproductive rate, we are in a better position to pinpoint the conditions of rise and decline in birth rates. This is what Davis and Blake have done in their discussion of what they call the "intermediate variables."[50] These are the social and cultural factors, present in all societies, that affect the probability of (1) intercourse, (2) conception and (3) successful gestation and bearing of the infant. The following outline of these variables gives us some conception of the many points at which rise or decline in fertility reflects social and cultural influences.

The Intermediate Variables
(factors through which varying cultural conditions
effect variation in fertility):

I. *Intercourse variables* (factors affecting exposure to intercourse):
  A. Those governing the formation and dissolution of unions in the reproductive period.
    1. Age of entry into sexual unions.
    2. Permanent celibacy: proportion of women never entering sexual unions.
    3. Amount of reproductive period spent after or between unions:
      a) When unions are broken by divorce, separation, or desertion.
      b) When unions are broken by death of husband.
  B. Those governing the exposure to intercourse within unions.
    4. Voluntary abstinence.
    5. Involuntary abstinence (from impotence, illness, unavoidable but temporary separations).
    6. Coital frequency (excluding periods of abstinence).

---

[50] Kingsley Davis and Judith Blake, "Social Structure and Fertility: An Analytic Framework," *Economic Development and Cultural Change,* published by The University of Chicago Press, Vol. IV (April, 1956).

II. *Conception variables* (factors affecting exposure to conception):
    7. Fecundity or infecundity, as affected by involuntary causes
    8. Use or non-use of contraception.
       a) By mechanical and chemical means.
       b) By other means.
    9. Fecundity or infecundity, as affected by voluntary causes (sterilization, subincision, medical treatment, etc.).
III. *Gestation variables* (factors affecting gestation and successful parturition):
    10. Foetal mortality from involuntary causes.
    11. Foetal mortality from voluntary causes.[51]

Consider, as an example, cultural prescriptions as to age of marriage (or, more generally, age of union—I, A, 1, above). In our nuclear family the age of union depends in some measure on the young people's command over minimal property, their independence of kin and elders. This is not the case where the group is organized on a clan basis. When the clan, immortal as it is, controls the property, "marriage is in no way made contingent on the possession of separate property by the newly married pair."[52]

Other cultural influences may press for early marriage. When marriages are arranged by the parents, they may do so before the puberty of the partners, thus lowering age of entry into sexual unions. Or, if the residence pattern is patrilocal, a mature but unmarried daughter may be regarded as disrupting the division of labor between her brother and his wife (or wives) and otherwise being in an anomalous position. Hence the inclination to see that she is married early.

On the other hand, in an agrarian group where marriage is neolocal and subdivision of land holdings is either prohibited or known to be injudicious, unions may be deferred until one son can inherit the farm, the others making their way elsewhere in other occupations. (This is the situation in Ireland, accounting, in part, for an average age at marriage for women, in 1926, of 29.1 years!)

In general, Davis and Blake suggest, where the marital bond is subordinate to the filial bond, marriage does not depend upon economic independence and occurs early. Where the marital bond has primacy, symbolized in neolocal residence, independence and marriage occur at later ages.

Celibacy operates in varying degree to lower fertility. While it

---

[51] *Ibid.*, p. 212.
[52] *Ibid.*, p. 212.

could not be the prevailing practice (in any group save religious orders who recruit "migrants" as new members), it is more widespread than might be assumed, even outside the religious realm. Among Irish women aged 45–49, one fourth, in 1946, had never married. Comparable data for a few other countries are given by Kingsley and Blake: a fifth of Swedish women (1945), a fifth of Swiss women (1941), and, earlier, 17 percent of the women in England and Wales in 1931 and 13 percent of the women in Belgium (1930).[53]

The practice and effectiveness of contraception vary widely. Again this intermediate variable depends upon social and cultural factors: limits of biological and chemical knowledge, theological prohibitions defining destruction of the fertilized cell as homicide, social theory that insists that population problems stem from the mode of organizing production and are, therefore, solvable through the reorganization of production, a changing view of woman's role that increasingly opens to her the (hitherto male) world of work *in addition to* her child-rearing task, divorce and post-widowhood practices. For most of the world the prevailing cultural traits are such as to lower the practice and effectiveness of contraception, operating in a way to increase fertility.

From the social perspective this is fortunate since such groups have, characteristically, high mortality rates. Indeed the conditions making for the one promote the other: elementary cultural development (limited physical and biological science and technology); hunting and gathering, pastoral or subsistence agriculture as the economic base; communal property, clan, or extended family organizations; a pervasive sense of the sacred supporting traditional patterns and militating against change.

The Reflection of Social and Cultural Influences in Population Pyramids

Such social features are revealed in the life table populations, by age and sex, given in Figure 8–13. Starting here with 100,000 females (and a somewhat larger number of males, since the sex ratio at birth is about 106 males to 100 females) we apply the prevailing age-specific mortality rates up to the point where the original cohort has disappeared. Here we see the Indian population continuously

---

[53] *Ibid.*, p. 218.

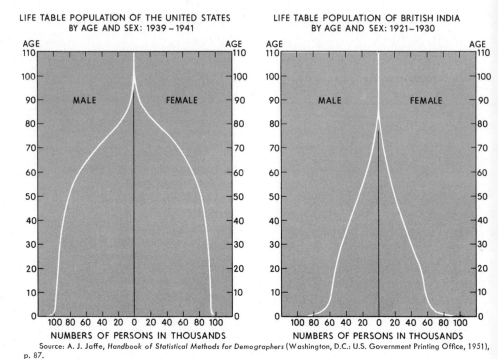

LIFE TABLE POPULATION OF THE UNITED STATES
BY AGE AND SEX: 1939 – 1941

LIFE TABLE POPULATION OF BRITISH INDIA
BY AGE AND SEX: 1921–1930

Source: A. J. Jaffe, *Handbook of Statistical Methods for Demographers* (Washington, D.C.: U.S. Government Printing Office, 1951), p. 87.

FIG. 8–13. Population pyramids constructed on the assumption of a continuation of the age-specific death (or survival) rates obtaining in the years indicated.

eroded by death, and with an average life expectancy clearly much below that of the United States. The crude death rate for India, in 1930, was 24.8, the infant mortality rate (deaths per thousand live births) was 180.0. These figures are about two and three times, respectively, the rates for the United States (11.3 and 64.6).[54] A comparison of expectation of life for the two societies is offered in the following figures.[55]

	EXPECTATION OF LIFE AT	
	BIRTH	AGE 20
India (1921–31)	26.9	29.6
United States (1929–31)	57.7	46.9

The life table population on the left in Figure 8–13, to speak metaphorically, reveals the prideful bulge of the affluent society.

[54] United Nations, *United Nations Demographic Yearbook, 1951*, Tables 14 and 19.
[55] *Op. cit.*, 1957, Table 24.

The near-vertical slope of the sides suggests effective control over death and a steady input to match a low output. We can fairly infer what we know to be true: an urban, industrial society strong on technology which, in turn, is buttressed by well-supported scientific work, a nuclear and neolocal family, a church informed with secular concerns, an economic system sufficiently effective to produce the surplus necessary for extensive investment in education, health, nutrition, shelter, and sanitation, a government that operates to reduce glaring discrepancies that might otherwise be registered in high mortality for a disadvantaged majority, etc.

Now if we look at a different sort of pyramid we can see, further, the way demographic data reflect the nature of the social order. These pyramids (see Figures 8–13, 8–14) are not projected by applying to a given cohort a set of age-specific death rates, but by simply depicting the distribution of persons, by age and sex—and sometimes, additionally, by race and nativity—characterizing a given group at some point in time. Age categories are represented vertically, numbers (or percent) of persons, by sex, in given age categories, horizontally.

Let me highlight two significant features of the Alaska pyramid that lead to useful inferences about the nature of this society: (1) the excess of males, especially between the ages of twenty and forty and (2) the fact that such a disparity must be attributed to in-migration. This is typical of what we might loosely call a pioneer community. Its effects are felt in the family, in relations between men and women (or their absence), in modes of governing and administering justice, in religious practices, in its economic system (work in extractive industry—fishing, mining, oil, agriculture—predominates).

The distribution of the German population, on the contrary, reveals an excess of women. They have survived, better than the men, the ravages of two world wars. Notice, in particular, the marked deficiency of both men and women who might have been expected to be born in the period 1917–1921. These children are missing because their parents are missing. And these are missing because of the disruption of the German family during the *first* World War. So do "the gods visit the sins of the fathers upon the children."[56] The demographic facts of life carry a delayed punch.

---

[56] Euripides, *Phrixus* (trans., Morris Hickey Morgan), fragment 970.

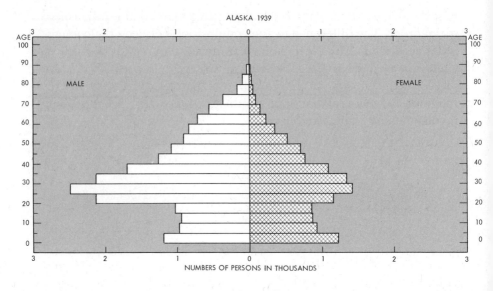

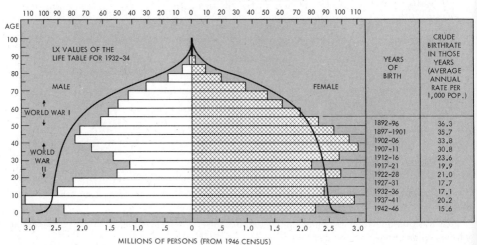

Source: A. J. Jaffe, *Handbook of Statistical Methods for Demographers* (Washington, D.C.: U.S. Government Printing Office, 1951), p. 88.

FIG. 8–14. Pyramids showing five-year age groups, by sex, for Alaska 1939, and Germany 1946.

Or, to put it more accurately, the characteristics of a given social order, registered in growth and composition of population, have social repercussions remote in time.

Let us look at some other intriguing population pyramids, focusing especially on what they suggest as to age and sex. An imbalance in sex and age may account for and promote marked aberrations in a social order. The difference in age composition between the communities represented by Newcomb's census tract pyramids is striking. Children are heavily represented in the first five pyramids, are scarce in the second set. Quite different patterns of family life, of religious behavior, delinquent conduct, concern for schools, civic involvement are suggested here.

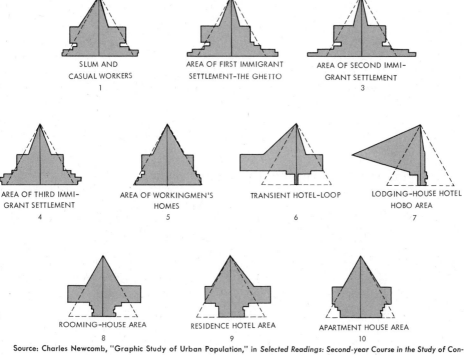

Source: Charles Newcomb, "Graphic Study of Urban Population," in *Selected Readings: Second-year Course in the Study of Contemporary Society* (Chicago: University of Chicago Bookstore, 1939), chap. xv, unpaged, Chart 5.

FIG. 8–15. Population pyramids for selected census tracts in Chicago, 1920, representing various types of age and sex distributions.

In the United States, taken as a whole, age composition has changed considerably in recent years. The exuberant vigor of a young nation, represented in a broad-based population pyramid (like that of Venezuela) has given way, through time, to a society with an ever larger proportion of persons in the older age categories. The data for the United States from 1900 through 1960 are shown in Table 8–6.

TABLE 8–6

Change through Time in Age Composition in the United
States: Population under 15 and over Age 65 (%)

	UNDER 15	OVER 65
1900	34.4	4.1
1910	32.2	4.3
1920	31.7	4.6
1930	29.3	5.4
1940	25.0	6.8
1945	25.2	7.2
1950	26.7	8.1
1960	31.3	9.1

Source: U.S. Bureau of the Census, *Historical Statistics of the United States,
1790–1945* (Washington, D.C.: U.S. Government Printing Office, 1945), Series
B 31–39, "Population, Annual Summary—Sex, Age and Color, Continental United
States: 1790 to 1945, p. 26 and *Continuation to 1952 of Historical Statistics of the
United States, 1790 to 1945*, Series B 18-B 109, p. 2; *United States Census of Pop-
ulation, 1960: United States Summary* (Washington, D.C.: U.S. Government Printing
Office, 1961), 1–146, Table 45.

The Venezuela pyramid, roughly triangular in its general outline,
resembles the typical distribution of a population predominantly
rural. This is, incidentally, the shape gradually taken by the
population of immigrant communities whose people, in our past,
have brought with them to the cities rural family ideals and
practices. We can see this in the progression of Newcomb's pyramids 2 through 5. (The erratic fringe of the Venezuela pyramid is
due to "age heaping," an addiction to the decimal system in the
misreporting of age! In these bars, spaced at ten-year intervals, we
have some clue to a type of error and its extent.)

Age and sex, as I pointed out in Chapter 6, are significant axes for
role differentiation. Since critical roles are geared to age and sex,
marked shifts in the demographic structure of a group mean shifts in
role structure, that is to say, in the social order. The peculiar social
character of certain of Newcomb's noncommunities is reflected in
their peculiar population composition.

In the Loop area of Chicago (1920) and in the lodging-house
hotel and hobo area (pyramids 6 and 7 in Figure 8–15) there is a
great excess of men. In the residence hotel area a great excess of
women (pyramid 9). This is some index of the transiency of such
communities (they cannot replace themselves through natural increase but must be fed by migrants), and of the effect on the
stability of all institutions, especially the family.

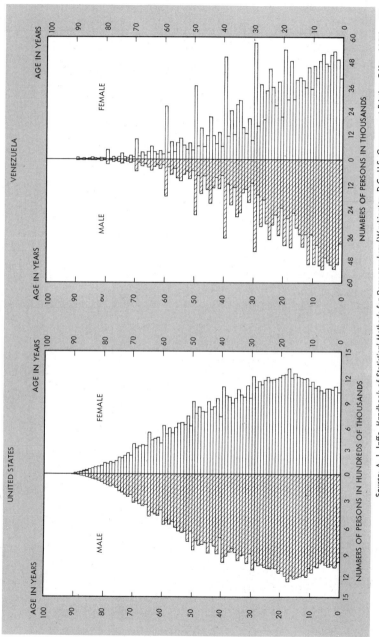

Source: A. J. Jaffe, *Handbook of Statistical Methods for Demographers* (Washington, D.C.: U.S. Government Printing Office, 1951), p 90.

FIG. 8–16. Pyramids showing single years of age by sex, United States 1940 and Venezula 1936.

Cultural Influences on the Sex Ratio

In a monogamous society some numerical balance between the sexes is necessary. Whether or not such a balance is achieved—and if so, how—is a matter of some interest to the sociologist. Do we achieve such a balance? The answer is, overall, yes. But the sex ratio varies considerably from group to group. (Cities tend to be on the female side, especially white-collar, commercial, governmental cities, like Washington, D.C., which had, in 1960, a sex ratio of 119.) But to suggest that we "achieve" a balance of sexes consonant with our monogamous pattern of courtship, marriage, and family life is to fly in the face of everyday experience: our impotence in determining the sex of our children. Indeed, we do not even know whether American parents do, somehow, come to prefer families in which both sexes are represented.

Raising this question allows me to place in evidence an ingenious piece of demographic detective work. It will also give us an example of empirical research. The case in point is a study of the extent to which the preference for at least one child of each sex influences the size of the family.[57] Or we could put it this way: Do parents achieve some control over the sex ratios in their families by altering family size? Or, a final formulation: Do parents prefer balanced-sex families, so acting as to achieve this balance within their families and thus providing for the larger group a sex ratio approximating 1.00, consonant with the legal, familial, and religious requirements in our social order?

The plausibility of such a preference ought first to be established since we do not come to understand our world through the random chasing of notions of zero plausibility. The notion of preference for at least one child of each sex might be supported by three assertions. First, each parent gets satisfaction from recapitulating, savoring, improving upon, his own childhood experiences through the agency of a child of his own sex. Second, although they might not be able to articulate it, each is aware, if dimly, that children are bridges to satisfying associations with other adults and children; but a boy leads to different interests, activities, and others than does a girl.

---

[57] Deborah and Ronald Freedman and Pascal K. Whelpton, "Size of Family and Preference for Children of Each Sex," *American Journal of Sociology,* published by The University of Chicago Press, Vol. LXVI, No. 2 (September, 1960), pp. 141–52.

Taken together, they expand the circle in which parents can be pleasingly implicated. Third, a parent may get compensatory satisfactions from enjoying, vicariously, a childhood much of which was denied him because he was of the other sex.

Now to test whether or not parents do prefer two-sex families, and the demographic effects of such a preference, the Freedman's and Whelpton raise these questions: what would people expect to do and how, in fact, would they act if this were their aim? The answer is given in their first formulation of the hypothesis: "If such differential satisfactions are enjoyed by couples with any given number of children, those with children all of the same sex will be more likely than will others to have an additional child."[58]

The first test of the hypothesis has to do with expectations. Table 8–7 reports the responses of 888 couples (345 with children of just

TABLE 8–7

Expectations of Additional Children of Two-, Three-, and Four-Child Couples, by Sex Distribution of Children Already Born

	COUPLES EXPECTING AN ADDITIONAL CHILD				
	FAMILIES WITH CHILDREN OF JUST ONE SEX		FAMILIES WITH CHILDREN OF BOTH SEXES		DIFFERENCES IN EXPECTATION OF ADDITIONAL CHILD BETWEEN ONE-SEX AND BOTH-SEX FAMILIES
NUMBER OF CHILDREN ALREADY BORN (1)	PERCENT (2)	N (3)	PERCENT (4)	N (5)	PERCENT (COL. 2 − COL. 4) (6)
Two	63	259	59	261	4
Three	61	69	53	197	8
Four	76	17	49	85	27
		345		543	

Source: Deborah and Ronald Freedman and Pascal K. Whelpton, "Size of Family and Preference for Children of Each Sex," *American Journal of Sociology*, published by The University of Chicago Press, Vol. LXVI, No. 2 (September, 1960). Adapted from Table 1, p. 143.

one sex and 543 with children of both sexes) as to whether they expected to have another child.[59] The differences, as we see, are small

---

[58] *Ibid.*, p. 141.

[59] These couples are a subsample of a national probability sample of families in the United States in which the wife was white, between ages 18 and 39 and living with the husbands (or temporarily separated because of military service). This subsample establishes additional limits and controls. It includes only fecund women, in their first marriage and having borne, to date, two, three or four children, all of them still living.

but consistent.[60] But let us turn from expectations to actual behavior. Let us compare the sex distribution of completed two-child families with that of the first two children whose parents went on to have a third. And we can do the same with completed three-child families and the first three children in families whose parents had a fourth. The results are summarized in Table 8–8. We see that with actual behavior as with expectations, having two or more children of the same sex is related both to expecting and having an additional child.

Now the investigators raise the question whether other factors known to be related to fertility might alter this apparent link

TABLE 8–8

A Comparison of the Sex Composition of Completed 2-Child Families with That of the First 2 Children in 3-Child Families; and of Completed 3-Child Families with That of the First 3 Children in 4-Child Families

TYPE OF FAMILY BY SIZE AND COMPLETION	SAMPLE SIZE	PERCENT HAVING CHILDREN OF THE SAME SEX	DIFFERENCE
Completed 2-child families	203	47%	
			8%
First two children in 3-child families	266	55%	
Completed 3-child families	119	23%	
			8%
First 3 children in 4-child families	102	31%	

Source: Deborah and Ronald Freedman and Pascal K. Whelpton, "Size of Family and Preference for Children of Each Sex," *American Journal of Sociology*, published by The University of Chicago Press, Vol. LXVI, No. 2 (September, 1960). Table built on data reported on p. 144.

between sex composition and having additional children. So they repeated the five comparisons I have reported above, holding constant the duration of the marriage, wife's religion and education, and the extent of her work experience (in years). In no case was the *direction* of the relationship altered and in only one case, religion, was the *extent* of the relationship affected. The relationship is more

[60] So are the *N*'s small, especially for the families having three and four children of one sex. The reason for this is given by the investigators. "Given the current norm of two, three, or four children in American families, it is inevitable that [the desire to have a child of each sex] will affect only a small percentage of the families by virtue of the nearly equal sex ratio at birth, most families will have children of both sexes in the course of having the moderate size of family they desire. On a chance basis, about 50 percent of the two-child families [note the *N*'s for two-child families in Table 8–7: 259 and 261!] 75 percent of the three-child families, and 87 percent of the four-child families will have at least one child of each sex." (Freedman and Whelpton, *op. cit.*, p. 142.)

tenuous for Catholics. "It seems that a desired sex distribution is more important to Protestants than it is to Catholics."[61]

So it is a fair inference that families in the United States prefer having both boys and girls among their children. And they seek, through the addition of children, to rectify a sex imbalance. So does modern man adapt himself to the dual character of a social order in which distinctive cultural prescriptions stipulate sex-linked roles. And so it is that the social order is reflected in demographic data.

Cultural Diffusion, Urban-Rural, and Effect on Fertility

Sociocultural influences on births and deaths and migration can be traced with some precision. One final illustration is seen in the inquiry of Nathan Keyfitz, an inquiry bearing on the cultural diffusion of urban influences tending to depress fertility.[62] As family size varies, Keyfitz argues, we get some index of exposure to, and the influence of, those social conditions and cultural characteristics that tend to depress birth rates. And when family size varies with some consistency along a given dimension, values along this dimension become useful indicators of degree of cultural diffusion: diffusion of knowledge and values and, in this case, the confrontation of traditional orthodoxy with urban heterodoxy. Distance (from cities over 30,000 in population) becomes the dimension, the independent variable, number of children the dependent variable.[63] "We suppose," he says, "that for a new element of culture the point of entry into a society is not only the rich, better-educated, urban population but also that, as among the rural population, those closer to cities are earliest affected."[64] His data show that

> . . . family size on French farms near cities, when all other accessible variables have been controlled [these were age at marriage, education, income, age and whether area was mixed French-English

---

[61] *Ibid.*, p. 145.

[62] Nathan Keyfitz, "A Factorial Arrangement of Comparisons of Family Size," *American Journal of Sociology,* published by The University of Chicago Press, Vol. LVIII, No. 5 (March, 1953), pp. 470–80.

[63] This is a shorthand statement. The distance from each county in Quebec to each of the five cities having a population greater than 30,000 was calculated. This city's population was divided by the square of the distance to a given county. Since there were five cities, there were five such quotients for each county. These five quotients were added to yield an index of closeness to or distance from urban influences.

I should also add, in explanation, that Keyfitz' chief interest was in the method of analysis rather than in the findings on which I concentrate here. Read the article for some sense of the care and sophistication of the method used.

[64] *Ibid.*, p. 478.

or not so mixed] is smaller than on French farms far from cities and we infer that the current of diffusion is from the city outward. On the other hand, no significant difference in family size is shown according to residence near or far away from English-speaking people. We infer that the influence of the English-speaking world upon the French-Canadian farmer is via the French cities.[65]

*   *   *   *

The task in this chapter has been to show how demographic data might be viewed as substructure of the social order. This is so since, without the individual, the organism, we lack the "makings" for a person. It is so because the physical and the biological—matters of life and death—are the materials upon which the social, the cultural, the psychic are overlaid. It is so because a regular input of persons-to-be is prerequisite for maintaining the social order.

But it is not a matter, simply, of balancing total output (dead and departing) with total input (infants and migrants). Certain sectors of the social order still overreproduce (rural dwellers, Catholics, miners, lower class) and others underreproduce (urban dwellers, upper class, professionals). And the ranks of the latter must be filled from those of the former. Thus we saw how differential fertility implies upward mobility if a given class structure is to be maintained.

Demographic factors also carry significant implications for the social order beyond the matter of staffing the system and its differentiated parts. Increased numbers entail an exponential increase in relationships, alter the give and take among men, promote social and cultural diversity, giving rise to different patterns of social control. Here Simmel and Terrien and Mills provided useful illustrations.

This was only one side of the coin, the other being the way social factors affect demographic variables. This effect is registered in the vital rates of different religious, occupational, class, and ethnic categories. It is reflected in the age and sex composition that we represent in population pyramids. Blake and Davis help us see the impact of social influences at the many points where they touch on intercourse, conception, and gestation. And unlikely as it might at first blush seem, we find couples in our society realizing a culturally conditioned preference for children of both sexes—through control of family size. Finally, we noted, in Professor Keyfitz' study, the

---

[65] *Ibid.*, p. 479.

influence of the city on family size in rural Canadian communities.

Thus demographic factors influence and are influenced by the social order. Just as ecological factors set spatial and temporal conditions for human relationships, so also can demographic factors be seen as substructure of the social order. But for the structure itself, and the means of sustaining it, we need to look at the problem of social integration. To this matter we turn in the following chapter.

SELECTED SUPPLEMENTARY READINGS

BERELSON, BERNARD, AND STEINER, GARY A. "Social Demography," in *Human Behavior: An Inventory of Scientific Findings,* pp. 588–604. New York: Harcourt, Brace & World, Inc., 1964.

*CRESSEY, PAUL FREDERICK. "Population Succession in Chicago: 1898–1930," *American Journal of Sociology,* 1938, pp. 59–69.

DAVIS, KINGSLEY. "The Sociology of Demographic Behavior," in Robert K. Merton, Leonard Broom, and Leonard S. Cottrell, Jr. (eds.), *Sociology Today,* ch. xiv. New York: Harper & Row—Harper Torchbooks, 1965.

*ECKLER, ROSS A., AND ZLOTNICK, JACK. "Immigration and the Labor Force," *The Annals of the American Academy of Political and Social Science,* 1949, pp. 92–101.

*FORD, RICHARD G. "Population Succession in Chicago," *American Journal of Sociology,* 1950, pp. 156–60.

FREEDMAN, RONALD (ed.). *Population: The Vital Revolution.* Garden City, N.Y.: Doubleday & Co., Inc.—Anchor Books, 1964.

———; WHELPTON, PASCAL K.; AND CAMPBELL, ARTHUR A. *Family Planning, Sterility and Population Growth.* New York: McGraw-Hill Book Co., 1959.

HANDLIN, OSCAR, *et al. The Positive Contribution by Immigrants.* Paris: UNESCO, 1955.

*KISER, CLYDE V., AND WHELPTON, P. K. "Résumé of the Indianapolis Study of Social and Psychological Factors Affecting Fertility," *Population Studies,* 1953, pp. 95–110.

*KUZNETS, SIMON, AND THOMAS, DOROTHY S. "Internal Migration and Economic Growth," in *Selected Studies of Migration Since World War II,* Milbank Memorial Fund, 1958, pp. 196–211.

LORIMER, FRANK, *et al. Culture and Human Fertility.* Paris: UNESCO, 1954.

MALTHUS, THOMAS. *Population: the First Essay.* Ann Arbor: Ann Arbor Paperbacks, The University of Michigan Press, 1959.

MURPHY, H. B. M., *et al. Flight and Resettlement.* Paris: UNESCO, 1955.

*PARK, ROBERT E.   "Human Migration and the Marginal Man," *American Journal of Sociology*, Vol. XXXIII (May, 1928) pp. 881–93.

*————.   "A General Typology of Migration," *American Sociological Review*, 1958, pp. 256–66.

PETERSEN, WILLIAM.   *Population.* New York: The Macmillian Co., 1961.

*STOUFFER, SAMUEL A.   "Intervening Opportunities: A Theory Relating Mobility and Distance," *American Sociological Review*, 1940, pp. 845–67.

THOMLINSON, RALPH.   *Population Dynamics: Causes and Consequences of World Demographic Change.* New York: Random House, 1965.

UNITED NATIONS, POPULATION DIVISION.   *The Determinants and Consequences of Population Trends.* New York: United Nations, 1953.

---

* Articles marked with an asterisk are available as reprints from the college division of the Bobbs-Merrill Company, Indianapolis, Indiana.

Chapter 9

Stabilizing

Human Relationships:

Means of

Group Integration

How are human relationships connected and controlled
for the effective maintenance of a social order?

In Part I the central question was this: How do people enter the group? In answer, we traced the induction of the child as, through family and school, this newcomer to the human group is first socialized. With passing years he enters and is "broken in" to particular subgroups: occupational, civic, religious, recreational . . . And for some, entering a national group not by birth but as immigrants, naturalization is the symbol of a second socialization.

To become a member of a group requires that we learn the culturally given sets of reciprocal expectations defining the roles we must take. Becoming a group member implies a process of introjecting, or internalizing the anticipated responses of others. We must acknowledge, then, the coercive influence of others, in particular the influence of two special agencies of induction, family and school. But while membership in the tribe is open to all the native born, no one joins all of its subgroups. Family membership and its relative position in the class hierarchy has much to do with which groups we subsequently enter. Thus a condition for entering groups is one's antecedent group membership. And throughout this process of entering groups the person's roles gradually crystallize. He gets a fix on his position, as it were—his position in the group, his role vis-à-vis others.

In the meshing of roles we build relationships, and relationships are connected to form the structures we call groups. By structure I mean a nonrandom or patterned arrangement of parts in some whole. Structure consists in an arrangement, in "a set of relations between entities"[1] so as to comprise some discernible whole.

When we focus on such a structure of human relationships we confront the central, generic issue of sociology: What is the nature of the social bond? What is it that sustains the group, that maintains its structure? I answered, first, that there is an ecological substructure, an ordering of human relationships in space and time, making for regularity and predictability in people's dealings with one another. Again, in Chapter 8, I pointed out that maintenance of a social structure depends on a more or less steady input of individuals through birth and immigration, providing the raw material for role formation and relationship-building; and that this input (and output, if we consider mortality and emigration) is linked with special characteristics of the subgroups being replenished.

Let us turn, now, to certain of the ways in which a group's integrity—the wholeness or unity of a structure of relationships—is sustained. It's useful to approach this problem by following Professor Landecker's distinction among types or means of integration: cultural, normative, communicative, and functional.[2] The first two emphasize similarities and refer, respectively, to consistency of group members' values and to the match of practice with profession. The last, functional integration, points to differences, the articulation of differentiated but complementary and interdependent roles. Communicative integration crosscuts the other forms. Communication promotes community. It makes for consistency of beliefs and behavior, and helps to fix agreements as to differentiated roles.

The maintenance of any group depends both upon likenesses and differences. But the relative significance of integration based on

---

[1] A. R. Radcliffe-Brown, *Structure and Function in Primitive Society* (New York: Free Press of Glencoe, Inc., 1952), p. 179. See also S. F. Nadel, *The Theory of Social Structure* (New York: Free Press of Glencoe, Inc., 1957), p. 4 *et seq.* Paul Tillich uses the term *gestalt* in parenthetical apposition to *structure:* a pattern in which the part takes its meaning from its connection with other parts. Form, pattern are common definitions of *gestalt*, an overall configuration emerging from relationship of figure and ground, part and all other parts. See Paul Tillich, *The Religious Situation*, trans. H. Richard Niebuhr (New York: Holt, Rinehart and Winston, Inc., 1956).

[2] Werner Landecker, "Types of Integration and their Measurement," *American Journal of Sociology*, Vol. LVI (January, 1951).

likenesses and that based on interlocking differences will depend on the size of the group and its cultural complexity. Using various terms sociologists have for many years explored the meaning of these two forms of integration. Durkheim saw an historical development from group unity based on likenesses ("mechanical solidarity," as he called it) to a unity growing out of the meshing of complementary differences ("organic solidarity").[3] Sir Henry Maine saw the nature of the social bond shifting as men's behavior came to be contractually defined, joining interdependent differences and displacing roles defined by their incumbents' inherited statuses as serfs, guildsmen, churchmen, and nobility.[4] Tönnies used the terms *gemeinschaft* and *gesellschaft* (roughly translated, "community" and "society") to describe somewhat parallel modes of integration.[5] Redfield's folk society gains its unity chiefly from common standards, generally acknowledged, in contrast to urban society with its interdependent specialties.[6] Similarly MacIver makes the contrast between groups in which men are bound by *common* and *like* interests. Common interests can be pursued and increasingly gratified without preventing their attainment by others.[7] Indeed, common interests, represented by words like love and patriotism, enhance others' well-being at the same time that one's own needs are ever more fulfilled. *Like* interests, on the contrary, are ones whose achievement prevents their realization by another. Thus for one merchant to preempt a sector of the market prevents another from fulfilling a like interest in maximizing profit.

Roughly speaking, we can say that integration based on common characteristics is a dominant source of unity in smaller, simpler groups, in microsocial systems, and, while it is not lacking in the macro system, this larger group of groups gains rather more of its unity from the interlocking of finely differentiated roles. In the first instance we see a structure of relationships in a single, bounded

---

[3] Émile Durkheim, *The Division of Labor in Society* (New York: Free Press of Glencoe, Inc., 1947).

[4] Sir Henry Maine, *Ancient Law* (New York: Henry Holt & Co., Inc., 1906).

[5] Ferdinand Tönnies, *Fundamental Concepts of Sociology* (Gemeinschaft und Gesellschaft), trans. and supplemented by Charles P. Loomis (New York: American Book Co., 1940).

[6] Robert Redfield, "The Folk Society," *American Journal of Sociology*, Vol. LII (January, 1947).

[7] Robert MacIver, *Society: A Textbook of Sociology* (New York: Rinehart & Co., 1937).

group; in the latter, a structure of structures. Insofar as beliefs and behaviors in one structure, one sector of the social system, mesh with those in another sector, the maintenance of the larger group is promoted. Again, this may be a matter of common and consistent standards (cultural and normative integration) as well as the interlocking of complementary differences (functional integration). Thus the affirmation of the Mosaic code through religious institutions promotes fidelity in the family, honesty at work, and the like.

We raise these questions about the linkages between sectors of a social structure because we want to know how they contribute to or detract from the maintenance of the social order. In general we assume that enduring patterns of behavior, *institutionalized* patterns, are those that persist because they tend to support, as they mesh with, other sectors of the system. "My basic postulate," says Kluckhohn, "is that no cultural forms survive unless they constitute responses which are adjustive or adaptive, in some sense, for the members of the society or for the society considered as a perduring unit."[8] And so we raise questions about the tie between educational institutions or the level of literacy, on the one hand, and the political posture of labor unions on the other; about the size of the professional middle class and the size and strength of liberal democratic parties; about the type of land tenure characterizing an economy and the political involvement of peasants.[9]

Now in the rest of this chapter let us concentrate on some of the mechanisms that promote cultural and normative integration, turning then to a further discussion of functional integration and introducing, finally, our discussion of those "frozen answers to fundamental questions" that we institutionalize—this latter as a prelude to the next four chapters.

---

[8] Clyde Kluckhohn, *Navaho Witchcraft* (Boston: Beacon Press, 1944), p. 79.

A good fit between parts of the social order is not, of course, to be construed as morally good. Adjustive or adaptive or supportive functions stemming from one pattern of behavior simply promote the maintenance of the system whether that is, in itself, desirable or not. It is clear, for example, that threat of war elicits a strong military posture and this, in turn, prompts enormous investment in the production of homicidal hardware. Sectors of the system are thus functionally integrated and this is good in the sense that it is seen as necessary. But the existence of such a necessity may be viewed as unfortunate. Domestic, like international crime presents a similar case.

[9] These connections are stressed by Ronald P. Dore in his "Some Comparisons of Latin American and Asian Studies with Special Reference to Japan," in *Items* (New York: Social Science Research Council), Vol. XVII, No. 2. (June, 1963), p. 14.

CONSISTENCY AMONG VALUES, BETWEEN BELIEF AND BEHAVIOR: CULTURAL AND NORMATIVE INTEGRATION

Common standards are sustained as traditional wisdom is imparted by the elders. In the family, through the church, from the lips of statesmen, the tribal heroes are celebrated (and the villains condemned) along with the events in which they figured. Christmas and Hannukah, Easter and Passover, the Fourth of July and Veterans Day—these and other memorial occasions offer opportunities to transmit and fix our "belief in the sanctity of immemorial traditions."[10] That such reaffirmations are commonly studded with cliches and platitudes is testimony to the extent to which traditional views are common currency. Judgments of fact and value come, through the authority of tradition, to be taken as gospel despite— indeed, because of—the fact that the individual does not and need not make a private determination for himself. These things are taken as natural, immutable.

> Individuals for the most part, without any authority of facts, single or multiplied, take their notion of things from report or prevailing opinion . . . Things again and again conceived, upon the authority of others [come to have] the same effect as to be experienced . . .
> From this source the bulk of people derive their conceptions on the point of honour, and on the constituents of rank or distinction, whether birth, fortune, or personal qualities. From this source they derive their veneration for the religion and their respect for the government of their country.[11]

Isolation, Ethnocentrism, Enmity, and the Boundaries Set by Language

The strength of tradition in promoting normative integration is multiplied when the group is small and isolated. Ignorance is the bulwark of conviction, and isolation guarantees a salutary ignorance of other, perhaps contaminating, ways. This explains why certain fundamentalist religious groups depreciate if they do not deride

---

[10] Max Weber, *Theory of Social and Economic Organization,* trans. Talcott Parsons (New York: Oxford University Press, Inc., 1950), p. 328.

[11] Adam Ferguson, *Principles of Moral and Political Science* (2 vols.; Edinburgh, 1792), Vol. I, p. 219.

education beyond the minimum essentials, and why groups like the Amish or the Mennonites withdraw their children from the public schools at the earliest possible moment. They are technically correct in seeing education as a seductive influence, leading one away from the road to salvation. For the integrity of their group depends upon likenesses in beliefs and behavior. And a secular or public education exposes people to differing—i.e., corrupting—standards. This is also why the church and the state have often been in conflict over the control of what is taught to the young.

Similarly, parents of college students sometimes discover the normatively disruptive influence of freshman exposures. This flesh of their flesh returns, for the holidays, an alien. It may be that his rejection of the elders' wisdom is a temporary ailment, a virulent bit of overprotestation from which he'll presently recover. But for the time being there's no doubt that the integrity of the family is threatened by beliefs and behavior distasteful to the group.

Parents and tribal leaders of American Indians found, likewise, that their cherished traditions were threatened as sons, returning from military service, sometimes derided tribal ways, preferring and promoting new ways of thinking and acting.

John Embree, in his study of Suye Mura,[12] a small, agricultural Japanese village, reports the same threat to cultural and normative integration from those who have been away, those who have known urban life, have had a college education or have served their stint in the army. On the one hand they have trouble adjusting to the old ways of a rural-agrarian community. On the other hand, they challenge these old ways with ideas of nationalism, of Shintoism and, engaging in modern businesses operating through a cash economy, undercut a system of social relationships based upon a rice and barter economy.

The significance of isolation and the disruptive effect of contact is powerfully brought home in the excellent film narrated by John Steinbeck, entitled "Forgotten Village." In this village, Santiago, it is the people from outside, from an urban, secular society who disrupt the even tenor of accustomed ways, offending local beliefs and derogating customary behaviors.

That is to say, the sustaining of cultural and normative integration —and to that extent the maintenance of the group—depends in

---

[12] John Embree, *Suye Mura, a Japanese Village* (Chicago: University of Chicago Press, 1939). Copyright 1939 by The University of Chicago.

large measure upon isolation. "Isolate," if you'll check its etymology, derives from the word for *island*. It means to insulate, to separate from others. The meaning of the word in chemistry is most appropriate here: "to separate from all foreign substances, to make pure." Thus one way of maintaining group integration is "to separate from all foreign substances," to isolate. With human groups, the isolation that promotes "purity" is cultural isolation. Physical barriers—mountains, rivers, oceans—promote cultural isolation. And so in a few remaining population pockets of the Southern Appalachians we can still find archaic remnants of seventeenth-century English speech, the strong blood ties that promote family feuding à la Hatfields and the Coys, and survival of old English dance forms such as the Kentucky running set. But here, too, as in Suye Mura, the outside world has penetrated. The CCC (Civilian Conservation Corps), the Resettlement Administration, the Department of Agriculture invaded these mountain fastnesses in the 1930's as the soft coal mining industry had before them, altering long-established patterns.

Group members often resist, both consciously and otherwise, these threats to the stability of the group. We use the term "ethnocentrism" to describe the self-centered appreciation of our own group which is intensified by a depreciation of other groups. Members of other groups are "wops," "dagos," "Kikes," "Micks," "Okies," "Arkies," "briar-hoppers," pagans, barbarians, aliens. Ethnocentrism, then, performs the function of reinforcing the isolation of a group from "impure" elements and thus promoting its integrity.

But beyond the excessive immodesty of ethnocentrism, there is the real or imagined enmity of outsiders. That others hate you or threaten you or wish you ill promotes reciprocal attitudes and behaviors. This is, of course, an effective way of maintaining isolation and of maintaining the group. For our safety depends upon identification with the group, with its beliefs and behaviors. Over 100 years ago Adam Ferguson made this observation:

> . . . it is vain to expect that we can give to the multitude of a people a sense of union among themselves without admitting hostility to those who oppose them.
> The sense of a common danger, and the assaults of an enemy have been frequently useful to nations, by uniting their members more firmly together, and by preventing the secessions and actual separations in which their civil discord might otherwise terminate. And this

motive to union which is offered from abroad, may be necessary, not only in the case of large and extensive nations, where coalitions are weakened by distance, and the distinction of provincial names; but even in the narrow society of the smallest states.[13]

The isolation imposed by hostility contributes to cultural and normative integration. Identity with the group and support of its ways become necessary for two reasons: First there is the enemy whose threats prompt us to tighten the drawstrings of the group. But second, since the group is being threatened from outside, any deviation from within would be regarded as collusion with the enemy. We are bound, then, to submerge differences and to conform even more meticulously to the group's standards when enmity isolates us from others. Finally, those tempted to see another group, the "enemy" group, as more attractive may find themselves inhospitably received and so thrust back into their own group. This is what Kurt Lewin emphasizes in Figure 9–1. B, the barrier, refers to acts and attitudes such as restrictive housing covenants, exclusive clubs, and the like.

The isolation that supports normative integration in a group is promoted, I've suggested, by immobility, by physical barriers—any factor, indeed, impeding communication—by ethnocentrism and by intergroup hostilities. Now language is another means of maintaining isolation. It is a means having the dual outcomes of enmity: (1) it isolates group members from nonmembers; and (2) it strengthens the identity of group members with one another. Every trade, every profession has its own jargon, largely incomprehensible to the outsiders. These terms are like passwords, like identification cards. With them you're in, a comrade, one of the elect. And as in a family

---

[13] Adam Ferguson, *An Essay on the History of Civil Society* (8th ed.; Philadelphia: A. Finley, Publisher, 1819), p. 38.

The German sociologist, Simmel, has written perceptively on the unity engendered in the process of conflict. See Georg Simmel, *Social Conflict* and *The Web of Group Affiliations,* trans. Kurt Wolff and Reinhard Bendix (New York: Free Press of Glencoe, Inc., 1957). Professor Lewis Coser, some fifty years later, elaborated on the Simmelian thesis in his book, *The Functions of Social Conflict* (1956). And Robert Murphy, analyzing the warfare patterns of a northeast Brazilian tribe, the Mundurucu finds that their warfare serves as an "effective means of promoting social cohesion in that it provides an occasion upon which . . . members . . . unite and submerge their differences in pursuit of a common purpose." See his "Intergroup Hostility and Social Cohesion," *American Anthropologist,* Vol. LIX, No. 6 (December, 1957), p. 1034. Currently a number of groups like that at Harvard under Sorokin's direction (the Center for the Study of Altruistic Love) and the University of Michigan's Center for the Study of Conflict Resolution are continuing the search for the meaning and significance of conflict.

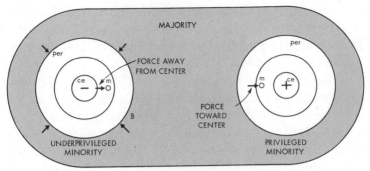

m = INDIVIDUAL MEMBER
per = PERIPHERAL STRATUM OF GROUP
ce = CENTRAL STRATUM OF GROUP
B = BARRIER PROHIBITING PASSING

Source: *Resolving Social Conflicts* (New York: Harper & Bros., 1948), p. 195. It should be pointed out, as Lewin does, that coerced group membership may generate frustration and aggressive responses *inimical* to the integrity of the group.

FIG. 9-1. **Kurt Lewin's schematic representation of the way a member of an underprivileged minority seeking identification with the majority may be driven back to his own group.**

that develops its own special words and jokes from situations not shared by anyone outside the intimate circle, the larger the number of such sayings, jokes, or terms the greater we may infer the unity of the group to be.

A case of emnity plus fear plus an exclusive language promoting group identity and isolating from the outside world is that of the criminal group. Sutherland writes of the significance of their language:

> Because the underworld is an exclusive society, it is necessary that the stranger be identified before he is admitted. The language of the underworld is both an evidence of this isolation of the underworld and also a means of identification. Criminal slang of 300 years ago is still being used today by criminals, though much of it is completely unknown to the general public . . . [such as being "nailed in the shed," or "pratting a man in"].[14]

Multiple Bonds through Overlapping Memberships

Of course the other side of the coin from isolation is exposure. To emphasize isolation resulting from immobility, physical and other

---

[14] Edwin H. Sutherland, *The Professional Thief* (Chicago: University of Chicago Press, 1956), pp. 16–18. © 1937 by The University of Chicago. Note also, on pages 35 and 36, the evidence of normative integration in what is apparently a clear-cut, clearly understood code of criminal behavior.

barriers, from ethnocentrism, intergroup hostility, and language is to stress the negative side, the preservation of "purity" through isolation from corrupting influences. The positive side is repeated exposure to others, especially when the group is small, exposure to others having the same views and ways of life. In such groups the person is bound to the same others by familial, religious, recreational, economic, political ties. Thus he is linked repeatedly to the same person, but in differing contexts. His circle of interaction is limited. His relationships are repetitive. This is the situation we may see in some small communities: every citizen a Pooh-bah—a variety of hats but under each a quite familiar face. This is the provincial, the immobile, the rooted.

We may find it in isolated population pockets, especially where low literacy and simple technology reinforce physical isolation. Such a pattern of repetitive relationships may be found in a utopian group, a self-acknowledged circle of arbiters of taste—any tight little knot of the elect, as well as in the physically isolated group of rustics. The thing to note, here, is that under these conditions there is constant reinforcement of the accepted ways—reinforcement through rewards and punishments. The person is exposed repeatedly to the same views. Affirming them, he gains others' approval, and is ever so much more vulnerable to punishment if he deviates from accepted norms. For to offend persons A, B, and C in situation *1* invites retaliation not only there and from them, but in situations *2, 3, 4 . . . n where he encounters the same others.* Furthermore, the word will have gotten around and the circle of censure will have expanded. This matter of overlapping memberships or multibonded relationships, relationships in which A and B are multiply bound, can be represented in the following scheme:

	ROSTER OF MEMBERS IN FOUR GROUPS GROUP NUMBER			
	(1)	(2)	(3)	(4)
Persons	A	A	A	A
	B	B	B	B
	C	C	C	C
	D	D	D	D

Contrast this with a different pattern of membership in four groups, one doubtless closer to a complex-society, large-city pattern.

	ROSTER OF MEMBERS IN FOUR GROUPS GROUP NUMBER			
	(1)	(2)	(3)	(4)
Persons	A	A	A	A
	B	E	H	K
	C	F	I	L
	D	G	J	M

Integration through Informal Controls: Rumor, Gossip, Embarrassment, Reciprocal Gift-giving

Let me make the point again. In the small, relatively isolated group, repetitive face-to-face relationships support cultural, normative, and communicative integration. They make for more effective control than segmental or transient relationships. These multi-bonded relationships multiply the occasions and extend the situations in which sanctions may be applied. Conversely, one-shot, segmental, or transient relationships reduce the possibility and the probability of punishment for deviant behavior and of reward for conforming behavior. The mores have control power, the crust of custom exerts effective constraint precisely because repetitive dealings with the same others constantly reinforce the norms. And although we must occasionally revert to law to control our deviants (as when Socrates is offered the cup of hemlock "Compliments of the Committee on Un-Athenian Activities") normally less stringent techniques are effective in maintaining a set of norms: disbarment, unfrocking,[15] or, in the ordinary course of events, the use of rumor and gossip, humiliation and embarrassment.

Of the literary arts, the one most practiced in Draperville was history. It was informal, and there was no reason to write it down since nothing was ever forgotten. The child born too soon after the wedding ceremony might learn to walk and to ride a bicycle; he might go to

---

[15] Under the headline "Heretic is Suspended," the *New York Times* (August 3, 1955), provides an illustration:

"A young Lutheran minister was suspended for heresy today. . . . The Rev. ———— found guilty last week on nine counts of 'doctrinal deviation,' was notified of his suspension. . . . Mr. ———— was convicted of falling into 'doctrinal deviation' by denying the virgin birth and physical resurrection of Jesus Christ; by abandoning 'fundamental principles of scriptural interpretation' that guided Martin Luther; by doubting some miracles and the transfiguration and ascension of Christ, and by denying that Adam was responsible for man's sinfulness."

PUNCH BRINGS A BIT OF HISTORY UP TO DATE

Source: The *New York Times*. © *Punch*, London.

"Compliments of the Committee on Un-Athenian Activities, Socrates."

school and graduate into long pants, marry, move to Seattle, and do well for himself in the lumber business; but whenever his or his mother's name was mentioned, it was followed inexorably by some smiling reference to the date of his birth. . . . *They say* was the phrase invariably used when a good name was about to be auctioned off at the block. *They say that before Dr. Seymour married her she was running around with.* . . . *They say the old lady made him promise before she died that he'd never.* . . . *.They say she has cancer of the breast.* . . .[16]

One can only speculate on the weight to be assigned rumor and gossip in promoting normative integration. The same is true of humiliation and embarrassment, the former springing from a real or fancied offense, the latter from a consciousness that one has misinterpreted the rules, or misplayed the role. Since even in simple groups a person will have several roles, there is always the possibility of so misinterpreting the situation that one plays the wrong role

---

[16] William Maxwell, *Time Will Darken It* (New York: Random House, Inc., Vintage Books, 1962), pp. 223–24.

for the given situation. Different situations, or different audiences imply what Goffman calls "audience segregation" (and a differentiation between roles appropriate to different audiences).

> In every social system . . . there are times and places where audience segregation . . . breaks down and where individuals confront one another with selves incompatible with the ones they extend to each other on other occasions. At such times embarrassment, especially the mild kind, clearly shows itself to be located not in the individual but in the social system where he has his several selves.[17]

Embarrassment, then, is a tormenting signal of failure to discriminate audience and role, a failure to recognize the norms, to meet others' expectations. It is a corrective warning to learn the rules that define the roles, to abide by the norms that sustain a system of relationships.

To maintain social relationships is to maintain the normative integrity of the group; for a relationship has a mandatory quality, an "oughtness." When Weber defines a social relationship, to paraphrase him, as one in which there is a high probability that a given act toward another will elicit a predicted response, the implication is clear that a failure to respond as anticipated will be disconcerting, if not disruptive. What is expected is what is normal, and what is normal is normative. Rumor, gossip, humiliation and embarrassment operate to reinforce norms of conduct. Conversely, the very maintenance of relationships implies normative integration.

Another way in which relationships are sustained, cultural and normative integration promoted, is through reciprocal gift-giving.[18] Because this practice is so common and is often activated by quite personal motives, its social function (integration of the group) is obscured. Gift-giving typically implies a return in kind and degree. In peasant communities and in our own rural-agrarian past it may be institutionalized as, in times of catastrophe or at pivotal points in the life cycle, a person joins his fellows in giving labor. There is, thus, a communal pool of time-and-energy gifts to which each contributes and from which each may draw on the appropriate occasions: when his house burns down, when he has a barn-raising, when the crops must be harvested, when there is a birth, a death, a

---

[17] Erving Goffman, "Embarrassment and Social Organization," *American Journal of Sociology,* published by The University of Chicago Press, Vol. LXII, No. 3 (November, 1956), p. 269.

[18] See, for example, Marcel Mauss's *The Gift: Forms and Functions of Exchange in Archaic Societies,* trans. Ian Cunnison (New York: Free Press of Glencoe, Inc., 1954).

marriage in the family. Often these are occasions for personal visits. And sometimes gift-giving occurs at a time of festival, a holiday time when the giving of a gift is linked with common commitments of group members.

A dramatic example of the social function, the bond-building function of gift-giving is seen in the Kula ring: a system of gift exchange among the peoples of a chain of islands northeast of New Guinea. There is among these peoples a regular, indeed a ritualized exchange of gifts having complex social consequences.

Around this ring of islands:

> . . . articles of two kinds, and these two kinds only, are constantly traveling in opposite directions. In the direction of the hands of a clock, moves constantly one of these kinds—long necklaces of red shell, called *soulava*. In the opposite direction moves the other kind—bracelets of white shell called *mwali*. Each of these articles, as it travels in its own direction on the closed circuit, meets on its way articles of the other class, and is constantly being exchanged for them.
>
> . . . though transacted between tribes differing in language, culture, and probably even in race, it is based on a fixed and permanent status, on a partnership which binds into couples some thousands of individuals. This partnership is a lifelong relationship, it implies various mutual duties and privileges and constitutes a type of intertribal relationship on an enormous scale . . . based on a specific form of credit which implies a high degree of mutual trust and commercial honour. . . . Finally, the Kula is not done under stress of any need, since its main aim is to exchange articles which are of no practical use.[19]

The Kula ring serves to identify friends, patrons and allies, to define rights and obligations and, probably unintentionally, to serve as a channel for diffusing culture traits.

> . . . In the long run, not only objects of material culture, but also customs, songs, art motifs and general cultural influences travel along the Kula route. It is a vast inter-tribal net of relationships, a big institution, consisting of thousands of men, all bound together by one common passion for Kula exchange, and secondarily, by many minor ties and interests.[20]

It is probable that gift-giving both reflects and reinforces changing patterns of human relationships. Under conditions of urbanism, a cash economy, the rationalism reflected in an ever refined technology and precise calculation (as in bookkeeping), we find changes in

---

[19] From Bronislaw Malinowski, *Argonauts of the Western Pacific* (New York: E. P. Dutton & Co., Inc., 1953).

[20] *Ibid.*, p. 370.

gift-giving. The gift certificate emerges and, in the calculated bookkeeping of Christmas exchanges, output must equal intake. If by mischance a Christmas card arrives from a person not sent one, there is always the possibility of a New Year's greeting to set the balance straight. Embree comments on the tendency in Suye Mura to balance output and input.

> People are very exacting about these exchanges. A *buraku* [hamlet] will come to the aid of a family whose child has drowned but later will complain to one another that the family was not at all generous with the wine it furnished to helpers. . . . Today, for funerals, each buraku has a *bancho* [a sort of bulletin board] on which is written the exact amount of food and drink a family is expected to give helpers. . . .
>
> The system of exchanges tends to become more rigid and less personal in the business *buraku*. Money frequently replaces rice and goods among village officials and shopkeepers. Whereas, formerly, on the festival of Bon, held in memory of all the dead, all members of a *buraku* called on each family who had suffered a loss during that year with gifts of cake and lanterns, today many *buraku* have a new custom whereby each member contributes 10 yen and one representative calls to present the money to the afflicted families.[21]

Embree's discussion of Suye Mura points out other ways in which the bonds of a small, rural group are strengthened. For example, there may be a responsibility that rotates through the community for celebrating certain religious festivals, for the "curing" of horses in the spring or for repairing irrigation channels. A second mechanism is what Embree calls "civic cooperation," as in the repair of an annually washed-out bridge.

> And so the work is finished. A bridge has been built at no cost in money. The expenditure in labor, besides giving the *buraku* a bridge has offered an occasion for the *buraku* to work together, talk together, party together. . . . The bridge is yearly washed away; the buraku yearly reunited.[22]

There is, third, "helping cooperation" as in cooperative housebuilding and, as a fourth sort of binder, the exchange of labor at planting and harvest time. Finally, there is a pattern of behavior that so well illustrates the distinction between manifest and latent functions, the latent function here being the group-binding effect, that I want to borrow extensively from Embree. It has to do with the credit club, a

[21] Embree, *op. cit.*, pp. 156, 157.
[22] *Ibid.*, p. 124.

device ostensibly set up to meet unexpected costs or to get rid of a debt, perhaps to buy some land. Almost everyone belongs to such credit clubs, many people to several. Embree's description of their operation will help us see how, quite unintentionally, such behavior contributes to the integration of the group.

> If a man needs, say, 160 yen, then a group of 20 friends can each contribute 8 yen toward the loan. This is repaid by him at the rate of 10 yen at stated intervals, in all 20 times. Thus, he pays 40 yen as interest on the loan. The kō (credit club) consisting of 20 lenders and the original borrower, meets as a rule twice a year thereafter in the eleventh and twelfth months by lunar calendar. At the meetings they each make a secret bid on a slip of paper. The man who bids lowest receives 10 yen from the original borrower and any other member who has already won, plus the amount he bid, say 4 yen, from each of the other members. People who have won cannot bid at future meetings and must pay 10 yen each time.
>
> Usually people bid high at first, desiring not to win, and bid low toward the end. For example, in a kō of 21 members the bids might run as follows:
>
> At the first meeting: everyone (20 people) pays 8 yen to the man in need = 160 yen.
> Second meeting: man who was in need pays 10 yen and others pay lowest sum bid, say 6 yen $(19 \times 6 + 10 = 124$ yen to winner).
> Sixth meeting: five men pay 10 yen and others lowest sum bid, say 5 yen $(15 \times 5 + 50 = 125$ yen to winner).
> Nineteenth meeting: 18 men pay 10 yen and others lowest sum bid, say I yen $(1 \times 2 + 180 = 182$ yen to winner).
> Twentieth meeting: 19 men pay 10 yen and others lowest sum bid, say 0 $(1 \times 0 + 190 = 190$ yen to winner).
> Last meeting: 20 men pay 10 yen, and the other automatically wins 200 yen.
>
> A large kō of 40 or 50 members *may last over 20 years*. If a member dies during this period, his eldest son usually inherits the rights and duties of membership. A son-in-law or widow less often inherits. While the interest the original borrower pays is high, he never has to pay out any large sum at once.
>
> At the last meeting . . . there is no real business on hand except drinking and *feeling sorry that the 20 years or so of the kō are finished.* The man for whom it was begun may present the company with a gift, say some fish delicacy, to add to the usual feast. The heads check over the books for the last payments and the kō is finished. . . .[23]

---

[23] *Ibid.*, pp. 139–41, *passim.* Italics mine.

Let me stress these three points: First, we have here a social invention admirably adapted to the need to redistribute the aggregate wealth of a community to meet extraordinary needs of its members. This is the ostensible or manifest function served by this device. Second, since the richer persons can afford (as the poorer cannot) to wait until the last meetings before winning, and since those who wait longest win most, these clubs have the effect of reinforcing the class structure of the group (insofar as wealth is a reasonable index of class in such a community). Such an outcome is a latent, an unintended function of the credit club pattern. But the most significant latent function is the contribution to cultural, normative, and communicative integration provided by the regular and recurrent interaction of group members as they cooperate to fulfill members' needs.

The integration I have been discussing is founded in what Professor Werner Landecker has distinguished as "communicative integration": the extent to which "communicative contacts permeate a group."[24] All the group-binding features I have mentioned contribute to communicative integration. Language—even dialect—defines group boundaries. Other characteristics intensify communication within the group, and with it, the sense of community: physical isolation, ethnocentrism, hostility toward outsiders. Communicative integration is served, too, by the sort of overlapping subgroup memberships we saw in Suye Mura. Repeated dealings (communication) with the same others promote conformity to approved standards of conduct (normative integration) and a fairly consistent pattern of views and values (cultural integration).

To maintain the group means to preserve those patterns of relationship that give it unity and identity. In their dealings with one another group members must have and act upon a sense of common cause. In the small, relatively isolated community, overlapping memberships may be so numerous as to weld the whole into a fairly coherent unit. But in a more complex society with many subgroups the problem of integration is more difficult. The coherence of the subgroup may depend upon its isolation, a "purity" promoted by ethnic homogeneity, language, ethnocentrism, and external pressures or hostilities that reinforce the sense of identity and special interest. But special interests may be divisive and threaten the integration of the larger group.

---

[24] Landecker, *op. cit.*, p. 336.

Conversely, when an encircling majority accepts a minority without hostility or discrimination—when anti-Negro or anti-Jewish or anti-Catholic prejudice abates, enabling minority group members to establish effective relationships with members of the majority group—then a potent source of group identity is lost. (To illustrate, with a decline of anti-Semitism the Jew may move from Orthodoxy, to the Conservative branch, to the Reform group, to Reconstructionism, to Ethical Culture, to the Society of Friends and so on . . . out.) The dilemma is this: the maintenance of a group depends in part on the social distance maintained between its members and those of other groups, but the maintenance of the larger group is threatened when this distance precludes effective integration.

The larger group is maintained to the extent that members view themselves as peers, as sharing a common citizenship. And this is promoted by the institutionalizing of conduct—in family and church, at the polls, through the school career—that symbolizes communal interests. In the small, relatively isolated community the several groups belonged to may represent the major, universal institutions: family, church, civic or tribal group, working group. But in a complex social order where there are many churches (denominations); two or more political parties; a variety of schools —public and private, well or poorly equipped and taught—it is quite possible that the institutional experiences of one person may not jibe with those of others. Indeed, they may be incompatible to a degree that induces schisms in the group, threatening to weaken the bonds of community. The southern Baptist democrat with an eighth grade education who has migrated to Willow Run may find himself deeply opposed to views and policies of a northern Episcopalian with an ivy league degree and a penchant for the Republican party. Living across the tracks may represent an institutional matrix so different from that of community members on the "right" side of the tracks that community integration becomes improbable.

The Binding Effect of Cross-Class, Cross-Institutional Affiliation

It is at this point that cross-class and cross-institutional organizations are of special significance. For these voluntary associations tend to fill in the interstices of the social order. Some, it is true, are restricted to narrowly defined memberships. But many associations, contrived to fill needs or interests not met within the regular institutional structure, draw their membership from a broad range of institutional affiliations. One can think of voluntary associations as interstitial groups, filling in the chinks in the institutional structure. They are a means for resolving the dilemma mentioned above: how to reconcile the conflicting requirements for identity and integration of the larger group and its constituent subgroups. For insofar as they build bridges between institutional sectors of the system, the norms guiding behavior, the values defining goals, and the standards for performance are likely to "leak" from one setting to another, from one person to another. Such a situation makes for a seamless web in the cultural system. So, also, it makes for stability in that network of roles and structure of relationships that constitute the social order.

W. Lloyd Warner's hypothesis about the social function of voluntary associations is one commonly held by sociologists. As to the voluntary assocation, Warner and his colleagues contend

> . . . that one of its basic functions was to integrate the larger structures of the society to the whole community . . . the Yankee City Second Church has surrounded itself with some twenty associations whose behavior consists largely of secular activities that cannot be included in the sacred programs to which the church restricts itself. One of these connected associations is the Second Church Men's Club. The group has virtually no connection with the sacred ritual of the church but *helps to integrate the Church with the larger society;* and, through the participation of its members in the club's activities, the Church is directly related to the larger community itself. At meetings of the Men's Club, a speaker, chosen from the community regardless of his religious affiliation, talks on some topic of current interest, and a discussion by members and their invited guests follows.[25]

Similarly, voluntary associations often cut across class lines again serving an integrating effect. Warner found that "those associations with members from three or four different classes accounted for . . . almost two-thirds of the associations and over three-fifths of all members [in Yankee City]."[26] The data from the Warner study shown in Table 9–1 give us some impression of the binding potential of the voluntary association.

These interstitial organizations provide flexibility, a kind of a safety valve against the rigidities of the institutional structure. For institutional membership is more likely to be ascribed than is the case with voluntary associations. One is more likely to inherit his

---

[25] W. Lloyd Warner (ed.), *Yankee City* (New Haven: Yale University Press, 1963).

[26] *Ibid.*, pp. 113, 114.

TABLE 9–1

Distribution of 12,876 Memberships (of 6,784 Persons) through 357 Associations

NUMBER OF MEMBERS	NUMBER OF ASSOCIATIONS	ASSOCIATIONS BY SIZE (PERCENT)	NUMBER OF MEMBERSHIPS	MEMBERSHIP DISTRIB'N (PERCENT)
0– 10	101	28	2,021	16
0– 20	194	26		
21– 80	131	37	5,260	41
81–312	32	· 9	5,595	43
	357	100	12,876	100

Source: W. Lloyd Warner (ed.), *Yankee City* (New Haven: Yale University Press, 1963), p. 107.

family (and its standing), his church, his political affiliation, than to fall automatically into his associational memberships. These latter provide a setting for his interest and achievements, sometimes revealing qualities and qualifications elsewhere irrelevant or hidden. This may lead to recognition on the basis of demonstrated ability. It is by this route that we have seen Negroes in American society achieving, gradually, equality of opportunity through a penetration of professional athletics. *Thus, where the institutional avenues to success are blocked, the voluntary association may absorb and deflect pressures that would otherwise threaten the stability of the larger group.*

Let us note, finally, that some voluntary associations—especially those serving the interests of a profession—may formulate ethical standards and codes of professional conduct in accord with the welfare of the larger group. So we have the Hippocratic Oath for physicians, a professional code of conduct for lawyers who may be disbarred for failure to adhere to it, a code of ethics for psychologists, and one in the making for sociologists.[27] In each case the code places the subgroup in support of the values of the larger group, enhancing its integration.

THE ARTS AND GROUP INTEGRATION

Up to this point, I have suggested ways in which the normative integration of the group is enhanced: isolation (through immobility, ethnocentrism, the exclusiveness of language, external hostility),

[27] See, for example, Benson Y. Landis (ed.), "Ethical Standards and Professional Conduct," *Annals of the American Academy of Social and Political Science*, Vol. 297 (January, 1955).

overlapping memberships entailing communicative contacts that permeate a larger group, various modes of cooperation, voluntary associations. The strands that bind the group are as numerous as the gossamer threads used by the Lilliputians to bind Gulliver to the ground. I've not exhausted them by any means. But let me only mention in passing the probable significance of the arts as reporters, reviewers, reprovers, and revisers of the social order. Essayists, troubadors, poets and composers, painters, sculptors and craftsmen are, like ordinary mortals, children of their times. It may be that because their crafts are eccentric to the mainstream of conventional life they have a power of transcendance not vouchsafed others. Even so, the critical posture itself may serve to signalize values disregarded, and so to prompt reaffirmation. Certainly where, as in Nazi Germany and in the U.S.S.R., the artist is seen as an agent of the state, the arts reflect and reassert the values of the tribe. It is no accident that nonrepresentational art was taboo with the Nazis and is scarcely tolerated in the Soviet Union. The messages conveyed through art must be, in totalitarian states, unambiguous bulwarks of the social order, praising leader and life as prescribed in official doctrine. Plan, discipline, and commitment are the bywords—not questioning, experimentation or criticism.

The arts provide objects for cathexis, affective targets on which A and B can triangulate and, in sharing their gratification, draw closer together. Nor need the outcome be wholly on the emotional side, although this is obviously a central feature of the artistic impact. Meanings, too, are conveyed. It may be that the artist seeking to convey meanings may sell his birthright for a pot of message—so the poet John Ciardi affirms. Yet whether intentionally or not, messages are conveyed. The arts write in vivid italics the cultural themes of a people, their time and place. Writing on the occasion of Hindemith's death, Harold Schonberg said:

> His early music often reflects the despair of Germany in the terrible period following World War I . . . the brilliant String Quartet No. 3, strong with vicious dissonances and wild rhythms, is not pretty music, but it reflects a period as only great art can. . . . Hindemith's early music was expressionalistic, almost the musical equivalent of a canvas by Nolde or Beckmann.[28]

It is easier to make such assertions than to demonstrate them. But certainly it seems plausible that the arts must speak to the social situation in which they are implicated. And they do this, as Tillich

---

[28] Harold Schonberg, "Musical Logician," *New York Times*, December 30, 1963.

suggests, in a manner different from science and philosophy which are limited by their very strengths, restrained from the daring, revelatory probing vouchsafed the arts.

> The immediate task [of art] is not that of apprehending essence but that of expressing meaning. Art indicates what the character of a spiritual situation is; it does this more immediately and directly than do science and philosophy for it is less burdened by objective considerations. Its symbols have something of a revelatory character while scientific conceptualization must suppress the symbolical in favor of a spiritual situation but art is the more important for its apprehension.[29]

Communicative integration, to continue with Landecker's classification, is strengthened by a complex set of factors such as those I have discussed. Communicative integration promotes cultural integration, a consistency in views and values; it also enhances normative integration to the extent that people's behavior conforms to commonly accepted standards. The integrative outcome is not, of course, the *purpose* of ethnocentrism, of isolation from the barbarians outside, of cooperative activities, of credit clubs, of voluntary associations or artistic effort. Such practices have the *latent function* of promoting group unity.

But as Durkheim pointed out in his *Division of Labor,* the unintended consequence, the latent function, may be far more significant than the intended outcome. (Thus, he argued, the economic efficiencies achieved through refined specialization, the increased production—these were far less important outcomes than the solidarity induced through the interlocking of interdependent roles.)[30]

These four sources of unity—communicative, cultural, normative, and functional integration—serve to maintain that network of relationships that is the group. I've implied that the chief source of integration in the small or elementary group stems from the first three types of integration: frequency of communication, reinforcing commonly shared beliefs and values, and making for a good match between profession and practice. The unity of the primary group is supported through human relationships that are direct rather than indirect, immediate rather than mediated, spatially bounded rather than limitless. Reflection on one's own personal experience will suggest how hard it is to deviate from professed values in a face-to-

---

[29] Paul Tillich, *op. cit.,* p. 85.
[30] Émile Durkheim, *op. cit.*

face situation. Our sense of obligation is aroused in others' presence. Conversely, it is hard to maintain a code of conduct outside the circle of those who profess the same beliefs. For example, we emphasize fair play, hearing both sides of a question, not talking behind the back of a person not present to defend himself. The reaction of embarrassment when, having made snide remarks about a person, he unexpectedly enters the room is some indication of how hard it is to lapse from the code in the presence of the other. The evidence indicates that face-to-face campaigning is more effective in selling war bonds or in sundry forms of political persuasion.

The greater persuasiveness, leverage, influence of the face-to-face situation in maintaining norms of human relationships is suggested in a modest "experiment" reported by Professor LaPiere. Anticipating a cross-country trip with a Chinese friend he wrote to a number of hotels and motels along the way requesting reservations for himself and his friend. Some 90 percent regretted that they could not provide accommodations. He then took the trip with his friend, calling systematically at each place to which he had previously written. When he applied for accommodations in person, the percentages were reversed: 90 percent of the innkeepers accepted them when the request was made in person.[31]

While normative integration is seen in the extent of the "fit" between profession and practice, revealing, in effect, the extent to which group members agree in views and values, cultural integration has to do with the compatibility of the things believed, the congruence between elements of their culture. Thus where people believe it desirable to renounce worldly things, to suppress appetites, to foresake the material world, a compatible belief is the conviction that men are irrevocably assigned by God to certain positions in life. In ancient India, acceptance of the caste system fitted in well with suppression of material desires and sensory gratifications. Max Weber points out the compatibility between the spirit and beliefs associated with capitalism and those characterizing the Protestant ethic: emphasis upon salvation through good works, the moral injunction to "work for the night is coming," the sense of stewardship ("well done, thou good and faithful servant, thou hast been faithful over a few things, I will make thee ruler over many"), the unremitting and conscientious application to the task,

---

[31] Richard T. LaPiere, "Attitudes vs. Actions," *Social Forces,* Vol. XIII (1934), pp. 230–37. For another, similar experiment, see Appendix at end of chapter.

and, withal, the ascetic discipline that uses gain not for personal self-gratification, but for multiplying God's gift—i.e., plowing profit back into production. There is a compatibility between the belief in exacting tests of physical fortitude, endurance to demonstrate manliness, and the rejection of corporal punishment of children. Belief in what we call nepotism, the according of privilege and political plums to friends and relatives, is compatible with a veneration of tradition, a social order that revolves about kinship ties and an elementary technology. With us an emphasis upon getting ahead fits well with our commitment to universal public education.

> In American higher education, the aspirations of the multitude are well reflected in and supported by generous admissions policies. Major cultural and social forces make for "open door" admission to public-supported colleges. The ethic of individual achievement, a central feature of American society, encourages individuals to seek the means of social mobility. The means of moving upward in status, and of maintaining high status, now include some years in college. . . .[32]

The "open-door" admissions policy is linked not only to our stress on upward striving, but also to our ideology of equal opportunity, to our dislike of arbitrary authority, and, therefore, to our rejection of devices to filter out those deemed unqualified for college. It is compatible with our acceptance of high income as a legitimate goal, with the public concern over national manpower, and, perhaps, with our fear of the U.S.S.R. and the threat to "bury us." All of these jibe with an emphasis upon extended, universal public education and, in their compatibility, promote cultural integration.

FUNCTIONAL INTEGRATION: THE INTER-LOCKING OF FINELY DIFFERENTIATED ROLES IN LARGE, COMPLEX GROUPS

Over time the unbroken fabric of common, traditional beliefs has been ruptured. Urban influences have penetrated to rural hinterlands; the Mexico Cities have invaded the Santiagos, the Tokyos have penetrated the Suye Muras, the Washingtons and New Yorks

---

[32] Burton R. Clark, "The Cooling Out Function in Higher Education," *American Journal of Sociology*, published by The University of Chicago Press, Vol. LXV, No. 6 (May, 1960), p. 570.

have imposed themselves, willy-nilly, on traditional patterns of life. Immigrants and migrants introduce values and attitudes eccentric to the patterns of the host. Improved communication and transport have brought strangers face to face. Military service engenders a strange mix of country boy and city boy, Indian and later American, Mormon and Methodist, Negro and white, wealthy and poor. The siren voice of the metropolitan huckster is heard throughout the land, over TV and through other mass media. The problem then becomes one of joining together those whom man has put asunder. In the secondary group, *functional integration* binds into a cohesive whole those who, by virtue of their numbers, mobility, and heterogeneity, no longer share so completely as they once did a common set of beliefs and behaviors.

> It is the division of labor which, more and more, fulfills the function formerly performed by the common conscience. It is the principal bond of social aggregates of higher types.[33]

This solidarity we refer to as functional integration is an integrity in the social order deriving from the connectedness of differentiated parts. In our social order, every man's fate is touched by others' activities; every man's behavior is vested with a public interest. Such interlocking of differentiated roles means that to touch one part of a social system is to send repercussions rippling to its remote edges. This form of integration is especially characteristic of contemporary mass society with its secondary, mediated relationships.

This is not to say that secondary groups—urban populations, for example—are quite without cultural and normative integration. Indeed functional integration itself assumes a certain minimum of fundamental agreements, often registered in law, that enable the meshing of diverse activities. But against the background of certain general commitments promoting a degree of integration there are many special interest groups, bound into a whole because of their *functional interdependence.* Or, to put it differently, a given function can be performed only if a host of other complementary actions are performed. This, of course, is why the strike has become such a potent weapon in our day and why the public, through its agent, the government, so often intervenes. It would never have been so in a rural agrarian past. For there, as in a simpler tribal group, a man more nearly resembled his fellows in capacities and conduct. Not

---

[33] Émile Durkheim, *op. cit.,* p. 173.

that there was not, then, a division of labor between man and wife, child and adult, between minister, judge, and physician. But each man was, to a degree seldom matched in the contemporary United States, independent and self-sustaining so far as life's necessities were concerned. Quite to the contrary, the secondary group organization of modern life means an intricate system of interlocking specialties, heterogeneity in contrast to homogeneity, and a social unity growing out of this interdependent differentiation. As Professor Kish's study shows, the closer one gets to metropolitan centers, the greater is this heterogeneity.[34]

While cultural and normative integration may join the public at large with special interest groups within it, so on the other hand may functional integration unite groups whose beliefs and values vary markedly. Indeed, as Honigmann points out,[35] the complementary diversities of 12 white Eurocanadians and 400 Indians bind them together in a trading relationship *despite* quite basic differences in belief. To the Eurocanadian, acceptance of public financial assistance is disgraceful, but to the Indian it is wise to accept assistance if needed. When the yield of a certain task is uncertain, the Eurocanadian believes that effort should be intensified while the Indian feels that effort should be discontinued. To the Indian, the point in owning personal property is a strictly utilitarian one, while to the Eurocanadian, personal property is a mark of prestige and should be sought beyond utilitarian needs. The Eurocanadian is future-oriented and will plan his life in terms of future goals. The Indian is oriented toward the present and gives little thought to the future. As a result, Eurocanadians consider the Indians lazy, even though the latter behave "logically in terms of their initial premises." There *were* certain common beliefs, some elements supporting cultural and normative integration: the concept of a universal God, the

---

[34] Leslie Kish, "Differentiation in Metropolitan Areas," *American Sociological Review*, Vol. XIX, No. 4 (August, 1954), pp. 388–98. This statement is an oversimplification. In the eleven metropolitan areas studied by Kish, differentiation (heterogeneity) among the communities surrounding the central city increased, with proximity to the city, for six characteristics. Differentiation did not increase for three: proportion of males in the population, proportion of males over age 14, and proportion of males over age 14 in the labor force. But for the following variables, differentiation did increase with closeness to the central city: proportion of professionals and of operatives and kindred workers in the male labor force, dwellings in need of major repairs, proportions of Democratic voters in a presidential election, proportion of dwellings occupied by nonwhites, and average monthly rental value of dwelling units.

[35] John J. Honigmann, "Interpersonal Relations and Ideology in a Northern Canadian Community," *Social Forces*, Vol. XXXV (1937).

notion of free will—making every adult responsible for his actions—
a repugnance for violence, and a belief in the desirability of working
cooperatively with others.

But the real mortar joining these two groups was that of functional integration. Despite their differing values, "an economic
dependence based on specialization united these two . . . groups
much as different cultural groups are united in the city. . . ."

> It is complementary diversities, i.e., detailed diversities of culture
> within broad uniformities that alone could give rise to social activities.
> No category of businessman could find anything useful to exchange
> . . . except with another whose use of resources was sufficiently spe-
> cialized within a broad similar economy.[36]

The concept of functional integration corresponds quite closely to
what Durkheim referred to as organic solidarity. In his *Division of
Labor in Society* he suggests that since law is in effect a codification
of socially specified relationships, it must reflect the principal forms
of social solidarity. Therefore, if we classify the law, sort out the
major types of law, we will be classifying forms of social solidarity
(or types of integration). Now there are, he observes, two principal
classifications of law: criminal and civil, as we would call them. The
first is a set of *repressive* laws, where suffering or loss is inflicted on
the violator. The second consists in *restitutive* laws requiring the
return of things to their antecedent state, a re-establishment of
untroubled relations. These latter are laws of contract, civil law,
commercial law.

Now the first type of law, repressive law, characterizes a group
bound in a "mechanical solidarity," the sort of integration we have
called cultural and normative. This sort of solidarity is maintained
through similarity of individual beliefs and behaviors. Under such
circumstances common values are informed with a religious principle. Their violation is reacted to with passion; for the most
abominable attacks are those against religion. This solidarity is one
of strong common commitments, one in which the individual is
bound directly to society without any intermediary. Society is an
organized totality of beliefs and sentiments *common to all* members
of the group. The individual personality is absorbed into the
collective personality. Thus, when an alien, a physician from Mexico
City, proposes injecting "horses' blood" (antityphoid vaccine) into

---

[36] *Ibid.*, pp. 365–66.

the children's arms, the reaction of the good people of Santiago is one of righteous outrage against blasphemers.[37]

Restitutive law, on the other hand, is an index of a different sort of solidarity, an integration based on the meshing of diverse and specialized activities. Durkheim calls it organic solidarity. Instead of persons resembling one another this sort of solidarity presumes their difference. Each person (and each group) has a sphere of action peculiar to him. Each person is simultaneously more individualized and yet more implicated in the social network.

Now if type of law is a valid index of type of relationship (or of the mode of social integration); and if law can be properly divided into two types, criminal and civil, then we may raise an interesting question. How has the proportion of all law which is criminal (or civil) changed through time? Which is to ask: how has the nature of the social bond changed through time? Durkheim's analysis of law persuades him that restitutive law has progressively supplanted repressive law, that organic solidarity has increasingly displaced mechanical solidarity. In our terms, functional integration has become increasingly the means by which the group, the larger group is maintained. We will return to this matter of change later (in Chapter 14). What needs to be clear at this point is the increasing significance, for the unity and maintenance of the group, of the linking of different patterns of behavior.

A social system, then, like other systems, is a unity of differentiated parts. The task of sociology can be seen as that of teasing out the not-so-obvious connections between the parts. Once he knows how the parts are connected, what function y is of x, he can both describe and predict. When we are able to specify with precision how much effect one pattern of behaving (or believing) has upon another in a social system we can say that the latter is a *function* of the former—i.e., that $y = f(x)$. Thus, certain aspects of police behavior are supported by (are functions of) certain types of criminal behavior. Level of employment is some function of the threat of war. Number of police per capita is some function of the density of population. Density of population is some function of agricultural productivity. Agricultural productivity is some function of average level of education achieved by group members. Democratic forms of government are functionally linked with universal

---

[37] Reference is to the documentary film "Forgotten Village."

education. Capitalism, or its central tenets, are seen by Weber to be functionally linked to the Protestant ethic. Level of fertility is an inverse function of literacy. Peaceful Negro-white relationships are some function of religious participation and narcotics addiction in Harlem—or so James Baldwin contends in a perceptive sentence.

> I remembered my buddies of years ago, in the hallways, with their wine and their whiskey and their tears; in hallways still, frozen on the needle; and my brother saying to me once, "If Harlem didn't have so many churches and junkies, there'd be blood flowing in the streets."[38]

Some functional connections are fairly clear, others not so at all, especially when, and because, the outcomes are in remote sectors of the system. Many Calloway County, Kentucky, farmers do not understand, today, why the bottom fell out of their tobacco-growing business with the passage of the prohibition amendment. (Their black tobacco was sold largely in Europe, especially in France and Italy. These countries paid for their tobacco imports through the export of wines and spirits. With the prohibition amendment, Calloway County lost its overseas market.)

Similarly, there was the mysterious case of the unwanted chicken. This lowly bird came to figure prominently in an extended social system embracing the European Common Market. To abbreviate a long and involved story, our large share of the defense costs of Europe has come largely from the chicken. High productivity has given the United States the world's highest standard of living. This involves a dietary shift from cereals to proteins. Beef and other meats are inefficient sources of protein. Whereas the cow "requires from 8 to 10 pounds of cereal to produce one pound of beef," the chicken can produce as much meat on two pounds of chicken feed.[39] We have almost automated the production of this creature. The chicken has become a virtual protein factory. One consequence is that the export of frozen poultry has "multiplied 20 times in value during five years"; and this bird has made up a sizable part of our

---

[38] James Baldwin, "Down at the Cross: Letter from a Region in My Mind," from *The Fire Next Time* (New York: The Dial Press, Inc., 1963), p. 90. If Baldwin's brother was right, then one would predict that where aggression was not siphoned off in such activities as religion and narcotics use, we would find Negroes overtly belligerent toward whites. This is precisely the case with the Black Muslims who stress an austere and abstemious way of life. They are as little deflected from their grim purpose by sublimations as were the Puritan forefathers.

[39] James Reston, "Foreign Affairs: The Case of the Unsick Chickens," *The New York Times*, July 1, 1963.

total agricultural exports upon which we rely to pay our share of European defense costs. But in the summer of 1963, the Common Market, countries whose leaders' tenure in office depends in considerable measure on their farm vote, wished to protect their own farmers against the flood of fowl from the United States.

> Thus the . . . American chicken, efficiently gobbling his grain, plays a significant international role. If he cannot be tidily frozen and cheaply exported, the U.S. soldiers that help preserve Europe's digestion may gradually be withdrawn. Then the whole Grand Design for NATO defense, interdependence and a tightening Western comity of nations, could scatter like feathers in a hen house.[40]

Functional integration is perhaps most clearly exemplified in the meshing of work roles in the economy. The interlocking of work roles is such that faint tremors in one part of the system send repercussions throughout the whole. You remember the chain reaction in the Mother Goose rhyme about the house that Jack built. (It involved the farmer who kept a cock which waked the priest who married the man who kissed the "maiden all forlorn. . . .") Contrast the rugged individualism of a Daniel Boone with that of the New Yorker when the Motormen's Benevolent Association pulled a subway strike at Christmas time some years ago:

> This is the motorman, now out on strike
> Whose income is rather less than he'd like.
> These are the shoppers who can't reach the store.
> These are the salesgirls of whom we've got more
> Than we need; while policemen in short supply
> Untangle the motorists, trapped where they lie.
> These are the Santas, with quite empty laps.
> No children they'll cozen until the collapse
> Is patched up by the Mayor, hizzoner, the boss
> Who's distraught about three hundred thousand, the loss
> In sales taxes each day from the people who would
> Be shopping for Christmas if only they could.
> These are the cop, the fireman, the clerk
> Who'll have a tough time getting home from their work.
>   etc., etc.

While the verse is poor, the idea is accurate: the tight functional integration of our social order is dramatically revealed in those times of crisis when one sector of the system goes out of whack. Consider another example. Given in Table 9–2 are estimates of losses to var-

---

[40] *Ibid.*

TABLE 9–2

Estimated Losses from Newspaper Strike, Winter and Spring, 1963
(Figures in Millions)

Losses to papers in sales and advertising revenue		$101.2
Salary losses		50.0
Merchants' losses:		25.0+
Including:		
Restaurants	16.0	
Department stores	6.5	
Hotels	2.0	
Theaters	?	
Florists (no obituaries to stimulate sales)	?	
Real estate: apartment rentals and home sales estimated to be off 50%		
Used car dealers who couldn't advertise their wares		
Employment agencies		
Losses to newsprint mills		28.7
Loss to federal and state governments in taxes		11.0
Loss of income to newsdealers (at least 30 blind dealers forced to go on relief)		11.0
Unemployment and other benefits paid		4.0
Loss to railroads from newsprint freight		2.4
Total		$233.3

Source: *Time* magazine, April 5, 1963, p. 80. Courtesy TIME; copyright Time Inc. 1963. These are crude estimates of apparent, gross losses. We should set over against them post-strike purchases simply deferred, the increased buying power of union members in future, and the like.

ious categories of persons affected by the newspaper strike in the winter and spring of 1963. The table includes, at that, only those most directly affected.

THE INCREASED SIGNIFICANCE OF COORDINATING ROLES

The prime problem in achieving functional integration is that of putting people—more precisely, minds, skills, knowledge—in touch with one another so that they may collaborate. The world's work—or, for that matter, its play, its worship, its governing, its education —is not achieved by persons acting in isolation. Nor is it achieved in simple, face-to-face cooperation. The complex social fabric of modern societies is a system of relationships binding together people remote in space and time, people who have not the faintest knowledge of each other's existence. To maintain the group, to sustain an infinitely complex network of interlocking relationships, an increasingly large sector of the labor force is employed in coordinating roles. By coordinating roles I mean all those roles that function so as to join two or more others in the fulfillment of some agreed-upon end. The incumbent, the go-between, is a mediating, arbitrating, facilitating, intervening third.

Relationships more immediate and direct in the smaller communities of the past—the dyadic relationship of owner-boss and worker, of ruler and ruled, of neighbor and neighbor, of teacher and taught —have been displaced by the triadic relationship as the modal form of social organization. All the mass media intervene between the doer and the learner of the deed, between entertainer and enjoyer, between producer and prospective buyer. Advertising, again, is a third element joining buyer and seller. The wholesaler links manufacturer and retailer. The banker joins lender and borrower. The administrator joins student and teacher. The whole of government, the largest enterprise by far in our country, is a third element mediating, arbitrating, joining different classes or categories of citizens. The police and courts stand between two parties making incompatible claims. Insurance companies ally those who lose with those who win, those suffering losses with their more fortunate fellows. The military are interposed between us and the enemy. Throughout the social order any role can be seen as a link between two other links in an endless chain of interdependencies. The scheme on p. 399 oversimplifies, but makes the point more clearly.

Such a list could be extended indefinitely. The coordinating role, or the coordinating aspects of a role constitute a sort of bridge between other roles that require linkage. In this way, disjunctures are reduced and the functional integrity (unity) of the system is promoted.

With this triadic model in mind as the social mechanism for promoting functional integration, we can highlight certain crucial characteristics of the coordinating role: the social distance and comparative objectivity with which it tends to be invested, the technical efficiency it promotes, the power vested in it and the growth and flexibility it enables by articulating skill A with skill B, surplus with short supply, haves with have-nots (a redistribution of wealth through taxation through the intervention of government), task with related task, etc.

Coordinating Role: the Role of the Intermediating Third Party	Parties Joined through the Offices of the Third	
	A	B
Trade union leaders	Management	Rank and file
Management	Employees	Stockholders
Lawyers	Plaintiff	Defendant
United Nations	Nation A (U.S.)	Nation B (U.S.S.R.)
Bankers	Depositors	Borrowers
National Association of Manufacturers	Manufacturers Manufacturer A	Public Manufacturer B
Chamber of Commerce	Businessmen Businessman A	Public Businessman B
American Medical Association	Physicians Physicians Physician A	Public Government Physician B
Board of Regents	School officials, teachers and, indirectly, students	Public
Librarians, editors, publishers	Writers	Readers
Stock and grain brokers	Buyers	Sellers

Objectivity may be increased in the role of the third. He deals with categories of persons, rather than with individuals: the banker with depositors, the physician with patients, the businessman with customers, the social worker (and the lawyer) with clients. On the other side they deal with borrowers, with professional colleagues, with suppliers. Dealing with categories of persons introduces some social distance, some diminution of affect, some objectivity in judgment. The larger the number of cases, the greater the probability of knowledge of the relevant attributes and the greater the insurance against loss or the assurance of success. It is because the salesman, mediating between his company and his customers, deals with them distantly and dispassionately that he can do so discerningly, efficiently. It is because the nurse, mediating between the physician and patient, deals with the latter *as a case*—that is, objectively—that she can achieve the end product, health, with technical efficiency.[41] In sum, the incumbent of the coordinating role, the third, dealing with two categories of others, can take a relatively dispassionate stance. The objectivity, the social distance implied in the suprapersonal coordinator's role promote both the knowledge and the emotional posture that mean power—power to achieve the goal and technical efficiency in reaching it.

The coordinator's role is crucial in functional integration because power tends to converge in it. Consider, for example, the power of the AMA, the NAM, the AFL-CIO, the government agencies by the hundreds. Each of these mediates between the member of the group and others whose activities affect his welfare. As in the case of major banking systems, wealth and power converge and are redistributed depending on the interests of the coordinating agency. Speaking of the power of the banks in this intermediary role, Walter Bagehot wrote:

> A million in the hands of a single banker is a great power; he can at once lend it where he will, and borrowers can come to him because they know or believe that he has it. But the same sum scattered in tens and fifties through a whole nation [lacking, that is to say, the co-ordination of a third party] is no power at all: no one knows where to find it or whom to ask for it. . . .
>
> Lombard Street [London's financial district, like Wall Street and LaSalle Street] is thus a perpetual agent between the two great divisions of England—between the rapidly-growing districts where almost any amount of money can be well and easily employed, and the stationary and the declining districts, where there is more money than can be used.[42]

Thus Bagehot, using money as a kind of radioactive tracer, reveals the functionally integrative role of the banker as a mediating third.

---

[41] Georg Simmel, writing about triadic forms of association, brings out the objectivity of the mediating third. But as always with Simmel, he stresses the possibility of an opposite outcome. ". . . among three elements, each one operates as an intermediary between the other two, exhibiting the *twofold function* of such an organ, which is to *unite* and to *separate*." (Georg Simmel, *The Sociology of Georg Simmel,* trans. Kurt Wolff [New York: Free Press of Glencoe, Inc., 1950], p. 135.) On the role of the nurse and the requirement of affective neutrality (objectivity) see Isidor Thorner's discussion. (Isidor Thorner, "Nursing: The Functional Significance of an Institutional Pattern," *American Sociological Review,* Vol. XX, No. 5 [October, 1955], pp. 531–38.)

[42] Walter Bagehot, *Lombard Street* (Reprinted from the 1873 edition in the Irwin Paperback Classics in Economics [Homewood, Ill.: Richard D. Irwin, Inc., 1962]).

THE INSTITUTING OF RELATIONSHIPS
ESSENTIAL TO GROUP MAINTENANCE

The major institutions of society can be viewed, also, as the third party in a triadic model. In them, we institutionalize (we fix and freeze) certain roles essential to the integration of society. In the family, parental roles mediate between past and present generations, and between the inner, nurturant circle and the outer, contractually demanding relationships of work and citizenship. In the school, the teacher mediates between the family (which provides an input of partially socialized persons) and the greater society whose numerous niches require further, specialized socialization. In the church, ideas and ideals are affirmed that bind man to God and man to man. (Consider the triad implied when we say that the brotherhood of man derives from the fatherhood of God.) At work, the employer's role is expressly designed to join producer with consumer. And in the institutionalizing of political roles, the role of governor mediates the common aspirations or conflicting interests of two or more classes of citizens.

And so we come to the integrating, the group-maintaining function of institutions, the routinizing of the rules and roles necessary to sustain a social order. Now in the final paragraphs of this chapter, I want to clarify the meaning of the concept and to discuss those functions that must be served through some institutional structure.

For a starter, consider institutions as "frozen answers to fundamental questions."[43] What are the fundamental questions? I want to

---

[43] This shorthand definition of institution comes from James K. Feibleman's book, *The Institutions of Society* (London: George Allen and Unwin, Ltd., 1956), p. 52. Sociologists have various ways of defining institution. Sometimes the emphasis is on the set of rules embodied in the culture, sometimes on the roles that reveal the rules in action, sometimes on both. "Institutions," say Kolb and Wilson, "are the rules of a society which directly condition the interrelated and organized activities of the members and give form to their social relations." Or again, "A social institution is a standardized set of rules and the machinery and authority for putting the rules into action" (Bogardus). A variant on the theme is E. A. Ross's statement: "Social institutions are sets of organized human relationships established or sanctioned by the common will." Lundberg, Schrag, and Larsen define institutions as "comparatively stable, permanent, and intricately organized system(s) of behavior formally enforced within a given society and serving social objectives that are regarded as essential for the survival of the group." A final definition stressing their fulfillment of social needs sees institutions as "the large systems of interrelated groups which all serve basic ends

develop the answer to this question presently; but let me say, for now, that the fundamental questions posed are such as these: How can we assure ourselves of that input of persons adequately equipped to man the role-structure of the group? How can we organize our efforts so as to provide group members with the foods, fibers, shelter, services and frivolities they deem appropriate? How shall we know the unknowable, especially when events of unknown nature and origin have profound influence on our welfare? How shall we know that which can be known, extending control over our destiny through the extension of our knowledge? How shall we reconcile the inevitable conflict of interest and inclination among group members? In short, how does the group assure its immortality despite the mortality, mobility, and mutability of men? (I don't mean to be excessively cryptic in posing the fundamental and universal questions in this way. The reader can anticipate that these are questions of rearing and training, of working and earning, of creed and morality, of the systematic pursuit of reliable knowledge and of accommodating citizens' like and diverse interests.)

What are the "frozen answers"? These are the roles, buttressed by the rules, established and organized in such a way as to provide answers necessary for group maintenance. Throughout England it is hard to find a village of any size without pub and church. Church and pub are words that stand for a set of roles defined and supported by expectations broadly shared by communicants and patrons. Patterns of behavior have been institutionalized, promoting communicative, cultural, and normative integration. And in connecting these behaviors with other sectors of the social system (patronage of the pub with the activities of brewers, bottle manufacturers, carpenters, printers, truck drivers, farmers, government agents, *et al.*), functional integration is achieved. In the United States, virtually every community has its school, and we know that it

in social life, such as the economic, political, socialization and reproductive institutions" (Bennett and Tumin). Sources of these definitions are as follows:

Logan Wilson and William L. Kolb, *Sociological Analysis* (New York: Harcourt Brace & Co., Inc., 1949), p. 513.

Emory Bogardus, *Sociology* (New York: Macmillan Co., 1949), p. 478.

E. A. Ross, *Principles of Sociology* (New York: D. Appleton Century Co., 1938), p. 190.

George A. Lundberg, Clarence C. Schrag, and Otto N. Larsen, *Sociology* (New York: Harper & Bros., 1958), p. 757.

John W. Bennett and Melvin M. Tumin, *Social Life: Structure and Function* (New York: Alfred A. Knopf, Inc., 1948), p. 69.

involves a standardized set of roles (board-of-education members, students, teachers, principals, superintendents), a set of rules (how and what to teach, teachers' and administrators' behavior outside as well as inside the school, etc.) and a public need (to provide the minimal skills, views, and values required by the group).

An institution, then consists in the routinizing of those critical roles and rules that support the social order. But what does "critical" mean here? Let it mean those institutions *without which a society could not sustain itself.* This brings us back, then, to the matter of "fundamental questions," the universal problems solved by all enduring groups through those "frozen answers" that we call institutions.

There is, first of all, the problem of replenishing the population: conceiving, bearing, and nurturing the infant and child through a period of dependency. To solve this problem some family system is everywhere institutionalized defining husband, wife, parental, child roles and those of kin at various removes. The pattern may differ: monogamous, polygynous, or polyandrous marriage; matrilocal, patrilocal or neolocal residence; matrilineal, patrilineal or bilineal inheritance; incest taboos variously defined; authority vested in father, in mother, in grandparent or some other. But always and everywhere the fundamental question of replacing lost members of the group is institutionalized in some sort of family arrangement.

But there are few if any groups—certainly not in Euroamerican cultures—that can rely on family induction and nurturance for the input of skills, knowledge, beliefs, and values needed to maintain the group. Universally, then, we find the institutionalization of roles committed to teaching and learning. Education, I alleged in Chapter 4, is the most powerful of the tools consciously and consistently used to bring the influence of the group to bear upon the person. Recall Durkheim's statement that education ". . . is above all the means by which society perpetually recreates the conditions of its very existence."[44]

So also must there invariably be some answer to the problem of meeting the basic subsistence needs of members of the group, and for the renewal of the material apparatus through which objects meeting such needs are produced. Food, clothing, shelter, transport, communication, services, recreation—these imply the institutionalization of a complex network of articulated roles and the common

---

[44] Émile Durkheim, *Education and Sociology*, trans. Sherwood D. Fox (New York: Free Press of Glencoe, Inc., 1956), p. 123.

understandings guiding conduct in such roles. Left to happenstance and given the scarcity of resources relative to need and demand, group members would be reduced to the war of each against all were it not for the standardizing of role and rule. Production is a collaborative affair. So is consumption, or the allocation of product to consumer. The preservation of a social order depends upon an orderly solution of the problem of need confronting limited resources.

In our society, one institutionalized means of solving such a problem is through the market place.[45] A host of intricately interlacing roles is involved through the interplay of which come decisions as to whether to employ, whom to employ, when to employ, whether, when and for whom to work; what, when and how much to buy or sell; how much, when, and where to invest. Such decisions are the result of the market mechanism with all its rational and nonrational accompaniments including the influence of government, the military establishment, advertising, transport and communication, regulatory agencies like the SEC, the FCC, the Pure Food and Drug Administration, and the like. "In a capitalist democracy," Arrow points out

> . . . there are essentially two methods by which social choices can be made: voting, typically used to make "political" decisions, and the market mechanism typically used to make "economic" decisions.[46]

No human group displays such consistency of conduct that alternative modes of behavior are unknown. And where there are alternatives there are preferences: there is the better and the worse. Which is to say, there are values. But values do not sustain themselves. Lacking their periodic affirmation, the new generation will not acquire them and the old will forget them. There must be, then, some system of ritual actions in which the ultimate value system is periodically reaffirmed. These rites and rituals are buttressed, characteristically, by a theology or a philosophy, a creed and a dogma often involving a conception of the source of ultimate sanction, i.e., of God. There must then be some institutionalization

---

[45] This is not true, of course, when government moves to meet demands that are not registered in the market place. Our war production and the TVA development stemmed from considerations outside the normal give and take, supply and demands of the market.

[46] Kenneth J. Arrow, *Social Choice and Individual Values* (N.Y.: John Wiley & Sons, Inc., 1951), p. 1.

of roles in support of ends deemed sacred and the means of achieving them.

If a social order is to be maintained, there must be institutionalized a set of roles to deal with disruptive elements, to reconcile competing claims, to define the boundaries of the group and thus the limits of allegiance. Above all, the function of such roles is to promote the public interest, the tribal welfare. Taken together, we call this set of roles the government. It puts the public in the position of the third as between two or more competing special interests, a third whose power is ultimate and whose interest transcends that of any member or any subgroup. In our society a primary function is to convert an aggregated distribution of preferences into an integral characteristic of the whole. I mean by this that, in the legislative process we aggregate individual decisions or choices, and having discovered where the weight of opinion lies, a decision is made *now binding on all members of the group.* There is now a single way, a single preference, a law binding all members of the group. If a group is to endure there must be an authoritative allocation of power. The authority may stem from tradition, from the supernatural power of a leader endowed with the gift of grace (charisma) or as the result of rational-legal considerations.[47] But a social order without the authority to preserve that order (or to alter it in orderly fashion) is a contradiction in terms.

What I have been contending, then, is that the integration of a social order—indeed, its very existence—depends upon a set of institutions. These can be crudely described as family and school, church, state, and economy. This is one way of cutting the pie of the *functional prerequisites for maintaining the group.*[48] Talcott Parsons takes a more formal and analytical approach. The preservation of any social system, he suggests, depends on an interplay with the outside world (the environing social system) such as to achieve its goals effectively. It also requires mechanisms for eliciting and affirming members' loyalties, and for reducing disruptive tensions.

---

[47] Max Weber, *Theory of Social and Economic Organization,* trans. Talcott Parsons (New York: Oxford University Press, Inc., 1947). See Part III on "The Types of Authority and Imperative Co-ordination," p. 324 *et seq.*

[48] For a more sophisticated and, as I think, a better statement, see D. F. Aberle, A. K. Cohen, A. K. Davis, M. J. Levy, Jr., and F. X. Sutton, "The Functional Prerequisites of a Society," *Ethics,* Vol. LX (January, 1950), pp. 100–111. I use a simpler and less abstract classification of prerequisites in order to tie in, more explicitly, with the four chapters that follow.

Take the family as an example of a social micro system. Achieving its standards of material welfare entails certain adaptations to the outside world: regular employment, a desire to "get ahead," collaboration of the wife, education of the children. And we can shift our attention to the American social order as a whole (the macro system) and still see this instrumental linking of ends and means. To "insure domestic Tranquility, provide for the common defence, promote the general Welfare, and secure the Blessings of Liberty to ourselves and our Posterity"—these goals prompt the instituting of such means as those embodied in the structure of government, in our military forces, in the apparatus of international trade, and in the elaboration of international organizations that effect adaptive compromises between competing national interests.

The affirmation of group unity is effected by rules, morals, creeds, symbols, uniforms, language, and a host of other mechanisms activated in the institutionalized roles of parent, priest, and politician. Again taking the family as a micro system, the family name, residence patterns, the obligations embodied in written law and unwritten tradition—such spouse-child-parent expectation sets unify and bound the group we call a family. And in this group there is institutionalized allowance for a range of emotional expression, from love to hostility, that makes it, as Parsons proposes, the prime setting for tension release and management. Similarly in the larger system—take, again, the United States as a social order—there are, necessarily, roles and relationships instituted to affirm loyalties and support the integration of the system. The rights, duties, and periodic affirmations of citizenship are obvious examples. So also do we fix roles to reduce the divisive effect of inevitable differences and antagonisms. Such roles are seen in the machinery of courts, police, and legislature, reducing tensions as they mediate conflicting claims.

Thus institutions can be viewed as principal means of meeting four needs of any social system: the specifying of goals, the fixing of appropriate means to achieve them, sustaining the group's integrity and reducing disruptive tendencies.

❖   ❖   ❖   ❖

In this chapter I raised the question: How are human relationships connected and controlled for the effective maintenance of the social order? I suggested four classes of answers: (1) a set of informal or unplanned behaviors contributing to cultural and normative (through communicative) integration. These were such things as isolation (topographically, linguistically, or ethnocentrically induced), gift-giving, endogamous marriage restrictions, sundry cooperative activities, the arts, etc.; (2) voluntary associations providing an interstitial mortar between the institutional bricks of the social order; (3) functional integration as, through the offices of the coordinating role, diverse but complementary activities are meshed; and (4) the central and indispensable role structures that are instituted to provide answers to fundamental questions of group survival.

Now we turn, in the next four chapters, to more detailed consideration of these institutions that constitute the core of the social structure.

APPENDIX

As another modest experiment in testing the power of communicative integration, the influence of face-to-face contact, in maintaining cultural and normative integration, you might try the following with any fairly large number of respondents—say 50 to 100. Instructions, the material of the experiment and mode of analysis follow:

I am going to tell you three stories, each of which ends with an unintended error or mishap. In each case, the person has the choice of correcting the error or letting it stand. I want you to indicate what, in your mind, *the likeliest outcome was*. Do this by putting three check marks, one for each story, in the following table:

		STORY		
		1	2	3
Does he rectify the error?	Yes			
	No			

Here are the stories:

1. An indigent New York boy suffering the pangs of the lovelorn is making a long-distance call—an expensive one, for him—to his girl in San Francisco. After he has deposited an exorbitant part of his weekly earnings and stuttered through the first three minutes of conversation, the operator intrudes to tell him that his time is up and to request an additional contribution to AT&T. This he does and proceeds until, finally, his funds are exhausted and he must, with loving regrets

and regretful love, hang up. It is at this point that a minor miracle occurs somewhere in the mechanical viscera of the machine. By some mischance, a flood of silver pours back into the change-return slot— several dollars in silver. Does he rectify the error? Yes or no?

2. Our same boy, wending his way toward the Golden Gate—and the girl—is now pacing a bus station in Chicago during a rest stop. Eyeing a sales counter in the station, he's reminded that he needs razor blades, a new toothbrush, and sundry other things. His bill comes to 87 cents and he hands the salesgirl a dollar bill. Her uncertain pecking at the cash register, and the fact that she puts his bill immediately in the tray and not on the shelf, suggests that she's a novice. She returns with his change, counting it out in his palm: "three is 90 and 10's a dollar," and, putting the bills in his hand one by one, "two, three, four, and five and thank you." Does he rectify the error? Or not?

3. Now the young man is back in the bosom of his family recalling with some chagrin that he neglected to buy his kid sister, three years old, the doll clothes hangers he'd promised her, for Christmas. He's down in the neighborhood store where he'd seen this item along with a display of dolls and toys before Christmas. He and the clerk pass the time of day, discuss the weather, and our friend reports on his trip to San Francisco. Finally, he tells the clerk what he needs to buy for the kid sister. The clerk remembers that Jane, whom he knows by name, had been in a couple of times with her parents and had wanted the tiny hangers for her dolls' clothes.

"But," says the clerk, "I dunno that we've got any of those left. They just about cleaned us out at Christmas time. Come on back and we'll look."

They look, but nothing doing.

"Well," the clerk says, "maybe we can rig something up. Let's try it with some No. 10 wire. Hand me those pliers."

The clerk then proceeds to bend together a reasonable facsimile of a clothes hanger, bending the curved part around a pipe to get a smooth loop. All in all, he contrives three of these. After a bit more conversation, the young man says he must go and asks how much it is.

"Oh, I dunno," the clerk responds. "The wire would be, say, maybe a dime for each and I'll call it a nickel's worth of labor: 35 cents."

The young man offers him a one dollar bill which the clerk stuffs thoughtlessly into the register while getting out the change: "Thirty-five and five is 40 and 10 is 50, 50's a dollar, two, three, four, and five." Does the young man rectify the error? Or not?

I would be very much surprised if the distribution of your data, as has always been the case when I tried it, did not move from lower left cell to upper right, in the six-celled table on the preceding page. A χ^2 analysis will let you know whether the distribution of your data departs significantly from a chance distribution. (See the discussion of the chi-square test in Chapter 3.)

SELECTED SUPPLEMENTARY READINGS

*ABERLE, DAVID F.; COHEN, A. K.; DAVIS, A. K.; LEVY, M. J., JR.; AND SUTTON, F. X. "The Functional Prerequisites of a Society," *Ethics,* Vol. 60 (Janaury, 1950).

BERELSON, BERNARD, AND STEINER, GARY A. "Organizations," in *Human Behavior: An Inventory of Scientific Findings,* pp. 363–80. New York: Harcourt, Brace & World, Inc., 1964.

GOULDNER, ALVIN W. "Organizational Analysis," in Robert K. Merton, Leonard Broom, and Leonard S. Cottrell, Jr. (eds.), *Sociology Today,* ch. xviii. New York: Harper & Row—Harper Torchbooks, 1965.

*LANDECKER, WERNER S. "Types of Integration and Their Measurement," *American Journal of Sociology,* Vol. LVI (January, 1951) pp. 332–40.

NEWCOMB, THEODORE M. "The Study of Consensus," in Robert K. Merton, Leonard Broom, and Leonard S. Cottrell, Jr. (eds.), *Sociology Today,* ch. xii. New York: Harper & Row—Harper Torchbooks, 1965.

*SHERIF, MUZAFER. "Superordinate Goals in the Reduction of Intergroup Conflict," *American Journal of Sociology,* Vol. LXIII, No. 4 (January, 1958), pp. 349–56.

---

* Articles marked with an asterisk are available as reprints from the college division of the Bobbs-Merrill Company, Indianapolis, Indiana.

Chapter 10

Family and School: Institutions of Induction

How do we maintain the input of skills, knowledge
and values necessary to maintain the social order?

The continuous supply of adequately socialized replacements for those dying, or otherwise departing,[1] requires a social mechanism. Such a mechanism we find in family and school, institutionalized agents of socialization that we discussed briefly in Chapter 4. The family as an institution is a system of rules generally shared, and of roles locally exhibited—in homes throughout the country. Look down from the air on any American community: converging arteries of traffic, tall buildings at the core, warehouses and light manufacturing plants, apartment houses, duplex and single-family dwellings stretching out, mile upon mile to suburbia. In each of these homes—whether "ticky-tacky little boxes" or the more sumptuous estates tucked away in copses—we find a similar set of roles, varying somewhat by class but within a given range of tolerance and supported by common understandings. The remarkable thing is that these roles and rules are so routinized that they are duplicated in other communities throughout the land.

---

[1] In the category of "otherwise departing," I include persons who leave their usual roles: the imprisoned, those hospitalized or chronically ill, people retiring and so moving out of the labor force, and out-migrants.

Learning the cultural score through institutions of induction.

A GLANCE AT THE INTERNAL STRUCTURE OF THE FAMILY

In each of these boxes there is a family, a social micro system, a "unity of interacting personalities" as Burgess called it. And each of these micro systems meshes with the external social order, the macro system, performing functions required for its survival. Thus we have two perspectives for looking at this institution: its internal structure and its linkage with the larger social order. Let's look first at some of the ideas and research bearing on the internal structure of the family. In the accompanying diagram the numbers represent the sequence in which we'll consider the interlocking set of relationships that constitutes the nuclear family. In each case we will consider one aspect of the relationship that varies, either as independent or dependent variable.

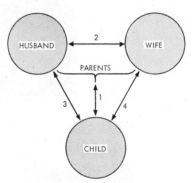

Parent-Child Relationships

A recurrent finding of sociological research is the way in which one attribute of the parents, class position, varies with or predicts to the patterns of child rearing. Our data have to do, chiefly, with middle- and lower-class parents. (Material on the upper class is most meager.) Child-rearing patterns differ because the lower-class American inherits a cultural tradition that stipulates a parental role peculiar to his conditions. Accustomed to dealing with things, under supervision, he stresses obedient response to orders, being neat, clean, and pleasing one's superiors, parents, and other adults. The middle-class parent deals with the child in a way that has been called "developmental."[2] Accustomed to more self-directed work

---

[2] Evelyn Millis Duval, "Conceptions of Parenthood," *American Journal of Sociology,* Vol. LII (November, 1946), pp. 193–203.

with ideas, symbols, and human relationships, this parent emphasizes inner states in the growth of his child: curiosity, happiness, sharing, and cooperation, eagerness to learn, confidence in parents, and the development of self-control. Professor Bronfenbrenner, summarizing twenty-five years of studies of parent-child relationships (up to 1958) says:

> Over the entire . . . period studied, parent-child relationships in the middle-class are consistently reported as more acceptant and equalitarian, while those in the working class are oriented toward maintaining order and obedience.[3]

These contrasts, by class, can be summarized as in Table 10–1. It is based on a perceptive essay by Melvin Kohn[4] in which he suggests that differences, by class, in child-rearing patterns cannot be explained simply by invoking differences in education. He argues persuasively that knowing is supported by valuing, that middle- and lower-class parental values stem from and reinforce quite different life conditions that have their reflection in different modes of child rearing. "The interpretive model, in essence, is: social class→conditions of life→values→behavior."[5]

Husband-Wife Relationships

Consider, now, the husband-wife relationship (relationship number 2 in the diagram on page 412) and the role of each. Some investigators have thought that husband and wife roles have changed through time, shifting from fairly fixed institutional forms toward an equalitarian and often transient companionship having

---

[3] Urie Bronfenbrenner, "Socialization and Social Class through Time and Space," in Eleanor E. Maccoby, Theodore M. Newcomb, and Eugene L. Hartley (eds.), *Readings in Social Psychology* (New York: Holt, Rinehart & Winston, Inc., 1958).

[4] Melvin L. Kohn, "Social Class and Parent-Child Relationships: An Interpretation" *American Journal of Sociology*, published by The University of Chicago Press, Vol. LXVIII, No. 4 (January, 1963), pp. 471–80. See also in this connection Martha Ericson, "Child-rearing and Social Status," *American Journal of Sociology*, Vol. LII, No. 3 (November, 1946), pp. 190–92. In this comparison of middle- and lower-class child-rearing practices she reports the middle-class parents as being more demanding, starting toilet training practices earlier, supervising more closely the child's activities, placing more emphasis on early responsiveness and on individual achievement. Her middle-class children were taken off the bottle earlier, (fewer were breast-fed), three times as many as among the lower-class children were thumb-suckers. Middle-class youngsters were expected to be back in the house earlier at night. They start later going alone to movies at night. They are expected to prepare themselves for some profession. In general, she found them more achievement-oriented and anxious.

[5] Kohn, *op. cit.,* p. 480.

TABLE 10–1

Contrasts, by Class, in Child-Rearing Patterns

CLASS	CHARACTERISTICS OF PARENTAL OCCUPATIONS	GENERAL ORIENTA- TION OF PARENTS	WANT CHILDREN TO BE	STRESS UPON	SOURCE OF CONTROL
Working and lower-middle	Dealing with things under supervision, getting ahead dependent on a collective orientation	Traditional	Neat, clean, obedient, respectful, please adults	Overt acts	External proscriptions and punishment stemming from the immediate consequences of an act
Middle	Working with ideas, symbols, relationships . . . self-directed, getting ahead dependent on one's own achievements	Developmental	Happy, sharing, cooperative, curious, eager learners, loving, self-controlled	Inner states	Self-direction and punishment stemming from the intent of the act

something of the character of a voluntary association.[6] Certainly the change from a rural-agrarian past to an urban-industrial present cannot fail to have penetrated every aspect of American life. If Alexis de Tocqueville's observations were correct, there is a marked contrast between the role of women and wives in the United States today and the situation as he saw it in 1840.

In no country has such constant care been taken as in America to trace two clearly distinct lines of action for the two sexes and to make them keep pace one with the other, but in two pathways that are always different. American women never manage the outward concerns of the family or conduct a business or take part in political life; nor are they, on the other hand, ever compelled to perform the rough labor of the fields or to make any of those laborious efforts which demand the exertion of physical strength. No families are so poor as to form an exception to this rule. If, on the one hand, an American woman cannot escape from the quiet circle of domestic employments, she is never forced, on the other, to go beyond it. Hence it is that the women of America, who often exhibit a masculine strength of understanding and a manly energy, generally preserve great delicacy of personal appearance and always retain the manners of women although they sometimes show that they have the hearts and minds of men.

Nor have the Americans ever supposed that one consequence of

---

[6] Ernest W. Burgess and Harvey J. Locke, *The Family: From Institution to Companionship* (New York: American Book Co., 1953).

democratic principles is the subversion of marital power or the confusion of the natural authorities in families. They hold that every association must have a head in order to accomplish its object, and that the natural head of the conjugal association is man. They do not therefore deny him the right of directing his partner, and they maintain that in the smaller association of husband and wife as well as in the great social community the object of democracy is to regulate and legalize the powers that are necessary, and not to subvert all power.

This opinion is not peculiar to one sex and contested by the other; I never observed that the women of America consider conjugal authority as an unfortunate usurpation of their rights, or that they thought themselves degraded by submitting to it.

It would seem in Europe, where man so easily submits to the despotic sway of women, that they are nevertheless deprived of some of the greatest attributes of the human species and considered as seductive but imperfect beings. . . .

It is true that the Americans rarely lavish upon women those eager attentions which are commonly paid them in Europe, but their conduct to women always implies that they suppose them to be virtuous and refined; and such is the respect entertained for the moral freedom of the sex that in the presence of a woman the most guarded language is used. . . .

Thus the Americans do not think that man and woman have either the duty or the right to perform the same offices, but they show an equal regard for both their respective parts; and though their lot is different, they consider both of them as being of equal value. They do not give to the courage of woman the same form or the same direction as to that of man, but they never doubt her courage; and if they hold that man and his partner ought not always to exercise their intellect and understanding in the same manner, they at least believe the understanding of the one to be as sound as that of the other, and her intellect to be as clear. Thus, then, while they have allowed the social inferiority of woman to continue, they have done all they could to raise her morally and intellectually to the level of man; and in this respect they appear to me to have excellently understood the true principle of democratic government.[7]

Eighty years after de Tocqueville wrote, both because of the changing nature of our labor force and as a result of women's seeking equality in the economic sphere, there was established in the United States Department of Labor a Women's Bureau to formulate "standards and policies for promoting the welfare of wage-earning women, improving their working conditions and

---

[7] Alexis de Tocqueville, *Democracy in America* (New York: Alfred A. Knopf, Inc., 1946), Vol. II, pp. 212–14.

advancing their opportunities for profitable employment." In the same year (1920) we passed an amendment to the Constitution of the United States, Article XIX, which reads: "The right of citizens of the United States to vote shall not be denied or abridged by the United States or by any state on account of sex." Clearly it has not been possible, in the years since de Tocqueville, to keep the American woman in her place![8]

But to think of the husband-wife relationship as shifting through time from husband-dominant to equalitarian is, doubtless, to project contemporary middle-class standards and to oversimplify matters. There are other possibilities: the wife-dominant relationship or one in which each dominates as he can, thus creating conflict. Professor Murray Straus has investigated the meaning of these four possible modes of husband-wife relationships for the achievement and anxiety levels of 287 juniors and seniors in the high schools of a Wisconsin county in 1959.[9] Acceptance-rejection of parents and active-future versus passive-present posture were also measured as variables depending on pattern of dominance in husband-wife relationships.

On the independent variable, dominance in husband-wife relationships, Straus found the following for parents of his 287 boys:

	PERCENT
Equalitarian (or "autonomic," relationship as Straus calls them)	40
Husband-dominant	25
Conflicting (both seeking to dominate)	23
Wife-dominant	12

---

[8] The phrase, "keeping (someone) in his place" suggests the possible parallel between women and Negroes as minority groups—minorities, not in a numerical sense but as being subject to adverse stereotypes that limit life chances. One might raise the question whether there is a sequence of liberation for women, as appears to be the case for Negroes. I have mentioned, above, the American woman's penetration of the world of work, a process of slow but gradual assertion of equality in the economic sphere; and the Nineteenth Amendment to the Constitution asserting equality in political sphere. It is suggestive to compare the sequence of *feminine liberation* with the order of demands by Negroes for full citizenship. (The following rank order of demands by Negroes is the same as the order of willingness on the part of whites to make concessions.)

1. Equal opportunity in the economic sphere.
2. Equality in justice and in political activities.
3. Equality in public services—restaurants, hotels, stores, bars, transportation.
4. Equality in the social sphere: clubs, voluntary associations, unions.
5. Intermarriage.

[9] Murray A. Straus, "Conjugal Power Structure and Adolescent Personality," *Marriage and Family Living*, Vol., XXIV, No. 1 (February, 1962) pp. 17–25.

Now for his dependent variables Straus asks: what consequences of husband-wife relationship are of some significance? He answers: those in particular that make for maintenance of the social order. Then, following Talcott Parsons' classification of the functional imperatives of social systems,[10] he seeks "one measure of adolescent personality to correspond with each of the four functional imperatives, thus revealing something about the "effectiveness with which [under conditions of these differing husband-wife relationships] the family performs these functional imperatives, and . . . the extent to which it has equipped the child to meet the problems associated with each of these functions."[11]

Using these four variants of the husband-wife relationship as points along the nominal scale of his independent variable, Professor Straus tests the following four hypotheses.[12] (Results of the tests are summarized in Table 10–2.)

1. The *wife-dominant* type of structure is associated with high-achieving but tense and rejecting sons.
2. An autonomic type of *equalitarian* spouse relationship is associated with boys who are well integrated into the family system and relatively anxiety-free, but also with boys who are low achievers in systems external to the family [for example, in school].
3. Sons from *husband-dominant* families occupy a position midway between the dominant and equalitarian type family.
4. Those families characterized by a *conflict* in power structure have sons with low levels of performance [on all measures: achievement, active-future orientation, anxiety and parental rejection].

Thus Straus does us the service of calling attention to different permutations of the husband-wife relationship along the dimension of dominance-submission; and the possible outcomes in personality attributes of the adolescent, outcomes having to do with internal and external system maintenance. His findings suggest that the impact within the family (rejection or acceptance of parents, and

---

[10] Recall our discussion in Chapter 9. Necessary for the maintenance of a social system, Parsons suggests, are: (1) the institutionalization of roles making for *adaptation*—i.e., roles whose incumbents must cultivate attributes necessary in the external social system. (Straus uses high school grade average as the adaptive dependent variable, here), (2) *goal attainment*, the institutionalization of roles that aim the person toward goals whose achievement is necessary for group, or system, maintenance (indexed here by scores on an active-future value orientation scale), (3) *pattern maintenance and tension management* for which Straus uses scores on "manifest anxiety scale, and (4) *integrative* roles, binding group members together. For this last, Straus uses scores on an acceptance-rejection scale.

[11] *Ibid.*, pp. 20, 21.

[12] *Ibid.*, pp. 19, 21, 22.

TABLE 10–2.   Straus's Findings as to Concomitants of Varying Patterns of
Husband-Wife Relationship

DEPENDENT VARIABLES: MEASURED CHARACTERISTICS OF 287 JUNIOR AND SENIOR HIGH SCHOOL STUDENTS, INDEXES LINKED WITH PARSONS 4 FUNCTIONAL IMPERATIVES OF A SOCIAL SYSTEM	INDEPENDENT VARIABLE: DOMINANCE-SUBMISSION IN THE HUSBAND-WIFE RELATIONSHIP			
	WIFE-DOMINANT	EQUALI-TARIAN	HUSBAND-DOMINANT	CONFLICTING
Having to do with the internal system (the family):				
Anxiety (Pattern maintenance and tension management)	Supported	Supported	Supported	Refuted (high but not highest: highest was wife-dominant)
Acceptance-Rejection of Parents (integration)	Supported	Supported	Supported	Refuted
Having to do with the environing system (larger social order):				
Grades as Measure of Achievement (Adaptation)	Refuted	Refuted	Refuted	Refuted (lowest, but not significantly lower than others)
Active-Future Orientation (Goal-Attainment)	Refuted	Refuted	Refuted	Supported

level of anxiety in the adolescent boy) is greater than the effect on the external order (level of achievement in school or on his orientation toward goals (active-future versus present-passive). His findings are suggestive but, as he notes, tentative, pointing the way to further inquiry into the significance of variations in family structure and their consequences.[13]

Mother-Child Relationships

Let us turn now to arrow number 4, the mother-child relationship in the diagram on page 412. I should like to call your attention to an intriguing piece of research carried out by Whiting, Kluckhohn, and Anthony.[14] Why, these investigators asked, do we find initiation rites

---

[13] Mirra Komarovsky in her study of *The Unemployed Man and His Family* (New York: Dryden Press, 1940), explores a related problem, the effect of unemployment on the authority of husband and father (relationships numbers 2 and 3 in the diagram on page 412). She found out that in about one out of five of her 58 families the husband's influence declined. This occurred chiefly in families (8 out of 12 of them) where acceptance of the husband's authority had been simply out of fear or as the necessary price for bed and board. Deterioration of the husband's authority occurred least where the authority was grounded in love and respect or where the wife was something of a traditionalist, accepting the dominance in the husband's role as natural, to be taken for granted.

[14] John W. M. Whiting, Richard Kluckhohn, and Albert Anthony, "The Function of Male Initiation Ceremonies at Puberty," in Eleanor E. Maccoby, Theodore M. Newcomb and Eugene L. Hartley, *Readings in Social Psychology* (New York: Holt, Rinehart & Winston, Inc., 1958), pp. 359–70.

for young men—emphatic, dramatic, sometimes sanguinary—in some groups while such ceremonies are lacking in others? What is the social function served by initiation rites? Under what conditions is this social function necessary? Or unnecessary? As they worked out their interpretation of this observed difference in patterns of behavior[15] their theoretical statement took this form: where boys are particularly dependent upon mothers and hostile toward fathers, then some sort of initiation rites are necessary to:

1. Put a final stop to his [the child's] wish to return to his mother's arms and lap.
2. Prevent an open revolt against his father who has displaced him from his mother's bed.
3. Ensure identification with the adult males of the society.[16]

The general hypothesis that follows is this: a protracted period of intimacy and dependence of male children upon their mothers will be associated with dramatic and sometimes violent initiation rites at puberty. Contrariwise, in societies not emphasizing dependence of male infants upon mothers and where the father exercises considerable authority, such initiation rites will be missing or extremely mild.

What we need, then, are measures on two variables: (1) some index of the male infant's intimacy with and dependence on the mother (the independent variable) and (2) some measure, for the dependent variable, of the existence or extent of celebration of initiation rites at puberty. For this latter the investigators use the simplest of nominal scales: the trait is either present or absent. For the independent variable, measures of son-mother intimacy and dependence, they ask whether the infant sleeps with the mother to the exclusion of the father, for at least a year ("long") or less ("short"); and whether, following the birth of the child, there is a taboo on sexual intercourse for at least a year ("long") or less ("short"). Thus, using these two measures on the independent variable (post-partum sex taboo and exclusive mother-son sleeping arrangements) there are four possible combinations: long-long and short-short, or long-short and short-long. The hypothesis predicts that the long-long combination, a lengthy period of post-partum sex

---

[15] Let me remind you again of our definition of the field. In the Komarovsky study, the Straus study, and in the one we are now treating by Whiting *et al.*, we are dealing with controlled observations and interpretations of differing patterns of human relationships: their sources and/or consequences.

[16] *Ibid.*, p. 8.

TABLE 10-3

The Relationship between Exclusive Mother-Son Sleeping Arrangements and Post-Partum Sex Taboo, Both of a Year or More Duration, and the Occurrence of Initiation Ceremonies at Puberty.

CUSTOMS IN INFANCY		CUSTOMS AT ADOLESCENT INITIATION CEREMONIES: INITIATION RITES	
EXCLUSIVE MOTHER-SON SLEEPING ARRANGEMENTS	POST-PARTUM SEX TABOO	ABSENT	PRESENT
Long	Long	Ganda Khalapur (Rajput) Nyakusa Tepoztlan Trobriander Yapese	Azande hgs* Camayura hs Chagga hgs Cheyenne ht Chiricahua ht Dahomean hgs Fijian gs Jivaro ht Kwoma hgs Lesu gs Neur hs Samoans g Tiv hgs
Long	Short	Ashanti Malaita Siriono	Cabaga ht
Short	Long	Araucanian Pilaga Pondo Tallensi	Kwakiutl s Ojibwa t Ooldea hgs

Source: John W. M. Whiting, Richard Kluckhohn, and Albert Anthony, "The Function of Male Initiation Ceremonies at Puberty," in Eleanor E. Maccoby, Theodore M. Newcomb and Eugene L. Hartley, Readings in Social Psychology (New York: Holt, Rinehart & Winston, Inc., 1958).

* Letters following the tribal names, in the right-hand column, indicate certain characteristics of the ceremony: h = painful hazing, g = genital operations, s = seclusion from women and t = tests of manliness.

taboo and of mother-son sleeping, will be associated with puberty initiation rites of varying degrees of severity. Contrariwise, the short-short combination should be associated with an absence of initiation rites at puberty. Either of the other combinations should lie in between, in presence or absence of such rites. The findings are presented in Table 10–3. The data are from fifty-five tribes selected

TABLE 10–3 (continued)

CUSTOMS IN INFANCY		CUSTOMS AT ADOLESCENT INITIATION CEREMONIES: INITIATION RITES	
EXCLUSIVE MOTHER-SON SLEEPING ARRANGEMENTS	POST-PARTUM SEX TABOO	ABSENT	PRESENT
Short	Short	Alorese Balinese Druz Egypt (Silwa) Eskimo (Copper) French Igorot (Bontoc) Japanese (Suye Mura) Koryak (Maritime) Lakher Lamba Lapps Lepcha Maori Mixtecans Navaho Ontong Javanese Papago Serbs Tanala (Menabe) Trukese U.S. (Homestead) Yagua	Hopi hs Timbira hst

for their geographic distribution, diversity of cultures, and because the data on puberty rites were adequate.

The analysis of these data suggest, then, that the social function of puberty rites, for the male, may be to overcome the influence of a tight mother-son relationship, establishing the youth in the role appropriate to adult males.

We can see the direction of the relationship—and the support of the hypothesis—more clearly if we collapse the table and convert the data into percentages (see Table 10–4).

Research is full of pitfalls. This is about the same as saying that rigorous thinking, the solution of difficult problems, is a hard and

TABLE 10–4

The Relationship between Mother-Son Intimacy/
Dependency and the Presence or Absence of
Adolescent Initiation Rites in 55 Tribes

MOTHER-SON INTIMACY AND DEPENDENCY	ADOLESCENT INITIATION RITES	
	ABSENT (%)	PRESENT (%)
Maximum	17	68
Intermediate	19	21
Minimum	64	11
	100	100
N =	36	19

$$\chi^2 = 72.6 - 55 = 17.6$$
$$d/f = 2$$
$$p < .001$$

hazardous undertaking. Having arrived at tentative interpretations, it is always necessary to assess sources of error (as these investigators do), couching one's conclusions in terms less pretentious than fundamental laws of nature. Thus we must recognize that the data from the Human Relations Area Files are uneven in accuracy and wealth of detail; and that coding such data always involves the chance of error—as does every step in research procedure. (The HRAF, developed over the years at Yale, is an extensive and intricately coded collection of data, from anthropologists' and others' reports, on tribes and societies around the world, better than 250 of them.) On the other hand, an excess of caution may deny us the occasional insights of a brave, imaginative sortie.[17]

It is just such a sortie that Whiting *et al.* make in concluding their study—one worth our consideration as it reveals the power of an

---

[17] There is reason in research for the self-conscious stalking of vagrant ideas. Without forsaking the hard-headed aspects of research, I must confess the appeal of Professor Jerome Bruner's statement when he prefaces a paper of his with the statement: "There is bound to be foolishness in such a preliminary exercise. But in the interest of clarity and *to render the foolishness more discernible* I [speak boldly] so that each theorem can stand on its own bottom. There is a minimum of qualification, for any proposition can be made to seem reasonable if enough qualifications are attached. *Better to be flat-footed and wrong than guardedly indeterminate.*" (Jerome S. Bruner, "Theorems for a Theory of Instruction," dittoed, n.d.; a working paper produced for the President's Committee on Education. Italics mine.) This is a statement from a position of strength and security. Unhappily for the development of any science, we are often so insecure in the face of research uncertainties that we hide behind the precision of the trivial and the obsurity of infinite qualifications. Needless to say the errors of undisciplined fantasy are equally damaging for effective inquiry.

idea, apparently supported by empirical research in one setting, through its extension to other groups and cognate behaviors.

Where, in our society, the investigators ask, do we find virtually ritualized violence among adolescent males? The answer: this occurs, if anywhere, among delinquent juveniles with their gangs, their rumbles, their rebellious defiance of authority, their assertion of independence, their anxious demonstration of virility. This isn't true, clearly, of all juveniles just as it is not true that all tribes have initiation ceremonies for adolescent males. A critical distinction between the delinquent and the nondelinquent may well be that the former must rip himself, metaphorically speaking, from an enveloping female world, asserting himself as an adult and finding his role as a male. And so the investigators suggest that

> . . . insofar as there has been an increase in juvenile delinquency in our society, it should be accompanied by an increase in the exclusiveness of mother-child relationships and/or a decrease in the authority of the father. It is not unreasonable [to suppose] that industrialization and urbanization has done just this.
> [If so] . . . then it can be countered either by decreasing the exclusiveness of the early mother-child relationship, increasing the authority of the father during childhood, or instituting a formal means of coping with adolescent boys functionally equivalent to those described in this paper [i.e., puberty rites, avuncular residence, moving to a "men's house," etc.][18]

Let us pursue this point a little further, paying attention to the contrast in American society between relationships 3 and 4 (see page 412). Parsons and Bales have stressed the fact that, for the boy, the socialization process requires readjustments not demanded of the girl. We get some intimation of the argument from the Figure 10–1.

During the socialization process in such a micro system the male child has the problem of straightening out sex relationships and three major indentifications. The relationships are F-M, M-D, S-D, F-S, M-S and F-D. Adequate socialization requires that S identify himself as being of the same generation as D, and of a different one from that of F and M; as a member of the family embracing all four persons; and as of the same sex as F. But in contrast with D, the son must at some point disengage himself from M, shifting his identification to F.

---

[18] Whiting, *et al., op. cit.,* p. 370.

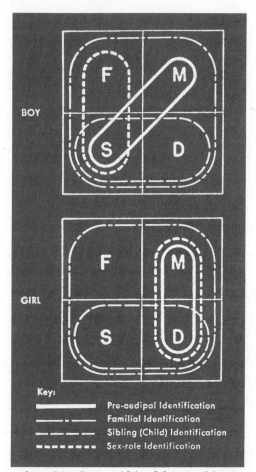

Source: Talcott Parsons and Robert F. Bales, in collaboration
with James Olds, Morris Zelditch, Jr., and Philip E. Slater, *Family,
Socialization and Interaction Process* (New York: Free Press of Glencoe, Inc., 1955), p. 99. Used by permission of The Macmillan Company.

FIG. 10-1. Basis of sex-role identification
in the nuclear family.

Then we can say that the boy has to undergo at this stage a *double*
"emancipation." In common with his sister he has to recognize that, in
a sense not previously so important, he must not pretend to adulthood,
he is unequivocally a child. But as differentiated from her, he must
substitute a new identification with an unfamiliar and in a very important sense threatening object, the father, at the expense of his
previous solidarity with his mother. He must renounce his previous
dependency in a more radical sense. The girl, on the other hand,
though she must internalize the father as object does so only in his

role as instrumental leader of the family as a system not in the dual role which includes sex-role-model as well . . . the boy must proceed farther and more radically on the path away from expressive primacy toward instrumental primacy. He is, therefore, subjected to greater strain.[19]

I have been offering some illustrations of problems touching the structure of the family viewed as a micro system. We can see this unity of interacting personalities as a structure of relationships: husband-wife, parent-child, mother-son and mother-daughter, father-son and father-daughter and brother-sister. The parent-child relationship has been shown to vary in significant ways by class. Professor Straus has pointed to possible concomitants of the locus of power in the husband-wife relationship: anxiety in the child, achievement in school, rejection of parents, and whether a passive or an active-future orientation. Parsons' discussion of problems peculiar to the mother-son, father-son relationship—and the cross-cultural study of male initiation ceremonies as linked with extent of mother-son intimacy and dependency—such studies highlight the promise and significance of analyzing the family as a micro system inducting the young.

The Woman's Role

Now let us shift our perspective from the double-headed arrows representing relationships (on page 412) to the roles that are joined in these relationships. Sociologists have long been interested in those changes in the woman's role that have altered the network of familial relationships. With radically new means of producing, packaging, distributing, preserving, and serving foods, technologically refined means of cleaning and maintaining a household, the shrinkage in lot sizes (hence the land to be maintained), the woman has increased leisure, as a housewife. In addition, with increased use of contraception, making children more nearly a matter of choice than chance, she has the opportunity for greater investment of self, per child, as well as the option of a wider range of activities.[20] She

---

[19] Talcott Parsons and Robert F. Bales, in collaboration with James Olds, Morris Zelditch, Jr., and Philip E. Slater, *Family, Socialization and Interaction Process* (New York: Free Press of Glencoe, Inc., 1955), pp. 98, 99. Used by permission of The Macmillan Company.

[20] In 1955 Freedman *et al.* drew a probability sample of the approximately 17 million wives in the United States, aged 18 to 39 inclusive. In interviews with 2,713 wives it was found that 70% of all couples and 83% of all fecund couples practiced contraception of some sort. (Recall that probability sampling allows us to bracket

exercises this option increasingly in the political and economic spheres. (M. de Tocqueville would scarcely recognize the modern American middle-class wife.) Women serve as senators and congresswomen. They preside over such businesses as Lord and Taylor's. They work in factories and business establishments. They own a tremendous amount in securities, controlling (*de jure*, if not *de facto*) major segments of business and industry—this, in part, by virtue of their longevity. Their increased participation in the world of work is suggested in Table 10–5.

TABLE 10–5

Percent of All Married Women Who Are Working and All Working Women Who Are Married, United States, 1890–1960

YEAR	PERCENT OF MARRIED WOMEN WORKING	PERCENT OF WORKING WOMEN MARRIED
1890	4.5	13.9
1900	5.8	15.4
1910	10.8	24.7
1920	9.0	23.0
1930	11.5	28.9
1940	16.7	36.4
1950	24.4	52.1
1960	31.4	59.9

Source: U.S. Bureau of the Census, *Historical Statistics of the United States* (Washington, D.C.: U.S. Goverment Printing Office, 1949), Table, Series D 1–10, p. 63, and *Statistical Abstracts, 1950,* Tables 207 and 27, pp. 172 and 21, respectively, and *Statistical Abstracts, 1963,* Tables 299 and 31, pp. 229 and 36, respectively.

As both cause and consequence, average educational achievement of women has increased, and in extrafamilial roles as in the marriage relationship itself, the woman achieves a more nearly equalitarian role.

---

these figures *within predictable limits of sampling error.*) Percent using contraceptive techniques varies by wife's age and husband's occupation. The proportion of contraceptive users declines, in general, with occupational status. By four age categories between 18 and 39, the percent of users for all couples is 68% (youngest wives), 73%, 73% and 65% (oldest wives). For fecund couples the figures are 71%, 84%, 90% and 90%. (Ronald Freedman, Pascal K. Whelpton, and Arthur A. Campbell, *Family Planning, Sterility, and Population Growth* (New York: McGraw-Hill Book Co., 1959), pp. 10, 11, 133.

The Role of Husband and Father

In sketching changes in the woman's role I have by implication noted changes in the role of husband and father. He no longer has a monopoly in the economic and political spheres. In American society there has been a steady decline in the importance of extractive industry (mining, fishing, forestry, agriculture), so reducing the realm of economic activity in which men had a monopoly. In the shift of our labor force from thing manipulation to symbol manipulation with an emphasis on psychic rather than physical strength, the male no longer has exclusive access to decision-making roles in politics and business. He no longer enjoys an unchallenged position as thinker-creator.

While the woman has been invading these spheres, the man has come to share in the hitherto motherly monopolies. Not only the increased career activity of woman but also certain views from psychology have led to a redefinition of the father's role. Especially in middle-class families, expressions of paternal care and affection are seen as necessary to the unfolding personality of the child. The father's involvement with the child may commence with clinics for expectant parents, ranging through participation at child-birth to occasional attendance at PTA meetings.

But on the whole, with the separation of work place from home place, and especially in middle-class families the commuting pattern has reduced the amount of father-child contact in many families leading to a not uncommon matricentric pattern. This, of course, is what Figure 10–1 suggests: an early orientation toward mother (and, in elementary school, toward female teachers) creating the greater probability of radical disjunctures in the socialization of the male child.

The Child's Role

Such disjunctures (to turn to the role of the child) are discussed in a perceptive analysis by Ruth Benedict.[21] The child's independence may not, in our society, be gradually achieved by small and easy increments. The shift to a heterosexual phase of development may be sudden, especially for the only child, or for the child having siblings of one sex only. Or, emerging from the protection of the

---

[21] Ruth Benedict, "Continuities and Discontinuities in Cultural Conditioning," *Psychiatry*, May, 1939.

small nuclear family, his apprehension of a world of duplicity and violence may hit the child suddenly and shockingly.

We have lengthened the period of the child's dependency by withdrawing youth, increasingly, from the labor market. While the exploitation of children has decreased it may be that the sense of adult self-sufficiency and responsible contribution to the family group has declined, concomitantly. It's probable that household and family duties of children are fewer than formerly. Along with this, there has been an extension of the period of formal education. And

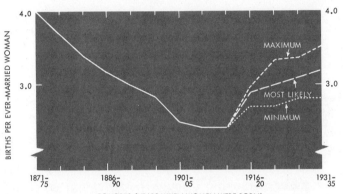

COHORTS (YEARS WHEN WOMEN WERE BORN)
Source: Ronald Freedman, Pascal K. Whelpton, and Arthur A. Campbell, *Family Planning, Sterility, and Population Growth* (New York: McGraw-Hill Book Co., 1959), p. 227.

FIG. 10–2. Average number of births by ages 45–49: Actual for ever-married women in cohorts of 1871–75 to 1911–15 and expected by wives in cohorts of 1916–20 to 1931–35.

at the other end we have thrust education toward the point of birth with cooperative baby pools, prenursery schools, nursery and kindergarten arrangements.[22] For some time, average family size has declined (although the postwar years show some recovery and a sort of convergence on a typical family size). These trends are recorded in the Figure 10–2.

The small nuclear family means, of course, a decline in number of

---

[22] If one thinks of American society as a three-layer cake, top and bottom being the dependent aged and the dependent young, it is clear that this sector is expanding in its proportion of the total, while the independent middle sector is contracting. This is a luxury that could be indulged only in a society marked by high achievement in science and technology with all that this may imply: a high average level of education, an instrumental orientation toward the biophysical—and probably the social—world, a high proportion of the labor force in distribution and service occupations, and the like.

siblings and increased dependence for peer relationships on outside associations. This may augur a decline in intimacy and perhaps in understanding between parents and children as they are separated through the interposition of external agencies—school, youth groups, commercial and other sorts of recreation. Or, as seems to me a likelier interpretation, social arrangements are being contrived to meet the requirements of independence training formerly met

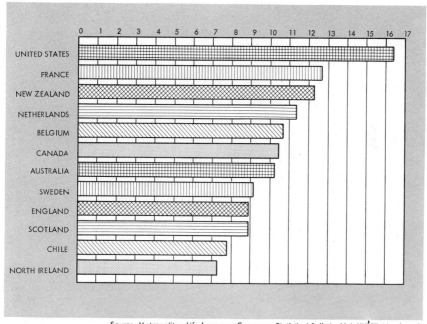

Source: Metropolitan Life Insurance Company, *Statistical Bulletin,* Vol. XXVIII, No. 6, p. 2.

FIG. 10–3. Marriage rate (marriages per 1,000 population) in the United States and selected countries, 1946.

within the household-as-a-farming-enterprise. But since such training may now occur in several contexts, the possibility of inconsistent if not incompatible expectations may be increased.

FORMATION AND DISSOLUTION OF FAMILIES IN THE UNITED STATES

Let us turn finally to some general features of the family in American society taken as a whole: data on its formation and dissolution, some examples of the way institutional characteristics interlock (family and religion, work patterns and family patterns), concluding with some remarks on probable changes in this institution.

Americans tend to be a much married and increasingly married people. Figure 10–3 compares our marriage rate with that for selected countries. These data are for an immediate postwar year, 1946, and therefore reflect a marriage boom stemming from deferred marriages. Actually there is a good deal of fluctuation in our

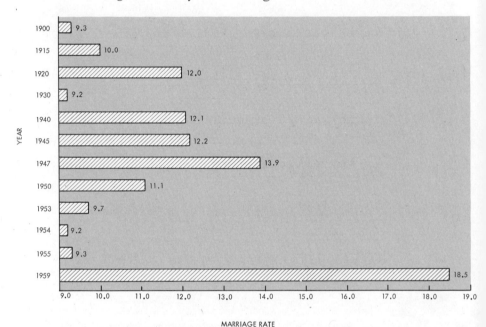

MARRIAGE RATE

Source: National Office of Vital Statistics, Public Health Service, U.S. Department of Health, Education, and Welfare.

FIG. 10–4.   Marriages in the U.S. per 1,000 population for selected years, 1900 to 1954.

marriage rates as Figure 10–4 reveals. (Note here that in 1947 the marriage rate had fallen to 13.9 and, by 1950, to 11.1 per 1,000 population.) Over a period of years the percent of the population over fifteen years of age that is married has increased quite consistently. By decades from 1890 to 1940, for example, the percent of males fifteen years of age and older, married, has moved this way: 53.9, 54.5, 55.8, 59.2, 60.0, and 61.2.[23] This may be due to the declining significance of economic barriers to marriage. It is doubtless due in part to the ability to control births, adapting family size to circumstance. It is at least conceivable that the marriage rate is

---

[23] U.S. Department of Commerce, *Statistical Abstract of the United States* (Washington, D.C.: U.S. Government Printing Office, 1941), p. 42.

related to the divorce rate in somewhat the same way as birth and death rates are connected. We can think of an institutionalized relationship, like marriage, being regularly broken by death and divorce and separation, and regularly replenished by newly married couples. Figures 10–5 gives the data on divorce. It suggests a long-term shift upward in the divorce rate. It is sufficiently regular so that we can say the divorce rate in the United States is a specific (mathematical) function of time. Thus if we plot a regression line

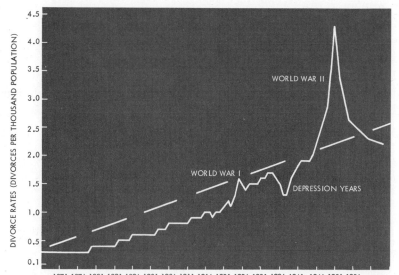

Source: U.S. Bureau of the Census, *Historical Statistics of the United States, 1789–1945* (Washington, D.C.: U.S. Government Printing Office, 1949) for data through 1945; and Murray Gendell and Hans L. Zetterberg (eds.), *A Sociological Almanac for the United States* (New York: Charles Scribner's Sons, 1961), Table 1.63, p. 46 for data for 1946, 1947, 1950, 1955, and 1959.

FIG. 10–5. Estimated divorce rates per 1,000 population, United States, 1867 through 1959. (Trend line fitted by inspection.)

through these data (a line of least mean squares) we can evaluate the formula $Y = a + bX$, describing divorce as a function of time and, through the slope of the line, b, getting some notion of the rapidity of change in the rate of family dissolution through divorce. While, of course, this is informative and allows us to predict by extending the regression line (on the assumption that conditions relevant to divorce remain the same), time taken by itself is not a very intelligible variable. We would wish to ask, additionally, what other social phenomena plausibly connected with an increasing divorce rate have changed through time: urbanization, a shift in the occupational structure from extractive industry, scientific advances, extension of education, etc.

LINKS BETWEEN INSTITUTIONS: FAMILY AND RELIGION, FAMILY AND WORK RELATIONSHIPS

There is no statement more basic to an understanding of the social order than that which asserts the interconnectedness of social things. So it is with the major institutions that form an interdigitating framework for the social order. Family, school, church, government, work while by no means perfectly orchestrated tend, nonetheless, to play in the same key and to resolve dissonances in favor of a common theme. To put it a different way, variations in one institutional theme are likely to be connected with variations in another.

Take as one example of interinstitutional connections the way in which dissolution of the family by divorce is linked with religious affiliation. Table 10–6 presents relevant data from three studies

TABLE 10–6

Percentage of Marriages of Mixed and Nonmixed Religious Faiths Ending in Divorce or Separation as Revealed by Studies of Marriages in Michigan, Maryland, and Washington*

RELIGIOUS CATEGORIES	LANDIS STUDY IN MICHIGAN (N = 4,108)		BELL STUDY IN MARYLAND (N = 13,528)	WEEKS STUDY IN WASHINGTON (N = 6,548)
	N	%	%	%
Both Catholic	573	4.4	6.4	3.8
Both Jewish	96	5.2	4.6	——
Both Protestant	2,794	6.0	6.8	10.0
Mixed, Catholic-Protestant	192	14.1	15.2	17.4
Both none	39	17.9	16.7	23.9
Protestant changed to Catholic	56	10.7		
Catholic changed to Protestant	57	10.6		
Protestant father–Catholic mother	90	6.7		
Catholic father–Protestant mother	102	20.6		
Father none–Mother Catholic	41	9.8		
Father none–Mother Protestant	84	19.0		

Source: Judson T. Landis, "Marriages of Mixed and Non-Mixed Religious Faith," *American Sociological Review,* published by The American Sociological Association, Vol. XIV, No. 3 (June, 1949), p. 403.

* Enter, here, a methodological caveat. First, the terms Catholic, Protestant, and Jewish are spongey ones. Protestant denominations vary widely, and some "Protestants" may, in fact, be atheists or agnostics, certainly noncommunicants. The same problem applies to Catholics and Jews. Thus, to an unknown extent, the high divorce rates for interfaith marriages may reflect *absence* of, rather than *difference* in, religious commitments. For some suggestive evidence on this point, see Lee B. Burchinal and Loren E. Chancellor, "Survival Rates among Religiously Homogamous and Interreligious Marriages," *Social Forces,* Vol. XLI, No. 4 (May, 1963), pp. 353–62.

Furthermore, we should note that while these data suggest a connection between two institutional spheres, family and church, divorce, like other aspects of family life, is touched by factors not controlled here: income, number of children, length of marriage, urban or rural residence, type of occupation, and the like.

while Figure 10–6 is a graphic summary of the Landis study of the families of 4,108 midwest college students.

Take another illustration of interinstitutional linkages, in this case the connection between family relationships and work relationships. It would seem reasonable that, both as a result of self-recruitment and employment policies, persons in quite different work settings might differ in personality and typical behaviors; and that such differences might be registered concomitantly in the familial (and other) spheres. Thus one might expect William H. Whyte's "organi-

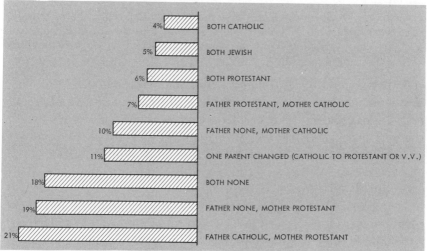

Source: Judson T. Landis, "Marriages of Mixed and Non-Mixed Religious Faith," *American Sociological Review,* published by The American Sociological Association, Vol. XIV, No. 3 (June, 1949), p. 403.

FIG. 10–6. Percentage of marriages of mixed and nonmixed religious faiths ending in divorce or separation among parents of 4,108 students of midwestern origin at Michigan State College.

zation man" in his anonymous gray flannel suit, an adaptive, accommodating, radar-responding, other-directed sort of person[24] to train his children in similar fashion. On the other hand the self-employed, or the person covering a variety of tasks in an entrepreneurial setting, might be expected to display a paternal pattern emphasizing drive, discipline, and self-reliance.

Some such notions as these prompted Professors Miller and Swanson to test whether there was a difference in parental behaviors between families whose fathers worked in bureaucratic settings and those whose fathers were entrepreneurs. The implicit assumption

---

[24] The last two terms are Professor David Riesman's. For a provocative study of the changing American character see his *The Lonely Crowd* (New Haven: Yale University Press, 1961).

that a change in style of working from the entrepreneurial to the bureaucratic organization was paralleled by a change in parent-child relationships accounts for the title of their work, *The Changing American Parent.*[25]

Entrepreneurial families were defined as those in which the husband was (1) self-employed, or (2) gained at least half of his income from fees, profits, or commissions, or (3) was employed by a small organization (having at most two levels of supervision, or (4) was farm-born or (5) was foreign-born. All other families were classified as "bureaucratic." In these families

> husbands work for someone else in organizations with three or more supervisory levels. Their income is primarily in the form of wages or salary. They are not taking entrepreneurial risks. Nor do most of them have entrepreneurial opportunities.[26]

This is a good illustration of a common methodological problem. We have here two quite abstract ideas, entrepreneurial and bureaucratic, ideas that must be cast in operational terms if we are to test the hypothesis. It is seldom a simple matter to contrive valid indexes of such terms. And we find Swanson and Miller shifting from characteristics of work setting to those of birthplace in their operational definition of "entrepreneurial."

Five hundred and eighty-two mothers having children under age nineteen were interviewed in an area probability sample of Detroit. After eliminating Negroes, families with adopted children or step-children, and those in which husband and wife were not living together, the sample numbered 479 families. Some of the investigators' findings are these:

Bearing on the development of strong self-control, entrepreneurial mothers were more likely than bureaucratic mothers to pay no attention, or delayed attention to the baby's crying, to feed the baby on a schedule, to begin urinary training before the baby was 11 months old, and to use symbolic punishments. For the development of an active and independent approach to the world, mothers from the entrepreneurial families were more likely than their bureaucratic counterparts to: use harsh means to prevent the child from sucking parts of its body, to deny that the child touched its sex organs, to approve leaving the child at home with a competent

---

[25] Daniel R. Miller and Guy E. Swanson, *The Changing American Parent* (New York: John Wiley & Sons, Inc., 1958).

[26] *Ibid.*, pp. 68–71, 78.

woman while the mother shopped or visited, to feel that a child should be on his own as soon as possible to solve his own problems, and to feel that only males should perform activities traditionally associated with their sex among adolescents.[27]

On a number of other beliefs and behaviors there were no statistically significant differences between the entrepreneurial and bureaucratic families. (I have reported only those on which the probability of the observed difference was less than .05.) Complex as the problem is and tenuous as are certain of the findings we are left with the conviction that there is an important connection between work relationships and parent-child relationships. There is, furthermore, the likelihood that both sets of relationships have changed over time. One has the sense of a moving equilibrium—an equilibrium always imperfectly achieved, of course.

We have looked at the family as a micro system, a system of relationships. With four persons—mother, father, daughter and son—we have six relationships. We might represent such a micro system, schematically, as in the accompanying illustration. For

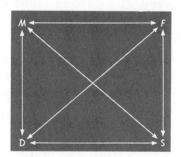

certain of these relationships I've illustrated the sociologist's approach: the significance of different permutations of power in the husband-wife relationships, the variations of parent-child relationships by class, and the significance, for achieving the role of adult male, of variations in the dependency dimension of the mother-child relationship.

In a discussion of the roles that comprise these relationships we see three changes heralding significant shifts in family structure: the extension of women's roles to realms hitherto exclusively men's, the redefinition of the man's role, with a reduction in his monopolies and some blurring of sex-linked roles, and, finally, the problem of

---

[27] *Ibid.,* paraphrased from pp. 99 and 105.

the child's—especially the son's—role with an extended period of dependency and the difficulty, in a feminine world, of achieving the role of adult, independent male.

Over the years the size of the family has declined, then recovered a bit with some evidence of an emerging modal family of just over three children. While marriage rates have gone up, so have rates of divorce and separation. The nuclear and neolocal family, modal in American society, has aspects of transiency and an air of convenient companionship to an extent probably not true in past centuries. And this is what we should expect for two reasons: (1) change in other sectors of the social order—in the accumulation of knowledge, in scientific discoveries and technological development, in the economy, in religion and government—have been great and rapid, and (2) since elements of the social order are interdependent, change in one sector exerts leverage for adaptive change in other sectors.

The connectedness of institutions has been illustrated in two ways. Family and church are linked, as is evidenced in the relationship between divorce rates and religious affiliation. (I skirt the obvious: the sacraments celebrating birth and death and christening, or the effect of the church on contraceptive practices.) Finally, there is the probable connection between relationships at work and those in the bosom of the family, a connection that Miller and Swanson tried to test when they suggested that work relationships in entrepreneurial and bureaucratic settings had their parallels in parent-child relationships.[28]

THE SCHOOL AS INDUCTING INSTITUTION

Along with the family, the school is the chief agency of socialization. With a greater relative emphasis upon the instrumental than the expressive, upon the cognitive in contrast to the affective, the institutionalizing of education guarantees a regular input of the knowledge, skills, attitudes, and values necessary to maintain the group. In the rest of this chapter I want to suggest answers to three

---

[28] In offering "illustrations" and using words like "finally," I may inadvertently have suggested a representative reporting of research on the family or, worse still, an exhaustive coverage of sociological inquiries into this institution. To put it mildly this is not the case: first, due to my ignorance of this field; and second, because to cover the sociology of the family would require many volumes. For current research see the indexes of the *American Sociological Review*, *Sociological Abstracts*, the *American Journal of Sociology*, the *American Journal of Orthopsychiatry*, and Harold T. Christensen, *Handbook of Marriage and the Family* (Chicago: Rand McNally, 1964).

questions: (1) What is the social function of education? (2) What sorts of evidence do we have that our schools perform this function? (3) What do we know about what is taught, by whom, and how?

The Social Function of Education

Education is the chief means of resolving a paradox: the fact of the group's immortality despite the continual loss of its constituent parts. Our nation, your town, the Ford Motor Company, your church, the Republican party—these groups persist over decades, generations, and longer despite withdrawal, death, and defection of citizens, residents, workers, communicants, members. This is a crude way of putting it; for it suggests that a group consists of people, some of whom are always leaving through death and migration, being regularly replaced by newcomers. This, as I've pointed out before, is not accurate. A group is an intricately woven fabric of relationships, the elemental units being the roles taken by people vis-à-vis one another: student-teacher, mother-child, boss-worker, priest and communicant. What is to be sustained, then, if the group—the organization—is to survive is this pattern of relationships. And this is the latent function of public education. Through sundry educational devices the newcomer is inducted into the secrets of society, taught the tribal lore so that he may take up his part in the complex orchestration of roles. The beliefs and behaviors that we institutionalize under the label, "education," are aimed at recruiting, developing, and sorting out the talents, attitudes, and values appropriate to the continuous fulfillment of the roles requisite for group survival.

Education involves three processes essential to any enduring organization: selective recruitment, indoctrination (or orientation, or in-service training), and separation of the maladapted. Failure in any one of these processes (and education is by no means totally effective) implies, to that degree, the transformation of the group. Education provides social insurance against such threats to the existing social structure. It recruits selectively. The children of professional parents it recruits early, keeps late. The children of subsistence farmers it recruits late, dismisses early. During the high school years, education recruits some for further training, allowing others to drop out. It sorts some into the college preparatory curriculum, some into the general curriculum, and others into the commercial curriculum. It recruits some for the High School of

Music and Arts, some for the Bronx High School of Science, others for Harlem Vocational. Thus through the educational process the group recruits and sorts its human input into the "right" preparatory experiences. It then transmits those elements of the culture deemed by powerful elders to be indispensable for the general welfare. And throughout the process it sorts and separates the maladapted, the misfits.

(Let me warn, again, about the metaphorical shorthand in such statements as "the group recruits . . . sorts . . . transmits." A group is not, of course, a sensate being. I mean that enduring groups are so organized as to perform these functions. And lest the investigator's perspective convey an over-rationalized picture, let us be clear, too, that these outcomes are, as often as not, unwittingly achieved.)

In our times there are three sorts of roles for which persons must be educated if the group is to survive: specialists' roles, coordinating roles, and integrating roles. A society as complex as ours obviously requires specialized training. For technical training, from plumber and printer to engineer and physicist, society fixes highly specific systems of induction. (For the elementary school's response to the increasing need for specialists in a complex society refer to Table 4–4 on the expansion of the elementary school curriculum from 1775 to 1900, on page 170.)

But beyond trained specialists our society requires, quite as much, training for the coordinating roles that bridge the specialties. This is the more necessary since, although strangers to most of our fellow Americans, each of us is implicated in their lives. In this intricate network every man's activities become vested with a public interest. Legal, clerical, and sales work are prime examples of this essential, intermediating function.

Finally, and especially because of its complexity, a modern society requires of its members a certain minimum of common skills, knowledge, allegiances. These enable minimal communication, provide an identity, and legitimize the demands of the group upon the person (as in the case of taxation and military service). For establishing personal and group identity society requires that we be trained in a commitment to our common cause.

Thus the sociologist sees education as a requisite of corporate life, a sort of official socialization assuring that as incumbents depart a role, others with comparable qualifications move in. And so the tendency is toward what I have called intergenerational repetition. For it is the powerful elders who stipulate how the young shall be recruited, indoctrinated, and allocated to the available social niches. The hirer has more power than the hired, the parent than the child, the Department of Justice more than the immigrant, the Board of Education more than teacher or student. The newcomer is always the vulnerable one confronting a prefabricated, ongoing organization. Generally the newcomer, knowing no alternatives, does not rebel against an induction process that seeks to fit him into the structure and processes of the organization. As the necessary means of group survival, public education is an intrinsically conservative

TABLE 10–7

Percent of Population in Specified Age and School Categories, Percent Enrolled and Dollar Amounts Invested in Schooling

SCHOOL CATEGORY AND AGE	PERCENT OF POPULATION IN THIS AGE CATEGORY	PERCENT IN THIS AGE CATEGORY ENROLLED	PERCENT OF GNP INVESTED IN THIS SCHOOLING	DOLLARS SPENT (IN MILLIONS)	EXPENDITURES PER STUDENT
Elementary and Secondary schools (ages 5–17)	24.8	95.6	3.69	$18,622	$ 436.11
Higher education (ages 18–21)	5.3	33.5	1.23	6.230	$1,747.00
Totals	30.1		4.92	$24,852	

Source: This table is based on data in Fritz Machlup, *The Production and Distribution of Knowledge in the United States* (Princeton, N.J.: Princeton University Press, 1962), pp. 71–79, *passim*, by permission of Princeton University Press. Copyright 1962, Princeton University Press; all rights reserved.

process, guaranteeing the future by recreating the past. The process is not, as Durkheim pointed out, one of simply teasing out of the person capacities lying latent within him. It is, rather, a process of creating a socially prescribed product. What is prescribed will, of course, change through time as conditions of the social order change.

Three conditions of our social order prompt expansion and proliferation in education: complexity, affluence, and danger. In the United States, public education responded to the challenge of Sputnik with greater emphasis on mathematics, foreign language, and the technical training deemed necessary to achieve parity in power. The complexity of our social order is reflected and reinforced by a complex educational structure (see Figure 10–7). And our affluence is reflected in the vast amounts we are able to spend for

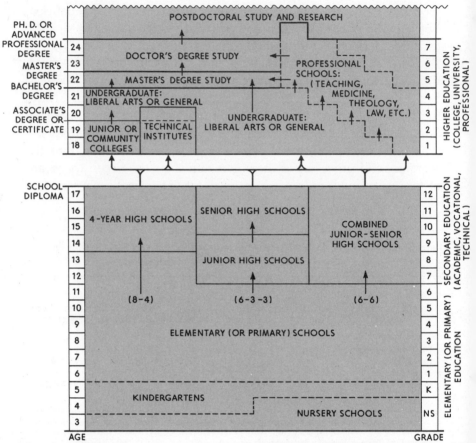

Source: Office of Education, U.S. Department of Health, Education, and Welfare, *Digest of Educational Statistics* (Washington, D.C.: U.S. Government Printing Office, 1962), p. 2.

FIG. 10–7.   **The structure of education in the United States.**

education, formal and informal (Table 10–8 and Figure 10–8); and the increased proportion of our population achieving various levels of education. Table 10–7 gives us some notion of the situation in 1960.

In Western societies, organized or official education has come to involve ever more people, ever more subjects over increasing time spans. In the United States most of our people now entering their productive years—more than three fourths of them—will have spent nearly a fifth of their lives in school. This is a minimum statement since I'm referring only to high school graduates. As Table 10–7 indicates, about one in four of our population fall in the 5–17 age category and of these, almost all are in elementary or secondary

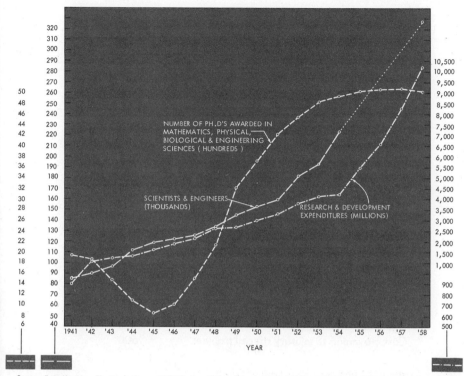

FIG. 10–8. Concomitants of higher education: number of scientists and engineers; number of Ph.D's awarded in mathematics, physical, biological, and engineering sciences; and research and development expenditures, U.S., 1941–60.

schools (data are for 1960). To keep them there we spent about 4 percent of our gross national product in 1960 or, in absolute numbers better than 18.5 billions. And an increasing proportion of our population is going beyond high school. The number of 18–21-year-olds was about the same in 1960 as in 1939. But in 1939 only 14 percent of them were in college whereas the figure for 1961 was 38 percent![29] To keep them there we spent another 1 percent of our gross national product or, actually, about $6.23 billion.

"Keeping them there" suggests a latent function of education: the withholding from the labor market of a large segment of our population—more than one fourth of it—that could not possibly be absorbed in our highly mechanized, automated economy. As John

---

[29] Martin Trow, "The Democratization of Higher Education in America," *European Journal of Sociology,* Vol. III, No. 2 (1962), p. 231.

TABLE 10–8

Total Cost of Education in the U.S., 1958
(Millions of Dollars)

Education in the home		
Income foregone by mothers staying home to educate their pre-school childern		$ 4,432
Training on the job		
Formal training programs operated by firms	$ 1,000	
Production loss and cost of training newly hired workers	2,054	
		$ 3,054
Education in the Church		
Current congregational expenses	$ 1,588	
New construction of churches and synagogues	879	
		$ 2,467
Education in the armed services		
Basic training	$ 1,810	
Special training schools and programs (including trainees' maintenance)	1,100	
Cash payments to military special trainees	500	
		$ 3,410
Elementary and secondary education		
Current expenditures, public schools	$ 10,716	
Current expenditures, nonpublic schools	1,642	
Plant expansion, public schools	2,853	
Plant expansion, nonpublic schools	437	
Implicit rent, public schools	2,392	
Implicit rent, nonpublic schools	352	
Cost of tax exemptions, public schools	890	
Cost of tax exemptions, nonpublic schools	132	
Earnings foregone by high-school students	13,519	
Transportation, supplies and clothing	406	
		$33,339

Updike's fey teacher put it: "School is where you go between when your parents can't take you and industry can't take you."[30]

In short, the great expansion of education in the United States is a response to the requirements of social survival.

---

[30]John Updike, *The Centaur* (New York: Alfred A. Knopf, Inc., 1963). The whole statement goes like this:

"The Founding Fathers . . . in their widsom decided that children were an unnatural strain on parents. So they provided jails called schools, equipped with tortures called an education. School is where you go between when your parents

TABLE 10–8 (Continued)

Higher education		
Current allowable expenditures, public institutions	$ 1,712	
Current allowable expenditures, nonpublic institutions	1,188	
Plant expansion, public institutions	711	
Plant expansion, nonpublic institutions	411	
Cost of tax exemptions, public institutions	181	
Cost of tax exemptions, nonpublic institutions	136	
Implicit rent, public institutions	464	
Implicit rent, nonpublic institutions	344	
Earnings foregone by college and university students	7,024	
Earnings foregone by medical interns and residents	165	
Transportation, supplies, and clothing	421	
		$12,757
Commercial, vocational & residential special schools		
Gross "sales" of commercial vocational schools	$ 223	
Current costs of residential special schools	30	
		$ 253
Federal funds for education		
Funds not elsewhere included (various training programs, etc.)	$ 342	
		$ 342
Public libraries		
Operating expenses	140	
Capital outlays	n.a.	
		$ 140
Total		$60,194 *

* Or the equivalent of better than $3,000 per household.

The function of education, then, is to enable the manning of the social order or, to put it in Durkheim's words, the social function of education

is to arouse and to develop in the child a certain number of physical, intellectual and moral states which are demanded of him both by the

can't take you and industry can't take you. I am a paid keeper of Society's unusables —the lame, the halt, the insane and the ignorant. The only incentive I can give you kid, to behave yourself, is this: if you don't buckle down and learn something, you'll be as dumb as I am, and you'll have to teach school to earn a living."

political society as a whole and the special milieu for which he is specifically destined.[31]

(A latent function of education, I've suggested, is to keep the unemployable young profitably occupied, or at least to prevent their being destructively occupied.)

Evidence That the Schools Perform This Function

Evidence that education acts to reinforce the social structure is found abundantly in the work of social anthropologists; and in the studies by Hollingshead and many other sociologists. You will recall from our discussion in Chapter 5 that Hollingshead's study, *Elmtown's Youth* yielded such findings as these: the lower the class of the high school student's family (1) the higher the drop-out rate, (2) the lower the vocational aspiration, (3) the lower the proportion planning on college, (4) the lower the course grades and the higher the number of failures, (5) the higher the proportion in commercial and vocational curricula, (6) the lower the education of the parents, (7) the lower the intelligence test scores, (8) the greater the number of recorded discipline problems. . . .

We have consistently found measures of class standing—occupation, income, education, and the like—to be effective predictors of belief and behavior. They are fair predictors not only as to whether the young person will go to college (and this among persons of comparable aptitude); but they predict, also, what sort of college will be attended among those who do go. Measures of parental status are related to the probability of attending a liberal arts college rather than a technical school or teacher's college; of attending private rather than public colleges or universities; and of fraternity membership.[32] Students whose fathers are farmers and blue-collar workers (in contrast to those whose fathers are in other occupations) show an interest in and enter teaching disproportionately.[33]

---

[31] Émile Durkheim, *Education and Sociology*, trans. Sherwood Fox (New York: Free Press of Glencoe, Inc., 1956), p. 71.

[32] See, for example, R. A. Mulligan, "Socio-Economic Background and College Enrollment," *American Sociological Review*, Vol. XVI, No. 2 (April, 1951), pp. 188–96; Ruth Strang, *Behavior and Background of Students in College and Secondary Schools* (New York: Harper & Bros., 1937); and W. Lloyd Warner, Robert J. Havighurst, and Martin B. Loeb, *Who Shall be Educated?* (New York: Harper & Bros., 1944).

[33] Mulligan, *op. cit.;* M. Moffett, *Social Background and Activities of Teachers College Students* (New York: Teachers College, Columbia, 1929); and Kate Mueller and J. H. Mueller, "Socio-Economic Background of Women Students at Indiana University," *Educational and Psychological Measurement*, Vol. IX (1949), p. 321–29.

On the other hand, students whose fathers are professionals appear to be interested in and to enter fields of law, medicine, dentistry, and music in disproportionate numbers. Years ago Cattell turned up a direct relationship between father's occupational status and the student's academic achievement in the physical sciences.[34] In short, the school tends to confirm the life chances, the mundane destiny with which the newcomer is endowed by the accident of birth.

These research data on the way an educational system reinforces the class structure of the group may lead to misconceptions. Like all facts, these do not speak for themselves. They require interpretation. How does it happen that the group assures its survival through the use of the institution of education, the prime effect being to train the children in parental roles? Perhaps the American nurtured on the Horatio Alger ideal and devoted to individual self-determination will resist this ultraconservative and static picture of the group endlessly perpetuating itself at the expense of individual differences, initiative, imagination, change. To the extent that it is true we might be disposed to think that middle-class teachers, a group Willard Waller once described as comprising unmarriageable women and unsalable men, are the witless stooges of dominant upper-class interests, favoring the children of the masters in their painful concern to please the powers and advance their own interests. This interpretation of the facts might be called the conspiratorial theory. Or it might be suggested that, since marriage and mating are selective matters, the rich and the well born are also the able. Thus genetic differentials parallel class lines and are reflected in differing levels of achievement. This we might call the *Drosophila* theory or the fruit fly fiction. More plausible than either the genetic gambit or the conspiratorial theory is a third interpretation, one that asserts: class differences in educability stem from family differences in stimulation, training, and motivation. The home of the lower-class child is no launching pad for upper-class orbiting. (Here again we see the interlocking of major social institutions.)

But of course there *is* upward mobility in the United States, and the school does deal a few children off the bottom of its deck—by no means surreptitiously, but triumphantly in affirmation of the American creed. One reason for this upward mobility is the failure of upper- and middle-class persons to reproduce themselves. As a result of such class differences in fertility, the schools must draw

[34] J. M. Cattell, "A Study of the Occupational Background of Men Listed in the First Edition of *American Men of Science*," *Science*, Vol. XXIV (1906), pp. 732–44.

from the lower strata, train in the necessary skills, values, and attitudes, and send into higher-class positions about a dozen out of every hundred adults. Furthermore, persons moving down and out of positions of power, prestige, and privilege must be replaced by others, trained out of lower-class backgrounds and moved up in the group structure. Thus for a minority of persons the school does act as a social escalator, and by this device preserves the structure of the group.

Other changes in populous, urban, industrialized societies have had emphatic effects on the part education plays in preserving the group. One of the most drastic of these changes has been our greatly increased capacity to provide foods, fibers, and frivolities. This is reflected in a redistribution of the labor force among the several classes of occupation. We have had, therefore, to institute adaptive changes in education. The data show that professional, managerial, clerical, sales, and various sorts of skilled workers increased in their proportion of the total labor force in the forty years following 1910. The range of the increase for these occupations was from 1 percent to 9 percent, the latter being the figure for clerical and sales workers. During the same period unskilled workers dropped, in their proportion of the labor force, by 4 percent, and farmers by 20 percent. These shifts in the labor force are seen clearly in Table 10–9.

The development symbolized by these figures has made for the obsolescence of youthful manpower. One tendency, then, as I have observed, is to convert the school into a custodial institution,

TABLE 10–9

Labor Force: Percentage Distribution over Broad Occupation Categories, 1900–1959

CATEGORY	1900	1910	1920	1930	1940	1950	1959
White-collar	17.6	21.3	24.9	29.4	31.1	36.6	42.1
Manual and service	44.9	47.7	48.1	49.4	51.5	51.6	48.0
Farm	37.5	30.9	27.0	21.2	17.4	11.8	9.9
Total	100.0	99.9	100.0	100.0	100.0	100.0	100.0

Source: Fritz Machlup, *The Production and Distribution of Knowledge in the United States* (Princeton, N.J.: University Press, 1962), p. 381. Reprinted by permission of Princeton University Press. Copyright 1962, Princeton University Press; all rights reserved. Data for 1900 to 1950: U.S. Bureau of the Census, *Working Paper No. 5*, "Occupational Trends in the United States, 1900–1950"; for 1959: *Current Population Reports*, Series P-60, No. 33, pp. 40–41.

Note: Figures do not always add up to total because of rounding. The 1959 data contain almost 4 million unemployed not distributed among occupation groups. In order to make the series comparable, these unemployed are here distributed among the three categories in the proportion in which the figures for "economically active" for 1950 exceeded those for "employed" in 1950, according to the *Current Population Reports*, Series P-60, No. 9 (April, 1951), p. 36.

extending its activities into spheres hitherto controlled by home, church, employer. Reinforcing the tendency toward lengthened school years has been the requirement of training specialists to man the increasingly particularized system of interlocking roles in an intricate division of labor. The outcome of increased numbers and inventive ingenuity, of spiraling population and technology has been to redefine the function of education in support of the social order, extending its realm and responsibilities.

This entailed, as a complementary aspect of the change, a contraction of youth's participation in activities of the family, market place, and church. It meant the increased isolation of the youth sector of our population from adult influence other than that of their teachers, and an enormously increased exposure to the influence of their peers. What the sociologist finds emerging, then, is an adolescent subculture with its own values and beliefs, its esoteric language and distinctive behavior. Insofar as the characteristics of the adolescent subculture are eccentric to the mainstream of the group's life, the school performs an important protective function. It acts as custodian until such time as its charges can be absorbed with impunity by the group. But if we emphasize, not the latent function of custodianship but the manifest function of staffing the social order with the best talent available, then the emergence of an adolescent culture, isolated from adult life, may militate against achieving this objective.

For some of the evidence shows that the mediocre rather than the talented student is rewarded in our public schools. Grades of "A," Professor Coleman found, go to students of exceptional ability *only where* the student population itself honors academic achievement.[35] Where the life of the intellect is not esteemed in the student subculture—and this seems often to be the case—students with high grade records are those of mediocre aptitude, the "squares" unable to achieve in activities honored by their peers. These activities are interscholastic athletics and social life. The abler students, sensitive to the sources of reward in the private world of the adolescent subculture, seek the plaudits of their peers in athletics and social popularity. Ability is not exploited when peers deride, or fail to recognize it. In Professor Coleman's study of ten high schools, the

[35] James S. Coleman, "The Adolescent Subculture and Academic Achievement," *American Journal of Sociology*, published by the University of Chicago Press, Vol. LXV, No. 4 (January, 1960), p. 337, *passim*.

. . . high performers, those who received good grades [were not] the boys whose ability was greatest but a more mediocre few. Thus the "intellectuals" of such a society . . . will not, in fact, be those with most intellectual ability. . . . In every school, without exception, the boys named as best athletes were named more often—on the average over twice as often—as members of the leading crowd than were those named as best students.[36]

Nor did the girls in Coleman's ten high schools wish to be remembered as brilliant students. Among them to an even greater extent than among the boys, the person named as "best student" had few friends and was not found in the leading crowd. "In all cases, the leading crowd [pulled] away from the brilliant-student ideal."[37]

The ingenuous might be inclined to mend mistakes with money, supposing that were the elders to provide students of high potential with better facilities they might work closer to their capacities. This appears not to be the case. Social, rather than physical factors seem to be critical. Investigators carrying out an extensive study in Connecticut found no relationship between achievement, as measured on standard tests, and educational expenditures per pupil. Coleman's research provides an answer to this peculiar finding:

Students with ability are led to achieve *only* when there are social rewards, primarily from their peers, for doing so—and these social rewards seem little correlated with [the facilities and equipment provided for students].[38]

Who Teaches What? And How?

Two points might be made here. First, the salutary effect of bricks and mortar—even laboratory equipment—upon teaching and learning, an effect that administrators and teachers and the rest of us often take for granted, is by no means certain. Second, the educational system is not, in fact, coterminous with the persons officially designated as teachers and students. This is one of the chief contributions of anthropologists whose cross-cultural studies show that the same or similar functions—teaching, for example—may be carried out by different agents and in different ways. (Thus the irreverent reference to the psychiatrist as a "head-shrinker" reflects the understanding that mental healing may be carried out, else-

---

[36] *Ibid.*

[37] *Ibid.*

[38] *Ibid.*

where, by the medicine man.) We are remarkably ignorant about the changes stemming from allegedly educational experiences, and from experiences not recognized as educational.[39] We can be sure that in settings we institutionalize as educational there are teachers other than those officially so designated. We can also be sure that there are social settings outside the school in which important learnings are regularly achieved.

We shall not have an adequate understanding of education until we renounce an exclusively psychological approach that obscures the significance of the social system, the adolescent subculture, the influence of peer groups, the significance of tribal rites, and the like. Psychology, and especially that brand called Educational Psychology (as though to distinguish it from other sorts of psychology that are mis- or un-educational!) focuses upon the individual. From the psychological point of view, as the pedagogical cliché goes, the function of education is to develop to the utmost the potential of the individual. This posture is consonant with many of our pieties—I do not deride them but mean only to call attention to certain plausible consequences—about the dignity of the individual, respect for the individual, the character of a democracy in contrast to totalitarian states, the Good Shepherd who would leave the ninety and nine to seek the single lost sheep.

Perhaps such an individualistic orientation stems also from our political and economic history, with its antiauthoritarian stance vis-à-vis the European elders,[40] its insistence upon the moral and legal

---

[39] I once asked fifty seniors in a liberal arts college what changes of some significance had occurred to them during their college careers. They reported 1,412 such changes induced by more than two dozen different sorts of "teachers." These reported learnings were rather evenly spread between the intellectual realm, the development of interest in new fields, changes in their world views and personal philosophies, personality changes and social development, career plans and choices and, finally, attitude toward the college itself. Insofar as they could identify the effective change agent, the "teacher," it was a fellow student in 10 percent of the cases, a work experience in 15 percent, the influence of a course in 17 percent of the cases of significant change. Just plain growing up, maturation or self-development, the teacher remaining obscure, seemed to account for 13 percent of the changes, teaching faculty in 8 percent of the cases, experiences in foreign countries in 5 percent, while husbands and wives, parents, employers, certain books, ministers, physicians, and administrative staff of the college figured in a few cases. I mention these details to underline the point: what is learned, who the effective teacher is, what the sanctions are that reinforce the learning, with what intensity it is learned, how long the learning is retained—about all these matters we are abysmally ill-informed.

[40] For an elaboration of this thesis that the American character is to be understood in part as a result of the children's revolt, in the New World, against the autocratic European father-figures, see Geoffrey Gorer's *The American People* (New York: W. W. Norton & Co., Inc., 1948).

equality of individuals, the rugged individualism fostered by the frontier. Perhaps it was given legitimacy by an unrecognized founding father, Adam Smith who endowed us with a special spirit of '76 in his *Wealth of Nations,* published in that year; or by Darwin's *Origin of Species* which, transferred from the biological to the social sphere, provided the rational and moral justification of an unremitting, competitive struggle among individuals. The individualistic orientation was doubtless reinforced by the successful spate of psychological testing going back at least to the alpha and beta tests of World War I and flowering through the marvelous elaboration of mental, attitudinal, aptitude, value, and personality inventories registered each year in Buros' encyclopedic survey of tests and measurements.

But what we have missed is the social conception of education, a view expressed by Durkheim when he said:

> . . . education, far from having as its unique or principal object the individual and his interests, is above all the means by which society perpetually creates the conditions of its very existence.[41]

Yet the "theory and practice of education remains focused on individuals; teachers exhort individuals to concentrate their energies in scholarly directions, while the community of adolescents [responding to the conditions of the social order] diverts these energies into other channels."[42]

What I am suggesting is that sociology has brought a late corrective to a one-sided view of education, a view resulting from an overpsychologizing, and overindividualizing, of the problems associated with learning. It is not surprising that an in-between discipline shared by sociology and psychology should have served as intermediary, providing fresh insights into the process of education. The work of social psychologists such as Sherif and Asch tells us how judgments, even of concrete and apparently invariant physical objects, are shaped by the person's group membership.[43] (Recall our

---

[41] Durkheim, *op. cit.,* p. 123.

[42] Coleman, *op. cit.,* p. 338.

[43] Reference here is to such works as the following:

Mustafer Sherif, "A Study of Some Social Factors in Perception," *Archives of Psychology,* No. 187 (1935).

Solomon E. Asch, "Group Forces in the Modification and Distortion of Judgments," chap. xvi in *Social Psychology* (New York: Prentice-Hall, Inc., 1952).

Theodore M. Newcomb, *Personality and Social Change: Attitude Formation in a Student Community* (New York: Dryden Press, 1957). First published in 1943.

Kurt Lewin, "Group Decision and Social Change," in Theodore M. Newcomb and

discussion of such work in Chapter 3.) Newcomb's pioneering study of attitudinal changes and group identity at Bennington College gave us important clues as to the way in which extra-class influences come to bear on the student and create a distinctive identity for the group. Lewin, Lippit, and White in their study of democratic, authoritarian, and laissez-faire group atmospheres, created through variation of the leadership role, tell us something about the *social* conditions of effective learning. In the attempt to formulate a set of propositions known as reference group theory, the social psychologists point to the significance of those groups that serve as benchmarks for the individual's identity, self-assessment, and aspirations. So also in the work of Piaget, Gordon Allport, and a number of other social psychologists do we get more insight into the significance of the group in the process of socialization, including the institutionalized processes of education.

If the corrective has been late in coming, perhaps it is the sociologists' own fault; for a social perspective on education has long been available in the work of anthropologists. Nowhere is the connection between education and other aspects of the social order more apparent than in their studies. They have often reported, for example, the way many Indian groups eschew corporal punishment. Lowie has written that "there is almost a direct ratio between rudeness of culture and gentleness with children."[44] This we understand when we link disciplinary prodecures with the methods used to induct youth into the status of adulthood: tests of strength, fortitude, endurance, suffering. The pain of corporal punishment cannot be used as an educational device when the group places a premium upon ability to withstand it, to suffer without flinching, to invite pain, to accept it not as demeaning, or as an index of reproach and disapproval, but as proper for the worthy. Nor are we likely to understand high school courses in driver training without some appreciation of the part played in American society by General Motors and automobile insurance companies. We cannot fully understand the teaching, disciplinarian relationship of the mother's brother to his nephew, anthropologists point out, except as we see

Eugene L. Hartley, *Readings in Social Psychology* (New York: Henry Holt & Co. Inc., 1947).

Ronald Lippitt, *An Experimental Study of Authoritarian and Democratic Group Atmosphere,* University of Iowa Studies in Child Welfare, No. 16.

[44] Lowie's statement is cited by George A. Pettitt in his *Primitive Education in North America* (Berkeley and Los Angeles: University of California Press, 1946), p. 6.

how it links with, supports, the culturally defined relationship between parents and child. Nor shall we understand the peculiar characteristics of our educational system except as we take into account the peculiarities of our husband-wife and parent-child relationships along with other social phenomena.

A second thing that anthropology clearly demonstrates is what I have stressed above: teaching occurs in vastly varying situations, under the auspices of many different teachers. Public ridicule, praise from the elders, punishment by the gods, hunting and warring exercises, derisive songs sung publicly by the best girl of a cowardly youth, instruction from his mother's uncle for the young boy, the pedagogical use of men's societies, brotherhoods, and so on. . . . Nowhere is the preeminently social function of education better illustrated than in the monographs of anthropologists.

* * * *

In this chapter we have focused on the two institutions which, above all others, fit newcomers to roles vacated by those departing, or no longer in, group-sustaining roles.

We looked first at the internal structure of the family, its institutionalized relationships and their constituent roles. Then we sketched some gross characteristics of the changing American family, moving on, finally, to consider the ties between family and other institutions (see the summary on pages 435–36).

Turning then to the agency formally charged with the second, collateral socialization, we stressed the social functions of education. This emphasis led us to pose problems rather different from those which, under the influence of psychology, we have posed in the past. Let us summarize briefly the notions that derive from this position.

To underline the point: the function of education is preeminently a social one. It is the principal means of promoting group survival. Since the group consists in a structure of relationships, these relationships and their constituent roles (not their incumbents) must be preserved. Education has the task of continuously filling these roles by training new incumbents.

Perhaps the strongest tendency is for son to replace father in the latter's roles. But such a simple, conservative pattern of intergenerational repetition is not completely possible: in part because of differing fertility rates between classes; in part because of the downward mobility of some, vacating roles that must be filled by the upwardly mobile; and in part because of new developments that create new roles for which the son's simple recapitulation of the father's role would be inadequate.

In a rapidly changing society such as ours, much of the old manpower has been rendered superfluous. Thus the school takes on a custodial function. In addition, new roles, new specialties require extended training. Both influences sweep an increasing proportion of our youth into the schools where they are held incommunicado, as it were, out of contact with the adult world. In this setting values emerge that sometimes make intellectual achievement a third and last choice for those of mediocre aptitude while the able, sensitive as we all are to the approval of our peers, find that approval in social and athletic prowess.

Thus we see the institutionalizing of educational processes as essential in maintaining the group. For a raw input of unsocialized creatures must be transmuted, becoming human beings with those skills and attitudes necessary to staff that role structure peculiar to a given group. The social function of education is an adaptive one, primarily.

The social function of religious institutions is somewhat different. It may also promote adaptation to the social order. But at base it is a social means of binding together those sharing common convictions and commitments. In the following chapter we shall consider the integrative influence of religion.

SELECTED SUPPLEMENTARY READINGS

BERELSON, BERNARD, AND STEINER, GARY A. "The Family," in *Human Behavior: An Inventory of Scientific Findings*, pp. 297–322. New York: Harcourt, Brace & World, Inc., 1964.

――――. "Educational Institutions," *ibid.*, pp. 436–43.

BRIM, ORVILLE. *Sociology and the Field of Education.* New York: Russell Sage Foundation, 1958.

COLEMAN, JAMES S. *The Adolescent Society.* New York: The Free Press of Glencoe, Inc., 1961. See also his "The Adolescent Sub-culture and Academic Achievement," *American Journal of Sociology*, Vol. LXV, No. 4 (January, 1960), pp. 337–47.

*GLICK, PAUL. "The Family Cycle," *American Sociological Review*, Vol. 12, No. 2 (April, 1947), pp. 164–74.

GOODE, WILLIAM J.   "The Sociology of the Family," in Robert K. Merton, Leonard Broom, and Leonard S. Cottrell, Jr. (eds.), *Sociology Today,* ch. vii. New York: Harper & Row—Harper Torchbooks, 1965.

GROSS, NEAL.   "The Sociology of Education," in Robert K. Merton, *et al.,* *op. cit.,* ch. v.

HALSEY, A. H.; FLOUD, JEAN; AND ANDERSON, C. ARNOLD.   *Education, Economy, and Society.* New York: The Free Press of Glencoe, Inc., 1961.

*PARSONS, TALCOTT.   "The Kinship System of the Contemporary United States," *American Anthropologist,* Vol. 45 (January-March, 1943), pp. 22–38.

*TURNER, RALPH H.   "Sponsored and Contest Mobility and the School System," *American Sociological Review,* Vol. 25, No. 6 (December, 1960), pp. 855–67.

WALLER, WILLARD, AND HILL, REUBEN.   *The Family: A Dynamic Interpretation.* New York: Dryden, 1951.

WINCH, ROBERT F., AND McGINNIS, ROBERT.   *Selected Studies in Marriage and the Family.* New York: Holt, Rinehart & Winston, Inc., 1953.

---

* Articles marked with an asterisk are available as reprints from the college division of the Bobbs-Merrill Company, Indianapolis, Indiana.

Chapter 11

The Church: Relationships Instituted to Sustain Group Values

How do we preserve our preferences, achieve consensus in our conceptions of the good, so providing guidelines for conduct and promoting predictable relationships within a social order?

You may find communities without walls; without letters, without kings; without money, with no need of coinage, without acquaintance with theaters or gymnasia; but a community without holy rite, without a God, that uses not prayer, without sacrifice to win good or avert evil—no man ever saw or ever will see.[1]

Western societies have been spectacularly successful in adapting to—indeed, recreating—their environments (perhaps more successful with the biophysical environment than the social milieu). This very technical proficiency may have led, as Merton suggests, to a preoccupation with means and to increased ambiguity as to the ends of life.[2] The truncating of tradition as the nuclear family supplants the extended family, the American emphasis on the bigger and better, the slant toward the future—in general, a proud instrumental orientation toward the world—these characteristics of our culture may lead us to underestimate the significance of religion.

But no sociologist can be cavalier in dismissing an institution with which, apparently, 96 percent of the adult population identify

---

[1] Plutarch (A.D., 46–120).

[2] Robert K. Merton, "Social Structure and Anomie," in *Social Theory and Social Structure* (New York: Free Press of Glencoe, Inc., 1957), chap. iv.

themselves.[3] Identification is not affiliation, to say nothing of participation. Yet restricting ourselves to membership, we still get something around 60 percent of the population who are members of some church group, perhaps 60 percent of them Protestants, a third Catholics, and 5 percent Jews.[4] A very large part of the U.S. population believes in some way in God, in the efficacy of prayer, in the Bible as the divinely inspired word of God, and in some version of heaven and hell. In any case it is clear that religious belief and behavior are prominent parts of our social order, and that the function of religion in that order must be investigated by the sociologist. Its universality in space and its persistence through time suggest that religion must be seen as playing an important part in maintaining the group, in promoting social integration. There is something to Durkheim's statement when he writes that

> . . . it is an essential postulate of sociology that a human institution cannot rest [solely] upon an error and a lie without which it could not exist. If it were not founded in the nature of things, it would have encountered in the facts a resistance over which it could never have triumphed.[5]

That is to say, however inadequate or archaic institutionalized patterns of thought and action may seem, their very persistence through time suggests that they must be supporting other, interlocked sectors of the social order. The task of the sociologist is to ferret out these connections, hidden from the casual observer.

A good academic discussion of religion should doubtless begin with definitions. But definitions are legion, and I am rather more concerned with the acts and beliefs that people themselves classify as religious. Yet for a point of departure we can accept Durkheim's definition of religion as a "unified system of beliefs and practices

---

[3] This is the percent of the nation's population over age fourteen who, when asked in a sample survey by the Bureau of the Census what their religion was, identified themselves with some faith. It is doubtless an overestimate of genuine religious commitment, by any definition. Yet the figure is so large, representing 119 million persons, that any credible reduction of it would still leave an impressive part of our population with clear religious identity and participation.

[4] See, for various estimates, Will Herberg, *Protestant, Catholic, Jew* (Garden City, N.Y.: Doubleday & Co., Inc., 1955) and Benson Landis, *The Yearbook of American Churches* (New York: National Council of Churches of Christ in the U.S.A., 1964).

[5] Émile Durkheim, *The Elementary Forms of the Religious Life,* trans. Joseph Ward Swain (New York: Free Press of Glencoe, Inc., 1947), p. 2.

What's
the link
between
work and
worship?

relative to sacred things, binding together those who adhere to these beliefs and practices in a single moral community."[6]

THE INTEGRATIVE FUNCTION OF RELIGION IN THE GROUP OF BELIEVERS

Such a definition points to the integrative effect of religion. We find such an effect to the extent that religion penetrates other spheres of life, rationalizing them and deflecting rebellious inclinations. It is integrative when its prescriptions are universalistic, applying to all believers. It promotes social unity when God and group are reflected in one another, when the church exerts pressure to match profession with practice, and when religion effectively bridges divisions within the group. Consider, for a bit, these group-maintaining functions of religion.

Group Unity Promoted as Religion Crosscuts Other Spheres of Life

Religious creeds and codes point often to a unifying aim; for religious commitments should (so we allege) permeate all aspects of life, rendering act consistent with act, thought with thought, and act with thought. Thus cultural and normative integration is promoted.

> God is concerned with the whole of men's lives: on at least this one point all the churches agree. He is not merely the Lord of the Sabbath, but is equally concerned with men's activities the other six days of the week: their work, their play, their politics, their family life.[7]

The penetration of religion throughout the social order is not peculiar to Western societies with their single God ruling all realms of life. C. K. Yang's study of religion in Chinese society shows us how the special functions of their temples—he classifies nearly 1,800 of them!—touch the myriad concerns of daily life (Table 11–1).

Among the 602 temples whose powers extend to the well-being and integration of social organizations, just over a fourth have to do with kinship groups, just under a fourth with community protection, and about one half promote the welfare of the state. These temples house gods, spirits, and authorities of various sorts. In support of the kinship group there are gods and goddesses of happy marriages, of

---

[6] *Ibid.*, p. 47.

[7] Gerhard Lenski, *The Religious Factor* (Garden City, N.Y.: Doubleday & Co., Inc., 1961), p. 1.

TABLE 11-1

A Classification of 1,768 Major Temples in Eight Localities in China,
According to the Nature of the Chief Gods in Each Temple
and the Function They Perform

FUNCTIONS	NUMBER OF TEMPLES	PERCENT
I. Integration and well-being of social organizations (kinship group, community protection, state welfare)	602	33.7
II. General moral order (heavenly deities and underworld authorities)	406	22.7
III. Economic functions (agricultural deities, patrons of crafts and trades, commerce and general economic prosperity)	143	8.1
IV. Health	19	1.1
V. General public and personal welfare (pantheons, devil dispellers, blessing deities, and temples with unspecified gods)	68	3.3
VI. Monasteries and nunneries	548	30.6
TOTAL	1,786	100.0

Source: Adapted from C. K. Yang, *Religion in Chinese Society* (Berkeley: University of California Press, 1961), pp. 8–11 and Appendix I, pp. 436–51. The data come from six different provinces and are for different dates ranging from 1923 to 1936.

mercy, child-giving, of flowers, protector of children against infanticide, spirits of chaste women, of filial sons and dutiful brothers, and spirits of martyrs for female chastity. Providing local community protection are gods of fire and flood, of the sea (controller of tidal waves), a god of bridges and protector against falling into rivers, of ferry docks, of roads, earth, and grain. Temples promoting civic and political virtues include those dedicated to civic and political figures, sanctuaries for "repaying distinguished service of officials and public leaders," for adoration of the virtuous and lingering affection for benevolent officials, for gods of righteousness, war, patriotism, justice, law, literature, and others.

Temples devoted to the general moral order include heavenly deities, and underworld authorities (judges and rulers over the spirits of the dead). The latter are represented in 55 percent of these 406 temples, the heavenly deities in 45 percent.

In the third category (temples whose gods promote economic, welfare) we find about three fourths supporting agricultural enterprise, 14 percent dedicated to crafts and trade, and 10 percent to commerce. Agricultural deities include the creator of agriculture; gods of thunder, rain, winds, clouds; the god of the sweet dew; the dragon god, river god, god of floods, of sluice gates, of insects, of trees, of domesticated animals, of fire. In crafts, trades, and commerce there are: the god of carpentry and construction, the goddess of sailing, the god of the rapids, the god of wealth, and the spirits of dead members of the dyestuff guild.

As to health, there is the patron of doctors and health, a goddess of the eyes, the Buddhist deity of healing, the god of herb medicine, the god of epidemics, the goddesses of smallpox and of the Bushel star.

Protecting the general public and promoting personal welfare are the temples of all gods, devil dispellers, and blessing deities; Taoist fairies, the goddess of mercy, the spirit of the general on a white horse, the spirit of the fox incarnate, and a number of temples with unspecified gods.

Yang's data do not specify the nature of the gods and spirits in monasteries and nunneries (of the 648, 90 percent are Buddhist, the remainder Taoist).

The classification of temples on the basis of the social functions they support may be an inaccurate reflection of the frequency with which people do in fact address their gods, soliciting their help in various enterprises. Not only does this table tell us nothing about frequency of use: it cannot reveal the extent to which the deity's help is asked in realms outside his nominal jurisdiction. If we could know what was in worshipers' minds as they addressed their gods, we would doubtless get a different picture of the connection between religion and other sectors of the social order. Some intimation of such connections is given in the content of people's prayers as recorded in 500 prayer slips. (But we should remember that the link between religion and other spheres is not properly represented by those in need who offer supplications to their gods.)

Thus functions necessary for system maintenance are performed through the instituting of such patterns of religious behavior. Goals to be sought, evils to be avoided, values to be cherished are celebrated through the heavenly deities who sustain the general moral order (category II, Table 11–1). Adaptive functions are performed through the agricultural deities and the patrons of crafts, trades, and commerce (category III, Table 11–1), whose help and guidance ensure successful enterprise. That requisite for maintaining the group, some patterning of roles so as to promote what Parsons calls *tension management,* is met through the agency of gods in all categories, perhaps especially those restoring health, the devil dispellers and blessing deities. The general integrative function is performed through the gods and temples dedicated to community protection, the celebration of benevolent leaders and the well-being of kinship groups.

Cutting across many spheres of life and offering solace or solutions in physical, mental, and emotional crises, religion contributes to the stability of the social order. The extent to which, in our

TABLE 11–2

Subjects of Prayers in 500 Prayer Slips Submitted
to Chinese Gods

SUBJECTS DEALT WTH	NUMBER OF PRAYER SLIPS CARRYING EACH SUBJECT	PERCENT (N = 500)
Healing of diseases	484	96.8
Marriage	459	90.2
Traveling mercies	440	88.0
Wealth	424	85.0
Lawsuits	391	68.2
Progeny	348	70.0
Family problems	348	70.0
Lost articles	346	69.2
Moving (household)	308	60.2
Business affairs	290	58.0
Crops	273	54.6
Domestic animals	266	53.2
Official position	246	50.0

Source: C. K. Yang, *Religion in Chinese Society.* Cited from L. Newton Hayes, *Gods of the Chinese,* Royal Asiatic Society, North China Branch, Vol. LV (1924), pp. 96–103 by way of Clarence B. Day, *Chinese Peasant Cults* (Shanghai, 1940), p. 13.

society, religion meshes with other sectors of social life, is seldom understood. Churches in the United States are active in education, child welfare, treatment and prevention of crime and delinquency, recreation, care of the aged, the placement of unemployed, medical care, political action, radio and television broadcasting and a wide range of social service activities. American churches spend millions annually on welfare and philanthropic activities. From the perspective of the social order, such services may be viewed as providing a safety net. For the disruptive, even explosive potential of a sense of unjust deprivation can be curbed through the welfare activities, the institutionalized "caring" of the church. When Marx spoke of religion as the "opiate of the people" he was referring to myth and dogma precluding a proper, active interest in one's own welfare, and in redressing the wrong of a maldistribution of wealth. The Marxist notion has been translated in terms both psychological (the soporific influence of religion) and conspiratorial (the calculated suppression of the masses through superstitions or resignation religiously induced). In reality, the welfare functions of religion are social and have tended, in the United States at any rate, to promote evolutionary rather than revolutionary change. The church's welfare activities have sometimes served as bellwether models for programs instituted later through legislation.

The Universality of Religious Prescriptions Promotes Integration

Religion performs a group-maintaining function not only because it cuts across a broad range of men's mundane activities but also because it establishes standards equally applicable to all believers, the high as well as the lowly. Through it we get a statement of the cultural universals. It is only because of an indignant sense of the universality of sacred principles that the pirate could reply to Alexander as Augustine reports him:

> . . . for elegant and excellent was that pirate's answer to the great Macedonian Alexander, who had taken him: the king asking him how he durst molest the seas so, he replied with a free spirit, "How darest thou molest the whole world? But because I do it with a little ship only, I am called a thief: thou, doing it with a great navy, art called an emperor."[8]

George Bernard Shaw expresses the same sense of a betrayal of common standards: If a thief "snatches a loaf of bread from the baker's counter [he] is promptly run into gaol. Another man snatches bread from the tables of hundreds of widows and orphans and simple credulous souls who do not know the ways of company promoters; and, as likely as not, he is run into Parliament."[9] The prescriptions of the group's religion bind together all members with universal imperatives.

---

[8] St. Augustine, *De Civitate Dei.*

[9] George Bernard Shaw, "Imprisonment," *The Prefaces* (London England: Constable and Company, Ltd., 1934), chap. xi, p. 302.

The Integrating Effect of Religion as It Exerts Pressure to Match Profession with Practice, and as It Bridges Subcommunities

The universality of religious prescriptions—in our society, the almost all-embracing sweep of the Judeo-Christian faith—makes it possible to exert pressure to match profession with practice. When practices are out of line (as they must be, inevitably falling short of religious counsels of perfection) and when such deviation is harmful to some group, its members can appeal to the violated universals. The church then becomes an instrument of justice, sometimes interpreting and applying God's law before the courts apply man's law to redefine and rectify human relationships. Prophetic jeremiads symbolizing a religious vigilance (more constant than the periodic assessment of morality by way of partisan politics) creates a strain toward consistency between words and deeds.

This has a special meaning for members of minority groups. With the American Negro, a common faith has provided a moral bridge into the white community. The church has often been the threshold to communication, hence to community: first, in identifying a company of the dispossessed and, later, in identifying a larger moral community embracing Negroes and whites. It was, Frazier suggests, the single agency through which such identity, such social cohesion could be wrought.

> The adventitious gatherings in which tribeless men and women without even the bones of kinship could find an ephemeral solidarity became regular meetings for religious services and a new bond of cohesion was established in the New World. Not only was a new bond with their fellow slaves established but as they joined in the religious services of their white masters their moral isolation in the white world began to break down.[10]

Thus the church can be regarded as a first force, an opening wedge in the drive toward equity, toward enhancing normative integration. But with such a depressed and dispossessed minority as the American Negro, integration required first of all a lifting of the level of life to the point where something approaching a peer relationship with majority members could emerge. Just as upstream traffic on river or canal is impossible until the water in the lock is raised to a higher level, so full equity in Negro-white relationships depended

---

[10] Reprinted by permission of Schocken Books, Inc., from *The Negro Church in America* by E. Franklin Frazier (New York: Schocken Books, Inc., 1963), pp. 82, 83.

on a lift in the Negro's life conditions. The church has sometimes served as such a lock in the stream of American society, not merely providing an emotional safety valve but generating collateral institutions to raise the level of life. The church was the source of organizations for economic cooperation, not only for buying and building churches, but for insurance companies and other forms of mutual assistance. It was through the internal organization of the church that the Negro's political impulses expressed themselves, a connection symbolized by the Reverend Representative Adam Clayton Powell. The church was critical in the development of educational opportunities for the Negro. And after generations of inching toward equity, it was through the church and its leaders (including an Indian Hindu-Christian pacifist) that the nonviolent civil rights movement made the breakthrough, initiating what has been called the revolution in race relations.

Social Integration through the Identity of Group and God

Religion is socially integrating, again, in the sense that gods are local, the unqualified Good is the God as defined within a given culture and by a given tribe. *Gott mit uns* reveals the common possessive posture of a nation toward its god. Official state doctrine invariably assumes that Providence is peculiarly receptive to its claims upon Him. National anthems disclose this conviction. These sometimes go beyond mere supplication and take on the tone of injunctions not to forget His contractual obligations to the tribal cause. A verse of the national anthem not often sung by Englishmen (the tune is the same as our "My Country 'tis of thee") goes this way:

> O lord our God, arise
> Scatter our enemies
> And make them fall.
> Confound their politics,
> Frustrate their knavish tricks,
> On thee our hopes we fix,
> God save us all.

This comes close to Durkheim's central thesis in a stimulating (and controversial) book entitled *The Elementary Forms of the Religious Life*.[11] For Durkheim, God must be seen as the more or

---

[11] Émile Durkheim, *The Elementary Forms of the Religious Life*, trans. Joseph Ward Swain (New York: Free Press of Glencoe, Inc., 1947). For a judicious appraisal

less ambiguous symbol of people's conception of the unqualified good. Notions of good and evil take on a transcendental character as they are commonly shared and reflected in the group's gods. And the persistence of moral and theological conceptions is not to be explained as due to God and His control over human affairs, but to men's creation of God, and of the church that institutionalizes the values they attribute to Him. Religion, then, is a social artifact—an artifact in the sense of creation, but not artificial; for it is an institution both natural to man and necessary for sustaining that continuing collective enterprise that is a society.

In an intriguing cross-cultural study of 50 societies, Professor Swanson accepts Durkheim's position in principle, that certain aspects or conditions of society generate responses we call religious.[12] In his study of the sources of monotheism, he suggests that the "high Gods," omnipotent or sovereign spirits (which he defines as "organized clusters of purposes") should be found in connection with sovereign groups. These are groups having original and independent jurisdiction over a given sphere of life: the nuclear family, the territorial unit, and the like. For one should anticipate some correspondence between characteristics of sovereign groups and sovereign spirits: group members' goals most purely represented in their gods, the immortality of high gods and the groups they symbolize, the means men use to achieve their ends and the God-prescribed modes of conduct, the distinctiveness of the group and the matchlessness of its god. For, on this last point, if the group is to have an identity, it must stem from a configuration of roles and relationships peculiar to it and establishing group boundaries. And this unique configuration is both exemplified and supernaturally legitimated in its God. Thus the unifying influence of God.

But to say that a high God has such a unifying effect is to imply that he transcends divisions in the group. Some order in human relationships is induced despite the differences that divide men and the subgroups in which they live and act. Thus we would expect a high God especially in groups having a number of relatively autonomous subgroups (the social parallel of the situation in which

---

of this important work see Imogen Seger, *Durkheim and His Critics on the Sociology of Religion* (New York: Columbia University Bureau of Applied Social Research, September, 1957).

[12] Guy E. Swanson, *The Birth of the Gods* (Ann Arbor: University of Michigan Press, 1964).

a number of individuals are, severally, *primus inter pares*, yet must collaborate to reach a common goal).

And so, Swanson argues, if we look for the social conditions appropriate to the "idea of a high god . . . we will focus our attention on those cases in which sovereign organizations have other groups subordinate to them."[13] For the need to build unity out of diversity should generate celestial echoes in the form of a unifying high God. And so Swanson predicts that, where we find three or more sovereign groups in a society we will also find a supreme God. The data testing this hypothesis are presented in Table 11–3.

TABLE 11–3

Number of Sovereign Groups and Presence of High God
in 39 Societies

	NUMBER OF SOVEREIGN GROUPS		
PRESENCE OF HIGH GOD	1 or 2	3	4 or More
Present	2*	7	10
Absent	17	2*	1*
Total	19	9	11
Percent present	11%	78%	91%

Source: Guy E. Swanson, *The Birth of the Gods* (Ann Arbor: University of Michigan Press, 1964), p. 65.
  * These starred groups represent negative cases. The two having a high God but with fewer than three sovereign groups are the Lengua of Paraguay and the Yahgan of Tierra del Fuego. The Lengua have two sovereign groups, as Swanson defines them, the household and the clan-village. There is no ready explanation for their being exceptions to the hypothesized relationships. The data on the Yahgan are a bit shaky and they may not, in fact, be an exception. Of the other three negative cases, the Orokaiva of Papua, New Guinea, and the Yokuts of California may have been misclassified due to the ambiguity of the data. (This is always a problem in the secondary analysis of data originally gathered for some other purpose.) The third group, the Timbira, appear to be a genuine exception to Swanson's thesis that the unification of sovereign groups generates the conception of a high God.

There is, then, some evidence that a supreme deity reflects and reinforces group unity. But if God is society writ large, the spiritual exemplification of ideals commonly shared in the group—and the means of their realization—what shall we infer from the presence of several Gods? Does this imply a fragmentation of the group, its various subdivisions having, each of them, its particular God? This may indeed be the case, as Swanson's discussion of "superior Gods" suggests. Superior Gods are those presiding over general functions or activities, rather than over particular people or places. The more clearly specific human aims and activities are distinguished, the more likely they are to be embodied in superior Gods. These are the special deities that go along with clearly differentiated roles repre-

---

[13] *Ibid.*, p. 62.

senting, as it were, a celestial division of labor paralleling the differentiation of earthly activities. (You'll recall that such a heavenly division of labor was revealed in Wang's data, Table 11–1.)

But there is a complication here: specialization may be seen in two dimensions, as it were, vertical and horizontal. Vertical differentiation of roles is illustrated in a sequence of specialties from chief, lieutenants, warriors, noncombatants, and those in supporting tribal (civilian) roles. A rough parallel is the CIO principle of industrial organization, from top to bottom (in contrast to the craft organization of the AFL). Group unity stems from a division of labor in

TABLE 11–4
Number of Noncommunal Specialties and Number of Superior Gods

NUMBER OF SUPERIOR GODS	NUMBER OF NONCOMMUNAL SPECIALTIES	
	NONE	ONE OR MORE
3 +	8	9
1 or 2	9	3
0	17	3
Total	34	15

Source: Guy E. Swanson, *The Birth of the Gods* (Ann Arbor: University of Michigan Press, 1964), p. 87.

support of a common enterprise. Horizontal differentiation of roles, on the other hand, is seen in the division of labor between carpenter, weaver, blacksmith, and medicine man.

Swanson calls the former "communal specialties" and the latter "noncommunal specialties." Where kinship is the central principle of social organization, providing the criteria for the vertical sort of role differentiation we have, as in the case of differentiated warmaking roles, communal specialties. Swanson's data suggest that the connection between number of specialties and the number of superior Gods obtains especially where kinship is *not* the overriding principle of organization. The presence of superior Gods, guiding specialized activities, appears to be linked with a stress on performance rather than, as in the case of kinship, on ascription. Table 11–4 gives the data for 49 societies on the connection between number of noncommunal specialties and the number of superior Gods.

Thus we find some support for the notion of an identity between group and God. For God appears both to reflect the social structure of the group and its central values. He promotes the cultural and normative integration of the group and, in the case of Swanson's superior Gods, validates its functional integration.

DISINTEGRATIVE EFFECTS OF RELIGION

For the individual, religion may lend purpose to life, providing more or less consistent guidelines for achieving that purpose. Thus from a personal standpoint, a man's life may gain a certain coherence or unity. So, also, at the social level, religion may serve an integrating function. I've been suggesting that religion promotes group unity as it celebrates standards supposed to apply across the range of life's activities, as it imposes these standards equally on all believers, stressing some correspondence between practice and profession and as, finally, its gods and goods define limits of allegiance, becoming identified with the group. Such an identification is both cultural and social, the gods exemplifying the group's values and reflecting its social structure.

But to use the plural (to speak of gods) and to say that they define the limits of allegiance is to suggest the potential divisiveness, or disintegrative effect of religion. For intragroup harmony is related to intergroup antipathy. If religion tightens the drawstrings of the group, it also accentuates the differences (and if the differences are religiously founded they may be intolerable differences) between the one group and others. If God promotes unity, gods often generate conflict. If it is true that the church has opened doors for a suppressed minority, so also has it barred and bolted them. For our southern God, and the South African God, faithfully reflecting group values, have generally validated segregation and white supremacy. The Holy Inquisition, the treatment of the Huguenots, the Mormons, the Quakers, Dachau and Buchenwald, St. Bartholomew's Day, Salem's witches, Marcus Aurelius' treatment of the minority sect called Christians—these bring to mind the intergroup divisiveness that feeds on religious absolutes that parallel group sovereignty. The church has often accepted St. Augustine's view: "When error prevails it is right to invoke liberty of conscience, but when on the contrary truth predominates, it is proper to use coercion."

In a complex society like ours with its great variety of subgroups we should, of course, expect to find differing, and potentially disruptive, religious commitments. To speak of Protestant, Catholic, and Jew is to understate the diversity of religion in American society. For religious divisions are much more numerous than this trichotomy would suggest. And other divisions may be more significant, as to doctrine and practice. Thus, for example, Professors Glock and Stark ask: "Is there an American Protestantism?"[14] and the answer, as Table 11–5 suggests, is no. Belief in the existence of God varies from 99 percent among southern Baptists to 41 percent among Congregationalists, with Catholics closer to American and Missouri Lutherans, Presbyterians, American Baptists, and Disciples of Christ than they are to fundamentalist sects and southern Baptists. Similarly, the belief in the virgin birth of Christ is more common among three Protestant groups than it is among Catholics.

It is a fair guess that religion is not more divisive than it is in the United States precisely because of its diversity. Differences, as these data suggest, follow continuous rather than discrete distributions, thus blunting the sharp edges of conflict, the black-and-white conflict of good versus evil, right versus wrong. And the formal divisions between Protestant, Catholic, and Jew are often spurious, since there is much overlapping of beliefs and behavior. Significant religious divisions sometimes fall along other lines. It is likely, too, that a strong secular orientation masks, if it does not displace, religious commitments, so reducing their *dis*integrative potential.

RELIGION'S ROOTS IN THE NATURE OF HUMAN RELATIONSHIPS

I've been pointing to two social effects of religious commitment: within the group, its integrating function; between groups an effect often divisive. Let's look further at the social implications of religion, or the religious implications of the social. For the generality of religious institutions can be understood as stemming in part from certain social imperatives: (1) the absolute requirement, for human relationships, of dependable—i.e., predictable—responses, and (2) the need to "know" beyond the realm of the demonstrable.

The requirement of dependable performance in role and, there-

---

[14] Charles Y. Glock and Rodney Stark, "Is There An American Protestantism?" *Trans-action*, Vol. III, No. 1 (November/December, 1965). The population sampled consisted of church members in four metropolitan counties in northern California. Key questions from this study, put to a national sample, yielded similar results.

TABLE 11–5

Rank Order, for 11 Religious Groups, of Percent of Members Holding Specified Beliefs: Four Metropolitan Counties in Northern California, 1964

	N	BELIEFS IN								
		EXISTENCE OF GOD (1)	DIVINITY OF JESUS (2)	THE VIRGIN BIRTH (3)	LIFE BEYOND DEATH (4)	EXISTENCE OF THE DEVIL (5)	THAT A CHILD IS BORN SINFUL (6)	JESUS AS SAVIOR REQUIRED FOR SALVATION (7)	GOOD WORKS REQUIRED FOR SALVATION (8)	BEING JEWISH PRECLUDES SALVATION (9)
Congregationalists	151	11.0	11.0	11.0	11.0	11.0	11.0	11.0	3.0	11.0
Methodists	415	10.0	10.0	10.0	10.0	10.0	9.0	10.0	4.5	9.5
Episcopalians	416	9.0	9.0	9.0	9.0	9.0	8.0	9.0	5.0	8.0
Disciples of Christ	50	6.0	6.5	7.0	8.0	8.0	10.0	4.5	1.0	6.0
Presbyterians	495	7.0	8.0	8.0	7.0	7.0	7.0	7.0	7.0	7.0
American Lutherans	208	8.0	6.5	6.0	6.0	5.5	3.0	6.0	8.0	4.5
American Baptists	141	5.0	5.0	5.0	5.0	5.5	6.0	4.5	9.0	4.5
Missouri Lutherans	116	3.5	3.0	3.0	3.0	3.0	1.0	1.5	10.0	1.0
Southern Baptists	79	1.0	1.0	1.0	1.0	1.0	5.0	1.5	11.0	2.0
Sects	255	2.0	2.0	2.0	2.0	2.0	4.0	3.0	2.0	3.0
Catholics	545	3.5	4.0	4.0	4.0	4.0	2.0	8.0	4.5	9.5

The full statement of belief, by column above, and percentage of respondents in first and last rank order are as follows:

	Percent of respondents in first and last rank order	
	1st	last
	99	41
	99	40
	99	21
	97	36
	92	6
	86	2
	97	38
	64	29
	31	1

(1) "I know God really exists and I have no doubts about it."
(2) "Jesus is the Divine Son of God and I have no doubts about it."
(3) "Jesus was born of a virgin" (response checked: "completely true").
(4) "There is a life beyond death" (response checked: "completely true").
(5) "The devil actually exists" (response checked: "completely true").
(6) "A child is born into the world already guilty of sin" (response checked: "completely true").
(7) For salvation, "Belief in Jesus Christ as Saviour is absolutely necessary."
(8) For salvation, "Doing good for others is absolutely necessary."
(9) "Being of the Jewish religion definitely prevents salvation."

Source: Based on data in Charles Y. Glock and Rodney Stark, "Is There An American Protestantism?" Trans-action, Vol. III, No. 1 (November/December '65), adapted from tables on pp. 9, 11, 13. Key questions from this study, put to a national sample, yielded parallel results.

fore, stability in human relationships is a moral one. For basic aspects of morality—its "oughtness," its impersonality, its generality, the stress on personal responsibility, the significance of the intent or spirit of the act—these are also requisites of a social order. The near universality of religion may be derived from these requisites for sustaining a social structure. Through holy writ and rite, religious institutions underly the law in the realm of morality. Rewards are promised for observance, punishment for infractions of the moral code—infractions, that is to say, of the rules that legitimate the expectations that define the roles that make for stable human relationships.

Consider the mandatory element in the moral and the social. A social relationship is something which, by its very nature, involves the dependence of one person upon another and a high probability that, given an action by one person, the other will respond with a predictable reaction. To describe one aspect of this interplay between persons we use adjectives like "responsible" and "dependable." If someone agrees to meet you at a given time, he does so. If he contracts to do a job, he comes on time and performs his work conscientiously. If he says he will sell you this sort of article, he does in fact do so and the article is as he claims it to be. Sometimes we use the stronger word "honesty" to describe the trust that can be placed in another to react as he is expected to. Of course, we are sometimes disappointed, not to say disillusioned—which is to say that performance is not always what it *should* be. Human conduct, in contrast to sheer behavior, carries connotations of better and worse, and the better is, of course, the preferred. In matters of any import, the preferred becomes mandatory. Performance in any significant role is informed with an "oughtness." Because of the common "oughtness" of our expectations, there is some leverage to guarantee that what ought, will be: that expectations will be met. And to meet expectations is to meet the prime requirement for sustaining a human relationship.

The stipulations for correct conduct are not aimed at any person. Religious sanctions for correct conduct apply equally to all communicants. Similarly with human relationships: they are defined by role, not by incumbent. They are impersonal (perhaps more correctly, suprapersonal) in the sense that the overarching rule prescribes the role. Core elements of role prescriptions, like religious prescriptions, have this characteristic: they are *impersonally* mandatory.

But while the rule is impersonal, responsibility is personal. Each person is accountable to others, and to the law, representing others. A parallel responsibility is to his gods who are typically and necessarily anthropomorphic conceptions. For men have always found it hard to conceive the inconceivable. Their closest approximation has been a god whose attributes are extensions, superior extensions, of the human. Man must create his gods in his own image. They are superhuman, of course, but in the same attributes that humans have: in power, benevolence, wrath, compassion, control.

> We Tibetans have a saying, "Gods, devils and men are alike in actions and thoughts," i.e., the same things will anger them and the same things will please them, and they will act accordingly."[15]

This extension to the gods of human attributes entails two consequences. We can understand the divine impulse; and we experience fear or guilt in our transgressions. The link of child to father is profoundly personal. An omniscient Father knows the communicant deeply and intimately. With the faculty of penetrating innermost thoughts comes a power, more terrible than that of the earthly father, to reward and punish. And this personal responsibility to a celestial Father is paralleled by responsibility to one's fellows: for a common father implies a sibling relationship with fraternal obligations. Thus impersonality in the rule, personal[16] responsibility in the role, contribute to the dependability of human relationships.

---

[15] C. A. Bell, *The People of Tibet* (Oxford: Clarendon Press, 1928), p. 72.

[16] Responsibility implies identification of the actor so that he may be held responsible. In this connection we may think of the name with which the child is christened, often in the church, as a sort of label on the package. It enables others to know whether the contents of this package are as specified, as expected. For the rest of his life the person's name, the label of the product, stands linked with performances enabling others to reward him for successes, punish him for failures. This is why the Mardi Gras, costume balls, are associated with liberation from the customary moral restraints and specified relationships of daily life. For some sort of identity is essential for pegging responsibility, for assuring the meeting of expectations. Conversely, anonymity is associated with amorality. This is in part why the transient, the migrant, the stranger whose identity is not established, may feel freer to act unresponsibly, and why others are disposed to view him with suspicion. (See in this connection Everett K. Wilson, "Mobility and the Maverick," *Antioch Review*, Vol. XVII, No. 1 [March, 1957].) This is why legislation has been passed against the hooded Ku Klux Klan who, in their anonymity, can flout conventional norms, fracture the law with impunity.

The impersonality of the rule, or its suprapersonal character implies a third characteristic of religion and an element essential for the social order, the generality of the rule. All communicants acknowledge a common Father, a common doctrine, share generally common aspirations. The general nature of the religious rule and of the rules for roles is linked with reciprocity of expectations. Given the role, any and all incumbents are expected to respond in a given way. If A responds to B . . . N in the appropriate way under conditions X, he may legitimately expect the same response from B *et al.* under similar circumstances. Anyone struck by disaster has certain legitimte expectations for help from his fellows; and he in turn must reciprocate when others are hurt. (This reciprocation is institutionalized in insurance programs in our society, a formalizing of reciprocity.)

As citizens having a common nationality we have certain minimal expectations that we reciprocate—willingness to be taxed for others' children's education and they for ours; to respect others' property, and they ours; to abide by a majority decision, even when we are in the minority; to serve the common cause in war and peace, so serving fellow citizens as they serve us. The moral equality among children of God supports this generality of reciprocal expectations and obligations wherever an enduring system of relationships is built. It promotes consistency through time (behavior in the role will be, tomorrow, quite as it was yesterday) and space (within the group these people, here, will fulfill role expectations just about as those people do, there). Reciprocal obligations thus impose general requirements for performance on all roles within a given category: husbands and wives, employers and employees, students and teachers, citizens, rulers and ruled, *et al.*[17] Both law and religion restrict the range of idiosyncratic conduct, channeling role performance in accord with legitimate expectations.

This may well suggest that to do unto others as you would have them do unto you is not merely a prescription. It is a description. It is an implicit proposition as to the conditions for maintaining stability in the human group. And it probably applies to hostile as well as to friendly relationships. It is necessary somehow to cut the

---

[17] It's instructive to note that our conception of good—i.e., morally correct—sportsmanship involves some element of this reciprocity. We match fighters and wrestlers by weight, put people into age classes, give one player a handicap in order to balance the relationship. Even in hunting there are mandates of good sportsmanship tending in the direction of reciprocity. One must give the prey a fighting chance.

other fellow down to one's own size, or else to inflate one's self to the adversary's size to carry on the conflict successfully.

Consider, finally, one more feature shared in common by the moral and the social, the spirit imputed to the person as he acts toward another. A social relationship exists, as Max Weber puts it, in ". . . the behavior of a plurality of actors in so far as, *in its meaningful content*, the action of each takes account of the other and is oriented in these terms."[18] Human relationships always involve the meaning or the intent of the actor. So also does moral conduct imply "good" or worthy intent. A few years ago the Undersecretary of Defense resigned when it was disclosed that his wife's company had garnered profits from big government contracts. His resignation was thought necessary because, however much he had kept to the letter of the law, he had neglected the *spirit* of the law, a spirit expected to inform the relationship of public servant to citizen. Human relationships always involve the spirit, the intent, the subjective aspect. We do not respond exclusively to the objective or external conditions of human behavior. We impute motives. All manner of cues are provided to reveal to the other what our intent, what our internal state is.

The fact that our symbols are not always exact makes it all the more necessary to code out of others' behaviors the meaning or intent of those behaviors. (When a person greets us by asking "How are you?" we do not impute to him a remarkable solicitude for our health.) And it is also an aspect of morality that we are concerned with what a person means by what he says and does. If we are constrained to make judgments on the basis of crude externalities of conduct, it is because we have poor cues or poor instruments for getting at motives or intent. Often the severity of punishment hangs upon whether the offending behavior was intentional. Goodness is to some extent a matter of motive rather than of performance. Indeed, to treat a person simply as an object, dealing only with the externalities of behavior is to suggest not only an inhuman or a nonhuman relationship: it may be deemed immoral. We do not treat a person from an impoverished background, ill-educated and guided by values different from our own, as evil if his behavior is not animated by, say, malice or vindictiveness. Or if we are

---

[18] Max Weber, *The Theory of Social and Economic Organization*, trans. A. J. Henderson and Talcott Parsons (New York: Oxford University Press, Inc., 1947), p. 118.

constrained to deal with persons who at first put us off, with time we sometimes find them to be tolerable if not genuinely likable. In such cases we've gotten beneath the surface of conduct and discovered something about the motive or intent of the behavior.

I've been suggesting that religious institutions serve a primary function of buttressing the moral order and that this moral order is fundamental in sustaining a social order. For human relationships are defined by certain dimensions that are intrinsically moral: the mandatory nature of reciprocal expectations, the impersonality or suprapersonality of the rules that govern roles, the acknowledgment that under like situations the rules apply to any and all members of the faith. Thus the moral code represents a sector of the culture generally shared by all members of the group. Each properly socialized member comes to feel a personal responsibility for fulfilling expectations of God and group. Indeed these expectations may be identical. And so there comes to be a sense of ". . . one body, and one Spirit . . . One God and Father of all, who is above all, and through all, and in you all."[19] It was this sense of generally shared, obligatory rules guiding and constraining the conduct of group members that led Durkheim to see God as a social creation incorporating, symbolically, the highest values of the group. Finally in sustaining a moral code—and beyond that, a structure of human relationships—religious doctrine typically stresses the subjective aspect, the meaning or intent of the actor.

ROOTS OF RELIGION IN THE NEED FOR KNOWING THE UNKNOWABLE

The identification of group with God, the universalistic character of religious prescriptions, the crosscutting of religious and other institutions or spheres of life—in these ways religion serves to sustain that network of relationships that constitutes the group. In a more profound sense, the requirements of morality and of a stable set of relationships are the same. Hence the ineluctable need for religious institutions of some sort. These are matters touching

---

[19] This statement is from Paul's Letter to the Ephesians, 4:4 and 6. This is not to overlook the fact that one group's gods may be another group's devils, that within a society there may be two or more social orders, incompatible or antithetical. These statements bear on relationships *within* a group of believers. On this point see Robert K. Merton, *Social Theory and Social Structure* (New York: Free Press of Glencoe, Inc., 1957), pp. 28–30.

mundane conduct, enabling men to realize their expectations of one another. Now there is another aspect of religion to which we should attend. This has to do with knowledge and control of the mysterious unknown.

Herbert Spencer alleged that religion was an outgrowth of fear or anxiety. (Quite to the contrary, Durkheim contended that fears and anxieties are necessary outcomes of religion!) In any case, it seems clear that men invariably confront the inscrutable. As we try to understand our worlds we are soon driven to the point where naturalistic or scientific explanations no longer suffice. A child of six, living close to the edge of mystery (a realm over which his intellectually docile elders have long since drawn the curtain of resigned agnosticism)—a child of six will pose questions that might stump an Einstein. That is to say, given the fact of our immense ignorance we soon come to the point where naturalistic explanations no longer provide answers. Often, then, rejecting agnosticism, we develop supranatural explanations or build up supernatural theory, dogma, and doctrine. In this sense religion provides a cognitive safety net. We find an illustration of this in Malinowski's discussion of science, magic, and religion among the Trobrianders. These people have, Malinowski reports,

> . . . a whole system of principles of sailing, embodied in a complex and rich terminology, traditionally handed on and obeyed as rationally and consistently as is modern science by modern sailors. . . .
> But even with all their systematic knowledge, methodically applied, they are still at the mercy of powerful and incalculable tides, sudden gales during the monsoon season and unknown reefs. And here comes in their magic, performed over the canoe during its construction, carried out at the beginning and in the course of expeditions and resorted to in moments of real danger. . . .
> . . . While in the villages on the inner lagoon fishing is done in an easy and absolutely reliable manner by the method of poisoning, yielding abundant results without danger and uncertainty, there are on the shores of the open sea dangerous modes of fishing and also certain types in which the yield greatly varies according to whether shoals of fish appear beforehand or not. It is most significant that in the lagoon fishing, where man can rely completely upon his knowledge and skill, magic does not exist, while in the open-sea fishing, full of danger and uncertainty, there is extensive magical ritual to secure safety and good results.[20]

[20] Bronislaw Malinowski, *Magic, Science and Religion* (Garden City, N. Y.: Doubleday & Co., Inc.–Anchor Books, 1954), pp. 30, 31. Reprinted by permission of George Braziller, Inc.

A four-celled table suggests the nature of the implied relationship without asserting the direction of causal influence. (With Spencer and Malinowski anxiety gives rise to rites for manipulating or propitiating the gods. But Durkheim and Radcliffe-Brown would reverse the relationship: the psychological state stems from the institutionalized behaviors, from religious rites).

	INNER LAGOON	OPEN SEA
Rites, accommodating to the supernatural (plus technical preparation)		XXX
Chiefly technical-scientific preparation	XXX	

What is implied, here, are two ways of "knowing," two modes of cognition, two metaphysics, two cosmologies, two epistomologies. Although the two modes can be found in any society, often incongruously interlaced, it is useful to separate them to clarify our analysis. The one may be thought of as belief and commitment, myth and dogma bearing on the mysterious and ultimate problems of our worlds, especially touching those crises over which our control is minimal. The other may be viewed as belief and practice, theory and its application, in realms increasingly susceptible to man's control.

Supernatural theory may be seen as a sort of cognitive safety net, helping men deal with problems insoluble in naturalistic terms. In his *Social Anthropology,* Professor Slotkin summarizes central features of supernatural theory embodied in religious institutions.[21] Most religions have, as aspects of supernatural theory, a rich heritage of myth, metaphorically conveyed. Stories of the founding of the faith, its meaning and mission are told, as in the New Testament. There is, furthermore, the formal statement of belief and doctrine typically found in the creed and periodically asserted in religious rites. Creed and myth imply forces, or power controlling events, good and evil. This power, itself immaterial, is called *mana.* It resides in spirits who may be gods, or, sometimes, in the ghosts of once animate beings: persons, plants, or animals. Studies in comparative religion reveal a great range of spirits: creator spirits, dualistic spirits (God and Satan), single Gods, or a Supreme Being presiding over a pantheon of lesser spirits, guardian spirits, nature spirits,

[21] See J. S. Slotkin, *Social Anthropology* (New York: Macmillan Co., 1950), chaps. vi, vii, and viii.

intercessor spirits. There are human incarnations of spirits and spirits residing in plants or in totemic animals.

Through dogma, or bodies of doctrine, groups provide their members means of meeting those recurrent problems for which their science and technology are inadequate. Through common conceptions of right conduct, of modes of propitiation and supplication, they can avert evil, allay anxiety, win through to the good. Since his spirits are projections of himself into the realm of the unknown, man's understanding of, and adjustment to the universe is made easier —or if not easier, at least credible. For he modifies his environment, controls his condition by the same sorts of conduct through which he tries to modify his relationships with other men. In the triad God (G), communicant (c_1) and fellow communicant (c_2), the relationship is

$$c_1 \leftrightarrow G = f(c_1 \leftrightarrow c_2).$$

(That is, the relationship between a communicant and his God is some function of his relationship to fellow communicant.) And conversely, the relationship $c_1 \leftrightarrow c_2 = f (c_1 \leftrightarrow G)$. This implies that the relationships of God to man and of man to man are governed by similar, commensurable imperatives. And this implies, as a further consequence, that religion performs a crucial function as a system of social control. Customary conduct fits into the scheme of the universe. For anthropomorphic projections of divinity must include the valued specifications of conduct. God in turn exemplifies and demands such conduct.

A naturalistic world view, on the other hand, seeks solutions not by invoking the beneficent intervention of a third, omnipotent party, but by attempting to induce environmental changes directly. The induction of change is guided by verifiable observations and procedures. It is based on several assumptions such as: (1) no event is uncaused, (2) given the same outcome on two or more occasions, the same causes are at work, (3) an idea, a proposition, may be regarded as true only when it can be walked down the abstraction ladder, tested, and confirmed empirically.

The naturalistic view, the scientific orientation toward the world, has led to remarkable achievements in the physical, biological, social, and psychological spheres. These achievements have fed on themselves, swelling the yield in technology, reducing our vulnerability in the face of the unknown or, put positively, extending the range of control. But it is not clear that such advances have contributed equally in the moral sphere: in promoting justice, happiness, goodness, or freedom. (Perhaps a case might be made that advances in goodness or increases in freedom depend on discriminating among various options and that knowledge multiplies the options and refines powers of discrimination.) In any event, moral issues persist, as do the ultimate questions of origin, destiny, and the meaning of life. Such questions, scientifically unanswerable, remain in the realm of religion.

SOME ASPECTS OF RELIGIOUS THOUGHT IN THE UNITED STATES

Seeing society as a system of interlocking elements, we would expect scientific triumphs to have an impact on religion. As men have gained more effective control over their environment we might anticipate, as a parallel development, a rejection of a resigned or passive posture toward life. Man becomes God's surrogate as performer of miracles, defeating gravity, erasing the boundary lines between matter and the energy it can be made to release, transforming the invisible into the visible, the inaudible into sounds heard, and, pushing hard on God's domain, transmuting the inanimate into viable matter.

The human condition, too, is seen as improvable, not irrevocably decreed by fate or the accident of birth. Especially in the Protestant countries of Europe and America the view has been, to paraphrase an insightful sixteenth-century "sociologist," that the fault lies not in heaven, but on earth, that we are underlings. Problems, then, become terrestial, not celestial matters. The issue of immortality is displaced by matters of mundane mortality. Nor does the religious theme of the social gospel restrict itself to after-the-fact patchwork represented in the parable of the good Samaritan. Not only does it deplore the indifference of the priest to earthly ills: it seeks to *prevent* wayside muggings. The church in the United States is legatee of a long tradition of increased involvement in man's bodily and psychic welfare. From Tawney House to Hull House, from the maladies of the Industrial Revolution through wars and depressions, the theme of the social gospel has been a prominent one in American religion. Thus its active engagement in other institutional spheres: the economy, politics and legislation, education, family and child care, publishing, radio and television.

If the social gospel can be viewed as a this-worldly antithesis of the other-worldly thesis, there is another theme that is a sort of synthesis. This theme is expressed in the neo-orthodox theology of such people as Reinhold Niebuhr and Paul Tillich and reaches back as far as Kierkegaard. Perhaps because man's mastery of his world seems not to have diminished but only to have changed the shape of pride, brutality, and squalor, the social gospel has come to seem a facile doctrine of overoptimistic perfectionism. A note of pessimism has crept in, not only in religion but also in its secular cousin, philosophy. There is an interesting parallel between religious neo-orthodoxy and the philosophical viewpoint known as existentialism; for both seem to stress the futility of conventional aspirations and achievements (so far as health of soul or moral gains are concerned). They stress the ambivalent nature of our deeds, and words, and worlds, vice and virtue being inextricably interwoven through the whole fabric of life. Man, nonetheless, is not excused from striving. Yet, being man, he must, in striving, sin. Salvation is God's benefaction, not man's achievement.

But this is to refer to the articulate exponents of religious orientations that speak to a new age dominated by the tangible triumphs of a naturalistic world view. The garden variety effects of this world view are seen in the common man's ignorance of, or indifference to theology, in ritualistic performance of his religious duties, in the shift in diagnoses from sin to sickness, in his commitment to science and his confidence in its capacity to solve whatever problems he may confront, in the practical test and justification of religion in the market place ("honesty is good business") and its translation into secular terms. Over the years, secular influences have had a powerful impact on religion.

Of course, the realms of the sacred and secular are not bounded with cartographic clarity. In a social system, the crosscurrents of influence are constantly flowing. And in a complex social order with its individual, group, and regional variations, and with great resources for generating change, we would expect a complex interplay of elements often incompatible. Old values and new collide. Rural and urban standards encounter one another, representing different, sometimes antithetical ways of acting and believing. The separation of home place from work place, a separation increasingly effected in the last 200 years, is paralleled by the rift between standards governing conduct in these two spheres. (But such standards meet in the commuter's person!) From various perspectives we can infer a tension between the spheres of sacred and secular life. The question is: Which sphere tends to dominate, which to accommodate?

Liston Pope studied the interplay between these spheres in his *Millhands and Preachers,*[22] the reciprocal influence of church and cotton mills in Gaston County, North Carolina. Over the years the church was sometimes source of change in local work arrangements, sometimes reflected changes in the mills. The church from time to time supported, or opposed the prevailing economic arrangements. On other occasions it was indifferent to workaday matters, or viewed them as irrelevant. Thus Pope suggests six modes of interplay between church and workplace, six postures as sacred confronts secular: opposition, support, initiating change, being changed, indifference to the other realm, or viewing it as irrelevant.

On the whole, Pope's study shows that more influence has flowed from workplace to church than in the other direction. Over the years religious doctrine and practice increasingly accommodated itself to the secular sphere. This tends to confirm a central thesis of Ernest Troeltsch's classic work on *The Social Teachings of the Christian Churches:*[23] a tendency in the Christian world for sects or evangelical bodies to change through time, accommodating themselves, as churches, to the secular establishment. "A sect is a religious group that rejects the social environment in which it exists,"[24] following Paul's injunction to the Corinthians: "Be ye not unequally yoked together with unbelievers: for what fellowship hath righteousness with unrighteousness? And what communion hath light with dark-

---

[22] New Haven: Yale University Press, 1942.

[23] Translated by O. Wyon (New York: Macmillan Co., 1931). Reinhold Niebuhr puts it this way in his *Does Civilization Need Religion?:*
"Since liberal Christianity is the product of an adjustment of the main tenets of orthodox Protestantism to the sophistication of the cities and the growing intelligence of the privileged and therefore educated classes, its whole moral atmosphere is much more determined by the special interests of these classes than it is willing to admit. . . . Religion can be healthy and vital only if a certain tension is maintained between it and the civilization in which it functions. *In time this tension is inevitably resolved into some kind of compromise.*" (New York: Macmillan Co., 1927), pp. 68, 69. Italics mine.

[24] Benton Johnson, "On Church and Sect," *American Sociological Review,* Vol. XXVIII, No. 4 (August, 1963), p. 542.

ness? . . .Wherefore come out from among them, and be ye separate, saith the Lord."[25] A church, on the other hand, "is a religious group that accepts the social environment in which it exists."[26] Thus the sect tends to be a small community apart, a voluntary fellowship of those who, feeling the impact of God's personal intervention in their lives, are converted and saved. The church is the sect grown large, interlocked with worldly affairs, its membership conferred at birth or ritually at—and the word is instructive—confirmation. Members of the sect are more likely to be among the poor and dispossessed, church members better established, having some standing in the political and economic structure of their communities. Teachings of the sect spring from a quite literal reading of holy writ while the church's teachings are based on a metaphorical interpretation of scripture. Differences in the treatment of holy writ are related to differences in leadership, in training, and means of certification. Fundamentalism and literalism are appropriately linked with a sense of the equality of all believers and a call to ministry by revelation, the descent of the Spirit. The church requires a trained ministry and fixes means of certification to assure leaders theologically more sophisticated than their laymen. Traditionalism, fundamentalism, ruralism are adjectives that might be applied, with rough accuracy, to sects. Modern, adaptive, urbane, more nearly describe the established church. (But this is not to imply that country and city are so neatly discriminable on religious grounds. The established church, smoothly meshing with the secular order, may be found in some rural areas. And the city embraces pockets of religious fundamentalism. But it is true that these tend to be imports from the rural hinterlands.) Finally, while the sect tends to be comparatively indifferent to worldly matters, emphasizing salvation of the soul and life after death—that is, eschatological concerns—the church is more likely to stress the Kingdom of God on earth. Thus Elinson, analyzing a Pentecostal evangelist's teachings, finds that they minimize the things of this world, minimize the relevance of science, minimize political engagement, and, in stressing personal election and salvation ("achievement," rather than ascription), oppose racism.[27]

---

[25] II Corinthians, 6:14, 17.

[26] Johnson, *op. cit.*, p. 542.

[27] Howard Elinson, "The Implications of Pentecostal Religion for Intellectualism, Politics, and Race Relations," *American Journal of Sociology*, Vol. LXX, No. 4 (January, 1965), pp. 403–15.

Let me offer a vivid, if extreme example of the translation of the sacred into secular terms. The following passages were written by Bruce Barton, formerly of the advertising firm of Batten, Barton, Durstin and Osborne, in his book about Jesus, *The Man Nobody Knows.*

> A physical weakling! Where did they get that idea? Jesus pushed a plane and swung an adze. . . .
> A kill-joy! He was the most popular dinner guest in Jerusalem!
> A failure! He picked up twelve men from the bottom ranks of business and forged them into an organization that conquered the world. . . . Nowhere is there such a startling example of executive success as the way in which that organization [the twelve disciples] was brought together.
> It has been remarked that "no astronomer can be an atheist," which is only another way of saying that no man can look up at the first, and greatest electric sign—the evening stars—and refuse to believe its message: "There is a Cause: a God."
> Take any one of the parables, no matter which—you will find that it exemplifies all the principles on which advertising textbooks are written. Always a picture in the very first sentence; crisp, graphic language and a message so clear that even the dullest can not escape it. . . . "Ten Virgins Went Forth to Meet a Bridegroom." A striking picture and a striking headline.[28]

RATIONALITY, THE PROTESTANT ETHIC AND THE SPIRIT OF CAPITALISM

Science and the secular orientation point to an increasingly rational orientation to life. For Max Weber, this word, rationalism, expressed the emerging *Weltanschauung* that was transforming the modern, Western world. Belief and behavior grounded in the sacred and traditional were progressively eroded as men were increasingly disposed and able both to pose and answer the question: what are the demonstrably most efficient means to achieve unambiguously stated ends? This *Rationalität*

> . . . driven by its own internal dynamic, has overthrown (or tamed) every form of resistance offered by pre-rational human nature, magic and tradition, instinct and spontaneity. Finally, with the Reformation, it has forced its way into the innermost temple wherein the motives behind human behaviour are generated, into the very heart of religious

---

[28] From *The Man Nobody Knows* by Bruce Barton, copyright 1925 by The Bobbs-Merrill Company, Inc., R. 1952 by Bruce Barton, reprinted by permission of the publishers.

belief, there to destroy all the dark, magical, mysterious tabernacles —image, cult and tradition—for which it substitutes the Bible as the authentic truth, supposedly unshakeable, accessible to critical examination, and susceptible of proof.[29]

This apparent opposition between sacred and secular, traditional and rational, leads us to one of the important inquiries in the sociology of religion, Max Weber's *The Protestant Ethic and the Spirit of Capitalism*. His study of the connection between two core institutions focuses on capitalism not merely as a particular mode of organization in the production and allocation of goods. Weber sees capitalism, "the most fateful force in our modern life," as the apotheosis of rationality. Rationality penetrates the rest of life, too: not only the market place, or science and technology, but political life, the arts, education, even the family and the church. Indeed if we ask: what are the prerequisites for the emergence of modern capitalism? Weber points out a necessary change in the home: the separation of business from the household, of the family budget from the financing of the enterprise. This is, in effect, a separation of the domain of the heart from that of the head, a distinction between the realm of warm sentimentality and that of coolly calculated cognitions.

Other prerequisites are noted by Weber. One such is the rational organization and use of labor drawn from a freely moving labor force. Labor becomes, then, a market commodity dealt with quite independent of ascribed traits. Furthermore, there must be some means, as in bookkeeping, for rational calculation of the outcomes of social action, measures that enable the continual improvement of means to maximize output. But above all Weber contended (virtually inverting the Marxist thesis) there must be some spirit or ethos that justifies and requires the institutionalized behaviors central in the social order.

> He was right against almost all his contemporaries, liberals and Marxists alike, who accepted the availability of capital and of labour force as adequate preconditions for economic progress. . . .[30]

Underlying these obviously necessary factors in production there is the commitment to ways of thinking, acting, and believing that make possible an enduring system of relationships. And if capital-

---

[29] Herbert Luethy, "Once Again: Calvinism and Capitalism," *Encounter*, Vol. XXII, No. 1 (January, 1964), p. 27.

[30] *Ibid.*, p. 27.

ism, as just such a system, is to endure, some such commitment, or spirit must inform these relationships. "The question of the motive forces in the expansion of modern capitalism," Weber writes," is not in the first instance a question of the origin of the capital sums which were available for capitalist uses, but, above all of the development of the *spirit of capitalism*."[31] What are the elements of this spirit?[32]

Central to the spirit of capitalism is an attitude toward work expressed in the word *vocation*, a calling. Work is not a necessary evil, not something merely to be tolerated, but a good in itself, an ethical imperative. We get the flavor of this orientation toward work in a Christian hymn whose injunction is "Work, For the Night is Coming." One of its stanzas goes:

> Work, for the night is coming. Work through the sunny noon.
> Fill brightest hours with labor. Rest comes sure and soon.
> Give every flying minute, something to keep in store.
> Work for the night is coming, when man works no more.

Work represents a necessary investment of God-given talents. Success provides at least a faint intimation of Providential approval.

A related element is the emphasis on production, rather than consumption. The investment of self in work is for the greater glory of God, not for self-gratification. Acquisition is not regarded as evil —quite the contrary—provided it leads to a reinvestment for more effective exploitation of resources and an increase in productivity. It is the man who fails to multiply the talents his lord has given him who is called wicked and slothful. This stress on productivity has as its corollary a degree of self-denial, of moderation in personal life, of rigorous self-discipline. And so it is that legend links names like that of Rockefeller, Sr., with the frugality, even abstemiousness, that is reflected in the homilies of Benjamin Franklin.

If work is a duty and a discipline, if the emphasis is on multiplying the yield, there follows another element of the spirit of capitalism, the celebration of shrewdness, ingenuity, inventiveness in devising more efficient means. This is one aspect of the rationalism that was, for Weber, the distinctive motif of modern society. Opposed to a traditionalism that revered established means, as well as ends, rationalism favored a separation of home place from workplace, the realm of sentiment from that of coolly calculated

---

[31] Max Weber, *The Protestant Ethic and the Spirit of Capitalism*, trans. Talcott Parsons (New York: Charles Scribner's Sons, 1952), p. 68.

[32] See "An Aside on Methods: Causal Explanations in Sociology," p. 486.

An Aside on Methods: Causal Explanations in Sociology

We should note here, that causal explanations in sociology require, Weber insists, both the observation of statistical regularities *and* a meaningful interpretation of such regularities. (Recall our definition of the field of sociology in Chapter 1.) Or, as the late Samuel Stouffer used to put it: to stop with a correlation coefficient— i.e., with a demonstration of statistical regularities—is an acknowledgment of defeat. In Weber's words:

"If adequacy in respect to meaning is lacking, then no matter how high the degree of uniformity and how precisely its probability can be numerically determined, it is still an incomprehensible statistical probability, whether dealing with overt or subjective processes. On the other hand, even the most perfect adequacy on the level of meaning has causal significance from a sociological point of view only in so far as there is some kind of proof for the existence of a probability that action in fact normally takes the course which has been held to be meaningful." (Max Weber, *The Theory of Social and Economic Organization,* trans., A. M. Henderson and Talcott Parsons [New York: Oxford University Press, Inc., 1947], pp. 99, 100.)

To get at the meaningful in human conduct, that which, at the level of motive and value is at the core of recurrent patterns of conduct, Weber devises what he calls the "ideal type." The ideal type is a kind of model, expressing in a pure—and therefore unreal—form, the core characteristics of a pattern of conduct. Herbert Luethy puts it very well when he speaks of Weber's

great and questioning mind [which was] never particularly interested in the facts of history, nor even in social and economic systems, but rather in the detection of the ultimate impulses behind man's attitudes and behaviour. What he analyzed were not the hybrid and wretched forms of an historically realised society (in which such ultimate impulses are never embodied in their purity), but rather the abstract and chemically pure "ideal types" which should provide the essences of a civilisation stripped of all the adulterations and accidents of actual history." (Luethy, *op. cit.,* p. 27.)

But so "stripped of all the adulterations" of actual social life, what use can the ideal type be? It is, first of all, an attempt to state certain psychic regularities that sustain an enduring system of relationships. Second, it points out a line of inquiry and offers a target for testing. The ideal type, says Robert Redfield referring to his own attempt to set up a conceptual model of the small, primitive society, "is there to point the way to the study of that which its use brings to notice." (Robert Redfield, *Peasant Society and Culture* [Chicago: University of Chicago Press, 1956], p. 13.) Third, it provides base points from which observed behavior deviates, raising the question as to why and under what conditions such deviations obtain. And if we can measure the "distance" between the ideal type and two patterns of observed conduct then we can solve for the "distance" or difference between the observed patterns, noting how they differ with respect to elements of the ideal type.

profit and loss. It encouraged a reorganization of men's relationships at work, and of work processes. It demanded meticulous accounting procedures. In the service of production and profit it would define roles with precision, treating incumbents impersonally.

If such views and values are core aspects of the spirit of capitalism, where do they come from? Surely, Weber argues, it is not wages alone, the material rewards or penalties of the system that prompts the capitalist worker to perform his work as though it were an absolute end in itself. This seems especially clear when we observe that profits are not used primarily to yield personal, material pleasures. Furthermore, such a way of acting and thinking must have institutional support. These are shared ways of believing and behaving, and they "had to originate somewhere, and not in isolated individuals alone, but as a way of life common to whole groups of men."[33] This way of life and the dictates supporting it Weber finds in certain of the Protestant sects.

The Protestant's propensity for trade and commerce had often been observed. "Even the Spaniards knew that heresy [i.e., the Calvinism of the Dutch] promoted trade."[34] And Weber cites Montesquieu's statement about the English (written 150 years before), that they "had progressed the farthest of all peoples of the world in three important things: in piety, in commerce, and in freedom."[35] He also cites one of his students, Martin Offenbacher, who studied the link between social class and religious affiliation in the Grand Duchy of Baden (about 60 percent Catholic at the time). Offenbacher said: "The Protestant prefers to eat well, the Catholic to sleep undisturbed."[36] The statement reflects Offenbacher's find-

---

[33] Weber, *The Protestant Ethic and the Spirit of Capitalism, op. cit.,* p. 55.

[34] *Ibid.,* p. 43.

[35] Cited from Montesquieu, *Esprit des Lois,* Book XX, chap. vii in Weber, *The Protestant Ethic and the Spirit of Capitalism,* p. 45.

[36] *Ibid.,* p. 41, and taken from Martin Offenbacher, *Konfession und soziale Schichtung: eine Studie über die wirtschaftliche Lage der Katholiken und Protestanten in Baden* (Tübingen and Leipzig, 1901), p. 58. The title of Offenbacher's work may be translated: *Religious Affiliation and Social Stratification: A Study of the Economic Role of Catholics and Protestants in Baden.*

Weber's thesis, briefly reported here, has stimulated a running controversy over the years. While I note in passing some exceptions that have been taken to his argument, it is left largely uncontested in order to lay it, in uncluttered fashion, next to some empirical tests of it made by Professor Lenski. But the student should know that a number of scholars express serious reservations. Kurt Samuelsson, for example, finds no support for the Weberian thesis and raises serious question about Offenbacher's data and Weber's use of them. He throws serious doubt on the alleged greater propensity of Protestants for schooling. (Protestants in Baden apparently

ings: marked secular ambition among the Protestants in contrast to the Catholics, and outstanding achievements not only in the realm of business, but also in the civil service, in academic life, in science and the professions. Thus we have a suggested link between two sets of values and two modes of conduct, the implication of a peculiar compatibility such that the one depends on the other. There is "the ethic of a religious belief and the spirit of an economic system, the cure of souls and the balancing of accounts."[37] And the former is seen as a necessary, though not sufficient cause of the latter, emphatically qualifying a Marxist position that would make the mode of economic production the fundament of the social order with religion, "the opiate of the people," altogether epiphenomenal. But what, precisely, was this ethic, this creedal catalyst that enabled a radical reordering of the relationships of men at work?

The appropriate ethic, the best "fit," the *Weltanschauung* that is a necessary precondition for the development of modern capitalism is discovered in the ascetic branches of Protestantism. Among these it is best exemplified in Calvinism, Weber contends. For in Calvinism we find a statement of spiritual imperatives that might well serve as a handbook for the "Compleat Capitalist." Here is the spirit of vocation,[38] of stewardship, of work as a good in itself, the approval of acquisition—but not for self-indulgence, the elaboration of more effective means of production.

> This rationalization of conduct within this world, but for the sake of the world beyond, was the consequence of the concept of calling of ascetic Protestantism.
> . . . Christian asceticism, at first fleeing from the world into solitude, had already ruled the world which it had renounced from the monastery and through the church. . . . Now it strode into the market-place of life, slammed the door of the monastery behind it, and undertook to penetrate just that daily routine of life with its

---

lived to a greater extent than Catholics in districts where advanced schools were available.) Samuelsson also finds Offenbacher's data on differentials in wealth both unreliable and misinterpreted. See Kurt Samuelsson, *Religion and Economic Action*, trans. E. Geoffrey French (Stockholm: Scandinavian University Books, 1961).

[37] Luethy adds a useful note. "The establishment of relationships between remote concepts is among the favourite games of the human mind, and perhaps one of its most fruitful, for it reveals surprising links and opens new perspectives—but also one of the most dangerous and seductively misleading ones." (Luethy, *op. cit.*, p. 26.)

[38] It is helpful to remember the etymology of this word. Those who studied Latin will remember *vocare* (*vocavi, vocatus*) meaning "to call," or "to summon," and *vocatio* (*vocationis*) meaning "a bidding," "a summoning," or "an inviting."

methodicalness, to fashion it into a life *in* the world, but neither *of* nor *for* this world.[39]

Above all there was in the doctrine of Calvinism the belief in predestination, the notion that an omniscient and omnipotent God had marked a man from birth for salvation or damnation. Such a terrifying belief, one might suppose, would lead to resignation, apathy—to anything but the commitment to an unremitting labor whose material fruits were not to be translated into personal pleasures. But the case was quite otherwise, Weber argues, and this for two reasons. There was, first, the awful anxiety about one's destiny compelling him, despite the fact that man's miserable achievements could not move the majesty of God's judgment, to seek through achievement whatever slight assurance he might get of Providential blessing. And second, there was the doctrinal injunction to have faith in God's beneficence. Indeed it was

held to be an absolute duty to consider oneself chosen, and to combat all doubts as temptations of the devil, since lack of self-confidence is the result of insufficient faith, hence of imperfect grace. . . .

. . . in order to attain that self-confidence, intense worldly activity is recommended as the most suitable means. It and it alone disperses religious doubts and gives the certainty of grace.[40]

Thus with the Protestant reformation and especially in Calvinism we see spiritual elements promoting capitalism. (Lutheranism, to say nothing of Catholicism, were still tradition-bound, emphasizing salvation through faith rather than good works, adequate performance in one's proper place rather than an improvement of position, celestial rewards rather than terrestial demonstration of God's approval.) Such elements include, as we have seen: dedication to incessant labor as a good in itself, asceticism, a faith that one is among the chosen and that labor's fruits give evidence of it, the individualism of a personal fate Providentially assigned and to be confirmed through personal effort, the endlessness of acquisition and the constant effort to improve the means to increased productivity.

We can summarize Weber's argument, schematically, in the simple model of research design, as in Figure 11–1

---

[39] Weber, *The Protestant Ethic and the Spirit of Capitalism, op. cit.,* p. 154.

[40] *Ibid.,* pp. 111–12.

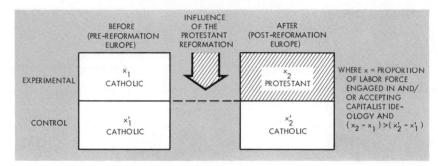

FIG. 11-1

Weber is asking the question often posed by historians—and indeed by ourselves in everyday life: what would have happened if . . . ? if things had been other than they were, if my decision had been different, if I had acted otherwise? The answer to this question requires us to set up something comparable to a control situation, precisely to tell us what would have happened in the absence of an alleged causal influence.

The control situation, for Weber, consists in Catholic Europe whose population remained uncommitted to the new doctrine, the supposed cause, necessary but not sufficient for the emergence of modern capitalism. In the context of his more general inquiries in the sociology of religion the control situation may be thought of as those patterns of economic organization and conduct seen in the orient, especially in China. For here if anywhere, Weber argues, we might reasonably expect to see the structure of relationships we call capitalism emerge. For the Chinese were not hedged about with religious prohibitions, the taking of interest was legitimate, and a hardheaded domestic economy was certainly aimed at maximizing the produce of soil and sea. Nor was there any nonsense about self-denial: the Chinese would have understood Irwin Edman when he spoke of the "genial life of the senses." Yet despite such predisposing characteristics, capitalism did not flower in China. Why? Because of the absence of a Protestant ethic. Thus through retrospective historical analysis we answer the question: what would have happened if . . . ? In effect, we contrive an *ex post facto* or retrospective study design.

But perhaps this is a little too easy—or so some scholars have alleged in a running controversy through the years. Richard Tawney in his *Religion and the Rise of Capitalism* suggests that we had better not lean too hard on the Protestant-ethic interpretation until we've taken account of such significant and plausibly capitalism-promoting factors as the voyages of discovery in the sixteenth and seventeenth centuries, the expansion of commerce, the tradition-challenging contact of countries and cultures. Furthermore, the difference between Protestantism and Catholicism may stem not so much from the compatibility of the former as from the incompatibility of the latter with the capitalist posture.

Perhaps, as Luethy suggests, it was not so much the Reformation as the counter-Reformation, an "appalling break . . . in the cultural history of Europe . . . the shadow cast by Inquisition and heresy trials across the lands . . ."[41] that accounts for the decline in power, wealth, intellectual and artistic life among Catholics, and the concomitant significance of non-Catholics.

Again, some evidence suggests that the contrast between areas commercially, industrially and financially active and those not so, corresponding to Protestant and Catholic dominance, respectively, were that way *before* the Reformation. And this in turn suggests another interpretation: one that the sociologist must always have in mind when he observes a connection between two variables. The necessary question is this: does some third factor underly or explain both of these? Conceivably the Protestant ethic itself, along with the spirit of capitalism is to be explained by some underlying characteristic.

It is instructive to remember that Luther sought to reform the church from within, not to establish a rival organization. His failure to do so thrust the protesters into a minority position, a defensive posture. And certainly many minority groups have demonstrated the hard-driving, intellectually oriented, success-achieving traits that Weber links with Protestantism: the west European Jew, the Parsees in India, the Chinese in southeast Asia (suggestively called the "Jews of the Orient"). It is at least conceivable that the identity given by discrimination and persecution may reinforce common religious commitments and stimulate the sorts of achievements registered in the successes of capitalism.

So we will take Weber's interpretation with some reservations. But we must not do him the injustice of naïvely misconstruing his argument. He was exploring what he regarded as *a necessary*, not *the sufficient* cause for the emergence of capitalism. He was

---

[41] Luethy, *op. cit.*, p. 31.

sensitive to the requirements of research strategy. Beyond the study of economic behavior before and after the advent of Protestantism he tried, through reference to Catholic Europe and non-Christian Asia, to answer the question: What would have happened in the absence of the Protestant ethic? In developing the notion of the ideal type he offers a tool to help us deepen our understanding of social phenomena. Perhaps above all we should heed the implicit allegation of this study: no significant social structure persists without supporting doctrine and creed. And this applies to the instrumentally oriented institutions of polity and economy, as well as to the expressively oriented institutions of kin groups and religious groups.

AN EMPIRICAL TEST OF WEBER'S THESIS

There is another way of checking Weber's ideas. Beyond asking what variables he has left uncontrolled, or what other factors might readily be thought to have contributed to the development of modern capitalism—beyond these questions we can ask: Does the Weberian thesis help us to predict to concrete situations? Take, for example, a major American city. Do Protestants, as Weber's thesis would predict, advance farther in the world of work than Catholics? Do they seek more actively than Catholics for work that offers advancement? Do they, to a greater degree than Catholics, value work for its own sake? Do they reject, more than Catholics, the collective, security-providing rewards of unionism? Are Protestants self-employed (suggesting the entrepreneurial, capitalistic spirit) to a greater degree than Catholics? Are they persuaded, more so than Catholics, that ability (rather than family connections) yields rewards, and that workingmen's sons do in fact have a good chance to advance in our system? Do Protestants, more than Catholics, think that God favors attempts to get ahead? Does installment buying—not paying, immediately, for what one gets—run more against the grain for Protestant than Catholic? Does greater devoutness characterizing family background mean, for Protestants, an orientation more rational, competitive, individualistic, and striving and for Catholics, less of such an orientation? An empirical study by Professor Gerhard Lenski offers answers to such questions as these, enabling us to check some of Weber's ideas.

But first, some preliminary intelligence about Lenski's study of religious behavior in Detroit. This inquiry, based upon a probability sample[42] of 750 families or dwelling units, succeeded in completing interviews with 87 percent of the sample. Among the 8 percent refusing to grant interviews a disproportionate number were over age 60 so that Lenski cautions us that "conclusions based on the responses of older people are slightly less reliable than those based on younger and middle-aged persons."[43] By religious affiliation or identification, the Detroit population breaks down as follows:[44]

	PERCENT
White Protestants	41
White Catholics	35
Negro Protestants	15
Jews	4

Comparable data for the United States (adults, age 14 and over) estimate Protestants (both Negro and white), Catholics and Jews as 66, 26 and 3 percent of the population, respectively.

Lenski's four independent variables include two measures of involvement in socioreligious groups and two measures of religious orientation. Here are his measures of communal and associational involvement.

MEASURES OF INVOLVEMENT	COMMUNAL (1)	ASSOCIATIONAL (2)
Active	Spouse of same socio-religious group with friends & relatives all or nearly all of whom are of the same group	Per month, attends service 2 or more times and, at least once, some church-related group
Marginal	All others	All others

---

[42] Let me remind students new to sociology that it is *only* with some variety of probability sampling that the investigator can calculate, adequately, an estimate of sampling error. To put it differently, it is only on the basis of probability theory that one can know the likelihood that his sample represents the whole, the population or universe of elements sampled. A fundamental difference between science and nonscience lies in this: in a scientific undertaking strenuous efforts are made not merely to eliminate sources of error but *to estimate the extent of the error* that invariably creeps in from various sources.

[43] From *The Religious Factor* by Gerhard Lenski. Copyright © 1961, 1963 by Doubleday & Company, Inc. Reprinted by permission of the publisher. The statement cited is from the revised edition, 1963, p. 17.

[44] *Ibid.*, p. 21.

TABLE 11–6

Strength of Religious Bonds, Associational and Communal, among Jews,
White Catholics and Protestants, Detroit, c. 1960

SOCIORELIGIOUS GROUPS	ASSOCIATIONAL INVOLVEMENT (%)				COMMUNAL INVOLVEMENT (%)		
	ATTEND WEEKLY	MINIMUM 1 PER MONTH	FEW TIMES PER YEAR	NOT AT ALL	REARED IN FAITH AND MARRIED SAME	CLOSE RELATIVES SAME FAITH	CLOSE FRIENDS SAME FAITH
Jews	12	20	56	12	100	96	77
Catholics (white)	70			5	70*	79	44
Protestants (white)	33	20	33	14	73	76	38

* Inferred from Lenski's data (op. cit., 1963 ed., p. 38). Data on associational involvement are based on H. L. Or-bach's findings on reported church attendance of nearly 7,000 Detroiters drawn from six sample surveys of the Detroit Area Study. In reporting these data, Lenski refers to Harold L. Orbach's study, "Aging and Religion," *Geriatrics* Vol. XVI (October, 1961), pp. 530–40. Apparently 25 percent of the white Catholics attended about once a month or, a few times per year.

Table 11–6 gives some notion of the differences among major religious groups in strength of associational and communal ties. (Negro Protestants are omitted from this summary since the communalism of race confounds the communalism of religion.)

Lenski's other two independent variables, measures of religious orientation, may be described as follows:

DOCTRINAL ORTHODOXY (CHRISTIANS) (3)	DEVOTIONALISM (4)
An orientation stressing acceptance of the following:	An orientation stressing personal and private communion with God:
Orthodox, when believing in a God who watches over one as a heavenly Father, who answers prayers and who expects weekly worship, in Jesus as God's only son and in punishments and rewards in a life after death	Scored as *high* in devotionalism when praying once or more daily and sometimes, or often, seeking God's guidance as to what to do
Unorthodox when unbelieving, disagreeing, or uncertain on any of the foregoing items	Otherwise, scored *low* in devotionalism

Lenski found that there was very little association between these two orientations. (He used the Kendall rank correlation coefficient to determine degree of association, τ, yielding a value of .05.) We may conclude, therefore, that doctrinal orthodoxy and devotionalism are two fairly independent dimensions of religious belief and behavior. The rank orders of the three largest socioreligious groups on these two dimensions Lenski found to be as follows:

PERCENT ORTHODOX, BY SOCIO-RELIGIOUS GROUP		PERCENT SCORING HIGH IN DEVOTIONALISM BY SOCIO-RELIGIOUS GROUP	
Catholics	62	Negro Protestants	68
Negro Protestants	38	Catholics	47
White Protestants	32	White Protestants	29

The dependent variables whose relation to these four independent variables was to be tested included measures of various aspects of family life, political and economic behavior. The focus, then, is upon interinstitutional connections: religion on the one hand, the family, polity, and economy on the other. If a social order must be understood as a system, then characteristic conduct in one sector must affect and be affected by conduct in another sector. Culturally prescribed roles (expectation sets), in their articulation, form relationships. Enduring patterns of relationship that sustain the group are institutionalized. These institutions are major elements in the structure of society. And the linkages between institutional elements of the system are prime matters of inquiry for the sociologist. Lenski himself puts it well when he says that "it is this *systemic* view of society which distinguishes the sociological view of political and economic behavior from that of the more narrowly circumscribed disciplines of political science and economics."[45]

Weber's thesis, of course, has to do with the connection between behaviors institutionalized, respectively, through church and market place. Let us turn now to some of Lenski's findings, for the Detroit population, that bear on this alleged connection. Certain very general findings about the relation between income and occupation on the one hand (summarized as class) and religious affiliation on the other are given in Table 11–7.

The data show clearly the economically preferred position of Jews in Detroit. But the figures of special interest to us are the 19 and 12 percent of upper-middle-class white Protestants and Catholics, respectively. For a sample size of better than 200 in each case, a

[45] Lenski, *op. cit.*, 1961 ed., p. 24.

TABLE 11–7

Percentage of Respondents in Various Classes, by Socioreligious Groups,
Detroit, 1958

SOCIORELIGIOUS GROUP	UPPER-MIDDLE*	LOWER-MIDDLE*	UPPER-WORKING†	LOWER-WORKING†	TOTAL	N‡
Jews	43	30	9	17	99	23
White Protestants	19	25	31	25	100	259
White Catholics	12	27	35	25	99	220
Negro Protestants	2	10	19	69	100	94

* Upper-middle-class respondents are those in families in which the family head was a businessman, a professional man, a clerk, or a salesman, and himself had an income of $8,000 or more in 1957. Those in families whose head was in a similar occupation, but earned less than $8,000, were classified as lower-middle class.

† Upper-working-class respondents are those in families in which the head was a manual worker or service worker who himself earned at least $5,000 in 1957. Those in families whose head was in a similar occupation, but earned less than $5,000, were classified as lower-working class.

‡ The income of the family head was not reported in 28 cases, and hence the Ns shown here are slightly lower than the total Ns for each of these groups.

Source: Gerhard Lenski, *The Religious Factor* (Garden City, N.Y.: Doubleday & Co., Inc., 1961), p. 80.

difference as great as 7 percentage points, and in the predicted direction (Protestants economically better off than Catholics) would be due to sampling error fewer than one in ten times.

This begins to answer our first question: whether Protestants advance farther in the world of work than do Catholics. All of Lenski's data lead him to conclude that "White Protestant men rise further in the class system than Catholics." He reports that "Catho-

TABLE 11–8

Occupational Level of White Males by Father's Occupational Level and
by Religion, in Percentages (Detroit Area Study Surveys:
1952–58, N = 1177)

RESPONDENT'S OCCUPATIONAL LEVEL	FATHER'S OCCUPATIONAL LEVEL							
	UPPER MIDDLE CLASS		LOWER MIDDLE CLASS		UPPER WORKING CLASS		LOWER WORKING CLASS	
	C	P	C	P	C	P	C	P
Upper middle class	32	49	28	38	28	27	16	26
Lower middle class	22	20	22	30	10	13	11	7
Upper working class	20	17	22	25	31	40	39	36
Lower working class	26	14	28	7	31	20	34	31
TOTAL	100	100	100	100	100	100	100	100
N =	99	157	36	40	202	205	276	162

Source: These data are from Table 10 in Neil J. Weller, "Religion and Social Mobility in Industrial Society" (unpublished doctoral dissetation, University of Michigan). Cited in Gerhard Lenski, *The Religious Factor* (rev. ed.; Doubleday & Co., Inc.–Anchor Books, 1963), p. 87.

lics wound up in the lower half of the working class more often than Protestants three out of four times."[46] He also cites material from a doctoral dissertation by Neil J. Weller summarizing data on inter-generational mobility (father's to son's occupational level) for Catholics and Protestants. Here again the greater upward mobility of Protestants is marked.

To help in reading Table 11–8, I have underlined the data on the diagonal representing the nonmobile categories. Data on the upper right of the diagonal represent the upwardly mobile, to the lower left, the downwardly mobile. We can see these differences between Protestant and Catholic mobility, upward and downward, in this summary:

NUMBER OF STEPS	PERCENT BY WHICH PROTESTANT UPWARD MOBILITY EXCEEDS CATHOLIC, BY NUMBER OF UPWARD "STEPS"		PERCENT BY WHICH CATHOLIC EXCEEDS PROTESTANT DOWNWARD MOBILITY BY NUMBER OF DOWNWARD "STEPS"	
1	Lower middle to upper middle	+10	Upper middle to lower middle	+2
	Upper working to lower middle	+3	Lower middle to upper working	−3
	Lower working to upper working	−3	Upper working to lower working	+11
2	Upper working to upper middle	−1	Upper middle to upper working	+3
	Lower working to lower middle	−4	Lower middle to lower working	+21
3	Lower working to upper middle	+10	Upper middle to lower working	+12

The relatively greater upward mobility of Protestants reflects underlying attitudes that differentiate Protestant from Catholic. For example, respondents were presented with five criteria for estimating the desirability of a job. These were: (1) high income, (2) no danger of being fired, (3) short working hours, (4) chances of advancement, and (5) the seeming importance of the work and the feeling of accomplishment it yields. Although differences were slight, the fourth criterion was picked most frequently by Jews, next by white Protestants, followed by Catholics and, last, Negro Protes-

---

[46] *Ibid.*, p. 77.

tants. Similarly in their attitudes toward work, white Protestants register an orientation more in accord with Weber's Protestant ethic than do Catholics.

Again, we can check on Protestant-Catholic differences in attitude toward work by asking about beliefs and behaviors bearing on labor unions. For the union posture opposes values embodied in the Protestant ethic. The unions stress security and aspire to prosperity

TABLE 11-9

Percentage of Male Detroiters Holding Positive, Neutral and Negative Attitudes toward Work, by Socioreligious Group

SOCIORELIGIOUS GROUP	ATTITUDE TOWARD WORK*					POSITIVE MINUS NEGATIVE
	POSITIVE	NEUTRAL	NEGATIVE	TOTAL	N	
Jews	42	50	8	100	12	34
White Protestants	30	50	21	101	111	9
Negro Protestants	24	54	22	100	41	2
White Catholics	23	57	21	101	106	2

* "Positive" means valuing work for its own sake or for the intrinsic rewards it provides. "Neutral" refers to a response that favors work, but for its extrinsic rewards, or because it's more acceptable than the alternative (not to work would be boring). "Negative" classifies a response indicating the person would be glad to give up work if he could. Percentages do not add to 100 due to rounding.
Source: Gerhard Lenski, *The Religious Factor*, 1961 ed., p. 85.

for the masses rather than exceptional rewards stemming from personal prowess and conscientious commitment to work as a good in itself. Lenski reports that slightly over a quarter of the male workers in the lower-middle class in Detroit are union members. White Catholics in the lower-middle class are far more likely to become union members (38 percent) than are white Protestants (15 percent).[47] Data on attendance at meetings and level of interest in their unions add confirmation.

Significant differences in subjective states are suggested in Lenski's data showing that Protestants are more likely to believe that those of humble origins have a chance to rise through their own efforts, and that ability is more important than family connections in getting ahead. Among middle-class respondents, 73 percent of the white Protestants and 61 percent of the white Catholics thought workingmen's sons had a good chance to advance. The comparable figures for working-class respondents were 62 percent and 51 percent. On the other question, whether ability was more important than family connections in achieving success, among middle-class

[47] *Ibid.*, p. 88.

respondents, 89 percent of the white Protestants and 71 percent of the white Catholics took this position. For the working-class respondents the figures are 82 and 70 percent for Protestants and Catholics, respectively.[48]

Now it might be argued that these are not, in fact, faith-linked differences in commitment to the get-ahead, Horatio Alger doc-

	ATTENDING ALL OR MOST OF THEIR UNION MEETINGS		EXPRESSING STRONG INTEREST IN THEIR UNIONS	
	%	N		%
Negro Protestants	29	24	Negro Protestants	75
White Catholics	26	46	Catholics	52
White Protestants	17	65	White Protestants	42

The unions deviate . . . from the traditional pattern of middle-class economic values with which businessmen have long been identified, and with which the Protestant Ethic is linked. Quite clearly, working-class Protestants have an affinity for middle-class economic values, while middle-class Catholics have an affinity for working-class values.

Source: Gerhard Lenski, *The Religious Factor*, 1963 ed., pp. 100 and 102.

trines. One might suspect that the success, and expectation of it, on the part of white Protestants simply reflects ethnic dominance in the American social order and the relatively unfavorable position of Catholics and Negroes. That is to say, it is a phenomenon of prejudice and ethnocentrism rather than one of religion. But Lenski points out that despite the clearly depressed situation of the Negro, differences between Negro Protestants and white Catholics on these attitudes toward work are negligible.

> . . . Similarly, if attitudes were merely reflections of objective conditions in the job market, we would expect Jews to be more pessimistic than Catholics. Yet neither of these relationships was found. Jews have much more confidence in ability than Catholics, and Catholics have little more than Negro Protestants. These findings indicate that such attitudes are partly independent of the extent of objective discrimination against groups. Whatever their origin, lack of confidence in ability and in chances for upward mobility almost certainly inhibit many Catholic youths who might otherwise rise in the system.[49]

Not only do Protestants believe, disproportionately, that effort pays off. They believe that God favors efforts to get ahead. Sixty percent of the white Protestants, followed by Jews (58 percent),

---

[48] *Ibid.*, p. 94.
[49] *Ibid.*, p. 94, 95.

white Catholics (55 percent), and Negro Protestants (33 percent) took this position.[50]

The juxtaposition of Jews and white Protestants in positions contrasting with those of Catholics and Negro Protestants is a consistent matter in Lenski's data. The last two repeatedly take positions that are less individualistic (or more collectivistic), more security-oriented, less striving and competitive. The first two take positions roughly consonant with the Protestant ethic as Weber described it.

But to assert is not to demonstrate. To describe differences between socioreligious groups—even such consistent ones as these —is not to explain them. To describe such differences between groups is not to tell us whether religion accounts for these differences; or whether the differences observed alter religious beliefs and behavior. In an attempt to determine whether religious orientations, or religious devoutness do in fact have an influence on behavior in the sphere of work, Lenski argues:

> If the churches do contribute to these differences between socio-religious groups, we should expect that the greater the degree to which white Protestants are involved in their churches, the more likely they will be to display the individualistic, competitive, rationalistic patterns of thought and action identified with the Protestant Ethic and with the middle class. Similarly, we would expect that the more Catholics and Negro Protestants are involved in their churches, the more they will display the collectivistic, security-oriented, anti-entrepreneurial working-class patterns of thought and action. If, however, the churches are irrelevant and have no effect on economic behavior and attitudes, we would expect to find no noticeable differences between those members of a given group who attend their church regularly, and those who do not, when other relevant factors are controlled.[51]

We might argue further that, if religion has the hypothesized effect, the devoutness of the parents, being antecedent in time to the movement of their children in occupational and class status, would lead to upward mobility for white Protestants and Jews and would have little or no effect for white Catholics or Negro Protestants. Because Lenski's N for Jews is small and because Negro Protestants are virtually nonmobile because of race, thus blocking out the effect of religion, let us consider only white Protestants and Catholics.

---

[50] *Ibid.,* p. 95.
[51] *Ibid.,* p. 103

Ordering Lenski's data in Table 11–10 we get some indication that "the relationship of the individual white Protestant to his church *antedates* upward mobility."[52] Chi-square tests of the existence of a relationship between devoutness of parents and mobility of children yielded a $p < .001$ for Protestants and $p > .99$ for Catholics.

TABLE 11–10

Percent of White Protestants and Catholics of Working-Class Background Who Moved, and Did Not Move, to Middle-Class Status, by Degree of Devoutness of Their Parents*

PARENTS' DEVOUTNESS	PROTESTANTS			CATHOLICS		
	UPWARDLY MOBILE	NOT UPWARDLY MOBILE	N	UPWARDLY MOBILE	NOT UPWARDLY MOBILE	N
Devout working-class or farm parents	51%	49%	43	31%	69%	84
Nondevout working class or farm parents	31%	69%	102	39%	61%	38

* For definitions of "working-class," see page 496. A respondent's parents were classified as devout if "(a) the respondent reported attending worship services every week and if he further stated that *both* his mother and father were at least as religious as he, or (b) if the respondent reported that he attended worship services less than once a week but at least once a month, and that *both* of his parents were *more* religious than he." (Gerhard Lenski, *The Religious Factor*, 1961 ed., p. 104, footnote.)

Thus we see that empirical tests tend to confirm the notion that religious commitments have a significant bearing on the system of relationships we call capitalism. Concluding this part of his study Lenski writes:

> With considerable regularity the Jews and white Protestants have identified themselves with the individualistic, competitive patterns of thought and action . . . historically associated with the Protestant Ethic or its secular counterpart, the spirit of capitalism . . . both faiths currently develop in their adherents attitudes, values, beliefs and behavior patterns which are in keeping with the spirit of capitalism to a greater degree than those developed by Catholicism.[53]

❀   ❀   ❀   ❀

The data support a principle repeatedly stressed: parts of a system are interdependent. Worship and work are linked, as are

---

[52] Lenski, *op. cit.*, 1963 ed., p. 117.

[53] Lenski, *op. cit.*, 1961 ed., p. 101.

other elements of the institutional framework of society. Religion in particular, sustaining preferred and obligatory modes of conduct, cuts across all spheres of life, interlocking with other institutions. It is, as I've contended, an institution crucial for the integration of society, the maintenance of the group. Through it, life goals are articulated. Through it, in creed and code, the means for reaching these goals are specified. Religion makes its mandates applicable to, required of, all members of the group. This exerts a strain to match profession with practice as offended members of the group can appeal to the violated universals to seek reparation. Through such moral universals the church may build bridges between subcommunities, again serving an integrative function. We know, too, that religion often reinforces tribal identity, supporting local loyalties, God Himself being typically supposed to have a preemptive concern for His chosen people.

But the contribution that religious institutions make toward maintaining the group lies basically in this: the church provides sanctions in support of the rules that legitimate those expectations that define, and reduce variance in, the roles that make, in their linkages, stable human relationships. Thus:

| THE CHURCH AS ENUNCIATOR AND GUARDIAN OF MORALITY | ARTICULATES THE RULES & THEIR SANCTIONS | PRESCRIBING EXPECTED PERFORMANCE IN ROLE & SO MAKING FOR | DEPENDABLE RELATIONSHIPS |

At the same time we must be clear about this. The very integrating effect of religion within the group means that, as between groups, differences may be intensified. Thus the *dis*integrative potential of religion from the intergroup perspective.

Finally, we have seen in passing how religion serves another function, providing knowledge of the unknown and unknowable, and "control" over circumstances where natural science and technology are unavailing.

But over time the realm of the supernatural has been eroded, the range of the awesome unknown whittled back, the sacred penetrated by the secular. In the abrasion of sacred and secular, the former has often been shaped to fit the latter, as we saw in Bruce Barton's statements about Jesus. Still, the interplay between these realms has not been so one-sided as some have thought. An ingenuous Marxism might allege a one-way street between material substructure and spiritual superstructure. But Weber, as we have seen, makes a plausible point when he insists that enduring patterns of conduct are sustained by a spirit and that patterned behavior in the production of material things is no exception. From this perspective, superstructure becomes substructure, the nonmaterial the foundation of the material, an ethic an indispensable ingredient in capitalism. Lenski's research on a sample of the Detroit population confirms the view that worship and work are not disparate and unconnected realms. It is not such a long step from church to office and factory, a step which, figuratively speaking, we are about to make as we consider the organization of men at work, in Chapter 12.

SELECTED SUPPLEMENTARY READINGS

BARBER, BERNARD. "The Sociology of Science," in Robert K. Merton, Leonard Broom, and Leonard S. Cottrell, Jr. (eds.), *Sociology Today*, ch. ix. New York: Harper & Row—Harper Torchbooks, 1965.

BERELSON, BERNARD, AND STEINER, GARY A. "Religious Institutions," in *Human Behavior: An Inventory of Scientific Findings*, pp. 384–86. New York: Harcourt, Brace & World, Inc., 1964.

DURKHEIM, ÉMILE. *The Elementary Forms of the Religious Life*. New York: The Free Press of Glencoe, Inc., 1947.

GOODE, WILLIAM J. *Religion Among the Primitives*. New York: The Free Press of Glencoe, Inc., 1951.

GLOCK, CHARLES Y. "The Sociology of Religion," in Merton, Broom, and Cottrell, Jr. (eds.), *op. cit., supra*, ch. vi.

*————, AND RINGER, BENJAMIN B. "Church Policy and the Attitudes of Ministers and Parishoners on Social Issues," *American Sociological Review*, Vol. 21, No. 2 (April, 1956), pp. 148–56.

YINGER, J. MILTON. *Religion, Society and the Individual*. New York: The Macmillan Co., 1957.

---

* Article marked with an asterisk is available as reprint from the college division of the Bobbs-Merrill Company, Indianapolis, Indiana.

Chapter 12

Work: Relationships Instituted to Sustain Standards and Style of Life

How do we order relationships among men in pursuit of goods and services, and in their allocation?

Institutions are the flywheels of society. Through them, rewards and punishments are set, thus confining deviant conduct within limits tolerable to the group. Each institution fixes means for achieving certain culturally prescribed values through the development of appropriate relationships, and their constituent roles.

The social requirement of inducting the young into the human group is met by instituting a system of relationships called the family. It is so organized as to fulfill our precepts about responsibility to the dependent young, as responsibility is defined in our culture. We institute a network of relationships that we call the educational system to transmit the values, attitudes, knowledge, and skills stipulated as necessary in our culture.[1] And as we institutionalize a system of relationships among Gods, priests, and communicants, we promote the realization of the unqualified good.

The last chapter stressed the social function of religion. Through this institution we get the regular reaffirmation of those moral

---

[1] Public education, as I have pointed out, must be a source of attitudes supporting the social structure. The historian Cobban notes—he is referring to the educational policy of the Guizot administration under Charles X—"The importance of the role of the teachers in *inculcating law and order and a proper respect for the powers that be* was recognized from the beginning." (Alfred Cobban, *A History of Modern France* [Harmondsworth, Middlesex: Penguin Books, 1961], p. 123.)

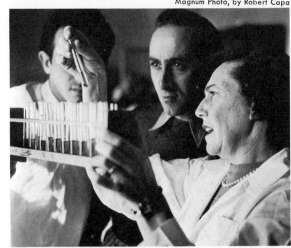

Four facets
of the
world of work.

commitments that make man's relations with his fellows dependable and responsible. It is inconceivable that the high probability of a given response to a certain action would in fact materialize were it not for the moral aspect of our relationships with one another. Sustaining these relationships—which is to say, maintaining the group—depends on a sense of obligation, of moral necessity in our dealings with others. And if the social order is to be maintained, this sense of moral necessity cannot be left to the vagaries of individual self-determination or the long chance of fortuitous consensus. It requires regular reaffirmation, such as that embodied in religious rites.

A second function of religion, I suggested, lies in its providing a cognitive safety net. It provides answers in supernatural theory that go beyond the very limited knowledge available to us in naturalistic theory. (Thus it was that Malinowski's Trobriand islanders (see page 476) sought answers and protection from their gods when mere technical knowledge, adequate in the inner lagoon, was insufficient for the hazards of the open sea.)

But if it is necessary to routinize rules and roles in support of group values through some sort of religious institution, so also must there be reliable means of getting and exchanging goods and services. If men do not live by bread alone, foods and fibers are something more than optional luxuries. And while we may consider with admiration the lilies of the field that toil not, neither do they spin, sinful descendants of Eve and Adam are not so automatically provided for. The old Persian poet is enjoying a fantasy life when he describes that idyllic situation with

> A Book of Verses underneath the Bough,
> A Jug of Wine, a Loaf of Bread—and Thou
> Beside me singing in the Wilderness—

For as all workers of the world would unite in pointing out, these valued things (goods and services for which demand exceeds supply) are nurtured in the soilbed of sorrowing toil. Few can indulge themselves in a nonchalant posture toward work. Given the scarcity of valued things and the lack of any instinctive guides for their production and consumption, we can avoid force, fraud, and the war of each against all only by instituting behaviors in the world of work. Thus the rules, roles, and relationships of men at work become grist for the sociologist's mill.

WORK AS A STRUCTURE OF ROLES AND RELATIONSHIPS WITH THEIR UNDERLYING RULES

Let us be clear what the sociology of work is about. Work—and the discipline of economics—is so often associated with the production exchange, and consumption of *things* that we overlook social dimensions. But having traveled this far in an exploration of sociology, you will appreciate that culture, knowledge of what is and what ought to be, penetrates the world of work as it does all other spheres of life. Thus attitudes toward work, toward unions, aspirations to get ahead, responses to various incentives—these are cultural products varying, as we saw in reviewing Lenski's study, by class, race, religion, and other social characteristics. They inform the differing patterns of relationships that we observe among work crews, between labor and management, production and maintenance workers, salesmen and customers, government and industry representatives. Industry and business are social enterprises. We sometimes err in our preoccupation with man-machine and machine-product relationships. Perhaps it is this fix upon the material product that has led to a misunderstanding of the best-known theorist of work relations.

For simply to link Marx with materialism is seriously to misconstrue his thesis. Certainly the production, distribution, and consumption of things (and services, as well) he saw as fundamental. And so do we. But the requirement of foods and fibers is to be taken for granted as a universal imperative. (There is no variance, here, and with no variance no variables and no problem; for there are no differences to explain.) Things, material things, were not, actually, the focus of Marx's inquiry, but the *mode of social organization* in the production of things. He was pointing to the way in which relationships between employer and employee, owner, manager, and worker, bourgeoisie and proletariat were patterned, and the way this patterning changed through history from periods of oriental despotism to European feudalism, the latter superseded by bourgeois capitalism and ultimately (and he thought inevitably) to be supplanted by socialism. One mode of organizing the relations of production gives way to another under the stress between roles that come to be seen as illegitimately differentiated by wealth and power. When workers become aware of their "alienation from the means of production," viewing themselves as a class wrongfully deprived, they will supplant the masters—by force, if necessary—initiating new relations of production. And since these relations of production constitute the real substructure of the social order, a necessary corollary must be a transformation in family, education, science, religion, polity—all other sectors of the social order that resonate to shifts in economic organization.

On many counts Marxist theory is inadequate from the viewpoint of historian, economist, and sociologist. The fantasy of a classless society is possible only on the basis of a simplistic theory of stratification quite at odds with sociologists' findings. Marx's staging of history, with its emphasis on the disenchantment of an urban proletariat does not accord with time and circumstance in the revolutions of Russia and China. Critically underestimated is the possibility of releasing a head of revolutionary steam through evolutionary devices. Such devices are social inventions, muting the impact of adventitious circumstance. Often legal and thus universalistic in their prescriptions, they may guarantee equality of opportunity (as through public education), rewards increasingly based on achievement (rather than on traits stemming from the accident of birth and ascribed to family, race, sex, or class), and protection against hazards to health and wealth (Old-Age, Survivors, and Disability Insurance, minimum wage laws, Medicare). Whether or not these social innovations are, as the late Senator Taft averred, "creeping socialism," they do not seem to constitute the revolutionary socialism that must, in Marxist strategy, be occasioned by the obdurate resistance of a favored few to the legitimate claims of the many. It is hard to imagine Ladybird Johnson echoing Marie Antoinette's "Let them eat cake."

And yet—I wince in saying it; for it seems a ponderous and preposterous pontificating on the obvious—Marx makes contributions of critical significance to sociology. Let me mention three of these at this point, pursuing one of them as it bears on the sociology of work. Marx brings home to us the fact that men's conceptions of the good, the true, and the beautiful (and the productions embodying these conceptions) are unintelligible apart from the social context from which they emerge. This is the fundamental insight still but partially plumbed in the field of the sociology of knowledge. Second, and despite the sometimes sinister connotations of Marxism, his was not a conspiratorial theory of society and history. The social order was a structure of relationships, immanent in which were quite impersonal, change-inducing forces. Individual actors there were, of course. But they were for the most part prisoners of their positions in the social structure and largely unaware of their roles in the social drama. This, of course, is a distinctly sociological posture. So, also, is his view of the economy in which the emphasis is not so much on indexes of production, the GNP (gross national product), discount rates, taxation, or the distribution of wealth, but on the structure of relationships in production as these relationships entail, or are represented by, such strictly economic variables as the foregoing.

We can look at work, then, as an extremely complicated *social* arrangement, the relationships of production, distribution, and consumption. It is an adaptive arrangement made by people with others, most of these being unknown, to exchange the product of brawn and brain. This exchange, symbolized commonly in cash, enables families, persons, groups to achieve some of their goals. In institutionalizing patterns of work we are offering an answer to the question: How can we garner, process, and allocate the things from soil and sea, the wisdom and skills from human hands and minds, that we need to satisfy our wants? Like other institutionalized answers, the organization of work consists in a generally shared set of *rules* (explicit and implicit, legal and customary) exemplified locally (in stores, factories, and offices) in a set of *roles* and *relationships:* boss-worker, lawyer or social worker–client, physician-patient, teacher-student, producer-wholesaler. . . . In studying the institutionalization of work patterns, the sociologist is likely to ask such questions as these:

1. How do men regard work (and leisure)? Has work an intrinsic virtue or is it to be viewed as a regrettably necessary means to desirable ends?
2. What views about the nature of man condition the authority structure of the workplace, the incentive system of rewards and punishments?
3. How are beliefs supporting work behavior buttressed or challenged in religion and other institutional spheres?
4. What is the standing of a given occupation in the status hierarchy of American society? Has it changed? And if so, how and why?
5. What is the occupational structure of a society? What are the chief occupational categories and how have they changed through time?

6. How are people recruited into these different occupations? How are the roles appropriate to each occupation created and sustained? What are the devices by which apprentices and novices are trained to conform to the life-style of their type of work?

7. How do beliefs and behaviors in the world of work articulate with those of other institutions? What, for example, are the occupational functions of an educational system? Why does education, in our society, tend to displace other criteria for vocational placement? What are the effects of working conditions, rewards, and habits upon the institution of the family? How are the occupational positions of women and children determined?

8. To what extent are occupations passed on from father to son? How much movement up the occupational ladder is there? Is there more or less rigidity in the occupational structure than there has been in the past?

9. What occupational characteristics—or, more generally, what social conditions—are linked with the development of labor unions and professional societies?

10. What variations among occupational groups do we find in political attitudes, life expectancy, interests, measures of intelligence, insanity rates, reading tastes, family size, and standards of conduct? How do we explain them? What consequences do these differences have for the community?

11. What are the characteristics of the work situation? How do they vary from occupation to occupation? What are the social factors affecting productivity, absenteeism, morale, the cohesiveness of work groups?

12. What accounts for workers' resistance—or easy adaptation—to changes in the work situation?[2]

We shall not find answers to these questions in this cursory introduction to the sociology of work. I list them as illustrations of problems pursued by sociologists. Note, furthermore, that we can ask questions such as these about the organization of work in any society, and this for several reasons. First, in their toil, men typically collaborate. Work is a social-cultural affair. Second, it is not a matter merely of means, but often of ends. True, we serve an instrumental purpose when, through the division of labor, we produce more, more efficiently. But economic activity often has social ends as well as social means.

---

[2] These questions are largely adapted and paraphrased from Theodore Caplow, *The Sociology of Work* (Minneapolis: University of Minnesota Press, 1954). See also William Foote Whyte, *Men at Work* (Homewood, Ill.: Dorsey Press, 1961), p. 5.

Aristotle was right: man is not an economic but a social being. He does not aim at safeguarding his individual interest in the acquisition of material possessions, but rather at ensuring social good will, social status, social assets. He values possessions primarily as a means to that end.[3]

But beyond the need for allies in production, beyond the social standing accorded on the basis of work's rewards, diversified work roles serve, in any group, an important unifying function. This is, of course, the burden of Durkheim's study of the *Division of Labor in Society:* the crucial function of men's collaboration at work, the unplanned end, is the solidarity of the group, the functional integration created by the interlacing of mutually dependent needs, interests, and capacities. Let me put it more generally. In all groups we find:

1. Understandings as to necessary and desirable goods. (Note that these are not necessarily "good" goods. Perhaps the sugar in soft drinks contributes to active careers in caries for the dental profession. Thalidomide was doubtless an effective tranquilizer, but pregnant women using it ran the risk of delivering monstrosities. And cigarettes, some evidence suggests, however far they "travel the smoke" and no matter what's "counting up front," may nonetheless be contributing to the development of lung cancer.)

2. A prescribed way of mobilizing social energy, of organizing effort in order to get these goods. These are the patterns of relationship reflected in the organizational chart of a business or industry, relations between union steward, workers, and management, between government representatives and company, and the like. (There are unofficial behaviors and informal relationships not formally prescribed.)

3. And finally, a set of beliefs, myths, symbols, rules that describe, prescribe, and justify our goods as goals, and the means of seeking these goals. All people, that is to say, define what is good, prescribe ways of getting these goods, and develop descriptive and normative statements about the ends and means of work. There are goods, roles (and relationships) for getting them and rules for the roles. As we would expect, work roles and the rules guiding them will differ from group to group through time and space.

---

[3] Karl Polanyi, "On Obsolete Market Mentality," *Commentary,* Vol. III (February, 1947), p. 112.

CULTURAL PERSPECTIVES ON WORK

People's words and deeds tell us what they know and believe. Some things they say and do reveal their orientation toward work, the cultural perspective on work. Let us consider first the rules of work. (I am using "rule" as a shorthand term for attitudes and value orientations—point 3, above—that guide men's conduct at work. We will then turn to roles and relationships, the organization of men at work—point 2, above.)

Attitudes toward Work

There are various conceptions of work. One view sees work as necessary, but scarcely sufficient for achieving the important ends of life. For some—and this may be part of the distinction between Weber's Protestant ethic and traditional Catholicism—the terrestial stint is mere prologue to celestial bliss. When the heavenly future is so certain and salient, ulcerous striving for kudos and cash in the here and now becomes an ill-advised if not immoral displacement of time and talent. For during the brief span of years allotted one on earth, the important thing is convivial amity with one's fellows, while paying one's decent devoirs to God.

This is the antithesis of the attitude toward work expressed by "Boss" Kettering when he wrote:

> I often tell my people that I don't want any fellow who has a job working for me; what I want is a fellow whom a job has. I want the job to get the fellow and not the fellow to get the job. And I want that job to get hold of this young man so hard that no matter where he is the job has got him for keeps. I want that job to have him in its clutches when he goes to bed at night, and in the morning I want that same job to be sitting on the foot of his bed telling him it's time to get up and go to work. And when a job gets a fellow that way, he's sure to amount to something.[4]

Such contrasting conceptions of what ought to be in the orientation toward work may have serious outcomes. So it was that after World War II, when the United States was heavily committed to reviving the economies of war-devastated allies, our government wished to stimulate the rationalization of French business and

---

[4] William Foote Whyte, *Men at Work* (Homewood, Ill.: Dorsey Press, 1961), p. 58; taken from *Coronet* (September, 1959), p. 72.

industry. This meant increased production, at lower unit cost, for distribution to a greater market. But as David Landes points out, French business had been typically a matter of family enterprise, geared to local markets and providing a modest but adequate living for a kin group.[5] Exhortations to expand, to boost production, to extend the market fell on quite indifferent ears.

One view of work, then, sees it as a good in itself and the person should be by work possessed. A second view makes work a worldly necessity in the trip toward otherworldly rewards. There is perhaps a third view of work found in some phases of finance capitalism. Work becomes a somewhat speculative enterprise, intriguingly touched by chance elements. The worker's role is that of the speculator operating through our great exchanges. E. B. White touched on this role when he commented on a transaction yielding the speculator a tidy profit of $300,000.[6] The case was that of a grader on the grain exchange whose knowledgeable buying and selling, some suspected, might be accounted for by a pipeline to the Department of Agriculture. White's words carry a gentle reproach for this third view of work, reproach tinctured with a bucolic nostalgia for elements of the Protestant ethic. For this work role is indifferent to the goods produced and sold, indifferent to satisfactions intrinsic to the making and using of things. For the work role of the speculator simply revolves about a change in price. And however the element of chance is reduced by the shrewdness of the "inside dopester," anticipating change in price is a kind of guessing game.

Three views of work—it's instrinsically virtuous, or an aspect of life secondary to social rewards and salvation, or a speculative game—do not exhaust the possibilities. But they do suggest significantly differing cultural perspectives on work, viewpoints that concern the sociologist as they influence work roles and relationships.

Attitudes toward Type of Work

Embedded in the culture we also find differing attitudes toward types of work (and workers), differing conceptions of property and rights in it, and differing assumptions about man's nature and what incentives, if any, prompt him to produce.

---

[5] David S. Landes, "French Business and the Businessman: A Social and Cultural Analysis," chap. xix, in Edward M. Earle (ed.), *Modern France* (Princeton, N.J.: Princeton University Press, 1951), pp. 334–53.

[6] See E. B. White, "The Talk of the Town," *The New Yorker*, February 21, 1948.

Under frontier conditions and where extractive industry dominates the economy, occupations requiring brawn may take precedence over brain-exploiting occupations, manipulation of things over manipulation of symbols. Men confined to the bowels of the social ship will, like Eugene O'Neill's stokers in *The Hairy Ape*, glorify their role as being heart and guts of the enterprise. Among the gypsum miners studied by Alvin Gouldner there was an air of death-defying, Dionysian daring and ego-enhancing independence, marking them off emphatically from the pedestrian factory workers on the surface. Type of work valued is likely to vary with level of social and cultural development.

That aspect of culture that we call technology will qualify attitudes toward work and its performance. With industry in an embryonic stage of development, there was a premium on unskilled labor, and the employment of children was widely approved. Even today where subsistence agriculture still obtains, the school year is foreshortened and children fill out the labor force at planting time and harvest. Thus the conditions under which it is proper to perform certain work are culturally differentiated in time and space. Barrie's admirable Crichton was top dog when, his English master and the family he served having been shipwrecked, he was the only person with the technical skills needed for suvival. But you'll recall that when, after a period of time, the family was rescued and returned to England, Crichton resumed his erstwhile role as a gentleman's gentleman. Furthermore, he did so not only without regret or recrimination but with pride in his position as butler and valet, an attitude toward such work that would doubtless be uncommon in the United States.

Even with similarities in the existential aspect of culture (knowledge of what is), normative elements may make for striking diversities. The Japanese are skilled in industrial technology, but their traditions dictate a mode of organizing men at work that contrasts sharply with ours.

Japanese workers are hired for life. They are practically never fired. Promotions go largely by seniority even at managerial levels. The incompetent executive moves up with advancing years to positions with titles appropriate to his age—even when this means devising types of duties that will keep him from interfering with the progress of the firm. The pay of workers bears no relation to their productivity. The pay envelope is the sum of a complex set of factors, in which length of service and number of dependents figure prominently. All management decisions are made on a group basis—at least nominally. If an individual were credited with a certain decision that turned out to be unwise, then the individual would lose face. To spare management people from such humiliation, to all appearances the group as a whole shares responsibility in all decisions.[7]

Overall contrasts in the culture of work are represented in the abstract labels that we apply to economies: a domestic economy, capitalism, state capitalism, socialism. A scheme summarizing these differing conceptions of what is and ought to be, in the world of work, is presented in Table 12–1.

Attitudes toward Distribution of Goods

Values, views, and rules vary, too, on the matter of distributing goods. For an interesting contrast, taken from anthropological literature, let us go with Margaret Mead to the land of the Arapesh, in northern New Guinea, the land of yams:

> The fortunate man who thinks he has a large surplus [of yams] will consult his elders, or they themselves may tell him that his supply is sufficient. He then gathers all his yams in one place . . . and after he and a series of associates—brothers, cousins, brother-in-law, etc.— have gathered together enough meat, he gives a large feast [an *abullu*] to which most of the locality come, and members of adjacent and related hamlets. Each guest family brings gifts, mainly meat, but also net bags, plates, etc., and takes away a part of the piled up yams to use as seed, seed from which the maker of the *abullu* can never eat again. He has the honor of having given the *abullu* . . . and his gardening luck has increased the food supply of the community. Although this is always phrased positively—that a man is "permitted" to make an abullu—it is actually an effective measure against any man's accumulating wealth disproportionate to the wealth accumulated by others.
>
> If there is meat on his smoking rack over the fire, it is either meat which was killed by another . . . and has been given to him, in which case he and his family may eat it; or, it is meat which he himself has killed and which he is smoking to give away to someone else, for to eat one's own kill, even though it be only a small bird, is a crime to which only the morally—which usually means in Arapesh, mentally— deficient will stoop. If the house in which he is living is nominally his, it will have been constructed, in part at least, from the posts and planks of other people's houses, which have been dismantled or temporarily deserted, and from which he has borrowed timber. He will not cut his

---

[7] Whyte, *op. cit*, p. 66. Whyte is summarizing material from a study by James Abegglen, *The Japanese Factory* (New York: Free Press of Glencoe, Inc., 1958).

TABLE 12-1

Examples of Overall Ways of Organizing Men at Work: Domestic, Capitalist, and Socialist Economies

TYPE OF ECONOMY	UNIT OF ECONOMIC ORGANIZATION	PRIME OBJECTIVE	PRINCIPAL MEANS OF COORDINATING DECISIONS ABOUT ALLOCATION OF GOODS AND SERVICES	OWNED BY	OPERATED BY
Domestic	Households	Satisfaction of a variety of familial needs/wants	Face-to-face product and service exchange within households and, at market, where agreements to exchange are consummated, between households	Family, or its representative	Head of family and its members
Capitalist	The privately owned firm or business enterprise	Money profit, "discounted for risk"*	Symbolic exchanges (paper transactions) in the market: Wall Street, LaSalle Street, Chicago grain exchange, etc.	Individual owner(s) or shareholders	Owners, self-employed executives, hired managers
State Capitalism	The publicly owned firm or business enterprise (e.g., the Renault car manufacturing company in France)	Money profit	Symbolic exchanges in the market—i.e., paper transactions as is the case with private capitalism	The state	State-appointed managers and their employees (e.g., the Canadian National Railways)
Socialism	The public service (e.g., postal service)	Satisfaction of community needs/wants	State planning agencies via official regulations, taxation, prescription of quotas, subsidies . . .	The state, or subsidiary public agencies	The state, or provincial governments, public service corporations, collectives, unions, co-operative associations.

* An important secondary objective, Oscar Lange points out, is safety, or the desire to minimize risk. Hence the primary aim of money profit is qualified by this secondary objective. See Oscar Lange, "What is Economics?" in *Review of Economic Studies* (London: London School of Economics, 1945–46) Vol. XII, No.1, pp. 19–32, *passim*.

rafters to fit his house, if they are too long, because they may be needed later for someone else's house which is of a different shape or size.[8]

Attitudes toward Property, Public and Private

So, also, do we find a great range of beliefs about property, its ownership and control. It is common for some sorts of property to be communally held, while other sorts are privately owned. But the types so owned, and the balance between public and private ownership vary broadly from group to group and time to time. The proportion of goods communally owned in the United States has increased markedly over the years. United States citizens own in common power-producing and flood control installations like TVA, thousands of miles of public highway, vast values in military installations, great resources in public parks and state and national forests, enormous reserves of grain and the storage facilities for it, schools and post offices and other government facilities in almost every community in the nation. Yet our ratio of private to public ownership is rather high, especially when compared with, say, the Hutterites or the Coronation Gulf Eskimos about whom Stefansson writes.

> Natural resources and raw materials were owned in common but made articles were privately owned. The blubber of a seal that was needed for light and heat, or lean or fat that were needed for meals, belonged no more to the man who secured them than to anyone else. . . . A meal that had been cooked was in a sense private property; but it was open to everyone under the laws of hospitality . . . it was very bad form to start a meal in any village without at the least sending a youngster outdoors to shout at the top of his voice that the family were about to dine.[9]

Beliefs about Work Incentives

Of all the cultural prescriptions touching the world of work, none embodies more fundamental assumptions about the nature of man, about "what makes Sammy run," than those bearing on incentives. In reporting on his Eskimos, Stefansson implies that the only incentive necessary was the pressure on the person from others' expectations. Thus he writes:

---

[8] Margaret Mead, "The Arapesh of New Guinea," in *Cooperation and Competition among Primitive Peoples,* Margaret Mead (ed.), (2d ed.; Boston: Beacon Press, 1961), pp. 29–31, *passim.*

[9] Vilhjalmur Stefansson, "Vilhjalmur Stefansson," in Clifton Fadiman, (ed.), *I Believe* (New York: Simon and Schuster, Inc., 1939), pp. 266, 267, *passim.*

I never knew even one who didn't try his best, although there were, of course, the same differences of energy and aptitude which we find among ourselves. If there had been a shirker, he would have received the same food; but even in a circle of punctilious courtesy he would have felt that he was not being fed gladly. It is the nearest thing to impossible, when you know how primitive society works . . . to conceive of anyone with that combination of indolence and strength of character which would make it possible for a well man to remain long a burden on the community . . . those who were selfish lost standing. Those who were altruistic rose in the public esteem.[10]

The common assumption in Euro-American capitalism seems to be that the carrot and the goad are required to stimulate mulish man to productive effort. The carrot is promotion and increases in pay. The goad is the threat of unemployment, demotion, reduction in income and, ultimately, starvation. This view has a long ancestry.

Professor Bendix writes about the rules underlying work roles in eighteenth- and nineteenth-century England.[11] The rules are *must* statements, linking the is's and ought's of culture. If it is true that a man will not work without rewards and punishments externally imposed, then certain ought's are, by implication, stipulated in the employer-employee relationship. The former *should* induce production through the prospects of promotions and raises. He *should* spur production through the threat of unemployment. Bendix describes how an emerging class of entrepreneurs and managers found such ideological support with the unfolding of the Industrial Revolution. A rising social class, a middle class of merchants and industrialists, were pitted against the landed aristocracy. They celebrated the promise of technology. They capitalized on a high birth rate and traditional conceptions of husband-wife and parent-child relationships to employ women and children under what would be regarded, today, as incredibly bad conditions. They were persuaded that the relationship between employer and worker was necessarily and properly that of the deserving rich to the undeserving poor, of wise to ignorant, of benevolent to needy, and that the appropriate and necessary incentive was the threat—the impersonal threat, to be sure—of destitution, even death.

Nor is such an ideology, such a set of rules backing work roles, altogether unknown in the United States today. That such rules do

---

[10] *Ibid.,* p. 267.

[11] Reinhard Bendix, *Work and Authority in Industry: Ideologies of Management in the Course of Industrialization* (New York and Evanston: Harper and Row, 1963).

exist is revealed when we are astonished to find workers casual about cutting work, cavalier about punctuality, careless despite the prospect of losing a job. Allison Davis gives us an example of this perhaps sizable category, a Negro factory worker in Chicago.

> . . . born in Mississippi, Ruth's parents were unskilled workers, . . . at the very bottom of the economic hierarchy. The family came to Chicago in 1935. For a long time, they were unable to secure either work or relief. Both then, and later when the father was given a job as an unskilled laborer on WPA, Ruth, her four sisters and brother, and her parents lived in the large cellar of an old tenement on the South Side. The cellar had been divided into nine rooms, one for each family. There was no kitchen, only an open corner at the back of the cellar, with a small gas stove and a faucet. The nine families shared this corner as their "kitchen." They shared their small stocks of furniture, their bedclothes, and their wearing apparel. Most important of all, they shared their food and even their money. When a family was both out of work and off relief, the other families put their money and food into a communal "pot," in which the destitute family shared. *This is a hard system to beat, for those who believe in the effectiveness of economic intimidation in making good workers.* When workers can survive at this level, and still have the social support and approval of their friends, they can scarcely be threatened or starved into better work habits.[12]

We might add that, if the punishment of deprivation doesn't work, neither, for the poorest category of worker, is the reward of upward mobility an incentive. For such rewards may not be genuine possibilities; they may provide no more incentive than in the case of a small Negro boy whose teacher held out to her pupils the possibility that one of them might become president of the United States. As the story goes, the Negro youngster whispered to a white classmate: "I'll sell you my chance for a quarter."

Note, finally, a small lesson that can be learned from these cursory comments on incentives. The vulgar proposition about human relationships (a man works under threat of punishment and/or

---

[12] Allison Davis, "The Motivation of the Underprivileged Worker," in William Foote Whyte (ed.), *Industry and Society* (New York: McGraw-Hill Book Co., 1946), p. 95. See also, on the matter of motivation and incentive, William Foote Whyte, *Money and Motivation* (New York: Harper & Bros., 1955).

A bit later in the chapter from which I've quoted, Davis helps us appreciate the ties between institutions, family, work, and school. He writes: "To the underprivileged adolescent, the words and the goals of his teacher—those words and goals to which middle-class adolescents react with respect and hard striving—mean very little. For the words of the teacher are not connected with the acts of training in his home, with the actual rewards in school, or with actual steps in moving toward a career." (*Ibid.*, p. 99.)

promise of reward) is typically too gross, disregarding *conditions under which it fails to hold true*. Water boils at 212° Fahrenheit *only* at sea level—i.e., only under specified conditions. The temperature of a gas is a given inverse function of pressure *only* at specified altitudes. The punishment-reward theory of incentives applies *only* when such incentives are relevant and meaningful for a given category of workers. And the evidence suggests that relevance and meaning vary widely by type of worker. Some people are moved to embrace a life of poverty and celibacy. Others are strongly motivated to pile up property in the here and now where moth and rust corrupt. Others may, like the Kwakiutl, accumulate goods not for their apparent uses but to gain status by destroying them in rivalry with other goods-destroyers. Culture permits and prescribes wondrously various conduct, at work as in other spheres of life.

Some Occupational Variations: Language and License

On a smaller scale there are cultural differences that distinguish and identify different occupational groups. Language, for example, not only discloses major value orientations ("free enterprise," "individualism," "the sanctity of private property") but provides occupational groups with distinctive technical argot and, in consequence, a sense of identity. Professors Miller and Form note that:

> The words "floor," "ceiling," "walls," "toilet," "right and left hand" are common words with rather exact referents. [But for the sailor these become] "deck," "overhead," "bulkheads," "head," "starboard and port."[13]

They also point to other cultural characteristics of occupational groups: the initiation rites for the newly hired; the "rites of intensification," cementing relationships among work group members; patterns of joking; gossip, rumor and stereotypical views of certain worker categories: Poles, Italians, French-Canadians, members of rival departments, *et al.*

Cultural variations on the theme of work are many and subtle. In a perceptive piece on occupations, Professor Hughes points out that occupations may vary in the degree to which license is accorded members by nonmembers of the occupational group. For example,

---

[13] Delbert C. Miller and William H. Form, *Industrial Sociology* (New York: Harper & Bros., 1951), p. 290.

members of some occupations are authorized to deal in "guilty knowledge" (priest, therapist, newsman, teacher). Some are given license to think, speak, and act dangerously. Physicians may speak among themselves in ways otherwise offensive. The cold, if not cavalier, talk of patients' ailments, the aseptically impersonal talk and treatment of clients' cases by lawyer or social worker, the "license of the doctor to cut and dose, of the priest to play with men's salvation, of the scientist to split atoms; or simply [license to run the danger] that advice given a person may be wrong, or that work done may be unsuccessful or cause damage"—such license, conferred through the culture of a group, is an intriguing dimension in the study of work patterns.[14]

Now let's back up for a running start. In considering the cultural aspects of work we noted three general views of work along the means-ends dimension. Sundry observations suggest how variously viewed and valued work may be, depending on time, place, and associated levels of technology (knowledge of what is). Slavery and work—at least heavy manual work—were conceptions wedded in the Greek mind. And there was the Biblical view of work as the sentence imposed upon man for his original sin, eating from the tree of knowledge (a curious view, since acquiring knowledge is itself so tough a task that a sentence to hard labor would seem a case of double jeopardy). The adverse view of work is seen, too, in the Christian stress on renunciation and the call to seek saintliness. At least from the time of the Reformation such attitudes toward work have come to seem, for most people of Euro-American culture, quaintly archaic. Clearly Christ's injunction to the rich man to "Give what thou hast to the poor, and come and follow me," is not the way to run a railroad.

Similarly, in synchronous comparisons—and even where, as between two groups, technical know-how (knowledge of what is) is comparable—differing conceptions of *what ought* to be will lead to differing work relationships. Thus James Abegglen has told us about Japanese–United States contrasts: for the former, lifetime hiring, the significance of seniority, the lack of a clear connection between productivity and pay. A chief dimension of our culturally variegated world lies in these differing views of work.

---

[14] Everett Cherrington Hughes, "The Study of Occupations," in Robert K. Merton, Leonard Broom and Leonard S. Cottrell, Jr. (eds.), *Sociology Today, Problems and Prospects* (New York: Harper Torchbooks, 1965), Vol. II, p. 449.

For the modern fascists, work is a social duty . . . the Soviets call themselves the republic of workers, peasants and soldiers, glorifying manual labor as the highest human dignity. Modern Protestant countries in the free West still draw on the liberal economics of yesterday in defense of the free market, private property, and (in America) minimum government as the formula for releasing the productive energies of the people. Catholic idealizations of labor continue to emphasize its roots in the natural order and its utility in the attainment of higher spiritual ends. French humanists define labor as man's confirmation of himself against nature (whatever it does to make life easier and longer or useful and beautiful).[15]

We mark different economies by words like capitalism and socialism. These abstract terms represent differing modes of organizing men's efforts at work, and the rules (by implication, the values) underlying them. The words imply differences in aims, means, and units through which work is carried out. We find, likewise, distinctive views of property, of appropriate ways of allocating scarce goods, and of the incentives deemed necessary to move men to work.

Finally, we observe that within a given economy, subsystems—work groups, occupational categories—register their own subcultures. These, too, are linguistically distinguishable, each with its own argot. And in the worker's self-image, in the license accorded group members to operate in a certain way, in the reciprocal obligations understood by members (and nonmembers), in patterns of recruitment, training, and separation, the sociologist finds intriguing points of inquiry.

Values Apparently Underlying Our Organization of Men at Work

From such observations we can infer general value constellations that undergird the ordering of men's work relationships. In societies like ours where science and technology enable marked mastery of man's environment, such convictions and commitments as the following seem reasonable inferences:

1. Man stands above all things and beings and so is justified in shaping them to gratify his ever increasing needs. Not only does he rule ocean, earth, and firmament: he rules himself. Assimilating human nature to other realms of nature, he believes it both possible and good to shape his destiny more precisely to desired ends. Levels of

---

[15] Harold L. Wilensky, "Varieties of Work Experience," in Henry Borow (ed.), *Man in a World at Work* (Boston: Houghton Mifflin Co., 1964), p. 129.

productivity and quality control apply to human as well as to non-human resources.

2. It is good "to strive, to seek, to gain and not to yield." We do not value the vegetable whose destiny is written in its genes. "The fault lies, not in our stars but in ourselves, that we are underlings." Our laurels go to the man who, despite limitations of birth and breeding, yet achieves the bigger and the better. We value demonstrable achievement.

3. Thus it is good to look forward, not backward. We have, as Professor Lynd once put it, a "tilt toward the future." And this faith (and beyond faith, hope, and beyond hope, confidence) is in a future not so far distant—not in some Beulah land of serene bliss, but in rewards to be realized, at least in part, within a man's lifetime.

4. If we fix on the near rather than the distant future, so must we be concerned with proximate rather than ultimate ends, and with concrete ways of achieving them. Since proximate goals (for example, getting a good grade) are but means to more distant ends (high grade point average, PBK, a flying start on one's career), we become, in fact, means-oriented, instrumentally oriented. Thus we value improved techniques. ("Let a man but build a better mousetrap and the world will beat a path to his door.")

5. A stress on achievement, a future orientation and an instrumental one, suggest as corollary the value placed on calculating reason, on knowledge that can be relied on to achieve our ends. There is implied some priority of head over heart, some control of impulse or affect in the service of efficient realization of our goals. Self-discipline, conscientious commitment to work, a degree of austerity, hardheadedness and a deprecation of sentiment—these characteristics come to be valued in the world of work.

6. Finally, degree of achievement is certified through verifiable measures of action and product. Teachers may lose their jobs because they fail "to produce," i.e., to write books and articles. In industry, men making time and motion studies set norms of production, providing yardsticks for measuring work performance. What is relevant is a man's performance and the product attesting that performance. Good intentions, facile justifications, simply won't do. Eliza Doolittle speaks the put-up-or-shut-up language of the world of work when she cries, "Show me!"

WORK RELATIONSHIPS IN BUREAUCRATIC STRUCTURES

Belief in man's supremacy in nature, and its justifiability, a stress on achievement, the reshaping of his world, a tilt toward the future, an emphasis on the constant improvement of means, control of impulse, an emphasis on action, performance, productivity—such cultural themes inform the world of work. These values (as is the case with all values) are realized in social structures. Today, in our society, there is a typical social structure, a pattern through which relationships at work are ordered. We call it *bureaucracy*.

The Meaning of Bureaucracy

Let me say three things about this concept. The sociologist uses the term for descriptive and analytical purposes. He does *not* use it in a prescriptive or derogatory sense. The term commonly carries connotations of time-serving, made possible by the anonymity of the worker in the vast reaches of bumbling mass enterprise. "Red tape" is the familiar epithet used to describe bureaucratic operations. Bureaucracy is thought to be found principally in government agencies and to be a form of organization shockingly costly because inefficient.

As the sociologist uses the word, this last belief, the tendency to link the adjective, "bureaucratic" exclusively to government, is wrong. Bureaucracy is found in private as well as public works. Indeed, wherever we have great numbers of persons, a complex social order with diverse needs to be met and capacities to be exploited, a money economy, an elaborate technology and a well-developed system of contract law, bureaucratic forms of work organization are invariably found. This mode of organizing men at work is an outgrowth of social conditions, not a straitjacket deliberately imposed by rulers.

As to its inefficiency and costliness, the time-serving of clerks enjoying sinecures, the red tape that hamstrings enterprise by a thousand trivial regulations, just as the Lilliputians restrained Gulliver—these allegations simply await empirical test. Without evidence we cannot be wholly confident that GE is more efficient than the Park Service, or TVA less efficient than TWA.

A second point is this: to state the aspects of bureaucracy is to outline a structure of relationships never corresponding, in detail, to any actual enterprise. It is an ideal type, the meaning and uses of which I touched on before (see page 486). The first significant formulation of this concept is found in the work of Max Weber. We will turn, presently, to his elaboration of this concept as background for discussing an empirical study of a mine and factory producing gypsum products.

Let me say, finally, why it seems reasonable to focus on this way of linking men's efforts at work. For there are other illustrations of the sociology of work that might be offered: inquiries into different levels of morale or cohesion in work groups, their sources and consequences, or the structure of unofficial relationships among workers, or the connections between beliefs and behaviors at work and those in other institutional spheres (family, religion, government), or effects on productivity of changes in relationship among workers, and between workers and supervisors or management, or effects of different leadership styles, and the like. But here, as elsewhere in this approach to sociology, we cannot cover the waterfront. Since we must be selective, to focus on this form of organization seems appropriate for the following reasons. First, the significance of bureaucracy is enhanced because of its generality: while its purest exemplification is to be found in the organization of work, we find it also in religion, in education—wherever the rational linking of many men's efforts is necessary. Second, it mirrors modern life. Although bureaucratic organization is not new—the organization of government in ancient China provides an excellent example —it is more fully elaborated in our time and place, and especially in the realm of work, than elsewhere, or in the past. Third, since it refers directly to a structure of statuses and interlocking roles, studies revolving about this concept are dead center for sociology.[16]

Characteristics of Bureaucratic Organization

Now let us get to the meat of the matter: what is the meaning, what are the characteristics of bureaucracy? For a definition, let us call bureaucracy a hierarchical form of social organization rationally

---

[16] This is not to say, obviously, that other approaches attack less significant problems. The economist, the business administrator, the industrial engineer simply confront different problems. Nor is it to suggest that we quite slip out of sociology's domain when we study psychological dimensions as they vary with aspects of bureaucracy. See, for example, Robert K. Merton's "Bureaucratic Structure and Personality," and the Miller and Swanson study of the connection between bureaucratic and entre-preneurial work settings, on the one hand, and the rearing of their children and their personality traits, on the other. (The references here are to Robert K. Merton, "Bureaucratic Structure and Personality," in *Social Theory and Social Structure* [New York: Free Press of Glencoe, 1957] and Daniel R. Miller and Guy E. Swanson, *The Changing American Parent* [New York: John Wiley & Sons, Inc., 1958]. See also the work of Merton's with Ailsa P. Gray, Barbara Hockey, and Hanan Selvin, *Reader in Bureaucracy* [New York: Free Press of Glencoe, 1952].)

geared to the achievement of precisely specified objectives by means of a division of labor based on demonstrated competence. This form of organization, Weber writes,

> . . offers above all the optimum possibility for carrying through the principle of specializing administrative functions according to purely objective considerations. Individual performances are allocated to functionaries who have specialized training and who by constant practice learn more and more. The objective discharge of business primarily means a discharge of business according to calculable rules and without regard for persons.[17]

This is a beginning. But the implications of the concept for the relationships of men at work will become clearer if we outline the characteristics of this form of organization. Professor Blau lists these as (1) specialization, (2) a clear-cut hierarchy of authority, (3) a clearly detailed system of rules, and (4) impersonality in allocating and coordinating roles.[18] Let me elaborate in the following enumeration of characteristics:

1. There is a finely refined differentiation of roles, a clear-cut division of interlocking activities regarded as duties inherent in a given position: eighth grade teacher, tech. sergeant, gaffer (the master craftsman in producing glassware), anaesthetist, first clarinet . . . *ad inf.*
2. These roles are dealt with *as roles,* quite regardless of who is performing in them.
3. Recruitment for these roles is on the basis of demonstrated capacity. Enter the personnel man. One may be appointed by a superior or assigned his role on the basis of a qualifying examination. Such roles are not filled by election, either of God or man.
4. There is a meticulous specification of these roles through job descriptions and rules that state, in terms as clear as may be, expectations defining the worker's relationship to a remote and anonymous management as well as to fellow workers and immediate supervisor.

    Such rules allow workers to accept demands made of them without implying, in the words of Peter Blau, a "personal submission to the supervisor that would betray their self-image as 'any man's equal.' "

    They also allow the supervisor to assess work performed without invoking any debatable claims as to his personal superiority. They also offer a basis for measures of work, measures which

---

[17] Max Weber, *From Max Weber: Essays in Sociology,* trans. Hans Gerth and C. Wright Mills (New York: Oxford University Press, 1946), p. 215.

[18] Peter Blau, *The Dynamics of Bureaucracy* (Chicago: University of Chicago Press, 1955). See also, Merton, *op. cit.,* pp. 151–52.

can, in turn, justify rewards (in pay and promotion) and punishments (docking the worker's wages or otherwise penalizing him).

Furthermore, they preclude the need for reissuing instructions in each particular case. It is the worker's responsibility to read and know the rules. *Caveat vendor laboris!*

5. Rules are written, not oral, emphasizing their impersonality and promoting continuity despite the fact that successive incumbents may be drawn from quite heterogeneous backgrounds. (The emphasis on writing and the whole clerical-recording apparatus of modern business enterprise is to be contrasted with oral transmission in simpler societies.)

6. There is an increased emphasis on evaluation, preferably a quantified assessment making comparisons possible. This includes accounting procedures, time-motion studies, the careful selection and continuous appraisal of the workers who are the instruments of production, and a check on the quantity and quality of their output.

7. Planning and control are carried out through a chain of command, a strictly ordered system of subordination and superordination following the distribution of authority.

8. Impersonality: This characteristic has been implied, above, in the emphasis on demonstrable achievement and the treatment of work roles without regard to particular incumbents. It means, also, that loyalty is to the organization, not the person. Sentiment affecting personal ties is appropriate only as it supports production, promotes organizational objectives. The realm of the family and all matters strictly idiosyncratic are to be separated from the realm of work.

9. As is suggested in points 6 and 7, above, coordinating roles become increasingly important, those roles in which the task is to articulate others' activities.

10. The worker progresses through the hierarchy of authority and rewards on the basis of sharpened skills and capacities.

A Research Example: Sorts and Sources of Bureaucratic Rules and Roles

Such characteristics as these make up the commonly accepted portrait of bureaucratic organization. But it remains to be seen when and if they apply in concrete cases. A study by Professor Gouldner helps us to refine and amplify this pattern of work organization.[19] His study hinges on a shift toward bureaucratic rules and roles attending the replacement of a plant manager in a factory and

---

[19] Alvin Gouldner, *Patterns of Industrial Bureaucracy* (New York: Free Press of Glencoe, Inc., 1954).

mine of the General Gypsum Company, studied by him and his students over a period of three years. Data come from three sources: (1) 174 interviews, 132 of these constituting a sample so stratified as to take into account workers' seniority, rank, and department, (2) direct observations in plant and mine (one of the research team was employed in the mine), and (3) documentary material including company correspondence, memoranda and reports, arbitrators' decisions and newspaper clippings.

The plant was located just outside a small community of some seven hundred souls, a farm-based, tradition-oriented community whose people emphasized friendly relationships; the importance of the family unit; interest in baseball, the volunteer fire department, and hunting; thrift, personal dignity, and equality among men, whatever their formal standing. They were reported as loyal to insiders, somewhat suspicious of outsiders, pro-Nordic and anti-Semitic. Community influentials were heads of old farm families and professionals such as ministers and physicians.

These local and traditional values were reflected in the gypsum factory and mine. Interview data tell us that before the advent of the new manager, rules were few and leniently enforced. There was little checking up. Workers seldom felt pushed. Their obligations to superiors were limited to the immediate and obvious technical requirements of the job. Nobody, one respondent said, was fired. A worker always got a second chance. It was quite usual for a worker to help himself to company equipment and materials. While asserting a sense of personal equality with anyone, workers yet applauded a solicitous posture on the part of the plant manager and his lieutenants, who not only tolerated minor deviations but acted in unrequired ways to care for the workers. Close family and community ties were reflected in the plant, where many workers were neighbors, friends, and relatives.

Thus before the arrival of a new plant manager, we find rules and roles somewhat at odds with the picture I have drawn of bureaucratic forms. Instead of precisely measured performance in a narrowly defined work role against standards impersonally administered and held to for all incumbents of that role—instead of this we find relationships emphatically tinctured by sentiment, roles diffusely and fuzzily defined, and such ascriptive qualities as kinship entering in. Two social spheres are fused here, that of home and community on the one hand and that of workplace on the other. Workers' descriptions of the plant under the old manager as being "like a family" confirm this analysis. And that is what they meant, in part, by referring to management as "lenient."

> "Leniency" is a judgment rendered by workers when supervisors temper the performance of their managerial roles by taking into account obligations that would be *relevant in other relationships*. Thus when workers lauded management for allowing the injured to do [physically undemanding] work in the sample room, or permitting workers to use Company material and tools for personal use, or giving those who violate managerial expectations a "second chance," they were employing criteria legitimately applicable to the relations among *friends* and *neighbors*, rather than in a *business* and *industrial* context.[20]

When the plant manager died, his successor felt an obligation, out of gratitude for his appointment (and in accordance with orders), to revise easygoing, haphazard methods, increase efficiency, and boost production. Symbolic of the change was the contrast between old and new personnel managers. The old manager was demoted and "a college educated, authority conscious, rule-oriented individual was substituted for an informal, 'lenient' man who had little taste for paper work," and preferred to hire farm boys whose qualifications he picked up through the local grapevine.[21] We see here the confrontation of two schemes: the rational, efficiency-enhancing values of bureaucratic organization versus the traditional indulgency pattern previously pervading the plant.

Stepping into others' shoes is seldom easy, and in this case the new manager stood at the point where these two forms of work organization collided. He faced problems common to all successors. He inherited commitments made by his predecessor. These must be honored or defaulted, either course being hazardous. He took with him the expectations of some friends to share the profits of his elevation. He inherited old lieutenants, not readily disposed of, whose loyalties might lie with the predecessor and whose position enabled them to make things tough for the successor. And he inherited workers who tended to idealize the past and disparage the present. (In this case "old Doug," the former manager was remembered as having faith in his men, being on intimate and friendly terms with them, and acting as an equal. He'd give a man a second chance, would wink at the personal use of plant property and

---

[20] Reprinted with permission of the Free Press of Glencoe from *Patterns of Industrial Bureaucracy* by Alvin Gouldner, p. 55. Copyright 1954 by The Free Press, a corporation. First italics mine.

[21] *Ibid.*, p. 63.

product. He was sincere, not feigning that folksiness that Merton has called "pseudo-gemeinschaft." He was a man who made his own decisions without everlastingly deferring until he could consult the main office.)

In this situation, bureaucratic rules became a personal and an organizational defense. They helped to deflect antagonism from the new manager (who merely mediated the rules) to the front office where they originated. The hierarchical organization of bureaucracy lowered the visibility of top echelons, blurring targets of antagonism. Strategic replacements in middle management created a cadre of the loyal and obligated, eliminated some dissidents while generating enough anxiety among others to prompt them to try, at least superficially, to stay in line.

Such an increase in bureaucratization is probably a function of frequent managerial shifts. In this plant Gouldner reports that average tenure for six managers was four years. The more frequent the shift of incumbents, the more necessary, for group stability, that rules and roles remain unchanged. Gouldner puts it this way:

> . . . Bureaucratization is . . . functional to a group subjected to an institutionally compelled high rate of succession while, in turn, a high rate of succession operates as a selecting mechanism, sifting out or disposing to bureaucratic modes of organization.[22]

And so the old rules were tightened up, new rules made and both enforced with dispassionate vigor.

This was easier among the factory workers, on the surface, than among the miners, underground. These latter were a spontaneous, profane, equalitarian, friendly, tough, hard-working, and cohesive group. (Miners were seen as proud of the quantity and quality of their work—although absenteeism was high—and surface workers as goldbrickers.) Instances of reveling and rebelling were regarded as naturally attending the danger of their work. The extension of bureaucratic rules was not, then, a marked success among the miners. Among them, supervisors found the no-absenteeism rule unworkable.

But distinctions are seen not only between the two work settings (surface and mine) but between types of rules—distinctions as to who initiates them, whose values are supported and whose violated by them, how violations of the rules are explained and how they

---

[22] *Ibid.*, p. 97.

affect the standing of workers and management. Such distinctions lead to the proposal that there are at least three types of bureaucracy: mock, representative, and punishment-centered bureaucracies. Gouldner uses the rule against smoking to illustrate the regulations of a mock bureaucracy, a rule that held only when the inspector from the insurance company appeared, and about whose coming everyone was warned. The complex set of safety rules in the development of which workers were highly involved is used as an illustration of representative bureaucracy. Finally, the rules bearing on unexcused absence are analyzed as an illustration of punishment-centered bureaucracy, management disciplining workers, or workers using grievance procedures against management. This elaboration of Weber's conception of bureaucratic organization is summarized in Gouldner's table, reproduced as Table 12–2.

We have here an extension and refinement of Weber's views on bureaucracy.[23] Where Weber saw expertise and discipline as compatible twin traits of rational organization, Gouldner finds contradictory tensions between them. In his "representative bureaucracy," the rules supporting expertise in differentiated roles are means toward common ends. In the "punishment-centered" bureaucracy— the stress here is on discipline—the rule is an end in itself, valued only by one party. In the first pattern, education is stressed as a remedy for defaulting on expectations. The second pattern metes out punishment. The first joins workers and management in a collaboration ostensibly to create safe work conditions, but having, additionally, the latent function of enhancing group cohesiveness. The second, the discipline-stressing pattern, entails an adversary relationship and is divisive.

If such distinctions are implicit in Weber's formulation, they are not brought out. And while the German sociologist would be the last to assert that there existed, anywhere, an actual example of his distilled form of bureaucratic organization, he does not offer, as Gouldner does, a concrete example of the "mix" of bureaucratic patterns. Gouldner also gives us some notion of how the effectiveness of a bureaucratic organization may vary, depending on whether rules are imposed from uppermost echelons or agreed to throughout the ranks (as in the case of the study by Coch and French that we

---

[23] This is the case, too, with Peter Blau's important study of bureaucratic organization in two government agencies. See his *The Dynamics of Bureaucracy* (Chicago: University of Chicago Press, 1955).

TABLE 12–2

Summary of Factors Associated with the Three Patterns of Bureaucracy

MOCK	REPRESENTATIVE	PUNISHMENT-CENTERED

1. Who Usually Initiates the Rules?

The rule or rules are imposed on the group by some "outside" agency. *Neither* workers nor management, neither superiors nor subordinates, identify themselves with or participate in the establishment of the rules or view them as their own.	*Both* groups initiate the rules and view them as their own.	The rule arises in response to the pressure of *either* workers or management, but is *not jointly* initiated by them. The group which does not initiate the rule views it as imposed upon it by the other.
e.g.—The "no-smoking" rule was initiated by the insurance company.	e.g.—Pressure was exerted by union *and* management to initiate and develop the safety program. Workers and supervisors could make modifications of the program at periodic meetings.	e.g.—Through their union the workers initiated the bidding system. Supervisors viewed it as something to which the Company was forced to adhere.

2. Whose Values Legitimate the Rules?

Neither superiors nor subordinates can, ordinarily, legitimate the rule in terms of their own values.	Usually, *both* workers and management can legitimate the rules in terms of their own key values.	*Either* superiors or subordinates alone consider the rule legitimate; the other may concede on grounds of expediency, but does not define the rule as legitimate.
	e.g.—Management legitimated the safety program by tying it to *production.* Workers legitimized it via their values on personal and bodily welfare, maintenance of income, and cleanliness.	e.g.—Workers considered the bidding system "fair," since they viewed it as minimizing personal favoritism in the distribution of jobs. Supervisors conformed to it largely because they feared the consequences of deviation.

3. Whose Values Are Violated by Enforcement of the Rules?

Enforcement of the rule violates the values of *both groups.*	Under most conditions, enforcement of the rules entails violations of	Enforcement of the rules violates the values of only one group, *either*

TABLE 12–2 (Continued)

MOCK	REPRESENTATIVE	PUNISHMENT-CENTERED
e.g.—If the no-smoking rule were put into effect, it would violate the value on "personal equality" held by workers and supervisors, since office workers would still be privileged to smoke.	*neither* group's values. e.g.—It is only under comparatively *exceptional* circumstances that enforcement of the safety rules interfered with a value held by management, say, a value on production.	superiors or subordinates. e.g.—The bidding rules threatened management's value on the use of skill and ability as criteria for occupational recruitment

4. What Are the Standard Explanations of Deviations from the Rules?

The deviant pattern is viewed as an expression of "uncontrollable" needs or of "human nature." e.g.—People were held to smoke because of "nervousness."	Deviance is attributed to ignorance or *well-intentioned carelessness*—i.e., it is an unanticipated by-product of behavior oriented to some other end, and thus an "accident." This we call a "utilitarian" conception of deviance. e.g.—Violation of the safety rule might be seen as motivated by concern for production, rather than by a deliberate intention to have accidents. If for example, a worker got a hernia, this might be attributed to his ignorance of proper lifting technique.	In the main, deviance is attributed to *deliberate* intent. Deviance is thought to be the deviant's *end*. This we call a "voluntaristic" conception of deviance. e.g.—When a worker was absent without an excuse, this was *not* viewed as an expression of an uncontrollable impulse, or as an unanticipated consequence of other interests. It was believed to be *willful*.

5. What Effects Do the Rules Have Upon the Status of the Participants?

Ordinarily, deviation from the rule is status-enhancing for workers and management *both*. Conformance to the rule would be status-impairing for both.	Usually, deviation from the rules impairs the status of superiors *and* subordinates, while conformance ordinarily permits both a measure of status improvement.	Conformance to or deviation from the rules leads to status gains *either* for workers or supervisors, but not for both, and to status losses for the other.

TABLE 12–2 (Concluded)

MOCK	REPRESENTATIVE	PUNISHMENT-CENTERED
e.g.—Violation of the no-smoking rule tended to minimize the visibility of status differentials, by preventing the emergence of a privileged stratum of smokers.	e.g.—The safety program increased the prestige of workers' jobs by improving the cleanliness of the plant (the "good housekeeping" component), as well as enabling workers to initiate action for their superiors through the safety meetings. It also facilitated management's ability to realize its production obligations, and provided it with legitimations for extended control over the worker.	e.g.—Workers' conformance to the bidding system allowed them to escape from tense relations with certain supervisors, or to secure jobs and promotions without dependence upon supervisory favors. It deprived supers of the customary prerogative of recommending workers for promotion or for hiring.

6. Summary of Defining Characteristics or Symptoms

MOCK	REPRESENTATIVE	PUNISHMENT-CENTERED
(a) Rules are neither enforced by management nor obeyed by workers. (b) Usually entails little conflict between the two groups. (c) Joint violation and evasion of rules is buttressed by the informal sentiments of the participants.	(a) Rules are both enforced by management and obeyed by workers. (b) Generates a few tensions, but little overt conflict. (c) Joint support for rules buttressed by informal sentiments, mutual participation, initiation, and education of workers and management.	(a) Rules either enforced by workers or management, and evaded by the other. (b) Entails relatively great tension and conflict. (c) Enforced by punishment and supported by the informal sentiments of *either* workers or management.

Source: Reprinted with permission of The Free Press of Glencoe from *Patterns of Industrial Bureaucracy* by Alvin Gouldner, pp. 216, 217. Copyright 1954 by The Free Press, a corporation.

shall presently consider). And he shows how the rules affect different sectors of a bureaucratic organization, to whose benefit or disadvantage the rules of work redound.

Now in summary, let's list a few tentative propositions that emerge from this research on the structure of work roles in gypsum factory and mine.

First, bureaucratic rules are set up and enforced when relationships break down. As we say when things go awry, "There oughta be a law." The sort of rule invoked depends on A's interpretation of B's failure to meet expectations. When this failure is thought to be due to technical inadequacy (carelessness or ignorance, as in the case of violating safety rules), the "response will take the form of developing a 'representative bureaucracy,' but when it is deemed a matter of intentional defaulting (insubordination), the organization of work moves toward a 'punishment-centered bureaucracy'."[24]

Bureaucratic rules are instituted when they are thought to be correct both as to what *is* and what *ought* to be in a given circumstance—when they are seen as technically correct and morally right. But when they are so defined depends, among other things, on the conditions of work. Danger is one such condition that may affect bureaucratic rules: such rules were relaxed for the gypsum miners, allowing absenteeism and drinking to a degree not tolerable in the factory. To do otherwise would have been technically incorrect, since such rules were virtually unenforceable. And a rule whose violation cannot be punished is not only a useless rule: it contaminates responses to other rules. It would have been morally incorrect since it was assumed that the hazards of mining required such Dionysian safety valves.

Worker resistance to bureaucratic rules depends on the solidarity of the work group and on the degree to which such rules and roles threaten or enhance the standing of workers and management. (Both of these variables come into play, as we shall see, in resistance to changes in work roles among operators in a pajama factory.) Resistance also depends on the compatibility of bureaucratic rules with workers' beliefs. On all these counts Gouldner's miners were a "tight little island," a unified group with particular beliefs and behaviors, making the application of bureaucratic rules impractical.

Such work rules have consequences, some of which Gouldner's research helps us see. Being public and general, bureaucratic rules take the curse out of supervision by making both boss and worker subject to the same requirements. Thus the dignity of the subordinate is safeguarded. "Impersonal and general rules serve in part to obscure the existence of power disparities which are not legitimate in terms of the group's norms"[25]—in this case, equalitarian norms. Being definitive and relatively unambiguous, they may be thought

---

[24] Gouldner, *op. cit.*, p. 233.
[25] *Ibid.*, p. 165.

to have been worked out with more deliberation than off-the-cuff orders. Seeming, then, less capricious or arbitrary, they may elicit less resistance, be more likely to win compliance. Obviously, they reduce the number of orders that need be given, thus the number of interactions between superior and subordinate in which the former will exhibit his authority. The control such rules exert is remote, from above and beyond. This is advantageous especially where immediate supervision is impossible. Again, where rules are public and general, sanctions for their violation became legitimate: otherwise not.

> . . . By and large, aggression and punishments directed toward in-group members are not preferred patterns of behavior in our culture and require especially unambiguous justification. Bureaucratic rules are thereby particularly functional in a context in which reliance upon the in-group has been shaken.[26]

Such rules also provide a base line for exceptions and favors, so supporting worker morale. As Gouldner put it: "Formal rules gave supervisors something with which they could 'bargain' in order to secure informal cooperation from workers."[27] Bureaucratic rules also promote apathy to the extent that they define minimum expectations and a level at which, therefore, workers are likely to perform. There is a yield for the worker as well as for management, for such rules "permit 'activity' without 'participation'; they enable an employee to work without being emotionally committed to it."[28] Finally, bureaucratic rules may reduce tension in the work group when they stipulate and clarify the chain of command and communication, support and legitimate reciprocal expectations, apply to all members of a category, bridging different belief and value systems, hold unofficial dealings to a tolerable minimum and support the need for close supervision. "Bureaucratic rules do not eliminate the need for close supervision but, instead, primarily function to reduce the tensions created by it."[29] The sequence, as Gouldner puts it is this: low motivation and inadequate performance in the work role lead to close supervision, creating tensions which are mitigated if not resolved through the development of rules that reinforce a low level of performance and lack of commitment to the job.

---

[26] *Ibid.*, p. 172.
[27] *Ibid.*, p. 173.
[28] *Ibid.*, p. 176.
[29] *Ibid.*, p. 177.

These are the suggested functions of bureaucratic rules that emerge from one piece of research on the social structure of a work group. Let us turn, now, from the matter of rules to that of roles, to work roles and the dimensions for their analysis.

WORK ROLES: SOME DIMENSIONS FOR ANALYSIS

When we talk about such a structure of relationships as Gouldner observed in the gypsum plant, we find ourselves thinking, on the one hand, about the rules (beliefs, standards, and regulations that guide conduct) and, on the other hand, about the roles that embody these rules, enabling men to work together. Underlying Weber's work, and Gouldner's extension of it, is the cultural emphasis that struck Weber as capturing the essence of modern societies, the *rule of rationality*. This means the calculating assessment and incessant improvement of means to reach unambiguously stated ends. It is an emphasis that leads to (1) a careful classification of things, persons, problems to be dealt with, (2) a treatment of members of each class in the same way (since they constitute the same problem), and (3) in terms of their observable—and preferably measurable—performances, by (4) workers who, as a result of specialization are distinctively competent (to produce or sell the article, cure the patient, handle the client's problem).

But as Gouldner's research instructs us, a narrow conception of rationality that disregards irrational components of conduct is misconceived. Applied research confronts precisely this problem in ferreting out the connections between productivity and work relationships: the needs of social beings at work, as they affect that work. From a shallow perspective such needs sometimes seem irrelevant to the task at hand. Yet the evidence shows that productivity is connected with work satisfaction, while the latter is linked with a number of aspects of worker relationships: extent to which machine-paced work is restricting, the sense of participation or helplessness in decision making, degree of knowledge of, or identification with, the end product, rate of change in status relative to others, spread and average length of time of interaction with other workers, with superiors and subordinates, cohesiveness of work group, and the like. Rationality in bureaucratic organization must, then, be redefined to include a complex cluster of social factors affecting work and workers. And the general research issue then becomes: what aspects of human relationships and their constituent roles are relevant to what sorts of work? Thus, in the illustration I used in Chapter 6, the nurse's work requires (as Thorner contends: it is a matter for empirical testing) affective neutrality, lest emotional attachment to one patient deprive others of deserved care. Here the worker must treat all members of a class (maternity cases, diabetics, appendectomies, arthritics) in the same way, *limiting* her dealings with the "customer" to interaction promoting the cure. These are Parsons' role characteristics of universalism and specificity.

Such characteristics as these provide analytic dimensions for studying the roles of men at work. If we were to rely on Parsons' scheme for analyzing the different ways in which work roles are patterned, or must be patterned if a set of work relationships is to be productive, we would characterize the roles in a bureaucratic setting as emphasizing specificity, universalism, performance, and affective neutrality. Consider some examples.

While the child's claims, to which the mother responds, may cover an enormous range—and this may be true of close-kin roles in general—business and industry bend the worker's role toward specificity. Through his union, the worker, too, has narrowed the range, or reduced the diffuseness of his role as contracts enumerate in ever greater detail the claims that may legitimately be made of him. This specificity attaches not only to a horizontal division of labor among peers at work but is also seen in the intricate, hierarchical division of statuses. Thus an automobile assembly line worker says of his foreman: "Since he [has become] a foreman I can't find myself at ease with him. It's not that exactly, but I feel uncomfortable some way. . . . Before I would kid and say things, but now I don't know how he would take it."[30]

Some relationships are determined by the particular set of characteristics of the person toward whom we act. To deal with another on the basis of traits peculiarly associated with his name is to do so *particularistically*. But at work the *universalistic* prescription reigns, at least if it is a matter of productivity and not one of subvention and sinecure. Perhaps in no setting so much as at work are men disposed to take the sociologist's perspective, thinking in

---

[30] Quoted from a worker's response to Arthur N. Turner when asked how often, on an average day, he talked with his foreman; from Whyte, *op. cit.*, p. 191.

terms of job descriptions or classifications—that is, in terms of roles —rather than the particular incumbent. Friendship, like kinship, becomes an irrelevant if not a detrimental criterion for arranging roles and relationships at work.

Again, while some roles are largely defined by such ascribed traits as age, or sex (men are seldom mothers), work roles are defined in our society on the basis of achievement in prescribed tasks. (This is not wholly true. In the factory, as in Congress, seniority—in effect, age—may confer laurels on some brows innocent of achievement.) There are, in any case, two inconsistent principles at work here. The contrast between these two modes of orienting work roles is nowhere clearer than in certain instances among the new nations. Here, in the organization of work or government, the emphasis on demonstrated performance rather than some ascribed quality may run counter to traditional criteria for assigning roles, conferring political plums, according rewards. Western-educated leaders in Ghana had to face antagonism, especially from northern tribesmen, in allocating offices on the basis of civil service ratings. By long established criteria, such assignments should be dictated by kin and tribal ties, ascriptive criteria.

The fourth of those variables in terms of which roles are patterned (Parsons calls them "pattern variables") is that of degree of affectivity. Some roles are suffused with emotion, especially familial and religious roles. But the world of work is for the head, not the heart. Not that the heart is irrelevant: it may be *used,* if such use is demonstrably profitable. (It is doubtful that a large New York department store is prompted solely by sentiment to buy a full-page advertisement in the *New York Times* to salute Casey Stengel on his birthday.) In the realm of work, more than in any other sector of society, quantity and quality of product and service can be assessed. Measures of worker productivity, quality control, the competition of the market place (for some, but by no means all, goods and services)—these encourage the suppression of sentiment and promote a consciously hardheaded manipulation of means to achieve the end of profit.

Thus the structure of relationships we call bureaucracy would seem to entail roles in which the orientation is toward specificity rather than diffuseness of role, toward a universalistic, rather than a particularistic posture in dealing with persons and problems, toward achievement or performance (rather than ascriptively oriented toward qualities imputed to the other), and with an emphasis on reducing "merely" sentimental considerations.

Two of these "pattern variables" you will notice, deal with cultural standards guiding performance in role: universalism-particularism, and achievement-ascription. The other two, while not independent of cultural prescriptions, yet have to do with personality factors affecting role performance: affectivity-affective neutrality, and the diffuseness or specificity which condition our readiness to respond to another's claims. If we crosscut these dimensions of role performance we get 16 possible combinations of variables describing role patterns.[31] Thus:

| | | PARTICULARISM | | UNIVERSALISM | |
		AFFECTIVITY	AFFECTIVE NEUTRALITY	AFFECTIVITY	AFFECTIVE NEUTRALITY
Ascription	Diffuseness	1	2	3	4
	Specificity	5	6	7	8
Achievement	Diffuseness	9	10	11	12
	Specificity	13	14	15	16

The cell numbered 16 combines those traits I have used to describe the worker's role in a bureaucratic social structure. (Perhaps the citizen's role might be correctly characterized by the combination in cell 3, or that of any mother by the role characteristics combined in cell 1.) But whether such abstract analysis of appropriate role performance in work, or other, roles is correct must depend, first, on clear operational definitions of these abstract terms and, second, their testing in actual work settings. Such tests would aim to discover whether certain combinations of role characteristics, in contrast to others, promoted productivity, worker satisfaction, worker-management conflict, and the like.

Such role dimensions as Parsons' pattern variables provide a kit of conceptual tools for analyzing a structure of work relationships. They also suggest the possibility of a temporal shift in the patterning of work relationships, one paralleling the notions of Tönnies,

---

[31] See Talcott Parsons and Edward A. Shils (eds.), *Toward a General Theory of Action* (Cambridge, Mass.: Harvard University Press, 1952), where this scheme is developed and discussed.

Durkheim, and others: *gemeinschaft* to *gesellschaft,* mechanical to organic solidarity, and the like. Traditional forms of work organization may have involved, to a greater degree than at present, a particularistic, affectively tinctured, diffusely defined and ascriptively oriented roles. But in a way this is scientific double jeopardy, for it adds unsupported historical speculation to an empirically ill-supported set of high-level abstractions.

Let us move to a more concrete level by considering the structure of the labor force, changes in it, and the corollary of labor which is leisure.

WORK ROLES: CHANGES IN LABOR AND LEISURE

Work roles are conditioned, in the large, by broad cultural currents that modify men's wants and capabilities. (In the economist's terms, there are changes in demand and supply of labor resources.) Underlying the great shift from work in extractive industry (agriculture, mining, forestry, fishing) is the upward sweep of technology and invention, the stress on science that enables an elaborate technology, and the commitment to education that promotes science. Differently put, changes in our knowledge of what is and what ought to be exert influences reflected in the changed structure of the labor force.

Through the centuries, modal occupational roles have changed more dramatically than we time-anchored children of one age can readily imagine. From hunting and gathering economies, man's work shifted to pastoral activity, herding, and then to the cultivation of the soil. Agricultural activities became increasingly complex and mechanized while commercial and industrial occupations took over ever larger sectors of the labor force. Now we are in a time when electronic communication, servomechanisms, and control systems displace old work roles and an increasing proportion of the labor force devotes itself to research, development, education, the professions, and sundry services. The changed distribution of work roles is suggested in Figure 12–1 and Table 12–3.

Advanced techniques greatly increasing productivity while reducing the required input of human energy have altered the distribution of work roles. And the direction of change suggests more of the same in the future. An undated Office of Education brochure estimates that employment in professional and technical occupations will increase by better than 40 percent between 1960 and 1970, in clerical and sales work by about 30 percent. Percentage increases, during this decade, in service workers, proprietors and managers, and skilled workers are all estimated at +20 to +30.

Such a shift implies a parallel change in schooling, for occupation and education are tightly linked institutional spheres. This is attested by the fact that in 1959, professional and technical workers

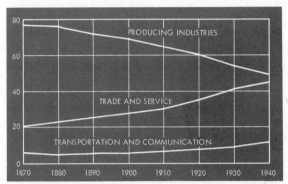

Source: Delbert C. Miller and William H. Form, *Industrial Sociology* (New York: Harper & Bros., 1951), Figure 21, p.138, and taken originally from Dewey Anderson and Percy E. Davidson, *Occupational Trends in the United States* (Stanford: Stanford University Press, 1940), p. 35.

FIG. 12-1. Changes in broad occupational categories as percentages of gainfully employed.

had completed 16.2 years of education, proprietors and managers 12.4 years, clerical and sales workers 12.5 years, skilled, semiskilled, and service workers 11.0, 9.9, and 9.7 years of education, respectively.

It is also commonly assumed that labor and leisure are linked, that leisure hours have increased and that, indeed, we face the awesome prospect of more free time than we know how to use. But the evidence suggests that the threat of leisure may be exaggerated.

There is no question that some people have more leisure, and some more leisure than they wish. Harold Wilensky writes (I am leaning heavily on his work): "There is a kind of forced withdrawal from work among three categories: (1) the involuntarily retired, (2) the intermittently unemployed, and (3) the chronically unemployed—all growing segments of the population."[32] The first category is that of the oldsters. Other sectors of the population enjoying,

---

[32] Wilensky, *op. cit.*, p. 131.

TABLE 12–3

Distribution of Occupational Roles in the U.S. Labor Force, 1900 to 1960, in Percent

OCCUPATIONAL CATEGORY	YEAR OF DECENNIAL CENSUS							CHANGE, 1900–1960
	1960	1950	1940	1930	1920	1910	1900	
Clerical and kindred workers	15.1	12.3	9.6	8.9	8.0	4.7	4.5	+10.6
Professional, technical, and kindred workers	11.8	8.6	7.5	6.8	5.4	4.7	4.3	+ 7.5
Operatives and kindred workers	19.4	20.4	18.4	15.8	15.6	14.6	12.8	+ 6.6
Service workers (except private household)	8.9	7.9	7.0	5.7	4.5	4.6	3.6	+ 5.3
Craftsmen, foremen and kindred workers	14.2	14.2	12.0	12.8	13.0	11.6	10.5	+ 3.7
Managers, officials, proprietors (except farm)	8.8	8.7	7.3	7.4	6.6	6.6	5.8	+ 3.0
Sales workers	7.5	7.0	6.7	6.3	4.9	4.7	4.5	+ 3.0
Farmers and farm managers	4.1	7.4	10.4	12.4	15.3	16.5	19.9	−15.8
Farm laborers and foremen	2.4	4.4	7.0	8.8	11.7	14.4	17.7	−15.3
Laborers (except farm and mine)	5.1	6.6	9.4	11.0	11.6	12.0	12.5	− 7.4
Private household workers	2.8	2.6	4.8	4.1	3.3	5.0	5.4	− 2.6

Sources: Donald J. Bogue, *The Population of the United States* (New York: Free Press of Glencoe, 1959), p. 475. His information is drawn from *Current Population Reports,* Series P-50, No. 85, June, 1958, Table F and from David L. Kaplan and M. Claire Dasey, "Occupational Trends in the United States, 1900 to 1950," *Bureau of the Census Working Paper No. 5* (1958). Data for 1960 are from U.S. Bureau of the Census, *United States Census of Population: 1960,* Vol. I, *Characteristics of the Population* (Washington, D.C.: U.S. Government Printing Office, 1964), p. lxxvii. I have added the final column and rearranged the sequence of categories from highest to lowest gains and losses.

or suffering, enforced leisure are the foreign born, Negroes, and the young.

It is clear, too, that if we use the nineteenth century as our base point for comparison, hours of work have declined from horrendous highs to what we now deem reasonable. In the century from 1850 to 1950 "we moved from a 70- or 72-hour workweek down to a 40-hour week—a 12-hour day, six-day week to an eight-hour day, five-day week."[33] But if we are less historically parochial we find that, based

---

[33] Harold L. Wilensky, "The Uneven Distribution of Leisure: The Impact of Economic Growth on 'Free Time,'" *Social Problems,* Vol. IX, No. 1 (Summer, 1961), p. 130.

on estimates of annual and lifetime leisure, "the skilled urban worker has now achieved the position of his *13th century* counterpart, whose long work-day, seasonally varied, was offset by many holidays, rest periods, and long vacations; annual hours of work now, as then, remain in the range 1900–2500."[34] Wilensky goes on to comment on the work role of women, and that of the "pace-setting elites":

> On balance, the female "work week" may be as long as it was a century ago . . . for women in all the rich countries, both opportunity and motivation to work run high. . . . It seems plain that emancipation, while it has released women for the labor market, has not to an equal extent released them from housewifery. Studies of the weekly round of women report a range of averages of 50 to 80 hours a week in housework, child care, and paid labor. If a woman takes a job today, she has to figure on adding her work week to a forty- or fifty-hour "homemaking" minimum [this especially at the two peak periods of extra-household work for women, ages 20–24 and over age 40].
>
> People in the upper strata have in fact lost out [in lifetime leisure]. Even though their work lives are shorter and their vacations longer than those of lower strata, they work many hours, week after week—sometimes reaching a truly startling lifetime total."[35]

Wilensky estimates that workers in the long-hours category will increase, in their proportion of the male labor force, from 20.5 percent in 1950 to 26.9 percent in 1970.

Our society, apparently, is one in which voluntary leisure is not, nor does it threaten to become, such an oppressive burden as we are sometimes led to think. But enforced leisure is another matter. Its uneven distribution can readily be seen as a practical as well as a research problem. For here "an old paradox becomes more prominent: those whose productivity is highest will work longer hours partly to support the forced leisure of men rendered obsolete by the activities of long-hour men."[36]

In a study from which most of the foregoing data were drawn, one based on a probability sample of six professional groups and a cross section of the "middle mass" in the Detroit area, Wilensky found that 10 percent of his 1,156 respondents were "moonlighters," holding more than one job. This worker had the following distinctive characteristics: an erratic work history, blocked mobility, a

---

[34] Wilensky, "Varieties of Work Experience," *op. cit.*, p. 130.

[35] *Ibid.;* the two quotations are from pp. 131 and 130, respectively.

[36] *Ibid.*, p. 133.

sense of being worse off than others he compared himself to, and, in addition, two crucial traits. The moonlighter was caught in a life-cycle squeeze, at that point in his career when support of dependents exerted most pressure and the gap between wants and resources was greatest. He also worked on a peculiar schedule, or a schedule that was more under his own control than is commonly the case.

Study of time devoted to work, leisure and changes in the proportion of each is a problem in accurate description for the sociologist. (So is the content of the leisure, the *way* members of the group spend their time.) Even as a descriptive problem it is not simple, since patterns of labor and leisure vary widely among different categories: age, sex, race, nativity, class, occupation, region, religion, and the like. Such differences may lead to intriguing questions. For example, Wilensky raises the question whether long hours are to entrepreneurial Jews what moonlighting is to ambitious Catholics. And of course you'll recall that the whole pursuit of the problem raised by Weber in the *Protestant Ethic and the Spirit of Capitalism* has to do with different orientations to work related to religious affiliation.

Another aspect of the work role—and the last we shall consider in this cursory introduction to the sociology of work—bears on the matter of incentives: inducements and resistances to work. An empirical study of resistance to change in the work role will provide a concrete example of social-scientific inquiry in this field.

WORK ROLES: REWARDS AND RESISTANCES

Perhaps a few are induced to work from a sense of obligation. (It has become almost a standard statement for some high-ranking government officials to say, in resigning, that continued government service is a sacrifice they can no longer impose on their families. They have been working, presumably, out of a sense of civic obligation which, in hours and income, conflicts with another obligation to take up work roles less demanding in time and more rewarding in income.) For a favored few, avocation and vocation are identical: the content of the work is rewarding in itself. (Teachers sometimes ruefully console themselves that their psychic income compensates for the limited largesse of the tax-minded citizenry. But for most, wages and salaries are a major inducement to perform in the work role.)

Income as Symbol of Relationships

Income is some index, however crude, of what we do to and for others. Represented in cash, it is an enormously flexible, symbolic medium for exchanging goods and services. Its use, following unimagined channels as it leaves the spender's hands, binds together

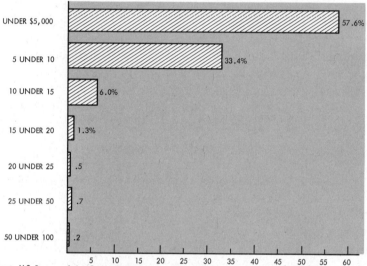

Source: U.S. Bureau of the Census, *Individual Income Tax Returns for 1960* (Washington, D.C.: U.S. Government Printing Office, 1961), Table 1, p. 15.

FIG. 12–2. Percent of 60,592,712 income tax returns for indicated gross income categories (000 omitted), United States, 1960. The percentage total for reported incomes under $100,000 is 99.7%. For the top three categories comprising .3%, the data are as follows (these are absolute numbers):

$100,000 under $150,000, 14,221 returns $ 500,000 under $1,000,000, 735 returns
$150,000 under $200,000, 4,413 returns $1,000,000 or more,   306 returns
$200,000 under $500,000, 4,848 returns

in a real if tenuous network great numbers of people unknown to one another. The rarity and value of each person's contribution to others is registered—not always in terms of stable or "correct" standards, equitably applied—in the distribution of income. For the United States this distribution (1960) is shown in Figure 12–2.[37]

---

[37] Another note on methods. Income distributions are typically skewed, as this one is. Since the mean $(\overline{X})$ is influenced by extreme values, its use on such a distribution would give a misleadingly high figure for average income. One should, then, fall back on a measure of central tendency less susceptible to extreme values. This is why the median is preferred as a summary figure for income distributions.

Some shift in the distribution of work rewards is suggested in Figure 12–3, a change probably stemming from the leverage of organized labor, and from legislation setting minimum wages for workers, providing income for the retired and, through the tool of taxation, redistributing gross national income.

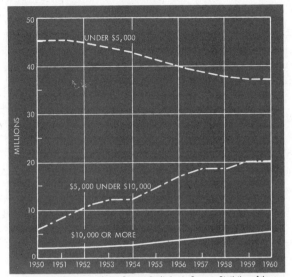

Source: U.S. Bureau of the Census, *Preliminary Report, Statistics of Income —1960, Individual Income Tax Returns,* (Washington, D.C.: U.S. Government Printing Office,1961).

FIG. 12–3. **Number of returns, by size of adjusted gross income, 1950–1960 ($N = 61,027,931$ returns).**

We are told almost daily in the press how people resist work when they deem their cash rewards inadequate (although strikes and slowdowns usually involve other demands in addition to wage increases). But certainly ever since the classic study at the Hawthorne plant of Western Electric in Chicago, no informed person could conceive of wages as the sole significant reward for the worker, especially in his day-to-day operations. (In this study, variations in lighting, in rest periods, in the provision of refreshments, and length of working day brought increased productivity. But so did a return to the original conditions with a regular working day, no refreshments, and no specified rest periods.)[38]

---

[38] See Elton Mayo, *The Human Problems of an Industrial Civilization* (New York: Macmillan Co., 1933), and F. J. Roethlisberger and W. J. Dickson, *Management and the Worker* (Cambridge, Mass.: Harvard University Press, 1939).

A Research Example: Rewards in, and Resistances to Work

An illuminating study of rewards in, and resistances to, work is that by Lester Coch and John R. P. French, Jr.[39] Work roles studied were those of employees in a Virginia pajama factory, about 600 of them, of whom 500 were women operators. Workers' average age was 23 and average number of years of schooling was 8.

Let's look at this research in some detail, for it helps us answer more adequately, and see more clearly the complexity of the question: What makes Sammy run? What induces us to work? Furthermore, it sharpens our appreciation of the social ends and means of work, the significance of group membership that we discussed in Chapter 4 and underlined in the statement of Karl Polanyi (page 511). Finally, it is a first-rate example of the fruitful interplay of deductive and inductive, theoretical and empirical, aspects of inquiry.

The investigators were trying to learn what accounts for resistance to—or conversely, for ease or flexibility in adapting to—changes in the work role. Such changes are common in competitive enterprises, especially those affected by a high rate of innovation. (The automobile industry with its annual transformations is a good example.) As in many work settings, adaptation to such changes can be measured by productivity—in the case of our pajama makers, before and after modifications in their work roles.

After a change in the pattern of work, the transfers (those whose work roles were altered) had to give up some familiar ways of behaving and learn new ones. While the drop in productivity entailed by transfer was compensated for so that, on the average, workers did not need to suffer a drop in income, Coch and French observed what we might call the Sysiphus effect. (Sysiphus was condemned by the gods to strive eternally to push, up a great hill, a gigantic boulder that incessantly rolled down.) A worker strove to push her production up to the standard level of 60 units an hour, and then, her work role altered, level of production rolled back on her again. The changed work role, with its new problems apparently induced a sense of failure, feelings of frustration and lowered aspiration. These, in turn, were reflected in expressions of resentment and aggression toward management, higher rates of absen-

---

[39] Lester Coch and John R. P. French, Jr., "Overcoming Resistance to Change," *Human Relations*, Vol. I (1948).

teeism and turnover (quitting). Among 198 operators whose work roles had not been changed in 34 weeks, mean rate of turnover was 4.5 percent per month. Among 85 who had been transferred within this period, mean turnover rate was 12 percent per month.

Attempting in a preliminary theoretical statement to explain resistance to change in work roles, Coch and French put it this way: Resistance to such change stems from frustration. The extent of frustration is a function of the relative strength of two forces, one toward, the other away from achievement of given production norms. The upward force depends in part on the difficulty of the job and the worker's skill. The downward or restraining force increases as number of units produced asymptotically approaches some limit. "Other things equal, the faster an operator is sewing the more difficult it is to increase her speed by a given amount."[40] If either of these forces is weak, frustration will be low, and "the strength of frustration is a function of the weaker of these two opposing forces, provided that the weaker force is stronger than a certain minimum necessary to produce frustration."[41]

Now such a formulation fits the facts about learning and relearning of work roles, It would lead us to predict just such learning curves as those in Figure 12–4. But it does not help us understand why workers transferred, in contrast to those not transferred, are unwilling to learn. That it is a matter of willingness—more precisely, of motivation—and not skill seems indicated, since skilled and unskilled operators had comparable recovery rates after modification of their work roles.

The investigators were led, then, to look for some other factor accounting for resistance to change (and, by implication, the rewards experienced in nonchange). They write that strong, group-anchored sentiments seemed to generate on the one hand negative attitudes toward management while, on the other hand, "changed groups with high we-feeling and positive cooperative attitudes [were those with the] best relearners."[42] The influence of such group standards is suggested in the record of one worker over a period of 40 days, the first 20 days as a member of a group with an apparent unofficial production norm of about 50 units (10 units below

---

[40] *Ibid.*, p. 517.
[41] *Ibid.*, p. 517.
[42] *Ibid.*, pp. 519, 520.

standard), and the last 20 days as a single worker. Here is the record.[43]

In the Group	
DAYS	UNITS PRODUCED PER DAY
1– 3	46
4– 6	52
7– 9	53
10–12	56
Scapegoating Begins	
13–16	55
17–20	48
Becomes a Single Worker	
21–24	83
25–28	92
29–32	92
33–36	91
37–40	92

Such evidence justifies the inference that group dimensions may help account for production-limiting characteristics of transferred workers. For while individual reactions to change (see Figure 12–4) may be understood as resulting from an interplay between two forces working for and against given levels of productivity, consistent differences between groups of workers in resistance to change appear to derive from characteristics of the groups themselves. Thus it seemed that "the most appropriate methods for overcoming the resistance to change would be group methods."[44] The dimension chosen as the independent variable in the experiment was the *level of group participation* in determining the change in work roles. The dependent variable was level of production and speed of recovery to prechange levels.

For the control group of hand pressers, the change in work

---

[43] *Ibid.*, pp. 519, 520.
[44] *Ibid.*, p. 520.

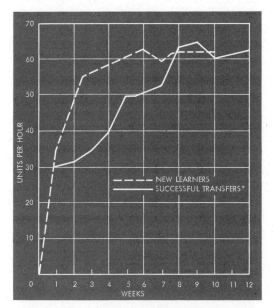

* Refers only to the percent of those whose work role was changed, who did not either quit or become chronic substandard operators.
Source: Lester Coch and John R. P. French, Jr., "Overcoming Resistance to Change," *Human Relations*, Vol. 1 (1948), p. 514.

FIG. 12–4. A comparison of the learning curve for new, inexperienced employees with the re-learning curve for only those transfers (38 percent) who eventually recover to standard production.

routines was made in the usual fashion, management determining the need, production department designing the change, and time study people setting the new piece rate. The record of these hand pressers then served as base point for assessing the significance of the experimental treatment. This treatment was of two sorts, both requiring worker participation in effecting a change in work pattern. The first (experimental group 1) included a presentation of the problem to all workers whose routine was to be changed, their designation of members of their group to be trained in the new pattern, and, finally, a retraining of all members of the group by their representatives who had learned the new techniques.

Experimental groups 2 and 3 raised the level of participation in these decisions by making all the operators direct participants in the whole process of change. The plan of the experiment is summarized in Table 12–4 and the results are given in Figure 12–5.

TABLE 12–4

Summary Scheme of the Coch and French Experiment in
"Overcoming Resistance to Change"

GROUP	CONTROLS	TREATMENT	EXTENT OF CHANGE INDUCED		OUTCOMES
			IN MINUTES ALLOWED FOR NEW TASK	AS PERCENT OF PREVIOUS TIME ALLOWANCE	
Exper'l$_1$ (N = 13)		Production problem presented, discussed and worker representatives participate in designing changes in work role, learn new process, then transmit to whole group at a second meeting	+1.8	9.4	Good relearning, at end of 14 days an average of 61 units/hour (60 being norm set) Cooperative, got on well with same supervisor as in control group. No quits in first 40 days. One act of aggression against supervisor
Exper'l$_2$ (N = 8)	Matched with respect to: 1. Previously established efficiency ratings 2. Degree of change in work role 3. Extent of cohesiveness observed in group	Same as above, except E$_2$ and E$_3$ are smaller groups, and all operators participate in designing changes in work roles	−1.2	8.0	Recovered faster than E$_1$, achieved efficiency ratings 14% above prechange level, worked well with supervisors, no acts of aggression, no quits in first 40 days
Exper'l$_3$ (N = 7)			−1.2	8.0	
Control		No change in way of altering work routines, production department changes work role, sets new piece rate, explains change, and new process is initiated (usual procedure)	+2.0	8.8	Little improvement, hostile, aggressive responses against supervisor, methods engineer, deliberate restriction of production, grievances filed, 17% quit in first 40 days

The control group in this first experiment was given the full participation treatment two and a half months later. The dramatic results of this second experiment are recorded in Figure 12–6.

The investigators tot up their findings in this paragraph.

The first experiment showed that the rate of recovery is directly proportional to the amount of participation, and that the rates of turn-

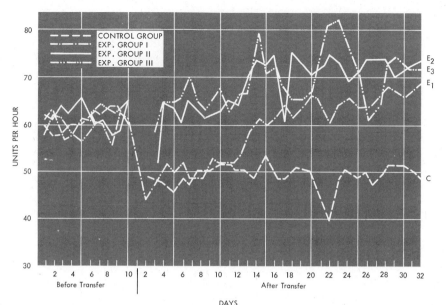

Source: Lester Coch and John R. P. French, Jr., "Overcoming Resistance to Change," *Human Relations*, Vol. I (1948), p. 522.

FIG. 12-5. The effects of participation through representation (group 1) and of total participation (groups 2 and 3) on recovery after an easy transfer.

over and aggression are inversely proportional to the amount of that participation. The second experiment demonstrated more conclusively that the results obtained depended on the experimental treatment rather than on personality factors like skill or aggressiveness, for identical individuals yielded markedly different results in the control treatment as contrasted with the total participation treatment.[45]

After summarizing their findings Coch and French look back, as good research people always do, to review and revise the theoretical position from which they started. They comment on the remarkable constancy of production levels over hundreds of individuals and groups in this factory. They suggest that where we find a situation like this, approximating a stable state in a work system, it is reasonable to infer roughly equivalent forces of opposite sign ($+$ and $-$), counterbalancing one another. This steady state was represented among the pajama factory workers by the standard production level of just over 60 units per hour achieved by all the groups (E_1, E_2, E_3, and C) just prior to their transfer. For the

---

[45] *Ibid.*, p. 524.

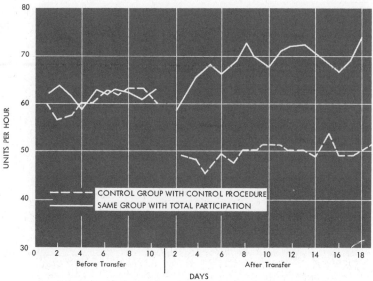

Source: Lester Coch and John R. P. French, Jr., "Overcoming Resistance to Change," *Human Relations*, Vol. I (1948), p. 523.

FIG. 12–6. Levels of productivity for workers (1) as controls in first experiment, and (2) two and a half months later, when given the full participation treatment.

control group, while production requirements remained the same (60 units per hour), the transfer entailed an increase in job difficulty confronted by workers less skilled in the new task than they had been in the old, familiar work roles. Thus the wish for a more comfortable situation (strain avoidance) should increase, depressing levels of production *unless* some countervailing force were to overcome this inclination toward strain avoidance. Coch and French describe level of strain avoidance this way.

$$\text{STRAIN AVOIDANCE} = \frac{(\text{JOB DIFFICULTY}) \times (\text{STIPULATED PRODUCTION LEVEL})}{\text{SKILL OF OPERATOR}}$$

Apparently the influence overcoming strain avoidance, for the experimental groups, consisted in forces induced by their acceptance of the change, an acceptance depending in large measure on workers' relationship to the change agent. For the control group the change agent was management, an adversary. One result was the setting of a group standard restricting production to 50 units per hour. There was little variation around this production mean: indeed, the standard deviation for number of units produced was lower for this group than for the other three. This points to the kind of group influence represented in the data on page 550.

But the change-inducing agent in the experimental situations was the worker himself, and his fellow workers, in addition to representatives of management. As Coch and French put it, "A force induced by a friend may be accepted in such a way that it acts more like an own force."[46] Furthermore, "the acceptance of an induced force sets up additional own forces in the same direction." Let me put it this way. The range and depth of a friend's characteristics that, in dealing repeatedly with him, we internalize, are much greater than those of an enemy. A friend, that is to say, carves out a greater sector of the self. Among friends, then, changes induced by others can be identified as one's own changes. This is precisely what is revealed in phrases used by members of the experimental groups. They spoke of the new job as "our job," and the new piece rates as "our rates." Thus a dyadic, adversary relationship between workers and management was transformed into a triadic relationship in which workers and representatives of management triangulated on a common problem of production.

❋   ❋   ❋   ❋

Clearly, the organization of men at work is a complex affair. The dimension of human relationships dealt with in the Coch and French study is only one of a host that may, depending on the problem, alter the patterns of men's behavior at work. How they may be altered depends in part on the prevailing rules of the game. (In the case we've been discussing, greater participation in decision making fits very well with our valuing of democratic process, although our rules for policy decisions seem to lean toward oligarchy in the private sphere, democracy in the public sphere. And this is worth more than a passing thought.)

We have seen how the rules governing production, distribution, and consumption of valued goods and services vary widely, depending on the cultural context. We have seen, too, that the world of work may—must, if it is to be fully apprehended—be viewed as a

---

[46] *Ibid.*, p. 529 (both quotations).

structure of relationships geared to the achievement of omnipresent needs. Thus the bureaucratic organization of great enterprises that typify our times may be seen both as a set of rules (values, and standards for achieving them) and as an intricate set of relationships.

It was Weber above all who gave impetus to the study of bureaucratic social structures. But it is doubtful that his formulation will stand without revision. One significant sequel to Weber's work we have seen in the research by Gouldner. Around the pivot of the problem of succession he illuminates the functions of bureaucratic rules, discriminates elements of the social structure of work (rather than treating it globally, as Weber did), and asks: what behaviors and beliefs have what effects on what parts of the structure, under what conditions? In the process he proposes three variations on the bureaucratic theme: mock, representative, and punishment-centered bureaucracies.

When we break down relationships into their constituent roles we look rather more microscopically at the social structure of work. There are many dimensions of roles which, depending on the problem, are appropriate for inquiry. Parsons offers such dimensions at a very general level of abstraction. These provide suggestive and stimulating take-off points for the study of work and other roles. At a more concrete level we have taken as an illustration the dimension of degree of participation in decision making as an aspect of the worker's role that had great significance for a group of women operators in a garment factory.

I've stressed, before, the interweaving of sectors of social life. In this chapter I noted in passing the study by Swanson and Miller that links the father's work role with patterns of child rearing. In the Gouldner study we saw how community and family relationships spilled over into the work setting of the gypsum factory. Work and family are not hermetically sealed and separated spheres. (If by no other means, the psychological mechanism of displacement builds a bridge between institutional domains: the disgruntled returning worker kicks the dog and maligns his wife.) Most of our discussion in Chapter 11 underlines the same theme: worship and work are not watertight compartments. The rules and roles instituted in one sphere condition belief and behavior in others. Institutions are elements of the social structure so interlacing as to form an organic whole. This is nowhere clearer than in the connections between economy and polity. Indeed, men govern in work settings and work at governing. An economist, Arthur F. Burns speaks of the interplay between these institutions:

> More than 12 million individuals are now working directly for government—Federal, state, or local. [This is nearly one in five persons in the civilian labor force.] Many others work in private firms that produce exclusively or mainly for the government. The prices charged by these enterprises are not set in free markets. They are commonly arranged by negotiation among experts, and they are sometimes determined years after the product has been delivered. The government controls the prices charged by railroads, airlines, pipelines, light and power companies, and even many motor carriers. It dominates the price-making process in agriculture. It controls the supply of petroleum by setting quotas on production and imports. It influences the supply of many other products by tariffs, subsidies, and its own stockpiling. It fixes minimum wages and intervenes in the collective-bargaining process. It fixes the price of gold and thus controls the foreign exchanges. It sets a ceiling on some interest rates, insures many private loans, and even engages in direct lending. It compels people to save for their old age and other contingencies on a collective principle. It uses the tax laws to encourage home ownership, good health, and philanthropy. It regulates the free market itself by stern anti-trust laws. And it uses its vast powers over the supply of money, the cost and availability of credit, the level of taxes, and the rate and direction of its own expenditures, to promote a high level of over-all production and employment.[47]

If, then, it was a short step from church to marketplace, and from home to work, so also is it an easy transition from economy to polity, from the relationships of men at work to those of men under the authority of law. In the next chapter, we will consider some of the issues dealt with as sociologists study the governing of some by others.[48]

---

[47] Arthur F. Burns, "Of Growth and Gain," a review of Adolf A. Berle's book, *The American Economic Republic* (N.Y.: Harcourt, Brace and World, 1963), published in *The Reporter*, Vol. 29, No. 4 (September, 12, 1963), p. 52. Copyright 1963 by the Reporter Magazine Company.

[48] This subfield is called political sociology. It seems to me an unfortunate label, misleading in its connotation. The same is true of subfields commonly called urban sociology, rural sociology, industrial sociology, and educational sociology. It suggests, erroneously, that sociology comes in different flavors, that there are various brands of sociology. More cumbersome terms would be more accurate: the sociology of urban, or rural life; the sociology of work; or the sociology of education.

SELECTED SUPPLEMENTARY READINGS

BERELSON, BERNARD, AND STEINER, GARY A. "Economic Institutions," in *Human Behavior: An Inventory of Scientific Findings,* pp. 397–417. New York: Harcourt, Brace & World, Inc., 1964.

*COCH, LESTER, AND FRENCH, JOHN R. P. JR. "Overcoming Resistance to Change," *Human Relations,* Vol. 1 (1948), pp. 512–32.

*DAVIS, ALLISON. "The Motivation of the Underprivileged Worker," in William Foote Whyte (ed.), *Industry and Society,* pp. 62–106. New York: McGraw-Hill Book Co., 1946.

HUGHES, EVERETT CHERRINGTON. "The Study of Occupations," in Robert K. Merton, Leonard Broom, and Leonard S. Cottrell, Jr. (eds.), *Sociology Today,* ch. xx. New York: Harper & Row—Harper Torchbooks, 1965.

KORNHAUSER, ARTHUR; DUBIN, ROBERT; AND ROSS, ARTHUR M. (eds.). *Industrial Conflict.* New York: McGraw-Hill Book Co., 1954.

*LANDES, DAVID S. "French Business and the Businessman: A Social and Cultural Analysis," in Edward Mead Earle (ed.), *Modern France,* pp. 334–53. Princeton, N.J.: Princeton University Press, 1951.

LIPSET, SEYMOUR MARTIN, AND BENDIX, REINHARD. "Social Mobility and Occupational Career Patterns: Stability of Jobholding," *American Journal of Sociology,* Vol. LVII, No. 4 (January, 1952), pp. 366–74.

———. "Social Mobility and Occupational Career Patterns: Social Mobility," *American Journal of Sociology,* Vol. LVII, No. 5 (March, 1952), pp. 494–504.

NOSOW, SIGMUND, AND FORM, WILLIAM H. (eds.). *Man, Work and Society.* New York: Basic Books, 1962.

SMELSER, NEIL J. *Social Change in the Industrial Revolution.* Chicago: University of Chicago Press, 1959.

*WILENSKY, HAROLD L. "The Uneven Distribution of Leisure: The Impact of Economic Growth on 'Free Time'," *Social Forces* (1961), pp. 32–56.

---

* Articles marked with an asterisk are available as reprints from the college division of the Bobbs-Merrill Company, Indianapolis, Indiana.

Chapter 13

The Ordering
of Relationships
under Law

*How do we solve problems of conflicting interest, setting and en-
forcing expectations defining one's relationships with fellow members of the group?*

Society is indeed a contract. . . . It is a partnership in all science;
in all art; a partnership in every virtue, and in all perfection. As the
ends of such a partnership cannot be obtained in many generations,
it becomes a partnership not only between those who are living, but
between those who are living, those who are dead and those who are
to be born.[1]

Men's institutions hang on a framework of rules. (We have just
been considering the rules that govern the roles that build into
relationships that constitute the work group.) But there is, as we
know, one institution whose end product is rules, and their enforcement. The rules we call laws. The institution is government.

THE GROUP-SUSTAINING CHARACTER
OF GOVERNMENT

Law makes explicit those sets of expectations that constitute the
citizen role. The relationships of citizen to citizen, governor to
governed are thus defined. A special network of relationships
enables and enforces the meeting of these expectations. Taken as a

---

[1] Edmund Burke *Reflections on the Revolution in France* (New York: Rinehart
& Co., 1959), p. 117.

whole, we call this network government: the lawmakers, the executives who carry out the law, the police and courts who enforce the law. In our society the lawmaking process aggregates individual preferences, registered in voting, transforming them into an integral characteristic of the group. When a majority has declared itself, the resulting decision is then applicable to all members.[2]

We often aggregate individual traits to derive a feature characteristic of the group: rates of birth, death, homicide, suicide, divorce and marriage, home ownership, gross national product, per capita income, and the like. But although their aggregation yields a value peculiar to the group (and often not characterizing any individual in it—no couple had 6.5 births, the average number of births per marriage between 1862 and 1869), such an aggregation retains its distributive character. The statement implies a range of values, each of them possible, if not plausible, and acceptable. But not so with the aggregation of political preferences. For a majority decision becomes binding, in our society, upon everyone. The law of the land applies equally to every citizen. And through the power funneling from the whole group to its representative agents, sanctions are applied to broken expectations. Through the agency of government, we try to resolve matters in dispute and achieve a common commitment despite inevitable differences.

Thus the group-sustaining, socially integrative character of government under law. It is an integrative institution as it underwrites reciprocal expectations. In our society it provides a means of so aggregating preferences that the will of a majority can be known. Expressed in law, this will states, and certifies as legitimate, the expectations that define the civic role. Government exacts fulfillment of these expectations by all who call themselves citizens.

The civic role is universal, as is its embodiment in some system of rule. Let's consider, briefly, the sources of this omnipresent institution, and its functions in the social order.

---

[2] Of course, this is an oversimplification. Some decisions require a simple plurality, some a two-thirds vote, etc. It is true, too, that a recalcitrant minority sometimes flouts the law of the land. But the very phrase, "law of the land," implies the integral, non-excepting nature of a legislative decision. And the arguments supporting the non-conformity of rebellious dissidents—the states' rights arguments of those opposing civil rights legislation, for example—are couched in terms of "the American tradition" of a federal government reserving rights of self-determination to the states. That is to say a single, group tradition, a general social value, is invoked.

Mart Studios Inc.

Mart Studios Inc.

Raleigh, N.C., News and Observer

Resolving differences through law. ▲
Treatment of deviants through law. ▶
The ordering of relationships through law. ▼

lic Law 88–352

AN ACT

enforce the constitutional right to vote, to confer juris-
ction upon the district courts of the United States to
ovide injunctive relief against discrimination in public
ccommodations, to authorize the Attorney General to
stitute suits to protect constitutional rights in public
cilities and public education, to extend the Commission on
ivil Rights, to prevent discrimination in federally assisted
ograms, to establish a Commission on Equal Employ-
ent Opportunity, and for other purposes.

*e it enacted by the Senate and House of Representatives of
United States of America in Congress assembled,* That
Act may be cited as the "Civil Rights Act of 1964".

TITLE I—VOTING RIGHTS

ɛc. 101. Section 2004 of the Revised Statutes (42 U.S.C.
), as amended by section 131 of the Civil Rights Act of
7 (71 Stat. 637), and as further amended by section 601
he Civil Rights Act of 1960 (74 Stat. 90), is further
nded as follows:

) Insert "1" after "(a)" in subsection (a) and add at
end of subsection (a) the following new paragraphs:
(2) No person acting under color of law shall—
    "(A) in determining whether any individual is qualified
nder State law or laws to vote in any Federal election,
apply any standard, practice, or procedure different from
he standards, practices, or procedures applied under such
aw or laws to other individuals within the same county,
arish, or similar political subdivision who have been found
by State officials to be qualified to vote;
    "(B) deny the right of any individual to vote in any
Federal election because of an error or omission on any
record or paper relating to any application, registration, or
other act requisite to voting, if such error or omission is
not material in determining whether such individual is
qualified under State law to vote in such election; or

SOURCES OF GOVERNMENT AND
THE FUNCTIONS IT SERVES:
INTEGRATION AND LIBERATION

The citizen role consists in a set of rights and duties vis-à-vis fellow members of the civic community. But right and duties are not self-evident, self-defining, or similarly perceived. Because people differ, the inculcation of common commitments is necessary: to vote, to abide by majority decision, to serve on juries and in other offices, in time of peril to defend the country, to resolve differences by means deemed legitimate.

Whence these inevitable differences that must be reconciled or transcended if a social order is to sustain itself? Let me suggest three sources: differences that stem (1) from genetic variations, (2) from the unique permutations of a person's contacts and affiliations, and (3) from those broader variations on the human theme embedded in different cultures. That is to say, the requirement of reconciling differences and establishing common rights and duties springs from biological, social, and cultural differences. With the exception of monozygotic (one-egg) twins, every person crosses the world's threshhold with a unique combination of biological traits. Whether these are differences entailing significant differences among men as human beings is perhaps debatable. But certainly, at the genetic extremes, problems are posed that no group can blink. The treatment of hereditary defectives is a case in point.

The social source of differences lies in the infinitely various permutations of social influence converging in each personality. Differing social sets generate differing views, values, and conduct. This is an inevitable source of sometimes abrasive differences; for no two persons confront or respond to the same set of others, the same constellation of kinfolk, friends, siblings, strangers. Differences— inadequacies, if you like—in the socialization process threaten the pattern of universal expectations that bind together all those called citizen. Similarly, in cases of upward or downward mobility, the person entering a different station or stratum may find both disposition and talents at odds with those of his new group. Such social differences may well generate incompatible claims, claims that might be socially disruptive but for the requirements built into the citizen role and enforced by government. So also with variant cultural themes typifying different religious, racial, regional, and nativity groups. Conflicting claims are accommodated or reconciled under law by prescribing those limits within which differences must be tolerated and beyond which corrective penalties are invoked.

I've been suggesting that government exercises an integrating influence by reconciling and transcending interpersonal and intergroup differences. The notion of government steming from conflicting claims is implicit in Rousseau who, at the beginning of his argument, declares: "Man is born free; and everywhere he is in chains."[3] There comes a time in man's history when, perhaps due to the pressure of population upon available resources—or at least to rival claims for scarce resources—aspirations, satisfactions, even survival are threatened. Under these conditions an agreement, a social contract is made in the service of survival, each person surrendering some aspect of his personal will to the general will. This latter becomes sovereign, and each citizen becomes subservient to that will. The elemental function of government, then (as with Hobbes) is to protect life, if not to promote liberty and happiness, when men who are relatively equal in physical and intellectual power and in moral claims confront limited resources. In fact, Hobbes explains the origins of the institution of government by starting with the assumption of the equality of men.

> Nature hath made men so equall, in the faculties of body, and mind; as that though there bee found one man sometimes manifestly stronger in body, or of quicker mind than another; yet when all is reckoned together the difference between man and man is not so considerable as that one man can thereupon claim to himselfe any benefit to which another may not pretend, as well as he. . . .[4]

And since men are not remarkably different in body, mind, and moral stature, differing views and values confronting scarce re-

---

[3] Jean Jacques Rousseau, *Le Contrat social ou principes du droit politique* (Paris: Pourrat Frères, 1838), p. 26.

In a brief introduction Rousseau justifies his writing on matters political. It is precisely his amateur standing that qualifies him, he argues. He goes on to say: "Were I a prince or a legislator I'd not waste time talking about what ought to be done. I'd put up or shut up!" (*"Je le ferois, ou je me tarois."*)

Then comes the famous statement, *"L'homme est né libre, et partout il est dans les fers."*

In Rousseau's *Émile, ou de l'education,* an important discussion of learning and teaching, we find a similar, startling opener when he writes: "From heavenly hands, all things are good. But in man's hands, all benefactions are corrupted." The original goes: *"Tout est bien sortant des mains de l'auteur des choses, tout dégénère entre les mains de l'homme."* (Paris: Ernest Flammarion, n.d.), Vol. I, p. 9.

[4] Thomas Hobbes, *Leviathan* (New York: E. P. Dutton & Co., Inc., 1931), p. 63.

sources lead to the war of each against all. Thus, man in a state of nature, without government, lived under conditions where his life was poor, solitary, nasty, brutish, and short. He was constrained, therefore, to contrive a compact with his fellows, agreeing to elevate one as governor.

There are several difficulties with these classical views of the sources of the institution of government.[5] Note three of them: the imputation of rational contrivance, the implication that government is a supererogation, and the notion of reluctant surrender to the necessary but evil restraints of law.

Quite aside from the fact that these notions on government's origin cannot be tested, for lack of data, they probably attribute a spurious rationality to man. One is not persuaded that this institution—or any other—grew out of an antique brainstorming session. Rather the likelihood is that it developed like Topsy, bit by arduous and mistaken bit.

A second difficulty, as MacIver put it, is that

> . . . by presenting government as something that supervenes in human society, something merely accessory to it, or something that actually perverts it, [such doctrines] misinterpret the service and minimize the necessity of government.[6]

For the control of human relationships represented in government responds to a fundamental need in human life. "Without law there is no order, and without order men are lost, not knowing where they go, not knowing what they do."[7] As with other institutional rules, the rules of family, school, church, and work, law promotes that predictability in others' responses without which our synapses would be in turmoil. And to say as much suggests that law, in a general sense, is already implicit in the folkways, in the mores, and in the family which long preceded the formal instituting of governing roles. In the family (which MacIver refers to as the "seedbed of government"), we find a host of rules governing eligibility for marriage (endogamous and exogamous regulations), incest, premarital and extramarital relationships, division of labor between sexes

---

[5] But I would agree with Hobbes that there is a general equality among men which, together with the differences cultivated in various social and cultural settings, generates stress in the rivalry for valued things.

[6] Robert MacIver, *The Web of Government* (New York: Macmillan Co., 1948), p. 31.

[7] *Ibid.*, p. 61.

and generations, control over property, descent of property, title to and distribution of the fruits of labor. All such rules constitute a chief bulwark of predictable interchange among men. In defining duties and rights of the citizen role, law enables people, even those otherwise unknown to one another, to build necessary relationships in support of common, civic interests.

A third error in these views of government might be called the fall-of-man notion. As the children of our colonial forebears intoned from their primers: "In Adam's fall / we sin-ned all." And so, cast out of an idyllic, ungoverned Garden, we became entrapped in the trappings of civilization. Thus, Rousseau sees the ordering of relationships under law as enslavement. (*L'homme est né libre, et partout il est dans les fers.*) To be free is to emancipate one's self *from* the restraints of government. The emphasis on freedom *from* disregards the social requirements of freedom *to* achieve one's ends. For such freedom is always contingent upon collaboration with others. There is no such thing as a "free individual." For a person's freedom is always related to his role and status vis-à-vis others. Freedom has this ambivalent aspect: to be free to achieve one's ends implies agreement on and adherence to reciprocal obligations. Freedom to love, to learn, to earn, to play, to worship—indeed, to live—depends on enforceable agreements with others. Freedom necessarily involves commonly accepted limitations. Only under such restrictions can one have confidence that given means will lead to desired ends. "The essence of freedom," DeGré suggests, lies in "its rationality, in the sense that it is defined according to the predictability of the probable expectations tied up with a course of action."[8] Or again:

> Freedom may be defined in terms of the probability that specific groups or individuals can formulate their ends of conduct and initiate a course of action with a minimum degree of constraint from other persons and with a high degree of predictability of the consequences within the institutional and associational structure of the community.[9]

Government, then, is not mere restraint. It extends the range of choice, opens up options hitherto closed, frees men to seek legitimate objectives by guaranteeing the order that is necessary if they

---

[8] Gerard DeGré, "Freedom and Social Structure," *American Sociological Review*, published by The American Sociological Association, Vol. XI, No. 5 (October, 1946), p. 530.

[9] *Ibid.*, p. 530.

are to reach their goals. If one function of government is social stability, another is to define and guarantee freedom.

The extent to which such correlates of governing emerge depends on the social conditions within which government operates and on the organization of government itself. In the suggestive essay from which I've quoted, Professor DeGré proposes a plausible link between concentration of power (one aspect of the governor-governed relationship) and the extent of freedom enjoyed by the individual. His thesis is summarized in Figure 13–1.

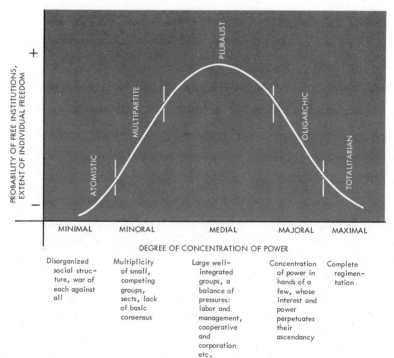

| Disorganized social structure, war of each against all | Multiplicity of small, competing groups, sects, lack of basic consensus | Large well-integrated groups, a balance of pressures: labor and management, cooperative and corporation etc. | Concentration of power in hands of a few, whose interest and power perpetuates their ascendancy | Complete regimentation |

Source: Adapted from Gerard DeGré, "Freedom and Social Structure," *American Sociological Review,* published by The American Sociological Association, Vol. XI, No. 5 (October, 1946), p. 534.

FIG. 13–1. A proposed relationship between degree of concentration of power and extent of freedom enjoyed.

Thus freedom is seen as a function of social—particularly, in this case, governmental—organization. It is puerile to echo Emerson: "the less government we have, the better. . . ." The institution of government fulfills its functions adequately when it meets the group's needs. Wartime needs, for example, shift us toward maximal concentration of power so that we can be free to prosecute a war. In peacetime and in a rapidly changing society, a more moderate concentration of power may make the best fit, promoting, through the interplay of differing preferences and interests, the emergence of new and adaptive solutions. In a complex society where every man's activities are vested with a public interest—in a society dominated by functional integration—the meshing of diverse skills and needs may require an extension of the governmental function. Burns's statement (page 557) points unmistakably to this development in our society.

The liberating and integrative functions of government are perhaps least understood when we think of courts, police, and punishment. We probably see these branches of government as operating to reduce aberrant behavior, bringing the deviant into line. If they confine the range of conduct within tolerable limits, as a thermostat restricts heat variation around the desired point, then we may view such agencies as sustaining the prevailing values and the system of relationships embodying them, that is, the group.

While this may be true, it is a partial truth that obscures the mechanism by which it occurs. Indeed, if we think of punishment simply as a device to deter wrongdoers it would be hard to persuade ourselves that various penalties, however swift, sure, and severe, have ever done much to discourage the criminal or reduce rates of recidivism. (In some statistical time series, crime rates vary *directly* with investment in law enforcement, and with frequency and severity of punishment.)[10] If punishment, then, does not so obviously serve its ostensible function of deterrence, what is its use? What is the social function of police and courts and the punishment they mete out? An answer to this question has been given that points to the lawabiding rather than the lawbreaker, to the offended rather than the offender. This is an answer that has appealed to sociologists, at least since Durkheim made the distinction between the *cause* of a pattern of behavior and the *function* it may serve. (The reason for instituting police, courts, and punishment is to deter from criminal activity. The function served by such a pattern may be

---

[10] Punishment may, in fact, deter, but we lack means for demonstrating it; for we cannot answer the question: What would happen in the absence of punishment? Law officers, not surprisingly, are disposed to think that in the absence of their increasingly costly efforts, crime would be higher yet. Of course, this whole question is too broadly posed, here. Controlled observation would require us to deal with specific types of offenses under specific conditions.

something else.) Let me summarize Durkheim's argument, as I have in another connection.[11]

The primary function of punishment is not to prevent recurrent offenses. If to some extent it achieves this end, it does so simply as a matter of guaranteeing overt and superficial propriety. It is a police procedure, in the narrow sense of the word, and in no sense a means of altering conviction and conduct. Nor is punishment a way of expunging the evil deed by a counteroffense that nullifes the former. This, Durkheim suggests, is as though a physician, in order to heal a diseased arm, began by amputating the other. The essential function of punishment is to offer the occasion for reaffirming the group's values, for a recommitment to conduct challenged by defections and delinquencies. He writes:

> This is the . . . moral evil caused by [illegal behavior]. It shatters . . . faith in the authority of . . . law.
>   . . . punishment is only the palpable symbol through which an inner state is represented: it is a notation, a language through which either the general social conscience or that of the [authorities] expresses the feeling inspired by the deviant behavior.
>   Punishment does not give discipline its authority; but it prevents discipline from losing its authority. . . . Severity of treatment is justified only to the extent that it is necessary to make disapproval of the act utterly unequivocal.

Perhaps the social function of punishment is especially visible when, as in the case of confession, it is self-imposed. The ex-communist Whittaker Chambers, offering what he calls an "accounting" in his book *Witness,* is a case in point. Beyond the punishment it exacts, such a public and voluntary confession of wrongdoing provides a dramatic affirmation of the forces of good over evil, of right beliefs and behaviors over wrong ones—that is, of ours over theirs. It is, of course, a means of bringing the once-deviant person, now purged and chastened, back into the fold. But here our attention is on the ninety and nine, not on the single lost sheep who has gone astray. As Professor Hausknecht points out in his discussion of the Chambers case, confession strengthens the hand of authority. Not only have official representatives of the group induced a confession, thus attesting their vigilance and technical competence. In addition, they have in the confession an inverted

---

[11] The following, including the quotations from Durkheim, is paraphrased from Émile Durkheim, *Moral Education,* trans. E. K. Wilson and Herman Schnurer (New York: Free Press of Glencoe, Inc., 1961), editor's introduction, p. xxvii.

manual for conformist behavior. This social function of the self-imposed punishment of confession is seen in the Inquisition, in the witch trials of England and America, and in the breast-beating *mea culpas* of trials of "deviationists" in the U.S.S.R. Hausknecht sums things up for us.

> Any deviant individual, whether he is an ordinary thief or a political nonconformist, severely damages the fabric of the social order. Those charged with maintaining order must not only prevent further damage but must also repair the damage already done. *Confession is a unique means for making the inevitable existence of nonconformist behavior a means for strengthening the tendencies toward conformity.*[12]

I've proposed that the need for instituting a system of rule making stems from those inevitable differences among men that arise from biological, social, and cultural variations. Rules commonly accepted channel conduct within bounds tolerable to the group. And the punishments linked to the rules offer opportunities for regular reaffirmation of shared values. Indeed, one may question whether values could be sustained without periodic challenges. But the rules of law mean more than this. For like the rules guiding conduct in other institutional spheres, they enhance freedom. They enable men to move more certainly toward chosen goals, provided, of course, that these goals fall within the range permitted by the common commitments of group members. Thus the paradox of law: simultaneously restricting and freeing.

THE STUDY OF THE POLITY

But such vagrant ruminations in political theory, you may have thought, must be poaching on the field of political science. In a sense it is true, although until recent years the empirical study of the allocation of power was a preserve so seldom penetrated by political science that infrequent invasion by sociologists seemed scarcely reprehensible. But if we take my definition of sociology in which the content of inquiry is differing patterns of human relationships, and if we recognize power as a crucial dimension of human relationships, then it is inevitable that sociology must inquire into matters political. Nor will we cavil when political scientists such as Robert Dahl define their field in a way that embraces ours. Political science

---

[12] Murray Hausknecht, "Confession and Return," *Antioch Review,* Vol. XIV, No. 1 (March, 1954), p. 79.

studies political systems, and a political system, Dahl writes, "is any persistent pattern of human relationships that involves, to a significant extent, power, rule, or authority."[13] "Significant," here, is a spongy term, but one might suppose that family, work, worship— all major institutional arrangements—"involve to a significant extent power, rule, or authority." In any case, problems are public property, and the power aspect of roles and relationships is a dimension that the sociologist cannot disregard. How *has* he regarded it? Let us look briefly at some of the problems posed by the sociologist in his study of the power dimension of human relationships. We will turn then to a study of the distribution and use of power in a union, so freeing ourselves from the conventional notion that governing occurs exclusively in government.

Democracy as a Function of Political Pluralism: Crosscutting Political Fault Lines as Requisite for Democratic Processes

One question we have already encountered: How does degree of concentration of power affect extent of freedom in a group? As we have seen, DeGré predicts that freedom will vary in a specified way (a curvilinear relationship) depending on the social structure: whether the system is atomistic, multipartite, pluralist, oligarchic, or totalitarian. But we can probe further and ask, as Professor Lipset does, what it is about a pluralist system that links with democratic patterns? What are the mechanisms involved in a pluralist society that sustain an engagement in issues, yet forestall such radical commitment that the stability of the system would be jeopardized? Under what conditions do ballots displace bullets? There are many conditions, but an important one is the mechanism for multiplying political fault lines and modes of dissent, a possibility only present in a pluralist society.

Professor Lipset points to the paradox that a stable democracy is impossible in the absence of mechanisms for revealing cleavage—as well as consensus.[14] But *how* the cleavages are made and revealed

---

[13] Robert A. Dahl, *Modern Political Analysis* (Englewood Cliffs, N. J.: Prentice-Hall, Inc., 1963). It seems to me significant that this book, defining the political scientist's object of inquiry as almost coterminous with the field of sociology, should be called *Modern* political analysis. See Heinz Eulau, *The Behavioral Persuasion* (New York: Random House, 1963).

[14] Seymour Martin Lipset, *Political Man: The Social Bases of Politics* (Garden City, N.Y.: Doubleday and Co., 1960), chap. i, "The Sociology of Politics," See also his chapter on "Political Sociology" in *Sociology Today*, ed. Robert K. Merton, Leonard Broom, and Leonard Cottrell (New York: Basic Books, Inc., 1959).

matters a great deal. The cleavages revealed in voting studies can threaten a democratic political system when they coincide precisely with class, race, religion, or region.[15] But when the social order is such as to permit or encourage political preference to cut across such categorical lines, common goals can be achieved by evolutionary rather than revolutionary means. Not all poor Catholics vote the Democratic ticket, nor do all wealthy Protestants plump for Republicans. Furthermore, a political party drawing some of its support from people whose *other affiliations* bind them to members of the

---

[15] Studies of political preference as registered in voting or survey responses, linked with such independent varibles as class, race, religious affiliation, region, age, sex, rural or urban residence, occupation, income—these appear to be the commonest subjects of inquiry for the sociologist.

For example, a probability sample of four census tracts in San Francisco, showed the following relationship between respondents' own class identification and political affiliation:

	Working Class	Middle Class	Total
Republican	25%	63%	44%
Democrat	75	37	56
Total percent	100%	100%	100%
N =	241	254	495

The same study disclosed this connection between occupational situs (clusters of related occupations covering about the same range of statuses) and political affiliation, holding constant subjective class identification.

	Commerce	Finance and Records	Manufacturing	Building and Maintenance	Total
Middle class					
Republican	72%	66%	56%	42%	63%
Democrat	28	34	44	58	37
Total percent	100%	100%	100%	100%	100%
N =	108	64	34	48	254
Working class					
Republican	54%	36%	26%	20%	25%
Democrat	46	64	74	80	75
Total percent	100%	100%	100%	100%	100%
N =	24	25	53	139	241

These data are from the study by Raymond J. Murphy and Richard T. Morris, "Occupational Situs, Subjective Class Identification, and Political Affiliation," *American Sociological Review*, Vol. XXVI, No. 3 (June, 1961), p. 390.

For a good summary of studies of political behavior sce Heinz Eulau, Samuel J. Eldersveld, and Morris Janowitz, *Political Behavior* (New York: Free Press of Glencoe, Inc., 1956), especially Sections III, IV and V.

opposition is under some pressure to make prudent concessions to selected views and values of that opposition.

> . . . considered from this perspective, the Tory worker or the middle-class socialist are not merely deviants from class patterns, but basic requirements for the maintenance of the [English] political system. A stable democracy requires a situation in which all the major political parties include supporters from many segments of the population. . . . The fact that Republicans have nominated Negroes and Jews even though most members of these groups in recent years have voted Democratic has undoubtedly had an important unifying effect and reduced the chance that party division along racial or religious lines could become permanent.[16]

Thus, important consequences flow from social pluralism, where there are many permutations on patterns of group affiliation, including party membership. From the person's perspective, this may mean pulls in different, sometimes opposing, directions. Lazarsfeld, Berelson, and Gaudet have analyzed the effects of such cross-pressures on political behavior in their study, *The People's Choice*.[17] One such effect is a delay in the decision whether and how to vote (see Table 13–1). Thus, under cross-pressures, unconditional party loyalty is less likely.[18] Rigid allegiances are challenged. A degree of independence and shifting is introduced. Hence voting becomes something more than a *pro forma* affair.

---

[16] Lipset, *op. cit.*, p. 31. Copyright © 1960 by Seymour Martin Lipset. Reprinted by permission of Doubleday & Co., Inc.

[17] Paul F. Lazarsfeld, Bernard Berelson, and Hazel Gaudet, *The People's Choice* (New York: Columbia University Press, 1948).

[18] **An Aside on Methods: The Problem of the Chemist in His Own Test Tube—Controlling Interviewer Effect**

The reference to the Erie county research offers a chance for another footnote on methods of inquiry. This was what is called a "panel study." The same respondents were interviewed seven times. This enabled the investigators to learn something about change, its extent and direction, for *the same person* over a period of time, and the influences accounting for such change.

From a visit to every fourth house in Erie County, Ohio, 3,000 respondents were chosen, closely resembling the total population in education, telephone and car ownership, age, sex, residence, and nativity. From this first group of respondents, four groups of 600 persons each were selected so that each group was "a miniature sample of the whole poll and of the county itself." Of these four groups, people in one constituted the panel and were repeatedly interviewed from May until election time in November.

We have here the old problem of the chemist in his own test tube. How would repeated interviewing affect people's responses? How might one estimate the error introduced by this extraneous influence? The answer was to use three control goups (A, B, and C, below), each of them being interviewed only once. Hence a com-

TABLE 13–1

The Relationship between Cross-Pressures* and Delay in Deciding How to Vote, by Level of Interest

	VOTERS WITH NO, OR ONE CROSS-PRESSURE (%)		VOTERS WITH 2 OR MORE CROSS-PRESSURES (%)	
TIME OF VOTE DECISION	GREAT INTEREST	LESS INTEREST	GREAT INTEREST	LESS INTEREST
September–November	7	21	21	33
June–August	20	29	35	41
May	73	50	44	26
	100	100	100	100
N =	92	117	34	94

* "Cross-pressures" refer to categories or groups pulling the person in different directions. For example, persons both rich and Protestant or poor and Catholic belong to categories known to vote, in disproportionate numbers, for Republican and Democratic candidates, respectively. Thus a poor Protestant or a rich Catholic was judged to be subject to cross-pressure. In addition, the following were seen as inducing cross-pressures: (1) family politically divided, (2) the person's vote in the previous election differed from his present inclination, (3) actual social standing differed from the person's perceived, or self-defined standing, (4) his stress on the importance of business or governmental experience for a candidate was inconsistent with his party preference, and (5) he senses a trend toward the other party. See pp. 56–60 passim.

Source: Paul F. Lazarsfeld, Bernard Berelson, and Hazel Gaudet, The People's Choice. Adapted from Chart 22, p. 63 (New York: Columbia University Press, 1948).

From the perspective of the social order, these interweaving cross- and counterpressures dilute extreme or radical positions, compromise revolutionary ardor, discourage convulsive change, permitting, rather, a more deliberate rate of change. To put it differently, the crosscutting of membership groups, while not precluding change, yet provides a sort of social gyroscope, slowing the rate of change but probably not affecting its direction.

parison of the control group with the main panel at a given point in time made it possible to estimate the effect that repeated interviewing might have on panel respondents. The general scheme of the study is provided below.

TIME OF INTERVIEWS AND NOMINATING CONVENTIONS	MAY	JUNE	JULY	AUGUST	SEPTEMBER	OCTOBER	NOVEMBER
			REPUBLICAN	DEMOCRATIC			
Interview No. (7 Waves)	1	2	3	4	5	6	7
	Total Poll	Main Panel	Main Panel	Main Panel	Main Panel	Main Panel	Main Panel
N =	(3,000)	(600)	(600)	(600)	(600)	(600)	(600)
Group Interviewed			Control A	Control B		Control C	
N =			(600)	(600)		(600)	

Democracy as a Function of Wealth, Urbanization, Industrialization, and Education

The effect, on political belief and behavior, of multiple affiliations in a pluralist society is one significant line of inquiry for the sociologist. There are many other aspects of the social structure whose putative effects on political patterns have been investigated. For example, it has long been thought that such factors as level of literacy, extent of diffusion of knowledge, and range of wealth bear significantly on mode of governing. In an intriguing study that asks about the social requisites for the form of government we call democratic, Lipset tests an old idea.

> Perhaps the most common generalization linking political systems to other aspects of society has been that democracy is related to the state of economic development. The more well-to-do a nation, the greater the chances that it will sustain democracy. From Aristotle down to the present, men have argued that only in a wealthy society in which relatively few citizens lived at the level of real poverty could there be a situation in which the mass of the population intelligently participate in politics and develop the self-restraint necessary to avoid succumbing to the appeals of irresponsible demagogues. A society divided between a large impoverished mass and a small favored elite results either in oligarchy (dictatorial rule of the small upper stratum) or in tyranny (popular based dictatorship). To give these two political forms modern labels, tyranny's face today is communism or Peronism; while oligarchy appears in the traditionalist dictatorships found in parts of Latin America, Thailand, Spain, or Portugal.
>
> To test this hypothesis concretely, I have used various indices of economic development—wealth, industrialization, urbanization, and education [selected aspects of the social order used as independent variables]—and computed averages (means) for the countries which have been classified as more or less democratic in the Anglo-Saxon world and Europe, and in Latin America.[19]

His classification of nations by degree of stable democracy is given in the following listing,[20] and the results of his inquiry, testing

---

[19] Lipset, *op. cit.*, pp. 48–50, *passim*.

[20] Professor Lipset settled on his classification of nations as follows. "The main criteria used to define European democracies are the uninterrupted continuation of political democracy since World War I *and* the absence over the past twenty-five years of a major political movement opposed to the democratic rules of the game. [This means] that no totalitarian movement, either fascist or communist received 20 per cent of the vote during this time. The somewhat less stringent criterion for Latin America is whether a given country has had a history of more or less free elections for most of the post-World War I period. Where in Europe we look for stable democracies, in South America we look for countries which have not had fairly constant dictatorial rule." (Lipset, *op. cit.*, p. 48.)

whether such a connection existed (between stable democratic forms and the diffusion of wealth and knowledge), and the strength of that connection, are given in Table 13–2.

Classification of European, English-speaking, and Latin-American Nations by Degree of Stable Democracy

European and English-speaking Nations		*Latin-American Nations*	
I	II	III	IV
Stable Democracies	*Unstable Democracies and Dictatorships*	*Unstable Democracies and Dictatorships*	*Stable Dictatorships*
Australia	Albania	Argentina	Bolivia
Belgium	Austria	Brazil	Cuba
Canada	Bulgaria	Chile	Dominican Republic
Denmark	Czechoslovakia	Colombia	Ecuador
Ireland	Finland	Costa Rica	El Salvador
Luxembourg	France	Mexico	Guatemala
Netherlands	Germany	Uruguay	Haiti
New Zealand	Greece		Honduras
Norway	Hungary		Nicaragua
Sweden	Iceland		Panama
Switzerland	Italy		Paraguay
United Kingdom	Poland		Peru
United States	Portugal		Venezuela
	Rumania		
	Spain		
	U.S.S.R.		
	Yugoslavia		

These findings lend support to the notion that there are specific features of the social order significantly linked to form of government. Certain demographic features (concentration of population in urban centers, itself a function of education and technological sophistication), and certain institutional characteristics (marked economic development, elaborate technology, high level of literacy and of education) appear to be buttresses for a stable democratic system.

We might note in passing that such findings have practical implications. This is as true of the sociologist's work as that of chemist or psychologist or economist. Should further research confirm these findings, certain principles seem to be suggested as guides for our foreign policy vis-à-vis the uncommitted nations.

Differentiating Forms of Rule by Role-Defining Values

Sometimes the sociologist shifts his attention from elements of the social structure, from roles and relationships, to the underlying rules that pattern conduct. They are revealed in norms of behavior and

TABLE 13-2

A Comparison of 4 Categories of Nations (European and English-speaking Nations: I—Stable Democracies, II—Unstable Democracies and Dictatorships; and Latin-American Nations: III—Democracies and Unstable Dictatorships, and IV—Stable Dictatorships), by Indices of Wealth, Industrialization, Education, and Urbanization

CATEGORY OF NATION	INDICES OF WEALTH (MEANS, IN U.S. $)						INDICES OF URBANIZATION (MEANS)		
	PER CAPITA INCOME	THOUSANDS OF PERSONS PER DOCTOR	PERSONS PER MOTOR VEHICLE	TELEPHONES PER 1,000 PERSONS	RADIOS PER 1,000 PERSONS	NEWSPAPERS COPIES PER 1,000 PERSONS	PERCENT IN CITIES OVER 20,000	PERCENT IN CITIES OVER 100,000	PERCENT IN METROPOLITAN AREAS
I	$695	.86	17	205	350	341	43	28	38
II	308	1.4	143	58	160	167	24	16	23
III	171	2.1	99	25	85	102	28	22	26
IV	119	4.4	274	10	43	43	17	12	15

CATEGORY OF NATION	INDICES OF INDUSTRIALIZATION (MEANS)		INDICES OF EDUCATION (MEANS)			
	PERCENTAGE OF MALES IN AGRICULTURE	PER CAPITA ENERGY CONSUMED	PERCENTAGE LITERATE	PRIMARY EDUCATION ENROLLMENT PER 1,000 PERSONS	POSTPRIMARY ENROLLMENT PER 1,000 PERSONS	HIGHER EDUCATION ENROLLMENT PER 1,000 PERSONS
I	21	3.6	96	134	44	4.2
II	41	1.4	85	121	22	3.5
III	52	.6	74	101	13	2.0
IV	67	.25	46	72	8	1.3

Source: Seymour Martin Lipset, *Political Man: The Social Bases of Politics.* Copyright © 1960 by Seymour Martin Lipset. Reprinted by permission of Doubleday & Co., Inc. Adapted from Table II, pp. 51–54. To save space I have omitted important data, his measures of deviation or spread. He uses the range, highest minus lowest values.

imply values that typify the group. Often, through interview or survey data, he taps people's values by way of their views on controversial issues: social security, the welfare state, Medicare, foreign policy, civil rights legislation, and the like. Seldom does he live as dangerously as Geoffrey Gorer, the free-ranging English social anthropologist who explores and explains English and American character.[21] Perhaps our prolific and provocative Professor Lipset comes close, although in a more theoretically disciplined, plausible, and stimulating fashion. Here is a sociologist whose whole work is devoted to comparative political analysis. In a suggestive essay he helps us see how one conceptual framework (a modification of Parsons' scheme of pattern variables that we discussed in the last chapter) can help us explore and describe variations on the democratic theme in terms of dominant values.[22] This is an especially difficult job, since he chooses for analysis four English-speaking democracies (Australia, Canada, England, and the United States), thus minimizing variance. (Contrasts, classification, and the discovery of relationships are easier when variance is great.)

The question is: Do democratic value patterns vary, and if so, how, as a result of what, and what are the consequences? Drawing on historical accounts and others' observations, Lipset organizes his analysis around three of Parsons' variables, adding one of his own. He asks whether the value systems in these countries stress: (1) demonstrable achievement or inherited qualities (achievement-ascription), (2) dealing with others in terms of general standards or in terms of the peculiarities of a special relationship (universalism-particularism), (3) relating to others in narrowly limited or broadly defined ways (specificity-diffuseness), and (4) regarding others as equals or making distinctions registered in deference, condescension, or *noblesse oblige?* I can convey some impression of his analysis in the summary given on page 579.

No claim is made that this analysis *demonstrates* the existence of such differentiated values among four democracies, however plausible they may seem from the limited data available. It is, of course, extraordinarily difficult to establish the existence, generality, and

---

[21] See Gorer's two books, *The American People* (New York: W. W. Norton & Co., Inc., 1943) and *Exploring English Character, a Study of the Morals and Behavior of the English People* (New York: Criterion Books, Inc., 1955).

[22] Seymour Martin Lipset, "The Value Patterns of Democracy: A Case Study in Comparative Analysis," *American Sociological Review,* Vol. XXVIII, No. 4 (August, 1963).

intensity of values formed through time and responding to the peculiarities of historical circumstance. (Canadian values probably cannot be understood, as Lipset intimates, apart from a defensive posture vis-à-vis the United States, or Australian values without recognizing the equalitarian and antiauthoritarian impulses of penal colonists, refugees from poverty and a rigid class system.)

But Lipset does suggest that such a conceptual framework may be useful in teasing out fundamental value assumptions that shape a nation's polity. Their existence seems the more likely as we can trace their impact in other sectors of the social order. The significance of equalitarian, universalistic, and achievement orientations is attested when we find "that almost seven times as large a group was attending [institutions of higher learning] in the United States as in England and Wales."[23] (This is percent of total population in the 20–24 age category, around 1956.) In the civic sphere, Australia's egalitarian values diminish the significance of leadership, and the "disdain for acquiring wealth for its own sake has made it difficult for wealthy classes to enter politics and serve as community leaders."[24] Some observations suggest that the two more equalitarian countries tolerate more lawlessness than do Canada and England. And the same equalitarian self-assertion may enable more radical assaults on the establishment than would be the case where a quite general (diffuse) deference to authority and its competence (ascription) permits "a more unified and powerful political elite to control the system."[25]

The Locus of Power, and Challenges from Right and Left

This last suggests another point of purchase for the sociology of politics. No system of authority, and least of all a democratic one, effectively controls the sources of the differences that produce the deviant. Movements that mobilize deviants and challenge existing power relationships concern the sociologist; for their study instructs us about conditions of social stability and change. (Lipset argues that while we have been much intrigued with such transient, extremist movements, we badly need to understand more about the factors that, in a democracy, operate to resist or curtail extremism.

---

[23] *Ibid.*, p. 524.
[24] *Ibid.*, p. 522.
[25] *Ibid.*, p. 525.

	United States	England	Australia	Canada
Equalitarian-Elite	Stress on equality of men. Source: break with past and traditional legitimation of a ruling class Necessary emphasis on equality of opportunity	Elitist, class a salient factor, hierarchical ordering of statuses	More equalitarian than the U.S. or Canada	In elitism, next to England, "repelled by the doctrine of the rights of man and all it implied." Effective, centralized legal and police system countered frontier influence, supported traditional orientations In part a reaction to American stress on equalitarianism
	Class consciousness not salient			
Achievement-Ascription	Competitive-dominant values legitimate upward striving, precluding need for revolutionary tactics, hence political goals and methods are moderate	Birth and class still ascriptive features of importance while not foreclosing claims of lower classes based on achievement, especially in economic and educational spheres, new elites in business and politics penetrate outer fringes of establishment	Success in conventional terms relatively unimportant in contrast to value placed on "mateship" and the reciprocal obligations of this relationship	Intermediate in value on achievement . . . among those aged 20–24, twice the proportion of the English in colleges and universities, but less than ⅓ the proportion for the U.S.
	General access to education	More restricted access to education		
Universalism-Particularism	All men expected and entitled to try to improve their positions; such a value allows upper classes to accept upward mobility as legitimate	Differentiated relationships to particular others	Particular relations to mates, or buddies	
	Every citizen entitled to penetrate government's operations/secrets	Particular status required for access to inner workings of government		
Specificity-Diffuseness	Specific achievements condition relationships	High birth and status accorded diffuse deference		

And, of course, one such factor, the crosscutting of group affiliations, we have already considered.)

About these movements of the left and right (the Birch Society, the Communists, the KKK), the sociologist asks questions such as these: What are their social roots, the social conditions generating fears, protests, hopes, and commitments of their members? What sort of person do they recruit? What sectors of society do they come from? How do we account for their rise and fall, their failures and successes? To what extent are they grass roots? How is the protest given form and force?

A summary of one such study is provided in Figure 13–2. The

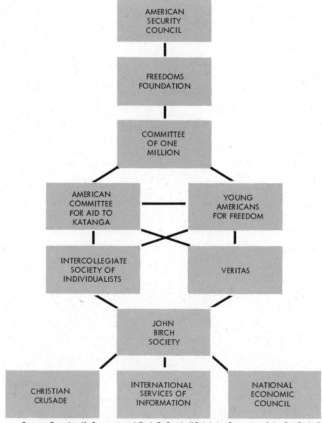

Source: Douglas K. Stewart and Ted C. Smith, "Celebrity Structure of the Far Right," *Western Political Quarterly*, Vol. XVIII, No. 2 (June, 1964), p. 353.

FIG. 13–2.   Interlocking control among 11 far-right organizations in which 50 percent or more of the top figures play similar roles in the indicated groups.

general problem underlying this research was the extent to which far-right movements were grass roots. A corollary query was whether there existed, and to what degree, a central nucleus to gather and shape protest. The figure presents certain organizations on the far (political) right, 50 percent of whose "celebrities" (trustees, directors, sponsors) played similar roles in the indicated organizations. Thus, more than half of the top people in the John Birch Society bridge into five other organizations: Christian Crusade, the National Economic Council, International Services of Information, Veritas, and the Intercollegiate Society of Individualists. This interlocking organizational control is also found in reform and philanthropic groups, in industry and business. Such analyses provide cues to the locus of power and the source of decisions. The investigators in this study conclude, reasonably enough, that, while a diffuse anxiety and resentment must be available to be mobilized, such a nucleus as that represented in this interlocking, rightist elite is also necessary to lend form and substance to an otherwise amorphous protest.

Where power resides, either in the establishment or among those opposed to it, is not easy to discern. Men in power are often in the wings, not on center stage. In Yankee City and Jonesville (studied by Warner and his associates) and in Regional City where Floyd Hunter did his research on community power structure,[26] late-coming professionals tended to be out in front while men of long, local lineage and wealth exerted, indirectly, disproportionate influence on community decisions.[27] Table 13–3 shows that, in Regional

---

[26] Hunter's study has provoked loud critical noises, chiefly from New Haven, and we might note some of the methodological problems posed by this sort of research. How shall we discover where in a community the power to influence others resides? Hunter was not so ingenuous as to assume that official position was an unerring indicator of power. He used presumably knowledgeable judges who came to agree in their selection of the 40 persons most influential in the spheres of business, government, civic associations, and "society" activities. This is the power-by-reputation technique. Unfortunately, people's knowledge may be inadequate and their judgments distorted. A third method is to estimate power by frequency of participation in decision making. But this rests on the hazardous assumption that participation equals power. A fourth method used by Professor Dahl to estimate influence was to score, for different sorts of decisions over a period of time, the frequency of successful initiation of, or opposition to a proposal. (See Robert A. Dahl, *Who Governs?* [New Haven: Yale University Press, 1961].)

[27] Reference here is to the study by W. Lloyd Warner, J. O. Low, Paul S. Lunt, and Leo Srole, *Yankee City* edited and abridged in the Yale University Press editior of 1963; to W. Lloyd Warner and associates, *Democracy in Jonesville* (New York: Harper & Bros., 1949); and to Floyd Hunter, *Community Power Structure* (Chapel Hill: University of North Carolina Press, 1953).

TABLE 13-3

Policy-Making Leaders in Regional City by Occupational Position

TYPE OF OCCUPATION	NAME OF LEADER	NAME OF ORGANIZATIONAL AFFILIATION	POSITION
Banking, Finance, Insurance	Hardy	Investment Company of Old State	President
	Mines	Producer's Investments	President
	Schmidt	First Bank	President
	Simpson	Second Bank	Vice-President
	Spade	Growers Bank	President
	Tarbell	Commercial Bank	Executive Vice-President
	Trable	Regional City Life	President
Commercial	Aiken	Livestock Company	Chairman, Board
	Black	Realty Company of Regional City	President
	Delbert	Allied Utilities	President
	Dunham	Regional Gas Heat Company	General Manager
	Graves	Refrigeration, Incorporated	President
	Parker	Mercantile Company	Executive Manager
	Parks	Paper Box Company	Chairman, Board
	Smith	Cotton Cloth Company	Manager
	C. Stokes	Oil Pipe Line Company	President
	Webster	Regional City Publishing Company	Managing Editor
	Williams	Mercantile Company	Chairman, Board
Government	Barner	City Government	Mayor
	Gordon	City Schools	Superintendent
	Rake	County Schools	Superintendent
	Worth	County Government	Treasurer
Labor	Gregory	Local Union	President
	Stone	Local Union	President
Leisure	Fairly	None	Social Leader
	Howe	None	Social Leader
	Mills	None	Social Leader
	Moore	None	Social Leader
	Stevens	None	Social Leader
Manufacture and Industry	Farris	Steel Spool Company	Chairman, Board
	Homer	Homer Chemical Company	Chairman, Board
	Spear	Homer Chemical Company	President
	E. Stokes	Stokes Gear Company	Chairman, Board
	Treat	Southern Yarn Company	President
Professional*	Farmer	Law Firm	Attorney
	Gould	Law Firm	Attorney
	Latham	Private Office	Dentist
	Moster	Law Firm	Attorney
	Street	Law Firm	Attorney
	Tidwell	Law Firm	Attorney

* Attorneys' affiliations not given. Without exception they are corporation lawyers.
Source: Floyd Hunter, *Community Power Structure* (Chapel Hill: University of North Carolina Press, 1953), p. 76.

City, few of the policy-making leaders were spotlighted by their official positions. Four out of 40 were in government positions. But over half were in business and industry. Six out of 40 were in the professions, all of them lawyers save one. Frequently, these men were directors of one another's corporations and belonged, many of them, to the same clubs. Decisions of some significance were often made informally, on ostensibly social occasions.

Hunter does us the service of underscoring the informal, and generally invisible, elements in a community power structure. But to think of a fixed structure is, in any complex community, to oversimplify matters. We can say that a person has power if he can so mobilize "influence resources" that, when he initiates or supports a proposal it wins, and when he opposes it, it loses. But is power so constant? Or does it shift, depending on the issue? Are issues alike, as to their valence or significance? fluoridation? a school bond issue? a city income tax? Are they commensurable? (Does a loss on the sewer issue precisely counterbalance a win on the appointment of a favored candidate to a post in the Treasurer's office?) Shall we estimate power without reckoning a person's level of interest in a given outcome? Such are the thorny questions that must be faced by the sociologist studying community power structures.

To speak of power is to imply resistance that must be overcome. To speak of rules is to imply their violation. We would not institute a system of rules with their concomitant sanctions were there not a fair probability that, upon occasion, they would be violated. Thus, the set of roles and relationships defining a group is preserved only through *constrained* adherence to the rules. But whatever the power vested in the authorities, this constraint is always imperfect, roughly as imperfect as the ratio of punishment to prevention. And so if deviance (due largely to cultivated human differences)[28] is to be expected, any enduring social system, like an organic system, has to be geared to ward off attack. If assaults on the system are fairly

---

[28] The *cultivated* character of deviant behavior is stressed by a sociologist who pioneered in the subfield of criminology, Edwin H. Sutherland. Presenting a theory of the process by which a person comes to engage in systematic criminal behavior he writes (in part): "Criminal behavior is *learned* . . . in [differential association and] interaction with other persons . . . [and the learning] includes (*a*) techniques of committing the crime, which are sometimes very complicated, sometimes very simple; (*b*) the specific direction of motives, drives, rationalizations, and attitudes." (Edwin H. Sutherland, *Principles of Criminology* [4th ed.; Philadelphia: J. B. Lippincott Co., 1947], p. 6.)

regular and actuarially predictable, then standing defenses can be established (the apparatus of law enforcement). But sometimes the threats are ambiguous, or unanticipated, or both. Under these circumstances, alarm spreads and members of the group may respond awkwardly, thrashing out in ways that violate their own cherished values. This was true under the proddings of the late Senator McCarthy of Wisconsin (not to be confused with the currently serving Senator McCarthy from Minnesota). Here was a situation in which many citizens felt threatened by alien values promoted by extralegal means. "Heresy, Yes! Conspiracy, No!" as Sidney Hook wrote in 1953.[29]

There is always the problem, then, of the degree of threat generated by different sorts of deviation. And there is the more refined question as to whether different subgroups or categories of society react differently to such a threat. The first amendment to our Constitution sustains a high level of tolerance for deviant views. ("Congress shall make no law respecting an establishment of religion, or prohibiting the free exercise thereof; or abridging the freedom of speech or of the press; or the right of the people peacably to assembly, and to petition the Government for a redress of grievances.") But what is written on paper may differ from what is inscribed in men's hearts and minds. And it is a question of interest to the sociologist what degree of tolerance for deviant behavior does in fact characterize the group, and subgroups within it.

This is the problem posed by one sociologist, Samuel Stouffer, in a study entitled *Communism, Conformity, and Civil Liberties*.[30] A discussion of this research will not only tell us something about tolerance of deviant beliefs and behavior; it will also acquaint us with a careful piece of empirical research having some novel features.

The dependent variable in this study is a measure of degree of tolerance of nonconformity along an ordinal scale. (Nonconformity in this case means Communism, Socialism or atheism.) There were three points along this scale called "relatively more tolerant," "in-between," and "relatively less tolerant." Stouffer was able to classify

---

[29] Sidney Hook, *Heresy, Yes! Conspiracy, No!* (New York: John Day Co., Inc., 1953).

[30] Samuel A. Stouffer, *Communism, Conformity, and Civil Liberties* (Garden City, N.Y.: Doubleday & Co., 1955). Copyright © 1955 by Samuel A. Stouffer.

his respondents in these categories by the method I describe, schematically, in Table 13–4.

TABLE 13–4

Scheme for Classifying Three Levels of Tolerance of Nonconformity in Stouffer's Study, *Communism, Conformity and Civil Liberties*

15 interview items arranged in sets of 3, from those indicating most tolerance to those showing least	Patterns of response indicating tolerance of nonconformity (giving 2, or 3 tolerant responses in five to no sets)	Classifying consistent patterns of response in 3 levels of tolerance of nonconformity
Sets of 3 items each	(+ = scored as tolerant)	Three-point ordinal scale
5th set (see below)*	+	relatively more tolerant = (scoring + on 5 or 4 sets of interview items)
4th set	+ +	
3rd set	+ + +	in-between = (scoring + on 3, or 2 sets)
2nd set	+ + + +	
1st set	+ + + + +	relatively less tolerant = (scoring + on 1, or 0 sets)
	Not giving 2 or 3 tolerant responses in any set	

Source: Samuel A. Stouffer, *Communism, Conformity, and Civil Liberties* (Garden City, N.Y.: Doubleday & Co., 1955.) Copyright © 1955 by Samuel A. Stouffer. Reprinted by permission of Doubleday & Co., Inc.

To make matters more concrete, let me reproduce the three interview items in the fifth set.[31] They were these (response scored as tolerant is indicated by an asterisk).

Now, I should like to ask you some questions about a man who admits he is a Communist. [Interviewer is addressing respondent.] (*a*) Suppose this admitted Communist wants to make a speech in your community. Should he be allowed to speak, or not?

          __ *Yes[32]

          __ No

          __ Don't know

---

[31] The preceding 12 items were similarly grouped in clusters of 3 questions each and scored in the same way.

[32] See "An Aside on Methods: The Guttman or Cornell Scale," p. 586.

An Aside on Methods: The Guttman or Cornell Scale

If a person gave tolerant responses on two out of the three items in this fifth set, we can be quite sure (and by "quite sure" I mean that 96 percent of the time we would be right) that he *would do likewise in each of the other sets of questions!* How can this be so? The answer to this question prompts another methodological detour to get a first acquaintance with the measure Stouffer is using here, a scale called the Guttman or Cornell scale. This sort of ordinal scale, or yardstick, has a special advantage that we call "unidimensionality." That is, it helps us deal with just one dimension at a time. This gives us more confidence in the *validity* of our measure. Now it may seem extraordinarily ingenuous for an investigator not to know what it is he is measuring, yet this is sometimes the case. What, for example, is represented by the independent variable when we find a high inverse correlation between density of population and age-specific birth rates? (The existence of a relationship may not tell us, in itself, what it is that we are measuring that accounts for the relationship.) The classic example is the intelligence test. How do we understand an inverse relationship between intelligence test scores and level of education achieved for a probability sample of Mississippi adults?

Professor Stouffer conveys very clearly the idea of the Guttman scaling procedure. Imagine, he says, a spelling test consisting of these three words: catastrophe, cattle, and cat.

This "test" has a very special kind of built-in internal consistency. If a person can spell the hardest word, he also is very likely to be able to spell the easier words. If he can spell only two words, we know *which* two words they are. If he can spell only one, we know *which* one that is. This is called a cumulative property of a test [or measure]. When we have only a few items, we *need some such built-in property in order to know whether we are measuring a single dimension.*

Unless our scale contains one dimension only, we cannot sensibly rank people in it. Consider a scale of "bigness" which mixes up both height and weight. Is a tall man who weighs 180 pounds bigger than a short fat man who weighs 220 pounds? One can rank people in terms of one *or* the other measure, but *not both on a single scale.* (Stouffer, *op. cit.,* p. 262; reprinted by permission of Doubleday & Co., Inc.; last emphasis in both paragraphs mine.)

The fact that we are dealing with a single scale, a single dimension, is revealed by the extent to which a given response (spells "catastrophe" correctly) implicates all others (also spells "cattle" and "cat" correctly). In the case of this tolerance-of-nonconformity scale, it is unidimensional to the extent that a person affirming 2 out of 3 tolerant responses in the 5th set, also does so in each of the 4 sets below. Similarly, a person who does not score as tolerant in the 5th set, but does on the 4th set of items must, if the scale is perfectly unidimensional, also give at least two out of three tolerant responses on the 3rd, 2nd, and first sets.

Not everybody, of course, will be wholly consistent. The degree of consistency is measured by a coefficient of reproducibility, which, by convention, must be at least .90. The coefficient [of reproducibility, the extent to which, knowing the person's score, we also know how he answered on each item] for this scale is a very satisfactory .96 and is exactly the same when the scale is constructed separately from the data from each of the two survey agencies. Moreover, separate tabulations by education showed that the reproducibility was approximately the same at all educational levels. (*Ibid.,* p. 266.)

(*b*) Suppose he wrote a book which is in your public library. Somebody in your community suggests the book should be removed from the library. Would you favor removing it, or not?

      __ Favor

      __ *Don't favor

      __ Don't know

(*c*) Suppose this admitted Communist is a radio singer. Should he be fired, or not?

      __ Should be fired

      __ *Should not be fired

      __ Don't know[33]

Other items, in the four other sets of three questions each, dealt with antireligionists (atheists, for example), socialists, and persons whose loyalty had been questioned before a Congressional investigating committee.

(A similar scale was developed for a second dependent variable, extent of perception of threat of Communism within the United States.)

Now the problem was to discover how adult citizens responded to the threat of nonconforming views and values and, if various subgroups of citizens differed in their responses, how they did so. To answer these questions *two* national probability samples of adult, U.S. citizens were drawn, independently, by two research agencies. These were the National Opinion Research Center (NORC) and the American Institute of Public Opinion (AIPO). This is a unique aspect of the study, for such a parallel but independent gathering of data had not hitherto been done nor, to my knowledge has it been done since. It allows an item-by-item comparison of the findings of two agencies, operating independently. (The data from NORC and AIPO are quite alike, often identical.) A combination of the two samples gave Stouffer data gotten by 537 competent interviewers on 4,933 cases.

Another sample was drawn, this of community leaders in those cities of 10,000 to 150,000, falling in the sample. Leaders were defined as persons in these roles:

. . . the mayor, the president of the Chamber of Commerce, the chairman of the Community Chest, the president of a . . . large labor-union local in the city, the chairmen of the Republican and Democratic county central committees, the commander of the largest American Legion post in the city, the regent of the D.A.R., the president of the

---

[33] *Ibid.*, Appendix C, p. 28; reprinted by permission of Doubleday & Co., Inc.

local Women's club, the chairmen of the school board and the library board, the president of the bar association, the publisher of the locally owned newspaper of largest circulation.[34]

Let me summarize certain central findings of this study by asking the reader to estimate which, in the paired categories that follow, tend to be more tolerant of the sort of nonconformity represented in atheism, Communism and Socialism.[35]

> Community leaders, or the rank and file of the national cross section?
> Younger people or older people?
> The better, or the less well educated?
> People living in the larger cities, or in smaller places?
> Northerners, or southerners?
> Men, or women?
> Non-church attenders or regular church attenders?
> Those viewing the internal communist threat as slight, or those seeing it as relatively great?

In each case, the first category is that of the more tolerant as classified (through use of the Guttman scale) in the scheme that I have just described. (Graphic illustrations of two sets of findings are shown in Figures 13–3 and 13–4).

Before leaving this study of leader and citizen response to deviant patterns (the tolerance dimension of civic relationships), let me add three comments.

First, this is a bare-bones, unqualified report of some of Stouffer's findings. It scarcely represents the care and clarity with which the investigator handles his data. The two-variable relationships listed above—for example, level of tolerance related to leadership-follow-ership—neglects other variables that Stouffer holds constant in making his analysis. (You will note in Figure 13–4 that he relates age of respondent to level of tolerance while holding education constant, and relates tolerance and level of education achieved while controlling age.) Furthermore, as the sociologist must do, Stouffer takes pains to point to sources of error. Sampling is one such source, but one well handled in this study. Slight changes in wording and inflection of voice on the part of interviewers may introduce error. Again, error may be introduced when a sizable part of the sample is not interviewed, persons who may differ in some

---

[34] *Ibid.*, p. 125.

[35] But, of course, you should consult the book itself to note variations in percentages for various items dealing with free speech, books in public libraries, the right to teach, and the like.

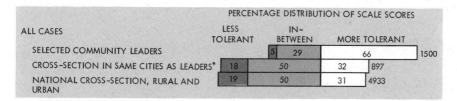

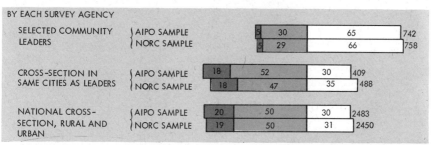

* For the definition of "community leader" see page 587, and for the method of developing the measure of level of tolerance, see "An Aside on Methods: The Guttman or Cornell Scale," p. 586.

Source: Samuel A. Stouffer, *Communism, Conformity, and Civil Liberties* (Garden City, N.Y.: Doubleday & Co., 1955), p. 51. Copyright © 1955 by Samuel A. Stouffer. Reprinted by permission of Doubleday & Co., Inc.

FIG. 13-3. A comparison of community leaders with rank and file of a national cross section of adult U.S. population on level of tolerance of nonconforming views (Communist, Socialist, and atheist).

consistent fashion from those who do respond. In this study, 84 percent of the sample interviews were completed. What of the other 16 percent? Stouffer turns his attention to these people: those not at home, despite five visits by the interviewer; people too sick to be interviewed; those cases where the respondent could not speak English (or the interviewer's second language, if he had one); those who refused to be interviewed (7 percent); and those (another 1 percent) who broke off the interview for one reason or another. A careful analysis of nonrespondents' demographic and other characteristics, so far as these could be gotten, led Stouffer to conclude that the loss of these respondents did not distort the findings.

Second, such findings do not speak for themselves. There is the matter of interpretation. Stouffer suggests, for example, that these observations may "reflect the operation of a factor which may be essential to tolerance; namely, that of contact with people with disturbing and unpopular ideas."[36] Another observation of interest: since level of education is positively related to the "relatively great

---

[36] *Ibid.*

tolerance" scores, and since average level of education is moving up, it seems reasonable to predict that expression of unpopular views may be more tolerated in future than it has been in the past. It would be well to read the book, obviously, for further interpretations of the findings.

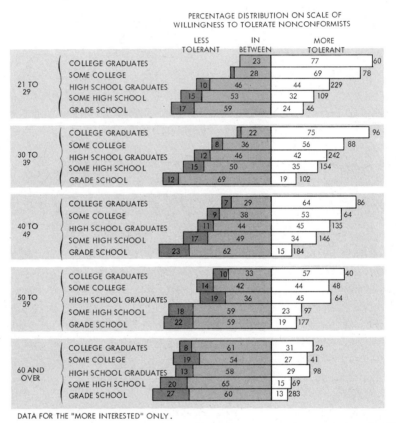

PERCENTAGE DISTRIBUTION ON SCALE OF
WILLINGNESS TO TOLERATE NONCONFORMISTS

DATA FOR THE "MORE INTERESTED" ONLY.

Source: Samuel A. Stouffer, *Communism, Conformity, and Civil Liberties* (Garden City, N.Y.: Doubleday & Co., 1955), p. 93. Copyright © 1955 by Samuel A. Stouffer. Reprinted by permission of Doubleday & Co., Inc.

FIG. 13-4. Relationship between level of tolerance of nonconforming views and (1) level of education achieved, holding age constant, (2) age of respondent, holding educational achievement constant.

But let's not miss the point, the forest for the trees. Communism, socialism, and atheism do have some intrinsic interest, and Stouffer's methodology does help acquaint us with the field. But our concern is a more general one: democratic process, the bill of rights, legitimate authority, and challenges to them. We noted the challenge to the establishment by such rightist groups as those studied by Stewart and Smith (see Figure 13–2). But this is not unique. The gauntlet is thrown down from left as well as right—and from intermediate points between these extremes. So, also, do criminal and other aberrant behaviors challenge group stability. But in our society certain challenges to authority—those touching belief and expression, in particular—are protected in law. This generates an interplay of challenge and response. And there are always the questions: How much challenge is tolerable? Which categories of citizens are more tolerant of such deviations, which least? What sorts of challenges are there, and how do they differ in gravity?

The problem is complex, for deviation has ambivalent effects. If not too novel and if the rate of incidence is fairly steady, deviation may enhance stability in the social order by providing the occasion, through trial and punishment, of reaffirming group values and authorized means for achieving them. (In this light, the courtroom is a secular church.) Like other systems, a group develops certain values and the norms of conduct that embody them. So also there emerges a range of behavior to "right" and "left" of norms, a range felt commonly to be tolerable. What this range is, by type of deviation, for differing social categories is, as we have seen, a problem of marked interest for the political sociologist.

We have been reviewing a quite arbitrary array of illustrative problems in the field of political sociology, problems bearing on the power dimension of human relationships—and the rules underlying the roles that define such relationships. In brief review, recall three problems bearing on requisites, in the social structure, for a democratic polity: (1) the probable connection between degree of power concentration and freedom, the latter being, it is suggested, a curvilinear function of the former, (2) the significance of crosscutting group affiliations in moderating radical and simplistic solutions, and producing a more measured rate of change, and (3) the significance of a quite general diffusion of wealth and knowledge as necessary for a democratic system. But there are permutations of the democratic theme. There is the possibility that differing value emphases may help us understand differing polities, even those as close as the four democratic nations dealt with in Lipset's study, in which he tested the usefulness of Parsons' patterns variables for analyzing value schemes.

In the interlocking directorates of eleven far-right groups, we saw how latent disaffection can be mobilized to protest and challenge the establishment. But the target for protest is not always clearly visible. For research on community power structures has revealed what C. Wright Mills called an unofficial "power elite," although this too may oversimplify the picture. For those whose influence is crucial may change depending on the issues at stake.

Sociologists have posed many other questions touching the power dimension of human relationships. How does the rationality of bureaucratic organization operate among interviewers in a public employment agency? (Or, to put a rhetorical question: Is there an irrationality in close adherence to bureaucratic rules?) How are people recruited for the role of professional politician? What attributes are peculiar to those who see politics as a vocation? What relationship obtains between work role (occupation) and political orientation? What are the sources and concomitants of different roles—spectator, citizen, and partisan—in an election? Who exert most influence on what kinds of community decisions? How can we describe and understand the social structure of the American military? What are the antecedents, and what power is wielded by military leaders? What social attributes are correlated with sentiments of white supremacy, so conditioning distribution of power?

These are all inquiries that have in fact been made.[37] Such a range helps us appreciate the generic character of the power dimension in human relationships. Law—although not, in the technical sense, legal—we find everywhere. Some type and degree of authority penetrates all social spheres. Rules govern roles throughout society and some degree and type of power invests most relationships. The size and might of government will not, then, delude us into thinking that there alone does governing take place. To pin down the point, let us as a final instance, look at the governing of a labor union, the

---

[37] These and related questions are dealt with in such studies as the following: Peter Blau, *The Dynamics of Bureaucracy* (Chicago: University of Chicago Press, 1955); Heinz Eulau and John D. Sprague, *Lawyers in Politics* (Indianapolis: Bobbs-Merrill Co., Inc., 1964); Duncan MacRea, Jr., "Occupations and the Congressional Vote, 1940–1950," *American Sociological Review*, Vol. XX, No. 3 (June, 1955), pp. 332–40; W. S. Robinson, "The Motivational Structure of Political Participation," *American Sociological Review*, Vol. XVII, No. 2 (April, 1952), pp. 151–56; R. E. Agger and Daniel Goldrich, "Community Power Structure and Partisanship," *American Sociological Review*, Vol. XXIII, No. 4 (August, 1958), pp. 383–92; Morris Janowitz, *The Professional Soldier: a Social and Political Portrait* (New York: Free Press of Glencoe, Inc., 1960); David M. Heer, "The Sentiment of White Supremacy: an Ecological Study," *American Journal of Sociology*, Vol. LXIV, No. 6 (May, 1959), pp. 552–98.

International Typographers Union, investigated in depth by Lipset, Trow, and Coleman.[38]

THE GOVERNING OF A UNION

Let me recount, quite briefly, the problem, the methods, and the findings of this inquiry.

The problem: How can we explain a persisting pattern of two-party, democratic government in a labor union? An answer to this will help us understand the conditions of democracy in other groups, and in society at large. The ITU is a case of special interest, for almost alone among labor unions—and, the author of the "iron law of oligarchy" might add, among organizations in general—it has successfully resisted oligarchic tendencies. The famous proposition of Robert Michels, to which the ITU seems an exception, is this:

> It is organization which gives birth to the dominion of the elected over the electors, of the mandataries over the mandators, of the delegates over the delagators. Who says organization says oligarchy.[39]

And indeed the power of office, together with passivity of a group's members does often lead to oligarchy, the persistence in control of a small and privileged elite who transform themselves into a permanent government. Why has this not been the case with the ITU? This was the problem.

This classic inquiry investigates a single deviant case in depth. It follows a method, or the first step in a method, sometimes referred to as analytic induction. With a provisional definition of the behavior to be studied, an hypothesis is stated and tested in the individual case. To the extent that our hypothesis fails to fit the data, we are required either (1) to revise the hypothesis so that it does fit our observations and/or (2) exclude the cases that fail to fit, reducing the generality of the original statement and redefining the range of phenomena under inquiry. Having made such revisions we can then approach a second case and so continue until the fit of hypothesis and observations is adequate.[40] The study of the ITU has

---

[38] Seymour M. Lipset, Martin A. Trow, and James S. Coleman, *Union Democracy* (New York: Free Press of Glencoe, Inc., 1956).

[39] Robert Michels, *Political Parties* (New York: Free Press of Glencoe, Inc., 1949), p. 401.

[40] See the lucid discussion of this procedure in W. S. Robinson, "The Logical Structure of Analytic Induction," *American Sociological Review,* Vol. XVI, No. 6 (December, 1951).

some features of analytic induction. But in the background of this intensive analysis of a single case, there is always implicit the existence of other union organizations whose government differs markedly, thus providing a base line for assessing the ITU's peculiarities. Thus it has features of the retrospective experiment, a study in comparative politics. And of course we ask: What accounts for the difference?

Most of the data for this study came from interviews with a random sample of printers who were active members of New York Typographical Union Number 6, working in shops employing three or more men. The investigators describe their two-stage sample (a sampling first of print shops, then of men within them) as follows:

Stage I	Stage II
(Stratified by shop size, three levels)	
3–20 men: ⅙ sample of shops	⅓ sample of men
21–99 men: ⅓ sample of shops	⅙ sample of men
100 + men: every shop	⅟₁₈ sample of men

Source: Seymour M. Lipset, Martin A. Trow, and James S. Coleman, *Union Democracy* (New York: Free Press of Glencoe Inc., 1956), p. 433.

The 434 interviews with printers were supplemented by 66 interviews with chapel (shop) chairmen, for a total of 500. Interview items were appropriately combined to yield the following indexes: liberal-conservative, extent of knowledge of union political issues, ideological sensitivity (coded from responses to open-ended questions about union policies and candidates for office), participation in printers' formal organizations, and informal relations.

Other sources of information included histories of unionization, and the background of the ITU in particular, comparative occupational studies, union voting records, and the like.

Now as to findings. One significant finding points to the remarkably tight occupational community formed by printers, and the social conditions contributing to it. There is the peculiarly intermediate position of printers (straddling manual and nonmanual occupations, working- and middle-class strata); their tradition of literacy, power, independence, and shop autonomy; their pride in the craft; a substitute system that ties a man seeking employment to a shop and his friends among the printers there; the peculiar isolation of night work, so common in this group—all features promoting interaction within the group, and generating a distinctive identity.

Together with, and stemming from, this sense of community, the investigators found a great elaboration of secondary organizations within the shop. Printers form social and athletic clubs, bowling leagues, even lodges and veterans' posts. They arise through the social relationships of men in the shop. Such interest groups have no formal connection with the union. Yet the higher the value of the index of social relations (referred to above), the greater the interest in, and discussion of, union politics, attendance at union meetings, and reading of the typographical journal. In the context of such subgroups, we have good ground for generating ideas, for the training (uncalculated, often) of potential opposition leaders, a springboard for participating in larger political settings and, sometimes, a seedbed for crystallizing discontent. The implications of these observations are extended in some powerful propositions.

> *Nonexistence of secondary organizations,* or a *mass society,* helps maintain a *conservative oligarchy,* such as is found in South American dictatorships, in Europe before the nineteenth century, or in the average stable American trade union.
>
> *Existence of secondary organization* [such as those elaborated in printers' shops]
>
> 1. *controlled* by the government, helps maintain revolutionary totalitarianism, intent on making changes within the society which it governs, as in Nazi Germany or Soviet Russia.
> 2. *independent* of the government, helps maintain *democracy* such as is found within the ITU, or in the United States or most European democracies.[41]

This study makes it crystal clear that nonconformity on significant issues depends on social support, on renforcing relationships with others sharing similar sentiments. (The larger shops more readily offer appropriate conditions for such support, both on and off the job.)

Another significant conclusion is this. The narrowness of the status gap between rank-and-file printer and union official enhances the former's power while reducing the tendency to cling tenaciously to union office as the sole source of standing.

> The chapels (shops) and printers' clubs are arenas of activity in which men can gain the status rewards of leadership without accepting the discipline of the administration machine and without being dependent on its approval. In this respect the existence of alternative sources of status in a union operates in similar and parallel fashion to the rough

[41] Lipset, Trow and Coleman, *op. cit.,* pp. 79, 80.

equality of status between working printer and union leader: *Both work to reduce the status stake that union activists have in holding union office, and by reducing that stake, reduce the dependency of officials on the incumbent administration and increase the chances of their supporting opposition groups.*[42]

There are important political consequences, too, from the traditional two-party system in the ITU. Members of groups having a legitimate two-party system are able, as is less likely in a one-party system, to discriminate between the organization and its administration, recognizing that the two are not identical and that there is a chance for the common will to effect changes. Furthermore:

> . . . the two-party system serves to deflect discontent among members and opposition leaders away from the union itself and toward the party in power. Thus in the ITU discontent works to maintain the party system . . . while at the same time serving to strengthen rather than undermine the unity and effectiveness of the union. . . .[43]

In larger organizations, the conditions promoting bureaucracy (technical complexities, power delegated to an incumbent administration) discourage democracy. Normally, members' occupations are not so much the nucleus of life, avocation and vocation will not merge to the extent they do among ITU members. Indifference and passivity result. Also, in large and bureaucratic organizations the democratic principle enabling membership to dethrone the leader is harder to support; for here the status differences between followers and leaders are great.

> Given the great emphasis placed by the social structure on achieving and maintaining high status, it is clear that the norms of democracy in trade unions and those of achievement in the larger society are often in sharp conflict. This may help account for the fact that democracy is found mostly in unions of high-status occupations or in small local organizations in which the status differentiation between leaders and followers is very small. Where the status gap is large, the leader is under strain from his position to institutionalize dictatorial mechanisms which will reduce the possibility that he may lose his office.[44]

*   *   *   *

Thus we get some sense of the universality of governing, the generality of power, the forms it takes and its intimate dependence on the nature of the social structure.

---

[42] *Ibid.*, p. 218.

[43] *Ibid.*, p. 269.

[44] *Ibid.*, p. 404.

Stemming from differences among men and the need to bridge them with common (and enforced) understandings, government functions to channel conduct within the bounds of common values. We invoke rules, we govern, lest the power investing human relationships destroy them. But we also invoke the constraints of law in order to achieve ends otherwise unattainable. Thus the paradoxical, dual outcome of government under law: it is at once restraining and liberating. And, from the perspective of the social order, it is an integrating institution linking citizen with citizen in common cause.

Since power is a significant dimension of human relationships, it becomes one focus for sociological inquiry. I've touched on a scattered few of these inquiries as examples of work in the field. One study suggests a complex connection between freedom and degree of concentration of power. Others point to the significance of political pluralism, affluence, urbanism, industrialism, and education as requisites for democratic modes of governing. Another study by Lipset was able to differentiate forms of rule in terms of values that imply different ways of dealing with others: elitism-equalitarianism, achievement-ascription, specificity-diffuseness, universalism-particularism. Another pair of studies suggests how, in a society like ours, the formal locus of power may be challenged from left and right; and how such challenges vary in force through different sectors of the population. Finally, the study of a union's government points to political mechanisms in support of democratic process, while reminding us that these matters are not peculiar to capitol, court, or congress.

Government is one among several of those "frozen answers to fundamental questions" that we call institutions. These constitute the gyroscope, the flywheel of society, maintaining the group, sustaining the system of social relationships that is the social order.

The other side of the coin, changes in the group, is the problem to which we now turn our attention.

SELECTED SUPPLEMENTARY READINGS

BERELSON, BERNARD, AND STEINER, GARY A. "Political Institutions," in *Human Behavior: An Inventory of Scientific Findings*, pp. 417–36. New York: Harcourt, Brace & World, 1964.

———— "Military Institutions," *ibid.*, pp. 443–49.

BIERSTEDT, ROBERT. "An Analysis of Social Power," *American Sociological Review,* Vol. 15, No. 6 (December, 1950), pp. 730–38.

EULAU, HEINZ; ELDERSVELD, SAMUEL J.; AND JANOWITZ, MORRIS (eds.). *Political Behavior.* New York: The Free Press of Glencoe, Inc., 1956.

KORNHAUSER, WILLIAM. *The Politics of Mass Society.* New York: The Free Press of Glencoe, Inc., 1959.

———. "Political Sociology," in Robert K. Merton, Leonard Broom, and Leonard S. Cottrell, Jr. (eds.), *Sociology Today,* ch. iii. New York: Harper & Row—Harper Torchbooks, 1965.

———. "Some Social Requisites of Democracy: Economic Development and Political Legitimacy," *American Political Science Review,* Vol. LIII (March, 1959), pp. 69–105.

———. "The Radical Right: A Problem for American Democracy," *British Journal of Sociology,* 1955, pp. 176–209.

LIPSET, SEYMOUR MARTIN. *Political Man.* New York: Doubleday & Co., Inc., 1960.

MacIVER, ROBERT M. *The Web of Government.* New York: The Macmillan Co., 1947.

SELZNICK, PHILIP. "The Sociology of Law," in Merton, Broom, and Cottrell (eds.), *op. cit., supra,* ch. iv.

*STRODTBECK, FRED L., AND HOOK, L. HARMON. "The Social Dimensions of a Twelve-Man Jury Table," *Sociometry,* 1961, pp. 397–415.

———.; JAMES, RITA M.; AND HAWKINS, CHARLES. "Social Status in Jury Deliberations," *American Sociological Review,* Vol. 22, No. 6 (December, 1957), pp. 713–19.

---

* Articles marked with an asterisk are available as reprints from the college division of the Bobbs-Merrill Company, Indianapolis, Indiana.

Part 3 Changes in the Group

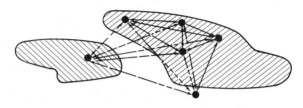

⬡ RULES (THE CULTURAL MATRIX)
● ROLES
⇄ RELATIONSHIPS (REENFORCING AND ATTENUATED)

Chapter 14

Sources of Change in Patterns of Human Relationships

What are some of the chief sources of change in a social system, especially in ours, and how do we interpret them?

In Part 2 we questioned the obvious: How is it that this marvelously intricate web of feeling, thought, and conduct—this social order—is maintained? In this chapter I want to point out that social change is the other side of the coin from group maintenance: that if forces making for integration promote maintenance, then in their absence, or in inverse form, they promote social change. After discussing the great-man theory and the culture-lag theory of social change, I shall go on to propose a third notion, the crossroads view of social change. After illustrating this perspective on social and cultural change, I would like to dwell for a bit on the city as locus and focus of social change, the most significant crossroads in Euroamerican societies.

First, then, to ask (and to answer) the question: How is the group maintained is also to ask and answer its opposite, How does it change? For if we know what holds it together we know, also, what weakens the ties that bind. If isolation promotes the integration of the group, then contact threatens that integration. If multibonded relationships promote cohesiveness, then single-bonded relationships erode it. If a real or alleged kinship network, or the threat of an external enemy, or the pervasive influence of the sacred, domi-

601

nating most of life's transactions—if these contribute to group unity and stability, then their opposites may promote change: declining significance of the blood bond, amicable relationships with outsiders, or an increasingly instrumental or secular orientation.

LACK OF INTEGRATION AND THE STRAIN TOWARD CHANGE

But integration, like some people and most concepts, profits from refinement. As we saw in Chapter 9, Professor Landecker has developed such a refinement of this idea.[1] His suggestion, you'll recall, was that group integration (and maintenance) depends upon: (1) consistency among the standards that guide people's conduct; (2) conformity, in conduct, to these standards; (3) extensive communication among group members—communication would of course tend to promote consistency among and conformity to standards; and (4) reciprocal rendering of differentiated services (functional integration).

As an example of the strain toward change arising from failure in the first form of integration (consistency among standards) we can think of any situation in which people have opposing or incompatible conceptions of things. Robert Lynd's statements cited in Chapter 2 illustrate such failures in cultural integration. The belligerent patriot in wartime versus the pacifist is a case in point. Senator Paul Douglas, himself a Quaker, says: "Thank God for the Quakers. And thank God there are not more of them." For if there were, he implies, the lack of cultural integration would do the group in. (While the Quaker's pacifism sustains *intra*group solidarity, it threatens *inter*group unity.) Richard Hofstadter writes about the

---

[1] Werner S. Landecker, "Types of Integration and Their Measurement," *American Journal of Sociology*, published by the University of Chicago Press, Vol. LVI, No. 4 (January, 1951), p. 332.

Professor Landecker's second paragraph is worth citing at length. He is contrasting the old and the new mode of formulating the problem of integration—and, from our point of view at the moment, of dis-integration, or social change. He writes:

"From the modern empirical point of view the problem of social integration is as challenging as it was from the older, more speculative point of view. However, a change has occurred as to the kind of question asked about integration. Nowadays it seems less pertinent to ask: What *is* integration? If this question is asked at all, then it is only in preparation for the more fruitful question: How can integration be measured? And again, this latter question is not of interest in itself but merely a preliminary step, which leads to genuine problems of research such as these: under what conditions does social integration increase? . . . decrease? What are the consequences of a high degree of integration? . . . a low degree of integration?"

Unplanned change: rural-agrarian past to urban-industrial present.

lack of cultural integration exemplified in anti-intellectualism in the United States. Those who celebrate the intellect are confronted by others characterized by ". . . a resentment and suspicion of the life of the mind and of those who are considered to represent it, and a disposition constantly to minimize the value of that life."[2] Consider the attitude toward books, literature, philosophy that we expect among university students, academicians, and intellectuals to say nothing of librarians, and the view expressed by this representative to the Georgia Assembly:

> Read the Bible. It teaches you how to act. Read the hymnbook. It contains the finest poetry every written. Read the almanac. It shows you how to figure out what the weather will be. There isn't another book that it is necessary for anyone to read, and therefore I'm opposed to all libraries.[3]

Currently the best example of a failure of Landecker's second type of integration (normative) is the discrepancy between practice and profession documented in Gunnar Myrdal's *An American Dilemma*, exposing the conflict between democratic ideals and actual practices of racial discrimination. Equality and liberty are keystones of the American creed: equality, both moral and civil; and liberty to the extent that the citizen does not abridge others' rights. Jefferson declared: "All men are created equal and from that equal creation they derive rights inherent and unalienable, among which are the preservation of life and liberty and the pursuit of happiness."[4] In further elaboration of the American creed, Charles Merriam writes:

> Democracy is a form of political association in which the general control and direction of the commonwealth is habitually determined by the bulk of the community in accordance with understandings and procedures providing for popular participation and consent. Its postulates are:
>
> 1. The essential dignity of man, the importance of protecting and cultivating his personality on a fraternal rather than upon a differential basis, of reconciling the needs of the personality within the framework of the common good in a formula of liberty, justice, welfare.

---

[2] Richard Hofstadter, *Anti-Intellectualism in American Life* (New York: Alfred A. Knopf, Inc., 1963), p. 7.

[3] *Ibid.*, p. 125.

[4] Cited by Gunnar Myrdal, *An American Dilemma* (New York: Harper & Bros., 1944), Vol. I, p. 9, from Ernest S. Bates, *American Faith* (New York: W. W. Norton and Company, Inc., 1940), pp. 274 ff.

2. The perfectibility of man; confidence in the possibilities of the human personality, as over against the doctrines of caste, class and slavery.
3. That the gains of commonwealths are essentially mass gains rather than the efforts of the few and should be diffused as promptly as possible throughout the community without too great delay or too wide a spread in differentials.[5]
4. Confidence in the value of the consent of the governed expressed in institutions, understandings and practices as a basis of order, liberty, justice.
5. The value of decisions arrived at by common counsel rather than by violence and brutality.[6]

In the United States none of these elements of the American creed has been realized for the Negro. His dignity is affronted, his race is used as a symbol of nonperfectibility, of inherent traits precluding the full realization of human potential. Whatever the "gains of the commonwealth," they are disproportionately meager in their distribution to the 10 percent of our citizens who are Negro. The restriction of Negro suffrage by conscious device and unwitting deprivation makes it impossible to gain the consent of the governed for this large sector of our population. And rather than arriving at decisions by common counsel, we have often resorted to violence and brutality in solving the problems attending the Negro's long haul from a depressed status to full citizenship.

Which is to say, in short, that practice has not matched profession. Conduct, failing to conform to our standards, threatens the integration of American society. This discrepancy, infinitely cruel in its individual impact and quite probably beyond the comprehension of even the most sensitive whites, drove Richard Wright to Europe;

---

[5] This was crucial to the position of Henry George who advocated a sole tax, that on land whose value was created socially ("mass gains") by growing population and improvements in *others'* real estate and in *their* productivity. This indigent seaman, reporter, and editor became preoccupied with the problem of poverty. Educating himself in economics—Malthus, Mill, Ricardo, Marx—he sought the solution to poverty. Capital and labor he saw as productive elements. But the landlord—and he meant almost literally the lord of the land—subsisted on unearned income, an income increasingly exploitative as, with increased population, its ownership devolved upon a smaller and smaller proportion of the whole. But this landed minority reaped the rewards of enhanced value, value that was a social product. (For example, a community grows and increased demand for land inflates real estate prices. Or a secondhand car dealer locates near or next to a competitor because his competitor brings potential buyers to the area. In each case the value of the land is a socially contributed value.) Increases in the value of land were, then, "mass gains" and should be "diffused . . . throughout the community" which created them.

[6] Charles E. Merriam, "The Meaning of Democracy," *Journal of Negro Education*, July, 1941, p. 309.

and also, James Baldwin who returned to warn us against *The Fire Next Time*.[7] Our social order shudders under this strain toward change, the costly shift from a pattern of relationships we label "segregation" to one that we call, significantly, "integration."

When there is a lack of both cultural and normative integration, it is a fair inference that there is a defect in communicative integration, Landecker's third type. Where opposing emphases upon individualism and collectivism go unreconciled, where we preach patriotism yet avoid civic duties, it is clear that communication must be garbled, impeded. Where differences are deep, having overtones of the sacred (the "system of free American enterprise" versus "national responsibility for minimum levels of welfare and security"), members of the warring camps withdraw to their own ranks, associating with the like-minded, "right-thinking" persons. Within the ranks communication is frequent, meaningful, reinforcing. Communication with the "enemy" then becomes infrequent, stereotyped, and officially conveyed in belligerent ultimatums.

We have an example of the disruption of communication in the case of the Hutterites and their more conventional fellow citizens: two groups within a larger whole, each being relatively consistent, internally, in behaviors and beliefs, but quite at odds externally, as they confront one another. A report of recent antipathies ran as follows:

> The communal farm colonies of the Hutterian brethren will be investigated this summer by a Montana state legislative committee. Some of the critics of the religious colonies have pledged money to a supplementary private investigation.
>
> It appears that the aim of both investigations will be the discovery of information on which to base yet another assault on the right of the Hutterites to live on communal farms as religious colonies standing aside from the mainstream of life. . . .
>
> When the legislative investigation begins, it will be directed by Representative Elmer Schye, a highway construction contractor and a Republican of White Sulphur Springs, a small town in the cattle country about 100 miles south of here. Two colonies of Hutterites have located recently in Mr. Schye's area.
>
> "They are no service to the community," said Mr. Schye. "They don't spend any money; they won't go to war; they just create social problems."
>
> A resolution directing the investigation was adopted but a companion bill providing $5,000 for expenses failed. It was at this point that

[7] James Baldwin, *The Fire Next Time* (New York: Dial Press, 1963).

Mr. (Ted) Sorenson, a wheat farmer near Dutton and his friends began to hold meetings and make phone calls to raise money. . . .

When asked what he wants from the Hutterites, Mr. Sorenson looked across a field of the 2,000 acres of wheatland he farms, in the direction of a Hutterite colony that adjoins his land, and said:

"I want them to contribute to society like the rest of us. I want their children to go to school. I want them to pay taxes. I want them to do their military service. I want them to vote. I want them to be like other people."[8]

Here, then, profession and practice are fairly consistent *within,* but incompatible *between* two groups. Communication is frequent; value and norms are enforced within, but not between groups. Change is being initiated by the conventional majority group in an attempt to bring a deviant minority into line. The intensity of the conflict will depend upon the cultural, normative, and communicative integration *within,* and the lack of it *between* these two groups.

Another illustration of the strain toward change initiated by social malintegration (situations in which practices and professions are consistent and conforming *within* but not *between* groups) is offered by Kurt Lewin in his discussion of "Self-Hatred among Jews."[9] He is contrasting the situation of privileged and underprivileged minorities (see p. 608). Their boundaries—their distinctiveness—are set by perceptible differences in patterned conduct supported by their respective subcultures. The minority group member ($\frac{m}{\sigma}$) seeking escape or relief from the restrictions imposed on members of his group is rebuffed at the boundary line (B). The central characteristics and the chief representatives of his group may have a negative valence for him. (To the extent that this is so, his group's integration is jeopardized.) Yet he finds it difficult if not impossible to escape his identification. With the privileged minority, on the other hand, the central stratum and its distinctive characteristics are positively attractive to its members, exerting pressure for identification with the central stratum of the group.

---

[8] Wallace Turner, "Hutterite Farm Groups Facing Inquiry by Montana Legislature," *New York Times,* Sunday, June 2, 1963. © 1965 by the New York Times Company. Reprinted by permission.

It should be noted that the Hutterites do in fact pay taxes, but as religious corporations, since no individual has any personal wealth. Their children do in fact go to school; but only through grade school, dropping out as soon as it is legally permissible.

[9] Kurt Lewin, *Resolving Social Conflicts,* ed. Gertrud Weiss Lewin (New York: Harper & Bros., 1948).

We have, then, one group enjoying the privilege of full majority membership *plus* the kudos of the elite; and a second group with majority membership *minus*, for example, free access to the full range of educational and occupational opportunities, to recreational facilities (hotels, resorts, and the like), and minus the dignity accorded full members of the group. But the role of majority group member is universalistically defined (*every* American citizen having reached majority is eligible to vote: ". . . *all* men are created equal [and] . . . are endowed by their Creator with certain unalienable rights"). Furthermore, the general rule for rewards-in-role is that they be warranted by demonstrable *achievement* rather than linked

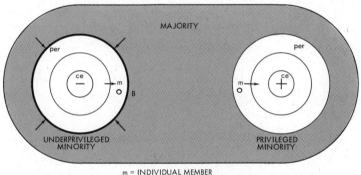

m = INDIVIDUAL MEMBER
per = PERIPHERAL STRATUM OF GROUP
ce = CENTRAL STRATUM OF GROUP
B = BARRIER PROHIBITING PASSING

Source: Kurt Lewin, *Resolving Social Conflicts*, ed. Gertrud Weiss Lewin (New York: Harper & Bros., 1948), p. 195.

FIG. 14–1.   Strain toward change as a result of tensions within and between two groups.

with qualities *ascribed* by virtue of birth and family. The tension between majority and minority principles is registered, then, in strain toward change. The channels of change may be through political or economic action or outbursts of aggressive protest.

The lack of community stemming from a lack of communication is perhaps exacerbated by extensive division of labor. For while the articulation of complementary differences does bind men in necessary alliances, it tends to emphasize these differences at the expense of the common cause. Preoccupation with the relationship of producer to supplier to wholesaler to retailer to customer may overshadow the common relationship of citizen to citizen, impeding cultural, normative, and communicative integration. Some sense of this is reflected in Robert Oppenheimer's statement:

> I have been much concerned that in this world we have so largely *lost the ability to talk with one another.* In the great succession of deep discoveries, we have become removed from one another in tradition, and in a certain measure even in language. We have had neither the time nor the skill nor the dedication to tell one another what we have learned, nor to listen, nor to welcome its enrichment of the common culture and the common understanding. *Thus the public sector of our lives, what we have and hold in common, has suffered,* as have the illumination of the arts, the deepening of justice and virtue, the ennobling of power and of our common discourse. We are less men for this. Our specialized traditions flourish; our private beauties thrive; but in those high undertakings where man derives strength and insight from the public excellence, we have been impoverished. We hunger for nobility; the rare words and acts that harmonize simplicity and truth. In this I see some connection with the great unresolved public problems: survival, liberty, fraternity.[10]

EXPLANATIONS OF SOCIAL CHANGE

What general ideas help us to understand the sources of change, the factors militating against cultural, normative, communicative, and functional integration? To answer this question we need to ask: What are the factors, the common denominators underlying the erosion of tradition, the challenge to the sacred, the declining significance of blood ties, the penetration of isolated population pockets, the glancing contacts with many in place of the repetitive relationships with a few?

The Hero as Agent of Change

One easy answer to the question of social change is the Hero in history, the man of superior endowment who shapes the course of events to his own ends. People have long been beguiled by such a theory, more often implicit than explicit, of social change. There are intimations of it when a vast potential for error or evil is attributed to a presidential nominee. (Deploring a party's selection of a presidential nominee, the *New York Times* headlines an editorial:

---

[10] The statement is by Robert Oppenheimer, quoted by Harold Taylor in an article, "What the Family Isn't Teaching," *Saturday Review of Literature* (May 18, 1963), p. 17. Italics mine.

"Disaster at San Francisco.") What the instinct theory is to individual conduct, the great-man theory is to patterns of social action. Not so long ago and perhaps throughout most of man's history, we interpreted individual conduct as a simple elaboration of instinctual drives. Similarly, social change is traced as the twisting path whose turns and detours are dictated by The Great Man, the Hero in History. This theory of social change errs as much in its oversimplification, in its fairy tale character, as does the instinct theory of individual development. Tolstoy spoke to this point, and tellingly, in his *War and Peace*.

> The higher a man stands on the social ladder, the more people he is connected with and the more power he has over others, the more evident is the predestination and inevitabilty of his every action.
>
> A king is history's slave. History, that is the unconscious, general, hive life of mankind, uses every moment of the life of kings as a tool for its own purposes.
>
> In historic events, the so-called great men are labels giving names to events, and like labels, they have but the smallest connection with the event itself.
>
> Every act of theirs, which appears to them an act of their own will, is in an historical sense involuntary and is related to the whole course of history and predestined from eternity.[11]

This is not, of course, to say that each man's influence equals every other's. People do differ. And significant personality differences may answer with peculiar appropriateness to the requirements of the social situation.

It is to say, however, that the variance in behavior in two different roles is less to be explained in personality terms than by the differing expectation sets defining the roles. Or, given the same role, performance in it, despite variations in personalities of incumbents, will be constrained (and stabilized through time) by virtue of the expectation sets defining that role. Furthermore, the higher in the social structure, or the more central the role, the greater the limits and restraints placed upon performance in that role. "A king is history's slave." It is in such terms as these that we can understand Republican presidents (whose party stresses individualism, local self-determination and opposes "creeping socialism") consistently supporting SEC, FDIC, OASDI, minimum wage laws and a host of other collectivist, welfare-state innovations.

---

[11] Leo Tolstoy, *War and Peace*, trans. Louise Maude and Aylmer Maude (New York: Oxford University Press, Inc.), Book 9, sec. 1.

Productive Power, Out of Phase with Economic Organization, Generates Social Change

In strong contrast to the psychobiological, great-man theory of social change is that of Marx. Based on shifts in the economic substructure of society (each economic stage providing the seed source of its transformed progeny), Marx provides a social theory of social change. Isolating this single, crucial sector of society and its supporting culture, he elaborates, in a powerful argument, the repercussions that transmute the superstructure: family, church, government—the whole network of interlocking institutions. But if the modes of production alter, converting peasant into factory hand, making a commodity out of labor, separating management from labor and owner from management, entailing the alienation of the worker from the means of production, we still have to ask: Why? How did it happen? What were the mechanisms of change? And we are driven to acknowledge the significance of urbanization and industrialization, the influence of religion and government, innovations in productive techniques arising at the intersection of ideas and roles.[12]

Two Cultures Out of Phase: The Culture-Lag Theory

Ogburn's culture-lag theory finds social change emerging from the stress between different change rates characterizing the material and the nonmaterial culture, the former tending always to outpace the latter.[13] Especially as a result of spiraling technological developments, adaptive changes are required in the major institutional spheres: household appliances alter the wife's role and marital and parental relationships; contraceptive devices entail reconsideration of the church's doctrinal position; computers, calculators, and probability sampling have repercussions in politics. But there are difficulties with this theory and its formulation. It is not always clear that changes in the nontechnological sphere follow rather than precede or act concurrently with technological change. (The women's suffrage movement may have lent impetus to the invention of laborsaving devices to liberate her from a more restricted, household-anchored role.) The terms of the proposition are not coordi-

---

[12] See Appendix, page 647, for further elaboration of this social theory of social change.

[13] William F. Ogburn, *Social Change* (New York: The Viking Press, 1938).

nate: all culture, being immortal, is nonmaterial, a condition of its transmissibility from generation to generation. (Recall our discussion of the meaning of culture in Chapter 2.) But what Ogburn points out is unquestionably true: when, among the interwoven aspects of the cultural fabric, some aspects change more rapidly than others, there is a strain toward change. But we have to ask: what accounts for burgeoning technology and the crescive curve of material culture? If we can contrive commensurable indexes of change, are those in technology faster than those in other spheres? And if so, why?

Social Change Stemming from Encounters at the Crossroads

Now I want to suggest that rate of change is a function of the way the social mix is altered by fluctuating rates of input and output. Perhaps Figure 14–2 will help us visualize this crossroads motion of social change.

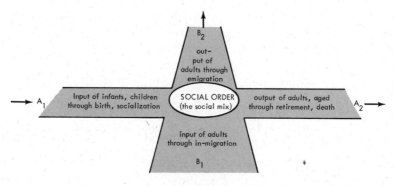

FIG. 14–2

The social order lies at a crossroads, at the intersection where different persons and ideas encounter one another. Change occurs at this intersection of experience. It is the result of a novel mix. Cultural change stems from a novel mix of ideas. Social change is rooted in discrepant role definitions. Cultural and social change have, then, two major sources: a change in the input-output balance as differing attributes are brought into the system through birth and subsequent socialization; and a shift in the input-output balance as different attributes or ideas are introduced into the system, either corporeally, as their bearers move, or as they travel via communication media.

Let us be clear about this. Change need not occur where there is a constant input and output in a social order, where one incumbent simply replaces another in a given role. Where input and output neatly balance one another, we have a homeostatic condition in the system. (This is close to being the situation among the Hutterites whom I shall mention again, presently.) It is, rather, when there is a marked change in the *rate* of input—or output—that we so alter the mix as to generate change.

Nor should we confuse social change with social disorganization. For example, a given rate of crime is a characteristic of our social order and as long as the crime rate remains steady we do not consider it an index of social change: quite the contrary. Only when there is a change in the rates of such social patterns do we have social change. And the same may be said of other phenomena usually conceived to be signs of disorganization: divorce, suicide, mental illness, and the like.

I've been arguing that social change is, in effect, an altered social "mix" and that the novelty of the social mix stems from a changing input/output ratio. Changes in this ratio may be seen both in terms of frequency (for example, births and deaths per unit population) and numbers, the former entailing the latter. Numbers are significant as they affect the character of social organization and the probability of change-inducing combinations (the "mix") of ideas and action. I mean, of course, numbers per unit space. It makes a difference that Nevada has about 3 persons per square mile and Manhattan, 76,156. Other things equal, increase in size means increase in range of attributes and the probability of their conjunction. It also means a necessary change in the social structure. Professor Hawley writes:

> The massing of population in cities has tremendously increased the potential size of the social aggregate. The average density of the 92 cities of 100,000 population or more in the United States in 1940 was 8,665. On this basis a circle with a 3-mile radius would contain 242,600 persons, and a 10-mile radius would embrace 2,720,800 individuals. Never before was it possible for an individual human being to come into physical contact in an hour's time, whether by walking or by riding a wheeled vehicle, with so many other individuals. And never before have the problems of organization, on the one hand, and of adjustment to the land, on the other hand, been so numerous and so difficult of solution.[14]

Such massing of population implies change: for it enables—indeed, requires—the confronting of differences. Ideas are generated,

---

[14] Amos H. Hawley, *Human Ecology: A Theory of Community Structure*, p. 102. Copyright 1950, The Ronald Press Company.

the intellect is stimulated, emotion is expressed, as Dewey suggested, when the smooth ongoing tenor of life is interrputed. It is at the point of some obstacle, some intrusion that we are faced with a problem and the need for its solution. The massing of population that Hawley speaks of guarantees a novel mix of ingredients and the problems, challenges, opportunities arising from them. The result is often change, for innovation is the fruitful union of complementary elements. If all units of a system were alike we would have that situation described by the preacher in Ecclesiastes: "The thing that hath been, it is that which shall be; and that which is done is that which shall be done: and there is no new thing under the sun."

A cultural innovation results from the intersection of two ideas whose combination, made possible by the state of their development and complementarity, gives issue to a solution meeting some need. The analogy with genetic innovations is not far off. Each child is a new product, unduplicated, except for the rare case of monozygotic twins, in time or space. Each child, that is to say, is a biological innovation derived from the differing but complementary germ plasm of his parents. In his organic makeup he develops unique attributes at the confluence of two genetic streams. The word confluence—or intersection, or conjunction—is the theoretically significant word. For inventive change is a crossroads phenomenon. And not only does the person represent an unique conjunction of genetic influences. He is a social crossroads, representing the unique conjuncture of an extraordinary number of influences.

Take as an example the incredibly simple case where people may have, or lack, each of two traits, X and Y. A person may have both, lack both, have X without Y or Y without X. To put it differently, with two traits that may be either absent or present (with no in-between degrees), the possible combinations or varieties of traits (and, thus, of men) would be represented by 2^2. Were there three traits and, again, if each could only be present or absent, we would have the following possible combinations, with $+$ representing the presence and $-$ the absence of the trait.

TRAITS	POSSIBLE COMBINATIONS							
	1	2	3	4	5	6	7	8
X	+	+	+	−	−	−	−	+
Y	+	+	−	−	−	+	+	−
Z	+	−	−	−	+	+	−	+

Thus with three traits, each present or absent, the possible combinations can be represented by 2^3. With ten traits, again either present or absent, 2^{10} gives us 1,024 different sorts of persons. If this seems to exaggerate the case, since not all combinations are equally likely, we need to remember that ten traits scarcely exhausts the attributes of a person. Using our stipulated present-absent scheme, for example, we might list such traits as: male-female, over-under age 20, U.S. citizen or not, Buddhist or not, blue-collar–white-collar, veteran-nonveteran, high school graduate or not, poor or not, southerner or northerner, etc. Clearly the range of attributes is not restricted, in reality, to such simple dichotomies. Even including sex there are intermediate grades or degrees. Human variables are typically continuous, not discrete. And ten such traits do not begin to reflect the spread of categories, affiliations and attitudes characterizing the person as an unique focus of a network of parent, sibling, kin, friendship, work, fraternal, play, religious, and civic relationships.

Lest this seem a far-spun digression, let me return directly to the question of social change. Social change is a change in the structure of the group—i.e., in the nature of the relationships, the roles that comprise them, and the definition of those roles given in the culture. What has interpersonal diversity got to do with changes in the structure of groups? If maintenance of the group depends on the maintenance of given relationships, if these relationships depend upon like performance in roles, if the same performance in roles depends on the same socialization, if the same socialization depends upon the same social and cultural exposures, and if, finally, there is no such thing as the same social-cultural exposure, then there must be a constant erosion of group-maintaining influences. This is the case and this is the point. Always and everywhere groups are replenished by persons whose background must differ, however slightly, from those they replace. The group's problems are constantly confronted by a changing collective "mix" that makes for changing solutions. Thus there is a constant tension in the system stemming from the shifting kaleidoscope of social configurations that characterize the human input, whether through the socialization of the native-born or the varying input of attributes of the in-migrant.

The Reduction of Encounter: A Condition of Relative Non-change. The most effective bulwark against change (I'm not referring to consciously contrived resistances) is that which obtains where input approximates output. We can better understand conditions of change if we examine a society where this is roughly true, a group existing under conditions of nonchange. By examining the factors promoting integration we can better see those tending toward dis-integration, or social change. One such stable, change-resisting group is that of the Hutterites, called by Joseph W. Eaton "an island of stability and security in a river of change."

In 1952 Eaton gave the following title to a study of this group: "Controlled Acculturation: A Survival Technique of the Hutterites."[15] It expresses the notion I've put forward: stability of the group depends upon control over input so as to make an effective match with output. Before discussing characteristics of the group permitting them to achieve this input-output balance, let me sketch a bit of their historical background as Eaton reports it.

Except for 108 converts and their children the descendants of this often-persecuted sect (originating in Switzerland around 1528) are the cultural legatees of about 50 Hutterite families who came to the United States between 1874 and 1877. In 1951 there were about 8,700 of them living in 93 communal groups, thus averaging about 94 per hamlet. From the beginning the religion of a small, threatened minority sect has been a strong integrating factor, promoting communication within the group and inhibiting communication between its members and outsiders. They believe themselves a chosen people living in the only way that is truly Christian: simply, pacifically, communally, and, so far as they can manage it, in isolation from the corrupting influences of the external social order. The economy is a communal, agrarian one with but few possessions personally owned. Since a colony numbers fewer than 100, their dealings with one another are of the primary sort, maximizing what I have called multibonded relationships. The family is chiefly an affectional and procreative unit (median number of children was ten per family around 1950), the induction of the young—their socialization—being a widely diffused community responsibility. In a way one may conceive the group as theocratically totalitarian. I do not use the word in a derogatory sense. I mean only that no gross deviations from the central value system are tolerated and that each generation is systematically indoctrinated to believe and behave in accordance with Hutterite traditions. There is little class differentia-

---

[15] *American Sociological Review*, Vol. XVII, No. 3 (June, 1952).

tion: the range of prestige, privilege, and power is quite narrow. In everything essential, members of the group share a common lot.

Observers have remarked the serenity of their lives,[16] the rarity of crime and—although this is less certain—of mental disorder, the virtual absence of suicide or divorce or quarreling—features whose rising rates signalize social change. The absence of these behaviors and the persistence of traditional ways point to an extraordinarily cohesive and stable community.

Input in this group has been almost exclusively through birth and effective socialization procedures. Social change is much less likely under these circumstances than where the input is through immigration. Contrast the situation of the Hutterite hamlet with that of New York City where, on the zero years of the decades 1870 through 1910, inclusive, there were .6, .6, .9, 1.3 and 1.9 million foreign born, respectively.[17] (Of these, in 1910, 13 percent were from Ireland, 14 percent from Germany, 17 percent from Italy, 23 percent from Russia, 12 percent from Austria-Hungary, with the rest coming from thirteen other sources.)[18]

But of course it is almost impossible to maintain the isolation that enables a group to retain complete control over the socialization process. The Hutterites are no exception. Military service, the pressure to attend public schools and to stay longer in them, the use of farm machinery and trucks entailing contacts with outsiders, dealings with agricultural experts and other government emissaries —these are influences that compromise effectively controlled acculturation. Such influences make it impossible to match performance

---

[16] See the study of Lee Emerson Deets, *The Hutterites: A Study in Social Cohesion* (Gettysburg, Pa.: Times and News Publishing Co., 1939) and his early study, "The Origin of Conflict in the Hutterische Communities," in *Publications of the American Sociological Society*, Vol. 25 (May, 1931), pp. 125–35.

[17] Moses Riskin, *The Promised City* (Cambridge, Mass.: Harvard University Press, 1962), Table 2, p. 271.

[18] Let me remind you that when I speak of input, it is an input of values, skills, attitudes, knowledge, manners that is at issue. People are their carriers (although with present means of communication the input need not be personally transmitted. The practice of jamming radio transmission of propaganda is evidence of the power of an incorporeal, ethereal input!) For example, we get an input of occupational knowledge and specialties among East Side, largely immigrant, Jews (1890). Forty-three percent were tailors, 11 percent peddlers, 9 percent cloakmakers, 6 percent clerks, 5 percent laundry workers, 4 percent cigar workers, 3 percent hat makers, 2 percent painters, another 2 percent carpenters, etc. (*Ibid.*, Table 3, p. 272). Riskin's data tell us, too, that the input of religious and political preferences as well as occupational skills, and of food and clothing habits—the input, indeed, of a way of life—by no means matched the output through retirement and death of the preestablished WASPS (white, Anglo-Saxon Protestants).

in the roles of departing incumbents. Social change is generated at the crossroads where Hutterite and alien ways intersect. It is at these crossroads that we confront the strange, the bizarre, the intriguing, the desirable, creating problems of choice and justification. (Five percent of the living Hutterite males over fifteen years of age had chosen, as of 1950, to leave their communal groups.)

The Usual Condition: Encounter and Change. The Hutterite case is unusual. Most groups are more permeable at their boundaries, less effective in their socialization. For example, Hutterite communities grow by "budding," sending out offshoots, or colonies. So they hold each agrarian community to a size roughly appropriate to "controlled acculturation." But in the usual American community, open migration and booming fertility with declining mortality often mean a marked increase in the input of newcomers, straining facilities for socialization, assimilation, maintenance. Neither home nor school, housing nor churches nor social work agencies, police and other protective services, may be equipped to handle such an input. This was emphatically the case with many mushrooming communities during and after World War II. Especially where input or recruitment is unselective it may represent immediately unassimilable cultural elements.

A great range of traits distinctive of newcomers, may stimulate change in the group: differences in language, in occupational skills, in education, in religion (even within Catholicism, Spanish Catholicism ≠ Italian Catholicism ≠ Irish Catholicism ≠ U.S. Catholicism), in moral positions (for example, positions on installment buying, the woman's role, the relationship of children to parents), in politics, etc. Where input differs markedly from output we find suspicion, exploitation of the newcomers, an irresponsibility—or unresponsibility—on the newcomers' part and a tendency toward segregation into homogeneous enclaves, further delaying assimilation of the person and stability in the group. Marked changes in output—as in the case of some countries suffering heavy male mortality in wartime—is reflected in the social mix at the crossroads in altered family structure, changes in the occupational structure. On the other hand, an emphatic decline in output through death means a change in the age composition of the social mix, posing the problem of support of the aged and their accommodation in familial systems now neo-local and no longer geared to three-generation families.

Changes in input may be impersonally conveyed through the

mass media. Magazines, radio, and television have allegedly exerted, with their national coverage, a leveling influence. This suggests that there is something to be leveled, that differences exist; and indeed rural and urban, north and south, east, midwest, and western United States do present differences. The impact of common media upon a noncommon base may well generate impulse toward change. These media constitute themselves a crossroads where differing views and values intersect. It is reasonable to assume that a hierarchy of values once unmistakably clear may be shaken when clean living is mysteriously linked with clean shaving; mink stoles are the unmistakable sign of deep affection *and* political corruption; the calculated winning of friends and influencing of people is the declared means of getting ahead; when the quantification of all things, including virtues, in cash terms strips them of their absolute values and makes the worth of everything relative to its price.

Patterns of parent-child relationship may be altered when the rate of change conveyed through the media is so great that the child lives in a world different from that of his parents. This is what happens with first- and second-generation migrants when the first-generation parents are in the position of marginal people, suspended between two worlds, while their children, the second generation, seek to identify clearly with one of these worlds, the new world. More generally, perhaps, this happens when the encounter of ideas promotes cultural accretion at such a rate as to transform the world between generations. From moon-shots to morals, communication may be impeded, parent-child relationships altered.

What I have been saying, to revise the scheme presented on page 620, can be summarized as in Table 14–1.

The City as Crossroads and Locus of Social Change. Now to be somewhat more concrete, consider one example and one argument, bearing, respectively, on social and cultural change as crossroads phenomena. These examples relate principally to cells *d* and *c* in the scheme above. The crossroads of contact, the point of intersection is the city, for in contemporary America this is preeminently the locus of a changing social mix.

The city is the crossroads for Negro-white contact. Here the "American dilemma" comes to a sharp focus, and the abrasive encounter exerts irresistible stress toward change. We know it lately as the revolution in race relations; but like the alleged population explosion, it has been long anticipated by sociologists. And it has been most apparent at the major urban crossroads.

Here there has been a tremendous input of Negroes, both by migration and birth. The German statement, *Stadt luft macht frei* suggests a reason for this input of Negroes. The city is the great

TABLE 14–1

	Social change, and the underlying cultural change represented in new:	
	Ideas	*Roles* (the expectation sets comprised in structures of relationships)
Find their sources, an input of attributes differing in degree and/or kind from output, in		
birth and socialization	a	b
and/or		
spatial transfers through the mass media or migration	c	d

market place. With its emphasis on impersonal competition, on the rational assessment of achievement, an ascribed trait like race becomes less relevant. And of course with its polyethnic mix fed by streams of immigrants, the city has somewhat immunized itself to an input of strangers. The city became for the Negro a destination of relative promise and opportunity. In the long trek from southern states Negroes have generally confirmed Stouffer's proposition: ". . . the number of persons going a given distance is directly proportional to the number of opportunities at that distance and inversely proportional to the number of intervening opportunities." [19]

[19] Samuel A. Stouffer, "Intervening Opportunities: A Theory Relating Mobility and Distance," *American Sociological Review,* Vol. V (October, 1940), p. 846.

"Opportunity" refers, chiefly, to employment and, as a correlate, income. In one test of Stouffer's theory of intervening opportunities, Professor Fred L. Strodtbeck defined opportunity—the opportunity characteristic of a given city—as "the number of persons living within a particular city in 1930 who were born outside the state in which the city is located [thus assuming that the number of such persons] is proportional to the number of opportunities the city has provided during the period of migration under study." The Strodtbeck study is "Equal Opportunity Intervals: A Contribution to the Method of Intervening Opportunity Analysis," *American Sociological Review,* Vol. XIV, No. 4 (August, 1949), p. 492.

This is not to say that the influx of Negroes was easily and painlessly accommodated. The migrants brought with them an impoverished background, a mother-centered–father-shifting form of family, a level of fertility characteristic of rural-agrarian settings, low educational levels, a narrowly limited spread of occupational skills and religious patterns functionally linked with a low ceiling on plausible aspirations. Compressed into Black Belts and Harlems, they are simultaneously exposed to *de facto* if not *de jure* discrimination, the more frustrating because, as with Tantalus, the grapes and water—the good things of their society—are exposed to them, and then withheld. But the myth of Tantalus is scarcely an adequate parallel. He was tantalized as punishment for a crime against the gods. The Negro is prejudged and punished not for a criminal act but simply for being. He is not teased or tantalized, but frustrated, and aggressive outcomes must be expected. Thus, given democratic doctrine, the irresistible drive for social change.

It becomes a formidable fact that major American cities are becoming, at their core, increasingly Negro and beyond the corpo rate limits, white. In the fourteen largest metropolitan areas in the country, with about a third of the nation's people, total population grew by 19 percent between 1940 and 1950, Negro population by 65 percent, more than four times the increase of the white population (15.6 percent).[20] Most of this growth was in the core of these metropolitan masses where Negro population grew 67.8 percent and white population 3.7 percent in the same decade. "An official census in New York City showed that nonwhites in the nation's largest city increased by 41 percent from 1950 to 1957 while the white population *decreased* by 6 percent."[21] The 1950–60 change for the fourteen Standard Metropolitan Statistical Areas having, in 1950, over one million population showed a total growth of 5,475,749, or 12.3 percent; white population growth was 3,491,695, or 8.7 percent, and nonwhite population growth (almost exclusively Negro) was 1,984,-054, or 47.0 percent.

Illustrative data are provided by Professor Grodzins (see Figure 14–3) who traces some of the changes to be anticipated. We can certainly expect deterioration in housing and a spread of slum conditions, for the input of Negroes typically outruns the housing

---

[20] Morton Grodzins, *The Metropolitan Area as a Racial Problem* (Pittsburgh: University of Pittsburgh Press, 1958), pp. 1, 2.

[21] *Ibid.*, p. 3.

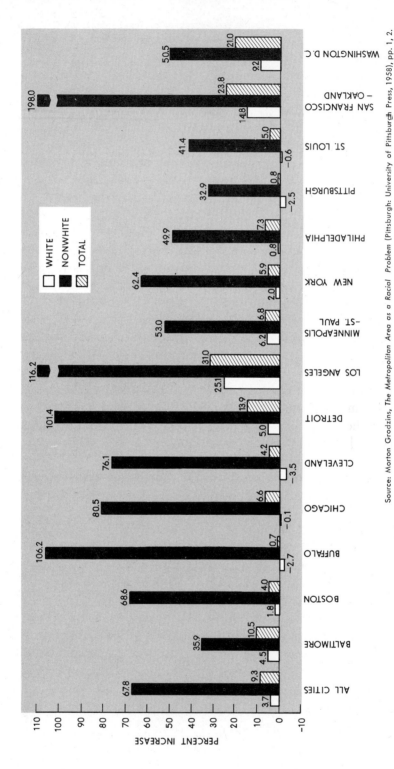

Source: Morton Grodzins, *The Metropolitan Area as a Racial Problem* (Pittsburgh: University of Pittsburgh Press, 1958), pp. 1, 2.

FIG. 14-3. Center cities: largest metropolitan areas population growth, by race, 1940–50.

available to them. Relatively unskilled in work, encountering resistance in labor unions, often exploited by landlords who capitalize on the pressure for housing, the Negro becomes the impotent instrument for spreading urban blight. Within the slum, dense occupancy adds relatives and strangers to the family, multiplies the frictions of daily discontents, precludes privacy for love and hate, and spills the surplus into the streets. Here aggressions often turn inward, within the group. But held almost literally incommunicando within the Black Belt the Negro is also at war between—between himself and "whitey." And with the flight of many middle-class whites to suburbia, the "whiteys" remaining on the Black Belt frontier are likely to be, like Puerto Ricans and southern white migrants, precisely those who are most threatened and feel most antagonistic. So the tensions at the crossroads build up to the tragic denouement that is the surface symptom of the undercurrents of change.

But since human institutions are interlocking, the effect of an input of Negro poor and an output of the well-to-do white is reflected not alone in the urban family and church. There are repercussions in the worlds of work and politics. Workers without realistic aspirations cannot, as Allison Davis has pointed out, be threatened into productivity.[22] Nor will they respond to incentives geared to the realizable aspirations of the white middle class. As consumers, slum area dwellers do not provide the market, in quality or quantity, that middle-class whites do. Slum housing has its counterpart in central business district slums. And while light manufacturing may remain in the urban pattern, drawing on an ever larger proportion of the dispossessed for its labor force, retail and nonindustrial activities remove to the white belt of suburbia depleting, as do the suburbanites themselves, the tax base of the city. From this flow economic consequences for schools, fire and police protection, streets, sewers, and a host of other urban amenities.

Nor is this the end of the change-inducing repercussions of the input of Negroes at the urban crossroads. Their power in politics is bound to increase. In concrete terms this means innovations in education destroying *de facto* segregation in the schools. It may mean a revision of zoning ordinances to extend housing opportu-

---

[22] Allison Davis, "The Motivation of the Underprivileged Worker," in William Foote Whyte (ed.), *Industry and Society* (New York: McGraw-Hill Book Company, 1946).

nities for Negroes. It may mean political conflict (for example, a place-of-work income tax) pitting Negro-dominated central city against white suburbs. It may mean, as Grodzins suggests, attempts by whites to regain political control by annexing the city to suburbs, or by gerrymandering urban areas so as to dilute Negro voting strength. It may mean an exacerbation of conflicts in the state legislatures, between downstate and upstate interests: New York city versus upstate New York, Cleveland and Cincinnati versus the rural middle-lands dominated by Columbus, Chicago versus down-state Illinois. And the same conflict of interests, freighted with racial antipathies, may register itself in the national legislature.

The city, I have argued, is a change-generating crossroads. But it is not the only one. Like the city, the new nations are points of encounter and change. Elements similar to those in the rural-urban encounter are at work here. And here, too, the alien input is enor-mously disruptive. An African writes:

> The white man is very clever. He came quietly and peaceably with his religion. We were amused at his foolishness and allowed him to stay. Now he has won our brothers, and our clan can no longer act like one. He has put a knife on the things that held us together and *we have fallen apart.*[23]

Kluckhohn notes the same effect at the crossroads of cultural contact. The erosion of commonly accepted standards means a lowering of the probability that a given act will elicit a predictable response. Relationships become undependable: *things fall apart.* "The absence of generally accepted standards of behavior among individuals constitutes . . . a definition of social disorganization."[24]

And so whenever and wherever complementary or contrary beliefs and behavior encounter one another there is the prospect of change. It need not be a desired or desirable innovation. Change, until accomplished, may mean a painful transition. When change is consummated we often forget the resistance at first pitted against it and the damage done to some in the process. Not only will Linton's patriot be unaware that he is thanking "a Hebrew God in an Indo-European language that he is a hundred percent (decimal system

---

[23] Chinua Achebe, *Things Fall Apart* (New York: McDowell, Obolensky, 1949), p. 183. (Italics mine.)

[24] Clyde Kluckhohn and Dorothea Leighton, *The Navaho* (Cambridge, Mass.: Harvard University Press, 1947), p. 217.

invented by the Greeks) American (from Americus Vespucci, Italian geographer)":[25] he forgets that the God, the language, the decimal system, and the establishment of America were all painfully resisted. The emergence of new elements in the social order is the painful counterpart of the infant's transition, himself the product of genetic encounter, from the intrauterine state to the outer world. Crudely put, change hurts.

Sometimes the hurt is a subtle effect registered in personal anxiety, uncertainty, and social unrest. If social disorganization means a breakdown in the structure of relationships, it also implies an ambiguity, an uncertainty in the roles that comprise the relationships. And ambiguity in the sets of expectations that constitute a role entails a degree of personal disorganization. The social order and the order of personality are linked. Disjunctures in human relationships have their counterpart in disjunctures of the synapses. Familiar paths no longer get us to our destinations. This potential for disruptive change is found whenever the customary patterns—traits, views, values—are challenged by unusual input or output.

Urban Crossroads, Information Exchange and Uncertainty. Pursuing this point, I would suggest that ambiguity of roles is a central feature of contemporary social change. Consider the city as a cultural crossroads. (Recall our definition of culture as knowledge, both of what is and what ought to be, symbolized in act and artifact.) The city, to a degree not true of other human aggregates, is the locus of information exchange, of trade in ideas, of the encounter of differing values. As Euroamerican culture has become increasingly urbanized, this attribute is diffused. In the United States most homes, villages, and towns become crossroads for cultural encounters. While most information exchange is trivial, yet in the course of an enormous and ever mounting interchange of information some novelties result, and this at an increasing rate. At the same time, ideas and values absolutely held are confronted with possible alternatives. The resulting permutation of ideas lies at the heart of social change. Let me be more explicit.

As never before we have the means of putting minds in contact with one another. Seventy-four million telephones in the United States (millions more than one per family) carried a *daily* average

---

[25] Ralph Linton, "One Hundred Per Cent American," *The American Mercury*, Vol. XL (April, 1937), p. 429.

of 219 million conversations in 1960.[26] (We need not dwell morbidly on the quality of the conversations, whether what was said was worth saying: my emphasis here is on the means of message transfer and encounter.) Each telephone is matched by one car, 74 million of *them* scudding about on 3½ million miles of highway in the United States, while overhead 52 million revenue passengers at home and 5½ million abroad soar from here to there and back again. Messages are transmitted almost as rapidly by letter mail. Sixty-two billion of them were conveyed in domestic interchange in 1960. From overseas we received another billion and responded with 500 million. Canned messages of various sorts debouched from 170 million radios and about 54 million TV receivers in 1960. In 1959 our newspaper circulation was about one copy for every three persons, daily. Our newsprint consumption (1960) was 37 kilograms per capita—about 80 pounds for every man, woman, and child in the country. (Runners-up in devouring newsprint were New Zealand, Australia, Canada, and the United Kingdom. It might seem that voracious consumption of news may go along with Anglo-Saxon forms of rule.) We produced 25,784 new books and new editions in 1963, a third of them in what is euphemistically called "literature."

We also have a meeting of minds—not consensus, but contact—through migration. In 1963, 306,260 immigrants were admitted to the United States. There were just under a million tourists to the United States in 1960, chiefly from Canada and Mexico. Imports and exports might be considered as messages of sorts. Value of exports in 1960, about a sixth of the world's total, amounted to 20 billions; and our imports, about 15 billions. Let me emphasize that this input of messages, especially that through the mass media, is chiefly an output from urban centers. The urban crossroads is reproduced, as it were, through the mass media in homes and communities throughout the country.

But in many ways more significant than such casual, unplanned and laissez-faire exchange of messages is the exchange that is consciously contrived to promote innovation. This is the exchange of messages by intellectuals: scientists and humanists. Their very existence is based on the premise of unimpeded interchange of

---

[26] These, and other data in this paragraph are from United Nations Office of Statistics, *Statistical Yearbook, 1961* (New York: United Nations Publishing Service, 1961), *passim.*

ideas. This is what professional journals are for. And so, as the chemists tell us, the discovery by a Canadian chemist that inert gases are not, in fact, inert at all, that they do enter into chemical combination with other elements—this discovery sends little tremors around the globe. With amazing rapidity laboratories in Rome and Moscow, Peiping, Stockholm, Paris, and London are replicating the experiment, extending it, ferreting out its implications, estimating new uses in novel compounds for Xenon and other of the erstwhile, allegedly inert gases. It is this matter of novel compounds, novel combinations, that I have been stressing as the crossroads phenomenon, central in a theory of social change.

Before going on to some of the implications of the increasing rate of spread and permutation of ideas, let me point out one other development of surpassing significance. This is the ability to store and retrieve, relate and manipulate ideas—or more accurately, the symbols representing them. We would be buried in our own effluence of ideas were it not for the development of electronic devices. These gadgets have the most explosive potential of any technological innovation in the twentieth century—which is to say, in all time. They are direct extensions or multipliers of the human mind. They allow us to solve the otherwise insoluble. They may produce sets of logically interconnected explanatory statements, together with testable deductions from such statements. In doing this, they will force an unprecedented rate of change, so generating in the process problems that they alone can solve. The computer is an electronic crossroads, the contemporary counterpart of the Stoa, the bazaar, the market place at the gate of the walled medieval city. It rationalizes the problem solution and decision making of the ballot box, the grain and security exchanges of the Lombard streets, the LaSalle and Wall streets of our day; and of the university, the research and development laboratories. And to return to our concern with expectation-sets (roles) and the structures of human relationships, this ever faster rate of exchange and permutation of ideas has meant (1) more uncertainties in knowing and (2) less certainty in conviction.

With so much more knowledge, why less certainty in knowing? This is a strange paradox of our times. The range of knowledge and our powers of discrimination have been vastly refined while, simultaneously, our ability or willingness to discriminate has been greatly blunted. If we had a cosmic yardstick giving readings on every dimension across the range of all things affecting human relationships, we'd have a hard time settling on the correct reading, pinning down the preferred set of values suiting ourselves. One reason for this I've been suggesting. The more numerous the points on a scale, the more finely graduated it is, the harder it is to get a precise reading. When our scale has just two values, big-little, many-few, good-bad, we can sort things, events, persons into these categories with deceptive ease. We make relatively few mistakes in assigning to the appropriate scale point. (But of course when we do make a mistake it's a 100 percent error.) When on the other hand the scale is finely graduated, with scores of points, then we often make an inaccurate reading, although the error is unlikely to be as great. Now what I have been contending is that, at our cultural crossroads (chiefly urban), the rate of information exchange has so increased, the permutation of ideas proceeding at such a rate that precisely this development has occurred. We have moved from the use of nominal scales, to ordinal, to equal-interval and ratio scales.[27] We have shifted from qualitative to quantitative slicings of our phenomenal pies, from discrete to continuous distributions, from conceptual to operational analyses of our problems. Cognitions cannot, therefore, have the simple certainty they once enjoyed. The probability of error is greater. The size of the error is, in probability, smaller. The greater refinement and accuracy in our knowing, the lesser certainty —these derive from the accelerating exchange of ideas at the crossroads. To put it the other way around, they vary inversely with isolation. Isolation and its concomitant ignorance are the great bulwarks of certainty.

Uncertainty in knowing is accompanied by uncertainty in believing. If instead of the dichotomy capitalism-socialism we have a gradient in which the one shades imperceptibly into the other, how can our convictions be as unqualified as would otherwise be the case? (If by socialism we mean a degree of control by the public over the major productive forces in a society, then the United States is clearly socialistic to some degree and England capitalist to some extent. What shall we say of a situation like that in Canadian railways where one line is run by the government, the other operated under private auspices?) The refinement of knowledge

---

[27] Recall our discussion of these matters—scale types, discrete and continuous distributions—in Chapter 1.

promoted by rapid information exchange has affected the certainty of our convictions as well as our cognitions.

This leads to the point. To know with less certainty is to weaken standards. To be uncertain about the standards embodied in rules is to make the roles and relationships they define ambiguous. Such ambiguity is both symptom and condition of social change. One source of such ambiguity, preeminently urban in origin, I've suggested: incessant permutations on the themes of life, the addition of points along an extended scale of experience, making it increasingly hard to get a sure fix on one's position. Thus the two paradoxically opposed outcomes: knowledge multiplies differences but decreases our knowledge—our certainty—in evaluating these differences.

The idea is metaphorically put in a poem by Phyllis McGinley when she reviews the news items on Sunday services reported "on page 27, just opposite Fashion Trends." On this page she finds God interpreted in a baffling variety of guises, and concludes in bewilderment that "God [only] knows which God is the God God recognizes."

Role-defining standards not only multiply with the gods. The simple erstwhile dualisms dissolve under the impact of more sophisticated thought, sometimes merging in an undifferentiated melange. To give unto Caesar the things that are Caesar's and unto God what belongs to Him has never been a very clear injunction. And certainly in our times, with secular influences suffusing the social order, the division between profane and sacred is very fuzzy. The church is in business, and business profits through religion. "Give us this day our daily bread," runs a bakery advertisement. Christmas and Easter become commercial windfalls. Christ, as Barton would have it (recall his statement in Chapter 11) becomes Chairman of the Board in the world's most successful enterprise.

Many old, sharp differences become obscured in "mergers." Work and play, day and night, hot and cold, even good and bad, or male and female—the sharp edges are worn off, the distinctions blurred.[28]

---

[28] Some blurring of male-female distinctions may be one index of contemporary social change. The range of work opportunities available to women has increased, consistently. The technology of domestic appliances has emancipated them from the home. The downward extension of schooling to ages three and four further releases them from home-bound duties. Among women ever married, 29.5, 30.6, 31.4, 32.1 and 32.6 percent were in the labor force in the years 1954–58, respectively. In 1958, among all women aged fourteen or over, 36 percent were in the labor force. Which is to say that the man's world of work is no longer exclusively his. And on his side, with

Ambiguity in rule and role stems also from the heterogeneous elements that crowd into our lives, elements juxtaposed without design, clouding communication, obscuring meaning. Leonard Bernstein comes to you courtesy of Ford cars, Lipton Tea (to make you brisk), and the conceivably carcinogenic Camels you are urged to "get with." On the same theme, Marya Mannes invites us to take a look at *Life* magazine.

> A magnificent full-page photograph of Etruscan tomb figures faces a rum-and-cola ad; a subtle and lovely Degas-like color photograph of a ballet is nullified by a full-page bowl of tomato soup. James Agee is sandwiched in between Falling Hair, Tums, and Choco-Cherry Spumoni; Sir Charles Snow is squeezed between constipation and Valentines, Professor Tizard between colored fruits and glue. Hurricane waves lashing at a Texas tower, which they ultimately destroyed along with its crew, compete for attention with a smiling full-page goddess in Formfit girdle and bra.[29]

Such bizarre juxtapositions confound the disparate elements of life. Secondary purposes impinge on primary interests. Levels of reality are confused. Across a wide spectrum of life's activities the old, relatively clear-cut distinctions between things, between classes of things, are obscured as the differences come to make little or no difference.

Thus the ever accelerating input of knowledge at the cultural crossroads shatters certainties in cognition and conviction.[30] The expectations defining roles are clouded. And the structure of relationships built on such roles must become unstable, shifting, both symptom and source of social change.

---

the regular decline of proportion of labor force in extractive industry (agriculture, mining, forestry, fishing, petroleum, and the like), there has been a shift of the labor force toward clerical, service, and professional occupations. The shift, in short, has been toward the more "feminine" occupations. If a changing social structure obscures traditional sex role distinctions we might well anticipate psychic change. I'm told by a professional social worker that a frequent finding with male clients is an extraordinary and incapacitating passivity; and that female clients commonly exhibit disabling guilt as they confront the home versus career dilemma.

[29] Marya Mannes, "The Intruders," *The Reporter,* August 16, 1962, p. 52.

[30] I'm not suggesting, of course, that the blurring of old distinctions is necessarily bad. Measured against the American creed, some such distinctions have been odious. The point is simply that unclarity in rules and roles is both symptom and source of social change. Perhaps it is unnecessary to add that I am not assessing social change as bad or good. It is doubtless both, in most instances, from any value perspective. And if it entails conflict, it is well to remember Simmel's point. Conflict promotes the integration of the group; for it strengthens bonds *within* the group and has as its end the resolving of differences *between* groups. (Georg Simmel, *Conflict,* trans. Kurt H. Wolff (New York: Free Press of Glencoe, Inc., 1955.)

The City as Symbol of Change through Time. We have been viewing the city as a social and cultural crossroads, hence as locus and source of change. As a crossroads of contact between white and Negro, the city can be seen to be one instance of social change in process. As a crossroads where ideas intersect—the editorial and publishing headquarters, the sites of great universities, museums, research centers—the city affords novel combinations, permutations of ideas, giving rise to cultural innovations. Such innovations extend our knowledge while, so I have argued, reducing the assurance of cognition[31] and conviction.

The city can also be seen as the culmination of social change, the current end product representing the latest, the newest in a number of spheres.

> . . . urbanism represents a revolutionary change in the whole pattern of social life. Itself a product of basic economic and technological developments, it tends in turn, once it comes into being, to affect every aspect of existence. It exercises its pervasive influence not only within the urban milieu strictly defined but also in the rural hinterland.[32]

For rural-urban implies not only spatial contrast but also temporal change in the social order. As we have seen before, this change from the then to the now has been signalized in different ways by various social thinkers. But all of them can be seen as dealing with some dimension of the shift from rural-agrarian past to urban-industrial present

> Society moves everywhere from a "rude" to a "polished" state, from *savage,* through *barbaric* to *civil* [i.e., urban] society. . . Savagery is characterized by fishing, hunting, and collecting, with property and political institutions little developed; [barbarism] by herdsmanship, property institutions, increasing strife, and the development of ranks and subordination (political institutions).[33]

---

[31] My argument emphasized the complexity of an increased body of knowledge and the difficulty in making accurate discriminations on our more finely refined scales. It has also been remarked that increased knowledge sensitizes one to the vastness of our ignorance, that it is the most knowledgeable who are, at the same time, most humble in the face of their ignorance. Better put: "The more the island of knowledge expands in the sea of ignorance, the larger its boundary to the unknown." (L. S. Rodberg and V. F. Weisskopf, "Fall of Parity," *Science,* Vol. CXXV [1957], p. 632.)

[32] Kingsley Davis, "The Origin & Growth of Urbanization in the World," *American Journal of Sociology,* published by the University of Chicago Press, Vol. LX (March, 1955), p. 429.

[33] W. C. Lehmann, *Adam Ferguson and the Beginnings of Modern Sociology* (New York: Columbia University Press, 1930), p. 81.

And civil society, Adam Ferguson's third stage, would be represented in the urban centers he knew, Edinburgh and London. Herbert Spencer saw the change through time, terminating in a society represented by his London, as one from simplicity, homogeneity, and slight role differentiation to one characterized by great complexity, heterogeneity and a highly developed division of labor. For Sir Henry Maine, change in patterns of human relationships was from those dominated by tradition and defined by the status of kin and clan, to relationships based on reciprocal interest, contractually sealed. Ferdinand Tönnies, using the two concepts we have used before, *gemeinschaft* and *gesellschaft*, emphasized the shift from a society whose members were bound by real or imagined kinship ties, a common ancestry and bonds of blood—roles and relationships being so defined; to the great society, more individualistically oriented, with political and economic interests superseding blood ties as determinants of roles. Durkheim describes social change from a mechanical articulation of social parts to their organic (functional) integration in a complex and highly differentiated system. Park, Burgess, Wirth, and Redfield are among the American sociologists who have seen social change in large measure along the rural-urban axis.

It is easy enough to document the change to an urban society: 72 percent of the labor force in agriculture in 1820 and now, something around 10 percent; over 300 times as many urban residents now as in 1790 and perhaps 10 times as many rural residents. (Reference is to the United States and under the rubric, "urban" I include the suburbanites in metropolitan areas.) The world trend is the same (Table 14–2).

TABLE 14–2

Percentage of World's Population Living in Cities

	CITIES OF 20,000 OR MORE	CITIES OF 100,000 OR MORE
1800	2.4	1.7
1850	4.3	2.3
1900	9.2	5.5
1950	20.9	13.1

Source: Kingsley Davis, "The Origin and Growth of Urbanization in the World," *American Journal of Sociology,* published by the University of Chicago Press, Vol. LX (March, 1955), p. 433.

But quite aside from sheer growth in numbers, how do the central characteristics of the city reflect major changes in our social order? Let us consider the unprecedented size, density, and heterogeneity of urban aggregates as they suggest basic changes in patterns of human relationships.

Increased Numbers: Changed Relationships. Bigness is something more than a physical fact, more than an increase in volume or external dimensions. It means a rearrangement of the component parts, a change in the nature of human relationships. We have illustrated this in one way by showing how the sheer number of potential, bilateral relationships increases, exponentially, with additions to the population base. [Where $y =$ the number of relationships and x the number of persons involved, $y = x/2 \ (x - 1)$]. Hence the impossibility of maintaining in the city the same character of human relationships as in the rural setting. In his essay "Die Grossstadt und das Geistesleben" Georg Simmel has pointed out:

> If, as in a small town where one knows almost everyone and has a positive relationship to each, the city dweller were to respond inwardly and deeply to the countless others whom he encounters, he would be atomized internally, reduced to an unimaginable psychic state.[*]

The first sentence of this essay suggests this contrast between the past and the present, a direction of social change from rural agrarian past to urban industrial present. It reads:

> The psychological basis of the city dweller's personality is the *intensification of nervous stimulation* flowing from the quick and uninterrupted change of external and internal impressions. . . . The metropolitan man—there are, of course, a thousand variations on the theme —develops a defense mechanism to protect himself from those crosscurrents and discrepancies in his external environment that threaten to uproot him: he reacts to them, in essence, with his head instead of his heart. . . . Thus the intellectual character of metropolitan life becomes comprehensible, in contrast with the rural which is based far more on deeply felt and emotional relationships.[†]

Sheer mass, the bigness of the city, lends itself to a qualitatively different type of personal relationship. With the thousands of people who fall within our field of vision, contacts must be largely transitory, superficial. There is an anonymity and remoteness of

---

[*] See Original Texts Note 1, at end of chapter.

[†] See Original Texts, Note 2, at end of chapter.

relationships that has been interpreted variously as callousness, a blasé attitude or sophistication. And so there is a tendency to convert people into things, social objects into physical objects.[34] Clearly we cannot treat the hordes whom we encounter daily with the intimacy and emotional tone characteristic of *human* relationships. People come to have no particular significance in and of themselves as unique and complex personalities.

Indeed the distinguishing characteristic of a physical as over against a social object lies in the paucity, clarity, and specific relevance to the user of its attributes. Thus we are likely to deal with people in terms of those symbols that define the utility of the relationship. Uniforms, badges, headgear, labels—these tell us it's the laundryman, the milkman, the mechanic, or the people from Brinks. More than this we need not know—nor do we want to know. On the contrary, in the rural setting we will know Mr. Jones, the grocer, not merely as a food retailer, but as a neighbor whose wife has the hives; and who, if his prices are sometimes exorbitant, makes recompense as deacon at the local church and whose boy has chosen this great university on the advice of a principal who was Eta Kappa Epsilon back in '37 when a brother, Tiger Turner, returned a last minute punt 80 yards.

This change in the structure of relationships, the dealing with others in a few, clearly defined aspects relevant to one's own interests entails a segmentalizing of personality, of relationships and allegiances. A deals with B on matter X, with C as to Y and with D on the matter of Z. This is obviously a concomitant of a highly refined division of labor promoting functional integration, the articulation of highly differentiated roles. Insofar as we relate ourselves to others only as they are of service to us and shrink from contact beyond a kind of contractual, *quid pro quo* relationship, others become preeminently means to our ends. To put it differently, roles tend to become instrumentally oriented.

In what has become a classic discussion of this tendency in modern (urban) American society, Robert K. Merton points to the

---

[34] The point was vividly made in a *New Yorker* cartoon some years ago. It was rush hour in the subway. Attempting to cram the last batch of bulging boarders into the car before the doors knifed shut, an attendant, both hands grasping the guard rails, had planted his foot against the derriere of a kindly little old white-haired lady. As he strained to wedge her in, she turned her head and, wagging a reproachful finger over her shoulder, said: "Gently, Sir, it's Mother's day." (I regret that I cannot remember the cartoonist's name.)

relative clarity and desirability of certain goals (wealth, power, winning the game) and the ambiguity, inaccessibility, or even the derogation of the institutionally appropriate means for reaching such goals. Coupled with the calculating instrumental orientation of many urban roles and the inventive potential at the urban cross-roads, this leads to the rapid increase in aberrant behavior which we regard as an index of social disorganization.

> . . . aberrant behavior may be regarded sociologically as a symptom of dissociation between culturally prescribed aspirations and socially structured avenues for realizing these aspirations.[35]
>
> The sole significant question . . . becomes, which available means is most efficient in netting the socially approved value? The technically most feasible procedure, whether legitimate or not, is preferred to the institutionally prescribed conduct. As this process continues, the integration of the society becomes tenuous and anomie ensues.[36]

Probably nowhere so much as in the city may goals of wealth and power be linked with an instrumental orientation (". . . which available means is most efficient . . .") leading to ingenious, technically efficient, but illegitimate, means for reaching those goals. And this is what we would expect if indeed the city is a change-inducing crossroads: an amoral inventiveness in contriving illegitimate as well as legitimate means to one's ends.

This inventive efficiency, this preoccupation with improved techniques is revealed in and made possible by an intellectual posture we describe as rational. This frame of mind is exactly that which assesses, preferably in quantitative and verifiable terms, the most efficient means for achieving a desired end. It is linked, again, with the inventive character of the urban crossroads; and with the requirement, where large populations are involved, of speed, careful organization, intricate timing, and new techniques to achieve success in competition. This is a feature of urban life that stands at the center of Simmel's analysis. Rationality is revealed in the quantification of things and services, especially in the elaborate network of exchange typical of great cities. The money economy is a mode of quantification providing a common denominator for, and enabling the exchange of, quite disparate things. The central position of the

---

[35] Robert K. Merton, "Social Structure and Anomie: Revisions and Extensions" (a new edition of the paper next cited), in *The Family: Its Function and Destiny*, ed. Ruth Nanda Anshen (New York: Harper & Bros., 1949), p. 24.

[36] Robert K. Merton, "Social Structure and Anomie," *American Sociological Review*, Vol. III (October, 1938), p. 674.

market place, located typically at points of maximum accessibility, is symbolic of the rational, calculating character of modern metropolitan life. Where land values are highest, where the most demanding hours of the day are spent—these are in the market place. In feudal days, the Cathedral dominated the community while buying and selling went on at the city gates. In the New England village, the

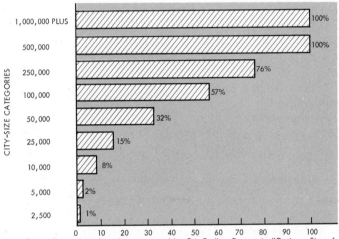

Source: Figure based on data presented by Otis Dudley Duncan in "Optimum Size of Cities," and drawn from National Recreation Association, *Municipal and County Parks in the United States, 1940* (New York: National Recreation Association, 1942). Reprinted with permission of The Free Press of Glencoe from *Cities and Society*, edited by Paul K. Hatt and Albert J. Reiss. Copyright 1951, 1957 by The Free Press, a corporation.

FIG. 14–4. **Percent of cities in given size categories having zoos, United States, 1940.**

church occupied the focal position on the green. These positions have been significantly reversed.

This rationality, this dispassionately calculating mode of dealing with men and things, is promoted by the fact that a person must deal *indirectly* with most of the others who affect his destiny. With vast numbers this must necessarily be the case. People are connected by representatives and intermediaries. The law and the police, the market place and the ballot box, symbolize the in-between roles in which men can act with less passion, with more rationality, than any two persons immediately involved.

Numbers promote rationality, finally, since people can and must be dealt with as members of categories: as patients, clients, customers, policemen, waiters, repairmen, *et al.* The category, then, provides an impersonal definition of the role and the relationship based on criteria more rational than those defining an intimate, personal relationship.

Diversity and Social Change. Bigness is intimately related to heterogeneity. The greater the number of people, the greater the potential differentiation. The city with its diverse input is a breeding ground for new biological and cultural hybrids. It consumes people produced, or reproduced, elsewhere, either in our own rural hinter-

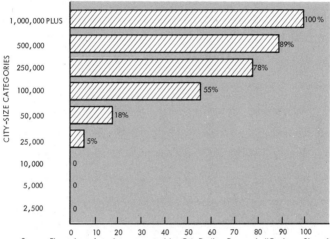

Source: Figure based on data presented by Otis Dudley Duncan in "Optimum Size of Cities," *Cities and Society*, p. 769, and drawn from "Symphony Orchestras in the United States and Canada," *The International Musician*, Vol. XLIV (June, 1946), pp. 7–8.

FIG. 14–5. Percent of cities in given size categories having symphony orchestras, United States, 1946.

lands or in foreign lands. It tolerates a diversity that rural areas do not. With its Bohemias and Bughouse squares it provides a range of choice—and in this sense a kind of freedom—not found in the pastoral fastnesses of the more homogeneous country communities. Yet it is not a matter of mere tolerance. In fact the city demands the diversity of tastes and services required to satisfy the needs of a motley population.

Some evidence on this score is provided in Figures 14–4, 14–5, and 14–6 showing the percent of cities in given size categories having zoos; symphony orchestras; colleges or universities; art museums; and AM radio stations. Let me stress, again, that this is not simply a contrast between small communities and large cities, but an index of temporal change in the social order. If you will

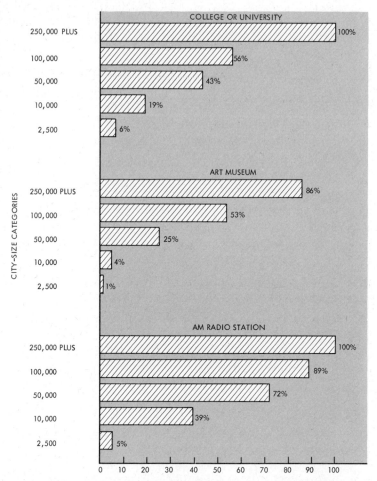

Source: Figure based on data presented by Otis Dudley Duncan in "Optimum Size of Cities," *Cities and Society*, p. 768. Duncan's sources were: U.S. Office of Education, *Education Directory, 1941, Part III, Colleges and Universities*, Bulletin 1941, No. 1 (Washington, D.C.: U.S. Government Printing Office, 1941); and Laurence Vail Coleman, *The Museum in America* (Washington, D.C.: The American Association of Museums, 1939), Vol. III; and "Directory of Broadcasting Stations of the United States," *Broadcasting*, 1946 Yearbook Number, pp. 71–190.

FIG. 14–6. Percent of cities in given size category having a college or university, an art museum, an AM radio station. Data are for 1940, 1938, and 1946 respectively.

accept my assumption that contemporary rural-urban contrasts represent a change through time, then certain changes taking place in our society are represented in these data. And the matching of diverse activities with the interests of a heterogeneous population does not stop here. The pimp and the numismatist, the gigolo and the couturier, the delicatessen and the Board of Public Welfare stand ready to serve. Here is a sanctuary for the person who might elsewhere be a misfit. Here are the most marked contrasts, from the sybaritic luxuries of the 400 and the penthouse plutocrats to the squalor of the slums. In the metropolitan complex we have the contrast between Beverly Hills, Burlingame, Brookline, and Wilmette on the one hand and the Harlems, the ghettos, the Little Sicily's on the other. Here one finds a whole spectrum of religious organizations, ranging from the most esoteric sects and cults dealing in ectoplasm and Ouija boards to the great conventional churches of America. Here is the greatest diversity of voluntary associations, ranging from the *Landsmanschaften* of foreign-born groups to the loosely knit American Hoboes' Association (of whom an estimated 300,000 drift through Chicago each year).

This heterogeneity has its own consequences. When an extremely diverse population must use the same schools, the same movies, listen to the same radio programs and view the same TV effusions, read the same newspapers and magazines, there is a tendency to seek common denominators. This leveling influence is partially offset by the great variety of urban media, many of them in the language or supporting the interests of small, particular groups.

Differentiation is conducive to segregation, especially when the variations are based upon imported culture traits such as language or religion. Thus it is that the city becomes a checkered mosaic of cultural islands, a "spatial pattern and a moral order."

Urban heterogeneity also implies a lack of common traditions. Relationships, no longer defined in custom, come to be prescribed by law. Without commonly held, internal controls built in through the socialization process, external controls must be imposed, transcending differences. This is not to suggest that the differences are suppressed. Quite to the contrary, these external, formal controls may provide occasions and channels for the expression of differences (and through their juxtaposition, the generating of innovation: through political activity, pursuit of labor union interests following the stipulations of federal and local law, etc.) But the nature of the civic relationship becomes quite different in the city. The person gains strength from the probability that there are others of like mind and interest. The contest for a favorable outcome becomes intergroup, not interpersonal. The individual's strength is multiplied because in a vast population there can always be found some with whom he can identify in promoting like interests. But his strength is limited as his group confronts those representing competing interests. With some group or organization typically mediating between the person and officialdom, the distance between governor and governed must necessarily increase. Furthermore, in the contest between interest groups the common welfare may sometimes come off second best. (Both of these circumstances favor change.)

The contest between private interest and public welfare is graphically illustrated in a study of the meat-packing industry in Detroit during World War II. In this study Professor Hartung tests the notion that the heterogeneity of the metropolitan social order (Durkheim's condition of "organic solidarity") weakens traditional commitments to the common cause, giving rise to an individualism, a pursuit of special interests sometimes at odds with the general welfare.[37] Hartung follows Durkheim's argument that the change in the nature of the social bond has been from mechanical to organic solidarity, from homogeneity to heterogeneity, from common interests, skills, and commitments to the complex accommodation of differences in modern, urban society.

The question is whether this transformation in the social order has in fact occurred, and whether as a result there are sometimes significant differences in response to threats to the public welfare and those to private interest. We can find out, Durkheim suggested, by looking at the rules that define men's relationships to one another, and most especially by looking at the sanctions that support the rules. These sanctions are of two kinds, retributive and restitutive. Rough parallels in contemporary law would be criminal and civil law with their respective sanctions. The first category of law (and sanctions) is invoked when the common conscience is offended, when generally shared commitments are violated. The

---

[37] Frank E. Hartung, "Common and Discrete Group Values," *Journal of Social Psychology* (August, 1953), p. 3 *et seq.*

Hartung writes: "Individualism . . . feeds upon a differentiated society. The person becomes conscious of himself as a member of groups because he is continually taking a succession of roles in *different* groups . . . Cooley remarks that there are two kinds of individuality, one of isolation and one of choice. Modern conditions, he says, foster the latter while they efface the former."

Speaking to the same point from the perspective of churchman and poet, T. S. Eliot asserted: ". . . when morals cease to be a matter of tradition and orthodoxy—i.e., of the habits of the community, formulated, corrected and elevated by the continuous thought and direction of the church—and when each man is free to elaborate his own, the personality becomes a thing of alarming importance." (*After Strange Gods: A Primer of Modern Heresy* [New York, 1934], p. 58.)

second comes into play to punish violations of contract between private parties. To the extent that sanctions of the second sort increase, relative to those of the first sort, we may infer that the social order, the nature of the social bond has changed.

Hartung makes a frontal attack on this problem, whether civil law sanctions are linked with differentiation, with special interests; and whether the public at large, in contrast to members of a special interest group, react differently to civil and criminal violations of the law. Given a set of civil and criminal violations by a special interest group (in this case, the wholesale meat industry in Detroit), his hypotheses were that:

1. The public should tend to disapprove both the criminal and the civil violations.
2. But public and industry should tend to differ significantly in the disapproval of civil cases, members of the industry being more indulgent of members of their own special interest group.
3. The public and the industry should disapprove criminal violations to about the same extent.
4. The industry should differ significantly in its disapproval of criminal and civil violations.

Aside from his work on the theoretical underpinning of the study (Durkheim, Cooley, MacIver, Redfield, *et al.*) Hartung's task involved the following: (1) reviewing all cases of violations by the Detroit wholesale meat industry of OPA regulations and selecting, with the help of two attorneys, five civil and five criminal cases as representing the range of violations. These ten cases were summarized, to be presented to respondents. (2) An approval-disapproval scale was developed with scores ranging from maximum approval (a score of 5) to maximum disapproval (a score of 25). (3) A probability sample was drawn of respondents from the industry and the public at large, the N's being 40 and 322 respectively. (4) Interviews having been completed, the data were analyzed and the findings discussed. The bare framework of the findings is presented in Table 14–3. (A more detailed analysis holds constant the variables of age, sex, occupation, and union membership.)

Hypotheses 2 and 4 seem clearly to be confirmed. (For lack of a statement on the sampling error we cannot be sure how safe it is to generalize to the populations as defined.) Industry goes along with the public on reactions to criminal violations; but the values of this special interest group are markedly different from those of the public on civil violations. The public does not make the same distinction as the industry between criminal and civil violations: they disapprove of both with approximately equal strength.

TABLE 14–3

Mean Score on Degree-of-Disapproval Test, for Criminal and Civil Violations of OPA Regulations by the Detroit Wholesale Meat Industry, by Public and Industry

| | NUMBER OF INTERVIEWS | CRIMINAL CASES | | | CIVIL CASES | | |
		MEAN	STAND. DEVIATION	STAND. ERROR	MEAN	STAND. DEVIATION	STAND. ERROR
Public	322	21.93	2.55	.142	20.77	3.29	.183
Industry	40	20.68	2.90	.459	12.98	3.85	.609

Source: Frank E. Hartung, "Common and Discrete Group Values," *Journal of Social Psychology* (August, 1953).

The point, then, is this: the heterogeneity of the urban social order is registered in a proliferation of special interest groups whose values may be eccentric to those of the public taken as a whole. This is a significant change from the relatively more uniform value system that, as we think, was characteristic of a more homogeneous rural society in the past. Let me add, finally, that the abrasive contact of heterogeneous values at the urban crossroads is both outcome and condition of social change.

Density and Social Change. The density of urban populations reinforces certain of the effects of size and heterogeneity. Specialization is one such consequence. When numbers increase and area is held constant, both interests and talents are available to maximize production through an intricate division of labor. Nowhere is this characteristic of contemporary society so vividly illustrated as in our great cities. One does not simply go to the dentist: he goes to the extractionist, or the prosthetic specialist or the X-ray technician, or the oral surgeon or the career man in caries. Whole areas are given over to specific activities, representing a minute division of labor within the city. Often a building—a medical arts building, for example—is devoted to a certain trade or occupation. It is as though a postmedieval street on which dwelt artisans of a given trade had been upended.

Obviously, density implies close physical contacts, reinforcing the tendency to insulate one's self from the importunities of others. Thus as Wirth has suggested, a primary characteristic of the city is physical proximity and social distance.[38] Propinquity implies the availability of diverse skills and interests to complement one's own. Social distance implies the possibility of choice in selecting among them. Both support the change-inducing character of the city.

Density also implies an intense, though rationalized, struggle for space. The minimizing of time-cost distance with fast suburban trains enables a considerable lateral expansion of the city. Yet there is a limit to lateral movement and the solution is to go up. The arched contour of the city skyline roughly reflects differential land values. Maximum competition for space occurs at points of maximum accessibility to the market. Other things equal, this is at the center of the city where the main arteries of urban life converge. And here the construction of skyscrapers results from the need to get most returns from limited (lateral) space.

Mobility and Social Change. Both heterogeneity and density are related in a very basic sense to mobility. Urban life enables one to be mobile (in a social and psychological sense) without moving (physically). For the urban dweller is exposed, willy-nilly to a great range of alternatives. Mobility in this sense is what Simmel refers to as the *Steigerung des Nervenlebens,* the intensification of nervous stimulation. The city, representing a society in flux, derives much of its change potential from this psychic and social mobility. But of course there is physical mobility also. There is the input of immigrants and of rural-urban migrants. There is the daily influx of shoppers and commuters. (In Chicago and New York this is a matter of hundreds of thousands, daily.) There are intercity movers and within-city shifts of residence. And there is the shifting population of our Skid Rows, thousands drifting in and out of American cities.[39]

---

[38] See Louis Wirth, "Urbanism as a Way of Life," *American Journal of Sociology,* Vol. XLIV (July, 1938), pp. 1–24.

[39] Donald J. Bogue, *Skid Row in American Cities* (Chicago: Community and Family Study Center, 1963), *passim.*

Professor Bogue distinguishes these categories of Skid Row men: physically disabled and elderly men, unskilled and daily laborers, migratory workers, transient and resident bums, criminals, and alcoholics. In 41 cities in the United States, about a third, on the average, have six or fewer years of schooling, just under half earn less than $1,500 a year. They live in city areas disproportionately male (sex ratio for the Skid Rows in these 41 cities is 172). In these same areas a fifth are nonwhite and a tenth are foreign born.

Bogue computes a socioeconomic status score based on education and income

What is the connection between mobility and social change? To the extent that the migrant's cultures of origin and destination differ, role definitions are at odds and relationships cannot be built. The social order is changed for lack of stable, predictable patterns of interaction. From the perspective of the receiving group the migrant may be ill-bred, strange in his ways, unattractive if not repulsive. He is often subject to the same sort of suspicious enmity bestowed upon the footloose person in the days of the repressive English Settlement Acts. The migrant does not know how to behave. Others do not know what to expect of him or how to respond to him. But beyond this—and as a consequence—they do not know how to control his conduct, what rewards and punishments to use to guide his behavior into appropriate channels. (In the ultimate case where a person is sufficiently mobile, sufficiently alienated from core elements of the group's culture to endure martyrdom, he is utterly beyond control. There is some subliminal sense of the impotence of the host majority when people observe that they had better not make a martyr of someone. For this is to put him beyond their control.)[40]

---

associated with an occupation. The special character of the urban input represented by Skid Row is suggested by the following data (*ibid.*, p. 322):

Socioeconomic Score	Chicago Skid Row 1958	U.S. Urban Males 1950
110 and above	1.4	19.8
100 to 109	5.1	27.5
90 to 99	3.3	9.2
80 to 89	9.6	21.7
70 to 79	17.2	8.2
60 to 69	52.8	6.3
Below 60	10.6	6.3

For Bogue's method of calculating his SES score see *ibid.*, p. 317, and Appendix B., p. 516 *et seq.* He presents here a most useful discussion and solution of the problem of contriving an adequate index of social and economic status.

[40] This argument is more fully developed in Everett K. Wilson, "Mobility and the Maverick," *Antioch Review* (Spring, 1957), pp. 60–71.

And from the point of view of the group he has left the migrant may be a defector, giving allegiance to alien standards and arousing the indignation of those whose standards are, by implication, rejected.

We get some sense of this view of the expatriate in a statement by Vladimir Nabokov. "Somewhere at the back of their glands," he writes, "the authorities secreted the notion that no matter how bad a state—say, Soviet Russia—might be, any fugitive from it was intrinsically despicable since he existed outside a national administration; and therefore he was viewed with the preposterous disapproval with which certain religious groups regard a child born out of wedlock." (Vladimir Nabokov, *Speak Memory* [New York: Grosset & Dunlap, Inc., Universal Library, 1951].)

We can see the matter a different way by suggesting that mobility always involves, in some degree, re-socialization. And quite aside from the resistance of previously inculcated views and values, the re-induction of an adult is likely to be thought a supererogation.

SUGGESTED DIRECTION OF CHANGE IN TERMS OF MODES OF INTERACTION

I have been trying to suggest certain aspects of urban society—great numbers, heterogeneity, density, and mobility—toward which the currents of social change have moved us. (I had argued, earlier, that the city itself exemplified the sort of crossroads most conducive to social and cultural change.) Let me conclude with a schematic representation of the direction of social change by plotting frequency of relationships against the modes of interaction embodied in them, the arrows representing the shift in emphasis through time. (See p. 646.)

While the evidence suggests that the direction of social change in our society is roughly that suggested in this scheme, I do not mean to suggest that the distribution of forms of interaction is in fact accurately described by a normal curve. (Nor would I hold that the position of *agape* and conflict are correctly represented at opposite ends of a continuum. They may be dimensions of relationships more often linked than either is with other forms of interaction.) But I would suggest that, in the universe of human relationships, an increased proportion have come to be the sort described in the center column.

❊   ❊   ❊   ❊

Social change is to be understood by inverting the interpretation of social stability. Group change is the other side of the coin bearing group maintenance on its face. Influences threatening cultural, normative, communicative integration lead to dis- or malintegration of the group—i.e., toward change.

Challenges to a given state of integration occur, I have argued, at social and cultural crossroads. The modern city is precisely such a crossroads where a shifting balance between input (birth, socialization, and in-migration) and output (death and out-migration) alters the social mix at the crossroads. Here the numbers involved require new forms of social organization, and the confrontation of differ-

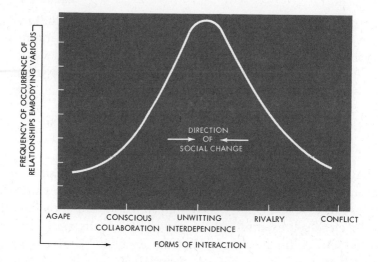

	Mutal aid and support without *quid pro quo* expectations	Coexistence through tight articulation of roles with those of many, unknown others (symbiosis)	Hostility toward personally identifiable others

Mutal aid and support without *quid pro quo* expectations

Coexistence through tight articulation of roles with those of many, unknown others (symbiosis)

Hostility toward personally identifiable others

Moving toward

Person-person

Social relationship

Relatively few persons involved

Rural

Integration: emphasis on cultural, normative, and communicative integration

Common interests

A "desirable" state

Objective: to maximize affect-expression sufficiently to provide support without creating overdependence

Differences between roles and incumbents qualitatively great but quantitatively few

Moving with

Person-intermediaries-person

A-social relationship

Virtually worldwide in terms of numbers involved

Urban

Integration: emphasis on functional integration

Like interests

A necessary state

Objective: to maximize instrumental effectiveness through widest possible collaboration of specialists

Differences between roles and incumbents qualitatively slight but quantitatively numerous

Moving against

Person-person

Social relationship

Relatively few persons involved

Rural

Integration: emphasis on cultural, normative, and communicative integration

Antithetical interests

An "intolerable" state moving toward its dissolution

Objective: to eliminate the relationship

Differences between roles and incumbents qualitatively great but quantitatively few

ences gives rise to problems—and, when they are complementary, to innovations. The great input of Negroes at the urban crossroads has generated that social change commonly dubbed the "revolution in race relations." The vastly increased input of ideas, with the aid of the mass media, professional journals, and devices like the computer have led to rapid and significant cultural change, again chiefly at the crossroads that is the city.

Finally we have looked at the city as the current end point of change in the social structure, pointing to some of the effects of numbers, heterogeneity, density, and mobility as they alter patterns of human relationships.

Two final comments. I have tried to describe social change in the structure of American society, not to evaluate it. If the reader detects a judgment, it was an unintended intrusion. Evaluation is crucial; but it is another problem. Second, our concern in this chapter has been with unplanned change. We use the fuzzy word "force" to refer to unknown influences conspiring to bring about a given outcome. We have been dealing with social forces, in this sense, influences leading, all unawares, to a different social order. In the next chapter let us look, briefly, at planned social change, and its assessment by the sociologist.

APPENDIX: A SOCIAL THEORY OF SOCIAL CHANGE

The truncated statement on page 611 obviously fails to do justice to Marx's erudition or the sophistication of his argument. Nor am I competent to do him justice. But I should point out that Marx does not overlook urbanization, the cosmopolitan nature of the bourgeois epoch, centralization of productive and political power (the latter deriving from the former), and the achievements of capitalism.

"The bourgeoisie, during its rule of scarce one hundred years, has created more massive and more colossal productive forces than have all preceding generations together. Subjection of Nature's forces to man, machinery, application of chemistry to industry and agriculture, steam navigation, railways, electric telegraphs, clearing of whole continents for cultivation, canalization of rivers, whole populations conjured out of the ground—what earlier century had even a presentiment that such productive forces slumbered in the lap of social labor?" (Karl Marx and Frederick Engels, *Communist Manifesto* [Chicago: Charles H. Kerr & Co., 1947], p. 19.)

Because his ideas, and their transformations, are so important in our world and because his insights are so often obscured by fighting slogans, it may be well to give the beginning student some notion of his thinking.

Here are a couple of excerpts. Note in particular (1) the keen sense of the functional interconnections of the social order and (2) his central proposition bearing on the sociology of knowledge: "It is not the consciousness of men that determines their being, but, on the contrary, their social being determines their consciousness."

"I was led by my studies to the conclusion that legal relations as well as forms of State could neither be understood by themselves, nor explained by the so-called general progress of the human mind, but that they are rooted in the material conditions of life. . . . In the social production which men carry on they enter into definite relations that are indispensable and independent of their will; these relations of production correspond to a definite stage of development of their material powers of production. The totality of these relations of production constitutes the economic structure of society—the real foundation, on which legal and political super-structures arise and to which definite forms of social consciousness correspond. The mode of production of material life determines the general character of the social, political and spiritual processes of life. It is not the consciousness of men that determines their being, but, on the contrary, their social being determines their consciousnes. At a certain stage of their development, the material forces of production in society come in conflict with the existing relations of production, or—what is but a legal expression for the same thing—with the property relations within which they had been at work before. From forms of development of the forces of production these relations turn into their fetters. Then occurs a period of social revolution. . . . In broad outline we can designate the Asiatic, the ancient, the feudal and the modern bourgeois modes of production as progressive epochs in the economic formation of society. The bourgeois relations of production are the last antagonistic form of the social process of production; not in the sense of individual antagonisms, but of conflict arising from conditions surrounding the life of individuals in society. At the same time the productive forces developing in the womb of bourgeois society create the material conditions for the solution of that antagonism. With this social formation, therefore, the prehistory of human society comes to an end." (Karl Marx, *Preface to a Contribution to the Critique of Political Economy* [Chicago: Kerr, 1904] pp. 11–13, *passim.*)

The bearing of Marx's theory of social change on the political struggle is best seen in the *Communist Manifesto*.

"The history of all hitherto existing society is the history of the class struggle . . .

"In the earlier epochs of history, we find almost everywhere a complicated arrangement of society into various orders, a manifold gradation of social rank. In ancient Rome we have patricians, knights, plebians, slaves; in the Middle Ages feudal lords, vassals, guild-masters, journeymen, apprentices, serfs; in almost all of these classes, again, subordinate gradations.

"The modern bourgeois society that has sprouted from the ruins of feudal society has not done away with class antagonisms. It has but established new classes, new conditions of oppression, new forms of struggle in place of the old ones.

"Our epoch, the epoch of the bourgeoisie, possesses, however, this distinctive feature; it has simplified the class antagonisms. Society as a whole is more and more splitting up into two great hostile camps, into two great classes directly facing each other: Bourgeoisie and Proletariat." (Karl Marx and Frederick Engels, *op. cit.*, pp. 12, 13.)

ORIGINAL TEXTS

1. Published in *Die Grossstadt,* Jahrbuch der Gehe-Stiftung zu Dresden, Band IX (Dresden: v. Zahn & Jaensch, 1903), p. 195. The German reads:

   Wenn der fortwährenden äusseren Berührung mit unzähligen Menschen so viele inner Reaktionen antworten sollten, wie in der kleinen Stadt, in der man fast jedem Begegnenden kennt und so jedem ein positives Verhältnis hat, so würde man sich innerlich völlig atomisieren und in eine ganz unausdenkbareseelische Verfassung geraten.

   This whole essay, a penetrating observation on the impact of the the city on mental life is beautifully translated by Kurt Wolff in Georg Simmel, *The Sociology of Georg Simmel,* trans. Kurt Wolff (New York: Free Press of Glencoe, Inc., 1950).

   Die psychologische Grundlage, auf der der Typus grossstädtischer Individualitäten sich erhebt, ist die *Steigerung des Nervenlebens,* die aus dem raschen und ununterbrochenen Wechsel äusserer und innerer Eindrücke hervorgeht . . . So schafft der Typus des Grossstädters— der natürlich von tausend individuellen Modifikationen umspielt ist— sich ein Schutzorgan gegen die Entwurzelung, mit der die Strömungen und Diskrepanzen seines äusseren Milieus ihn bedrohen: statt mit dem Gemüte reagiert er auf diese im wesentlichen mit dem Verstande . . . Daraus wird vor allem der intellektualistische Charakter des grossstädtischen Seelenlebens begreiflich, gegenüber dem kleinstädtischen, das vielmehr auf das Gemüt and gefühlsmassige Beziehungen gestellt ist.

SELECTED SUPPLEMENTARY READING

ANDERSON, C. ARNOLD. "Trends in Rural Sociology," in Robert K. Merton, Leonard Broom, and Leonard S. Cottrell, Jr. (eds.), *Sociology Today,* ch. xvi. New York: Harper & Row—Harper Torchbooks, 1965.

BERELSON, BERNARD, AND STEINER, GARY A. "Social Change," in *Human Behavior: An Inventory of Scientific Findings,* pp. 613–40. New York: Harcourt, Brace & World, 1964.

BERELSON, BERNARD, AND STEINER, GARY A. "Social Geography," *ibid.*, pp. 604–10.

*BOGUE, DONALD J. "Urbanism in the United States, 1950," *American Journal of Sociology,* Vol. LX, No. 5 (March, 1955), pp. 471–86. (See whole issue)

COHEN, ALBERT K. "The Study of Social Disorganization and Deviant Behavior," in Merton, Broom, and Cottrell (eds.), *op. cit., supra,* ch. xxi.

*DAVIS, KINGSLEY. "The Origin and Growth of Urbanization in the World," *American Journal of Sociology,* Vol. LX, No. 5 (March, 1955), pp.429–37.

*FREEDMAN, RONALD AND DEBORAH. "Farm-Reared Elements in the Non-farm Population," *Rural Sociology,* 1956, pp. 50–61.

GIBBS, JACK. *Urban Research Methods.* Princeton, N.J.: D. Van Nostrand Co., Inc., 1961.

HATT, PAUL K., AND REISS, ALBERT J., JR. (eds.) *Cities in Society: Revised Reader in Urban Sociology.* New York: The Free Press of Glencoe, Inc., 1957.

*KISH, LESLIE. "Differentiation in Metropolitan Areas," *American Sociological Review,* Vol. 19, No. 4 (August, 1954), pp. 388–94.

*MERTON, ROBERT K. "Social Structure and Anomie," *American Sociological Review,* Vol. 3 (October, 1938), p. 672–82.

———, AND NISBET, ROBERT A. (eds.). *Contemporary Social Problems.* New York: Harcourt, Brace & World, Inc., 1961.

*MINER, HORACE. "The Folk-Urban Continuum," *American Sociological Review,* Vol. 17, No. 5 (October, 1952), pp. 529–37.

MUMFORD, LEWIS. *The Culture of Cities.* New York: Harcourt, Brace & World, Inc., 1938.

———. *The City in History* New York: Harcourt, Brace & World, Inc., 1961.

*REDFIELD, ROBERT. "The Folk Society," *American Journal of Sociology,* Vol. LII, No. 4 (January, 1947), pp. 293–308.

SIMPSON, GEORGE E., AND YINGER, J. MILTON. *Racial and Cultural Minorities.* 3d ed. New York: Harper & Row, 1965.

———. "The Sociology of Race and Ethnic Relations," in Merton, Broom, and Cottrell (eds.), *op. cit., supra,* ch. xvii.

SJOBERG, GIDEON. "Comparative Urban Sociology," in Merton, Broom, and Cottrell (eds.), *op. cit., supra,* ch. xv.

*WALLACE, ANTHONY F. C. "Revitalization Movements: Some Theoretical Considerations for their Comparative Study," *American Anthropologist,* 1956, pp. 264–81.

*WIRTH, LOUIS. "Urbanism as a Way of Life," *American Journal of Sociology,* Vol. XLIV (July, 1938), pp. 1–24.

---

* Articles marked with an asterisk are available as reprints from the college division of the Bobbs-Merrill Company, Indianapolis, Indiana.

Chapter 15

Planned Change in the Patterning of Human Relationships

*How do we devise desired social change?
And how do we know whether—and
to what extent—change has in fact been achieved?*

M an is a valuing animal, and in every social order he seeks so to modify behavior and belief as to achieve his values. A dramatic example of this was the Civil Rights Act of 1964, redefining the roles of white and Negro: the citizen role, the worker role, the customer role, and secondarily, the whole complex of roles and relationships linked with, or affected by, these. All legislation may be seen in this light: the prohibition amendment, the amendment according suffrage to women, the minimum wage law, the income tax amendment. This is, indeed, the legislator's daily task: writing new rules, or revising old ones, and so changing the roles and relationships that constitute the social order.

But purposive change is not restricted to legislators. In our personal lives each of us, in more modest ways, tries to induce change. This is the whole aim of the socialization process, the task of parents and teachers (although in this case the aim is to induce changes in support of the social order, rather than to alter it: and the change is registered in the person, rather than in the total structure of relationships). Similarly priest, minister, and rabbi direct their efforts to individual and collective changes in support of professed values.

And in business, producers, salesmen, advertisers attempt to alter the consumer role in their favor.

TWO BASIC REQUIREMENTS FOR PLANNED SOCIAL CHANGE

What prompts efforts to induce change? What is basic in the notion of planned change? Two requirements underlie efforts at social change: first, an awareness that there are alternatives, different ways of doing things, and second, a conviction that one way is better than another. Calculated social change grows, first of all, from an awareness of differences. This means that we must have points of comparison, in space or time. "If there were only one moon, it might just as well be made of green cheese," Louis Wirth used to say. If there were only one of something it wouldn't make any difference what we called it: we couldn't discriminate between it and anything else. And there would be no question of better and worse. "If there isn't any difference it doesn't make any difference."

> I was thinking the day most splendid
> till I saw what the not-day exhibited,
> I was thinking this globe enough till
> there sprang out so noiseless
> around me myriads of other
> globes.[1]

An awareness of differences leads to the need for evaluating the differences. As between two means, one may be the more efficient and less costly way of achieving a given end. As between two ends, one may be the more ultimate, the less qualified, being therefore the more desirable or having higher priority. As between means and ends, or practice and profession, the one may not be consonant with the other.

There is something more than a mordant humor in Sarah Cleghorn's "Quatrain." She uses ironic contrast to sensitize our synapses to social inequity.

> The golf links lie so near the mill
> That almost every day
> The laboring children can look out
> And watch the men at play[2]

---

[1] Walt Whitman, "Night on the Prairies", in Walt Whitman, *Complete Poetry and Selected Prose and Letters,* ed. by Emory Holloway (London: The Nonesuch Press, 1938), p. 407.

[2] Sarah Norcliffe Cleghorn, "Quatrain," *New York Tribune,* January 23, 1915.

AP Newsfeatures Photo

Two examples of efforts to reshape the social order: A Peace Corps worker in Togoland and the March on Washington, part of the campaign to alter the Negro's role and Negro-white relationships.

Magnum Photo by Bruce Davidson

RESISTANCES TO PLANNED CHANGE

If there is a gap between what is and what ought to be in a social order it is implied that there are resistances, obstacles to closing that gap. This is, of course, the case. Changes can't be made without harming some sector of the social order. Resistance to change is, therefore, inevitable. To live in a peaceful society, today, would be to invite profound disruption in our economy. Peace would, in some ways, be harmful. To change our society by abiding by the Mosaic code would be to subvert great sectors of business and civic enterprise: the insurance industry, public and private police and their apparatus, the Yale & Townsend Lock Company, etc. For an apparently modest change in England, the shift to a decimal currency with 100 pennies to the pound, the cost is estimated at a minimum of £100,000,000.[3] A committee appointed by the Chancellor of the Exchequer was asked, in 1961, to advise on the most efficient means of achieving the change-over. Three years of planning plus the time required for the change-over suggest how, in a social system, one change ripples out to induce others. In this case it is not merely a matter of printing and minting new money, but of converting business machines such as cash registers and price computers and coin-operated machines. About 4 million of these machines must be converted or modified. Price adjustments will have to be made on various commodities as the half-penny, worth about $\frac{1}{480}$ of a pound is displaced by the new half-cent piece, worth about $\frac{1}{400}$ of a pound.

Resistance to change is implicit in the routinizing of relationships in institutional structures. What we mean, when we refer disparagingly to "the establishment" is that modes of behavior have become so routinized as to have lost their *raison d'être*. When roles become ritualized, preoccupation with traditional means blocks out sensitive apprehension of the ends sought. So, likewise, do organizations tend to become rigid, the structure of relationships sustained through time, safeguarded if not embalmed in printed rules, printed policies, manuals and guides covering all imaginable contingencies. This flood of printed material may, as Willard Waller once perceptively pointed out, defeat itself, may result in defective communication.

One aspect of age in the social organism is a disorder of communication, an "excess of the organ of language" attended by a lack of real

[3] *New York Times*, Tuesday, September 24, 1963, p. 1 *et seq.*

communication, a growth of verbiage and a failure of that inner contact upon which communication depends. . . .

. . . this breakdown of communication is most clearly visible when one generation is succeeded by another. It is easy to communicate duties, and it is easy to find men to do duties, but it is difficult to communicate a mission. So that it often happens that what is passed on to the newer generation is not a living insight into function, but dead information about duties.[4]

But whatever the resistances to change—and some of the resistances, themselves, induce even greater strain toward change—we continue to plan and work toward a transformed future. That is, we contrive change. Many of our plans have a quantitative air about them—we plan for more of the same thing. In this sense:

"Many of our plans are not really plans but are detailed rationalizations of the status quo, projected a bit into the future. We build more automombiles according to plan; then more highways, also according to plan; then more cars; more highways and so on ad infinitum. This may be planned change, but it is . . . in danger of becoming a synonym for rigidity and conformity and helplessness. . . ."[5]

Plans to extend *what is,* as in Professor Bennett's illustration, are unlikely to meet much resistance. In the world of work it is almost routine. "Better things for better living—through chemistry" or any other means, enlists the effective efforts of planners in business and industry. More for less, or newer products to accomplish the same ends more efficiently—these are ideals that prompt endless planned changes with minimum resistance. Professor March has described such ideals as limitless, represented by an upsweeping curve asymptotically approaching the vertical.[6]

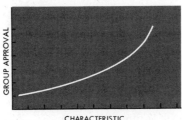

CHARACTERISTIC

[4] Willard Waller, *The Sociology of Teaching* (New York: J. Wiley & Sons, Inc., 1932), p. 442.

[5] John W. Bennett, "Planned Change in Perspective," an introduction to a symposium on planned change, *Human Organization,* Vol. XVIII, No. 1 (Spring, 1959), pp. 2–4.

[6] James G. March, "Group Norms and the Active Minority," *American Sociological Review,* Vol. XIX, No. 6 (December, 1954), pp. 733–41.

But when we attempt to change the social order and its supporting culture so as to make practice more closely approximate
profession, we may find that our norms are not so unqualified as
might be thought. All men are created equal; but some more equal
than others. Honesty is an indubitable virtue; but an excess of
honesty is intolerable. Cleanliness is next to Godliness: but there is
such a thing as being "mean clean." Which is to say that the
optimum, the "best," may not (in practice) be the most of the good
or the least of the bad. Less cryptically, acceptable behavior and
belief may lie somewhere between the best and the worst, the most
and the least. March represents it this way:

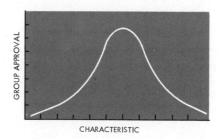

Thus as we try to induce changes that shift practice closer to
profession, we are likely to encounter resistances. The same is true,
in a way, as the industrial chemist tries to develop an anticaries
toothpaste, as the business man tries to reduce costs and enlarge his
market, as the industrialist tries to establish quality control, cutting
his losses from defective parts.

But there are these differences between change in things and
social change. First, as I've indicated, *more* is likely to be seen as
better in the one case and as questionable in the other. Second, the
effectiveness of the change-inducing efforts (the input of energy)
will often be assessed with care and precision in the one case and
seldom in the other. The sophistication and precision with which
Coch and French studied the problem of "Overcoming [people's]
Resistance to Change" is fairly recent and relatively rare;[7] and here,
again, the change to be induced in persons is linked with an increase
in productivity.

---

[7] Lester Coch and John R. P. French, Jr., "Overcoming Resistance to Change,"
Human Relations, Vol. I, No. 4 (August, 1948).

ACTION RESEARCH: MEN OF KNOWLEDGE IN LEAGUE WITH MEN OF ACTION

Increasingly, however, change-agents decline to work in the dark. The NAACP employs a sociologist and institutes an action research program to evaluate the success of its change-inducing efforts. The military must ask: what are the effects on human relationships, on morale and efficiency when we are able, for the first time, to keep a submarine crew submerged for months at a time, or planes in the air for protracted periods? The Quakers raise the question: What in fact are we accomplishing through the program of the American Friends Service Committee workcamps as we try to educate (change) people toward the Friends' ideals? The Federal Reserve Board, through periodic national surveys, seeks information on the spending-saving habits of Americans so that it may better plan adaptive changes in credit policy. Perhaps the major effort in linking research with planned change is that of the U.S. Bureau of the Census. In social work and education, as well as in business and industry, the planning of new programs is, increasingly, linked with research to assess the adequacy of the program in achieving its objectives.

The interplay between attempted social change and its evaluation will be clearer if we consider both the meaning and some examples of action research. As persons, or through organizations, we act quite continuously to achieve preferred outcomes. The outcome desired is often a change in others' behavior. Lobbyists, philan-thropic agencies, political parties, organizations in social work, PTA's, reform groups—these and scores of others seek to change patterns of human relationship in ways deemed desirable. And, as I mentioned before, changing the rules, and the roles they govern, is the continuing task of the gentlemen in Congress. Yet frequent reversal or revision of legislation suggests that theirs are often trial and error methods. Outcomes are more, or less, or other than intended. Groaning mountains of reform sometimes deliver a very small mouse. Or yet again we may achieve results opposed to those we sought. Activists are often amateurs at social change. They illustrate the futility, in the sphere of human relations, of action not grounded in verifiable knowledge. Illustrations of the unfortunate divorce of action from research are legion.

Here for example, is a settlement school in an isolated mountain area. It draws youngsters from poor homes to a well-equipped boarding school. Many of the children arrive with intestinal parasites that, in their initial stages, enter the body through bare feet. The children are wormed, shod with proper shoes, introduced to the flush toilet, taught the elements of sanitation and given a conventional education with some emphasis on vocational training. Excepting the summer vacation they remain at the school for a period of four to six years. Yet one might find, within weeks after graduation, that a student has undergone a fairly complete reversion. He might be barefoot again, or defecating on a slope above the well outside his family's mountain cabin. What change has been induced by the school? Much of the honestly motivated and well-intentioned effort to induce change may add up to little more than this. Not that such efforts are without consequence. But the results may not be what we anticipate, or less or more than we expect. It is well to ask about the adverse outcomes of well-intentioned action; and the good that is blown by ill winds.

Take the pattern of parole from federal prisons. These are perhaps the best of our prisons, trying to do an enlightened job in rehabilitating (inducing change in) criminals. The social workers, the chaplains, the parole officers and a host of others combine to direct the inmate toward constructive and law-abiding behavior. Yet one of the conditions for parole has been that the prisoner return to the community he came from: often the setting, the social contacts, the influences most conducive to recidivism.

The point, I trust, is clear. However generously motivated, action without the check of controlled observation of consequences is likely to go far astray. Which raises one of Max Weber's questions: "whether the intrinsic value of ethical conduct—the 'pure will' or the 'conscience' as it used to be called—is sufficient for its justification, following the maxim of the Christian moralists: 'the Christian acts rightly and leaves the consequences of his action to God.' "[8] One may doubt, however, whether it's reasonable further to burden the Deity with man's inanities. It would seem the moral as well as the scientific obligation of the man of action—the teacher, the penologist, rabbi, priest or social worker—to evaluate with all possi-

---

[8] Max Weber, "The Meaning of Ethical Neutrality," in *The Methodology of the Social Sciences*, trans. and ed. by Edward A. Shils and Henry A. Finch (New York: Free Press of Glencoe, Inc., 1949), p. 16.

ble precision the consequences of his deeds (or misdeeds as they may turn out to be). The actions of people professionally committed to induce changes in people's behavior demand correlative research.

When we turn to examine the last half of the term "action research," we encounter the notions of lofty detachment, "purity," the desire to avoid the value-laden view. But this posture may neglect certain elementary facts in research. As Professor Arnold Rose has pointed out, and Max Weber before him, the data of the social sciences are infinitely numerous. It follows, then, in determining which problem is to be pursued, that we must select. And selection implies criteria, stated or not, that guide the choice. It is not a random affair: there is some purpose, perhaps more often implicit than explicit in the reports of social scientists.

> Probably most of the investigators who deliberately withhold a statement on the basis of their selection of data do so because they believe that this is not proper in a scientific document. Yet it is one of the basic canons of science that all steps in the collection and analysis of data be specified.[9]

To try to escape the value implications of sociological inquiry may lead, then, to the self-deception that certain kinds of research problems are value-free. But even when the value honestly espoused is the advancement of knowledge, we must ask: knowledge for what? And having stated the end, we are constrained to evaluate knowledge in contrast to alternate means to the desired end. Wherever there are differences there are, with respect to given ends, preferences.

But beyond this, some research purists might contend that preoccupation with action programs or problems impedes the discovery of universal propositions or principles. Yet some first-rate research is produced by sociologists working under the auspices of applied agencies (for example, at the Bureau of Applied Social Research at Columbia University, at the Socio-Environmental Laboratory of the National Institutes of Health in Washington, D.C., and at the Bureau of the Census). And on the other hand, it is not clear that sociologists (or other scientists) enjoying the purer sanctuary of the academic groves are, in their selection of problems or means of attacking them, austerely immune to the practical

---

[9] Arnold Rose, "The Selection of Problems for Research," *American Journal of Sociology,* published by the University of Chicago, Vol. LIV, No. 3 (November, 1948), p. 219.

immediacies of the moment, to the kudos and cash that flow from inquiries into current crises. In short, the distinction between "pure" and "applied" is less than crystal clear. It is not immediately obvious that research on practical problems precludes broadly generalizable findings.

In any case, two assertions seem justified. First, only as people who are practically concerned with altering patterns of human relationships can guide and check their work against the systematic findings of research will they be able to validate their efforts. Second, only to the extent that the social scientist's predictions are ultimately compatible with mundane experience can we be confident in a body of propositions that claim to illuminate patterns of human relationship.

PLANNED CHANGE WITH SOCIOLOGIST AS ALLY: THREE EXAMPLES

Changes Induced by the Encampment for Citizenship

Now let us look at three instances in which men of action, attempting to induce change, collaborate with the sociologist, the latter evaluating results of the effort. One such example is an appraisal of the Encampment for Citizenship by the Bureau of Applied Social Research of Columbia University. Under the auspices of the Ethical Culture Society, the Encampment aims, through its six-week summer program, to help its campers identify, clarify, and understand central issues of our social order, and, in confronting them, to increase will, skill, and commitment to democratic principles.

The population, campers in the summer of 1955, was heterogeneous in religion, race, and region and in income and education. While not selected for their views and values, they tended, in joining this group, to select themselves for certain attributes: in contrast to other youth they wanted to work in the public service and they were disposed to express their altruistic sentiments in action.

The design of this study may be translated into the scheme we have used before (see Table 15–1).

The experimental influence was, of course, the summer program of the Encampment for Citizenship. The formal program, aimed at economic, international, and political-social problems, consisted of lectures, discussion groups, field trips, and films. The informal influences stemmed from living with fellow members of the encampment for six weeks, participating in the governing of the community, and

TABLE 15–1

	BEFORE	AFTER		CHANGE
		6 WEEKS	1 to 8 YEARS*	
EXPERIMENTAL (Encampment subjects, 1955)	x_1†	x_2	x_3	$x_2 - x_1 = d$
CONTROL₁ (Comparable group not exposed to Encampment for Citizenship program)	x'_1	x'_2		$x'_2 - x'_1 = d'$
CONTROL₂ (Comparable group of American Friends Service Committee campers)	x''_1	x''_2		$x''_2 - x''_1 = d''$
CONTROL₃ (Comparable group of persons this age subject to changes normally occurring in a six week period and registering those changes attributable to general impact of events during such a period)	x'''_1	x'''_2		$x'''_2 - x'''_1 = d'''$

*Encampment alumni, 1946–54.   † x = measures of knowledge and attitudes characteristic of good citizenship.

$$\text{Hypotheses: } d > \begin{cases} d' \\ d'' \\ d''' \end{cases} \simeq p < .01$$

in common recreational activities. Some apparently worshipped together.

What were the outcomes? ($x_2 - x_1$ or d, in contrast with d', d'' and d'''?) Eight out of ten thought the encampment experience had changed them either "moderately" or "a great deal." These perceived changes were about evenly divided four ways: greater awareness of social problems, a greater respect for and understanding of others, a decline in prejudice toward other ethnic groups, and a greater interest in social problems along with a disposition to do something about them.

The immediate effects of the encampment were an increased commitment to traditional civil rights for nonconformists and minorities. The campers also became more sanguine about solving pressing social problems (through group, rather than individual effort) through the use of established legal and social means. They did not suffer reverse prejudice, nor did they become more unrealistic or radical in their approaches to these problems. And while the immediate outcome did not disclose an elitist sense, a little later, after the Encampment members returned home, there was some indication of disenchantment. There was

> . . . some increased sense that the larger society is unbound by moral imperatives . . . of alienation from the average American (and a) considerable attrition on the scene of action due to lack of desire to act, lack of trying despite desire, or lack of clarity in the course of action.[10]

Such findings are similar to those of Henry Riecken in his American Friends Service Committee-sponsored study of *The Volunteer Workcamp*,[11] a Friends' summer work project in Mexico. But I do not mean to overemphasize the slippage effect—the tendency toward reversion upon return to campers' home communities. Findings indicated a quite substantial change apparently induced by the Encampment for Citizenship, change that persisted, even among Encampment alumni who had undergone this experience from one to nine years previously. "Despite the passage of time, the alumni furthest removed show no marked lessening of sentiments on behalf of tolerance and civil liberties."[12]

A final point should be made. Although the effects of the formal and informal programs were not separated, greatest change was induced in attitudes developed and reinforced by the informal patterns of daily life. Thus while there was significant change in level of tolerance and in attitudes on civil rights, there was virtually no change in political and economic orientations. It is in the former rather than the latter sphere that daily, *informal* intercourse with those of differing regional and ethnic background may be supposed to have had its effect. Informal peer influence was, apparently,

---

[10] Encampment for Citizenship, "Summary of an Evaluation Study of the Encampment for Citizenship Made by the Bureau of Applied Social Research of Columbia University" (New York: Encampment for Citizenship, March, 1956), mimeographed, p. 9.

[11] Henry Riecken, *The Volunteer Workcamp* (Reading, Mass.: Addison-Wesley Publishing Co., Inc., 1952).

[12] Encampment for Citizenship, *op. cit.*, p. 12.

potent in effecting change. There is strong evidence, the research summary states, that

> . . . the most salient feature of the total Encampment . . . what was psychologically central to the campers, was the group experience in democratic living which they enjoyed so much.[13]

Here, then, we have a good instance of contrived social change: first through inducing a change in the aggregate distribution of traits in the group and then, presumably, a change induced by a different input of attitudes into their several communities as members of the Encampment returned home. Having left his home community with a constellation of attributes, X, he returns with the personality mix slightly altered (X'). Thus some slight change in the whole is induced. This kaleidoscopic process, an incessantly altered mix of attributes, goes on constantly in human communities. The thing distinctive of our example is that it is a consciously contrived process and program aimed at changing patterns of human relationship for the fuller realization of democratic values.

Changing Fertility Levels

Consider a second example of contrived social change, a change in all those relationships linked with rise or decline in fertility: husband-wife, parent-child, governor-governed, buyer-seller. . . . With declining mortality, especially in the new nations, and with rates of natural increase far outstripping increases in production, some have felt an urgent need to lower fertility rates. Under these circumstances we want to know (1) whether groups or governments have as official policy a reduction in the birth rate, (2) whether people do in fact desire to control the size of their families, and (3), if the answer to these questions is yes, whether "the control of fertility [can] actually be implemented on a large scale, [especially] in the developing areas."[14]

As to the first question we know that in India, in Puerto Rico, in China (although official policy has vacillated, there) and, for the case in point, in Taiwan, official agencies have encouraged family limitation to achieve a decline in the birth rate. And in Taiwan, where mortality rates have been dropping (to less than 8 per 1,000: see Figure 15-1) and where the birthrate in 1960 was about 37 per

---

[13] *Ibid.*, p. 6.

[14] Bernard Berelson and Ronald Freedman, "A Study in Fertility Control," *Scientific American*, Vol. 210, No. 5 (May, 1964), p. 29.

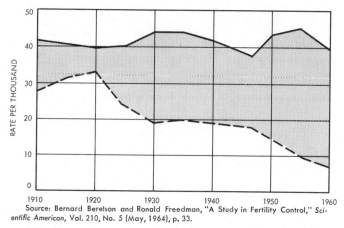

Source: Bernard Berelson and Ronald Freedman, "A Study in Fertility Control," Scientific American, Vol. 210, No. 5 (May, 1964), p. 33.

FIG. 15-1. **Rate of increase in Taiwan's population** (shaded area) **has grown because the birthrate** (solid line) **has remained high while the death rate** (broken line) **has fallen.**

thousand yielding a rate of increase that would double the population in 25 years, there is evidence that people do wish to control the size of their families. The data show that as the number of living children goes beyond three or four, the percent who would have

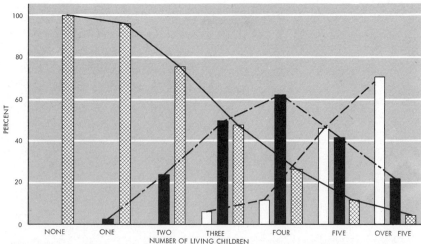

Source: Bernard Berelson and Ronald Freedman, "A Study in Fertility Control," Scientific American, Vol. 210, No. 5 (May, 1964), p. 34.

FIG. 15-2. **Family preferences are charted for Taichung wives according to the number of children they have. The chart shows the percent of wives in each group who said they would have preferred fewer children** (white bars) **or more children** (shaded bars) **than they had or were satisfied with the number of children they had** (black bars).

Courtesy, G. D. Searle & Co.   Courtesy, The Ford Foundation

A dramatic example of planned change: control of fertility. (The Ebers Papyrus provides an early prescription for control of fertility—1550 B.C. Birth control education was assisted in Singapore by the Ford Foundation.)

preferred fewer children mounts from more than 40 percent (those having five children) to better than 70 percent for those having more than five.

In the Taiwan study, an initial survey with public health nurses interviewing about 2,500 married women between ages 20 and 39— this in the capitol city of Taichung—established a base line from which change might be measured. Their responses, in addition to the suggestive data on number of children preferred (above) give a clear answer to the second question:[15]

. . . these women as a group wanted to have a moderate number of children, were having more children than they wanted, approved of

---

[15] The figure suggests that a desire for fewer children—not a total, but fewer on the average—is not a conscious imposition of Western values. If women in the older age groups wish to call a halt to reproduction it may be because (1) a declining mortality rate allows them to achieve the desired family size without additional births, or (2) because other desires are competing with that for children.

the idea of family limitation and were trying—ineffectively—to limit the size of their families. . . . It seems clear that if, throughout the world, unwanted children were not conceived, a large part of the "population problem" would disappear.

. . . To study how best to enable the people of Taiwan to do what they themselves said they wanted to do, the provincial health authorities undertook to develop a program of action to make the practice of family planning more readily available in the city of Taichung. This effort, we think, is one of the most extensive and elaborate social science experiments ever carried out in a natural setting.[16]

The problem, then, was this: What means might be used, and at what cost, to increase the level of effective family planning in

TABLE 15–2

Information and Persuasion Treatments by Degree of Intensity in Three Sectors of Taichung

TREATMENT	HEAVY (13,908)	MEDIUM (11,154)	LIGHT (11,326)	TOTAL (36,388)
Nothing	232	243	292	767
Mail	232	244	292	768
Everything (Wives Only) (Wives and Husbands)	232 232	122 122	73 73	427 427
Total *lin's*	928	731	730	2,389

Source: Bernard Berelson and Ronald Freedman, "A Study in Fertility Control," *Scientific American*, Vol. 210, No. 5 (May, 1964), p. 34. Matrix shows the allocation of various "treatments" among the *lin's* in the three density sectors. The figures in parentheses give the total number of women 20 to 39 years old.

Taichung, a city of about 300,000 with about 36,000 married women between ages 20 and 39 (60 percent of these having had three or more children)? Under the auspices of the provincial health authorities the Population Study Center of the University of Michigan tested the effects of different "treatments" to induce the desired change. These treatments, in addition to community-wide announcements (through posters) and meetings with community leaders) were as follows: (1) no contact or information dispensed, (2) a direct-mailing to parents with two or more children and to newlywed couples, (3) "everything": wives only, entailing visits by

---

[16] Berelson and Freedman, *op. cit.*, pp. 31, 32.

trained nurse-midwives to every married woman in the neighborhood (the *lin*), conveying information and setting appointments for them at health stations where contraceptives could be supplied and questions answered, and (4) "everything": wives *and* husbands. The intensity of the "everything" treatments was varied: in one of three sectors of the city it was applied to half of the *lins,* in a second sector to a third of them and in the third sector to a fifth of them. These are the "heavy," "medium," and "light" treatments shown in Table 15–2. The other *lins* in each sector were divided equally between the "mail" and "nothing" treatments. The distribution of the various treatments, the independent variable, is indicated in Table 15–2.

The design of the study may be represented as in Table 15–3.

TABLE 15–3

	BEFORE	EXPERIMENTAL TREAT-MENT: FEBRUARY '63 THROUGH OCTOBER '63	AFTER	CHANGE
Experimental$_1$ ("Everything": Wives + Husbands)	x_1		x_2	$x_2 - x_1 = d$
Experimental$_2$ ("Everything": wives only)	x'_1		x'_2	$x'_2 - x'_1 = d'$
Experimental$_3$ (Mail)	x''_1		x''_2	$x''_2 - x''_1 = d''$
Control (The "nothing" treatment)	c_1		c_2	$c_2 - c_1 = d'''$

How much change was induced? At the time of writing the outcomes were necessarily uncertain since the promptest results require a time lag of nine months to disclose themselves. But there is some evidence of outcomes from two sources: case records of couples accepting information or contraceptive devices and a sample survey of 2,432 women of child-bearing age. The sample survey revealed a drop in pregnancy of about a fifth between the end of 1962 and the end of 1963 (from 14.2 percent to 11.4 percent pregnant in the samples). The case records show that 11 percent of the married women between ages 20 and 39 accepted information and contraceptive devices, about 4,000 women in the city of Taichung. But the figure 11 percent is probably an underestimate of the success of the program since not all women in that age group were "eligible" to accept family planning through this program.

> About 16 per cent were already practicing contraception to their own satisfaction. Another 16 per cent had been sterilized or were believed to be sterile. Nine per cent were pregnant, 3 per cent lactating and 1 per cent experiencing menstrual irregularities of one kind or another. If these women are eliminated, only about 55 percent of the 36,000 in the age group were "eligible." Of these 20,000 or so women, the program secured about 20 per cent as family planners. Included in that definition of eligibility, however, are women who actively want another child—young wives who have not completed their families or those who want a son. If they are considered not really eligible for contraception at this time, the "currently eligible" category is reduced to some 10,000 women, and those who have taken up contraception in the first 13 months come to about 40 per cent of this truly eligible population.
>
> This arithmetic helps to define a "success" in the spread of family planning in the underdeveloped countries.[17]

The full assessment of this effort at contrived change must wait until the population treated moves beyond the child-bearing age. But in the meantime we have some intimation of the relative effectiveness of several means for contriving social change. We know that level of education achieved, number of children already born and desire for various gadgets of contemporary life—radios, bicycles, refrigerators—affect the degree of change induced. We know that there is a remarkable word-of-mouth diffusion of information beyond the experimental population (nearly 25 percent of the acceptances in the Taiwan program came from women who lived outside the city). We know that the heavy saturation treatment ("everything" applied to half of the *lins* in one sector of the city) did not seem to yield results proportionately greater than the less concentrated effort in two other sectors. And we know that the nature of the contraceptive device has much to do with the success of the program: "nearly 75 per cent of the new devices were accepted without the necessity of a home visit, compared with only 15 per cent in the case of the traditional methods."[18] Such precise

---

[17] *Ibid.*, p. 34.
[18] *Ibid.*, p. 37.

and carefully controlled observations enable the man of action to move, literally, with intelligence in programs of planned change. In this case the issue is one of great significance as world population soars, and precisely in those countries whose efforts to improve the general standard of living are vitiated by the multiplication of mouths.

Changing Negro-White Relationships

Perhaps the most dramatic instance of contrived change in American society is the redefinition of the Negro's role, eliminating the adventitious link between race and chances for working, voting, learning, and the use of tax-supported facilities. Symbolized in the Supreme Court's 1954 ruling on forced segregation in the schools, this change has been in process for some years as the steady decline in Negro illiterates from 95 percent in 1865 to 11 percent in 1947 suggests. In the past generation—indeed since the end of World War II—the rate of change in the Negro's role has accelerated greatly. And the shift has been from change sporadically achieved through voluntary associations like the Urban League and the NAACP to change contrived through government intervention.

In this process, research has increasingly accompanied action. Representing these two aspects of change in the Negro's role and coincidentally appearing in the same year, 1947, were the report of President Truman's Committee on Civil Rights and Professor Williams' monograph reviewing research on problems of ethnic, racial, and religious group relations.[19] In addition to appraising various programs aimed at improving intergroup relations, Williams provides a list of 102 propositions on intergroup hostility and conflict, propositions selected for their probable truth and their use in research and action programs. Pointing to further possibilities for research, he also summarizes (in Table 15–4) representative studies of changes in intergroup attitudes.

Williams' summary tells us how frequently the subjects in these studies were students, and how often the experimental influence was some contrived, classroom operation.

---

[19] These two publications are: The President's Committee on Civil Rights, *To Secure These Rights* (Washington, D.C.: U.S. Government Printing Office, 1947), and Robin M. Williams, Jr., *The Reduction of Intergroup Tensions* (New York: Social Science Research Council, 1947). For a more recent summary of research on a related problem, see Melvin Tumin, *An Inventory and Appraisal of Research on American Anti-Semitism* (New York: Freedom Books, 1961).

TABLE 15–4

Representative Studies of Changes in Intergroup Attitudes: Before-and-After Testing

INVESTIGATOR	TYPE OF STUDY		NUMBER OF CASES	SUBJECTS	INFLUENCES TESTED	TECHNIQUES OF OBSERVATION OR MEASUREMENT	FINDINGS
	BEFORE-AND-AFTER TESTING OF EXPERIMENTAL GROUPS	EXPERIMENTAL AND CONTROL GROUPS					
1. D. Young	X		450	College undergraduates	Course in race relations	Ranking of ethnic groups	No change in relative position of groups ranked
2. D. Young	X		16	Graduate students	Visit to Negro Hospital; participation in activities there	Own questionnaire; psychological examination	Slight increase in tolerance, but results inconclusive
3. Schlorff		X	425	High-school students	15 weeks course aimed to increase tolerance toward the Negro	Paired comparisons (Thurstone method) of 20 nationalities; social distance scale	No change in control group. Experimental group ranked the Negro higher at end than at beginning of course
4. Droba	X		30	College students	Course on the Negro	Hinckley scale, A and B	No change (slight favorable tendency)

			N	Subjects	Course	Tests	Results
5. Wanger		X	40	High-school students	Course including material on Negroes	Written testimony; direct observation (no objective tests)	More favorable toward Negroes at end of course
6. Campbell and Stover	X		48 (24 with paired controls)	9th grade girls	Study of Negro; experimental factor: use of opaque projector	Tests: Bogardus, Hinckley, Neumann-Kulp-mann-Davidson	More favorable on Bogardus test, but not on the Hinckley scale
	X		28 (14 with paired controls)	9th grade boys	Instruction on 10 races for one group; other group studied 10 other races	Bogardus	Positive for one group; inconclusive for the other
7. Manske		X	661	High-school students	"Non-indoctrinating" lessons by teachers with "liberal" and "prejudiced" attitudes	Hinckley	Of 22 classes tested, only 2 changed in direction of the teacher's attitude; 8 changed in opposite direction
8. Bolton	X		162	Women college students	Study of Negro education	Hinckley	No significant change
9. Ford		X	26	College students	Course in immigration and race relations	Bogardus; Hinckley; own scale of experience	Positive shift in attitude; no change in reported experience

TABLE 15–4 (Continued)

INVESTIGATOR	TYPE OF STUDY			NUMBER OF CASES	SUBJECTS	INFLUENCES TESTED	TECHNIQUES OF OBSERVATION OR MEASUREMENT	FINDINGS
	EXPERI-MENTAL AND CONTROL GROUPS	BEFORE-AND-AFTER TEST-ING OF EXPERI-MENTAL GROUPS						
10. Billings		X		26	College students	Seminar on social problems	"Scale of Belief"	Slight increase in "favorable" attitudes
11. M. Smith	X			81 (46 in one group; 35 in other)	College students	Course in immigration and race problems	Bogardus; Hinckley	Slight "favorable" gain; considerable shifting of individuals, positive and negative
12. F. T. Smith	X			354 (exp. and control groups, 46)	Graduate students	Tour and visit in Harlem	Battery of tests, including Hinckley	Significant gain in favorableness of attitudes toward Negroes
13. Brooks		X (Quasi-control group)		238	Sociology students (college)	Course with special study of race	Modified Bogardus (on 12 ethnic groups)	No significant change. Tests showed preference for better-educated members of ethnic groups

14. Remmers	X		300	High-school students	One class period of pro-Negro indoctrination	Generalized scale of attitude toward any social group	More favorable to Negro
15. Chen		X	662 (3 control and 6 exp. groups)	College students	Pro-Chinese, pro-Japanese and neutral propaganda (oral)	Agreement with 20 statements on Manchurian issue	Significant changes in direction of each propaganda appeal
16. Peterson and Thurstone	X		130	School children (grades 7–12)	Motion picture: "Four Sons" (pro-German)	Thurstone tests	More favorable to Germans
17. Idem	X		180	School children (grades 9–12)	Motion picture "Son of Gods" (favorable to Chinese)	Thurstone tests	More favorable to Chinese
18. Idem	X		434	School children (grades 6–12)	Motion picture "Birth of a Nation" (anti-Negro)	Thurstone tests	Less favorable to Negroes

A very different study was reported in 1951 by Morton Deutsch and Mary Evans Collins, a study of the effects of interracial housing on the attitudes of white housekeepers, the base point for comparison being segregated biracial public housing. The experimental effect lay in the greater frequency of interaction characterizing integrated interracial housing.[20]

The experimental design would look somewhat as shown in Table 15–5. The aim was to test the hypotheses that the integrated,

TABLE 15–5

Experimental Design in the Deutsch and Collins Study

	BEFORE	EXPERIMENTAL TREATMENT	AFTER	CHANGE
Experimental	$x_1{}^*$	Admission to and living in integrated interracial public housing	x_2	$x_2 - x_1 = d$
Control	$x_1{}'$	In contrast to admission to and living in a segregated biracial housing project	$x_2{}'$	$x_2{}' - x_1{}' = d'$

* x refers to values on the distribution of scores describing respondents' (white housewives') attitudes toward Negroes.

interracial (in contrast to the segregated biracial) housing pattern would yield: (1) more social give and take, (2) friendlier attitudes on the part of white housewives, and (3) more equalitarian standards of behavior.

There were two projects in New York City providing low-income public housing on an integrated, interracial basis. These were matched with two projects in Newark operating on a segregated biracial basis. While the match on race of project residents was reasonably good (two-to-one Negro in New York I and Newark I, and 60–40 Negro/white in New York II compared with 50–50 in Newark II), on other factors there was marked variation. For example, there was a much higher proportion of Jews in the New

[20] Morton Deutsch and Mary Evans Collins, *Interracial Housing* (Minneapolis: University of Minnesota Press, 1951). My comments are based on the abridged version in William Petersen, ed., *American Social Patterns* (Garden City, N.Y.: Doubleday–Anchor Books, 1956).

York than in the Newark projects and the New York residents tended to be more liberal than their Newark counterparts. Such differences had to be taken into account in the analysis. In one such analysis, residents in the four projects who reported having no neighborly relations with Negroes were compared by education, religion, and political attitudes to see if these characteristics accounted for differences in white-Negro relationships. But the data show that

> it seems to make little difference what type of person you are, or what kind of background you have, or what type of attitudes you possess; if you live in a segregated project, almost inevitably you will have no neighborly relations with the Negroes in the project.[21]

The figures in Table 15–6 show the consistent differences in favor of the integrated project in promoting friendly contacts (holding one attribute constant).

Again, holding constant three attributes (political leaning, religion, and education) we find the same differences persisting between integrated and segregated housing projects. In the segregated projects none of the 28 Catholic, politically conservative white housewives having an elementary school education had neighborly

TABLE 15–6

Percentages of White Housewives Having No
Neighborly Relations with Negroes in Project

ATTRIBUTES	NEW YORK I (INTEGRATED)	NEWARK I (SEGREGATED)	DIFFER-ENCE (%)	NEW YORK II (INTEGRATED)	NEWARK II (SEGREGATED)	DIFFER-ENCE
Political attitudes						
Liberal	36% (31)	100% (18)	64%	60% (35)	92% (26)	32%
Middle-of-road	22 (23)	100 (37)	78	59 (32)	95 (36)	36
Conservative	26 (35)	97 (45)	71	61 (31)	100 (38)	39
Education						
Only public school	39 (26)	100 (50)	61	68 (47)	93 (42)	25
Some high school	30 (30)	100 (33)	70	50 (28)	100 (34)	40
Completed high school						
or had some college	16 (31)	100 (14)	84	53 (15)	93 (14)	40
Religion						
Protestant	31 (16)	100 (23)	69	25 (4)	100 (16)	75
Catholic	38 (39)	98 (66)	60	58 (19)	98 (40)	40
Jew	13 (23)	100 (7)	87	67 (72)	95 (41)	28

Source: William Petersen (ed.), *American Social Patterns* (Garden City, N.Y.: Doubleday–Anchor Books, 1956), Table 2, pp. 26, 27. Figures in parentheses stand for number of cases.

---

[21] Petersen, *op. cit.*, p. 26.

relations with Negro women. In the integrated projects, 9 out of 14 housewives, having the same attributes, had developed such relationships with Negro women.

These differences, very probably related to the occupancy pattern (propinquity and frequency of contact) were supported by different views or judgments about the housing projects and about Negroes. In the segregated Newark projects such views were more like those of the broader (extra-project) community than was the case with residents of the integrated New York projects. In the latter case, because of the greater divergence from the outside community, housewives felt more cross-pressures—as, for example, when they dealt with visitors, relatives, *et al.*

When asked to recall what their attitudes toward Negroes had been before entering the project and to indicate how these attitudes had changed—if at all—the effect of occupancy pattern came out, again. "The *net gain* (percentage of housewives reporting favorable changes minus the percentage reporting unfavorable changes) was 56 percent and 55 percent for the integrated projects: for the segregated it was 5 percent and 20 percent."[22]

Since we are considering planned or contrived change, and the relationship between the sociologist and action agencies, the following statement by Louis Danzig, executive director of the Housing Authority of the City of Newark is apposite (the date is 1950).

> A new policy for locating tenants is now in effect in Newark's eight public housing projects. . . . As a result, the partial segregation that has characterized public housing in Newark will no longer obtain. . . .
>
> In large measure this change in fundamental policy reflects the impact of the study reported here. The study has served as a catalyst to the re-examination of our basic interracial policies in housing and as a stimulus to their change. . . . In supplying us with an objective picture of race relations in our projects . . . [the study by Deutsch and Collins] dramatically focused our attention and that of the community at large on matters which, under the press of other business, we had tended to ignore.
>
> The study did more than help to focus attention on the basic question of segregation in housing. Perhaps its most important consequence was its usefulness to those community groups concerned with intergroup relations and civil rights, such as the Essex County Intergroup Council. To such groups the study was an invaluable tool in creating

---

[22] *Ibid.*, p. 42.

the atmosphere that made it possible for the housing authority to adopt and execute a policy of non-segregation.[23]

Here we have an example of applied research in which, to put it grossly, the man of action and the man of knowledge are collaborators. While there is a difference in their roles, each contributes to the other's goal. The housing administrator has information useful to him in making decisions. And the sociologist has additional data on the effects of propinquity on interaction and the effects of interaction on prejudice.

In the case just described we can think of the Housing Administrator as a social engineer, Deutsch and Collins as engaged in applied research. Thus, with the person engaged in pure research, we now have three categories, the characteristics of which are distinguished by Professor Hauser as shown in Table 15–7.

In these three illustrations we have seen how the sociologist's skills were used to determine the extent to which certain planned changes had in fact been accomplished: the development of democratic skills and attitudes, a reduction in Taichung's fertility and, finally, friendly relationships between whites and Negroes. In such instances the sociologist is cast in the role of an outside examiner. The change agent's values may, or may not be his. His task is chiefly that of providing the methodological sophistication that will allow the change agent to answer the question: To what extent am I doing what I think I'm doing? Sometimes the sociologist may be a full-time employee of the change agent: in business, industry, government or a private, nonprofit organization. In this case it seems reasonable to infer that his values are consonant with the aims of his employer. Here again his role is to bring knowledge and skills to bear, a facility in controlled observation and interpretation of differing patterns of human relationships, so promoting the change-inducing efforts of his organization.

✻   ✻   ✻   ✻

In sum: By virtue of his symbol storing and manipulating prowess, man contrasts *then* with *now,* and *there* with *here.* Differences discerned lead to choices. He prefers one way to another. And when things valued are less than fully realized, he acts to shape the world closer to his heart's desire. His world, in its most

---

[23] *Ibid.,* pp. 57, 58.

TABLE 15–7

	PURE RESEARCH	APPLIED RESEARCH	SOCIAL ENGINEERING
Auspices	Organizations given to transmission and extension of knowledge: foundations, universities, and some work in government and private business	Any organization concerned with some practical problem	Any organization seeking to effect changes in behavior, in human relationships
Purpose	Extension of knowledge at the most general level possible	Knowledge immediately relevant to solution of a practical problem	To effect desired change as efficiently as possible
Manner of selecting problem	Problem grows out of antecedent research and is so selected as to promise fruitful extension of knowledge, or to resolve differences between theories yielding different predictions	Problem specified by client	Problems emerge, continuously (as in lawmaking, resolving international issues) in effort to achieve organizational ends
Procedures	Testing hypotheses to establish high-level generalizations, typically involving probability statements	Testing hypotheses to establish low-level generalizations guiding client in achieving his objectives	Formulating policy, predicting outcomes, taking into consideration uncontrollable contingencies, making decision, implementing decision in action programs
Outcomes	Another step taken in endless cycle of formulating theory, testing hypotheses, analyzing data, reformulating theory. . . . Propositions of the order: "If a, b, and c are observed in situations L and M, X will occur in situation L, p out of n times, and Y in situation M, p_1 out of n times, ceteris paribus"	Solution of immediate problem at which point work may end although findings may be relevant to pure research. . . . Propositions of the order: "Given a and b and given situation M, Y will occur p out of n times if c is brought into the situation, ceteris paribus."	Propositions of the order: "Having decided on Y, c is to be brought into the situation to supplement a and b in situation M, and situation L is to be avoided to preclude X."

Source: Philip M. Hauser, "Social Science and Social Engineering," *Philosophy of Science*, Vol. XVI (July, 1949), p. 211.

crucial aspects, is a complex pattern of relationships. That he often bumbles in reshaping this pattern—in his efforts at planned change —testifies to the amateur in all of us. Skills in planned social change are scarcely common currency. Increasingly the men of action seek allies among men of knowledge. In this alliance the sociologist is enlisted to help find some answers to the question: What are the outcomes of these efforts to reshape a sector of our world?

This is one facet of the sociologist's expanding role. That role merits some attention, and to that matter we now turn in a brief epilogue.

SELECTED SUPPLEMENTARY READINGS

*EMPEY, LaMAR T., AND RABOW, JEROME.   "The Provo Experiment in Delinquency Rehabilitation," *American Sociological Review*, 1961, pp. 679–95.

See also, EUGENE P. SCHWARTZ, "Discussion," on the following 2 pp. of same issue and, in *American Sociological Review*, 1962, p. 256, WHITNEY H. GORDON's query, "Communist Rectification Programs and Delinquency Rehabilitation Programs: a Parallel?" together with the author's reply on the following two pages of the same issue.

*HAUSER, PHILIP M.   "Social Science and Social Engineering," *Philosophy of Science*, Vol. 16 (July, 1949), pp. 209–18.

---

* Articles marked with an asterisk are available as reprints from the college division of the Bobbs-Merrill Company, Indianapolis, Indiana.

Epilogue

Chapter 16

Sociology and Sociologist: Their Uses and Abuses

What are some special uses of sociology?
In retrospect, what's the route we've traveled?
How has sociology developed in the United States?

SOCIOLOGY IN THE UNITED STATES: A THUMBNAIL SKETCH

The Early Years

A newcomer to the academic scene, sociology is today a flourishing, far-flung enterprise. It is always hard to pinpoint the inception of ideas, so remote and varied are their forebears. But certainly, in the United States, we cannot date the advent of sociology much before 1900.[1] We can think of a first phase of the discipline's development running from then to the end of World War I.[2] Against a background of bourgeoning industrial and urban growth, turn-of-the-century sociologists sought to build a science of society whose

---

[1] The American Sociological Society (now, *Association*) was founded as recently as 1905. While the *American Journal of Sociology* first appeared in 1896, it was not until 1907 that the first official publications of the Society were issued. In 1936 the *American Sociological Review* became the official medium for interchange among sociologists.

[2] I am borrowing, here, from the discussion by Roscoe C. Hinkle, Jr., and Gisela J. Hinkle, *The Development of Modern Sociology* (Garden City, New York: Doubleday & Co., Inc., 1954).

laws of social evolution would point to prescriptions for the better world. Many of them, religious and rural in their backgrounds, reformist in their inclinations, sought solutions to social problems: crime, poverty, alcoholism, child labor, unemployment, immigrant adjustment, and the like.[3]

Roscoe and Gisela Hinkle divide the years since 1918 into two later periods in the development of modern sociology, up to· and after 1935. World War I, they speculate, had a disenchanting effect on social scientists who, from Condorcet and Comte through Lester Ward and Albion Small had high hopes for the reformation of society, guided by the science of society. If problems posed still revealed a fix on social issues, the central concern became scientific rather than reformist. The task became, increasingly, the identification, unscrambling, and assessment of multiple causes of patterned conduct. During this period, 1918–1935, there were major contributions to social psychology (Cooley, Mead, Dewey, Baldwin) and, with the contributions of Park, McKenzie, and Burgess the field of human ecology emerged. But it has been in the years since 1935 that sociology exhibited its most remarkable growth. This can be documented in terms of professional identification and the development of subfields.

Rapid Growth, High Demand, Short Supply

A count of the 1959 membership of the American Sociological Association totaled 6,345 sociologists, an 80 percent increase over the 1950 membership of the Association.[4] By 1962 there were an estimated seven to eight thousand persons professionally employed as sociologists in the United States.[5] The recency of sociology's

---

[3] As to rural backgrounds, the Hinkles write: "Of the 19 presidents of the American Sociological Society who had been born prior to 1880, who had completed their graduate studies before 1910, and who had achieved some prominence before 1920, not one had experienced a typically urban childhood." *Ibid.*, p. 3. The same might be said, perhaps, of other academic disciplines, although in these—physics, for example—the background would not have had so direct an influence on the selection of research problems.

[4] Matilda White Riley, "Membership of the American Sociological Association, 1950–59," *American Sociological Review*, Vol. XXV, No. 6 (December, 1960), p. 914.

[5] U.S. Department of Labor, Bureau of Labor Statistics, *Employment Outlook for Social Scientists* (Washington, D.C.: U.S. Government Printing Office, 1964), p. 172.

The *Directory of the American Sociological Association* records a membership of 7,368. Their distribution, by classes of membership in the Association, was as follows:

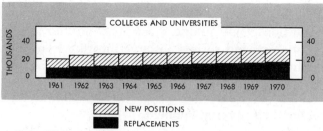

NEW POSITIONS

REPLACEMENTS

Source: U.S. Department of Health, Education, and Welfare, Office of Education; and U.S. Department of Labor, Bureau of Labor Statistics.

FIG. 16-1. Estimated annual recruitment need for teachers.

growth in numbers is brought home to us by the following fact. Among the 1,888 members of the Association who, in 1959, had doctorates, 61 percent were awarded the degree within the preceding ten years.[6] Yet this apparently rapid growth in numbers scarcely matches demand. "Perhaps as many as 300 new sociology teachers will be needed each year, on the average, to fill new positions and to replace college faculty members who leave the profession."[7] But the supply of sociologists—those trained in doctoral programs—averaged only 116 per year in the decade 1950 through 1959.[8] Sibley's data would put the annual average somewhat higher (see Table 16-1) but still about 50 percent short of meeting the demand. It is

Fellow	25.0%
Active	13.3
Associate	32.7
Student	29.0
	100.0%

Definitions of the first three classes of membership are these:
"To be eligible for Active membership an applicant must have: (*a*) a Ph.D. or equivalent professional training in Sociology or (*b*) substantial professional achievement in Sociology, or (*c*) a Ph.D. or its equivalent or substantial professional achievement in a closely related field, provided that the applicant's interest and activities have sociological emphasis or implication. . . . On completion of five years of Active membership, a member shall automatically become a Fellow, provided that those whose eligibility for Active membership rested upon criterion (*c*) above shall have a major commitment to the field of Sociology . . . Any person interested in study, teaching, research or practice in Sociology, or in closely related fields of scientific interest, may be admitted to Associate membership in the Association. . . ." (Washington, D.C.: American Sociological Association, 1755 Massachusetts Ave., NW, 1963), p. 174.

[6] Riley, *op. cit.*, p. 920.

[7] U.S. Department of Labor, *op. cit.*, p. 173.

[8] This figure is inferred from a table in Riley, *op. cit.*, p. 919.

conceivable that the complexities of our society will require that a larger proportion of all American scientists go into sociology. But the immediate demand springs in large measure from the increase and changing composition of our population, swelling enrollments in colleges and universities.

Multiplication of Interests, Subfields

I called sociology a far-flung enterprise. It is this, geographically. At the meetings of the Fifth World Congress of Sociology in 1962,

TABLE 16–1

Average Number of Doctoral Degrees Conferred Annually in Sociology and Certain Other Fields, 1926–62

PERIOD	SOCIOLOGY	ANTHRO-POLOGY	ECONOMICS	POLITICAL SCIENCE	PSYCHOLOGY	ALL ACADEMIC FIELDS
	ANNUAL AVERAGE NUMBER OF DEGREES CONFERRED					
1926–29	31	5	103	35	71	1,583
1930–34	45	8	130	45	97	2,332
1935–39	48	21	108	54	111	2,700
1940–44	54	22	108	61	103	2,919
1945–49	64	20	119	76	141	3,168
1950–54	156	43	306	166	545	7,737
1955–59	156	53	277	195	621	8,887
1960–62	173	68	257	211	708	10,675
	Indices of Relative Growth (1926–1939 Annual Average = 100)					
1960–1962	412	566	225	469	745	475

Sources: 1926–1935—C. S. Marsh, (ed.), *American Universities and Colleges.* American Council on Education, Washington, D.C., 1936, Table XI, p. 74; 1936–1953—Office of Scientific Personnel, National Research Council, *Doctorate Production in United States Universities 1936–1956.* Washington, D.C., 1958, Publication 582, Table 1, p. 7; 1954–1962—U.S. Office of Education, *Earned Degrees Conferred by Higher Educational Institutions.* (Annual). Taken from Elbridge Sibley, *The Education of Sociologists in the United States* (New York: Russell Sage Foundation, 1963), Table 1, p. 45.

forty-nine countries, in addition to the United States, were represented. But more indicative of its development is the number of subfields that have emerged, and the range of occupations engaged in by sociologists.

Look at a 24-page pamphlet[9] announcing the complex schedule

---

[9] There were also 48 pages of advertising by book publishers!

for the annual meeting (in 1964, at Montreal) of the American Sociological Association. It lists two or more sessions at which professional papers were read and discussed for 33 subfields of sociology.[10] Tables 16–2 and 16–3 give us a good idea of this proliferation of special interests within the field.

Professional Preparation

Their professional training in these specialties takes aspiring sociologists to such schools at those listed in Table 16–4. Those earning the doctorate are about 32.5 years old when it is conferred. This is about ten years (median interval is 9.9 years) after receiving their A.B. degree, although only about half this period is spent in full-time graduate study.[11]

The emergence of new subfields, more than the sheer increase in numbers, attests the development and significance of sociology. But aside from an enumeration of specialties, it is instructive to consider

---

[10] These were: criminology, comparative social structures, demography and population, deviance, economy and society, family, kinship and marriage, formal organization, history of sociology, industrial sociology, international organization, medical sociology, methodology, occupational sociology, political sociology, popular culture and mass society, public opinion and mass communications, race and ethnic relations, research in the sociology of education, federal data sources, rural sociology, social change, social disorganization, small groups, social history, social movements and collective behavior, social psychology, social work and welfare, sociology of knowledge, sociology of art, sociology of education, sociology of law, sociology of religion, stratificaton, teaching in the social sciences in high school, theory, and urban sociology.

There were, additionally, scores of council and committee meetings devoted to the business of the Association itself.

[11] Elbridge Sibley, *The Education of Sociologists in the United States* (New York: Russell Sage Foundation, 1963), p. 100. Using data from the Office of Scientific Personnel, Sibley makes some interesting comparisons between fields as to length of time between receiving A.B. and Ph.D. degrees.

Median Intervals between A.B. and Ph.D.: Recipients of Ph.D. Degrees in 1958 and 1959

Field of Study	Years	Field of Study	Years
History	9.9	Anthropology	9.4
Sociology	9.9	Psychology	8.4
Political science	9.8	Life sciences	8.1
Economics	9.5	Physical sciences	7.1

Source: Data from Office of Scientific Personnel, National Research Council, by courtesy of Lindsey R. Harmon.

TABLE 16–2

Fields of Special Competence Reported by Sociologists in 1959, Rank Order of the Most Frequently Reported and Those Showing Greatest Increase in Interest, 1950–59

RANK ORDER	FIELD	N	PERCENT
	*Aging, problems of	45	0.5
	Area studies	95	1.1
	*Art, music and literature, sociology of	28	0.3
11	Community	326	3.6
9	Criminology	361	4.0
10	Cultural anthropology	341	3.8
14	Disorganization, deviance	253	2.8
	Educational sociology	111	1.2
6	General sociology	419	4.7
	History, sociology and/of	52	0.6
13	Industrial sociology	307	3.4
	Knowledge, sociology of	40	0.4
	*Law, sociology of	35	0.4
3	Marriage and family	605	6.7
	*Medical sociology	188	2.1
	*Mental health, sociology of	113	1.3
2	Methodology, techniques and methods of research	662	7.4
	*Occupations, work, sociology of	103	1.2
4	*Organization, sociology of	464	5.2
	Political sociology	177	2.0
7	Population	380	4.2
12	Public opinion and communication	318	3.5
8	Race and ethnic relations	373	4.2
	*Religion, sociology of	209	2.3
17	Rural sociology	199	2.2
	*Small groups	112	1.2
	Social change	81	0.9
	Social control	9	—†
1	Social psychology	901	10.0
	Social welfare, sociology and	114	1.3
	*Stratification	193	2.1
5	Theory	434	4.8
16	Urban sociology and ecology	201	2.2
	Other fields, not sociology	732	8.2
	Total fields mentioned	8,981	99.8

Source: Matilda White Riley, "Membership of the American Sociological Association, 1950–1959," *American Sociological Review*, published by the American Sociological Association, Vol. XXV, No. 6 (December, 1960), adapted from Tables 11, 12 and 13, pp. 924, 925.

* These are fields whose frequency of mention as one of special competence increased more than 400 percent between 1950 and 1959.

† Less than .12 percent. Percentages do not sum to 100 due to rounding.

the general posture, or orientation of the contemporary sociologist as he approaches his work. We lack hard data on this matter, but I think Professor Bressler's summary reproduced in Table 16–5 is roughly accurate (see p. 693). Much of the vitality of modern sociology stems from a productive tension between the scientific, humanistic, and action-oriented emphases.

What Sociologists Do

But what, more specifically, do sociologists do? Over half (59 percent) are employed in liberal arts colleges. Most of these are teachers, and many, in addition to teaching, are engaged in research. Another 11 percent are employed in professional schools: schools of education, law, medicine, social work, business administration, agriculture, and the like. About 5 percent are in government service: health, education, corrections, justice, the military, information services, welfare, commerce, agriculture. And 21 percent are in business, industry, and private organizations dealing with problems of education, health, welfare, law, religion, and the like. These three figures, 70 (59 + 11), 5, and 21 percent employed in educational institutions, government, and private enterprise may be compared with the figures for all scientists holding Ph.D degrees: 47, 13, and 32 respectively.[12]

In size and scope, then, sociology is flourishing. There may be something to Professor Talcott Parsons' statement: ". . . perhaps we may say that, ideologically, a 'sociological era' has begun to emerge, following an 'economic' and, more recently, a 'psychological' era."[13] I suspect that sociology's remarkable growth—along with that of the social sciences generally—is due to two factors: liberation from the soil (a once necessary preoccupation with our biophysical environment) and the problems generated by large and dense populations whose activities are functionally interlocked. Now the *necessary* study of mankind becomes man. The sheer survival of his social order—to say nothing of improvements in it— demands the controlled observations and interpretations that are the task of the sociologist.

---

[12] National Science Foundation, *American Science Manpower, 1960* (Washington, D.C.: U.S. Government Printing Office, 1962), p. 10 Data on sociologists are from Riley, *op. cit.*, p. 923

[13] Talcott Parsons, "Some Problems Confronting Sociology as a Profession," *American Sociological Review*, Vol. XXIV, No. 4 (August, 1959), p. 553.

TABLE 16–3

Specialties List for Use with National Register of Scientific and Technical
Personnel

SOCIOLOGY

B001—Applied Sociology
(specify)

B101—General Sociology

Methodology

B201—Computer techniques
B202—Experimental sociology
B203—Field data collection
B204—Measurement and index con-
struction
B205—Model building
B206—Qualitative analysis
B207—Statistical analysis
B208—Survey design
B209—Other (specify)

Population

B301—Internal migration
B302—International migration
B303—Labor force
B304—Population characteristics
B305—Population trends
B306—Vital statistics
B309—Other (specify)

Rural-Urban Sociology

B401—Community studies
B402—Human ecology
B403—Rural sociology
B404—Urban sociology
B409—Other (specify)

Social Change and Development

B501—Invention and innovation
B502—Social control
B503—Social process
B504—Social mobility
B505—Socio-economic development
B505—Other (specify)

Social Organization, Structure, and Institutions

B601—Bureaucracy
B602—Cultural—the Arts

B603—Educational
B604—Family
B605—Industrial
B606—Intergroup
B607—Knowledge
B608—Legal
B610—Medical
B611—Occupational
B612—Political
B613—Religious
B614—Scientific
B615—Stratification
B609—Other (specify)

Social Problems, Social Disorganization

B701—Criminology
B702—Deviance
B703—Poverty and dependence
B704—Social conflict
B709—Other (specify)

Social Psychology

XB01—Attitudes
XB02—Collective behavior and so-
cial movements
XB03—Culture and personality
XB04—Group interaction
XB05—Leadership
XB06—Public opinion
XB07—Reference groups
XB08—Role behavior
XB10—Social perception
XB11—Symbolic communication
XB09—Other (specify)

6405—Sociology of language

B909—Sociology, other
(specify)

4021—Raman spectrometry
4022—Titrimetry
4023—X-ray and electron diffraction
4009—Other (specify)

Inorganic Chemistry

4101—Alkalies and alkaline earths
4102—Atomic structure
4103—Boron and silicon compounds

4104—Building materials
4105—Coordination compounds
4106—Electronic materials; semicon-
ductors, ferroelectrics, fer-
romagnetics
4107—Explosives, rocket fuels
4108—Gaseous elements
4110—Glass, fused silica
4111—Halogen family
4112—Industrial carbon, graphite,
carbon black
4113—Inner-transition elements, lan-
thanide series and actinide
series
4114—Inorganic equilibria and
phase relationships
4184—Inorganic nomenclature and
symbolism
4115—Inorganic reaction kinetics
and mechanisms
4116—Metals and alloys
4117—Molecular and crystal structure
4118—Nonmineral products; asbes-
tos, vermiculite, etc.
4119—Pigments and industrial minerals
4120—Radiochemistry, minerals and
products
4121—Solutions and solvent theory
4122—Synthetic inorganic chemistry
4123—Theoretical inorganic chemistry
4124—Transition elements
4125—Water chemistry
4109—Other (specify)

Organic Chemistry

4201—Adhesives
4202—Agricultural chemicals
4203—Aliphatic chemistry
4204—Alkaloids
4254—Amino acids and proteins
4258—Antibiotics
4205—Aromatic hydrocarbons, de-
rivatives
4263—Carbohydrates
4206—Coal

Source: National Science Foundation, *American Science Manpower*, 1960 (Washington, D.C.: U.S. Government Printing Office, 1962), p. 10.

TABLE 16–4

Number of Resident Graduate Students and Faculty Members (1960) in Each Institution That Conferred More Than 10 Ph.D. Degrees in Sociology between 1950 and 1960.

INSTITUTION	Ph.D. DEGREES CONFERRED, 1950–1960[a]	GRADUATE STUDENTS IN RESIDENCE, 1960	FACULTY MEMBERS, 1960[b]
University of Chicago	198	73	17
Columbia University	128	109	18
Harvard University	103	47	12
Cornell University[c]	84	43	19
University of North Carolina	73	55	15
University of Wisconsin	72	65	20
Ohio State University	71	32	22
University of Minnesota	59	53	14
New York University	56	196	10
Yale University	54	28	12
University of Southern California	53	53	9
University of Pennsylvania	52	43	18
Michigan State University	50	59	23
University of Washington	50	58	17
University of California (Berkeley)[d]	42	132	22
University of Michigan	40	84	25
Catholic University	35	46	6
State University of Iowa (Ames)	35	39	9
University of Pittsburgh	35	31	9
University of Illinois	30	36	15
Louisiana State University	28	33	11
New School for Social Research	28	108	6
Pennsylvania State University	24	22	10
Washington University (St. Louis)	21	30	12
Duke University	19	18	13
Indiana University	19	41	13
Northwestern University	19	27	9
Washington State University	18	20	10
Iowa State University	16	23	10
University of Texas	16	34	14
Stanford University	15	31	12
Vanderbilt University	15	11	5
University of Kentucky[d]	14	19	15
University of Missouri[c]	14	34	15
American University	13	30	6

TABLE 16–4 (Continued)

INSTITUTION	Ph.D. DEGREES CONFERRED, 1950–1960[a]	GRADUATE STUDENTS IN RESIDENCE, 1960	FACULTY MEMBERS, 1960[b]
Boston University	13	21	10
University of Nebraska	13	16	7
Fordham University	12	43	3
St. Louis University	11	25	5
Syracuse University	11[e]	[f]	[f]
University of Calif. (Los Angeles)	10	44	16
Florida State University	8	14	9
University of Florida[d]	8	10	8
University of Notre Dame[d]	8	23	8
University of Utah	8[e]	[f]	[f]

[a] Data for 11-year period, except as indicated by note e.
[b] Assistant professorial and higher ranks only, including part-time members.
[e] Combined data for general and rural sociology departments.
[d] Ph.D. program inaugurated since World War II.
[e] Data for 1950–1959 only.
[f] Figures not available.
Sources: Degrees conferred, 1950–1956, National Research Council, *Doctorate Production in U.S. Universities, 1936–1956,* Publication 582, Washington, 1958; degrees conferred, 1957–1959, U.S. Office of Education, *Earned Degrees Conferred* (Annual); degrees conferred, 1960, Schedule I. Students and faculty, Schedule I.
Taken from Eldridge Sibley, *The Education of Sociologists in the United States,* p. 65. Sibley's table includes 28 additional institutions, some of them of very high quality, conferring ten or fewer doctorates during the indicated interval.

SOME LINGERING FICTIONS

The Nature of the Field and Dimensions Appropriate to It

Perhaps because of the recency and rapidity of its growth, the aims and methods of the field remain obscure for many. Flanked by the biological and physical sciences on the one side, the humanities on the other, sociology, in its intermediate no-man's land sometimes suffers the most naïve misconceptions. Perhaps the most serious of these is misconstruction or ignorance of the boundaries and units of analysis in sociology. It is, apparently, hard to see that a group does not consist in a collection of people, that the sociologist is dealing with a structure of *relationships,* and their constituent roles, and that the dimensions of analysis are quite different from those used in the study of personality systems. Even thoughtful people are likely to fall into the nominalist fallacy: only the concrete individual has reality. This is reinforced by the strong position psychology has enjoyed in our intellectual tradition. It has deflected our attention

TABLE 16–5

Three Orientations or Emphasis in Sociology: Scientific, Humanistic and Action-Oriented

CHARACTERISTICS COMPARED	SCIENTIFIC		HUMANISTIC	ACTION-ORIENTED
	THEORY	EMPIRICAL RESEARCH		
Role model	Natural scientist		European intellectual	Engineer
Primary goal	Social knowledge		Social criticism	Solution of social problems
Value perspective	Ethically neutral		Challenges dominant American value orientations	Guided by dominant American value orientations
Criterion for problem selection	Theoretical importance		Social importance of fundamental issues	Social importance of segmental problems
Theoretical perspective	Functionalism		Humanism	Pragmatic liberalism
Methodology	Logic and mathematics	Rigorous statistical analysis	Disciplined insight	Statistical and qualitative analysis
Criteria of adequacy	Coherence	Correspondence	Perceptiveness	Usefulness
Intellectual product	Analytical schemes	Empirical generalization	General trends and tendencies	Implications for action

Source: Adapted from Marvin Bressler, "The Conventional Wisdom of Education and Sociology," in *Sociology and Contemporary Education*, edited by Charles H. Page (New York: Random House, Inc., 1964), p. 99. © Copyright 1964 by Random House, Inc. Reprinted by permission. I have reversed his second and third columns and substituted the word "humanistic" for his heading, "significance." For students—and others—whose interests bridge sociology and education, this short essay makes extraordinarily pleasant and profitable reading.

from relationships *between* self and other to those *within:* emotional, cognitive, neurological.

. One result has been that some people (like the journalist–political philosopher Russell Kirk, and even some professional academicians like Jacques Barzun) understand neither the unit of analysis nor the boundaries of the discipline. Kirk, for example, sees sociology as being a grab bag made up of the leftovers from other fields, especially economics and political science. Thus sociology can have no logical identity for lack of determinate boundaries. And, for lack of a distinctive unit of analysis, a discipline has only a spurious claim to independent identity.[14] If one takes the position, as Barzun seems to, that the individual or his attribute is, or ought to be, the ultimate reality for the inquirer, then sociology is ruled out. This indefatigable defender of the humanistic faith sees neither sense nor necessity in statements about groups—statements which, when applied to an individual, must be nonsensical. Ingenuous about the nature of the field, Barzun and Graff, in their occasionally defensive essay, fall into the vulgar superstition that certain "absurd" findings, apparently contrary to common sense, must be corrected by the concrete individual instance.[15] They fulminate against the quantitative and abstract character of sociology (and other social sciences) while taking hope in the occasional acknowledgment by sociologists of the significance of history, the discipline from which, as they see it, sociology sprang. Let me illustrate their confusion about disciplinary boundaries and units of analysis by referring to their book.

> . . . wherever the counting professes to correct the ordinary man's or the historian's generalizing from a single instance or from "mere observation," two cautions have to be kept in mind. One is that the

---

[14] See Russell Kirk's "Is Social Science Scientific?" in the *New York Times Magazine* for June 25, 1961, pp. 11f. Kirk's article reflects a point of view often found among those who would have us rely, for definitive statements about society, on the wisdom of the seers, especially those whose pronouncements are hallowed by antiquity. It is among theologians, historians, writers, and philosophers that such people— Joseph Wood Krutch is another example—find the omniscience, prescience, and precision needed to describe and explain patterns of human relationships. No more is necessary for an adequate understanding of group characteristics. Indeed, for writing articles like Kirk's, any more knowledge would be a distinct handicap; for he might then hesitate to say what sociology means to "the typical college student," or to make sweeping statements on the basis of an N of 1 or 2, or to damn a whole discipline and its seven thousand practitioners by quoting approvingly from one of them, "perhaps the best-known of American sociologists" (Sorokin), or to define Durkheim's "*anomique*" as "the masterless man," or to assume he knows who is the most widely read of living French sociologists, or to cite the latter, acceptingly, when he describes "the typical American sociologist," or so casually to contradict himself: "If man were predictable . . . he would cease to be truly human . . . of course there can be ascertained certain general rules concerning human behavior in community. . . ."

You will profit from reading Kirk's article *if* you balance it with Robert K. Merton's rejoinder, "Now the Case *for* Sociology," this appearing in the *New York Times Magazine* for July 16, 1961, pp. 14f. It should be noted that Kirk confuses social science with sociology. While he writes, presumably, about economics, anthropology, psychology, political science, and sociology, his reference is repeatedly to sociology as though it were synonymous with social science.

A similar confusion reflected in loose terminology is the interchange of the words "social" and "sociological."

[15] Jacques Barzun and Henry F. Graff, *The Modern Researcher* (New York: Harcourt, Brace & World, Inc., 1962).

"correction" may produce results that are in conflict with the known reality, and thus have to be corrected again in making particular judgments: the demographer, for instance, declares that the American family of today has 3.6 children.[16]

Now one can wring a good deal of irony out of this sort of nonsense so characteristic of the sociologist. (Of course it would not be hard to find historians citing such facts as they describe the social context of historical events!) But why is it nonsense, if indeed it is? Clearly there is no family with three and six tenths children. Never since Solomon forced a tearful mother to quail at the prospects of five tenths of a baby have we even approached a fractional child. It must, then, be nonsense to speak in such unrealistic terms.

But what Barzun and Graff misunderstand is the referent. The sociologist does not refer to *an* American family but to *the* American family. The 3.6 refers, clearly, to United States society. *It is an attribute of the group, not an attribute of a family.* Groups can be characterized decimally, fractionally. There is a realm of inquiry having dimensions peculiar to it and not to be found in its parts. Barzun and Graff do not seem to know what the sociologist (the demographer, above) is talking about. Like the sensible man in the street with whom they ally themselves, they have trouble in emancipating themselves from the immediate, corporeal case. This is the myopia of a raw, empirical nominalism.

It is precisely because of this historical-psychological prejudice that we extrapolate directly from person to group, falling into egregious errors—errors ranging from the projection on a national scale of biases shaped through the person's atypical experience, to assessing a national budget in individual terms. These worthies may read Durkheim, but they do not grasp his statement that the group represents a set of phenomena *sui generis*. Of course no individual ever had a median rate of income. None ever had an average level of grade achieved, a birth or a death rate, a net reproduction rate, a distribution of scores combining attitude toward something with intensity of feeling. None ever had a delinquency or recidivism rate, a percent voting the Socialist ticket, a psychosis rate, or percent belonging to the Church of the Latter Day Saints. None ever had a measure of density, or of cohesion, or of moral integration. But groups do.

---

[16] *Ibid.*, p. 224.

When our point of inquiry is the group, then we must deal in dimensions appropriate to it, not in dimensions suitable to other classes of phenomena. Barzun, Graff, Krutch, Kirk, *et al.* miss the boat because they do not know the nature of the field, its boundaries and units.

The Forced Choice: Science *or* Art

They also miss the boat—to cite a second abuse of sociology—through a spurious split between the sciences and the humanities. Not only is it alleged that there are "two cultures" suffering lack of communication: they are, as these people see it, antithetical. They fail to see that craftsman and madman are joined in scientific as well as poetic enterprise. They miss the science in art—and the art (the imaginative, creative aspects) in science. In sociology as in every fruitful scientific enterprise, there is an interplay between theory and its empirical testing, a two-way street between interpretation and observation, between imagination and knowledge. "There is, it would seem, in the dimensional scale of the world, a kind of delicate meeting place between imagination and knowledge, a point arrived at by diminishing large things and enlarging small ones, that is intrinsically artistic."[17] There are the trees and the forest, the immediate, concrete, sensible reality and the more remote, interpretive conceptualization, moving beyond perception to a higher level of abstraction. As I suggested in the first chapter, to celebrate the one by damning the other is to truncate the process of inquiry. We do not need to depreciate sociology to appreciate the humanities, or vice versa. It may indeed be questioned whether this academic distinction between realms of inquiry makes sense. This is the question raised by Professor Stanley Garn, President of the American Association of Physical Anthropologists.

---

[17] Vladimir Nabokov, *Speak Memory* (New York: Grosset & Dunlap, Inc., Universal Library, 1951), p. 118. Charles Horton Cooley spoke to the same point in his journal. He wrote:

"Our common way of talking and thinking greatly exaggerates the difference between science and art. Science is nothing without an ideal—that is, a theory—which it strives to verify and perfect through facts. So art is nothing unless it is grounded in a minute study of nature. Both call for a union of patient observations and experiment with creative imagination. The difference is in the character of the ideal which is sought . . . or rather in the means through which the ideal can be realized. Art seeks a harmonious organization of emotional impressions, such as those from form, sound and color; while science seeks a more intellectual harmony, which also, in its way, appeals to emotion. It is impossible, I think, to say where science ends and art begins." (*Journals* [Vol. 11, 1896], p. 57.)

We know of their civilizations [Greece and Rome] through written works and through the efforts of archaeologists. Must we make a distinction between these sources of knowledge? Was the Rosetta stone a contribution to the sciences or the humanities once it unlocked the hieroglyphics of pre-dynastic Egypt?

Consider the ancient human interest in the origin of man and the origins of life on earth. Given this interest, was Darwin's contribution more to the sciences and less to arts and letters? Can Australopithecus then be named exclusively as a "scientific" discovery? Is the evidence for ongoing evolution in living man of interest only to scientists? . . .

We know now why smells smell and how tastes taste. We know why the apple falls and how the gull soars. We understand the rainbow and the eclipse and the tornado, the reasons why swallows migrate and what makes the leaves turn orange and red and brown. Is such knowledge beyond the pale for the properly cultivated man? . . .

There was a time when the sciences and the humanities were correctly viewed as one. Mechanics gave new insight into the beauty of the universe. Exploration opened new wonders for man to view. Men gazed at the stars and dreamed of visiting them. Have we hurt poetic feelings by traversing the atmosphere instead of wandering about on a donkey? . . .

Who first wrote about the sciences *and* the humanities? How narrow he was, how uneducated to believe that human knowledge and human experience could ever be stuffed into separate trunks, divided and compartmentalized. How unscientific. And how untrue to the meaning of the humanities.[18]

Man, Mercurial and Idiosyncratic

Sometimes the abusers of sociology allege that reliable knowledge about human behavior is impossible, that man's conduct is idiosyncratic, unpredictable, controlled if at all by ineffable, intangible, and erratic forces. "It is a rather pitiful assumption," says Congressman Reece's report, "that the springs of human behavior can be reduced to formulae."[19] This same report of a congressional com-

---

[18] Stanley Marion Garn, "The Sciences Are Humanities," *Antioch Notes,* Vol. XLII, No. 3 (Yellow Springs, Ohio: Antioch College, November, 1964).

[19] Special Committee to Investigate Tax-Exempt Foundations and Comparable Organizations, *Report* (House of Representatives, 83rd Cong. 2d sess., House Resolution 217 [Washington, D.C.: U.S. Government Printing Office, 1954]), p. 73.

Membership of the committee, in addition to Congressman Reece, was as follows: Congressmen Jesse P. Wolcott (R), Michigan; Angier L. Goodwin (R), Massachusetts; Wayne L. Hays (D) Ohio; and Gracie Pfost (D) Idaho. Rene A. Wormser was General Counsel, Arnold Koch, Associate Counsel, Norman Dodd, Research Director, Thomas McNiece, Asst. Research Director, Karl Ettinger, part-time research consultant, Kathryn Casey, Legal Analyst, John Marshall, Jr., Chief Clerk, Mildred Cox, Asst. Clerk.

The posture of the committee is suggested as they express the fear that when

mittee's investigation of tax-exempt foundations (especially those supporting the social sciences) asserts:

> Human beings are motivated by a complex of factors: by goals . . . by ethical and moral concepts: by exercises of free will. Some of the social sciences seem to have wholly rejected the concept of free will.[20]

To this statement we need to counterpose Max Weber's: "The characteristic of 'incalculability' [i.e., unpredictability] . . . is the privilege of—the insane . . . we associate the . . . feeling of freedom [the freedom to will] with those actions which we are conscious of performing rationally—that is . . . in which we pursue a clearly perceived end by means which are the most adequate in accordance with the extent of our knowledge. . . ."[21]

The unpredictability of human behavior is of course belied, daily, by the classification of actions and attributes that each of us makes in dealing with others and anticipating their responses.[22] It is belied, also, by the propositions about conduct and culture that lace the work of members of the clan most captious about the sociologist's generalizations.

The writer's function, Mr. Allen Tate says in his essay "The Man of Letters in the Modern World," is "to render the image of man as he is

---

Foundations' activities "spread into the field of the so-called 'social sciences' or into other areas in which our basic moral, social, economic and governmental principles can be vitally affected, the public should be alerted to these activities and be made aware of the impact of Foundations' influence on our accepted way of life."

Or again, "There is . . . a concentration of Foundation power in the United States, operating in the social sciences and education. . . . There is no conclusive evidence that this interlock, this concentration of power, having some of the characteristics of an intellectual cartel, came into being as the result of an over-all, conscious plan. Nevertheless it exists." *Ibid.*, pp. 3, 4.

[20] *Ibid.*, p. 73.

[21] Max Weber, *The Methodology of the Social Sciences*, trans., ed. by Edward A. Shils and Henry A. Finch (New York: Free Press of Glencoe, Inc., 1949), pp. 124–25.

[22] What makes gambling such a pleasant retreat from the patterns of mundane life is that it offers *un*predictable outcomes. (I mean to suggest, of course, that in daily life the outcomes are typically predictable.) Insofar as gambling is transformed so that the outcome *is* predictable, it has been converted from recreation to work, from an escape from daily life's requirements to an extension of them. It's instructive to note our tendency—a virtual mandate in business—to convert a situation in which outcomes are unknown into one where we can predict, hence control, the outcome. Control of income is what John Le Carré had in mind when he protested against the manipulation of the writer by "that great apparatus which was set up in order to drown the critics' protests and convert the public taste into the plaything of Hollywood and Madison Avenue. . . . It is engaged in turning the writer into an institution which will underwrite and where necessary supplement his faltering talent. *It is there in fact to take the chance out of his future.* He has become a property." (*New York Times Book Review*, June 27, 1965, p. 2. Italics mine.)

in his time" . . . I wish to emphasize the centrality of literature . . . for all who seek to be aware of the human in his changing world.[23]

Anthony Trollope writes about one of his characters, Lord Fawn, that:

> Being a poor man, filling a place fit only for rich men, he had been driven to think of money, and had become self-denying and parsimonious—perhaps we may say hungry and close-fisted. *Such a condition of character is the natural consequence of such a position.*[24]

Or consider Albert Guerard's statements about Joseph Conrad's novels:

> For they seem to say, and indeed do say, important things about our puzzled and striving human nature: about our capacity for idealism and our capacity for deterioration; about our desire for brotherhood and our propensity to solitary crime. These stories . . . nearly always suggest long vistas of experience beyond themselves. . . .[25]

So the humanists do not write as though they believe what they say about the futility of general statements about human behavior. One might more accurately infer a jealous guarding of a preserve thought to be exclusively theirs, against the poaching of the sociologist.

There are other abuses. I pass over the once fashionable, now trite charge of jargon, a necessary characteristic of all specialties while pointing out that among my clansmen there are some superb stylists. (Indeed, Professor Bierstedt insists that their literary grace and style is a special reason for including some sociological studies in a general education program.) But let us turn to two final indictments, the issues of complexity and collectivism.

Social Phenomena: Their Inscrutable Complexity

It is alleged that social phenomena are so complex that man's mind and methods of problem solution are simply inadequate. "Every adjective that may be applied to mankind is thought to denote a variable. And many other variables . . . lurk beneath the level of language proficiency. Variables are uncountable; they

---

[23] Francis Fergusson, *The Humane Image in Dramatic Literature* (Garden City, N.Y.: Doubleday & Co., Inc.–Anchor Books, 1957), p. vii.

[24] Anthony Trollope, *The Eustace Diamonds* (London: Oxford University Press, 1953), p. 74. Italics mine.

[25] Albert Guerard's introduction, in Joseph Conrad, *Heart of Darkness and The Secret Sharer* (New York: The New American Library, 1957), pp. 7, 8.

march in endless disarray."[26] This is a hoary chestnut, long discredited at three levels. Our daily experience, if we reflect on it, reveals how we select, from a host of social cues, those successfully predicting others' responses. First, then, we must and do cope with complexity every day. At a second level, the methodology of the social sciences suggests ways of making manageable a complex set of data. Theory isolates the crucial variables bearing on our problem. (Not all variables are relevant in understanding given behaviors.) Among these, one may be selected for study while others are controlled by means such as those discussed in Chapter 1. And occasionally we can explain much of the variance in behavior with two or three independent variables. At a third level, sophisticated mathematical techniques (now supported by computer technology) permit the manipulation of many variables simultaneously.

In short, complexity of social phenomena is not an insuperable roadblock, barring solutions in sociology. Of course there are endless ways of slicing the pie of social phenomena. The task is to discover which way of looking at the problem is fruitful, which variables, or combinations of them, make good predictors.

Sociology Implies Collectivism = Socialism, Hence Subversion

Both more and less serious are the accusations that the sociologist's orientation is exclusively quantitative, smacking of materialism and leading to Marxism. In a statement that might be improved, if tainted, by quantification, the Reece report says: "It is not surprising that so many of the social scientists tend to collectivism."[27] The same report asserts that the sociologist promotes "moral relativism and the culture-lag theory [which] strike at the very roots of the average American's traditional values."[28] Such allegations are less serious for being ludicrous, but more serious to the extent that they reveal apprehension and misapprehension about the sociologist's role. It is a grave matter for the sociologist to be seen in such a sinister light as systematically subverting American values. Perhaps some unease is inevitable since the sociologist may investigate traditional patterns of human relationships that are vested with an air of the sacred. And it is of course true that the sociologist refuses to rule out of bounds,

---

[26] Amos H. Hawley, "Social Science and the Humanities," *Michigan Alumnus Quarterly Review*, Vol. LXV, No. 21 (August 8, 1959), p. 281.

[27] Special Committee to Investigate Tax-Exempt Foundations, *op. cit.*, p. 73.

[28] *Ibid.*, p. 88.

as an object of inquiry, any class of social behavior that stimulates scientific curiosity. Parent-child, man-woman, worshiper and priest, labor and management—none of these or countless other relationships is immune to inquiry as searching as the investigator's wisdom and skill permit. And for some, the findings or interpretation may make unpleasant reading. But the sociologist's role is not that of uncritical booster or perennial optimist. (No more is he an inveterate knocker or pessimist.) His task is to discover what is and to explain why it is that way.

SOME SPECIAL USES OF SOCIOLOGY

By virtue of its subject matter, its methods of problem solving and its position between biophysical science and the humanities, sociology can be extraordinarily useful. Let me suggest a few special uses of sociology before concluding with a thumbnail review of our work in this book.

The scope of sociology, cutting across all sectors of social life, means an extended range of relevance. Its findings have much to say to many. Professor Page puts the point well when he says that undergraduate work in sociology

> is an especially appropriate educational preparation for a large number and variety of post-collegiate roles . . . sociological knowledge and sensitivity are needed more and more in public affairs, law, medicine, social work, journalism, architecture and engineering, teaching, and, with its increasing semi-professionalization, a growing segment of business; moreover, this knowledge and awareness are highly advantageous for women, not only with respect to their roles as wives and mothers—as major strategists of family life, but also with reference to their participation in local and national community affairs—where many female college graduates also occupy strategic positions.[29]

In another way sociology has a peculiar personal relevance. It helps us to discover our identity and, in doing so, to resolve the old and ever recurring dualism between self and society. Perhaps this is especially useful in our day. For I would guess that there are circumstances converging on young people that make the study of sociology a tough but useful corrective. Let me suggest certain

---

[29] Charles H. Page, "Sociology as an Educational Enterprise," in *Sociology and Contemporary Education,* edited by Charles H. Page (New York: Random House, Inc., 1964), pp. 22, 23. © 1964 by Random House, Inc. Reprinted by permission.

circumstances that may make for a spuriously isolated and impoverished conception of self.

Social inventions now provide a level of security (and, therefore, independence) never before enjoyed. At the same time there is an understandable sense of impotence—an alienation from the sources of control—in the face of always impending international disaster. The popular allegations of sheep-like conformity in contrast to some supposed past of free-wheeling self-determination justify defiance of the establishment and its witless conventionality. For some, fashionable corruptions of Zen and existentialism challenge any loyalty save to immediate sensory experience. Thus one is isolated from others, unable to share in a suprapersonal common cause. Even in the courageous commitment to civil rights there is an incongruous, and temporary, juxtaposition of atheist and religious, the zealous and the reluctant fearful, educated and illiterate, young and old, transients and deep-rooted, lifelong residents. Here, too, is a rejection of established change agencies like NAACP, to say nothing of the sluggish legal devices of the establishment. And so, even in its missions, the youthful self may cut its moorings in the past and isolate itself from the current social context.

Especially at the point of transition from dependence to independence these conditions converge, I suspect, to produce the *culte de moi*, an obsessive preoccupation with the self and a misconception of that self. It becomes the product of some parthenogenetic miracle, a creation without creator. Perhaps delusions about self and illusions about society are not wholly deplorable. But if there is something to the Socratic injunction about knowing one's self, then insensibility to that self's social genesis is harmful.

Here sociology can offer significant help. To discover with some precision the ways in which, the extent to which, the means by which man becomes a social animal is to gain a fuller sense of self and society. To the ingenuous this seems sometimes to imply resignation—or require rebellion. For the data are clear on the impact of reference groups, the significance of socialization, the bonds and bounds of community. But the shaping of a person is the making of a person. To know the extent and conditions of this creation has important outcomes. We can appreciate how personal strength is a social benefaction. Knowing the conditions that contribute to an outcome we know what must be done to reshape them for getting better outcomes. And we must know ourselves better for the explicit identification of the self in society.

A third use of sociology lies in its sharpening our ways of thinking, of solving problems, in the intriguing realm of human relationships. If it suffers the limitations of a marginal discipline, sociology also profits from its position. Its study stimulates a critical appreciation of logic and tools of inquiry characteristically lacking in the realms that bracket it. "For in the humanities the scientific method plays no part and in the sciences it is taken for granted. It is especially in sociology that it rises to the level of awareness and becomes a matter of conscious application and employment."[30] While there's a touch of hyperbole in this statement of Professor Bierstedt's, the emphasis is correct. If, in the humanities, the branch of philosophy we call epistomology is preeminently concerned with the *strategy* of inquiry, it typically shortchanges the grubbery of *tactics*, the artful collection and meticulous analysis of data. If, on the other hand, the biological and physical sciences are long on tactics, on the hardware of inductive research, they tend in their training, to short-suit problems of strategy, the epistomological underpinnings of inquiry.[31] Sociology (and other of the social sciences) offers a special opportunity for cultivating sensitivity to problems both of strategy *and* tactices of disciplined inquiry.

Let me mention two other uses of sociology, playing variations on themes suggested by Bierstedt.[32] First, sociology is extraordinarily useful in promoting the liberation of the mind that is, presumably, the prime aim of a liberal arts education. Excepting anthropology, sociology has no peer in opening the mind's door to the deceptively familiar world of men's social arrangements. It enables a responsible questioning of the customary. It encourages us to entertain alternatives. (This is, indeed, implied when we define the field and design our studies in terms of *differing* patterns of human relationships.)

---

[30] Robert Bierstedt, "Sociology and General Education," in Page, *op. cit.*, p. 45.

[31] Practitioners in these older disciplines are likely to pick up their epistemological assumptions, all unwittingly, in osmotic exposure to laboratory work. Perhaps, as Bierstedt suggests, the tardy emergence of their discipline requires sociologists to confront more challenging epistemological questions than is true of the biophysical sciences whose roots press deeper into the past. So it may be that sociology profits from what Trotsky called "the privilege of historical backwardness." (Leon Trotsky, *The History of the Russian Revolution* [Ann Arbor: University of Michigan Press, n.d.], p. 4.)

[32] Bierstedt, *op. cit.*

And in the process we achieve a better understanding of why what is, is. "This sort of liberation, in a world beset by provincialisms, by the ethnocentrisms of place and the temporocentrisms of time . . . is no mean . . . accomplishment."[33] A number of disciplines, of course, have the virtue of puncturing provincialisms. But sociology not only reveals, as history does, differing social structures in space and time. It transcends space and time themselves, seeking those isomorphisms characterizing groups, under specified conditions, anywhere and any time.

A final use of sociology is in mending the intellectual fissures induced by an artificial opposition of science and the humanities—the spurious split decried by Stanley Garn in the passages I quoted. Sociology is dead center in the tradition of the liberal, the liberating, arts, joining the so-called two cultures, putting together in our minds matters not meant to be disjoined. It "spans two cultures, the scientific and the humanistic, using as it does the method of science to explore the concerns and affairs of humanity."[34]

*   *   *   *

I've offered this abbreviated list of sociology's uses, not as paean to past accomplishments but to point to possibilities. Of course, it would be pleasant to think that in small measure some of these uses have been realized through this book. Now it is time for a final, backward look. Let us review the role of the sociologist as I have described it in the chapters past.

A BACKWARD LOOK, ONCE OVER LIGHTLY

The sociologist fixes his attention on those structures of relationships that we call groups. But since men are mortal and groups, especially those institutionalized, are immortal, he has to explain their continuous re-creation as newcomers enter the group. In Part I we saw that the individual enters the human group, articulating his behavior with others' only as he picks up the culturally prescribed expectation sets transmitted to him through the socialization process. Like the musician, he joins the orchestra, comes to play his part adequately, as he learns the score. In this process, self and other, individual and group are joined; for becoming self-conscious means

---

[33] *Ibid.*, p. 43.
[34] *Ibid.*, p. 54.

becoming other-conscious. The group assimilates the person as he assimilates the group.

But the sociologist cannot take this mundane process for granted. He must ask: how does this remarkable transmutation occur? Thus he inquires into that social process of induction in which the chief institutionalized agents are family and school. With his peers, kinfolk and teachers are partners in the arduous task of person building. With them we engage in an intricate dialectic. The significant outcome is the elaboration of a self, the realization of self through others. We do not grow directly, but only indirectly. A person becomes an object to himself, becomes self-conscious (and so, himself, a collaborator in the process) through the responses of others. From their vantage point he is able to get a fix on his position, to participate in the process of becoming a person. As others act toward him, as he estimates the judgments of him implied in their responses, his self-conception, at first wavering and uncertain, crystallizes.

But infant, youth, and immigrant are not uniformly socialized. Culture is not uniformly transmitted. Hence the sociologist must ask what accounts for the differential transmission of role definitions. We find that such differences stem from several sources. First, in a few cases basic biological attributes may condition ability to learn and perform in role. Second, since the inner ring of influences—kin, gang, and teachers—is unique to each person, none will be subjected to precisely the same constellation of influences. These groups contrive an idiosyncratic mask for each of us. The sociologist finds a third significant source of differing role definitions, the expectation-sets differentially transmitted through the subcultures called classes. These categories may not be so simply discrete as is suggested by the old Protestant hymn:

> The rich man in his castle, the
> poor man at his gate,
> God made them, high or lowly,
> and order'd their estate.[35]

Yet if class lines are somewhat more blurred today, we nonetheless find everywhere differences in prestige, privilege, power—in style of

---

[35] This is the hymn buoyantly entitled "All Things Bright and Beautiful," by Mrs. C. F. Alexander. In their new *Anglican Hymnbook,* the Church of England will drop the lines I have quoted as being out of tune with the times and smacking overmuch of feudalism (report in the *New York Times* for September 20, 1963).

life—reflecting differences in securing things valued by the group. The meaning of his class position for the person entering the group is suggested by research findings of sociologists: the connection between class and the extent, types, and treatment of mental illness, between class and fertility, class and longevity, class and sexual behavior, class and child-rearing patterns, class and religious conduct, class and ideology—in short, class and style of life. Class has been an effective predictor because it captures a complex cluster of variables that create

> different basic conditions of life at different levels of the social order. Members of different social classes, by virtue of enjoying (or suffering) different conditions of life, come to see the world differently—to develop different conceptions of social reality, different . . . hopes and fears, different conceptions of the desirable.[36]

And so the sociologist studies the shaping of personality and the constant renewal of the group as the culture is differentially transmitted to various sectors of the incoming population.

The role of the sociologist requires that he ask not only how roles are shaped and meshed with others to build relationships, but how relationships themselves are articulated to form and maintain groups. This was our concern in Part II where we raised the question: How are groups, how is society itself, integrated? What are the sources of cohesion? Since the probability, and frequency of human interaction affect group unity, the sociologist must look into the spatial-temporal patterning of behavior. Hence his inquiries in the realm of human ecology, the unplanned ordering of human relationships largely as a result of competitive processes. He finds a moral—i.e., a social—order revealed, in time and space, in a nonrandom distribution of attributes and activities. And since the group consists in a structure of relationships and their constituent roles, its maintenance depends on a regular input and allocation of role incumbents (through birth and in-migration) to replace those departing (through death and out-migration). Hence his inquiry into population problems, the realm of demography.

These are fundamental considerations. But he must also ask what behaviors and beliefs must be institutionalized to maintain the group. As he pursues his inquiry, the sociologist finds several types and various sources of group integration. Common views and values

---

[36] Melvin Kohn, "Social Class and Parent-Child Relationships," *American Journal of Sociology*, Vol. LXVIII, No. 4 (January, 1963), p. 471.

promote cultural integration. Common standards and the behaviors reflecting them point to normative integration. Frequent dealings among group members promote communicative integration. And the interlocking of differentiated but complementary roles enhances functional integration.

But common values, shared standards of behavior, frequency of social interaction, the harmonious meshing of differentiated roles, the allocation of goods and power and authority, mating, marriage, and the rearing of newcomers to meet the group's role requirements —these things do not happen automatically or as the result of individual inclination. The group institutionalizes behaviors, structures of relationships, to achieve these ends. And we call these "frozen answers to fundamental questions" institutions. Now the sociologist must ask: how in fact do these institutions contribute to social integration? What is the structure of roles and relationships characterizing each: family, church, economy, and polity? How do they recruit their members and officials? How does each link with the rest of the institutional structure? How does the social structure of an institution vary from place to place and time to time? What are the effects of differences in institutional structure? Hence the interest of the sociologist in kinship, marriage, family, and child rearing. Hence, also, the sociology of religion, of work, of political behavior, of education, of military organization, and the like.

But there would be no problem of group maintenance without its corollary of social change, deducible from differing inputs of knowledge and values and the differing inputs (and outputs) of population. I have stressed the word "differing" in my definition of the field. When the past confronts the present, or the "there" confronts the "here" we have just such a change-generating juxtaposition of differences. Change, then, can be seen as a crossroads phenomenon, a confrontation generating a novel "mix." The encounter of rural with urban, immigrant with native, an encounter occurring above all in the city, suggests both locus and focus for an analysis of changes in the group. This is a principal reason for the emergence of such subfields as the sociology of rural life and the sociology of urbanism. The city is a crossroads for ideas, hence of cultural innovation. It intrigues the sociologist because such a large part of its input must be migrant; for it typically fails to replenish its ranks through natural increase. The urban order provides a perfect setting for stress and change.

Changes such as those induced by migration, or race prejudice and shortage of adequate housing (as in the development of a Harlem) are unplanned. They evolve through the reinforcing actions and decisions of many individuals. On the other hand, and perhaps especially in the city, change may be contrived. Here the sociologist plays a somewhat different part. It requires not so much an addition to the fund of reliable knowledge as an application of what he knows in order to promote a change deemed good; or he may apply his methods of inquiry in order to assess the outcomes of efforts at contrived change. As in other fields, there is an applied as well as a "pure" aspect of the sociologist's role.

Were there a way to measure it, I expect that we would find both aspects of his role more important today than ever before: the extension of knowledge and its application in the cryptic domain of the social order. It might be contended that since man's humanity stems from the fact that he is a social animal, the study of society must always have been crucially significant. But there is a difference, in degree if not in kind, in our day. Our control over land, sea, and space, over life and death, has been enormously extended. This liberates us for the effort at more effective management of our personal and social destinies. It seems clear that such management is needed. Contemporary life is more and more a matter of groups and their intertwining. While we have always had "organization men," their number, variety, and interdependence are certainly greater today than ever before. If the penalty of ignorance of history, as Santayana asserted, is to be fated to repeat it, ignorance of sociology means, at best, provincialism and at worst, disaster. For now the crucial part of nature is human nature, and human nature is preeminently social. Both woe and weal depend on our knowledge of this nature. And this knowledge must come from the controlled observation and insightful interpretation of differing patterns of human relationship: their sources and their consequences.

SELECTED SUPPLEMENTARY READING

Sibley, Elbridge. *The Education of Sociologists in the United States.* New York: Russell Sage Foundation, 1963.

Indexes

Name Index

A

Abegglen, James, 521
Aberle, David, x, 405, 409
Achebe, Chinua, 624
Adams, Gene L., 64
Agger, R. E., 592
Alexander, Mrs. C. F., 186, 705
Allport, Gordon, 63, 88
American Institute of Public Opinion, 587
American Sociological Association, 32
Amory, Cleveland, 188
Anderson, C. Arnold, 217, 454, 649
Anderson, Dewey, 542
Angell, Robert C., x
Anthony, Albert, 418, 420
Arrow, Kenneth J., 404
Asch, Solomon E., 143–45, 450
Auchincloss, Louis, viii
Auden, W. H., 39
Augustine, St., 462

B

Back, K., 275
Bacon, Francis, v, 29
Bagehot, Walter, 400
Bain, Read, v
Baker, Harry J., 337
Baldwin, James, 395, 606
Bales, Robert F., 21, 161, 423–25

Barber, Bernard, 127, 503
Barlow, Nora, 29
Barnett, James H., 88
Barrie, J. M., 514
Barton, Allen H., 41
Barton, Bruce, 483, 629
Barzun, Jacques, 693–95
Bates, Ernest S., 604
Beard, Charles, 19
Becker, Howard S., v, 41, 130
Bell, C. A., 472
Bellamy, Edward, 99
Bendix, Reinhard, 207, 210, 225, 250, 374, 518, 558
Benedict, Ruth, 27, 48, 59, 73, 76, 92, 130, 228, 427
Ben Gurion, David, 119
Bennett, John W., 402, 655
Berelson, Bernard, 41, 130, 163, 225, 241, 365, 409, 453, 503, 558, 572–73, 597, 649, 663–64, 666
Berle, Adolf A., 557
Bierstedt, Robert, 18, 41, 598, 703
Blake, Judith, 307, 351–53, 365
Blau, Peter, 526, 531, 592
Blumer, Herbert, v
Bogardus, Emory S., 159, 401–2
Bogue, Donald J., 643–44, 650
Bossard, James H. S., ix, 158, 275, 336
Boulding, Kenneth, 8, 310

Subject Index

This book is set in 11, 10, and 8 point sizes of the celebrated Caledonia typeface created by W. A. Dwiggins, probably the most renowned of contemporary American type designers. Bernhard Modern and Venus Medium Extended types are used for display.